COBOL

Fundamentals of COBOL Programming

Second Edition

Carl Feingold, C.P.A., C.D.P.

West Los Angeles College

WM. C. BROWN COMPANY PUBLISHERS

Dubuque, Iowa

Copyright © 1969, 1973 by Wm. C. Brown Company Publishers

Library of Congress Catalog Card Number: 72-98007

ISBN 0—697—08107—9

Seventh Printing, 1976

Printed in the United States of America

Contents

Preface

COBOL has emerged as one of the leading programming language in use today. COBOL enjoys support from its users: computer manufacturers and governmental agencies which assure that the programming language will meet the needs of the user today as well as in the future. The wide and popular acceptance of COBOL as a standard business programming language has made it essential that more COBOL programming courses be offered at the various institutions of learning.

The relative ease of COBOL programming with its self-documentary feature makes it an ideal introductory programming course for students whether they be programmers, business students, accountants, or any other person interested in learning computer programming.

The purpose of the text is to provide the general reader with a broad and comprehensive coverage of all the features of the latest American National Standard (ANS) COBOL which has been universally adopted by all computer manufacturers. No prior programming knowledge is required as the introductory chapters will serve as a review for continuing students and programmers, as well as provide a sufficient background for the beginning student.

The second edition represents a total revision including all the features of the latest American National Standard COBOL. Extremely comprehensive, it provides the user with introductory concepts of data processing through the basic components of COBOL programming and advanced COBOL programming concepts. It is a step-by-step problem-oriented approach to COBOL programming covering both basic and advanced COBOL topics. The text contains a wealth of illustrated examples helping the student to progress from problem definition to solution.

All chapters have been carefully and extensively revised with expanded explanations, numerous examples and illustrations and new programming problems. Every COBOL entry is described and illustrated in great detail. The text is meant to be all inclusive, with little or no need for reference to computer manufacturers reference manual. The text is so arranged that the first half may be used as an introductory COBOL programming course while the second half may be used in an advanced COBOL programming class.

Some additions to the second edition include:

BASIC COMPUTER COMPONENTS—This *chapter* serves as an introduction to data processing demonstrating the importance of data processing in our economy and the role the computer plays in this ever changing field. The hardware and storage devices are explained and illustrated so that the student has a complete understanding of the physical operation of a computer. Brief explanations of functions and operations of input and/output and storage devices are presented.

INTRODUCTION TO PROGRAMMING—This *chapter* introduces the student to the programming phase of data processing. The student is shown how to prepare for the programming effort from the problem definition to the final program execution. Numerous simplified flowcharting problems are presented so that the reader will become familiar with some of the important tools of programming.

A thorough knowledge of the preparation stage of computer programming will be an invaluable aid to the actual programming of a COBOL program.

TABLE HANDLING—The Table Handling feature provides a capability for defining tables of contiguous data items and accessing an item relative to its position in the table. Language facility is provided for specifying how many times an item is to be repeated. The definition of tables and making reference to them is through the use of a subscript or an index-name. This feature enables the programmer to process tables and lists of repeated data conveniently. A table may have up to three dimensions, i.e., three levels of subscripting or indexing can be handled. A convenient method for searching a table is provided. This feature also provides additional facilities for specifying ascending or descending keys and permits searching of a table for items to satisfy a specified condition.

Sample table handling programs and procedures are illustrated and explained in this section.

MASS STORAGE—The Mass Storage devices allow the records of file to be read or written in a serial manner or to be read or written randomly in a manner specified by the programmer. In sequential accessing of records, the sequence is implicitly determined by the position of the logical record in the file whereas in random accessing of records in a mass storage file, the retrieval or writing of logical records is specifically defined by keys supplied by the programmer. Techniques of creation and updating of sequential, index sequential, and random (direct) file organization are explained and illustrated.

JOB-CONTROL LANGUAGE—Job-control statements describe the jobs to be performed and specify the programmers requirements for each job. Job-control statements are written by the programmer using the job-control language. Job-control statements request facilities and schedule program execution from the system. The job is identified to the system and execution is called for. The function and purposes of job-control statements are explained in this section. Examples of compilation and execution of COBOL programs are illustrated here as well as samples of job control statements.

SEGMENTATION—COBOL segmentation is a facility that provides a means by which communication with the compiler to specify object program overlay requirements can be accomplished. COBOL segmentation deals only with segmentation of procedures. As such, only the Procedure Division and Environment Division are considered in determining the segmentation requirements for a program.

The segmentation feature allows large problems to be split into segments that can be designated as permanent or overlayable core storage at object time. Sample segmented programs are illustrated.

LIBRARY—The library feature provides a capability for specifying text that is to be copied from a library. The COBOL library contains text that is available to a source program at compile time. The effect of the compilation of the library text is the same as if the text were actually written as part of a source program. The COBOL library may contain text for the Environment Division, the Data Division, and the Procedure Division available through the COPY statement.

The library feature supports the retrieval and updating of the prewritten source program text entries from a users program library for inclusion in the users COBOL program at compile time. Samples of uses of the Library facilities are explained and illustrated.

COBOL DIFFERENCES—This section summarizes the differences between D/E/F COBOL and the new American National Standard COBOL. It also summarizes new features to be found in the ANS COBOL.

In addition to the above items, the chapter on programming techniques has been greatly expanded. A new section on debugging COBOL programs has been added presenting the tools and techniques that can be used to discover and eliminate errors in the program.

I am indebted to the IBM Corporation for gratuitously granting permission to use the numerous illustrations, charts, photos, and diagrams that made the text more meaningful.

My special thanks to the Burroughs Corp. for permitting me to use their excellent problems and illustrations in the book.

My last special thanks is to my wife Sylvia, who served as the chief typist, confidante, proofreader, and without whose encouragement, the book would never have been written.

Acknowledgment

The following information is reprinted from *COBOL Edition 1965,* published by the Conference on Data Systems Languages (CODASYL), and printed by the U. S. Government Printing Office.

"Any organization interested in reproducing the COBOL report and specifications in whole or in part, using ideas taken from this report as the basis for an instruction manual or for any other purpose is free to do so. However, all such organizations are requested to reproduce this section as part of the introduction to the document. Those using a short passage, as in a book review, are requested to mention "COBOL" in acknowledgment of the source, but need not quote this entire section.

"COBOL is an industry language and is not the property of any company or group of companies, or of any organization or group of organizations.

"No warranty, expressed or implied, is made by any contributor or by the COBOL Committee as to the accuracy and functioning of the programming system and language. Moreover, no responsibility is assumed by any contributor, or by the committee, in connection therewith.

"Procedures have been established for the maintenance of COBOL. Inquiries concerning the procedures for proposing changes should be directed to the Executive Committee of the Conference on Data Systems Languages.

"The authors and copyright holders of the copyrighted material used herein

FLOW-MATIC (Trademark of Sperry Rand Corporation), Programming for the Univac (R) I and II, Data Automation Systems copyrighted 1958, 1959, by Sperry Rand Corporation; IBM Commercial Translator Form No. F28-8013, copyrighted 1959 by IBM; FACT, DSI 27A52602760, copyrighted 1960 by Minneapolis-Honeywell

have specifically authorized the use of this material in whole or in part, in the COBOL specifications. Such authorization extends to the reproduction and use of COBOL specifications in programming manuals of similar publications."

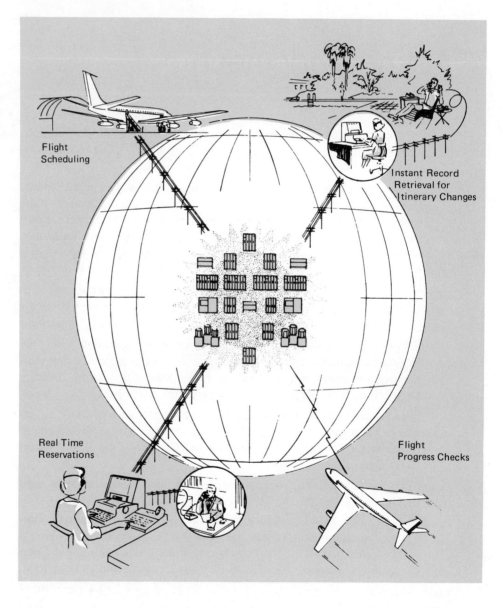

Figure 1–1. Data Processing System Applications.

1

Basic Computer Concepts

INTRODUCTION

The dynamic introduction of the computer in the last quarter-century has entirely changed man's information needs. Since the resources of society are limited, man has developed methods of compiling and analyzing large quantities of data with a minimum of human intervention. The methods of applying data processing systems to information needs are boundless. With each new application, data processing systems have demonstrated still newer ways in which they can be used to help man increase his productivity and advance civilization a little further. Data processing is not just another new industry or innovation, but a giant step forward in man's utilization of science and knowledge as a means of progress.

Computers are perhaps the most useful tools ever invented by mankind. In this, the era of computers, they are used to figure our bank statements, help plan new buildings and bridges, and guide our astronauts in space. Our lives are affected each day in some manner by computers. Life as we know it would not be possible without computers.

In addition, patterns of consumer spending have changed. Credit cards have become a way of life. Almost any of man's needs can be satisfied with a credit card. Daily interest on bank savings would be an impossibility without the present rapid methods of processing data. Service industries have greatly increased, providing numerous services to the consumer, making life more convenient and pleasant. All that is required is to reach for the telephone to make reservations for some distant hotel or to plan a trip to another part of the world. Each individual is touched by the computer in some manner—some unhappily by the Internal Revenue Service.

All of the aforementioned activities illustrate ways that data has become part of our community life. Clerical operations have greatly increased to handle the large quantities of paper to be processed. It seemed that the paper handling alone would overwhelm all our enormous productive capabilities if clerical mechanization had not kept pace with the technological advances in the factory. Great opportunities lie ahead in the data processing field with the addition of the computer. Expanded markets, greater productivity, corporate growth, and increased governmental activity provide the data processor with new challenges each day.

BASIC COMPONENTS OF DATA PROCESSING

Data processing is a planned series of actions and operations upon information which uses various forms of data processing equipment to achieve a desired result. The data processing equipment came into being primarily to satisfy the need for information under increasingly complex conditions. Programs and physical equipment are combined into data processing systems to handle business and scientific data at high rates of speed with self-checking

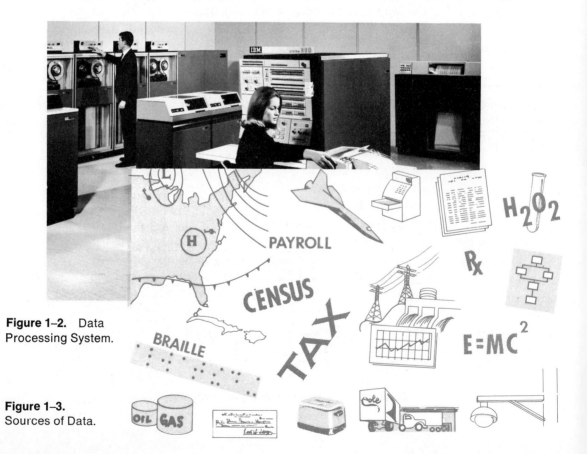

Figure 1–2. Data Processing System.

Figure 1–3. Sources of Data.

accuracy features. The physical data processing equipment consists of various units, such as input and output devices, storage devices, and processing devices to handle information at electronic speeds.

The computer is a major tool for implementing the solution to data processing problems. In brief, the computer accepts data, processes the data, and puts out the desired results. There are many computer systems varying in size, complexity, costs, levels of programming systems, and applications, but regardless of the nature of the information to be processed, all data processing involves these basic considerations.

1. *Input.* The source data entering the system.
2. *Processing.* The planned processing necessary to change the source data into the desired result.
3. *Output.* The finished result, the end product of the system.

The processing operation is carried out in a preestablished system of sequenced instructions that are followed automatically by the computer. The plan of processing is of human origin, involving calculations, sorting, analysis and other operations necessary to arrive at the desired result.

The basic elements of a computer data processing system are its software and hardware features.

Software consists of the totality of programs and routines that are used to extend the capabilities of the computer, such as compilers, assemblers, subroutines, etc. The COBOL compiler is an example of software.

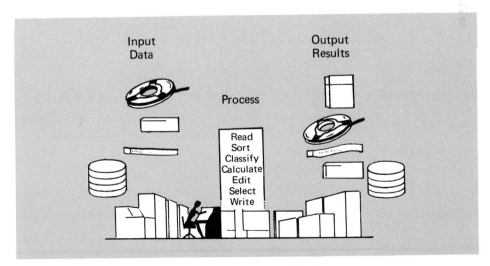

Figure 1–4. Data Processing by Computer.

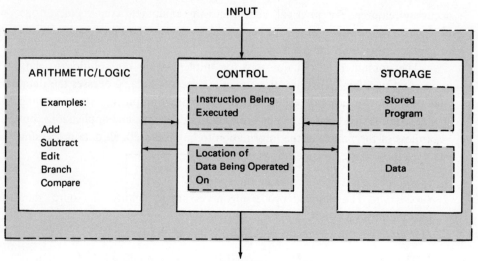

Figure 1-5.   Basic Data Processing Pattern.

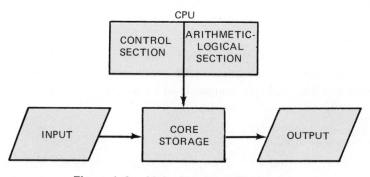

Figure 1-6.   Major Hardware Elements.

Hardware is defined as the physical equipment or devices of a system forming a computer and its peripherial equipment. It includes all the necessary equipment for the input, processing, and output functions.

The major hardware elements of the computer are:

1. *Input Devices* that are used to enter data into the data processing system.
2. *Central Processing Unit* that accepts the data for processing and makes the results available to the output devices.
3. *Output Devices* that accept the data from the processing unit and record it.

Data processing systems are divided into three types of functional units: Input/output devices, central processing unit, and storage.

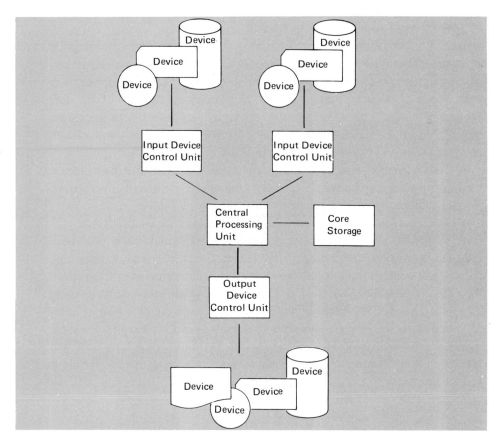

Figure 1–7. Input/Output Units in a Data Processing System.

The data processing system requires input/output devices, linked directly to the system, as part of its information-handling ability. These devices can enter data into and record data from a data processing system. The data for input may be recorded in cards, in paper tape, in magnetic tape, as characters on paper documents, or as line images created by a light pen.

Output devices record and write information from the computer into cards as punches, as holes in a paper tape, or as magnetized spots on magnetic tape. These devices may also print information in the form of reports, generate signals for transmission over telephone lines, produce graphic displays on cathode tubes, or produce microfilm images.

The number and types of input/output devices will depend on the design of the particular system and the type of computer used.

An input/output device is a unit for putting or getting data out of the storage unit. The device operation is initiated by a program instruction that generates a command to a particular input or output device. A *control unit* acts as an intermediary between the command and the input/output device. The control unit decodes the command and synchronizes the device with the data processing system. The information is read by the input reader as the record moves through the input device. The data is then converted to the particular computer code and transmitted to its main storage area.

The output involves the transferring of the data from the main storage area to the particular output device. The computer code must be transcribed into the individual output medium.

The input/output devices perform their functions automatically and continue to operate as directed by the program until the entire file is processed. Program instructions select the required device, direct it to read or write, and indicate the storage locations into which the data will be entered or from which the data will be taken. Data may also be entered directly into storage by using a keyboard or switches. These input/output devices are used for manual entry of data directly into a computer without any medium for recording the data. The manual devices used are console keyboards, transmission terminals, and graphic display terminals. These terminals may be used at remote locations and the information transmitted over teleprocessing lines.

Control Unit

Because of the many types of input/output devices that can be attached to a data processing system, a unit is needed to coordinate input/output operations with the central processing unit. The control unit performs the function by acting as a traffic cop directing information to various input/output devices as they are read into or out put by the system.

Channel

A channel is a separate piece of equipment devoted exclusively to managing the input/output control unit and devices assigned to it. Once the channel is activated, it carries out its own program independent of the central processing unit. This permits the overlapping of input/output operations in computer processing. Sometimes this is performed in a interweaving pattern working with several input/output control units at one time and maintaining the proper destination for storage allocation (input) or the control unit and device (output).

The channel thus performs the important function of permitting the simultaneous operation processing input/output devices with computer processing of data.

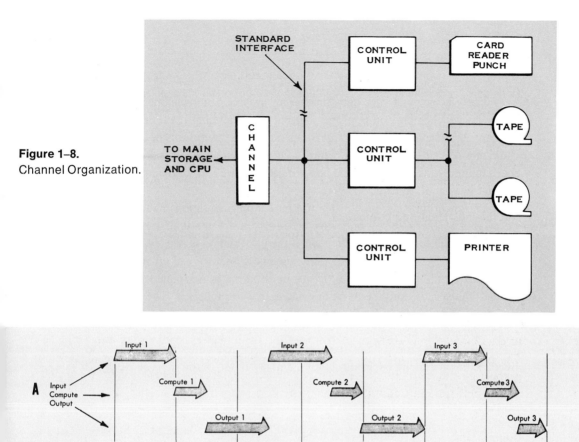

Figure 1–8.
Channel Organization.

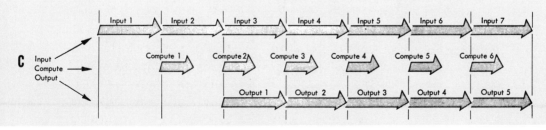

Figure 1–9. Channel Processing.

Buffer

The efficiency of any data processing system can be increased to the degree to which input, output, and internal data-handling operations can be overlapped and allowed to occur simultaneously. The usefulness of a computer is directly related to the speed at which it can complete a given procedure. The speed of input/output units should be arranged so as to keep the central processing unit busy at all times.

To synchronize the processing of input/output operations and to provide an overlap of operations, a buffering system is used. Data is first entered into an external unit known as a buffer. When the information is needed, it is transferred to main storage in a fraction of the time necessary to read the information directly from the unit. Likewise, output information is assembled in a buffer unit at high speeds until the output device is free to process it. The output device then proceeds to write the data while the central processing unit is free to continue its processing.

Large computer systems have many buffers and buffering techniques to overlap the processing operations with the many input/output devices attached to the system.

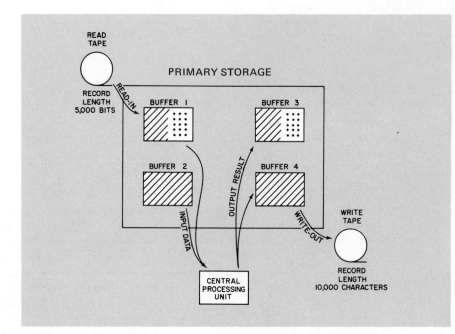

Figure 1–10.   Buffer Operations.

Card Reading and Punching Devices

Card Readers

Card-reading devices introduce punched-card records into a data processing system. The cards move past a reading unit that converts the holes into a machine-processable format.

Card Punches

The card-punch device punches the output from the computer as a series of coded holes into a blank card.

Card-reading and card-punching devices are one of the slowest means of getting information into and out of a computer.

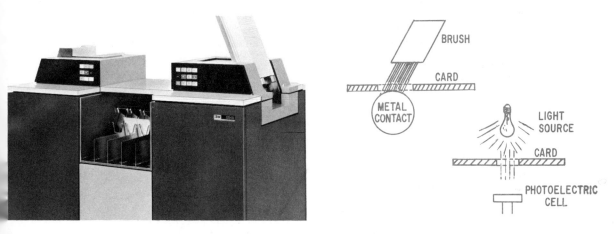

Figure 1–11. Card Read Punch—Card Reading Methods.

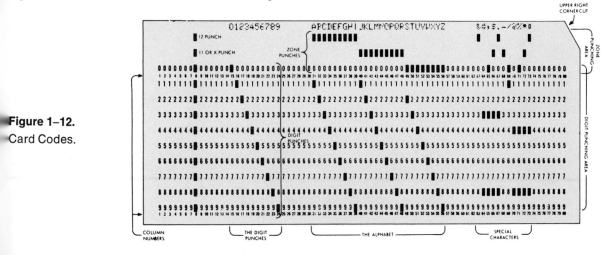

Figure 1–12. Card Codes.

Magnetic Tape Devices

Magnetic tape devices, with their dual capacity of input and output, record information on tape through a read/write head by either reading the magnetized spots or by magnetizing areas in parallel tracks along the length of the tape. The writing on magnetic tape is destructive in that the new information erases the old information on the tape.

Magnetic tape records are not restricted to any fixed record size (cards are restricted to 80 columns of data), words, or blocks. Blocks of records (which

Figure 1–13. Magnetic Tape Operation.

may be a single record or several records) are separated on the tape by an interblock gap, a length of blank tape averaging about .6 to .75 of an inch. This interblock gap is automatically produced at the time of the writing on the tape and provides the necessary time for starting and stopping the tape between blocks of records. Blocks of records are read into or out of buffer units.

Magnetic tape provides high-speed input and output of data to a computer.

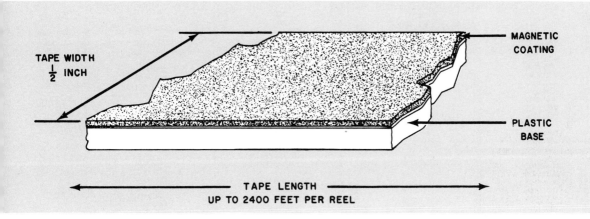

Figure 1–14. Magnetic Tape.

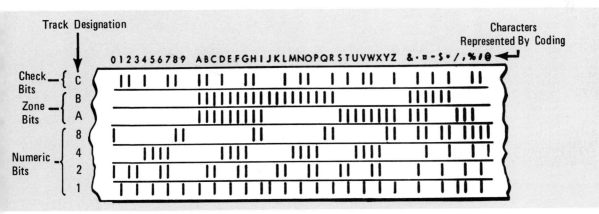

Figure 1–15. Magnetic Tape Character Code.

EBCDIC	Bit Configuration
NUL	0000 0000
SOH	0000 0001
STX	0000 0010
ETX	0000 0011
PF	0000 0100
HT	0000 0101
LC	0000 0110
DEL	0000 0111
	0000 1000
RLF	0000 1001
SMM	0000 1010
VT	0000 1011
FF	0000 1100
CR	0000 1101
SO	0000 1110
SI	0000 1111
DLE	0001 0000
DC1	0001 0001
DC2	0001 0010
TM	0001 0011
RES	0001 0100
NL	0001 0101
BS	0001 0110
IL	0001 0111
CAN	0001 1000
EM	0001 1001
CC	0001 1010
CU1	0001 1011
IFS	0001 1100
IGS	0001 1101
IRS	0001 1110
IUS	0001 1111
DS	0010 0000
SOS	0010 0001
FS	0010 0010
	0010 0011
BYP	0010 0100
LF	0010 0101
ETB	0010 0110
ESC	0010 0111
	0010 1000
	0010 1001
SM	0010 1010
CU2	0010 1011
	0010 1100
ENQ	0010 1101
ACK	0010 1110
BEL	0010 1111
	0011 0000
	0011 0001
SYN	0011 0010
	0011 0011
PN	0011 0100
RS	0011 0101
UC	0011 0110
EOT	0011 0111
	0011 1000
	0011 1001
	0011 1010
CU3	0011 1011
DC4	0011 1100
NAK	0011 1101
	0011 1110
SUB	0011 1111
SP	0100 0000
	0100 0001
	0100 0010
	0100 0011
	0100 0100

EBCDIC	Bit Configuration
	0100 0101
	0100 0110
	0100 0111
	0100 1000
.	0100 1001
¢[	0100 1010
.	0100 1011
<	0100 1100
(	0100 1101
+	0100 1110
|	0100 1111
&	0101 0000
	0101 0001
	0101 0010
	0101 0011
	0101 0100
	0101 0101
	0101 0110
	0101 0111
	0101 1000
	0101 1001
!]	0101 1010
$	0101 1011
*	0101 1100
)	0101 1101
;	0101 1110
¬	0101 1111
—	0110 0000
/	0110 0001
	0110 0010
	0110 0011
	0110 0100
	0110 0101
	0110 0110
	0110 0111
	0110 1000
	0110 1001
7/12 ,	0110 1010
	0110 1011
%	0110 1100
_	0110 1101
>	0110 1110
?	0110 1111
	0111 0000
	0111 0001
	0111 0010
	0111 0011
	0111 0100
	0111 0101
	0111 0110
	0111 0111
	0111 1000
6/0 :	0111 1001
	0111 1010
#	0111 1011
@	0111 1100
'	0111 1101
=	0111 1110
"	0111 1111
	1000 0000
a	1000 0001
b	1000 0010
c	1000 0011
d	1000 0100
e	1000 0101
f	1000 0110
g	1000 0111
h	1000 1000
i	1000 1001

EBCDIC	Bit Configuration
	1000 1010
	1000 1011
	1000 1100
	1000 1101
	1000 1110
	1000 1111
	1001 0000
j	1001 0001
k	1001 0010
l	1001 0011
m	1001 0100
n	1001 0101
o	1001 0110
p	1001 0111
q	1001 1000
r	1001 1001
	1001 1010
	1001 1011
	1001 1100
	1001 1101
	1001 1110
	1001 1111
—	1010 0000
	1010 0001
s	1010 0010
t	1010 0011
u	1010 0100
v	1010 0101
w	1010 0110
x	1010 0111
y	1010 1000
z	1010 1001
	1010 1010
	1010 1011
	1010 1100
	1010 1101
	1010 1110
	1010 1111
	1011 0000
	1011 0001
	1011 0010
	1011 0011
	1011 0100
	1011 0101
	1011 0110
	1011 0111
	1011 1000
	1011 1001
	1011 1010
	1011 1011
	1011 1100
	1011 1101
	1011 1110
	1011 1111
PZ 7/11	1100 0000
A	1100 0001
B	1100 0010
C	1100 0011
D	1100 0100
E	1100 0101
F	1100 0110
G	1100 0111
H	1100 1000
I	1100 1001
	1100 1010
	1100 1011
⌐	1100 1100
	1100 1101
⌐	1100 1110

EBCDIC	Bit Configuration	ASCII-8
	1100 1111	
<	1101 0000	
J	1101 0001	
K	1101 0010	
L	1101 0011	
M	1101 0100	
N	1101 0101	
O	1101 0110	
P	1101 0111	
Q	1101 1000	
R	1101 1001	
	1101 1010	
	1101 1011	
	1101 1100	
	1101 1101	
	1101 1110	
	1101 1111	
†	1110 0000	
	1110 0001	a
S	1110 0010	b
T	1110 0011	c
U	1110 0100	d
V	1110 0101	e
W	1110 0110	f
X	1110 0111	g
Y	1110 1000	h
Z	1110 1001	i
	1110 1010	j
	1110 1011	k
	1110 1100	l
	1110 1101	m
	1110 1110	n
	1110 1111	o
	1111 0000	p
1	1111 0001	q
2	1111 0010	r
3	1111 0011	s
4	1111 0100	t
5	1111 0101	u
6	1111 0110	v
7	1111 0111	w
8	1111 1000	x
9	1111 1001	y
	1111 1010	z
	1111 1011	
	1111 1100	
	1111 1101	
	1111 1110	ESC
	1111 1111	DEL

Figure 1–16. EBCDIC Codes.

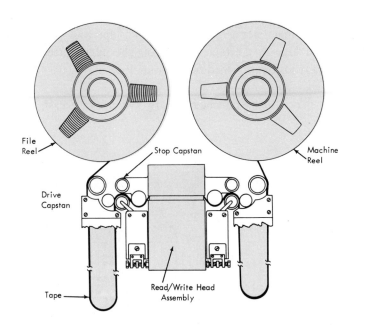

Figure 1–17. Magnetic Tape Operation.

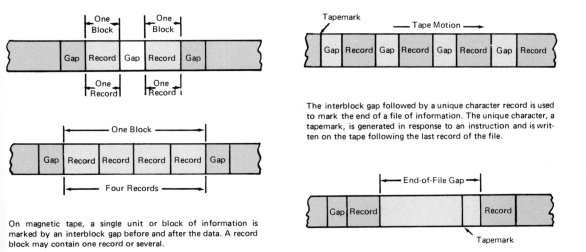

On magnetic tape, a single unit or block of information is marked by an interblock gap before and after the data. A record block may contain one record or several.

The interblock gap followed by a unique character record is used to mark the end of a file of information. The unique character, a tapemark, is generated in response to an instruction and is written on the tape following the last record of the file.

Figure 1–18. End-of-Block and End-of-File Indicators on Tape.

Paper Tape Devices

The data from main storage is converted to a tape code and is punched into a blank paper tape as the tape moves past the punch mechanism. The paper-tape reader reads the punched holes as the tape moves past the reading unit.

Paper tape may also be punched as a by-product of a cash register or some other device.

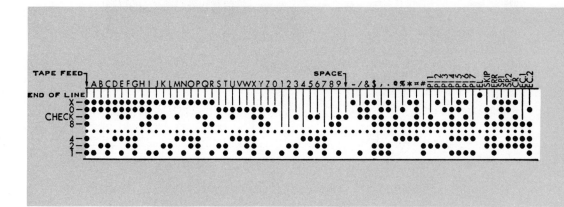

Figure 1–19.   Paper Tape Channel Code 8 Track.

Character-Recognition Devices

Magnetic Ink-Character Readers

These machines read card and paper documents inscribed with magnetic ink characters. The special magnetic ink characters are read by a reader at high speeds and interpreted for the system.

Magnetic ink character readers are used extensively in banking operations to process checks at electronic speeds.

Optical-Character Readers

An optical character reader can read some hand-printed or machine-printed numeric digits and certain alphabetic characters from paper and card documents. The read-and-recognition operation is automatic and takes place at electronic speeds.

Optical-character reading is used extensively with utility bills, insurance premiums, notices, and invoices.

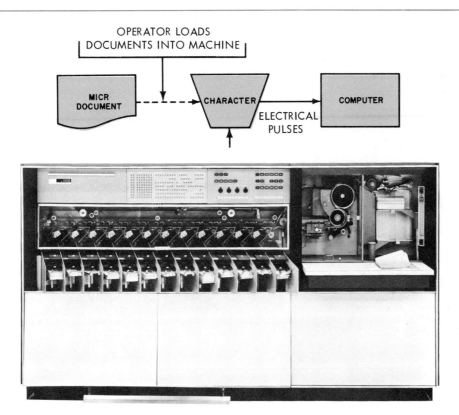

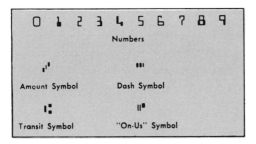

Figure 1–20.   IBM 1419 Magnetic Ink Character Reader and Magnetic Ink Characters.

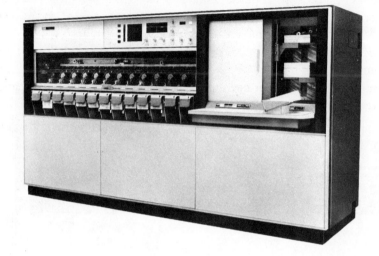

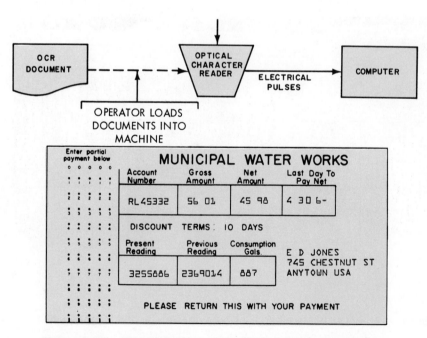

Figure 1–21.   IBM 1428 Alphameric Optical Character Reader.

Visual Display Unit

A visual display unit permits the transfer of information to and from a computer. All input information to the unit is through a keyboard where the input is displayed on a video screen. Before the data is released to the computer, the operator can backspace, erase, or correct an entire input and re-enter it.

Output information is written on a cleared display or added to an existing display on the tube face under operator or program control. Once information is displayed, it is available for as long as needed.

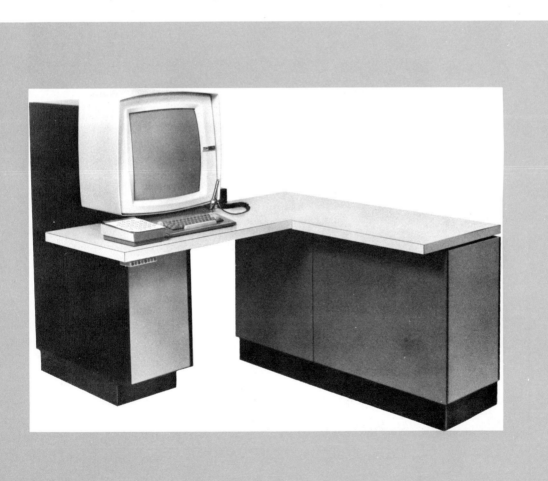

Figure 1–22.   IBM 2250 Visual Display Station.

Printers

The printers provide the permanent visual record (hard copy) from a data processing system. As an output device, the printer receives data from the computer and prints the report. A paper transport automatically spaces the form as the report is being prepared.

There are many types of printers available, depending upon the needs of the user. Printing mechanisms can achieve speeds as high as 2,000 to 3,000 lines per minute.

ACCOUNT NUMBER	BALANCE DUE	DATE OF LAST PAYMENT	
8332	$ 308.65	6/09/62	*
9818	$ .02	12/08/62	*
10003	$1,803.17	6/14/63	
10015	$ .89	10/13/62	*
11007	$1,000.56	6/01/63	
20005	$ 756.79	5/18/63	

Figure 1–23.   IBM 1403 Printer and Printed Report.

Consoles

The console of a data processing system is used by the operator to control the system and monitor its operations. Keys, switches, audible tone signals, and display lights are some of the manual controls available to the operator for manipulation and checking of the program.

Typewriter consoles can be attached to a data processing system for communication between the operator and the system, such as operator-to-program or program-to-operator communication as program checking, and job logging.

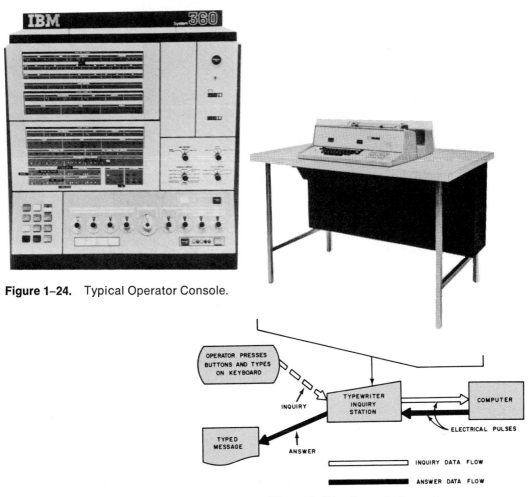

Figure 1–24.   Typical Operator Console.

Figure 1–25.   Console Operation.

Figure 1–26.   Terminal Operation.

Terminals

Terminals are used in telecommunications within a data processing system. Terminal units at the sending location accept data from cards, magnetic tape, or data entered manually into a system through a keyboard, and partially conditions the data for transmission over telephone, telegraph, radio, or microwave circuits. At the receiving station, the data is punched into cards, written on magnetic tape, printed as a report, or entered directly into a data processing system. Automatic checking features insure the validity of all transmitted data.

Figure 1–27. Remote Terminals.

CENTRAL PROCESSING UNIT

The Central Processing Unit is the heart of the entire data processing system. It supervises and controls the data processing components and performs the arithmetic and logical decisions.

The Central Processing Unit is divided into two sections: the Control Section and the Arithmetic and Logical Section.

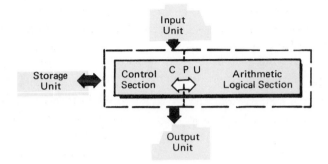

Figure 1–28.   Central Processing Unit.

Figure 1–29.   Control, Arithmetic and Logical Sections.

Control Section

The control section acts as a traffic manager directing and coordinating all operations called for by the instructions of the computer system. This involves control of input/output devices, entry and removal of information from storage, routing of information between storage and the Arithmetic and Logical section.

The control aspect of the processing unit comes from the individual commands contained in the program. These commands are instructions to the various devices to perform a function as specified. Each time a card is read or punched, or a line is printed on the output printer, or two amounts are added together, it is because an instruction in the processing unit caused it to happen. An instruction tells the computer what operation is to be performed (add, subtract, multiply, move, read a card) and where the data is that will be affected by this operation.

This section directs the system according to the procedure and the instructions received from its human operators and programmers. The control section automatically integrates the operation of the entire computer system.

Arithmetic and Logical Section

This section contains the circuitry to perform the necessary arithmetic and logical operations. The arithmetic portion performs operations such as addition, subtraction, multiplication, division, shifting, moving, and storing under the control of the stored program. The logical portion of the section is capable of decision-making to test various decisions encountered during the processing and to alter the sequence of the instruction execution.

STORAGE

All data to be processed entering a computer must be placed in storage first. Storage can be compared to a great electronic file cabinet, completely indexed and available for instant accessing. Information is entered into storage by an input device and is then available for internal processing. Storage is arranged so that each position has a specific location, called an address. The stored data may then be referenced by the computer as needed. For example, consider a group of numbered mail boxes in a post office. Each of these boxes is identified and located by its number. In the same manner, storage is divided

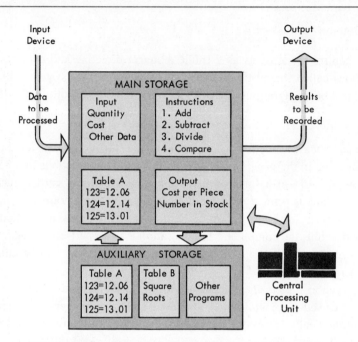

Figure 1–30.   Schematic Main and Auxiliary Storage.

into locations, each with its own assigned address. Each location holds a special character of information. In this way, the stored data can be located by the computer as it needs it.

Data may be rearranged by sorting and collating different types of information received from the various input units. Data may also be taken from storage, processed, and the result placed back in storage. The size and capacity of storage determines the amount of information that can be held within a system at one time. The larger the capacity, the more powerful and expensive the computer.

Storage may be classified as main and auxiliary storage.

Main Storage

Main storage is usually referred to as core or primary storage. Core storage consists of doughnut-shaped ferro-magnetic-coated material vertically aligned. Electric current is sent through these tiny cores. The direction of the current determines the polarity of the magnetic state of the core and gives each core a value of 0 or 1. All programs and data is translated into 0s and 1s and stored in the computer.

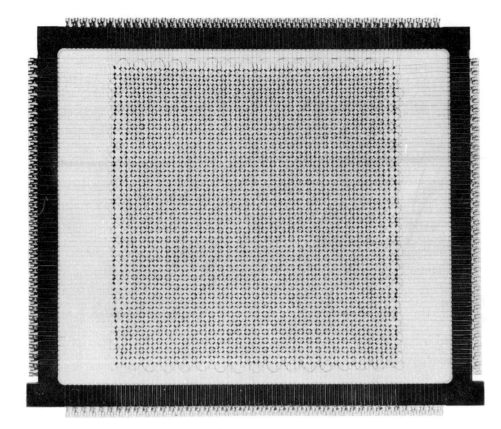

Figure 1–31. Magnetic Core Plane.

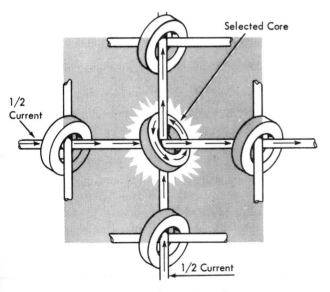

Figure 1–32. Selecting a Core.

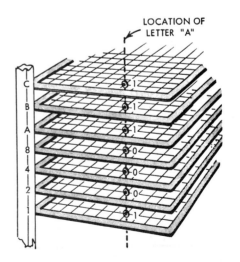

Figure 1–33. Magnetic Core Location.

All data to be processed must pass through main storage. Main storage accepts data from the input unit, holds processed data, and can furnish data to an output unit. Since all data passes through main storage, the unit must therefore have the capacity to retain a usable amount of data and all necessary instructions for processing.

If additional storage is required, the capacity of main storage is augmented by auxiliary storage units; however, all information to and from auxiliary storage must be routed through main storage.

Auxiliary Storage

There are two types of auxiliary storage.

A. *Random-Access Units.* Drum, disk, and data cell devices can be accessed at random. That is, records can be accessed without reading from the beginning of a file to find them.

B. *Sequential-Access Unit.* The magnetic tape unit is the chief type of sequential-access unit. This type of processing indicates that the tape reels must be read from the beginning of the tape to find the desired record.

RANDOM ACCESS:

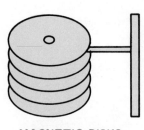

MAGNETIC DISKS

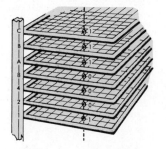

PRIMARY STORAGE

Figure 1–34. Types of Storage.

SEQUENTIAL ACCESS:

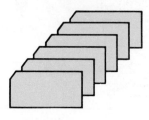

PUNCHED CARDS

MAGNETIC TAPE

Magnetic Drum

A magnetic drum is a constant-speed rotating cylinder with an outer surface coated with a magnetic material. The chief function of the drum is to serve as a high-capacity, intermediate-access (store results temporarily for future processing) storage device. Data is recorded as magnetized tracks around the drum. The primary uses of a magnetic drum are the storage of data that are repetitively referenced to during processing (tables, rates, and codes) or as a supplementary storage for core storage. Another important use today is to serve as a random-access device to provide program storage, program modification of data, and as a temporary storage for high-activity random-access operations involving limited amount of data.

The outer surface of the cylinder can be magnetized and read repeatedly as the drum rotates at a constant speed. Each time new data is read into the area, the old data is automatically erased. The data is read or written by a read/write head that is suspended at a slight distance from the drum.

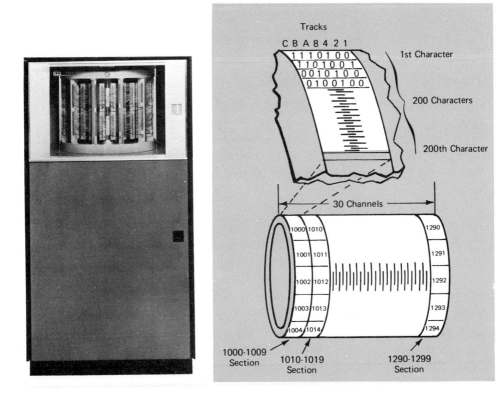

Figure 1–35.   Magnetic Drum Storage.

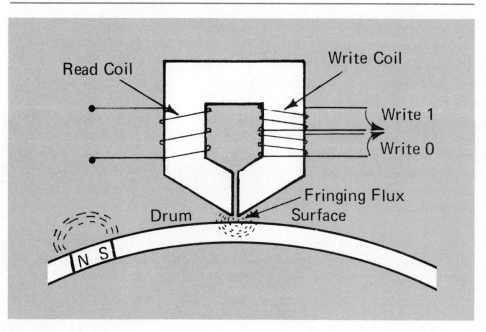

Figure 1–36.   Drum Recording.

Magnetic Disk

A magnetic disk, like drum storage, provides data processing systems with the ability to read or retrieve records sequentially or randomly. The magnetic disk is a thin metal disk coated on both sides with magnetic recording material. Data is stored as magnetic spots on concentric tracks on each surface of the disk. These tracks are accessible for reading by positioning the read/write heads between the spinning disks.

Disks provide the data processing systems with the ability to read and retrieve records randomly or sequentially. They permit the immediate access to specific areas of information without the need to examine each record, as in magnetic tape operations. Independent portable disks can be used with interchangeable disk packs. Six disk packs are mounted on a single unit (on some units) which can be readily removed from the disk drive and stored in a library of disk packs. Read/write heads are mounted on an access arm arranged like teeth on a comb that moves horizontally between the disks. Two read/write heads are mounted on each arm with one head servicing the bottom surface of the top disk and the other head servicing the top surface of the lower disk. Thus it is possible to read or write on either side of the disk. Each disk pack has a capacity of over seven million characters.

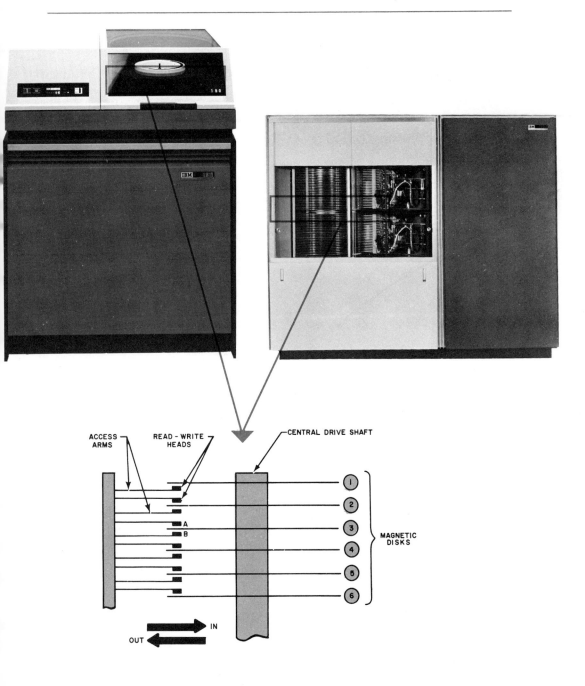

Figure 1–37. Magnetic Disk Schematic Drawing.

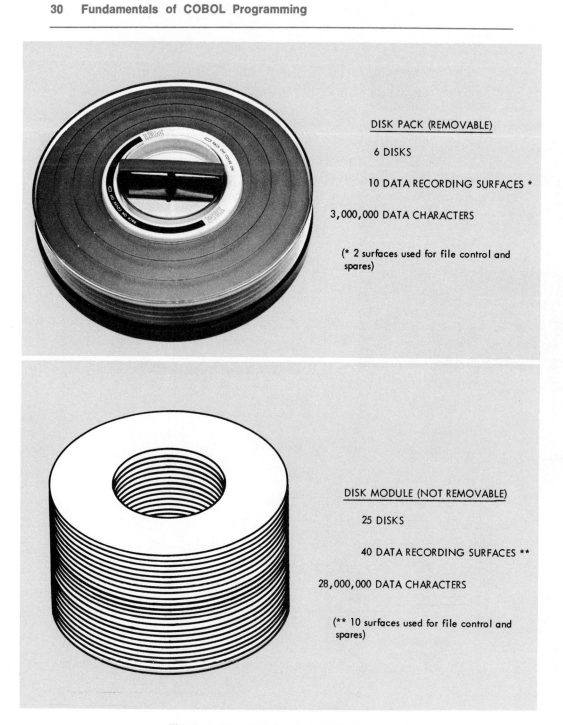

DISK PACK (REMOVABLE)

6 DISKS

10 DATA RECORDING SURFACES *

3,000,000 DATA CHARACTERS

(* 2 surfaces used for file control and spares)

DISK MODULE (NOT REMOVABLE)

25 DISKS

40 DATA RECORDING SURFACES **

28,000,000 DATA CHARACTERS

(** 10 surfaces used for file control and spares)

Figure 1–38.   Disk Packs and Modules.

Data Cells

The data cell drive economically extends the random storage access storage capabilities to a volume of data beyond that of other storage devices. Each data cell device contains from one to ten data cells, each having a capacity of forty million characters. The data cells are removable and interchangeable, permitting an open-ended capacity for libraries of data cells.

The storage medium is a strip of magnetic film 2¼ inches wide by 13 inches long. Each data cell contains 200 of these strips divided into 20 subcells of 10 strips each. A rotary position aligns the selected subcell beneath the access station.

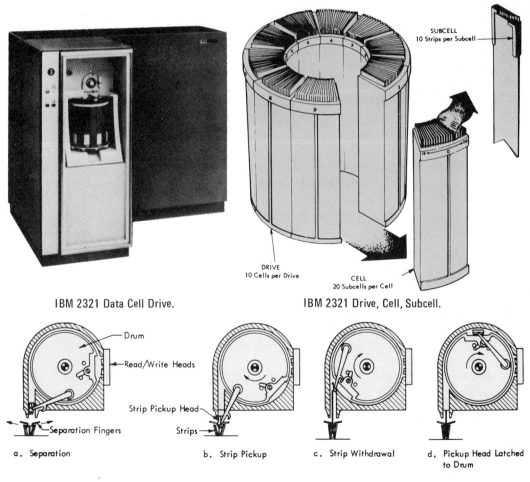

IBM 2321 Data Cell Drive.   IBM 2321 Drive, Cell, Subcell.

a. Separation   b. Strip Pickup   c. Strip Withdrawal   d. Pickup Head Latched to Drum

Figure 1-39. Data Cells.

Exercises

Write your answer in the space provided.

1. The computer was introduced in the last _____ century.
2. _____ industries have greatly increased to make life more pleasant and convenient.
3. Data processing is a planned series of actions and operations upon _____ using various forms of _____ equipment to achieve a desired _____.
4. A data processing system consists of _____ and _____.
5. The physical data processing equipment consists of _____, _____, and _____ devices.
6. The source data entering a computer is known as _____.
7. The totality of programs and routines that are used to extend the capabilities of a computer is known as _____.
8. The _____ unit accepts the data for processing and makes the results available to the output device.
9. Data for input may be recorded in _____, _____, _____, as _____, or _____.
10. An _____ device is a unit for putting or getting data out of the storage unit.
11. A _____ unit decodes the command and synchronizes the input/output devices with the data processing system.
12. A _____ is a separate piece of equipment devoted exclusively to managing the _____ control unit and devices assigned to it.
13. A _____ system provides the overlap operations necessary for high speed data processing operations.
14. _____ and _____ devices are the slowest means of getting information into and out of a computer.
15. Magnetic tape is not restricted to any _____ record size and is the _____ input and output device.
16. _____ readers are used extensively with utility bills, insurance premiums, etc.
17. _____ character readers are used extensively in banking operations.
18. The permanent (hard copy) record from a data processing system is provided by a _____.
19. The _____ of a data processing system is used by an operator to control the system and monitor its operations.
20. _____ are used in telecommunications within a data processing system.
21. The heart of the data processing system supervises and controls the data

processing components and performs the necessary arithmetic and logical operations in the _____ unit.

22. The _____ section directs the system according to the procedures and instructions received from its operators and programs.

23. The _____ portion of the _____ and _____ section is capable of decision making to test various conditions encountered during the _____ of the data and to _____ the sequence of the instruction execution.

24. All data entering a computer to be processed must be placed in _____ _____ first.

25. The _____ the capacity of storage, the more _____ and _____ the computer.

26. _____ storage is usually referred to as core storage.

27. All data to be processed must pass through _____ storage.

28. _____ storage augments main storage.

29. _____ units can process records without the necessity of reading from the beginning of the file to find them.

30. The main types of auxiliary storage are _____, _____, and _____.

Answers

1. QUARTER
2. SERVICE
3. INFORMATION, DATA PROCESSING, RESULT
4. PROGRAMS, PHYSICAL EQUIPMENT
5. INPUT/OUTPUT, STORAGE, PROCESSING
6. INPUT
7. SOFTWARE
8. CENTRAL PROCESSING
9. CARDS, PAPER TAPE, MAGNETIC TAPE, CHARACTERS ON PAPER DOCUMENTS, LINE IMAGES
10. INPUT/OUTPUT
11. CONTROL
12. CHANNEL, INPUT/OUTPUT
13. BUFFERING
14. CARD READING, CARD PUNCHING
15. FIXED, FASTEST
16. OPTICAL CHARACTER
17. MAGNETIC INK
18. PRINTER
19. CONSOLE
20. TERMINALS
21. CENTRAL PROCESSING
22. CONTROL
23. LOGICAL, ARITHMETIC, LOGICAL, PROCESSING, ALTER
24. STORAGE
25. LARGER, POWERFUL, EXPENSIVE
26. MAIN
27. MAIN
28. AUXILIARY
29. RANDOM ACCESS
30. MAGNETIC DRUM, MAGNETIC DISK, DATA CELLS

Questions for Review

1. List the three ways our daily lives are affected by the computer.
2. What physical units constitute a data processing system?
3. What are the basic considerations in all data processing systems?
4. What is meant by "hardware"? "software"?
5. What are the major "hardware" elements of the computer?
6. What is the main function of the input/output device?
7. What main purpose does a control unit serve?
8. How does a channel perform within a data processing system?
9. How do the buffers increase the efficiency of input/output operations?
10. How is information recorded on magnetic tape?
11. What is an interblock gap and what is its purpose?
12. What are the uses of paper tape?
13. What are the two types of character recognition devices? Give examples.
14. What is a visual display device?
15. What is the main function of the printer?
16. What purpose does a console serve?
17. What is the main function of the central processing unit?
18. What are the sections of the central processing unit and what is the primary function of each section?
19. How is storage used in a data processing system?
20. What constitutes main storage? Auxiliary storage?
21. What is the difference between random access units and sequential access units?
22. Describe the following storage units and their main functions within a data processing system: magnetic core, magnetic drum, magnetic disk, data cells.

Problems

1. *Fill in the Labels of the Following Units:*

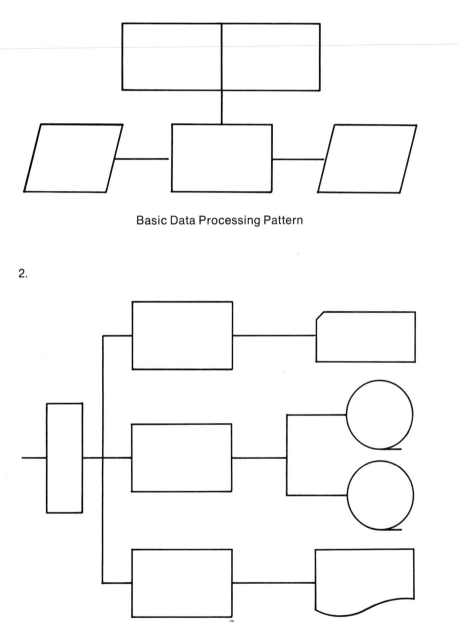

Basic Data Processing Pattern

2.

Channel Organization

3.

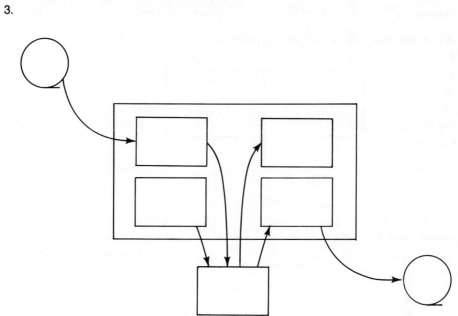

Buffer Operation

4.

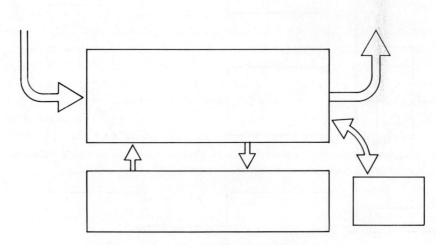

Schematic-Main and Auxiliary Storage

2

Introduction to Programming

A computer program is a set of instructions arranged in a proper sequence to cause the computer to perform a particular process.

The success of a computer program depends upon the ability of the programmer to do the following:

1. Analyze the problem.
2. Prepare a program to solve the particular problem.
3. Operate the program.

ANALYSIS

A problem must be thoroughly analyzed before any attempt is made at a solution. This requires that boundary conditions be established so that the solution neither exceeds the objectives of management nor be too narrow to encompass all the necessary procedures. Output needs should be clearly stated, and the necessary input to produce the desired results should be carefully studied. If necessary, the source documents (input) should be revised so that they can be more readily converted into machine language for data processing operations. The relationship between the inputs and the outputs must be clearly shown. Flowcharts are prepared to depict the orderly, logical steps necessary to arrive at the computer solution to the problem.

PREPARATION

After a careful analysis of the problem and after flowcharting, the computer program should be written. Instructions are coded in the particular computer language using the program flowchart as a guide. The sequence of instructions will determine the computer program.

STEP	GENERAL TERMS	PROGRAMMING TERMS
1	Defining the problem	Preparing job specifications
2	Planning the problem solution	Flowcharting (the program)
3	Describing the problem solution	Coding (the program)
4	Executing the problem solution	Program 'Translation' Program Testing Production Run
5	Documenting the problem solution	Documentation

Figure 2–1.   Steps in Problem Solving.

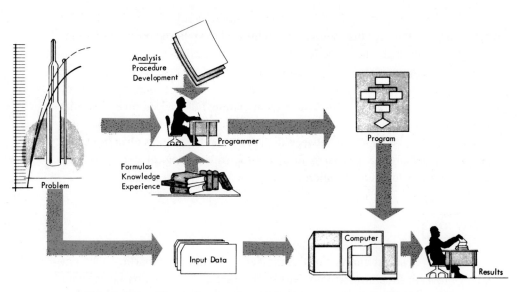

Figure 2–2.   Direct Conversion of Problem to Machine Program.

STEP 1. Preparation of Job Specifications consisting of:

A. Job Description

1. Job title

2. Summary of what is to be accomplished in run

3. System flowchart for the run

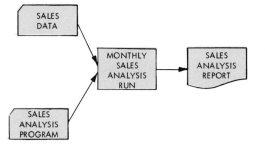

B. Input Files Description

C. Processing Requirements

D. Output Files Description

STEP 2. Flowcharting the Problem

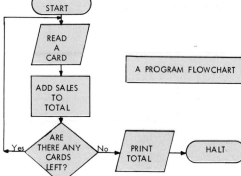

A PROGRAM FLOWCHART

STEP 3. Coding the Program

COBOL PROGRAM SHEET

```
PROCEDURE DIVISION.

START-RUN.
     OPEN INPUT MASTER-FILE; OUTPUT CREDIT-LETTERS.

READ-MASTER
     MOVE SPACES TO OUTPUT-LINE
     READ MASTER-FILE;
         AT END; CLOSE MASTER-FILE, CREDIT-LETTERS; STOP RUN.
     MOVE CUSTOMER-NAME TO DATA-AREA.
     WRITE OUTPUT-LINE AFTER ADVANCING 0.
     MOVE STREET-ADDRESS TO DATA-AREA.
     WRITE OUTPUT-LINE AFTER ADVANCING 1.
     MOVE CITY TO DATA-AREA.
     WRITE OUTPUT-LINE AFTER ADVANCING 1.
     GO TO READ-MASTER.
```

PROGRAMMING FORM

Figure 2–3.   Documentation.

STEP 4. Program 'Translation'; Program Testing; and Production Run

A. Program Translation

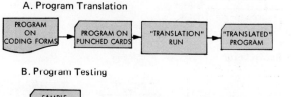

B. Program Testing

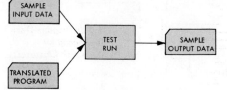

C. Production Run: execution of <u>translated program</u> on <u>actual</u> input data to produce <u>final</u> results.

NOTE: The systems flowchart, prepared as part of the Job Specifications, diagrams the production run.

STEP 5. Documentation

Preparation of a permanent job file containing all documents produced in previous steps.

Figure 2–3.   Documentation—Continued.

OPERATION

The next step is usually the placing of the program and data into the storage unit of the computer. The program must be prepared on punched cards or other media for entry into the machine through an input device. The data must also be made available to the computer through some input unit. The program must be thoroughly checked with the test data and all necessary debugging accomplished before the program is ready for operation upon actual data.

The following items should be checked to insure that the proper analysis and coding was made and that the computer will operate properly.

1. *Precise Statement of the Problem.* This statement must be exact, specifying what the program is to accomplish. "To compute social security tax, multiply gross pay by social security rate to arrive at the FICA tax, etc."

2. *List of inputs.* All sample copies of inputs to be used together with the size of the fields, type (alphabetic or numeric), control fields, etc., should be included.

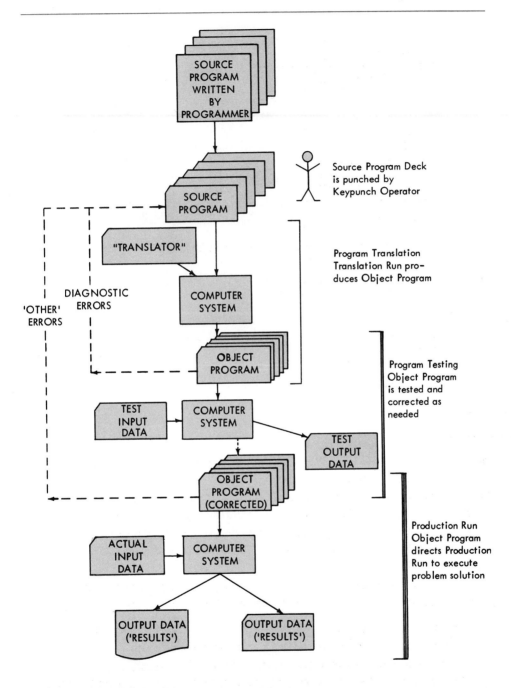

Figure 2–4. Execution: Program Translation and Testing and Production Run.

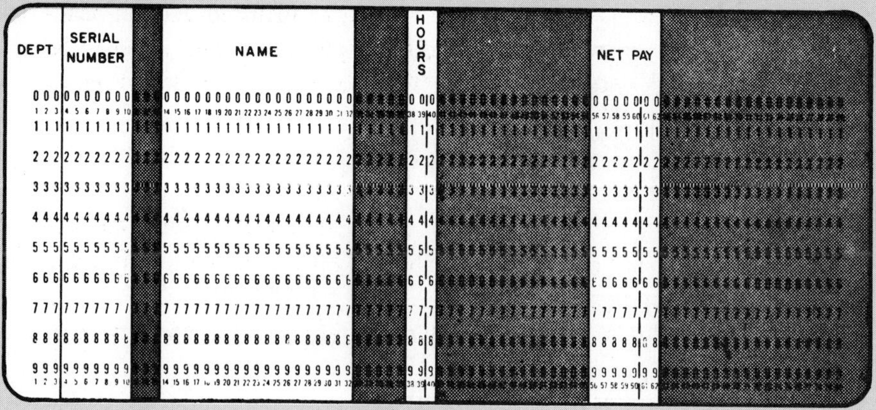

DEPT.	SERIAL NUMBER	N A M E		HOURS WORKED	NET PAY
1	1234560	SMITH	JW	40.1	285.15
1	1892750	JONES	RA	39.6	152.16
1	8929016	MAUS	JB	62.5	182.55
				$	619.86
2	0238648	GOLDMAN	H	31.7	100.25
2	0333367	WOLFE	DJ	9.5	26.60
				$	126.85

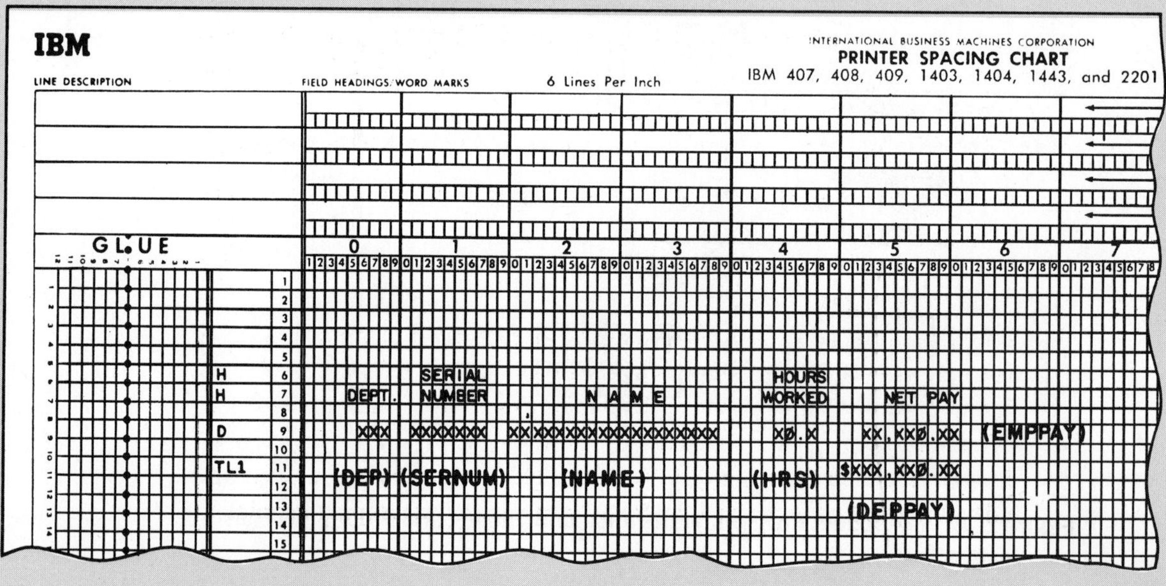

Figure 2–5. Example—Card Design and Printer Layout.

3. *Outputs Desired.* Samples of all outputs should be included with all headings indicated. The number of copies desired, type and size of paper to be used, tape density (if used), is some of the information that should be included in this section.

4. *Flowcharts.* All necessary system flowcharts, program flowcharts, and block diagrams should be included. A system flowchart represents the flow of data through all parts of a system, and a program flowchart places the emphasis on computer decisions and processes. A block diagram is a detailed breakdown of a program flowchart.

5. *Program.* A printed copy of the computer program with all necessary comments.

6. *Test data.* Sample data to be used to test programs.

7. *Job-control cards.* All job-control cards necessary to load the program and the data into the computer. Job-control cards tell the computer what kind of job it is about to do, how to go about performing certain operations involved in doing that job, and how to recognize the end of the job. Job-control cards might vary from one program to the next as well as from one computer to another.

8. *Test results.* Output listings and/or cards used to test the accuracy of the program.

PLANNING A PROGRAM

A computer program is the outcome of a programmer's applied knowledge of the problem and the operation of the particular computer. Problem definition, analysis, documentation, and flowcharting are just the initial steps in the preparation of a program.

The following must be considered even in the simplest of programs:

1. The allocation of storage locations for the storing of data, instructions, work areas, constants, etc.

2. The necessary input procedures to convert the source data into machine processable media.

3. The various reference tables and files that are essential to the program.

4. The checking of the accuracy of the data and the calculations.

5. The ability to restart the system in case of unscheduled interruptions, machine failures, or error conditions.

6. The necessary housekeeping procedures to clear storage areas, register, and indicators prior to the execution of the program. Housekeeping pertains to

those operations in a program or computer system which do not contribute directly to the solution of the user's program, but which are necessary in order to maintain control of the processing.

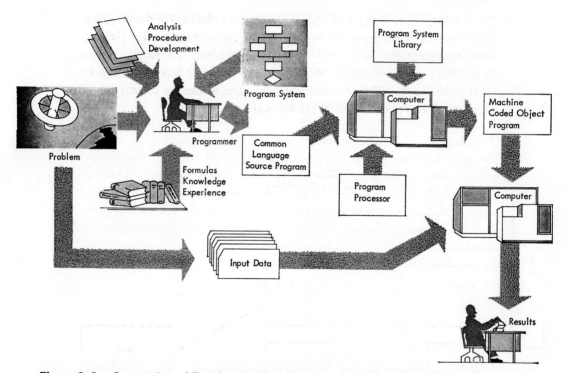

Figure 2–6.   Conversion of Problem to Machine Program Using Programming Symbols.

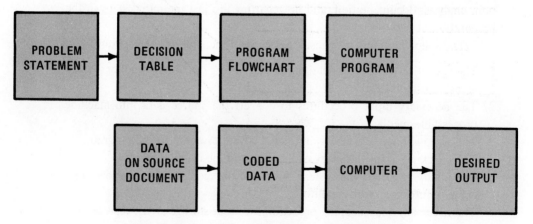

Figure 2–7.   Problem Solving Using a Computer.

7. A thorough knowledge of the arithmetic and logical procedures to be used in the program.
8. The output formats of cards, printed reports, displayed reports, magnetic tapes, etc.
9. The subroutines available from other procedures to be used in the program. A subroutine is a subprogram consisting of a set of instructions that perform some subordinate function within the program. A *closed* subroutine is stored in one place and connected to the program by means of linkages at one or more points in the program. An *open* subroutine is inserted directly into a program at each point where it is to be used.

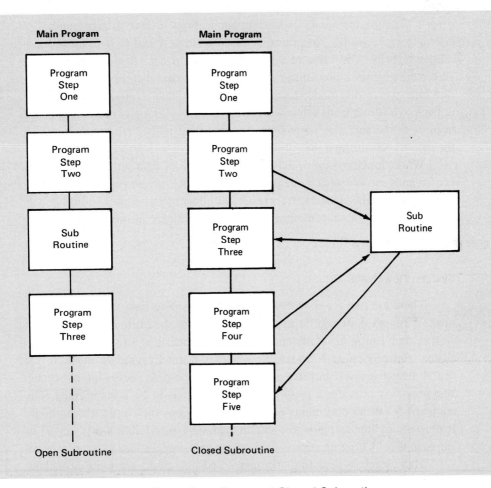

Figure 2–8.   Examples—Open and Closed Subroutines.

FLOWCHARTS

The increased use of data processing has focused attention upon the need for the logical representation of data flows. Once the problem has been defined and the objectives established, the next step is the orderly presentation of procedures so that the objectives can be realized. Any successful program depends upon well-defined steps prior to the actual program. The steps involve the processes to be performed and the sequence of these processes. The processes must be precisely stated before any programming can begin.

The analysis is normally accomplished by developing flowcharts. *The flowchart is a graphic representation of the flow of information through a system in which the information is converted from the source document to the final reports.* Because most data processing applications involve a large number of alternatives, decisions, exceptions, it would be impractical to state these possibilities verbally. The value of a flowchart is that it can show graphically at a glance the organized procedures and data flows so that their apparent interrelationships are readily understood by the reader. Such relationships would be difficult to abstract from a detailed narrative text. Meaningful symbols are used in place of the narrative statements. The flowchart is the "roadmap" by which the data travels through the entire system.

While flowcharts are widely used in the field of data processing, they are occasionally misinterpreted due primarily to the lack of uniformity in the meanings and use of the symbols. As a result, a uniform set of flowcharting symbols was prepared by a subcommittee of the United States of America Standards Institute.

System Flowcharts

There are two types of flowcharts widely used in data processing operations: a system flowchart, representing the flow of data through all parts of a system, and a program flowchart, where the emphasis is on the computer decisions and processes. A system flowchart is normally used to illustrate the overall objectives to data processing as well as non-data processing personnel. The flowchart provides a picture indicating what is to be accomplished. The emphasis is on the documents and the work stations they must pass through. It presents an application where source media is converted to a final report or stored in files. A brief mention is made of the actual operations to be performed.

Many symbols depicting documents and operations are used throughout the system flowchart. The symbols are designed so that they are meaningful

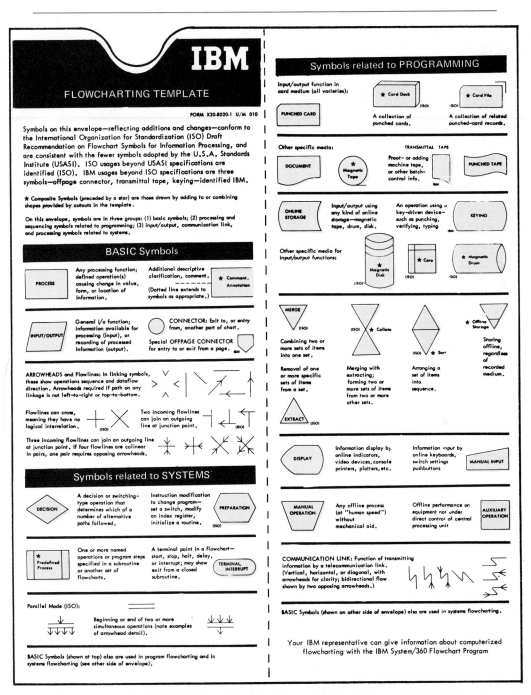

Figure 2–9. Flowchart Template Symbols.

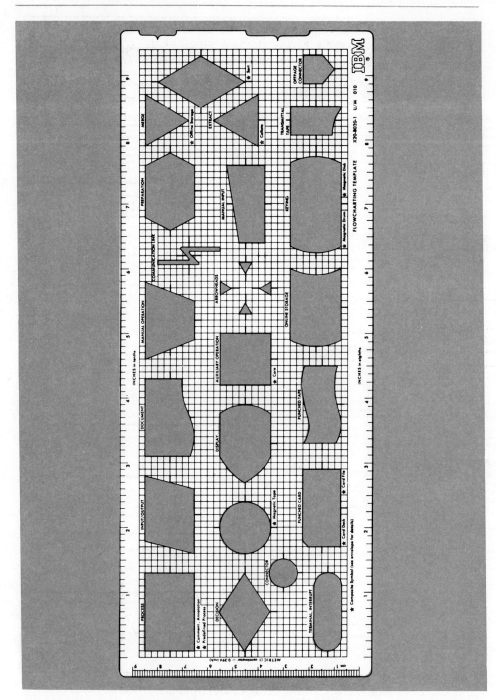

Figure 2–10.   Flowcharting Template.

without too much further comment or text. Card symbols are used to indicate when the input or output may be a card. Document symbols are used to represent the printed reports.

The system flowchart is usually prepared on one sheet of paper to present the overall picture of the system to administrative personnel and executives. It indicates the job to be done without detailing the steps involved.

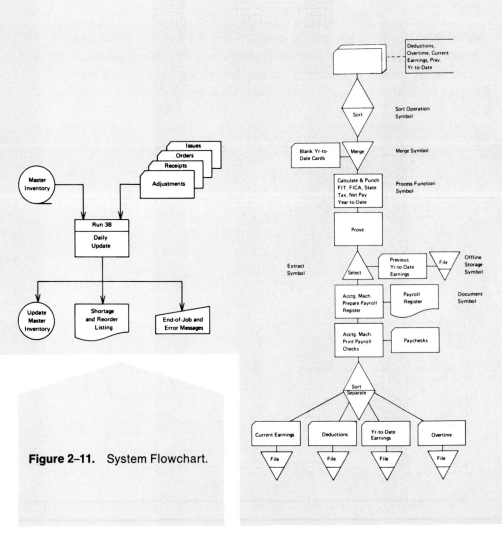

Figure 2–11.   System Flowchart.

Figure 2–12.   System Flowchart Punched Card Symbols.

Program Flowchart

A program flowchart is a graphic representation of the procedures by which data is to be processed. The chart provides a picture of the problem solution, the program logic used for coding, and the processing sequences. Specifically, it is a diagram of the operations and decisions to be made and the sequence in which they are to be performed by the machine. The major functions and sequences are shown, and if any detail is required, a *block diagram* is prepared.

The program flowchart shows the relationship of one part of the program to another. The flowchart can be used to experiment or verify the accuracy of different approaches to coding the application. Where large segments of the program are indicated, a single processing symbol may be used and the detail for the segment shown in a separate block diagram which would be used for

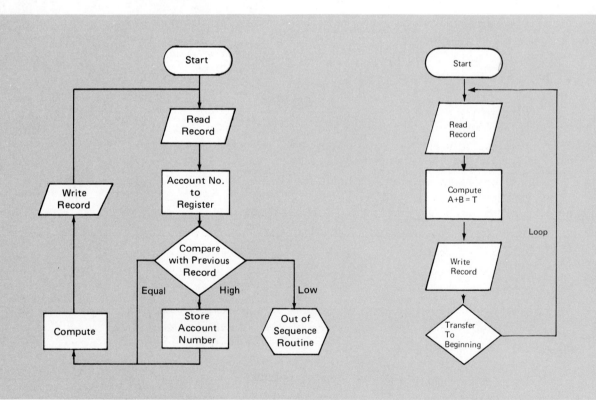

Figure 2–13.   Program Flowchart—Sequence Checking.   **Figure 2–14.**   Program Flowchart—Loop.

the machine coding. Once the flowchart has been proven sound and the procedures developed, it may be used for coding the program.

A program flowchart should provide:

1. A pictorial diagram of the problem solution to act as a map of the program.
2. A symbolic representation of the program logic used for coding, desk checking, and debugging while testing all aspects of the program.
3. Verification that all possible conditions have been considered and taken care of.
4. Documentation of the program. Documentation is necessary to give an unquestionable historical reference record.
5. Aid in the development of programming and coding.

The important points in program flowcharts are the following:

1. It provides the programmer with a means of visualizing the entire program during its development. The sequence, the arithmetic and logical operations, the input and outputs of the system, and the relationship of one part of the program to another are all indicated.
2. The system flowchart will provide the various inputs and outputs, the general objective of the program, and the general nature of the operation. A program flowchart will be prepared for each run and will serve as means of experimenting with the program to achieve the most efficient program.
3. Starting with symbols representing the major functions, the programmer must develop the overall logic by depicting blocks for input and output, identification decisions, etc.
4. After the overall logic has been developed by the programmer, he will extract the larger segments of the program and break them down into smaller, detailed block diagrams.
5. After the flowchart has been proven sound, the coding for the program will commence.
6. Upon completion of the coding, the program will be documented for further modification, which will always occur after the testing, installation, and operational stages.
7. Final documentation should involve the overall main logic, system flowcharts, program flowcharts, and the detailed block diagrams. The general system flowcharts help in the understanding of the more detailed program flowcharts.

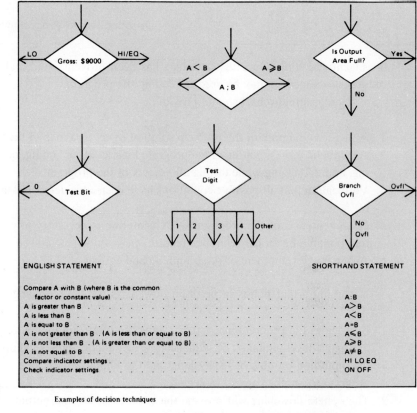

Examples of decision techniques

Figure 2–15.   Decision Technique.

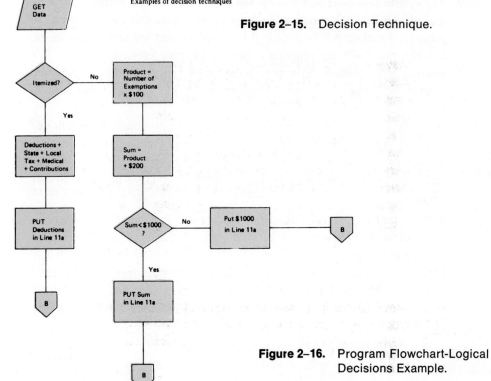

Figure 2–16.   Program Flowchart-Logical
Decisions Example.

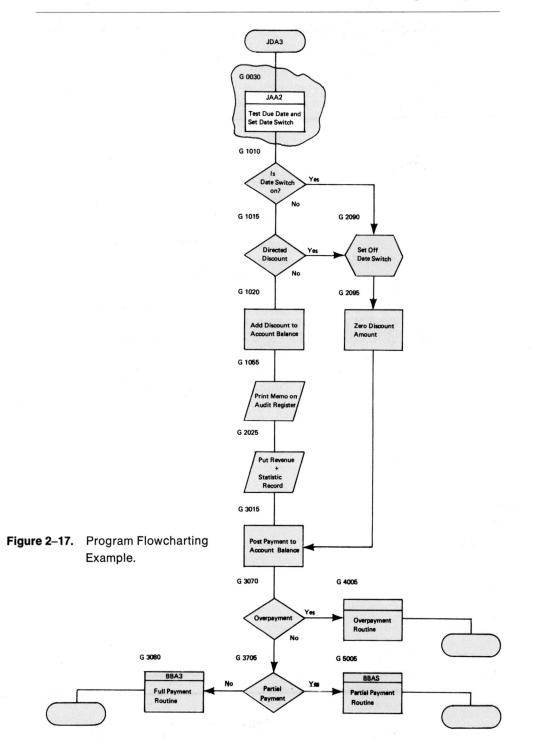

Figure 2–17. Program Flowcharting Example.

The use of standard techniques for the preparation of flowcharts for data processing systems will greatly increase the effectiveness of the programmer's ability to convert the problem into a meaningful program. It will reduce the time necessary to program the applications and, if properly done, will provide a proper communication between the analyst and the many groups with whom he must deal.

Flowcharts are used extensively in the field and are the fundamental basis for all operations in data processing. A clear understanding of flowcharting techniques is a must for everyone who becomes involved with data processing at any level.

Exercises

Indicate your answer in the space provided.

1. The success of a computer program depends upon the ability of the programmer to _____, _____, _____, _____, and _____.
2. Boundary conditions should be established so that the solution _____ _____ nor be _____.
3. The relationship between _____ and _____ must be clearly shown.
4. The _____ will show the orderly _____ steps to arrive at the _____ solution to the problem.
5. _____ are coded in the particular _____ language using the _____ as a guide.
6. The program must be prepared on _____ or _____ before entry into the machine.
7. The _____ must be thoroughly checked with the _____ and all necessary _____ accomplished before the program is ready for operation upon _____.
8. Samples of all _____ desired should be included with all _____ indicated.
9. _____ cards are necessary to load the _____ and the _____ into the computer.
10. A computer program is the outcome of a _____ and the _____.
11. _____, _____, _____, and _____ are the initial steps in the preparation of a program.
12. The steps involved in flowcharting are _____ and _____.
13. The flowchart is a _____ representation of the flow of

_____ through a _____ in which the _____ is converted from the _____ to the _____.

14. The flowchart is the _____ by which the _____ travels through the entire _____.

15. A _____ flowchart represents the flow of data through all parts of a _____ while in a _____ flowchart the emphasis is on the _____ and the _____.

16. A system flowchart indicates the job to be done without _____.

17. The system flowchart is usually prepared to present the _____ of the system to _____ and _____.

18. The program flowchart is a _____ representation of the _____ by which data is to be processed.

19. The program flowchart is a diagram of the _____ and the _____ to be made and the _____ in which they are to be performed by the machine.

20. The program flowchart can be used to _____ and _____ the accuracy of different _____ to coding the application.

21. Once a program flowchart has been proven sound, it may be used to _____ the program.

22. _____ is necessary to give an unquestionable historical reference record to the program.

23. A program flowchart should provide _____ that all possible conditions have been considered and taken care of.

24. The flowchart will provide a proper _____ between the _____ and the many groups he must deal with.

25. The use of flowcharts will greatly increase the _____ of the _____ ability to convert the _____ into a meaningful solution.

Answers

1. ANALYZE THE PROBLEM, PREPARE A PROGRAM, SOLVE PROBLEM, OPERATE THE PROGRAM
2. DOES NOT EXCEED OBJECTIVES OF MANAGEMENT, TOO NARROW TO ENCOMPASS ALL NECESSARY PROCEDURES
3. INPUT, OUTPUTS
4. FLOWCHARTS, LOGICAL, COMPUTER
5. INSTRUCTIONS, COMPUTER, PROGRAM FLOWCHART
6. PUNCHED CARDS, OTHER MEDIA
7. PROGRAM, TEST DATA, DEBUGGING, ACTUAL DATA
8. OUTPUTS, HEADINGS
9. JOB CONTROL, PROGRAM, DATA
10. PROGRAMMERS APPLIED

KNOWLEDGE OF THE PROBLEM, OPERATION OF THE PARTICULAR COMPUTER

11. PROBLEM DEFINITION, ANALYSIS, DOCUMENTATION, FLOWCHARTING

12. THE PROCESSES TO BE PERFORMED, THE SEQUENCE OF THESE PROCESSES

13. GRAPHIC, INFORMATION, SYSTEM, DATA, SOURCE DOCUMENT, FINAL RESULT

14. ROADMAP, DATA, SYSTEM

15. SYSTEM, SYSTEM, PROGRAM, COMPUTER DECISIONS, PROCESSES

16. DETAILING THE STEPS INVOLVED

17. OVERALL PICTURE, ADMINISTRATIVE PERSONNEL, EXECUTIVES

18. GRAPHIC, PROCEDURES

19. OPERATIONS, DECISIONS, SEQUENCE

20. EXPERIMENT, VERIFY, APPROACHES

21. CODE

22. DOCUMENTATION

23. VERIFICATION

24. COMMUNICATION, ANALYST

25. EFFECTIVENESS, PROGRAMMERS, PROBLEM

Questions for Review

1. Describe the steps involved in programming.
2. List the steps that are necessary to insure that the proper analysis and coding was made and that the computer will operate properly.
3. What are the important considerations in planning a program?
4. What is a flowchart and what is its importance?
5. Explain the two types of flowcharts widely used in data processing and their purpose.
6. List the important points in program flowcharting.

Problems

1. *Identify the following flowcharting symbols.*

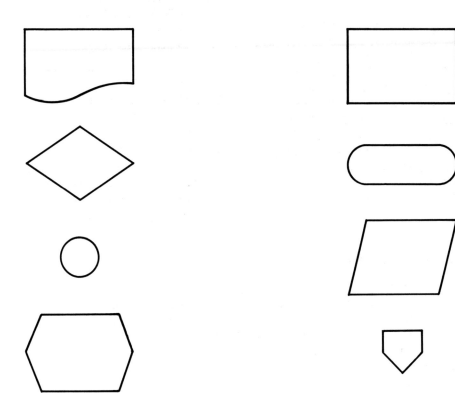

2. *In registering for classes, prepare a flowchart of the procedures and de-cisions necessary to enroll in the correct courses.*
3. *Given a file of records of students containing the following information:*

Student ID Number
Names
Sex
Age
Class code: Freshman, sophomore, junior, senior.
Grade point average.

a. Prepare a program flowchart which will list the freshman female students between the ages of 18–20.
b. Prepare a flowchart that will list all 21 year old junior students with a grade point average of (B) 3.0 or better.

4. *Prepare a system flowchart showing the following:*

Inputs   Magnetic tape — Inventory file.
          Punched cards — Transaction cards.

Outputs Magnetic tape — Updated Inventory file.
          Printer report — Transaction register.

5. *In an Inventory file containing quantity, class of stock, stock number and amount. Prepare a program flowchart that will*

   a. Print all items of the file.
   b. Accumulate all the amounts in class stock 34.
   c. Count the number of items in the file.

6. *Prepare a program flowchart to calculate FICA tax in a payroll procedure. Some of the information in the payroll record include the following:*

   a. Social Security Number.
   b. Employee Name.
   c. Accumulate Earnings—previous week.
   d. Current Weekly Earnings.

   Required:

   a. Read all records.
   b. Check to see if accumulated earnings exceed $9,000 this week or last week.
   c. Calculate FICA tax for

      (1). Employees who have not exceeded FICA limit this week or last week.
      (2). Employees who have reached FICA limit this week.
      (3). Employees who have reached FICA limit last week.

3

Introduction to COBOL

COBOL is defined as COmmon Business Oriented Language. As such it is the result of the efforts of computer users in both industry and government to establish a language for programming business data processing applications. The committee was formed in 1959 at the insistence of the Department of Defense with the express purpose of producing a common business language that could be processed on the various computers without any reprogramming. The federal government, one of the largest users of data processing equipment, was faced with the enormous task and expense of reprogramming each time a different type of computer was installed.

As data processing installations grew in size and complexity, it became apparent that a new programming tool was necessary, one in which the source language was the language of the business man. None of the existing compilers could be used since they were mathematical in nature and not geared for business applications. However, experience gained in the creation of the algebraic compilers pointed the way for the creation of the more complex data processing compilers.

Could a language be created for existing computers that could also be utilized on future computing systems?

Could a language be developed that would fit the rapidly changing and expanding requirements of management?

With the need to produce a large number of computer programs in a short period of time, could a language be developed that would permit existing programming staffs to be augmented with relatively inexperienced programmers?

Figure 3–1. Questions to be Answered.

The initial specifications for COBOL were presented in a report by the *CO*nference on *DA*ta *SY*stems *L*anguage (CODASYL) in April of 1960. The group consisted of computer professionals representing the U.S. Government, manufacturers of computer equipment, universities, and users. This group was inspired by the difficulty of program exchange among users of computer equipment. At the first meeting the conference agreed upon the development of a common language for the programming of commercial problems that was capable of continuous change and development. The proposed language would be problem oriented, machine independent, and would use a syntax closely resembling English-like statements, thus avoiding the use of special symbols as much as possible. The combined effort of the group was utilized to produce a business-oriented language that would permit a single expression of a program to be compiled on any computer presently operative or contemplated in the future. This would reduce the reprogramming costs and provide an interchange of computer programs amongst the users.

COBOL is especially efficient in the processing of business problems. *Business data processing is characterized by the processing of many files, used repeatedly, requiring relatively few calculations and many output reports.* A payroll application is a good example of a business application, since with the limited amount of input, such as time cards and personnel records, many output reports are produced, such as updated personnel files, payroll checks, payroll registers, deduction reports, and various other internal and external reports. Business problems involve relatively little algebraic or logical processing; instead, they usually manipulate large files of similar records in a relatively simple manner. This means that COBOL emphasizes the description and handling of data items and input and output records.

The first special specifications for COBOL were written in 1960 and improved, refined, and standardized by subsequent meetings of the CODASYL committee. In 1970, a standard COBOL was approved by the American National Standards Institute (ANSI), an industry-wide association of computer users and manufacturers. This standard is called American National Standard (ANS) COBOL and includes the following processing modules:

Nucleus defines the permissable character set and the basic elements contained in each of the four COBOL divisions: Identification, Environment, Data, and Procedure divisions.

Table Handling allows the creation and reference to tables through subscripts and indexes. Convenient facilities for table search are provided.

Sequential Access allows records of a sequential organized file to be written or read in a serial manner. Each record is referred to by its physical position in a file.

Random Access allows records of a file stored on a direct-access device to be read or written in a manner specified by the programmer. Specifically defined keys, supplied by the programmers, control successive references to the logical records.

Sort provides the capability of manipulating records within files and sorting these records either in ascending or descending sequence. Procedures for handling such files before and after sorting are provided.

Report Writer allows the programmer to produce a list type report by describing the report format specifications in the Data Division thereby minimizing the amount of Procedure Division coding.

Segmentation allows a large problem program to be split into segments that can be overlaid in the Procedure Division at object time. These can be designated as permanent or overlayable core storage. This would assure the more efficient use of core storage at object time.

Library supports the retrieval and updating of prewritten source program entries from the user's library through the use of a COPY verb, for inclusion in a COBOL program at compile time. The effect of the compilation of the library text is the same as if the program were written at the same time as the source program, thus eliminating the necessity of recopying an existing program definition.

COBOL has emerged as the leading processing language in the business world and is enjoying a wide and popular acceptance in the data processing market.

POPULARITY

COBOL is a high-level computer language that is problem oriented and relatively machine independent. COBOL was designed with the programmer in mind in that it frees him from the many machine-oriented instructions of other languages and allows him to concentrate on the logical aspect of a program. The program is written in an English-like syntax that looks and reads like ordinary business English. Organization of the language is simple in comparison to machine-oriented language—that it is much easier to teach to new programmers thus reducing training time.

The following are some of the reasons advanced for the popularity of COBOL today.

1. COBOL has been continuously standardized by repeated meetings of the

CODASYL committee to improve the language and to guarantee its responsiveness to the data processing needs of the community.

2. COBOL has been designed to meet the needs of users today and in the future at decreasing costs.

3. COBOL is the only language translator supported by the users, including the Federal Government.

4. COBOL users will be skeptical of any new equipment without COBOL capabilities; therefore, it is incumbent upon the computer manufacturers to participate wholeheartedly in all technological progress in COBOL.

5. COBOL is the major data processing language available today. It is included in more software packages of computer manufacturers than any other language.

6. COBOL has proven that it is machine independent in that it can be processed through various computer configurations with the minimum of program change.

7. Although COBOL was primarily designed for commercial users, it has evolved as a highly sophisticated language in other areas of data processing.

8. COBOL is not plagued by computer obsolesence since it is constantly revised to accommodate the newer computers.

9. COBOL has a self-documentary feature in that the English language statements are easily understood by managers and nonprogramming personnel.

After a decade of dedicated effort by a small group of data processing professionals, COBOL has emerged as the leading language in the data processing community. The continued voluntary efforts at standardization and technological improvements in the COBOL language will guarantee its responsiveness to the needs of information by management and its ability to survive the ever-changing data processing field.

```
SUBTRACT DEDUCTIONS FROM GROSS GIVING NET-AMOUNT.

MULTIPLY UNITS BY LIST-PRICE GIVING BILLING-AMT.

IF ON-HAND IS LESS THAN MINIMUM-BALANCE GO TO
REORDER-ROUTINE.
```

Figure 3–2. Typical COBOL Statements.

COMMON LANGUAGE

A great deal of controversy arises when considering whether COBOL is truly a common language—that is, a programming language that can be compiled on any configuration of any computer. COBOL programs are written for computers of a certain minimum storage capacity. Certain small computers are thus eliminated from using COBOL.

Can a programmer write a more efficient program in COBOL if he is familiar with the hardware? The answer of course is yes. He can take advantage of many programming approaches offered by the different computer manufacturers to reduce programming time and the number of storage positions required.

COBOL is not completely common as yet, but it is rapidly approaching this objective. It offers more commonality than any other processor presently in use. It is hoped that the continuing meetings of the CODASYL committee will make COBOL a more useful tool in the future.

The efficiency of COBOL has steadily increased to the point whereby a COBOL program is more efficient than that of a new programmer who codes a program on a one for one basis in some assembly language for a particular machine. However, the COBOL program is not as efficient as an object program produced by an experienced programmer in the symbolic language of the individual computer.

ADVANTAGES

1. The principal advantage of the COBOL system is the establishment of communication. The ability to use English-like statements solves language difficulties that have often existed between the advanced programmer and decision-making management.
2. The program is written in the English language, thus removing the programmer from the individual machine or symbolic language instructions required in the program. Although a knowledge of the individual instructions (symbolic and machine) are not required in COBOL programming, it is very useful to the writing of an efficient program if the programmer possesses some knowledge of the hardware and coding of the particular computer.
3. Pretested modules of input and output are included in the COBOL processor which relieve the programmer of the tedious task of writing input and output specifications and testing them.

COMPATIBILITY—COBOL makes it possible for the first time to use the same program on different computers with a minimum of change. Reprogramming can be reduced to making minor modifications in the COBOL source program, and re-compiling for the new computer.

STANDARDIZATION—The standardization of a computer programming language overcomes the communication barrier which exists among programming language systems which are oriented to a single computer or a single family of computers.

COMMUNICATION—Easier communication between decision-making management, the systems analyst, the programmer, the coding technician, and the operator is established.

AUTOMATIC UNIFORM DOCUMENTATION—Easily understandable English documentation, provided automatically by the compiler, facilitates program analysis and thus simplifies any future modifications in the program.

COMPLETELY DEBUGGED PROGRAMS—Programs produced by the COBOL compiler are free from clerical errors.

CORRECTIONS AT ENGLISH LEVEL—Corrections and modifications in program logic may be made at the English level.

EASE OF TRAINING—New programming personnel can be trained to write productive programs with COBOL in substantially less time than it takes to train them in machine coding.

FASTER AND MORE ACCURATE PROGRAMMING—The English language notation expressed by the user and the computer-acceptable language produced by the COBOL computer ensure greater programming accuracy and a reduction in programming time.

REDUCTION IN PROGRAMMING COSTS—The ability to program a problem faster reduces the cost of programming. Also, reprogramming costs are greatly reduced since a program run on one system may be easily modified to run on another without being entirely recoded.

Figure 3–3.   Benefits Derived from Using COBOL.

4. The programmer is writing in a language that is familiar to him, which reduces the documentation required since the chance for clerical error is diminished. Generally, the quality and the quantity of documentation provided by the COBOL compiler is far superior to that of other language processors. The printed output resulting from the compilation provides an added improvement in the communication problems of man to man and man to machine.

5. While COBOL is not completely machine independent, a program written for one type of machine can be easily converted for use on another with minimum modification. The standardization of a COBOL program provides this benefit.

6. Because of the separate divisions in COBOL, a large program can be broken down into various segments, and each programmer may write one division. The format definition can be made available to all programmers engaged in the problem.

7. Nonprogrammers and managers can read the COBOL program in English, which provides them with the opportunity of judging the logic of the program.

8. During the compilation phase, the COBOL language processor generates a list of diagnostics. A diagnostic is a statement provided by the compiler indicating all errors in a source program, excluding the logic errors. Because diagnostics effect the measurement of compiling efficiency, these as well as compiling speed become important conditions for measuring the superior attributes of COBOL. This advantage derived from the attribute of COBOL can materially reduce the "debugging" time.

DISADVANTAGES

Most of the disadvantages arise with the failure of personnel to fully understand the language and its use.

1. The expectation that a single COBOL program will provide a permanent solution without ever reprogramming.

2. Assuming that the programmer need be taught only the COBOL language without any knowledge of the hardware or the operation of the computer.

3. COBOL will not generate a sophisticated program similar to one written in the actual language of the particular computer.

4. COBOL processors will operate only with a computer having a certain storage capacity. The newer COBOL compilers have drastically reduced the

storage requirements. With the introduction of larger and larger storage units, this problem has been greatly reduced.

OBJECTIVES

1. To provide standardized elements in entry format that can be used on all computers regardless of make or model—a single common language that can be used by all.
2. To provide a source program that is easy to understand because it is written in the English language. Nonprogrammers can understand the logic of the program as well as the programmers themselves.
3. To provide a language that is oriented primarily toward commercial applications. Thus the opportunity is provided for business people to participate in the programming.

Although COBOL is oriented toward a problem rather than a particular machine, there are major differences in computers that have to be allowed for and adjusted to within the framework of the common language. These adjustments are usually minor, and the programmer with a COBOL knowledge can learn these on the job.

Because it uses English-language descriptions of application requirements, COBOL is especially designed for those who can best define their data processing needs. With a minimum of training and only a basic familiarity with the computing system as a prerequisite, accountants, systems and procedures analysts, and many other members of operating management can use COBOL and the computer.

Exercises

Write your answer in the space provided.

1. COBOL is defined as _____.
2. The initial specifications for COBOL was presented in a report by the _____ committee in _____.
3. COBOL is a _____ oriented and machine _____ programming language.
4. COBOL is especially efficient in the processing of _____ problems.
5. Business data processing is characterized by the _____, used repeatedly, _____ and _____.

6. The standard COBOL adopted in 1970 is called _____.
7. The _____ processing module defines the permissable character set and the _____ contained in each of the COBOL divisions.
8. The processing module that allows creation and references to tables through _____ and _____ is known as _____.
9. The _____ access allows records to be written or read in a serial manner while _____ access allows records stored on direct access devices to be read or written in a manner specified by the programmer.
10. The _____ feature provides the capability of manipulating records within files.
11. COBOL is written in _____ syntax.
12. COBOL is included in more _____ packages of computer manufacturers than any other programming language.
13. COBOL is the only language translator supported by the _____.
14. COBOL statements are easily understood by _____ and _____ personnel.
15. A programmer can write a more efficient program in COBOL if he is familiar with the _____ of the particular computer.
16. Pretested modules of _____ and _____ are included in the COBOL processor.
17. A COBOL program written for a particular type of computer can be easily converted for use on another with a _____.
18. A _____ is a statement provided by the compiler indicating all _____ in a source program excluding the _____ errors.
19. COBOL will not generate a _____ program similar to one written in the _____ language of the particular computer.
20. COBOL _____ will operate only with computers having certain _____ capacity.
21. _____ can understand the logic of COBOL programs as well as the programmers themselves.
22. COBOL provides the opportunity for _____ people to participate in the programming.

Answers

1. COMMON BUSINESS ORIENTED LANGUAGE
2. CODASYL, APRIL 1960
3. PROBLEM, INDEPENDENT
4. BUSINESS

5. PROCESSING OF MANY FILES, REQUIRING FEW CALCULATIONS, MANY OUTPUT REPORTS
6. AMERICAN NATIONAL

STANDARD COBOL

7. NUCLEUS, BASIC ELEMENTS
8. SUBSCRIPTS, INDEXES, TABLE HANDLING
9. SEQUENTIAL, RANDOM
10. SORT
11. ENGLISH-LIKE
12. SOFTWARE
13. USERS
14. MANAGERS, NONPROGRAMMING
15. HARDWARE
16. INPUT, OUTPUT
17. MINIMUM MODIFICATION
18. DIAGNOSTIC, ERRORS, LOGIC
19. SOPHISTICATED, ACTUAL
20. COMPILERS, STORAGE
21. NONPROGRAMMERS
22. BUSINESS

Questions for Review

1. Why was the federal government interested in developing a common business language?
2. When did the first CODASYL committee meet and what was their major objectives?
3. List and briefly describe the following processing modules of the American National Standard COBOL; Nucleus, Table Handling, Sequential and Random Access, Sort, Report Writer, Segmentation, and Library features.
4. List the main reasons for the popularity of COBOL.
5. What is a common language? Is COBOL a common language?
6. Why can a programmer write a more efficient COBOL program if he is familiar with the hardware of the particular computer?
7. Why has COBOL emerged as the leading programming language in the data processing community?
8. What are the main advantages of COBOL as a programming language?
9. Why isn't COBOL as efficient as a program written in a symbolic language tailored for a particular computer?

4

Components of COBOL

COBOL is similar to the English language in the use of words, sentences, and paragraphs. The programmer can use English words and conventional arithmetic symbols to direct and control the operations of a computer.

```
ADD QUANTITY TO ON-HAND.
MULTIPLY GROSS-EARN BY SS-RATE GIVING SS-TAX.
IF Y-T-D-EARN IS LESS THAN SS-LIMIT, GO TO SS-PROC.
```

Each of the above sentences is understandable by the computer, but they must be first translated into the particular machine language of the computer before the program can be executed. During the compilation stage, a special system program known as a compiler is first entered into the computer.

The COBOL system consists of two basic elements; the *source program,* which is a set of rules or instructions that carry out the logic of the particular data processing application; and the *compiler,* the intermediate routine that converts the English-like statements of COBOL into the computer-acceptable instructions. Since the COBOL language is directed primarily at those unfamiliar with machine coding, terms common to business applications rather than to computing systems are used in the language.

THE COMPILER

Obviously, neither the computer nor the method of operating it is an end in itself. Rather, the purpose of a data processing system is to achieve, in the most efficient and economical way possible, solutions to the various applications that occur in the normal functioning of any business, educational, or governmental installation. With the advent of larger, more complex data processing systems, the burden of the programmer could conceivably increase to the point where problem solution becomes subordinate to the intricate methods

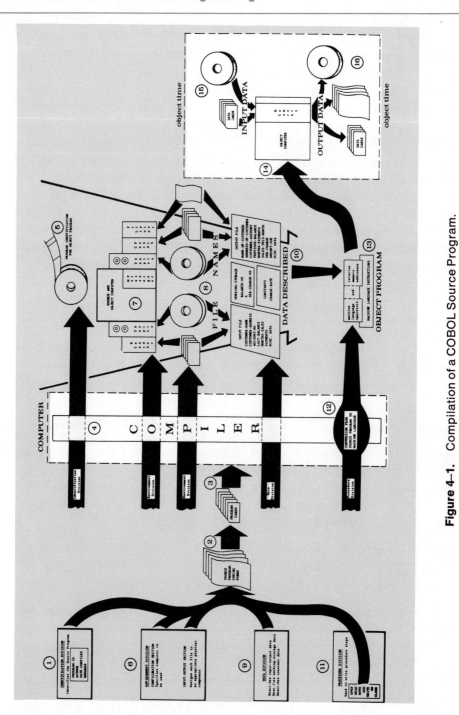

Figure 4–1.   Compilation of a COBOL Source Program.

of computer operation and direction. To preclude this possibility, innovations are constantly being made in an area that has come to be known as *software*.

Precoded software programs, which in large measure are often considered extensions of hardware capabilities, free the programmer from exacting machine considerations and allow him to devote more time to the logic of the problem. These routines, which may vary from simple input-output and diagnostic routines to the more sophisticated routines that effect mass conversions of data being fed to the computer, are provided as special software packages with each data processing system. Certainly, the software packages effect a great saving in coding time and in problem preparation by performing many jobs normally undertaken by the programmer. Furthermore, because many sources of programming errors are removed, costly machine time is conserved.

The compiler, the most intricate of the software routines, is a master routine which takes a program, one written in some elementary form of problem statement (e.g., COBOL English-like statements), and translates it to instructions acceptable to the computer. The translated program is then fed back to the computer to be processed. The initial program that the compiler translates is called the *source program*. The machine-coded program produced from the translation is referred to as the *object program*.

The source program (COBOL symbolic program) is read into the computer and translated into a usable set of machine instructions. Thus the combination of COBOL reserved words and symbols are transformed into a machine language program (object program). This object program will be used to process the data at execution time to provide the desired outputs. The machine language program produced may be used at once or may be stored on an external medium where it may be called in when needed. This object program may be used repeatedly to process data without any further compiling.

In order to write a COBOL program, the programmer should familiarize himself with the basic components of COBOL programming. There are many terms, rules, entry formats, and program structures to be learned before any attempt at COBOL programming is made.

TERMS

Source Program. The problem-solving program written in the COBOL language which will be later compiled and translated into the machine language of the particular computer.

Object Program. The machine language program that resulted from the compilation of the COBOL source program which will be used to process the data.

Compiler. A program supplied by a computer manufacturer that will translate the COBOL source program into the machine language object program.

Source Computer. The computer that is used to compile the source program. Usually the same computer is used for the object computer.

Object Computer. The computer upon which the machine language program will be processed.

Character Set. The complete set of COBOL characters consists of 51 characters. These are the characters (alphabetic, numeric, and special characters or symbols) the manufacturer has included in the COBOL programming package.

CHARACTER SET

Digits 0 through 9
Letters A through Z
Special characters:

  Blank or space
  + Plus sign
  − Minus sign or hyphen
  * Check protection symbol, asterisk
  / Slash
  = Equal sign
  > Inequality sign (greater than)
  < Inequality sign (less than)
  $ Dollar sign
  , Comma
  . Period or decimal point
  ' Quotation mark
  (Left parenthesis
) Right parenthesis
  ; Semicolon

The following characters are used for words:

  0 through 9

A through Z
- (hyphen)

The following characters are used for punctuation:

  ' Quotation mark
  (Left parenthesis
) Right parenthesis
  , Comma
  . Period
  ; Semicolon

The following characters are used in arithmetic expressions:

  + Addition
  − Subtraction
  * Multiplication
  / Division
  ** Exponentiation

The following characters are used in relation tests:

  > Greater than
  < Less than
  = Equal to

Figure 4–2. COBOL Character Set.

NAMES

Names are a means of establishing words to identify certain data within a program. A symbolic name is attached to an item that is being used in the program. All reference to the item will be through the name, although the value may change many times throughout the execution of the program. The name must be unique or identified with the particular group of which it is a part.

Types of Names

Data-Names

Data-names are words that are assigned by the programmer to identify data items in the COBOL program. All items used in the Data Division must be identified by a unique or qualified name.

```
                    DISBURSEMENTS
                        QUANTITY
                        RECORD-DATE
                        DOCUMENT-NUMBER
                        CLASS-STOCK
                        STOCK-NUMBER
                        UNIT-PRICE
                        AMOUNT
                        UNIT
                        DESCRIPTION
```

Figure 4–3.   Data-Names.

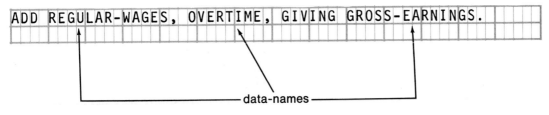

Figure 4–4.   Example—Data-Names.

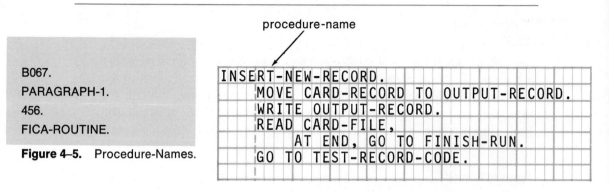

B067.

PARAGRAPH-1.

456.

FICA-ROUTINE.

Figure 4–5. Procedure-Names.

Figure 4–6. Example—Procedure-Name.

Procedure-Names

Procedure-names are symbolic names that are attached to the various segments of the Procedure Division. These names are used for reference by the program in a decision-making operation. The basic concept of computer programming is the ability of the program to leave the sequential order to another part of the program for further processing. A procedure-name may be either a paragraph-name or section-name. The procedure-name may consist entirely of numerals.

Condition-Names

Condition-names are assigned to an item that may have various values. The data item itself is called a condition variable and may assume a specified value, set of values, or a range of values. Condition-names are often used in the Procedure Division to specify certain conditions for branching to another part of the program.

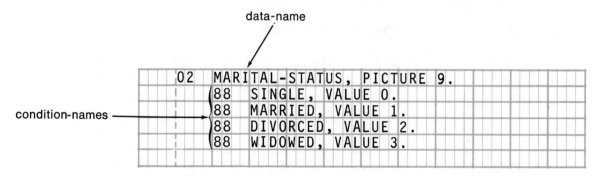

Figure 4–7. Example—Condition-Names.

Special-Names

Special-names are the mnemonic-names that are assigned to various components in the Environment Division. The term special-name refers to the mnemonic-name that is associated with a function-name. Function-names are fixed for each different type of computer. In the Procedure Division, the special-name can be written in place of the associated function-name in any format where substitution is valid.

```
SPECIAL-NAMES.
     SYSIN IS CARD-READER.
     SYSOUT IS PRINTER.
```

Figure 4–8. Example—Special-Names.

Rules for the Assignment of Names
1. Names may range from one to thirty characters in length.
2. No spaces (blanks) may appear within a name.
3. Names may be formed from the alphabet, numerals, and the hyphen. No special characters may appear in a name except the hyphen.
4. Although the hyphen may appear in a name, no name may begin or end with a hyphen.
5. The procedure name may consist entirely of numerals, but all other names must have at least one alphabetic character.
6. Names which are identical must be qualified with a higher level name (see qualification rules).

Qualification of Data-Names

Every data-name used in a COBOL program must be unique. Qualification is required where a single data-name has been used to name more than one item. Qualification is the process by which such a name is made unique. This is accomplished by placing a data-name or a paragraph-name, one or more phrases, each composed of the qualifier preceded by IN or OF (IN and OF are logically equivalent). Thus, if an item in MASTER-RECORD is called STOCK-NUMBER, and an item in DETAIL-RECORD is also called STOCK-NUMBER, then the data-name must appear in a qualified form, since

```
01   OLD-MASTER                    01   NEW-MASTER
     02   CURRENT-DATE                  02   CURRENT-DATE
          03   MONTH                         03   MONTH
          03   DAY                           03   DAY
          03   YEAR                          03   YEAR
```

The above example illustrates nonunique data-names. The names can only be referred to through qualification.

```
     MOVE MONTH OF CURRENT-DATE IN NEW-MASTER . . .
     MOVE MONTH IN CURRENT-DATE OF OLD-MASTER . . .
     MOVE MONTH OF OLD-MASTER . . .
     MOVE MONTH OF NEW-MASTER . . .
```

The above example illustrates a number of points.
1. Either connector (IN or OF) may be used.
2. The order in which the qualifiers appear must proceed from lower level to higher level.
3. It is not necessary to include all intermediate levels of qualification unless a data-name could not be uniquely determined if such intermediate levels were omitted.

Figure 4–9.   Example—Qualification of Names.

the data-name STOCK-NUMBER is not unique. All references to this name must appear as STOCK-NUMBER OF MASTER-RECORD or STOCK-NUMBER IN DETAIL-RECORD, whichever name is intended.

Rules for Qualification of Data-Names
1. If any data-name, paragraph-name, or condition-name is assigned to more than one item in a program, it must be qualified whenever it is referred to in the Environment, Data, or Procedure Division.
2. The name may be qualified by writing IN or OF after it followed by the name of the group which contains the item being qualified.
3. A qualifier must be of a higher level of the group which contains the item being qualified.
4. The name must not appear at two levels in the same hierarchy in such a manner that it would appear to be qualifying itself.
5. The name of an item to which condition names have been assigned may be used to qualify any of its condition-names. For example, SINGLE OF STATUS is permitted where STATUS is the item and SINGLE is the condition-name associated with it.
6. Qualifications when not needed are permitted.

7. The highest-level qualifier that is permitted to qualify a data-name is a file-name.
8. No matter what qualification is available, a data-name cannot be the same as a procedure-name.
9. A procedure-name may be qualified only by a section-name. When this is done, SECTION must not appear as part of the qualifier.
10. A procedure-name must not be duplicated within the same section.
11. Qualifiers must not be subscripted, but the entire qualified name may be subscripted.
12. The highest-level qualifier must be a unique name.
13. No duplicate section names are allowed.
14. Similar data-names are not permitted where the data-name cannot be made unique by qualification.

WORDS

A COBOL word consists of one or more COBOL characters chosen from the character set. A word is followed by a space or by a period, right parenthesis, comma, or semicolon.

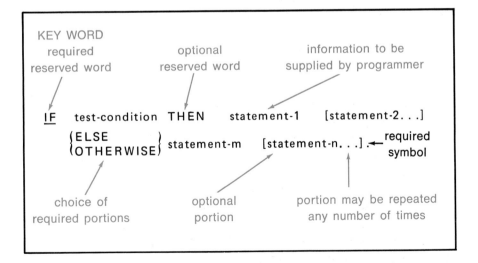

Figure 4–10. COBOL Words.

Reserved Words

Reserved words have preassigned meanings and must not be altered, misspelled, or changed in any manner from the specific purpose of the word. Each of these COBOL reserved words has a special meaning to the compiler; hence, it should not be used out of context. COBOL reserved words may appear in nonnumeric literals (enclosed in quotation marks). When appearing in this form, they lose their meanings as reserved words; therefore they violate no syntactical rules.

A list of reserved words is available for all computers and must be checked before attempting to program, since there are slight differences in the lists for different computers.

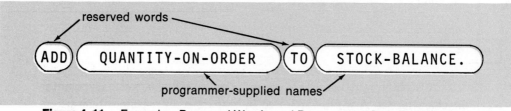

Figure 4–11.   Example—Reserved Words and Programmer Supplied Names.

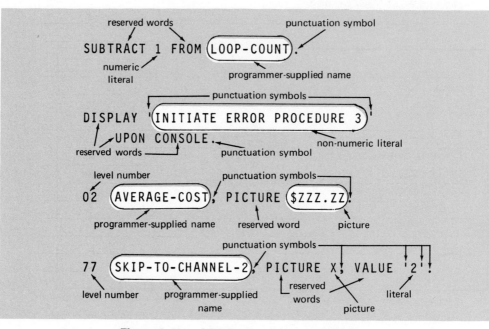

Figure 4–12.   COBOL Symbols and Words.

Interpretation of Words Used in COBOL Statements

The foregoing are used in describing the format of the COBOL statements and are not used in the actual programming of the statements.

Reserved Words. Reserved words are printed entirely in capitals.

Key Words. A key word is a reserved word that is required in a COBOL entry. The use of reserved words is essential to the meaning and structure of the COBOL statement. All key words are underlined and must be included in the program.

Optional Words. Reserved words become optional words in the format in which they appear if they are not underlined. These words appear at the users option to improve the readability. The presence or absence of an optional word does not affect the compilation of the program. However, misspelling of an optional word or its replacement by another word is prohibited.

Lower Case Letter Words. Words printed in lower-case format represent information that must be supplied by the programmer.

Bracketed Words [ ]. Words appearing in brackets indicate that the enclosed word must be included or omitted depending on the requirements of the program.

Braced Words { }. Words appearing in braces indicate that at least one of the words must be included.

Ellipsis (. . . . . . .). Ellipsis immediately following the format indicate that the words may appear any number of times.

CONSTANTS

A constant is an actual value of data that remains unchanged during the execution of the program. The value for the constant is supplied by the programmer at the time the program is loaded into storage.

There are two types of constants used in COBOL programming—literals and figurative constants.

Literals

Literals are composed of a string of characters where the value is determined by the set of characters of which the literal is a part of. A literal may be named or unnamed. A named literal has a data-name assigned to it with a fixed value stipulated in the Working-Storage Section of the Data Division.

Example 1.   77   FICA-RATE   PICTURE V999   VALUE .052.

MULTIPLY GROSS BY FICA-RATE GIVING FICA-TAX.

Example 2.   MULTIPLY GROSS BY .052 GIVING FICA-TAX.

In example 1, we are using a named numeric literal which must be described in the Working-Storage Section of the Data Division before it can be used in the Procedure Division.

In example 2, we are using an unnamed numeric literal which need not be described anywhere as it is used exactly as written.

One of the principal advantages of using a named numeric literal is that it can be changed easily. For example, if the rate of FICA-TAX changes, as it often does in a payroll application, all that need be changed is the description in the Working-Storage Section. If an unnamed numeric literal was used, it would have to be changed in every procedural statement that it appeared which may be rather cumbersome.

Figure 4-13.   Examples—Named and Unnamed Literals.

An unnamed literal has the actual value specified at the time it is being used in the Procedure Division and does not require any separate definition in the Data Division.

There are two type of literals—numeric and nonnumeric.

Numeric Literal

A numeric literal is composed of a string of characters chosen from the digits 0–9, the plus or minus sign, and the decimal point. The value of the literal is implicit in the character themselves. Thus, 842 is both the literal as well as its value.

Rules for Numeric Literals

1. A numeric literal may contain from 1 to 18 digits.
2. It may contain a sign only in the leftmost character position. If no sign is indicated, the compiler will assume the value to be positive. No space is permitted between the sign and the literal.
3. It may contain a decimal point anywhere in the literal except as the rightmost character. Integers may be written without decimal points. The decimal point is treated as an assumed decimal point.
4. It may contain only one sign and/or one decimal point.
5. It must not be enclosed in quotation marks.

VALID NUMERIC LITERALS

-857394867.9842

+7583902.87

-.0006

5849245

205

INVALID NUMERIC LITERALS

2,678.56	Incorrect because it contains a comma.
- 294.84.	Incorrect because of the space between the minus sign and the first digit.
-30984378953592.87485	Incorrect because it contains too many digits.

Figure 4–14. Examples—Valid and Invalid Numeric Literals.

ADD 150.50 TO AMOUNT.

MOVE -8967 TO BALANCE.

MULTIPLY GROSS BY .01 GIVING SDI-TAX.

Figure 4–15. Examples—Usage of Numeric Literals.

Nonnumeric Literal

A nonnumeric literal is composed of a string of any character in the computer's character set except the quotation marks. Non-COBOL characters may be included.

Rules for Nonnumeric Literals

1. A nonnumeric literal must be enclosed in quotation marks.
2. It can only be used for display purposes. The literal must not be used for computation. Only numeric literals may be used in computation.
3. It may contain from 1 to 120 characters.
4. It may contain any character in the character set of the particular computer, including blanks, special characters (except quote marks), and reserved words.

(*Note:* Signs and/or decimal points are not included in the size count of a numeric literal but are counted in the size of a nonnumeric literal. Quotation

'7%'
'JANUARY, 1972'
'NOT IN FILE'
'THIS IS A COBOL PROGRAM'
'123456'

Figure 4–16.   Examples—Valid Non-Numeric Literals.

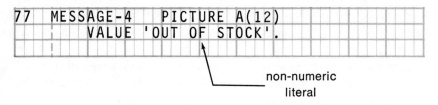

Figure 4–17.   Example—Non-Numeric Literal.

HIGH-VALUE(S)	are assigned the highest value in the computer collating sequence
LOW-VALUE(S)	are assigned the lowest value in the computer collating sequence
ZERO ZEROS ZEROES	are assigned the value 0
SPACE SPACES	are assigned to one or more spaces (blanks)
QUOTE QUOTES	are assigned to one or more quotation mark characters (apostrophes)

ALL "any literal" will represent a continuous sequence of "any literal."

The singular and plural forms of figurative constants are interchangeable.

Figure 4–18.   Figurative Constants.

marks are not considered part of a nonnumeric literal and therefore are not included in the size count. A figurative constant may be used in place of a literal wherever a literal appears in the format.)

Figurative Constant

A figurative constant is a reserved word that has a predefined value recognized by the COBOL compiler. These words are frequently used in programming so that the programmer is relieved of the responsibility of assigning names for commonly used constants. A MOVE ZEROS TO WORK statement will fill the entire area WORK with zeros. Similarly MOVE SPACES TO OUT will blank out the entire area OUT. ZERO, ZEROS, ZEROES may be used interchangeably when singular or plural forms are desired. Usage of singular or plural forms does not affect the execution of the statement. They are only used to improve the readability of the statement.

Assume that GRAND-TOTAL is defined as an 8 character data area. If we use the MOVE verb (to be explained fully in another section), which results in a transfer, the results will be:

COBOL STATEMENT	GRAND-TOTAL WILL CONTAIN
MOVE ZERO TO GRAND-TOTAL.	00000000
MOVE SPACES TO GRAND-TOTAL.	(all spaces)
MOVE QUOTE TO GRAND-TOTAL.	''''''''
MOVE ALL "9" TO GRAND-TOTAL.	99999999
MOVE ALL "ZERO" TO GRAND-TOTAL.	ZEROZERO

Figure 4-19. Example—Figurative Constants.

OPERATORS

Operators are used in the COBOL language to specify some sort of action or relationship between items in the program. Symbols are special characters that have a specific meaning to the compiler. The type of operators and their symbolic forms are as follows:

Arithmetic Expression Operators

The characters used in arithmetic expressions are as follows:

Meaning	Character	Name
ADDITION	+	Plus
SUBTRACTION	−	Minus
MULTIPLICATION	*	Asterisk (times)
DIVISION	/	Slash (divided by)
EXPONENTIATION	**	Double asterisk (raise to the power of)
EQUAL	=	Make equivalent to
PARENTHESIS	( )	To control sequence of calculations

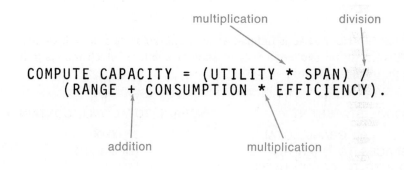

Figure 4–20.   Example—Arithmetic Expression Operators.

Sequence Rules for Processing Arithmetic Expressions
1. The innermost sets of imbedded parentheses are processed first, then the outermost pair.
2. Exponentiation of data is processed next.
3. Multiplication and division calculations are then processed from left to right.
4. Addition and subtraction calculations are then processed from left to right.

Arithmetic expression operators are used in the COMPUTE statement and in relational conditions. The uses and examples of these operators are discussed in greater detail in the Procedure Division section of the text.

Relational Expression Operators

The logical flow of a program frequently depends on the ability to make comparisons of the current value of the data-name and/or to compare this value with another or predetermined value. The expression can be reduced to a true or false statement. If the statement is true, the remainder of the statement is executed. If the statement is false, the program is directed to the next sentence unless an alternative action is specified. The following are the symbols used in relational expressions together with their meanings.

Meaning	Symbol	Name
EQUAL	=	"IS EQUAL TO"
GREATER THAN	>	"IS GREATER THAN"
LESS THAN	<	"IS LESS THAN"
PARENTHESIS	( )	To control sequence of statements to be evaluated.

```
IF PAYMENT < PREVIOUS-BAL GO TO PART-PAYMENT.

IF PAYMENT > PREVIOUS-BAL GO TO OVER-PAYMENT.

IF PAYMENT = PREVIOUS-BAL GO TO PROCESS.
```

Figure 4–21.   Example—Relational Operators.

Relational expression operators may be used in place of their names in relation conditions. The uses and examples of these operators are discussed in greater detail in the Procedure Division section of the text.

Logical Expression Operators

These three logical operators are used to combine simple statements in the same expression for the purpose of testing the condition of the expression. The following are the operators used in logical operations together with their meanings.

Operator	Meaning
AND	Used to evaluate both statements.
OR	Used to evaluate either or both statements.
NOT	Used to negate a positive condition.
( )	Used to control the sequence of enclosed statements.

```
IF A > B OR A = C AND D IS POSITIVE, GO TO PROC-1.
```

Figure 4–22. Example—Logical Operators.

Sequence Rules for Processing Logical Expression

1. Parenthetical expression are evaluated first, from the innermost pair to the outermost pair.
2. AND expressions are evaluated next, starting at the left of the expression and proceeding to the right.
3. OR expressions are evaluated last, starting at the left of the expression and proceeding to the right.

Logical expression operations are discussed in greater detail in the Procedure Division portion of the text.

Punctuation Symbols

Punctuation symbols are important to the successful execution of a COBOL program. Unless the correct usage of symbols are used, many diagnostic errors can be generated during the compilation phase. The following are the symbols and their meanings as used to punctuate entries.

Name	Symbol	Meaning
PERIOD	.	Used to terminate entries.
COMMA	,	Used to separate operands, clauses in a series of entries.
SEMICOLON	;	Used to separate clauses and statements.
QUOTATION MARK	'	Used to enclose nonnumeric literals.
PARENTHESIS	( )	Used to enclose subscripts.

Rules for the Use of Punctuation Symbols

The following general rules apply to the use of punctuation in writing COBOL entries.

1. At least one space must be between two successive words or parenthetical expressions. More than one space will not affect the execution of the program.

2. A period, comma, or semicolon, when used, must not be preceded by a space but must be followed by a space.

3. When any punctuation is indicated in the format, it is required in the program.

4. An arithmetic, relational, or logical operator must always be preceded and followed by a space.

5. Each sentence must be terminated by a period and a space.

6. Parentheses should be used to resolve potential ambiguity in a statement.

7. A left parenthesis must not be immediately followed by a space. A right parenthesis must not be preceded by a space.

8. Semicolons or commas may be used to separate a series of clauses. Semicolons and commas are not required for correct COBOL execution of a program. They are included only to improve the readability of a program.

9. When a quotation mark double (") or single (') (permitted for IBM computers) is used, all entries between quotation marks are considered part of the entry even spaces.

STATEMENTS

A statement is a syntactically valid combination of words and symbols written in the Procedure Division used to express a thought in COBOL. The statement combines COBOL reserved words together with programmer-defined operands.

A COBOL statement may be either a simple or compound expression. A *simple* statement would specify one action while a *compound* statement, usually joined by a logical operator, will specify more than one form of action.

The statement may be either imperative or conditional. An *imperative* statement directs the program to perform a particular operation under *all* conditions, while a *conditional* statement specifies the operation to be performed only if the condition is satisfied (true) or not (false).

```
GO TO READ-RECORD.
```

Figure 4–23.   Example—Simple Imperative Statement.

```
IF SCORE > 84 AND SCORE < 93,
    MOVE 'B' TO GRADE.
```

```
IF CONTRIBUTION = 100.00
    OR CONTRIBUTION > 100.00,
    DISPLAY 'GOOD SHOW' UPON CONSOLE.
```

Figure 4–24.   Example—Compound Conditional Statement.

Exercises

Write your answers in the space provided.

1. COBOL is similar to the English language in the use of _____, _____, and _____.
2. The _____ program is a set of instructions that carry out the _____ of a particular application.
3. The translation of the _____ program into _____ instructions of a particular computer is performed by a special program known as a _____.

4. Precoded _____ programs free the programmer from exacting machine considerations.

5. The machine coded program produced from the translation of a source program is known as the _____.

6. _____ are a means of establishing words to identify certain data within a program.

7. The different types of names used in COBOL programming are _____, _____, _____ and _____ names.

8. All items used in the Data Division must be identified by a _____ or _____ name.

9. A procedure name may either be a _____ or _____ name.

10. Names may range from _____ to _____ characters in length.

11. Names which are identical must be _____ with a higher level name.

12. An identical name is made unique by preceding the qualifier by the words _____ or _____.

13. A _____ name must not be duplicated within the same paragraph.

14. The highest level qualifier must be a _____ name.

15. A COBOL word is followed by a _____, _____, _____, _____ or _____.

16. Reserved words have _____ meanings and must not be _____, _____ or _____ in any manner from the specified purpose of the word.

17. Reserved words are printed entirely in _____.

18. A _____ word is a reserved word that is required in a COBOL entry.

19. An actual value of data that remains unchanged during the execution of a program is known as a _____.

20. A numeric literal is composed of a string of characters chosen from _____, _____ or _____, and the _____.

21. A numeric literal may not exceed _____ digits.

22. A numeric literal may contain only _____ and/or _____.

23. A nonnumeric literal must be enclosed in _____.

24. A nonnumeric literal may contain _____ characters in the character set of the particular computer and may be up to _____ characters in length.

25. A _____ is a reserved word that has a predefined value recognized by the COBOL compiler.

26. Operators are used in the COBOL language to specify some _____ or _____ in a program.

27. The types of operators used in COBOL programs are _____, _____ and _____ operators.
28. Arithmetic expression operators are used in the _____ statement and in _____ conditions.
29. Relational expression operators reduce an expression to a _____ or _____ statement.
30. Logical expression operators are used to _____ simple statements in the same expression for the purpose of _____ the condition of the expression.
31. The incorrect use of _____ can generate many diagnostic errors during the _____ phase of the program.
32. Each operator must be preceded and followed by at least _____.
33. Each COBOL sentence must be terminated by _____ and _____.
34. A _____ is a syntactically valid combination of words and symbols written in the Procedure Division used to express a thought in COBOL.
35. A COBOL statement may be either a _____ or _____ expression usually joined by a _____.
36. A statement that directs the program to perform a particular procedure under all conditions is known as a _____ statement while a _____ statement specifies the operation to be performed only if the condition is satisfied (true) or not (false).

Answers

1. WORDS, SENTENCES, PARAGRAPHS
2. SOURCE, LOGIC
3. SOURCE, MACHINE LANGUAGE, COMPILER
4. SOFTWARE
5. OBJECT PROGRAM
6. NAMES
7. DATA, PROCEDURE, CONDITION, SPECIAL
8. UNIQUE, QUALIFIED
9. PARAGRAPH, SECTION
10. ONE, THIRTY
11. QUALIFIED
12. OF, IN
13. PROCEDURE
14. UNIQUE
15. SPACE, PERIOD, RIGHT PARENTHESIS, COMMA, SEMI COLON
16. PREASSIGNED, ALTERED MISSPELLED, CHANGED
17. CAPITALS
18. KEY
19. CONSTANT
20. DIGITS 0–9, PLUS, MINUS SIGN, DECIMAL POINT
21. 18
22. ONE SIGN, ONE DECIMAL POINT
23. QUOTATION MARKS
24. ANY, 120
25. FIGURATIVE CONSTANT

26. ACTION, RELATIONSHIP
    BETWEEN ITEMS
27. ARITHMETIC EXPRESSIONS,
    RELATIONAL EXPRESSIONS,
    LOGICAL EXPRESSIONS
28. COMPUTE, RELATIONAL
29. TRUE, FALSE
30. COMBINE, TESTING

31. PUNCTUATION SYMBOLS,
    COMPILIATION
32. ONE SPACE
33. A PERIOD, A SPACE
34. STATEMENT
35. SIMPLE, COMPOUND,
    LOGICAL OPERATOR
36. IMPERATIVE, CONDITIONAL

Questions for Review

1. Define the terms, Source Program, Object Program and Compiler and explain how they are used in COBOL programming.
2. What should the programmer familiarize himself with before attempting to write a program in COBOL?
3. Explain the different types of names used in COBOL programming and their expressed purpose.
4. What are the rules for assigning names?
5. What is a Reserved word and how is it used?
6. What are the rules for the use of words?
7. Name seven rules for qualification of data names.
8. What is a literal?
9. What are the rules for the use of numeric literals?
10. What are the rules for the use of nonnumeric literals?
11. What is a figurative constant? What is its main advantage to a programmer? Give an example of a figurative constant.
12. What is an operator and how is it used in COBOL programming?
13. What are Relational expression operators?
14. What is the purpose of Logical expression operators?
15. What are the important rules of punctuation?
16. What is the difference between an imperative and conditional statement?

Problems

1. *Identify the Following:*

Compilation of a COBOL Source Program

2. *Match Each Item With Its Description.*

_____ 1. Hardware   A. A program used to translate a symbolic program to instructions acceptable to the computer.

_____ 2. Software   B. Any magnetic, electronic, or electrical component of a computer.

_____ 3. Source Program   C. A program used to process data.

_____ 4. Object Program   D. Any technique for utilizing computer components.

_____ 5. Compiler   E. A program written in a symbolic language.

3. *Indicate the* incorrect *numeric literals in the following list.*

    a. −8573956894183456.98
    b. −.00015
    c. 2,900.56
    d. −192.85
    e. .5
    f. SIX

4. *Rewrite the following entry correctly.*

    COMPUTE GROSS,ROUNDED= (HOURS*RATE)+OTPAY.

5. *Correct the following data-names.*

    a. SPACE
    b. JOB 1
    c. 12345*
    d. LEVEL−1
    e. −10T4
    f. TAX/RATE

6. *Identify the following operators.*

Operator		Name of Operator	Type of Operator
a.	=		
b.	>		
c.	*		
d.	**		
e.	AND		
f.	/		

5

Writing COBOL Programs

COBOL PROGRAM SHEET FORMAT

The source program is written by the programmer on a COBOL Program Sheet Coding Form. The program sheet provides the programmer with a standard method of writing COBOL source programs. Despite the necessary restrictions, the program is written in rather free form. However, there are precise rules for using this form. Unless these rules are followed, especially in respect to spacing, many diagnostic errors will be unnecessarily generated.

The program sheet is so designed so that it can be readily keypunched. Each line on the form requires a separate card. The form provides for all columns of a card. Unnumbered boxes will not be punched.

Care should be taken in the sequence of the instructions as the COBOL compiler will execute the program exactly as written. Punched cards from the program sheet serve as the initial input medium to the COBOL compiler. The compiler accepts the source program as written in the prescribed program sheet reference format and produces an output listing in the same format. Ample room in sequence numbers should be left for possible insertion of additional or "patch" instructions.

All characters should be written distinctly so that there aren't any questions as to the nature of the instructions. A key punch operator will punch them exactly as written. Punctuation symbols, especially periods, can cause numerous errors when incorrectly used. Such characters as Z and 2, zero and O (letter), should be clearly indicated in the punching instructions of the form so that there will be no doubt as to what characters were intended.

Sequence Number (1–6)

The sequence numbers are written in columns 1 through 6 of the form.

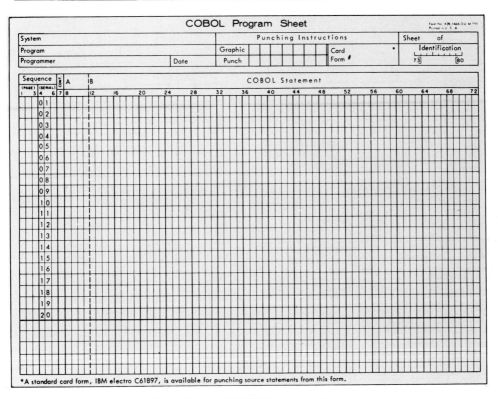

Figure 5–1. COBOL Program Sheet.

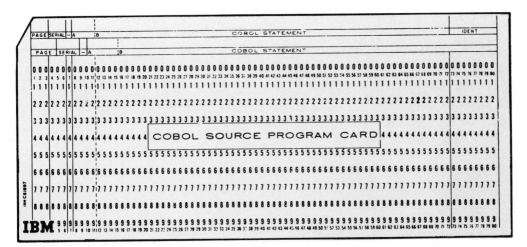

Figure 5–2. COBOL Program Card.

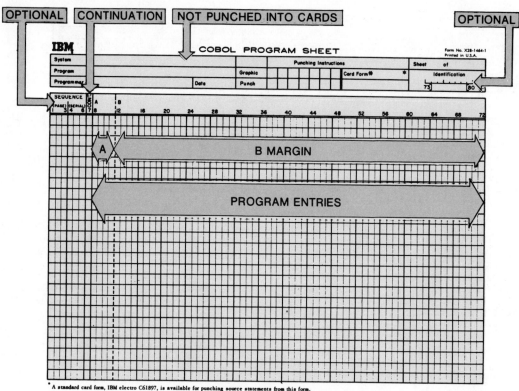

Figure 5–3.   COBOL Program Sheet Entries.

The sequence number consisting of six digits is used to identify numerically each card to the COBOL compiler. The use of these sequence numbers is optional and has no effect on the object program. It is a good practice to use these sequence numbers since they will provide a control on the sequence of the cards if the cards are scattered or if an insertion is to be made into the program. The single-character insertion permits one or more lines of coding to be inserted between existing lines. Column 6 normally contains a zero except where insertions are made.

If sequence numbers are used, they must be in ascending sequence. The compiler will check the sequence and indicate any sequence errors. No sequence check is made if the columns are left blank.

Continuation Indicator (7)

A coded statement may not extend beyond column 72 of the coding form. To continue a statement on a succeeding line, it is not necessary to use all spaces up to column 72 on the first line. Any excess spaces are disregarded by the compiler. If a statement must be continued on a succeeding line, the continuing word must begin at the B margin (column 12 or any column to the right of column 12). A continuation indicator is not necessary.

Words and Numeric Literals Continuation

When splitting a word or numeric literal is necessary, a hyphen is placed in column 7 of the continuation line to indicate that the first nonblank character follows the last nonblank character of the continued line without an intervening space. If the hyphen is omitted, the compiler will assume that the word or numeric literal was complete on the previous line and will insert an automatic blank character after it.

Nonnumeric Literal Continuation

Unlike the word or numeric literal, the nonnumeric literal, when continued, must be carried out to column 72, since spaces are considered part of the literal. To split a nonnumeric literal, the last character must be written in column 72, a hyphen placed in column 7 of the continuation (next) line, and a quotation mark placed in the B margin (Column 12 or anywhere to the right of column 12) and the literal continued. A final quotation mark at the end of the literal terminates the entry.

SEQUENCE																

```
     02  TITLE,  PICTURE  A(38),  VALUE  'LISTING OF DATA RECORDS IN F
  -     'ILE NUMBER'.
```

Figure 5–4. Continuation Nonnumeric Literal.

Program Statements (8–72)

These columns are used to write the source program entries. These columns are grouped as to margins. A margin begins at column 8 and continues through column 11. Any information between these two columns is considered to be written at the A margin. The B margin begins at column 12 and continues through column 72. Any information written between these two columns is considered to be written at the B margin. A blank is assumed to appear in the column following column 72 except where the continuation indicator (hyphen in column 7 on succeeding line) is present. The assumed blank will terminate a word ending in column 72. If it is necessary to place a period beyond column 72 to terminate a sentence, a period should be written on the succeeding line at the B margin with a hyphen in column 7.

```
SEQUENCE   CONT. A    B
(PAGE)(SERIAL)
1   3 4   6  7   8    12  16  20  24  28  32  36  40  44  48  52  56  60  64  68  72
                 MULTIPLY AMOUNT OF CLIENT-PURCHASES BY TRADE-DISCOUNT, GIVING
```

```
      -REDUCTION.
        REDUCTION.
           REDUCTION.
      -            REDUCTION.
```

The third line is the only correct method to complete the entry. If an element ends in column 72, it is treated by the compiler as if it were followed by a space. Therefore, the continuation of such an entry may be written right at the beginning of the B-margin.

The first two lines show the continuation of the entry written in the A-margin, which is illegal. The first and fourth choices have hyphens in column 7, also illegal. The fourth line is correct, except for the hyphen in column 7.

```
SEQUENCE   CONT. A    B
(PAGE)(SERIAL)
1   3 4   6  7   8    12  16  20  24  28  32  36  40  44  48  52  56  60  64  68  72
                 READ SERVICE-CALL; AT END, CLOSE SERVICE-CALLS-FILE, STOP RUN
```

The entry is incorrect.

The period used to end an entry *must not* be preceded by a space. Since the reserved word RUN ends in column 72, it is treated as if it were followed by a space—and that space precedes the period written on the next line. The simplest correction is to write the word RUN on the second line instead of the first, and write the period directly after it.

Figure 5–5. Examples—Program Statements.

Rules for Margin Entries

1. The division header must begin at the A margin and be the first line in a division. The name of the division must be on a line by itself followed by a space then the word DIVISION and a period.
2. The section header must begin at the A margin followed by a space then the word SECTION and a period. If program segmentation is used, a space and priority number may follow the word SECTION; otherwise, no other text may appear on the same line as the section header except the USE or COPY sentence.
3. Paragraph headers must begin at the A margin and are followed by a period and a space. These headers need not be on a line by themselves. Statements may start on the same line at the B margin. Succeeding statements must be written starting at the B margin.
4. The level indicator FD (two letter reserved word for file description) found in the Data Division must be written at the A margin, but the remainder of the file description entry must be written at the B margin.
5. Level numbers 01 and 77 found in the Data Division must be written at the A margin, but the remainder of the entry must begin at the B margin.
6. Special declarative headers in the Procedure Division, DECLARATIVES, and END DECLARATIVES must be written at the A margin on a line by themselves.

```
A    B
8    12   16   20   24   28   32   36   40   44   48
ENVIRONMENT DIVISION.
CONFIGURATION SECTION.
SOURCE-COMPUTER.
      IBM-360-F40.
OBJECT-COMPUTER.
      IBM-360-D30.


FD   SALES-MASTER-FILE,
     BLOCK CONTAINS 30 RECORDS,
     LABEL RECORDS ARE STANDARD,
     DATA RECORD IS SALES-MASTER-RECORD.
```

Figure 5-6. Sample Entries.

All other entries must be written at the B margin (except as noted in the succeeding statement).

Level numbers (01–49, 66, 77, 88) of the data description entries in the Data Division may begin at the A margin if so desired. Usually 01 and 77 level numbers, which are required to be written at the A margin, are written at the A margin with the other level numbers indented at the B margin to improve readability.

An entry that is required to start at the A margin must begin on a new line.

If an entry is too long to be completed on one line and must be continued on another line, the continuation of the entry is written at the B margin of the next line (see continuation indicator rules).

Good practice dictates the writing of short entries leaving the remainder of a line blank. Individual statements on separate lines aid in the debugging of the COBOL program and increase the readability of the program. Insertions and corrections of programs are simplified by using short entry statements on single lines.

Identification Code (73–80)

These columns are used for the names of the program for identification purpose. Any character, including blanks, in the COBOL character set may be used. These codes are particularly useful in keeping programs separate from each other. A group of COBOL program cards could be sight checked in colums 73–80 to assure that there are no other program cards in the deck. This code has no effect on the object deck or compilation, and may be left blank.

Blank Lines

A blank line is one that contains nothing but spaces from columns 7 through 72 inclusive. These blank lines are usually used to separate segments of a program and may appear anywhere in the source program, except immediately preceding a continuation line.

PROGRAM STRUCTURE

COBOL programs are arranged in a series of entries that comprise divisions, sections, and paragraphs. A division is composed of a series of sections, while a section is made up of paragraphs. Paragraphs are composed of a series of sentences containing statements.

COBOL PROGRAM STRUCTURE

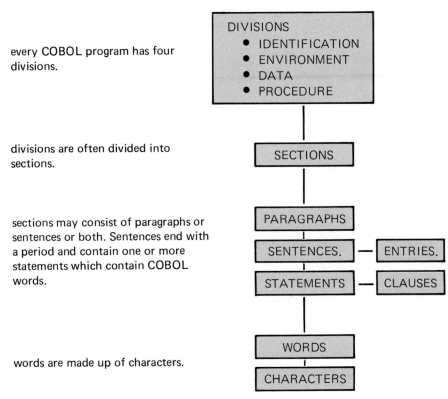

every COBOL program has four divisions.

DIVISIONS
- IDENTIFICATION
- ENVIRONMENT
- DATA
- PROCEDURE

divisions are often divided into sections.

SECTIONS

sections may consist of paragraphs or sentences or both. Sentences end with a period and contain one or more statements which contain COBOL words.

PARAGRAPHS

SENTENCES. — ENTRIES.

STATEMENTS — CLAUSES

words are made up of characters.

WORDS

CHARACTERS

Figure 5–7. COBOL Program Structure—Schematic.

Divisions

Four divisions are required in every COBOL program. They are the Identification, Environment, Data, and Procedure. These divisions must always be written in the aforementioned sequence. A fixed name header consisting of the division name followed by a space, the word DIVISION, and a period must appear on a line by itself.

Sections

All divisions do not necessarily contain sections. The Environment and Data Divisions always contain sections with fixed names. Sections are never found in the Identification Division, while the Procedure Division sections are optional and are created by the programmer if needed.

The beginning of each section is preceded by the name of the section followed by a space, the word SECTION, and a period. The header must appear on a line by itself unless otherwise noted. (See rules for margin entries.)

Paragraphs

All divisions except the Data Division contain paragraphs. In the Identification and Environment Divisions, the paragraphs all have fixed names. The paragraph names in the Procedure Division are supplied by the programmer.

Each paragraph is identified by a paragraph name followed by a period and space. Paragraph headers *do not* contain the word PARAGRAPH. The paragraph header need not appear on a line by itself; however, it must be the first entry, and can be followed on the same line by a series of entries.

A paragraph header entry consists of either a reserved word or a data-name and a period.

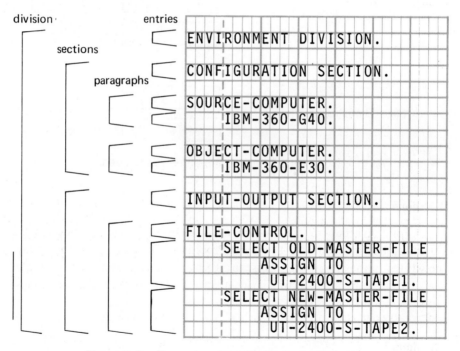

Figure 5–8. Example—COBOL Program Structure.

Entries

Entries (sentences) consist of a series of statements terminated by a period and a space. These statements must follow precise format rules as to sequence.

DIVISIONS OF COBOL

Every COBOL source program is divided into four divisions. Each division must be placed in its proper sequence, begin with a division header, and abide by all the format rules for the particular division. The four divisions listed in sequence with their main functions are:

Identification Division	Identifies the program to the computer.
Environment Division	Describes the computer to be used and the hardware features to be used in the program.
Data Division	Defines the characteristics of the data to be used, including the files, record layouts and storage areas.
Procedure Division	Consists of a series of statements directing the processing of the data according to the program logic as expressed in the detailed flowchart.

Identification Division

The Identification Division contains the necessary information to identify the program that is written and compiled. A unique data-name is assigned to the source program.

The Identification Division must appear first at compile time. The intended use of the division is to supply information to the reader. Usually it contains information as to when the program was written, by whom, and any security information relative to the program. The REMARKS paragraph usually contains the purpose of the program, a brief description of the processing to be performed, and the outputs produced. This information will serve as documentation for the program.

Environment Division

Although COBOL is to a large degree machine independent, there are some aspects of programming that depend upon the particular computer to be used and the associated input and output devices. The Environment is the one division that is machine dependent since it contains the necessary information about the equipment that will be used to compile and execute the source program. To exchange a COBOL program from one computer to another, the

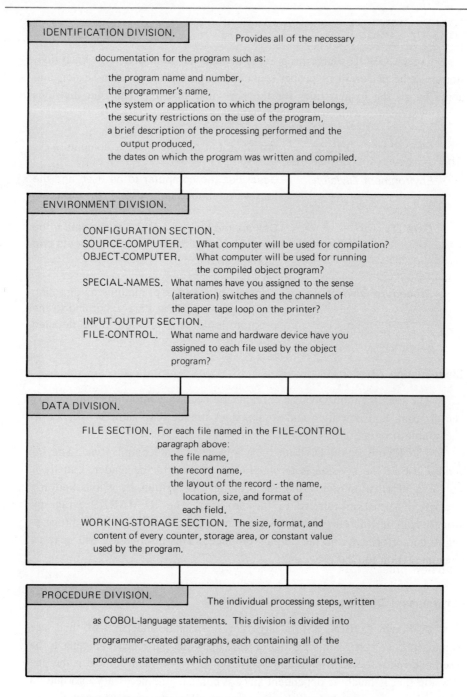

Figure 5–9. The Four Divisions of a COBOL Program.

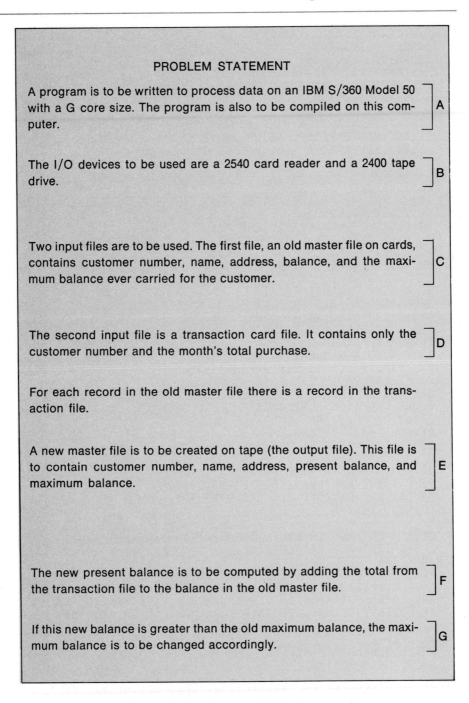

PROBLEM STATEMENT

A program is to be written to process data on an IBM S/360 Model 50 with a G core size. The program is also to be compiled on this computer. **A**

The I/O devices to be used are a 2540 card reader and a 2400 tape drive. **B**

Two input files are to be used. The first file, an old master file on cards, contains customer number, name, address, balance, and the maximum balance ever carried for the customer. **C**

The second input file is a transaction card file. It contains only the customer number and the month's total purchase. **D**

For each record in the old master file there is a record in the transaction file.

A new master file is to be created on tape (the output file). This file is to contain customer number, name, address, present balance, and maximum balance. **E**

The new present balance is to be computed by adding the total from the transaction file to the balance in the old master file. **F**

If this new balance is greater than the old maximum balance, the maximum balance is to be changed accordingly. **G**

Figure 5–10. Sample COBOL Programs.

```
       SEQUENCE  C
       (PAGE) (SERIAL) O A    B
        1  3 4   6 7 8    12  16  20  24  28  32  36  40  44  48  52  56  60  64  68  72
          100    IDENTIFICATION DIVISION.
          101    PROGRAM-ID. LESSON-1-EXAMPLE.
          102    ENVIRONMENT DIVISION.
          103    CONFIGURATION SECTION.
   A      104    SOURCE-COMPUTER. IBM-360-G50.
          105    OBJECT-COMPUTER. IBM-360-G50.
          106    INPUT-OUTPUT SECTION.
          107    FILE-CONTROL.
          108        SELECT TRANSACTION-FILE ASSIGN TO UT-2400-S-TAPE1.
   B      109        SELECT MASTER-FILE ASSIGN TO UR-2540R-S-CARD1.
          110        SELECT NEW-MASTER-FILE ASSIGN TO UT-2400-S-TAPE2.
          111    DATA DIVISION.
          112    FILE SECTION.
          113    FD  MASTER-FILE
          114        LABEL RECORDS ARE OMITTED.
          115    01  CUSTOMER-RECORD.
          116        02 CUSTOMER-NUMBER PICTURE X(6).
   C      117        02 NAME PICTURE X(20).
          118        02 HOME-ADDRESS PICTURE X(30).
          119        02 OLD-BALANCE PICTURE 9999V99.
          120        02 MAXIMUM-BALANCE PICTURE 9999V99.
          121        02 FILLER PICTURE X(12).
          122    FD  TRANSACTION-FILE
          123        BLOCK CONTAINS 10 RECORDS,
          124        LABEL RECORDS ARE STANDARD.
   D      201    01  PURCHASE-RECORD.
          202        02 CUSTOMER-NUMBER-T PICTURE X(6).
          203        02 TOTAL-PURCHASE PICTURE 9999V99.
          204        02 FILLER PICTURE X(68).
          205    FD  NEW-MASTER-FILE
          206        BLOCK CONTAINS 4 RECORDS
          207        LABEL RECORDS ARE STANDARD.
          208    01  NEW-CUSTOMER-RECORD.
   E      209        02 CUSTOMER-NUMBER PICTURE X(6).
          210        02 NAME PICTURE X(20).
          211        02 HOME-ADDRESS PICTURE X(30).
          212        02 PRESENT-BALANCE PICTURE 99999V99.
          213        02 MAXIMUM-BALANCE PICTURE 99999V99.
          214    PROCEDURE DIVISION.
          215    BEGIN.
          216        OPEN INPUT MASTER-FILE, TRANSACTION-FILE,
          217            OUTPUT NEW-MASTER-FILE.
          218    MAIN-ROUTINE.
          219        READ MASTER-FILE AT END GO TO EOJ.
   F      220        MOVE CORRESPONDING CUSTOMER-RECORD TO NEW-CUSTOMER-RECORD.
          221        ADD TOTAL-PURCHASE TO OLD-BALANCE GIVING PRESENT-BALANCE.
          222        IF PRESENT-BALANCE GREATER THAN MAXIMUM-BALANCE OF
   G      223            NEW-CUSTOMER-RECORD COMPUTE MAXIMUM-BALANCE OF
          224            NEW-CUSTOMER-RECORD = PRESENT-BALANCE.
          301        WRITE NEW-MASTER-RECORD.
          302        GO TO MAIN-ROUTINE.
          303    EOJ.
          304        CLOSE MASTER-FILE, TRANSACTION-FILE, NEW-MASTER-FILE.
          305        STOP RUN.
```

Figure 5–10. Sample COBOL Programs—Continued.

Environment Division would have to be modified or even replaced to make the source program compatible to the new computer.

The Environment Division describes the hardware features of the source as well as the object computer. Each data file to be used in the program must be assigned to an input or output device. If special input or output techniques are to be used in the program, they have to be specified in this division. Any special-names assigned to hardware devices must be stipulated here.

Data Division

The Data Division describes the formats and the detailed characteristics of the input and output data to be processed by the object program. The programmer attaches unique names to the files, the records within the files, and the items within the records. All files that are named in the Environment Division must be described therein.

In addition to the file and record descriptions of data, work areas and constants to be used in the program must be described in the Working-Storage Section of the division.

Entries in this division will describe how the items are grouped and organized into records to be used in the processing. Information, such as the type of data and usage of the data, will be found in the division.

The Environment Division describes the computer upon which the source program will be compiled and the computer that will be used to execute the object program, the Data Division describes the characteristics of the data, and the Procedure Division will describe the logical steps necessary to process the data.

Procedure Division

The Procedure Division specifies the actions expected of the object program to process the data to achieve the desired outputs. The division indicates the sequential order of the processing steps and also any alternate paths of actions where necessitated by decisions encountered during the processing.

This division is usually written from the program flowchart. The names of the data described in the Data Division are used to write sentences, employing program verbs to direct the computer to some action. The main types of action that may be specified are input and output, arithmetic, data transmission, and sequence control. All sentences are imperative even though they may be preceded by IF, since they direct the computer to perform some action.

Examples of Program Verbs

Input and output	OPEN, READ, WRITE, CLOSE, ACCEPT, DISPLAY
Arithmetic	ADD, SUBTRACT, MULTIPLY, DIVIDE, COMPUTE
Data Transmission	MOVE, EXAMINE
Sequence Control	GO TO, PERFORM, ALTER, STOP

These program verbs and other verbs are explained later in the text with the formats for each.

Exercises

Write your answers in the spaces provided.

1. The _____ is written by a programmer on a COBOL Program Sheet Coding form.
2. Each line of the coding form must be punched on a _____.
3. _____ in sequence numbers should be allowed for the possible insertion of additional instructions.
4. The use of sequence numbers is _____ and has no effect on the object program.
5. The compiler will check the _____ of the program instructions.
6. A coded statement may not extend beyond column _____ of the coding form.
7. If a statement must be continued on a succeeding line, it must begin at the _____ margin.
8. A _____ in column _____ is used when a statement must be continued on a succeeding line.
9. The continuation indicator is used when it is necessary to _____, _____, or _____.
10. The A margin begins at column _____ and continues through column _____.
11. A _____ is assumed to appear in the column following column _____ unless a _____ in column _____ appears on the succeeding line.
12. A _____, _____, or _____ header must begin at the _____ margin followed by a _____ and a _____.

13. Level numbers _____ and _____ are required to begin at the A margin.

14. An entry that is required to start at the _____ margin must begin on a new line.

15. Identification codes are punched in columns _____ through _____ and are particularly useful to keep programs separate from each other.

16. A _____ is composed of a series of sections.

17. A section is composed of a series of _____.

18. The divisions of COBOL in sequence are _____, _____, _____ and _____.

19. The _____ and _____ divisions always contain sections with _____ names.

20. All divisions except the _____ division contain paragraphs.

21. The _____ header need not appear on a line by itself.

22. Entries consist of a series of _____ terminated by a _____ and a _____.

23. The _____ division must appear first at compile time.

24. The _____ paragraph of the Identification Division usually contains a brief description of the purpose of the program.

25. The Environment Division is the one division that is _____ dependent since it contains the necessary information about the _____ that will be used to _____ and _____ the source program.

26. The Data Division describes the _____ and detailed characteristics of the _____ and _____ data to be processed by the _____ program.

27. The Procedure Division specifies the _____ expected of the _____ program to _____ the data and to achieve the _____ results.

28. _____ verbs direct the computer to perform some action at _____ time.

Answers

1. SOURCE PROGRAM
2. SEPARATE CARD
3. AMPLE ROOM
4. OPTIONAL
5. SEQUENCE
6. 72
7. B
8. HYPHEN, 7

9. SPLIT A WORD, CONTINUE A NUMERIC LITERAL, CONTINUE A NON NUMERIC LITERAL
10. 8, 11
11. BLANK, 72, HYPHEN, 7
12. DIVISION, SECTION, PARAGRAPH, A, PERIOD, SPACE
13. 01, 77

14. A

15. 73 , 80

16. DIVISION

17. PARAGRAPHS

18. IDENTIFICATION, ENVIRON-
    MENT, DATA, PROCEDURE

19. ENVIRONMENT, DATA, FIXED

20. DATA

21. PARAGRAPH

22. STATEMENTS, PERIOD,
    SPACE

23. IDENTIFICATION

24. REMARKS

25. MACHINE, EQUIPMENT,
    COMPILE, EXECUTE

26. FORMATS, INPUT, OUTPUT,
    OBJECT

27. ACTIONS, OBJECT, PROCESS,
    DESIRED

28. PROGRAM, EXECUTE

Questions for Review

1. Explain the purpose and use of a COBOL program coding sheet.
2. What is the importance of the sequence number on a programming coding sheet?
3. What is the purpose of the continuation indicator? What are some of its principal uses?
4. List the rules for A and B margin entries.
5. Explain the major program structure of COBOL.
6. What are the main functions of each of the COBOL divisions?
7. What are the four types of program verbs? Give examples of each.

Problems

1. *Identify the purposes and uses of numbered items.*

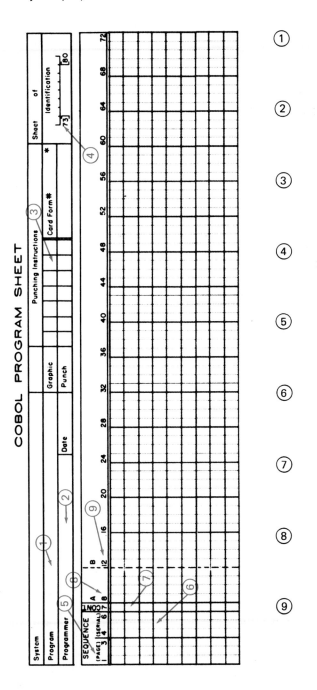

1
2
3
4
5
6
7
8
9

2.

SEQUENCE			

```
          MULTIPLY AMOUNT OF CLIENT-PURCHASES BY TRADE-DISCOUNT, GIVING
```

Which of the lines below shows a correct way of completing this entry?

```
a.        -REDUCTION.
b.         REDUCTION.
c.         REDUCTION.
d.     -       REDUCTION.
```

3. *Number the following in their proper sequence of appearance in a COBOL source program.*

   _____ a. DATA DIVISION.
   _____ b. ENVIRONMENT DIVISION.
   _____ c. PROCEDURE DIVISION.
   _____ d. IDENTIFICATION DIVISION.

4. *Number the following in an ascending to descending order.*

   _____ a. Data-name.
   _____ b. Division headers.
   _____ c. Paragraph-name.
   _____ d. Section-name.

5. *Match each item with its description.*

   _____ 1. Procedure Division

   _____ 2. Identification Division

   _____ 3. Data Division

   _____ 4. Environment Division

   A. Describes the computer to be used and the hardware features to be used in the program.

   B. Describes the characteristics of the information to be processed.

   C. Identifies the program to the computer.

   D. Specifies the logical steps necessary to process the data.

6. *Identify each of the following types of program verbs as INPUT/OUTPUT, ARITHMETIC, DATA TRANSMISSION or SEQUENCE CONTROL.*

_____ GO TO
_____ MOVE
_____ OPEN
_____ ACCEPT
_____ MULTIPLY
_____ EXAMINE
_____ ALTER
_____ DISPLAY
_____ COMPUTE
_____ READ
_____ STOP
_____ SUBTRACT
_____ PERFORM

6

Identification and Environment Divisions

IDENTIFICATION DIVISION

The Identification Division is the first and simplest of all four divisions to write and must be included in every COBOL program.

Function. The function of the Identification Division is to identify both the source program and the resultant output listing. In addition, the user may include any other information that may be considered vital to his program, such as the date the program was written, the date of the compiliation of the source program, etc.

```
IDENTIFICATION DIVISION.

PROGRAM-ID.  program-name.
[AUTHOR.  [comment-entry]...]
[INSTALLATION.  [comment-entry]...]
[DATE-WRITTEN.  [comment-entry]...]
[DATE-COMPILED.  [comment-entry]...]
[SECURITY.  [comment-entry]...]
[REMARKS.  [comment-entry]...]
```

Figure 6–1. Identification Division Format.

The required entries are:

1. Division Header—Identification Division.
2. Program-ID.
3. Program-Name. The program-name is used to identify the object name to the control program and must be given in the first paragraph.

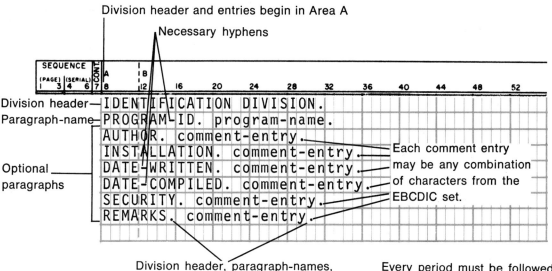

Figure 6–2. Guide for Coding Identification Division Entries.

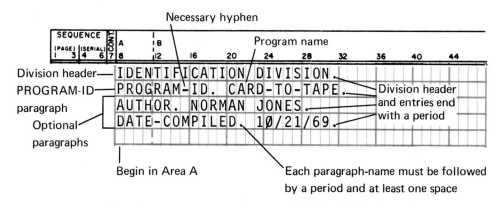

Figure 6–3. Format Requirements for Sample Identification Entries.

```
IDENTIFICATION DIVISION.
PROGRAM-ID.
    EXPENSES.
AUTHOR.
    CHARLES BROWN.
INSTALLATION.
    DYNAMIC DATA DEVICES, INC.
DATE-WRITTEN.
    NOVEMBER 9, 1972.
DATE-COMPILED.
    NOVEMBER 10, 1972.
SECURITY.
    COMPANY-CONFIDENTIAL; AVAILABLE TO
    AUTHORIZED PERSONNEL ONLY.
REMARKS.
    PRODUCES A WEEKLY LISTING OF ALL
    OPERATING EXPENSES, BY DEPARTMENT.
```

Figure 6–4. Example—Identification Division.

Rules for the Formation of the Program-Name are
1. The name *must not* be enclosed in quotation marks.
2. The name must conform to the rules for the formation of a procedure-name, such as

   a. A unique data-name.
   b. No special characters permitted.
   c. No reserved words, etc.

The other paragraphs are optional and may be included at the user's option. The six additional fixed named paragraphs are AUTHOR, INSTALLATION, DATE-WRITTEN, DATE-COMPILED, SECURITY, and REMARKS. These optional paragraphs, if used, must be presented in the order shown in the format. The sentences may contain any numerals, letters, blanks, special characters, or reserved words organized to conform to sentence and paragraph structure.

The programmer has complete freedom in what he chooses to write in each of these optional paragraphs. Entries in the REMARKS paragraph usually stipulate the purpose and what the program is to accomplish.

(*Note:* Regardless of what date is placed in the DATE-COMPILED paragraph, the actual compilation date will be printed on the source program listing.)

> ENVIRONMENT DIVISION.
> CONFIGURATION SECTION.
> SOURCE-COMPUTER paragraph
> OBJECT-COMPUTER paragraph
> [SPECIAL-NAMES paragraph]
> [INPUT-OUTPUT SECTION.
> FILE-CONTROL paragraph
> [I-O-CONTROL paragraph]]

Figure 6–5.   Environment Division Format.

ENVIRONMENT DIVISION

All aspects of a data processing problem that depend upon the physical characteristics of a specific computer are expressed in the Environment Division. This division is the one division of COBOL that is machine dependent, and the programmer must familiarize himself with the characteristics and special name of the machine upon which the particular source program is to be run. Any changes in a computer requires many changes in this division. A link is provided between the logical concept of the files and the physical aspects of the devices upon which the files will be processed and stored.

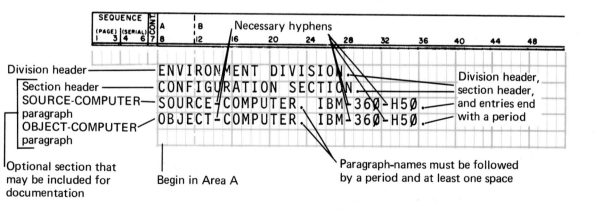

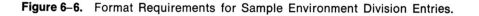

Figure 6–6.   Format Requirements for Sample Environment Division Entries.

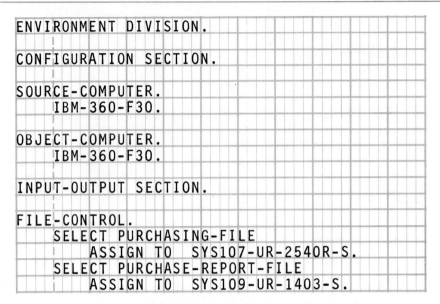

```
ENVIRONMENT DIVISION.

CONFIGURATION SECTION.

SOURCE-COMPUTER.
    IBM-360-F30.

OBJECT-COMPUTER.
    IBM-360-F30.

INPUT-OUTPUT SECTION.

FILE-CONTROL.
    SELECT PURCHASING-FILE
        ASSIGN TO  SYS107-UR-2540R-S.
    SELECT PURCHASE-REPORT-FILE
        ASSIGN TO  SYS109-UR-1403-S.
```

Figure 6-7. Example—Environment Division Entries.

Function. The function of the Environment Division is to specify the configuration of the computer that will be used to compile the source program and also the configuration of the computer that will execute the object program. In addition, all input and output files will be assigned to individual hardware devices. Any special input and output techniques that will be used in the processing of data will be defined here.

The Environment Division must be included in every COBOL source program. The Environment Division must begin at the A margin with the heading ENVIRONMENT DIVISION followed by a period on a line by itself.

The Environment Division is divided into two sections, the Configuration Section and the Input-Output Section. The sections and paragraphs, when used, must appear in the sequence as shown in the format.

Configuration Section

The Configuration Section specifies the overall characteristics of the computer involved in the compilation and execution of a COBOL program. The section is divided into three paragraphs: SOURCE-COMPUTER, OBJECT-COMPUTER, and the SPECIAL-NAMES paragraphs.

The SOURCE-COMPUTER paragraph describes the computer upon which the compilation of the source program is to take place.

Figure 6–8. Configuration Section—Format.

CONFIGURATION SECTION.

SOURCE-COMPUTER. source-computer-entry

OBJECT-COMPUTER. object-computer-entry

[SPECIAL-NAMES. special-names-entry]

Figure 6–9. Example— Configuration Section.

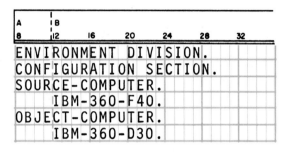

Division header, section header, and paragraph names begin in Area A

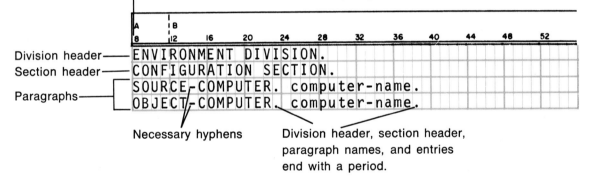

Division header ── ENVIRONMENT DIVISION.
Section header ── CONFIGURATION SECTION.
Paragraphs ── SOURCE-COMPUTER. computer-name.
OBJECT-COMPUTER. computer-name.

Necessary hyphens   Division header, section header, paragraph names, and entries end with a period.

Core Size for Source and Object Computer Paragraphs

F   64k
G   128k
H   256k*
I   512k

* minimum for Model 65

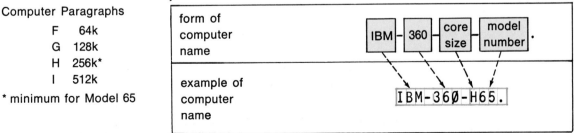

form of computer name	IBM – 360 – core size – model number .
example of computer name	IBM-360-H65.

Figure 6–10. Guide for Coding Environment Division-Configuration Section Entries.

The OBJECT-COMPUTER paragraph describes the computer upon which the object compiled program is to be executed. Also the specifications as to size and range of main storage to be used may be stipulated.

In both the SOURCE-COMPUTER and the OBJECT-COMPUTER paragraphs, the computer name must include the model number and conform to the rules for COBOL names.

The SPECIAL-NAMES paragraph is used to equate user specified mnemonic-names with function-names used by the compiler. This paragraph may also be used to exchange the functions of the comma and period in PICTURE character strings and numeric literals. If a currency symbol other than the $ is used in a PICTURE clause, the user must specify the currency substitute character in this paragraph. (Discussed in greater detail later in text.)

The SOURCE-COMPUTER and the OBJECT-COMPUTER paragraphs are required in all COBOL programs, while the SPECIAL-NAMES paragraph is optional and is included only when necessary in the program.

Input-Output Section

The Input-Output Section must be included in any COBOL source program if there are any input and ouput files required. As most programs involve the processing of files, this section is required in most programs.

The Input-Output Section is concerned with the definition of the input and output devices as well as the most efficient method of handling data between the devices and the object program.

This section is divided into two paragraphs, FILE-CONTROL and I-O-CONTROL paragraph. The individual clauses that comprise these paragraphs may appear in any sequence within their respective sentences or paragraphs but must begin at the B margin.

File-Control Paragraph

The File-Control paragraph names and associates files with external media. The names of files given in the file description entries in the Data Division are assigned to input/output devices. There is a relationship between the file entries in the three divisions. The Data Division entries specify the characteristics and the structure of the data within these files. The Procedure Division will specify the READ and WRITE entries for these files. The input/output device that will be used to read or write will be determined by the Environment Division entry which names the input/output devices assigned to the particular file.

The coding guide shows column positions A (8), B (12), 16, 20, 24, 28, 32, 36, 40, 44, 48, 52, 56, 60 with "Necessary hyphens" noted.

Division header ——— ENVIRONMENT DIVISION.   Headers, paragraph names,
Section header ——— CONFIGURATION SECTION.   and entries end with a period.
SOURCE-COMPUTER. computer-name.
Paragraphs ——— OBJECT-COMPUTER. computer-name.
(optional) SPECIAL-NAMES.
        system-name IS mnemonic-name.
Section header ——— INPUT-OUTPUT SECTION.
Paragraph name ——— FILE-CONTROL.
Statement to link ——— SELECT file-name ASSIGN TO system-name.
file name to device
(as many as
necessary)

SELECT clause is contained in Area B

Division header, section headers, and
paragraph names begin in Area A

More than one space is allowed whenever a space is indicated.

Figure 6–11. Guide for Coding Environment Division-Configuration and Input-
Output Section Entries.

Select Clause

The Select clause is used to name files within a COBOL source program.
The Select entry must begin with the word SELECT followed by the file-name,
and must be given for each file referred to by the COBOL source program. A
separate SELECT clause is required for each file name in the Data Division.

File-Name. The unique name of the file assigned in the file description
entry in the Data Division of the source program. This name will also be used
in entries in the Procedure Division.

Optional. A key word that may be specified only for input files accessed
sequentially that may not be present each time the object program is executed.
If this option is used and the file is not present at object time, the first READ
statement causes the control to be passed to the imperative statement following
the key words AT END.

Figure 6–12. Select Clause
Format.

```
SELECT [OPTIONAL] file-name
```

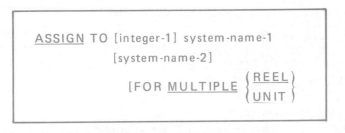

Figure 6–13. Assign Clause Format.

Assign Clause

The Assign clause is used to assign files to external media.

Integer. Indicates the number of input/output devices that may be used for a given medium assigned to file-name. Since the number of units is automatically assigned by the operating system, this integer is rarely used.

System Name. Identifies the device class, the particular input/output device, the organization of the data upon the device and the external name of the file. The external name is a 1-to-8-character field by which the file is known to the system.

Device Class. Two character field that specifies the particular category of devices to be used. Each file must be assigned to a device class.

DA. The *Direct-Access* class is composed of mass storage devices that can read and write records randomly—disks, drums, data cell devices. The same devices may also appear in the Utility class.

UT. The *Utility* class is composed of devices that can read and write records sequentially. They include such devices as magnetic tape, disk, drum, and data cells.

UR. The *Unit-Record* class is composed of devices that can read and provide data, such as printers and card read/punch devices.

(*Note:* Files that are assigned to UT or UR device class must have a standard sequential organization, and records can only be accessed sequentially. Files that are assigned to DA devices may have both standard sequential or direct organization. When the organization is specified as direct, access may be either sequential or random.)

Device Number. A four- or five-character field used to specify a particular device within a device class. If device independence is specified, the device class must be UT; therefore, no device number is given, and no END-OF-PAGE class is associated with the file. At execution time, such a file may be assigned to any device including unit record devices.

DOS ASSIGN Clause Guide‡

Device name	Class indicator*	Device number	Organization indicator†
card reader	UR	2540R	S
card punch	UR	2540P	S
printer	UR	1403	S
tape drive	UT	2400	S
disk drive	UT or DA	2311, 2314	S I
data cell	UT or DA	2321	S I

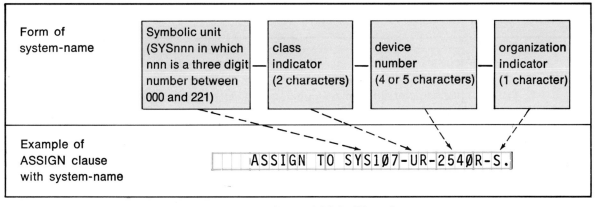

* Class indicator UR stands for Unit-Record, UT for Utility, and DA for Direct Access.
† Organization indicator S stands for Sequential and I for Indexed sequential.
‡ This Guide is applicable to both the complete and subset ANS COBOL compilers.

Figure 6–14.   IBM-360 DOS Assign Clause Guide.

The allowable device numbers for the IBM 360 and 370 computers are:

Direct-Access	DA	2301, 2302, 2303, 2311, 2314, 2321.
Utility	UT	2301, 2302, 2311, 2314, 2321, 2340, 2400.
Unit-Record	UR	1403, 1404, 1442R, 1442P, 1443, 1445, 2501, 2520P, 2520R, 2540P, 2540R. (R indicates reader; P indicates punch)

OS ASSIGN Clause Guide

Device name	Class indicator*		Device number	Organization indicator†
card reader	UR		254OR	S
card punch	UR		254OP	S
printer	UR		1403	S
tape drive	UT		2400	S
disk drive	UT or		2302, 2311, 2314	S
	DA			I
drum	UT or		2301	S
	DA		2301, 2303	I
data cell	UT or		2321	S
	DA			I

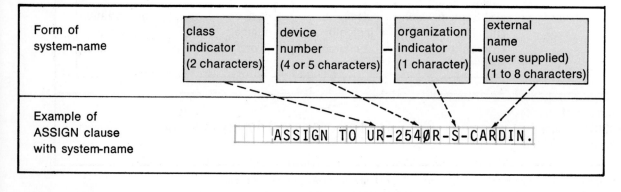

*Class indicator UR stands for Unit-Record, UT for Utility, and DA for Direct Access.
†Organization indicator S stands for Sequential and I for Indexed sequential.

Figure 6–15.   IBM-360 OS Assign Clause Guide.

Organization. A one character field indicating the type of organization used for a particular file.

S. Is used for files with standard sequential organization. When standard sequential organization is specified, the logical records of a file are positioned and read sequentially, in the order in which they were created. If the RE-VERSED option is specified, these records within these files may be sequentially reversed for read and write operations. The type *S* organization must be used for magnetic tape or unit record files and may be used for files assigned to direct-access (mass storage) devices. No actual keys are associated with records on a sequentially organized file.

D. Is used for files with direct organization. A direct-organization file specifies that the records are organized in a random sequence. The addressing scheme is determined by the programmer whereby the positioning of the logical records within the file is determined by keys supplied by the actual user in the Environment Division. The ACTUAL KEY is used to locate records within the file.

Name. The external file-name by which the file is known to the control program. The name may consist of one to eight characters.

I-O-Control Paragraph

The I-O-Control paragraph defines special control techniques to be used in the object program. It may specify certain conditions in a object program, such as which checkpoints are to be established, which storage areas to be shared by different files, the location of files on multiple-file reels, and the optimization techniques.

If special techniques or conditions need be defined in the program, the I-O-Control paragraph is used; otherwise, the entire paragraph and its associated clauses may be omitted.

The features of the I-O-Control paragraph and other features of the Environment Division are discussed later in the text.

Exercises

Write your answers in the space provided. The following relate to the IDENTI-FICATION DIVISION.

1. The Identification Division is the _____ and _____ of all four divisions to write.
2. This division must be included in every COBOL program and is used to identify both the _____ and the resultant _____.
3. The required entries are _____, _____, and _____.
4. The program name must not be enclosed in _____ and must conform to the rules for the formation of a _____.
5. The six optional fixed named paragraphs in order of sequence are _____, _____, _____, _____, _____, and _____.
6. The entries in the REMARKS paragraph usually stipulates the _____.

The following relate to the ENVIRONMENT DIVISION.

7. This division is the one division of COBOL that is _____ dependent.

8. The programmer must familiarize himself with the _____ and _____ names of the machine upon which the particular _____ is to be run.

9. A link is provided between the _____ aspects of the files and the _____ characteristics of the devices upon which the files will be processed and stored.

10. The configuration of the computer that will be used to _____ the object program must be specified in this division.

11. All input and output files must be assigned to individual _____ devices.

12. The Environment Division is divided into _____ sections.

13. The _____ section specifies the overall characteristics of the computer involved in the compiliation and execution of a COBOL program.

14. The _____ paragraph is used to equate user specified _____ names with _____ names used by the compiler.

15. The Input-Output section is concerned with the definitions of the _____ _____ and _____ devices as well as the most efficient method of handling data between the _____ and the _____ program.

16. The File-Control paragraph _____ and _____ files with external media.

17. The _____ clause names _____ within a COBOL source program.

18. The Assign clause assigns _____ to _____.

19. The System-Name identifies the _____, the particular _____ devices, the _____ of the data and the _____ name of the file.

20. The I-O-Control paragraph specifies specific _____ to be used in the object program.

Answers

1. FIRST, SHORTEST
2. SOURCE PROGRAM, OUTPUT LISTING
3. DIVISION HEADER, PROGRAM-ID, PROGRAM NAME
4. QUOTATION MARKS, PRO-CEDURE-NAME

5. AUTHOR, INSTALLATION, DATE-WRITTEN, DATE-COM-PILED, SECURITY, REMARKS
6. PURPOSE OF THE PROGRAM
7. MACHINE
8. CHARACTERISTICS, SPECIAL, SOURCE PROGRAM

9. LOGICAL, PHYSICAL

10. COMPILE

11. HARDWARE

12. TWO

13. CONFIGURATION

14. SPECIAL-NAMES, MNEMONIC, FUNCTION

15. INPUT, OUTPUT, DEVICES, OBJECT

16. NAMES, ASSOCIATES

17. SELECT, FILES

18. FILES, EXTERNAL MEDIA

19. DEVICE-CLASS, INPUT/OUTPUT, ORGANIZATION, EXTERNAL

20. CONTROL TECHNIQUES

Questions for Review

1. What is the function of the Identification Division?
2. What are the required entries in the Identification Division?
3. What is the importance of the REMARKS paragraph in the Identification Division?
4. What are the six additional optional paragraphs in sequence that may be included in the Identification Division?
5. What is the importance of the Environment Division and what is its main function?
6. What are the sections of the Environment Division and what is the main function of each of these sections?
7. What are the main functions of the Select and Assign clauses?
8. What are the components of the System-Name and what is the function of each of its segments?
9. What is the purpose of the I-O-Control paragraph and what is it customarily used for?

Problems

1. *In the following entries, which one is correctly written?*
   a. IDENTIFICATION DIVISION.
      PROGRAM-ID.SALES-ANALYSIS.
   b. IDENTIFICATION DIVISION
      PROGRAM-ID. CARD-TO-TAPE.
   c. IDENTIFICATION DIVISION.
      PROGRAM-ID. PAYROLL-MASTER.

2. *Which of the following PROGRAM-ID names is written correctly?*

   a. DATA
   b. 'INVENTORY-CONTROL-REPORT'
   c. INVENTORY-MASTER
   d. PAYROLL*

3. *In the following list of Identification Division paragraph names, which one is incorrect?*

   AUTHOR, TITLE, INSTALLATION, SECURITY, REMARKS

4. *Match each item with its proper paragraph name.*

_____ 1. Program-Id.	A. Non-Military.
_____ 2. Author.	B. May 17 1972.
_____ 3. Date-Written.	C. J Morse.
_____ 4. Date-Compiled.	D. This program calculates payroll.
_____ 5. Installation.	E. Payroll 04.
_____ 6. Security.	F. District Office.
_____ 7. Remarks.	

5. *In the Environment Division, indicate with a check mark which of the following must be written at the A margin.*

   _____ SOURCE-COMPUTER.
   _____ CONFIGURATION SECTION.
   _____ SPECIAL-NAMES.
   _____ SELECT Clause.
   _____ FILE-CONTROL.
   _____ ASSIGN Clause.

6. *Match each item with its proper device class.*

_____ Utility	A. Magnetic disks and data cells.
_____ Unit Record	B. Magnetic tape and magnetic drum.
_____ Direct Access	C. Card Readers, Card Punches and Printers.

7. *Write the Identification Division, using all the required and optional entries for the following:*

   The Acme Manufacturing Company is initiating an inventory control system. You are the programmer assigned to writing the program. The program is restricted to production control personnel and is to be run at the Boston center.

8. *Write the Environment Division for the following systems flowchart. The program will be compiled and executed on an IBM 370 model 155 computer with the following hardware assignments:*

SYS005	1403	Printer
SYS009	2540R	Card Reader
SYS006	2540P	Card Punch
SYS011	2400	Magnetic Tape
SYS012	2400	Magnetic Tape

SYSTEMS FLOWCHART

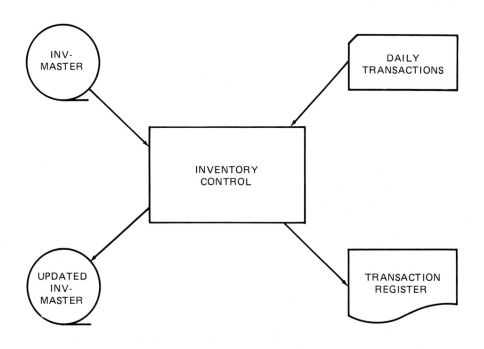

9. *Write the Environment Division for the following systems flowchart using the same hardware assignments as problem 8.*

SYSTEMS FLOWCHART

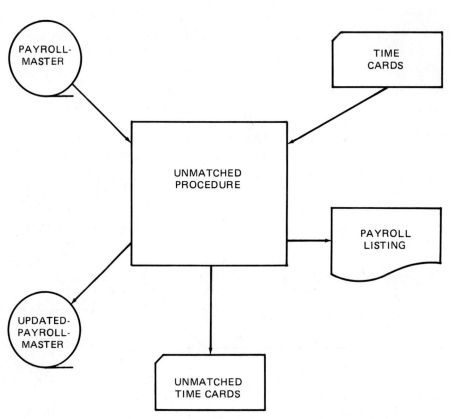

7

Data Division

The Data Division of a COBOL source program describes the characteristics of the information to be processed by the object program. The separation of divisions provides the programmer with flexibility as the Procedure Division is interwoven with the Data Division. The manner in which data is organized and stored has a major effect upon the efficiency of the object program. Data to be processed falls into three categories.

1. The data in the files that are entering or leaving the internal storage areas of the computer.
2. The data in the work areas of the computer that have been developed internally by the program.
3. Constant data that is to be used by the program.

The structure of each record within a file is usually shown with the items described in the sequence in which they appear in the record.

The Data Division begins with the header DATA DIVISION at the A margin followed by a period on a line by itself. *Each of the sections within the Data Division have fixed names.* The sections are followed by the word SECTION and a period, and are on a line by themselves. These sections consist of entries rather than paragraphs. Each entry must contain:

1. A level indicator or level number.
2. A data-name or other name (FILLER).
3. A series of clauses defining the data that may be separated by commas. The clauses may be written in any sequence by the programmer (except the REDEFINES clauses). Each entry must be terminated by a period and a space.

```
DATA DIVISION.
FILE SECTION.
FD   TRANSACTION; BLOCK CONTAINS 25
     RECORDS; LABEL RECORDS ARE STANDARD;
     DATA RECORD IS TRANSACTION-RECORD.
01   TRANSACTION-RECORD.
     02   ACCOUNT-NUMBER, PICTURE X(10).
     02   TRANSACTION-CODE, PICTURE X.
     02   AMOUNT, PICTURE 9(6)V99.
WORKING-STORAGE SECTION.
77   PREVIOUS-NUMBER, PICTURE X(10).
01   MESSAGE.
     02   ACCOUNT, PICTURE X(10).
     02   FILLER, PICTURE XX, VALUE SPACE.
     02   TOTAL, PICTURE $ZZZ, ZZZ.99.
     02   FILLER, PICTURE XX, VALUE SPACE.
     02   COMMENTS, PICTURE X(30).
```

Figure 7–1. Example—
Data Division.

Data in COBOL source programs are referred to by various names. They are:

Item. An item is considered a field and is an area used to contain a particular type of information.

Elementary Item. The smallest item available that is not divided into smaller units.

Group Item. A larger item that is composed of a named sequence of one or more elementary items. A referral to a group item applies to the entire area of elementary items.

Independent Item. An elementary item appearing in the Working-Storage Section of the Data Division that is not a record or a part of a record. These items are usually used as work areas or to contain constant data.

Data Record. The data record is usually considered to be the group item comprising several related items. It is also referred to as the "logical record." The "logical record" is normally the unit that each program processes in input and output operations.

File. A file is composed of a series of related data records. The data records may have the same or varying lengths.

Block. A block is referred to as the "physical record" consisting of a series of "logical records." When data is stored on magnetic tape or direct-access devices, the logical record are grouped in blocks. Each read or write operation may transfer an entire block of data to or from main storage at one time to or from an input/output device. Each logical record within the block is then processed separately.

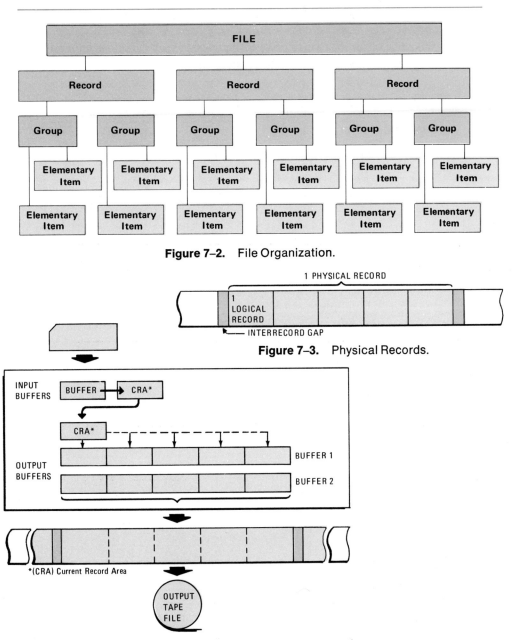

Figure 7–2.   File Organization.

1 PHYSICAL RECORD

1 LOGICAL RECORD

INTERRECORD GAP

Figure 7–3.   Physical Records.

INPUT BUFFERS

BUFFER → CRA*

CRA*

OUTPUT BUFFERS

BUFFER 1

BUFFER 2

*(CRA) Current Record Area

OUTPUT TAPE FILE

Figure 7–4.   Physical Record Operation—Input/Output Buffer.

COBOL source language statements provide a means of describing the relationship between physical and logical records. Once this relationship is established, only logical records are made available to the program.

Label Records. Label records are normally used for files that are stored on magnetic tape or direct-access devices. The record usually contains information relative to the file. Card files do not contain any label records.

Figure 7–5.   Label Records.

ORGANIZATION

The Data Division is divided into three fixed sections: File, Working-Storage, and Report. The File Section defines the contents of the data files that are stored on the external medium. The Working-Storage Section describes record or noncontiguous data items which are not part of the external data files but which are developed and processed internally, or data items whose values are assigned in the source program and do not change during the execution of the program. Both logical records and noncontiguous items may be specified in the Working-Storage Section. The Report Section describes the content and format of all reports that are generated by the Report Writer Feature. The Report Section is discussed and described in greater detail later in the text.

The sections must appear in the above-mentioned sequence. If the section is not required in the source program, it may be omitted along with its name.

```
DATA DIVISION.
FILE SECTION.
{file description entry
{record description entry }...}...
WORKING-STORAGE SECTION.
[data item description entry]...
[record description entry]...
REPORT SECTION.
{report description entry
{report group description entry }...}...
```

Figure 7–6.   Structure of the Data Division.

```
DATA DIVISION.
FILE SECTION.
FD  file-name-1.
    LABEL RECORDS ARE OMITTED.
Ø1  record-name.
    Ø2 data-name-1 PICTURE picture-of-data-name-1.
    Ø2 data-name-2 PICTURE picture-of-data-name-2.
    ⋮
FD  file-name-2.
    LABEL RECORDS ARE STANDARD.
Ø1  record-name.
    Ø2 data-name-1 PICTURE picture-of-data-name-1.
    Ø2 data-name-2 PICTURE picture-of-data-name-2.
    ⋮
WORKING-STORAGE SECTION.
77  data-name-1 PICTURE picture-of-data-name-1.
⋮
Ø1  record-name-1.
    Ø2 data-name-1 PICTURE picture-of-data-name-1.
    Ø2 data-name-2 PICTURE picture-of-data-name-2.
    ⋮
Ø1  record-name-2.
    Ø2 data-name-1 PICTURE picture-of-data-name-1.
    Ø2 data-name-2 PICTURE picture-of-data-name-2.
    ⋮
```

File description entry

Record description entry

Data description entries (as many as necessary)

Entries to define an input or output area and link it to a file name (as many as necessary)

Independent data description entries (as many as necessary)

Data description entries (as many as necessary)

Record description entries (as many as necessary)

Form of LABEL RECORDS clause required for card and printer files, may be used for tape files

Form of LABEL RECORDS clause required for disk drum, and data-cell files; may be used for tape files

Must follow the File Section

Each entry ends with a period

File name, LABEL RECORDS clause, record names, and level number 02 are contained in Area B

Division header, section headers, FD, and level number 01 begin in Area A

FILE SECTION must precede WORKING-STORAGE SECTION if both are included in a program. Within the Working-Storage Section, any level 77 entries must precede any record description entries.

Figure 7–7. Guide for Coding the Data Division with the File Section and the Working-Storage Section.

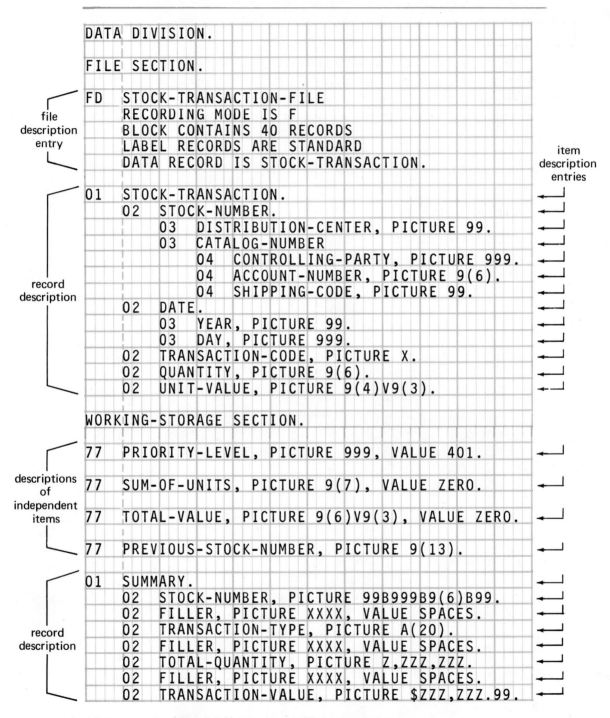

```
DATA DIVISION.

FILE SECTION.

FD   STOCK-TRANSACTION-FILE
     RECORDING MODE IS F
     BLOCK CONTAINS 40 RECORDS
     LABEL RECORDS ARE STANDARD
     DATA RECORD IS STOCK-TRANSACTION.

01   STOCK-TRANSACTION.
     02   STOCK-NUMBER.
          03   DISTRIBUTION-CENTER, PICTURE 99.
          03   CATALOG-NUMBER
               04   CONTROLLING-PARTY, PICTURE 999.
               04   ACCOUNT-NUMBER, PICTURE 9(6).
               04   SHIPPING-CODE, PICTURE 99.
     02   DATE.
          03   YEAR, PICTURE 99.
          03   DAY, PICTURE 999.
     02   TRANSACTION-CODE, PICTURE X.
     02   QUANTITY, PICTURE 9(6).
     02   UNIT-VALUE, PICTURE 9(4)V9(3).

WORKING-STORAGE SECTION.

77   PRIORITY-LEVEL, PICTURE 999, VALUE 401.

77   SUM-OF-UNITS, PICTURE 9(7), VALUE ZERO.

77   TOTAL-VALUE, PICTURE 9(6)V9(3), VALUE ZERO.

77   PREVIOUS-STOCK-NUMBER, PICTURE 9(13).

01   SUMMARY.
     02   STOCK-NUMBER, PICTURE 99B999B9(6)B99.
     02   FILLER, PICTURE XXXX, VALUE SPACES.
     02   TRANSACTION-TYPE, PICTURE A(20).
     02   FILLER, PICTURE XXXX, VALUE SPACES.
     02   TOTAL-QUANTITY, PICTURE Z,ZZZ,ZZZ.
     02   FILLER, PICTURE XXXX, VALUE SPACES.
     02   TRANSACTION-VALUE, PICTURE $ZZZ,ZZZ.99.
```

file description entry

item description entries

record description

descriptions of independent items

record description

Figure 7–8.   Example—Data Division Entries.

FILE SECTION

Every program that processes input or output files is required to have a File Section. Since most programs employ files in the processing, a File Section appears in most programs. The File Section describes the characteristics of the file, the overall organization of the file, and the record descriptions of the data contained in these files.

For every file named in the SELECT clause in the Environment Division, a file description entry must appear in the Data Division.

File Description Entry

The file description entry describes:
1. The name of the file.
2. How the information is recorded.
3. The size of the blocks and records in the file.
4. Information about the label records.
5. The names of the data records within the file.

The file description entry consists of a level indicator (FD) followed by the file-name, followed by a series of independent clauses. The entry is terminated by a period.

Format   FD   file-name

[RECORDING MODE IS   mode]

[BLOCK CONTAINS integer-1 {CHARACTERS} {RECORDS}]

[RECORD CONTAINS [integer-2 TO] integer-3 CHARACTERS]

{LABEL RECORD IS   } {STANDARD }
{LABEL RECORDS ARE} {OMITTED }
                    {data-name }

[VALUE OF Clause]

{DATA RECORD IS   }
{DATA RECORDS ARE} record-name . . .

Figure 7-9. Format—File Description.

```
FD  OPINION-SURVEY,
    RECORDING MODE IS V,
    BLOCK CONTAINS 5 RECORDS,
    RECORD CONTAINS 120 TO 200
        CHARACTERS,
    LABEL RECORDS ARE STANDARD,
    DATA RECORD IS RESPONSE.
```

Figure 7-10. Example—File Description Entry.

Level Indicator

The file description entry always begins with the level indicator "FD" which is a reserved word. The indicator must be written at the A margin.

File-Name

The file-name always follows the level indicator. The name is supplied by the programmer and must be the same as stipulated in the SELECT clause in the Environment Division. The name must begin at the B margin.

The clauses that follow the name of the file are optional in many cases, and the order of their appearance is insignificant to the program.

Block Contains Clause

The Block Contains clause specifies either the number of records in a block or the number of characters in a block. When the number of characters per block is given, the clause specifies the largest number of characters that the longest block in storage will occupy. If both Integer-1 and Integer-2 are shown, they refer to the minimum and maximum size of the physical records respectively.

The Block Contains clause states the number of logical records or characters per physical record. The clause may be omitted when there is only one logical record per block. In all other instances, the clause is required.

$$\text{BLOCK CONTAINS [integer-1 TO] integer-2} \begin{Bmatrix} \text{CHARACTERS} \\ \text{RECORDS} \end{Bmatrix}$$

Figure 7–11. Block Contains Clause Format and Example.

```
BLOCK CONTAINS 20 RECORDS
```

Record Contains Clause

The Record Contains clause specifies the size of the logical records contained in the file. If the record does not range in size, this clause will specify how many characters will appear in the longest record. If the record has a range of record sizes, Integer-1 will indicate the size of the smallest record, and Integer-2 will indicate the size of the largest record.

Whether this clause is included or omitted, the record lengths are determined by the compiler from the record description entries. Since the size of each record is completely defined within the record description entry, this clause is never required.

RECORD CONTAINS [integer-1 TO] integer-2 CHARACTERS

Figure 7–12. Record Contains Clause Format and Example.

RECORD CONTAINS 80 CHARACTERS

Recording Mode Clause

The Recording Mode Clause is used to specify the format of logical records within a file. If the computer has more than one recording mode for data, this clause must be written. The IBM/360 and IBM/370 computers use the following recording modes.

RECORDING MODE IS mode

RECORDING MODE IS F;

Figure 7–13. Recording Mode Clause Format and Example.

F (Fixed Length). F recording mode assumes all records to be of the same length, and each is wholly contained within the block. No length or block length fields are necessary in this mode. The size of all logical records is fixed, and the logical records are not preceded by any control words. When these records are blocked, there is usually more than one record per block. The number of records per block is usually also fixed.

V (Variable Length). V recording mode assumes that records may be either fixed or variable in length and are preceded by a control word that specifies the length of the record. This is the only mode where blocks of two or more variable length records may be handled. Each record contains a control word length field and each block contains a block length field. The control word is not described in any record entry in the Data Division and cannot be referred to by the program.

U (Undefined Length). A U recording mode assumes that all records may be either fixed or variable in length. There are no record or block length fields, and there is only one record per block. Unlike the recording mode V, there are no control words preceding the logical record indicating the size of the record. The COBOL compiler considers the files with recording mode U as containing one record per block. The READ statement in the Procedure Division makes only one block available for processing (one record).

S (Spanned). In the S recording mode, the recording may be fixed or variable and may be larger than the block. If the record is larger than the block, a segment of the record is written in the block and the remainder is stored in the next block or blocks. Only complete records are made available to the user since each segment of a record in a block contains a control word, and each block contains a control word. These control words are automatically provided by the compiler and need no descriptive entries in the Data Division. These words cannot be referenced by the user.

(*Note:* If the Recording Mode clause is omitted, the default option is determined by an algorithm which does not always give V [variable length] recording mode).

Label Records Clause

The Label Records clause specifies whether labels are present and, if present, identifies the labels. Usually, magnetic tape files are labeled at the beginning to identify the file and the tape unit and another label at the end of the file to provide a control to signal the end or indicate if there are more tapes in the file.

The Label Records clause specifies the presence of standard or nonstandard labels in a file or the absence of labels. This clause is required to appear in every file description entry. The clause may indicate that the label records are omitted or standard, or it may give a name for the label record.

Omitted. This option is used where there are no explicit labels for the file or where the existing file labels are nonstandard. The Omitted option is used for files assigned to unit record devices. This option may also be specified with nonstandard labels that the user wishes not to be processed by a label declarative.

Standard. The Standard option is used for labels that exist for a file and have the standard label format for the particular computer.

Data-Name. The Data-Name option indicates either the presence of user labels in addition to the standard labels or the presence of nonstandard labels. Data-Name is a programmer-supplied name of a storage area in which the labels will be processed. Data-Name will be defined in the File Section of the Data Division, where it must be associated with the appropriate FD entry.

$$\text{LABEL} \begin{Bmatrix} \underline{\text{RECORD}} \text{ IS} \\ \underline{\text{RECORDS}} \text{ ARE} \end{Bmatrix} \begin{Bmatrix} \underline{\text{OMITTED}} \\ \underline{\text{STANDARD}} \\ \text{data-name-1 [data-name-2]} \dots \end{Bmatrix}$$

Figure 7–14.   Label Records Clause
Format and Example.

`LABEL RECORDS ARE OMITTED;`

Value Of Clause

The Value Of clause particularizes the description of an item in the label records associated with the file and serves only as documentation. To specify the required value of identifying data items in the label record for the file, the programmer must use the Value Of clause.

VALUE OF data-name-1 IS

$\left\{ \begin{array}{l} \text{literal-1} \\ \text{data-name-2} \end{array} \right\}$

[data-name-3 IS

$\left\{ \begin{array}{l} \text{literal-2} \\ \text{data-name-4} \end{array} \right\}$] . . .

Figure 7–15. Value Of Clause Format and Example.

```
VALUE OF IDENT IS DESC
```

Data Records

The Data Records clause informs the compiler what the name or names of each record or records in a file are. The name of each record is the data-name supplied by the programmer. There must be at least one record in each file so that this clause will appear in every file description entry. The presence of more than one name indicates that the file has more than one data record. Two or more record descriptions may occupy the same storage area for a given file. These records need not have the same description.

Below the file description entry, each record-name must also appear in the level 01 entry in the record description clauses. This Data Records clause is never required in the file description entry.

Report Clause

The Report clause is used in conjunction with the Report Writer Feature. A complete description and use of this clause can be found in the "Report Writer Feature" section.

DATA $\left\{ \begin{array}{l} \underline{\text{RECORD}} \text{ IS} \\ \underline{\text{RECORDS}} \text{ ARE} \end{array} \right\}$ data-name-1 [data-name-2] . . .

Figure 7–16. Data Record Clause Format and Example.

```
DATA RECORDS ARE EXPENSE-DETAIL,
    DEPARTMENT-TOTAL.
```

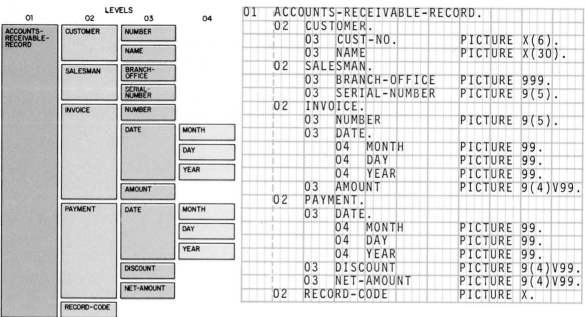

```
01  ACCOUNTS-RECEIVABLE-RECORD.
    02  CUSTOMER.
        03  CUST-NO.              PICTURE X(6).
        03  NAME                  PICTURE X(30).
    02  SALESMAN.
        03  BRANCH-OFFICE         PICTURE 999.
        03  SERIAL-NUMBER         PICTURE 9(5).
    02  INVOICE.
        03  NUMBER                PICTURE 9(5).
        03  DATE.
            04  MONTH             PICTURE 99.
            04  DAY               PICTURE 99.
            04  YEAR              PICTURE 99.
        03  AMOUNT                PICTURE 9(4)V99.
    02  PAYMENT.
        03  DATE.
            04  MONTH             PICTURE 99.
            04  DAY               PICTURE 99.
            04  YEAR              PICTURE 99.
        03  DISCOUNT              PICTURE 9(4)V99.
        03  NET-AMOUNT            PICTURE 9(4)V99.
    02  RECORD-CODE               PICTURE X.
```

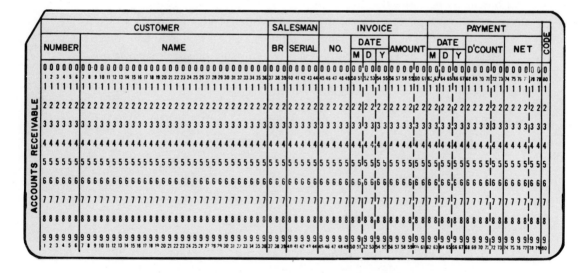

Figure 7–17.   Example Record Description Entries and Levels.

RECORD DESCRIPTION ENTRY

At least one record description entry is found below each file description entry. A record description entry specifies the characteristics of each item in a data record. Every entry must be described in the same order in which the item appears in the record and must indicate if the items are related to each other. Each record description entry consists of a level number, a data-name or FILLER, and a series of clauses followed by a space. The entry must be terminated by a period.

level number
$\begin{Bmatrix} \text{data-name} \\ \underline{\text{FILLER}} \end{Bmatrix}$

[REDEFINES Clause]
[BLANK WHEN ZERO Clause]
[JUSTIFIED Clause]
[OCCURS Clause]
[PICTURE Clause]
[SYNCHRONIZED Clause]
[USAGE Clause]
[VALUE Clause].

Figure 7–18. Record Description Format.

Some records may be divided into smaller units as follows:

1. Each entry must be given a level number beginning with a 01 for the record, and succeeding entries are given higher-level numbers.
2. In subdividing an entry, the level numbers need not be consecutive. Level numbers 01–49 may be used for entries in the File Section.

Elementary Items are not further subdivided. Elementary items may be part of a group, but may be an independent item (not part of a group).

Group Items consist of all items under it until a level number equal to or less than the group number is reached.

Indentation. Item descriptions are usually indented to show the reader the relationship of the items within the group. Indenting is not required. If one entry at a given level is indented, then all similar entries should be indented for consistency.

Level Numbers

Level numbers are used to structure a logical record to satisfy the need to specify subdivision of data record for the purpose of data reference. The system of level numbers shows the organization of elementary and group items.

Level numbers are the first items of a record description entry.

1. Level number 01 and 77 must begin at the A margin followed by data-names and associated clauses beginning at the B margin. All other level numbers may begin at the A or B margin, with the data-names and associated clauses beginning at the B margin.
2. At least one space must separate a level number from its data-name.
3. Separate entries are written for each level number.
4. A single-digit level number may be written as a space followed by a digit or as a zero followed by a digit.

01 Level number indicates that the item is a record. Since records are the most inclusive data items, the level number for a record must be 1 or 01. A record is usually composed of related elementary items, but may be an elementary item itself.

Level numbers 02–49 are used for subdivisions of group record items (not necessarily successive).

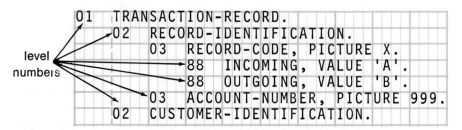

```
01   TRANSACTION-RECORD.
     02   RECORD-IDENTIFICATION.
          03   RECORD-CODE, PICTURE X.
               88   INCOMING, VALUE 'A'.
               88   OUTGOING, VALUE 'B'.
          03   ACCOUNT-NUMBER, PICTURE 999.
     02   CUSTOMER-IDENTIFICATION.
```

level numbers

Figure 7–19.   Example—Level Numbers.

```
01   PLANT-2-PRODUCTS        PICTURE X(200).
WORKING-STORAGE SECTION.
77   WHEELBARROW             PICTURE 9(12)
          VALUE  309463552078.
77   PICKUP-TRUCK            PICTURE 9(12)
          VALUE  790084659302.
```

Figure 7–20.   Example—Level Numbers 01 and 77.

66 Level number is used for names of elementary items or groups described by a RENAMES clause for the purpose of regrouping data items (see RENAMES clause section for an example of the function of the clause).

77 Level number is used to identify an independent elementary item in the Working-Storage Section. The item is not part of any record and is not related to any other item. Level 77 is usually used for noncontiguous items to define a work area or to store constant data.

88 Level number designates a condition entry and is used to assign values to particular items during execution time. A name is furnished to values that the preceding item assumes. It does not reserve any storage area. Level 88 is only associated with elementary items (see Condition-Name clause section for examples of the use of level 88 entries.)

---

88 condition-name <u>VALUE</u> Clause.

Figure 7–21. Condition Name Clause Format and Example.

```
02  MARITAL-STATUS, PICTURE 9.
    88  SINGLE, VALUE 0.
    88  MARRIED, VALUE 1.
    88  DIVORCED, VALUE 2.
    88  WIDOWED, VALUE 3.
```

Data-Name or FILLER

Data-Name. Each item in the record description entry must contain either a data-name or the reserved word FILLER immediately following the level number beginning at the B margin. The data-name permits the programmer to refer to items individually in procedural statements. The data-name must be unique (not a reserved word) or must be properly qualified if not unique. The data-name can be made unique by either spelling the data-name differently from any other data-name used in the program, or through qualification of a nonunique name (see Qualification of Names section).

The data-name refers to the name of the storage area that contains the data, not to a particular value; the item referred to may assume numerous values during the execution of the program.

In addition to the rules mentioned earlier in the Qualification of Names section, the following rules apply to data-names in the Data Division.

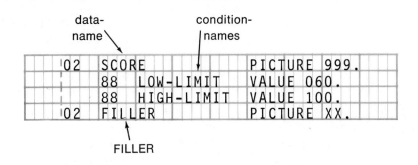

Figure 7–22. Example—Data-Names, Condition-Names and Filler.

1. The highest possible qualifier would be the name of the file; thus it is possible for two records to have the same name.
2. The highest possible qualifier in the Working-Storage Section would be the record-name; thus all record-names in this section must be unique. The data-names for all independent items (level 77) must be unique since they can never be qualified.

FILLER. The reserved word FILLER may be used in place of a data-name. The name cannot be referenced by any procedural statements. Its primary use is in the description of items that will not be referred to because the information contained is not necessary for the processing of the program. FILLER *does not always represent a blank area.*

Independent Clauses

Each record description entry may consist of one or more clauses that provide information about the data item. The most commonly used clauses are the USAGE, PICTURE, and VALUE clauses.

Usage

The USAGE clause describes the form in which the data is stored in main storage of the computer.

Rules for USAGE clauses are
1. The clause may be written at any level.
2. If the clause is written at a group level, it applies to each elementary item within the group.
3. The usage of an elementary item must not contradict the explicit usage of the group item of which the item is a part.

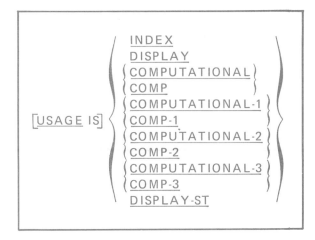

Figure 7–23. Usage Clause Format.

4. The usage of an elementary item is assumed DISPLAY if some other usage clause is not specified at the group or elementary level.

DISPLAY. This option specifies that one character is stored in each byte of the item. This corresponds to the form in which the information is represented for initial card input or for final printed or punched output. If the item is used to store numeric data, the rightmost byte may contain an operational sign in addition to the digit.

COMPUTATIONAL CLAUSE. All items in computational clauses represent values to be used in arithmetic operations, and they must be numeric. If a group USAGE clause is used, it is only the elementary items that have that usage, since the group item cannot be used in computation.

The SYNCHRONIZED clause must be added to all definitions of COMPUTATIONAL clauses that require alignment or the level 01 descriptions that contain such items.

Figure 7–24. Example—
Elementary Usage Clause.

```
01   STOCK-TRANSFER.
     02   STOCK-NUMBER      PICTURE  X(7).
     02   DESCRIPTION       PICTURE  X(15).
     02   UNITS-OF-STOCK    PICTURE  S9(8)
                    COMPUTATIONAL.
```

When the SYNCHRONIZED clause is specified for an item that also contains a REDEFINES clause, the data item that is redefined must have the proper boundary alignment for the data item that REDEFINES it. For example, if the programmer writes:

```
05 A                PICTURE X(4).
05 B   REDEFINES A  PICTURE S9(9) COMP SYNC.
```

he must ensure that A begins on a fullword boundary.

Figure 7-25. Synchronized Clause.

```
  02  PAYMENT, COMPUTATIONAL-3.
      03  AMOUNT-DUE, PICTURE S9(6)V99.
      03  AMOUNT-PAID, PICTURE S9(6)V99.
```

Figure 7–26. Example—Group Usage Clause.

Item	Value	Description	Internal Representation*
External Decimal	−1234	DISPLAY PICTURE 9999	|Z1|Z2|Z3|F4| ⏜ byte
		DISPLAY PICTURE S9999	|Z1|Z2|Z3|D4| ⏜ byte Note that, internally, the Dr, which represents −4, is the same bit configuration as the EBCDIC character M.
Binary	−1234	COMPUTATIONAL PICTURE S9999	|1111|1011|0010|1110| ↑S byte Note that, internally, negative binary numbers appear in two's complement form.
Internal Decimal	+1234	COMPUTATIONAL-3 PICTURE 9999	|01|23|4F| ⏜ byte
		COMPUTATIONAL-3 PICTURE S9999	|01|23|4C| ⏜ byte
External Floating-point	+12.34E+2	DISPLAY PICTURE +99.99E-99	|+|1|2|.|3|4|E|b|0|2| ⏜ byte
Internal Floating-point		COMPUTATIONAL-1	|S|Exponent|Fraction| 0 1 7 8 31
		COMPUTATIONAL-2	|S|Exponent|Fraction| 0 1 7 8 63

*Codes used in this column are as follows:

   Z = zone, equivalent to hexadecimal F, bit configuration 1111

   Hexadecimal numbers are their equivalent meanings are:
      F = non-printing plus sign (treated as an absolute value)
      C = internal equivalent of plus sign, bit configuration 1100
      D = internal equivalent of minus sign, bit configuration 1101

   S = sign position of a numeric field; internally,
         1 in this position means the number is negative
         0 in this position means the number is positive

   b = a blank

Figure 7–27. Internal Representation of Numeric Items.

COMPUTATIONAL. This option is specified for binary data items. One binary digit is stored in each bit of the item, except the leftmost bit of the item, which will contain the operational sign. Such items have the decimal equivalent consisting of the decimal digits 0 through 9 plus the operational sign.

The amount of storage to be occupied by a binary item depends on the number of digits in its PICTURE clause.

Digits in PICTURE clause	Storage Occupied
1 through 4	2 bytes (halfword)
5 through 9	4 bytes (fullword)
10 through 18	8 bytes (2 fullwords not necessarily a doubleword)

The PICTURE clause of an item having COMPUTATIONAL usage may contain only 9s, the operational sign character S, the implied decimal point V and one or more Ps. An operational sign character S must appear in COMPUTATIONAL usage items.

Items are aligned at the nearest halfword, fullword, or doubleword boundary.

COMPUTATIONAL-1. This option specifies that the item is stored in short precision internal floating-point format. Such items are 4 bytes in length and aligned on the next fullword boundary.

The data code is internal floating point, short (fullword) format.

COMPUTATIONAL-2. This option specifies that the item is stored in long precision internal floating-point format. Such items are 8 bytes in length and are aligned on the next double-word boundary.

The data code is internal floating-point long (doubleword) format.

Both COMPUTATIONAL-1 and COMPUTATIONAL-2 options have special formats designed for floating-point arithmetic operations. Part of the item may be stored in binary form, and part may be stored in hexadecimal format.

No PICTURE clauses are associated with internal floating-point items.

COMPUTATIONAL-3. This option is specified for an item that is stored in packed decimal format (2 digits per byte) with the low-order 4 bits of the rightmost byte containing the operational sign.

The PICTURE clause of COMPUTATIONAL-3 usage may contain only 9s, the operational sign S, the assumed decimal point V, and one or more Ps.

The data code is internal decimal (packed decimal).

INDEX. This option is discussed in the Table-Handling Section of the text.

If the usage is	Then the data code is	Which means that
display	external decimal—also called BCD (binary-coded decimal), or EBCDIC (extended binary coded decimal interchange code)	one character is stored in each byte of the item; if the item is used to store a number, the rightmost byte may contain an operational sign in addition to a decimal digit
computational	binary	one binary digit is stored in each bit of the item, except the leftmost bit, in which the operational sign is stored
computational-1	internal floating-point, short (fullword) format	the item has a special format designed for floating-point arithmetic operations; part of the item is stored in binary code, and part in hexadecimal code
computational-2	internal floating-point, long (doubleword) format	
computational-3	internal decimal—also called packed decimal	two decimal digits are stored in each byte of the item, except the rightmost byte, in which one digit and the operational sign are stored

Figure 7–28.   IBM-360/370 Chart—Usage Clause.

PICTURE Clause

The PICTURE clause specifies the general characteristics and the detail description of an elementary item.

$$\left\{ \begin{array}{l} \underline{PICTURE} \\ \underline{PIC} \end{array} \right\} \quad IS \text{ character string}$$

Figure 7–29.   Picture Clause Format.

If the picture contains	and also (possibly)	For example . . .	Then the item is called	And will be used to store
one or more Xs		XXX	alphanumeric	characters of any kind; letters, digits, special characters, or spaces
one or more As		A(35)	alphabetic	only letters or spaces
one or more 9s, but no editing symbols	S V P	S9(7)V99	numeric	only digits, and possibly an operational sign
one or more editing symbols; Z * $. , DB CR + — 0 B	9 V P	$ZZ,ZZZ.99	report	numeric data that is edited with spaces or certain special characters when the data is moved into the item
an E, in addition to 9s	+ — . V	+.9(8)E+99	external floating-point	a decimal quantity in an edited floating-point format that includes spaces or certain special characters

Figure 7–30. Identification of an Item by Its Picture.

Rules for the Use of PICTURE Clause are

1. This clause is required in the description of every elementary item except those whose usages are COMPUTATIONAL-1 or COMPUTATIONAL-2. (Floating-point items have definite storage formats.)
2. The clause tells how many characters will be stored and describes the types of characters through the use of various symbols.
3. The clause is forbidden at the group level.
4. Numeric literals enclosed in parenthesis is a shorthand method of expressing the repetition of a consecutive occurrence of a character. For example, X(10) is another way of writing XXXXXXXXXX.
5. All characters except P, V, and S are counted in the total size of any item.

6. CR and DB occupy two character positions in storage and may not both appear in the same PICTURE clause.
7. A maximum of 30 characters is permitted in the clause. For example, PICTURE X(60) consists of 5 PICTURE characters, since only the actual characters appearing in the PICTURE clause are included in the count.
8. The characters S, V, CR, and DB may appear only once in a clause.

X	Each X stands for one character of any kind—a letter, digit, special character, or space. The picture X(12) indicates that the item will contain twelve characters, but gives no indication of what characters they will be; all twelve could be spaces, or all could be digits, or there could be a mixture of various kinds of characters.
A	Each A stands for one letter or space.
9	Each 9 stands for one decimal digit. Numbers are always described in terms of the *decimal* digits they are the equivalent of—even when the data code is *binary*.
S	S indicates that the number has an operational sign. An "operational" sign tells the computer that the number is negative or positive; it is *not* a separate character that will print as "+" or "−".
V	V shows the location of an assumed decimal point in the number. An "assumed" decimal point is *not* a separate character in storage.
P	Each P stands for an assumed zero. Ps are used to position the assumed decimal point away from the actual number. For example, an item whose actual value is 25 will be treated as 25000 if its picture is 99PPPV; or as .00025 if its picture is VPPP99.

Figure 7–31. Meaning of Some Common Picture Characters.

Categories of Data

The categories of data that can be described with a PICTURE clause are

1. Alphabetic.
2. Numeric.
3. Alphanumeric.
4. Alphanumeric Edited.
5. Numeric Edited.

Level of Item	Class	Category
Elementary	Alphabetic	Alphabetic
	Numeric	Numeric
	Alphanumeric	Alphanumeric Alphanumeric Edited Numeric Edited
Group	Alphanumeric	Alphabetic Numeric Alphanumeric Alphanumeric Edited Numeric Edited

Figure 7–32. Class and Category of Elementary and Group Data Items.

Alphabetic. An alphabetic item may contain any combination of the 26 letters of the alphabet and the space. No special characters are permitted in an alphabetic item. The permissible character in an alphabetic picture is A.

Numeric. A numeric item may contain any combination of the numerals 0–9; the item may have an operational sign. Permissable characters in a numeric picture are 9, V, P, and S.

Alphanumeric. An alphanumeric item may contain any combination of characters in the COBOL character set. A permissable character in an alphanumeric picture is X.

Alphanumeric Edited. An alphanumeric edited item is one whose picture clause is restricted to certain combinations of the following characters: A, X, 9, B, 0. To qualify as an alphanumeric edited item, one of the following conditions must exist. The PICTURE clause must contain at least:

1. One B and at least one X.
2. One 0 and at least one X.
3. One 0 and at least one A.

Numeric Edited. A numeric edited item is one whose PICTURE clause is restricted to certain combinations of the following characters: B, P, V, Z, 0, 9, ., *, +, −, CR, DB, $. The maximum number of digits in a numeric edited picture is 18.

Figure 7–33. Examples—Editing Applications of Picture Clauses.

	Source Area		Receiving Area	
	PICTURE	Data Value	PICTURE	Edited Data
1.	S99999	12345	-ZZ,ZZ9.99	12,345.00
2.	S99999V	00123	$ZZ,ZZ9.99	$ 123.00
3.	S9(5)	00100	$ZZ,ZZ9.99	$ 100.00
4.	S9(5)V	00000	-ZZ,ZZ9.99	0.00
5.	9(5)	00000	$ZZ,ZZZ.99	$ .00
6.	9(5)	00000	$ZZ,ZZZ.ZZ	
7.	999V99	12345	$ZZ,ZZ9.99	$ 123.45
8.	V99999	12345	$ZZ,ZZ9.99	$ 0.12
9.	9(5)	12345	$**,**9.99	$12,345.00
10.	9(5)	00123	$**,**9.99	$***123.00
11.	9(5)	00000	$**,***.99	$******.00
12.	9(5)	00000	$**,***,**	**********
13.	99V999	12345	$**,**9.99	$****12.34
14.	9(5)	12345	$$$,$$9.99	$12,345.00
15.	9(5)	00123	$$$,$$9.99	$123.00
16.	9(5)	00000	$$$,$$9.99	$0.00
17.	9(4)V9	12345	$$$,$$9.99	$1,234.50
18.	V9(5)	12345	$$$,$$9.99	$0.12
19.	S99999V	-12345	-ZZZZ9.99	-12345.00
20.	S9(5)V	12345	-ZZZZ9.99	12345.00
21.	S9(5)	-00123	-ZZZZ.99	- 123.00
22.	S99999	12345	ZZZZ9.99	12345.00
23.	S9(5)	-12345	ZZZZ9.99-	12345.00-
24.	S9(5)	00123	------.99	123.00
25.	S9(5)	-00001	------.99	-1.00
26.	S9(5)	12345	+ZZZZZ.99	+12345.00
27.	S9(5)	-12345	+ZZZZZ.99	-12345.00
28.	S9(5)	12345	ZZZZZ.99+	12345.00+
29.	S9(5)	-12345	ZZZZZ.99	12345.00
30.	S9(5)	00123	+++++.99	+123.00
31.	S9(5)	00001	------.99	1.00
32.	9(5)	00123	+++++.99	+123.00
33.	9(5)	00123	------.99	123.00
34.	9(5)	12345	BB999.00	345.00
35.	9(5)	12345	00099.00	00045.00
36.	S9(5)	-12345	ZZZZZ.99CR	12345.00CR
37.	S9(5)	12345	$$$$$.99CR	$12345.00

Picture Characters

Nonedited PICTURE Clauses

A nonedited PICTURE clause may contain a combination of the following characters.

Character	Meaning
9	The character 9 indicates that the position contains one decimal digit. Numbers are always described in terms of the decimal digits that they are equivalent to, even when the data is binary.
X	The character X indicates that the position can contain any type of character in the COBOL character set; a letter, digit, or special character.
V	The character V indicates the presence of an assumed decimal point. Since a numeric nonedited

item may not contain an actual decimal point, an assumed decimal point provides the compiler with information concerning decimal alignment involved in computations. An "assumed decimal point" is not counted in the size of an elementary item and does not reserve any storage space.

P
    The character P indicates the presence of an assumed zero. The Ps are used to position the assumed decimal point away from the actual number. For example, the actual value in storage is 15. It would be treated as 15000 if the PICTURE clause is 99PPP, or as .00015 if the PICTURE clause is VPPP99.

    The character V may be used or omitted when using the P character. When the V is used, it must be placed in the position of the assumed decimal point, to the left or the right of P or Ps that have been specified.

    The scaling position character P is not counted in the size of the data item.

S
    The character S indicates the presence of an operational sign to the computer, either a positive or a negative number. It is not a separate character that will be printed as + or −. If used, S must be written as the leftmost character of the PICTURE clause. The presence of S is required where the USAGE clause is indicated as COMPUTATIONAL, since a sign appears in all binary numbers.

    The absence of S in a PICTURE clause will indicate a positive value. The operational sign is not counted in the size of an item.

A
    The character A indicates the presence of a letter or space in an item. No special characters are permitted in a PICTURE clause with A picture.

Edited PICTURE Clauses

    An edited PICTURE clause is used to describe items to be out put on the printer (alphanumeric and numeric edited items).

Rules Governing the Use of Edited PICTURE Clauses

1. There must be at least 1 digit position character in the clause.
2. If a fixed or floating string of plus or minus insertion characters are used, no other sign control character may be used.

3. The character to the left of an actual or assumed decimal point in the PIC-TURE clause (excluding the floating string of characters) are subject to the following restrictions.

   a. A Z may not follow 9, a floating string, or *.
   b. * may not follow 9, Z, or a floating string.

4. A floating string must begin with 2 consecutive characters (+, −, or $).
5. There may be only one type of floating string characters.
6. If the PICTURE clause does not contains 9s, BLANK WHEN ZERO is implied unless all the numeric positions contain asterisks. If the PICTURE clause does contain asterisks, and the area is zero, the area will be filled with asterisks.
7. The following restrictions apply to the characters to the right of the decimal point up to the end of the PICTURE (excluding insertion characters of +, −, CR, DB, if present).

   a. Only 1 type of digit character is permissable.
   b. If any of the characters appearing to the right of the decimal point is represented by +, −, Z, *, or $, then all the numeric characters in the PICTURE must be represented by the same characters.

8. The PICTURE character 9 can never appear to the left of the floating string or replacement character.
9. There cannot be a mixture of floating or replacement characters in an editing picture. They may appear as follows:

   a. An * or Z may appear with a fixed $.
   b. An * or Z may appear with a fixed leftmost + or fixed leftmost −.
   c. An * or Z may appear with a fixed rightmost + or fixed rightmost −.
   d. $ (fixed or floating string) may appear with fixed rightmost + or −.

   The characters and meanings of allowable editing characters in edited PICTURE clauses are as follows:

Character	Meaning
Z	The character Z represents a digit-suppression character.
	1. Each character Z represents a digit position.
	2. All leading zeros appearing in positions represented by Zs are suppressed, leaving the positions blank.
	3. Zero suppression is terminated when the actual or assumed decimal point is encountered.

4. A Z may appear to the right of the decimal point point only if all positions to the right are represented by Zs.

5. If all digit positions are represented by Zs, and the value of the data is zero, the entire area will be filled with blanks.

6. A Z character may not appear anywhere to the right of a 9 character.

7. Each Z is counted in the size of the item.

The character (.) represents an actual decimal point to be inserted in the printed output.

1. The decimal point is actually printed in the position indicated.

2. The source data is decimal aligned.

3. The character that appears to the right of the actual decimal point must consist of characters of one type (Z, *, 9, +, $, or −).

4. The character is counted in the size of a data item.

5. The actual decimal point may not be the last character in the PICTURE clause.

The asterisk (*) in the edited PICTURE clause is primarily used for protection of the amount in the printing of checks.

1. Each asterisk represents a digit position.

2. Leading nonsignificant zeros are replaced by asterisks.

3. Each field so defined will be replaced by asterisks until an actual or assumed decimal point is encountered.

4. An asterisk may appear to the right of the decimal point only if all digit positions are represented by asterisks.

5. If all digit positions are zero, the entire area will be filled with asterisks, except the actual decimal point.

6. The BLANK WHEN ZERO clause does not apply to any item having an asterisk (*) in its PICTURE.

7. An asterisk is counted in the size of an item.

CR DB

These character symbols are used as editing sign control symbols. These character symbols

are printed *only if an item is negative.* They are
called credit and debit symbols.

1. They may appear only at the right end of a
PICTURE.
2. A positive value will blank out the characters,
and only spaces will appear.
3. These symbols occupy 2 character positions
and are counted in determining the size of an
item.

Picture character	Data type	Specification	Additional explanation
X	alphanumeric	The associated position in the value will contain any character from the COBOL character set.	
A	alphabetic	The associated position in the value will contain an alphabetic character or a space.	
9	numeric or numeric edited	The associated position in the value will contain any digit.	
V	numeric	The decimal point in the value will be assumed to be at the location of the V. The V does not represent a character position.	
	numeric edited	The associated position in the value will contain a point or a space.	A space will occur if the entire data item is suppressed.

Figure 7–34.   Picture and Edit Characters.

$	numeric edited	a. (simple insertion) The associated position in the value will contain a dollar sign. b. (floating insertion) The associated position in the value will contain a dollar sign, a digit, or a space.	The leftmost $ in a floating string does not represent a digit position. If the string of $ is specified only to the left of a decimal point, the rightmost $ in the picture corresponding to a position that precedes the leading nonzero digit in the value will be printed. A string of $ that extends to the right of a decimal point will have the same effect as a string to the left of the point unless the value is zero; in this case blanks will appear. All positions corresponding to $ positions to the right of the printed $ will contain digits; all to the left will contain blanks.
	numeric edited	The associated position in the value will contain a comma, space, or dollar sign.	A comma included in a floating string is considered part of the floating string. A space or dollar sign could appear in the position in the value corresponding to the comma.
S	numeric	A sign ($+$ or $-$) will be part of the value of the data item. The S does not represent a character position.	

Figure 7–34. Picture and Edit Characters—Continued.

Editing Symbol in PICTURE Character String	Result	
	Data Item Positive or Zero	Data Item Negative
+	+	—
—	space	—
CR	2 spaces	CR
DB	2 spaces	DB

Figure 7–35. Editing Sign Control Symbols and Their Results.

Insertion Characters

Insertion characters are counted in determining the size of an item and represent the position into which the character will be inserted.

The characters and meanings of the insertion characters are as follows.

Character	Meaning
, (comma) B (space) 0 (zero)	1. The insertion character does not represent a digit position 2. Zero Protection (Z) and Check Protection (*) indicates the replacement of insertion characters with spaces or asterisks if a significant digit or decimal point has not been encountered. 3. The comma, blank, or zero may appear with floating strings.

PICTURE	Value of Data	Edited Result
99,999	12345	12,345
9,999,000	12345	2,345,000
99B999B000	1234	01 234 000
99B999B000	12345	12 345 000
99BBB999	123456	23 456

Figure 7–36. Examples—Simple Insertion Editing.

PICTURE	Value of Data	Edited Result
999.99	1.234	001.23
999.99	12.34	012.34
999.99	123.45	123.45
999.99	1234.5	234.50

Figure 7–37. Examples—Special Insertion Editing.

PICTURE	Value of Data	Edited Result
999.99+	+6555.556	555.55+
+9999.99	- 5555.555	- 5555.55
9999.99-	+1234.56	1234.56
$999.99	- 123.45	$123.45
-$999.99	- 123.456	- $123.45
$9999.99CR	+123.45	$0123.45
$9999.99DB	- 123.45	$0123.45DB

Figure 7–38. Examples—Fixed Insertion Editing.

Floating Strings

Floating string are a series of continuous characters of either $, or +, or −, or a string composed of 1, or a repetition of 1, such characters may be interrupted by 1, or more insertion characters (, 0, B) and/or V, or an actual decimal point.

1. The floating string characters are inserted immediately to the left of the digit position indicated.
2. Blanks are placed in all positions to the left of the singly floating string character after insertion.
3. The presence of an actual or assumed decimal point in a floating string is treated as if all digit positions to the right of the decimal point where indicated by the PICTURE character 9 and BLANK WHEN ZERO clause were written for them.
4. A floating string need not constitute the entire picture.

```
$$,$$$,$$$
++++
--,---,--
$$$B$$$
+(8)V++
$$,$$$.$$
```

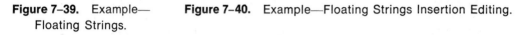

PICTURE	VALUE	Edited Result
$$$$.99	12.34	$12.34
$$$$.99	1234	$234.00
$$$$.99	.1234	$.12
----.99	+12.34	12.34
----.99	- 1.234	- 1.23
$$99.99	1.234	$01.23

Figure 7–39. Example— Floating Strings.

Figure 7–40. Example—Floating Strings Insertion Editing.

5. When B (blank) or , (comma) or 0 (zero) appears to the right of the floating string, the character floats there to be as close to the leading digit as possible.

6. A comma may not be the last character in a PICTURE clause.

The characters and meanings of floating strings are as follows:

Character	Meaning
B (blank)	The character B indicates that an imbedded blank is to appear in the indicated position unless the position immediately precedes a non-significant zero. Embedded blanks need not be single characters.
, (comma) 0 (zero)	The characters comma and zero operate in the same manner as the blank except that the character themselves appear in the output instead of blanks.
$ (Dollar Sign) + (plus) — (minus)	These characters may appear in an edited PICTURE clause either in a floating string or singly as a fixed character.

1. As a fixed sign character, the + or − must appear as the first or last character (not both).
2. The plus sign (+) indicates that the sign of an item may be either plus or minus, depending on the algebraic values of the item. The plus or minus sign will be placed in the output area.
3. The minus sign (−) indicates that a minus sign for items will only be placed in the output area. If the item is positive, a blank will replace the minus sign.
4. As a fixed insertion character, the character $ may appear only once in a PICTURE clause.
5. Each character symbol is used in determining the size of the item.

PICTURE	VALUE OF DATA	Edited Result
ZZZZ.ZZ	0000.00	
******.**	0000.00	******.**
ZZZZ.99	0000.00	.00
****.99	0000.00	****.00
Z,ZZZ.ZZ+	+123.456	123.45+
*,***.**+	−123.45	**123.45−
*,***,***.**+	+12345678.9	2,345,678.90+
$Z,ZZZ,ZZZ.ZZCR	+12345.67	$ 12,345.67
$B*,***,***.**BBDB	−12345.67	$ ***12,345.67 DB

Figure 7–41. Example—Zero Suppression and Replacement Editing.

Relationship Between PICTURE and USAGE Clauses

The usage of an item must be compatible with the PICTURE clause. The following kinds of items can have only DISPLAY usage: alphabetic, alphanumeric, alphanumeric edited, numeric edited, external decimal, and external floating-point. Digits may have any usage: DISPLAY COMPUTATIONAL, COMPUTATIONAL-1, 2, or 3, or INDEX. DISPLAY items may have any PICTURE clause; other than DISPLAY usage can have only numeric PICTURE clauses.

USAGE clause   PICTURE clause

```
02   Y-T-D-DEMAND, COMPUTATIONAL, PICTURE S9(6)V99.
```

Figure 7–42. Example—Picture and Usage Clauses.

VALUE IS literal

Figure 7–43. Value Clause Format.

Value Clause

The VALUE clause defines the condition-name values in the initial value of an item in the Working-Storage Section. This clause is used mainly in the Working-Storage Section to assign values to constants at the elementary level. The value assigned to the item remains constant during the execution of the object program unless it is changed by a procedure in the program.

Rules Governing the Use of the Value Clause

1. The size of the literal in the VALUE clause must be less than or equal to the size of an item as given in the PICTURE clause. All leading or trailing zeros reflected by Ps in a PICTURE clause must be included in the VALUE clause.

2. This clause is not permitted in the description of data items in the File Section other than condition-name entries at the 88 level.

3. When an initial value is not specified for an item in the Working-Storage Section, no assumption should be made regarding the original contents of the item.

4. A numeric literal must be used if the PICTURE clause designates a numeric item.

5. A nonnumeric literal should be used if the item is alphabetic or alphanumeric.

6. A Figurative Constant ZERO may be used in place of numeric or nonnumeric literal. The number of zeros generated will be the same as the size specified in the PICTURE clause.

7. A Figurative Constant SPACE may be used as an initial value in the place of a nonnumeric literal. The number of blanks generated will depend upon the size of the item in the PICTURE clause.

8. The VALUE clause can only be specified for elementary items.

9. The VALUE clause must not be specified for any item whose size, explicit or implicit, is variable.

10. The VALUE clause must not be written in a record description entry that contains an OCCURS clause or REDEFINES clause or an entry which is contained in an OCCURS or REDEFINES clause.

11. If the VALUE clause is written in an entry at the group level, the literal must be a Figurative Constant or nonnumeric literal, and the group area is initialized without consideration for the usage of the individual elementary or group items contained within this group. The VALUE clause cannot be specified at subordinate levels within this group.

Figure 7–44. Example—Value Clause Numeric Literal.

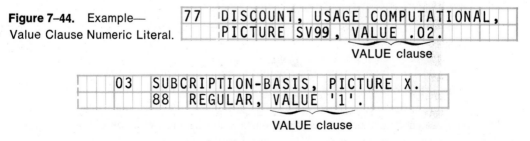

```
77   DISCOUNT, USAGE COMPUTATIONAL,
       PICTURE SV99, VALUE .02.
```
                                    VALUE clause

```
     03   SUBCRIPTION-BASIS, PICTURE X.
          88   REGULAR, VALUE '1'.
```
          VALUE clause

Figure 7–45. Example—Value Clause—Conditional Name—Nonnumeric Literal.

Condition-Name Clause

A condition-name is a name assigned by the programmer to a particular value that may be assumed by a data item.

Rules Governing the Use of Condition-Name Clauses

1. The condition-name is the name of the value of an item, not the name of the item itself. The item description entry complete with a PICTURE clause is required to describe the item.
2. A level 88 must be used in any condition-name entry.
3. A condition-name may pertain to an elementary item in a group item except a level 66 item; a group containing items with description which include JUSTIFIED, SYNCHRONIZED, or USAGE other than DISPLAY; or an index data item.
4. The condition-name is used in the Procedure Division simple relational test statements.
5. The VALUE clause is the only clause required in a condition-name entry.
6. The condition-name must immediately follow the item with which it is associated.
7. The type of literal used must be consistent with the data type of the condition variable. For example, a numeric literal must be used if the item has a numeric picture or a nonnumeric literal for alphabetic or alphanumeric pictures. The Figurative Constant zero may be used in place of a numeric or nonnumeric literal.

Figure 7–46.   Format—Condition-Name Clause.

```
88   condition-name   VALUE IS   literal .
```

```
         02  SALESMAN.
             03  REGION, PICTURE A.
                 88  EASTERN, VALUE 'A'.
                 88  CENTRAL, VALUE 'B'.
                 88  WESTERN, VALUE 'C'.
             03  OFFICE-NUMBER, PICTURE 999.
             03  BADGE-NUMBER, PICTURE 9999.
             03  INDUSTRY, PICTURE 99.
                 88  PETROLEUM, VALUE 20.
                 88  METALS, VALUE 21.
                 88  CHEMICALS, VALUE 26.
                 88  UTILITIES, VALUE 32.
```

SALESMAN

REGION
A = EASTERN
B = CENTRAL
C = WESTERN

OFFICE-NUMBER
999

BADGE-NUMBER
9999

INDUSTRY
20 = PETROLEUM
21 = METALS
26 = CHEMICALS
32 = UTILITIES

Figure 7–47.   Example—Condition-Name Clauses.

Other Independent Clauses

Redefines Clause

The REDEFINES clause specifies that the same area is to contain different data items. The entry gives another name and description to an item previously described. That is, the REDEFINES clause specifies the redefinition of a storage area, not of the items occupying the area.

The same area may be called by different names during the processing of the data. The area may contain different types of information and may be processed in a different manner under changing conditions.

Rules Governing the Use of the Redefines Clause

1. The word REDEFINES must be written right after the data-name followed by the name of the item being redefined.
2. The level numbers of the two entries sharing the same area must be the same.
3. The 01 level must not be used for redefinition.
4. The usage of data within the area can be redefined.
5. The redefinition starts at data-name-2 and ends when a level number is less than or equal to that of data-name-2 is encountered. Between the data description of data-name-2 and data-name-1, there may be no entries having lower-level numbers than data-name-1 or -2.
6. A new storage area is not set aside by the redefinition. All descriptions of the area remain in effect.
7. The entries giving new descriptions of the area must immediately follow the entry that is being redefined.
8. A REDEFINES clause may be used for items subordinate to items who are themselves being redefined.
9. This entry should not contain any VALUE clauses.

Figure 7–48. Redefines Clause Format.

level number data-name-1 REDFINES data-name-2

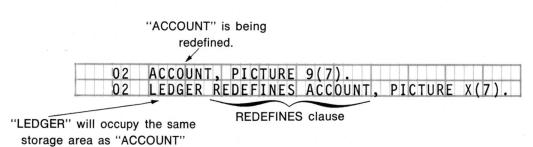

"ACCOUNT" is being redefined.

```
02   ACCOUNT, PICTURE 9(7).
02   LEDGER REDEFINES ACCOUNT, PICTURE X(7).
```

"LEDGER" will occupy the same storage area as "ACCOUNT"

REDEFINES clause

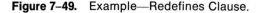

Figure 7–49. Example—Redefines Clause.

```
05  NAME-2.
    10  SALARY      PICTURE XXX.
    10  SO-SEC-NO   PICTURE X(9).
    10  MONTH       PICTURE XX.
05  NAME-1   REDEFINES    NAME-2.
    10  MAN-NO      PICTURE X(6).
    10  WAGE        PICTURE 999V999.
    10  YEAR        PICTURE XX.
```

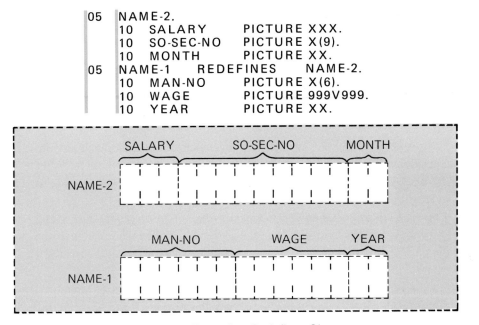

Figure 7–50. Example—Redefines Clause.

```
05  REGULAR-EMPLOYEE.
    10  LOCATION   PICTURE A(8).
    10  STATUS   PICTURE X(4).
    10  SEMI-MONTHLY-PAY   PICTURE 999V999.

05  TEMPORARY-EMPLOYEE   REDEFINES REGULAR-EMPLOYEE.
    10  LOCATION PICTURE A(8).
    10  FILLER  PICTURE X(6).
    10  HOURLY-PAY   PICTURE 99V99.
    10  CODE-H REDEFINES HOURLY-PAY   PICTURE 9999.
```

Figure 7–51. Example—Redefines Clause.

Blank When Zero Clause

The **BLANK WHEN ZERO** clause is used when an item is to be filled with spaces when the value of the item is zero. The clause may be specified only for an item whose PICTURE is numeric at the elementary level. The clause may not be specified for level 66 or 88 items.

Figure 7–52. Blank When Zero Clause Format.

Justified Clause

The JUSTIFIED clause is used to override the normal positioning of alphabetic or alphanumeric data when it is moved to a larger area. If an item is moved to a location that is larger than itself, it may be necessary to specify the position that the data is to occupy in the new area. In the absence of the JUSTIFIED clause, normal justification will be performed on the movement of data as follows:

Numeric Data will be *right justified* after decimal alignment with any unused positions at the right or left being filled with zeros. The rightmost character will be placed in the rightmost positions in the new area (if no decimals are involved), with zeros being supplied to the unused positions at the left.

Alphabetic and *Alphanumeric* data will be *left justified* after the move, and any unused character positions at the right will be filled with blanks. If the sending field is larger than the receiving area, excess characters at the right will be truncated.

If the programmer *wishes to alter* the normal justification of alphabetic or alphanumeric items, he could do so with the JUSTIFIED clause. If the JUSTIFIED clause is used, it affects the positioning of the receiving area, as follows:

1. If the data being sent is larger than the receiving area, the leftmost characters will be truncated.
2. If the data being sent is smaller than the receiving area, the unused positions at the left are filled with spaces.

The JUSTIFIED clause may only be used at the elementary level and must not be specified for level 66 or level 88 data items.

The standard rules for positioning within an area are:

1. When the receiving item is NUMERIC, the data is right-justified with zero-fill. For example:

Sending	Receiving
146 ⟶	ØØØØ146

2. When the receiving item is ALPHABETIC or ALPHANUMERIC (nonedited), data is left-justified with space fill. For example:

Sending	Receiving
JOE-JONES ⟶	JOE-JONES

Figure 7–53. Normal Justification Rules.

Figure 7–55. Justified Clause Format.

Sending   Receiving

Figure 7–54. Example—Justified Right Clause.

Synchronized Clause

The SYNCHRONIZED clause is used to specify alignment of an elementary item in the natural boundaries of the computer memory. This clause specifies that the COBOL processor, in creating the internal format for this item, must arrange the item in contiguous units of memory in such a way that no other data item appears in any of the memory units between the right and left natural boundary delimiting these data items. If the size of the item is such that it does not itself utilize all of the storage area between the delimiting natural boundaries, the unused storage positions (or portion thereof) may not be used for any other data item.

Rules Governing the Use of the Synchronized Clause

1. SYNCHRONIZED not followed by RIGHT or LEFT specifies that an elementary item is to be positioned between the natural boundaries in such a way as to effect utilization of the elementary data items. The specific positions are determined by the implementor.

Figure 7–56. Synchronized Clause Format.

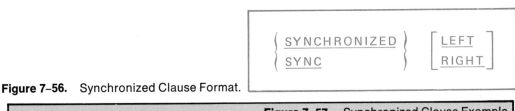

Figure 7–57. Synchronized Clause Example.

```
01  WORK-RECORD.
        05  WORK-CODE              PICTURE X.
        05  COMP-TABLE OCCURS 10  TIMES.
            10  COMP-TYPE          PICTURE X.
        [   10  IA-Slack-Bytes     PICTURE XX. Inserted by compiler]
            10  COMP-PAY           PICTURE S9(4)V99 COMP SYNC.
            10  COMP-HRS           PICTURE S9(3) COMP SYNC.
            10  COMP-NAME          PICTURE X(5).
        [   10  IE-Slack-Bytes     PICTURE XX. Inserted by compiler]
```

2. If SYNCHRONIZED LEFT is specified, the leftmost character will occupy the leftmost position in the contiguous memory area. The right-hand positions of the area will be unoccupied.

3. If SYNCHRONIZED RIGHT is specified, the rightmost character will occupy the right-hand position in the contiguous memory area with the leftmost positions of the area unoccupied.

4. Whenever a SYNCHRONIZED item is referenced in the source program, the original size of the items, as shown in the PICTURE clause, is used in determining any action that depends on size, such as justification, truncation, or overflow.

5. In the data description for an item, the sign appears in the normal operational size position regardless of whether the item is SYNCHRONIZED LEFT or SYNCHRONIZED RIGHT.

6. This clause is hardware dependent and, in addition to the rules stated above, the implementor must specify how elementary items associated with this clause are handled. The user should consult individual reference manuals for particular computers for further information relative to this clause.

Occurs Clause (See Table Handling Section)

The OCCURS clause is used to define tables and other homogeneous sets of data, whose elements can be referred to be subscripting or indexing. The clause specifies the number of times that an item is repeated with no change in its USAGE or PICTURE clauses. The clause is used primarily in defining related sets of data such as tables, lists, matrixes, etc.

OCCURS clause

Figure 7–58. Example—Occurs Clause.

Rules Governing the Use of the Occurs Clause

1. Record description clauses associated with an item that contains an OCCURS clause, apply to each repetition of the item being described.

2. Whenever the OCCURS clause is used, the data-name that is the defining name of the entry must be subscripted whenever used in the Procedure Division.

3. If the data-name is the name of a group item, then all data-names belonging to the group must be subscripted whenever used.

4. The OCCURS clause may not be used in the 01, 77, or 88 level of a record description entry.

5. The clause cannot describe an item whose size is variable.

Subscripting

The need arises to have tables of information accessible to a source program for referencing. Subscripting provides the facility for referring to data items in a list or a table that has been assigned individual values.

Like all data tables, the tables must be described in the Data Division with an OCCURS clause to indicate the number of appearances of a particular item. The subscripts are used in the Procedure Division to reference a particular item in the table. If subscripting were not used, each item would have to be described in a separate entry.

Rules Governing the Use of Subscripts

1. A subscript must always have a positive nonzero integral value whose value determines which item is being referenced within a table or list.
2. The subscript must be represented either by a numeric literal or a data-name that has an integral value.
3. Subscripts are enclosed in parenthesis to the right of the subscribed data-name with an intervening space. If the subscripted data-name is qualified, the subscripts must appear to the right of all qualifiers.
4. If more than one level of subscript is present, the subscripts are separated by commas and arranged from right to left in increasing order of inclusiveness of the grouping within the table. Multiple subscripts are written with a single pair of parentheses separated by commas and followed by a space. A space should also separate the data-name from the subscripted expressions. A *maximum of three levels of subscripts is permitted.*
5. A subscripted data-name must be qualified when it is not unique in accordance with rules for qualification.
6. A subscript must always be used to reference an item that has an OCCURS clause or belongs to a group having an OCCURS clause. *Subscription may not be used with any data-name not described using an OCCURS clause.*
7. A programmer may refer to blocks (sets) of data within a table. The data-name is written, followed by the subscript of the particular block plus any other subscript necessary to locate it. A complete table may be referenced just by using the name of the table.
8. Subscripts may not themselves be subscripted.

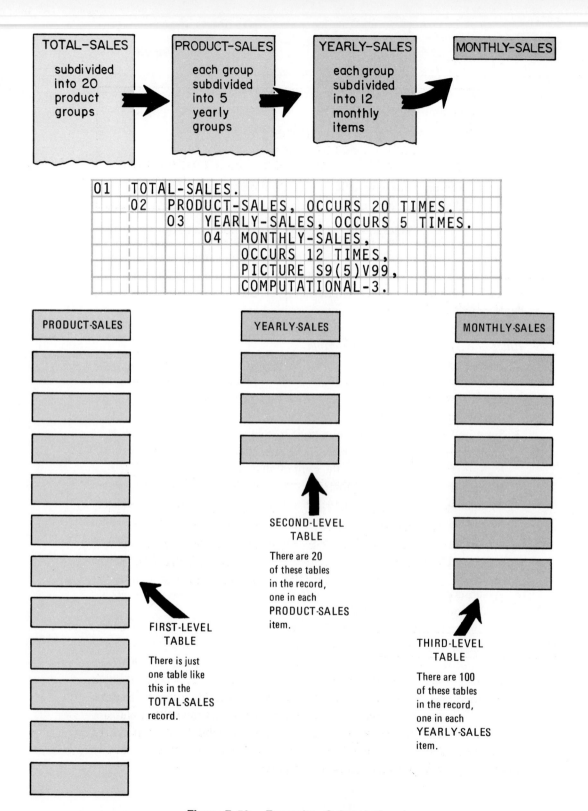

Figure 7–59. Example—Subscripting.

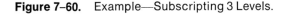

```
01     GROUP.
   02     ARRAY OCCURS 2 TIMES.
      03     VECTOR OCCURS 2 TIMES.
         04     ELEMENT OCCURS 3 TIMES USAGE
                 COMPUTATIONAL PICTURE S9(9).
```

Figure 7–60. Example—Subscripting 3 Levels.

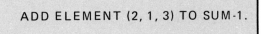

ADD ELEMENT (2, 1, 3) TO SUM-1.

Figure 7–61. Example—Procedure Division Entry.

9. A data-name may not be subscripted when it is being used as
   a. A subscript or qualifier.
   b. A defining name of a record description entry.
   c. Data-name-2 in a REDEFINES clause.
   d. A data-name in a LABEL RECORDS clause.
   e. A data-name in the DEPENDING ON option of the OCCURS clause.

Additional examples of subscripting will be found in the Procedure Division PERFORM statements and the Table Handling Section of the text.

Qualification and subscripting are entirely different. Qualification involves appending additional data-names to a name which has been used to represent different items. Subscripting is used to refer to one item amongst a group organized in a table or list.

WORKING-STORAGE SECTION

The Working-Storage Section may contain descriptions of records which are not part of external data files but which are developed and processed internally. This section is used to describe areas where intermediate results are stored temporarily at object time. The section is also used for descriptions of data to be used in the program. The section may be omitted if there aren't any constants or work areas needed in the program.

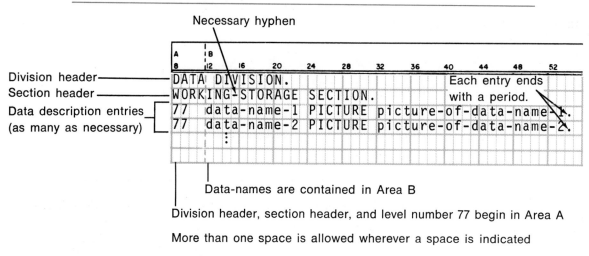

Necessary hyphen

Division header ——
Section header ——
Data description entries
(as many as necessary)

```
A    B
8    12    16    20    24    28    32    36    40    44    48    52
DATA DIVISION.                              Each entry ends
WORKING-STORAGE SECTION.                    with a period.
77   data-name-1  PICTURE  picture-of-data-name-1.
77   data-name-2  PICTURE  picture-of-data-name-2.
```

Data-names are contained in Area B

Division header, section header, and level number 77 begin in Area A

More than one space is allowed wherever a space is indicated

Figure 7–62. Guide for Coding 77 Entries in the Working-Storage Section.

The Working-Storage Section is often used to provide headings for a report. Since this is the only section that is permitted to have VALUE clauses (outside of condition-name entries), report headings can be designed and moved to an output file description prior to a write operation. Output formats for detail lines to be printed can also be provided for in this section. In many programs, the Working-Storage Section is the largest unit in the Data Division.

Structure

The Working-Storage Section must begin with the header WORKING-STORAGE SECTION followed by a period and a space on a line by itself. The section contains data entries for independent (noncontiguous) items and record items in that order.

Independent Items are items in the Working-Storage Section that bear no hierarchical relationship to one another and need not be grouped into records, provided that they do not need to further subdivide.

1. These items must not be subdivided or themselves be a subdivision of another item.
2. These entries must precede record item entries (level number 01–49).
3. Each item must be defined in a separate record description as follows: Level number 77, Data Name, USAGE Clause (optional), VALUE clause (optional), and a PICTURE clause (required).
4. An OCCURS clause must not be used in describing an independent item.

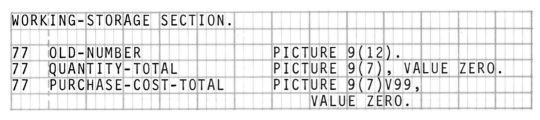

Figure 7-63. Example—77 Entries Working-Storage Section.

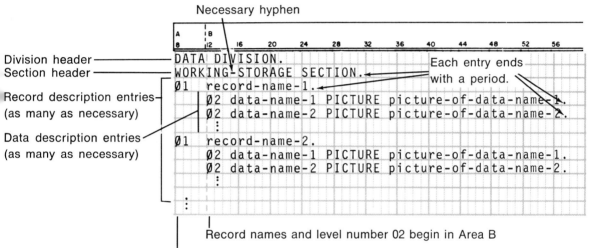

Figure 7-64. Guide for Coding Level 01 and 02 Entries in the Working-Storage Section.

These items are used primarily as temporary storage of an item pending the completion of a calculation or to define a constant to be used in the program.

Record Items are data elements in the Working-Storage Section among which there is definite hierarchical relationship; they must be grouped together into records according to the rules for the formation of record descriptions.

1. These items are subdivided into smaller units and bear a definite relationship to each other.
2. The entries used to describe these record items are identical to those used to describe a record in the File Section. However, one difference exists between records in the File Section and the entries in the Working-Storage Section. The entries in the File Section may be elementary items, but entries at the record level in the Working-Storage Section must be group items.

```
DATA DIVISION.
WORKING-STORAGE SECTION.
01  INPUT-DATA.
    02  FIELD-1, PICTURE X(10).
    02  FIELD-2, PICTURE X(5).
01  OUTPUT-DATA.
    02  FIELD-A, PICTURE X(5).
    02  FILLER, PICTURE X(19), VALUE SPACES.
    02  FIELD-B, PICTURE X(10).
```

Figure 7–65. Example—01 and 02 Entries in Working-Storage Section.

```
DATA DIVISION.
WORKING-STORAGE SECTION.
77  TOTAL, PICTURE 9(8), VALUE ZERO.
01  NUMBERS.
    02  SMALLER, PICTURE 9999.
    02  LARGER, PICTURE 9999.
```

Figure 7–66. Example—77, 01 and 02 Entries in Working-Storage Section.

Record entries are often used for output heading and detail formats because of the ability to use the VALUE clause in the Working-Storage Section.

An internal value of an item in the Working-Storage Section may be specified by using the VALUE clause. The value is assumed by the item at the time of the execution of the program. *No assumption can be made of the initial value of an item that has not been defined with a VALUE clause.*

Additional Data Division clauses, entries, examples, and uses will be found later in the text.

ACCOUNTS RECEIVABLE PROBLEM

INPUT

Field	Card Columns
Entry Date	1–5
Entry	6–7
Customer Name	8–29
Invoice Date	30–33
Invoice Number	34–38
Customer Number	39–43
Location	44–48
Blank	49–62
Discount Allowed	63–67
Amount Paid	68–73
Blank	74–80

CALCULATIONS TO BE PERFORMED

1. Calculate Accounts Receivable = Amount Paid + Discount Allowed.
2. Final Totals for Accounts Receivable, Discount Allowed and Amount Paid.

OUTPUT

Print a report as follows:

ACCOUNTS RECEIVABLE REGISTER

CUST. NO. CUST. NAME INV. NO. ACCTS. REC. DISCT. ALLOW. AMT. PAID

TOTALS

ACCOUNTS RECEIVABLE PROBLEM

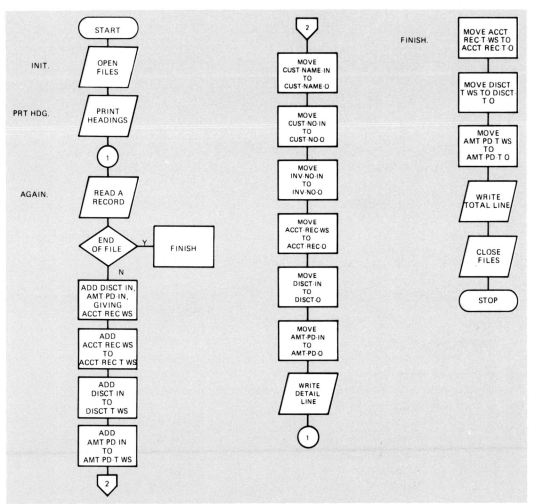

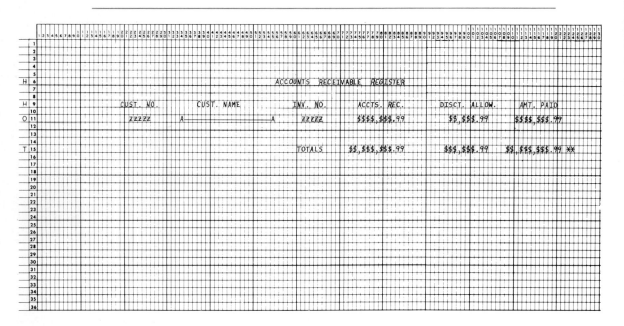

```
00001    001010 IDENTIFICATION DIVISION.                                      ACCTSREC
00002    001020 PROGRAM-ID. ACCTS-REC.                                        ACCTSREC
00003    001030 AUTHOR. C FEINGOLD.                                           ACCTSREC
00004    001040 DATE-WRITTEN. JUNE 14 1972.                                   ACCTSREC
00005    001045 DATE-COMPILED. 10/27/72                                       ACCTSREC
00006    001050 INSTALLATION. WEST LOS ANGELES COLLEGE.                       ACCTSREC
00007    001060 REMARKS. THIS PROGRAM PREPARES AN ACCOUNTS RECEIVABLE         ACCTSREC
00008    001070     REGISTER.                                                 ACCTSREC
00009    002010 ENVIRONMENT DIVISION.                                         ACCTSREC
00010    002020 CONFIGURATION SECTION.                                        ACCTSREC
00011    002030 SOURCE-COMPUTER. IBM-360-H50.                                 ACCTSREC
00012    002040 OBJECT-COMPUTER. IBM-360-H50.                                 ACCTSREC
00013    002045 SPECIAL-NAMES. C01 IS SKIP-TO-ONE.                            ACCTSREC
00014    002050 INPUT-OUTPUT SECTION.                                         ACCTSREC
00015    002060 FILE-CONTROL.                                                 ACCTSREC
00016    002070     SELECT FILE-IN ASSIGN TO SYS009-UR-2540R-S.               ACCTSREC
00017    002080     SELECT FILE-OUT ASSIGN TO SYS005-UR-1403-S                ACCTSREC
00018    002085     RESERVE NO ALTERNATE AREA.                                ACCTSREC
00019    003010 DATA DIVISION.                                                ACCTSREC
00020    003020 FILE SECTION.                                                 ACCTSREC
00021    003030 FD  FILE-IN                                                   ACCTSREC
00022    003040     RECORDING MODE F                                          ACCTSREC
00023    003050     LABEL RECORDS OMITTED                                     ACCTSREC
00024    003060     DATA RECORD IS CARD-IN.                                   ACCTSREC
00025    003070 01  CARD-IN.                                                  ACCTSREC
00026    003080     02 ENTRY-DATE-IN        PICTURE 9(5).                     ACCTSREC
00027    003090     02 ENTRY-IN             PICTURE 99.                       ACCTSREC
00028    003100     02 CUST-NAME-IN         PICTURE X(22).                    ACCTSREC
00029    003110     02 INV-DATE-IN          PICTURE 9(4).                     ACCTSREC
00030    003120     02 INV-NO-IN            PICTURE 9(5).                      ACCTSREC
00031    003130     02 CUST-NO-IN           PICTURE 9(5).                     ACCTSREC
00032    003140     02 LOC-IN               PICTURE 9(5).                     ACCTSREC
00033    003150     02 FILLER               PICTURE X(14).                    ACCTSREC
00034    003160     02 DISCT-IN             PICTURE 9(3)V99.                  ACCTSREC
00035    003170     02 AMT-PD-IN            PICTURE 9(4)V99.                  ACCTSREC
00036    003180     02 FILLER               PICTURE X(7).                     ACCTSREC
00037    004010 FD  FILE-OUT                                                  ACCTSREC
00038    004020     RECORDING MODE F                                         ACCTSREC
00039    004030     LABEL RECORDS OMITTED                                     ACCTSREC
```

```
                2

00040   004040     DATA RECORD IS PRINTOUT.                                      ACCTSREC
00041   004050  01 PRINTOUT          PICTURE X(133).                             ACCTSREC
00042   004060 WORKING-STORAGE SECTION.                                          ACCTSREC
00043   004070  77 ACCT-REC-WS       PICTURE 9(6)V99.                            ACCTSREC
00044   004080  77 ACCT-REC-T-WS     PICTURE 9(7)V99   VALUE ZEROS.              ACCTSREC
00045   004090  77 DISCT-T-WS        PICTURE 9(5)V99   VALUE ZEROS.              ACCTSREC
00046   004095  77 AMT-PD-T-WS       PICTURE 9(7)V99   VALUE ZEROS.              ACCTSREC
00047   004100  01 HDG-1.                                                        ACCTSREC
00048   004110     02 FILLER         PICTURE X(56) VALUE SPACES.                 ACCTSREC
00049   004120     02 FILLER         PICTURE X(30)                              ACCTSREC
00050   004130        VALUE 'ACCOUNTS  RECEIVABLE  REGISTER'.                    ACCTSREC
00051   005010  01 HDG-2.                                                        ACCTSREC
00052   005020     02 FILLER         PICTURE X(20) VALUE SPACES.                 ACCTSREC
00053   005030     02 FILLER         PICTURE X(9)  VALUE 'CUST. NO.'.            ACCTSREC
00054   005040     02 FILLER         PICTURE X(10) VALUE SPACES.                 ACCTSREC
00055   005050     02 FILLER         PICTURE X(10) VALUE 'CUST. NAME'.           ACCTSREC
00056   005060     02 FILLER         PICTURE X(11) VALUE SPACES.                 ACCTSREC
00057   005070     02 FILLER         PICTURE X(8)  VALUE 'INV. NO.'.             ACCTSREC
00058   005080     02 FILLER         PICTURE X(7)  VALUE SPACES.                 ACCTSREC
00059   005090     02 FILLER         PICTURE X(11) VALUE 'ACCTS. REC.'.          ACCTSREC
00060   005100     02 FILLER         PICTURE X(8)  VALUE SPACES.                 ACCTSREC
00061   005110     02 FILLER         PICTURE X(13) VALUE 'DISCT. ALLOW.'.        ACCTSREC
00062   005120     02 FILLER         PICTURE X(5)  VALUE SPACES.                 ACCTSREC
00063   005130     02 FILLER         PICTURE X(9)  VALUE 'AMT. PAID'.            ACCTSREC
00064   005140  01 DETAIL-LINE.                                                  ACCTSREC
00065   005150     02 FILLER         PICTURE X(22) VALUE SPACES.                 ACCTSREC
00066   005160     02 CUST-NO-O      PICTURE Z(5).                               ACCTSREC
00067   005170     02 FILLER         PICTURE X(7)   VALUE SPACES.                ACCTSREC
00068   005180     02 CUST-NAME-O    PICTURE X(22).                              ACCTSREC
00069   005190     02 FILLER         PICTURE X(6)   VALUE SPACES.                ACCTSREC
00070   005200     02 INV-NO-O       PICTURE Z(5).                               ACCTSREC
00071   005210     02 FILLER         PICTURE X(8)   VALUE SPACES.                ACCTSREC
00072   005220     02 ACCT-REC-O     PICTURE $$$$,$$$.99.                        ACCTSREC
00073   005230     02 FILLER         PICTURE X(10) VALUE SPACES.                 ACCTSREC
00074   005240     02 DISCT-O        PICTURE $$,$$$.99.                          ACCTSREC
00075   005250     02 FILLER         PICTURE X(6)  VALUE SPACES.                 ACCTSREC
00076   006010     02 AMT-PD-O       PICTURE $$$$,$$$.99.                        ACCTSREC
00077   006020  01 TOTAL-LINE.                                                   ACCTSREC
00078   006030     02 FILLER         PICTURE X(61) VALUE SPACES.                 ACCTSREC


                3

00079   006040     02 FILLER         PICTURE X(6)  VALUE 'TOTALS'.               ACCTSREC
00080   006050     02 FILLER         PICTURE X(6)  VALUE SPACES.                 ACCTSREC
00081   006060     02 ACCT-REC-T-O   PICTURE $$,$$$,$$$.99.                      ACCTSREC
00082   006070     02 FILLER         PICTURE X(9)  VALUE SPACES.                 ACCTSREC
00083   006080     02 DISCT-T-O      PICTURE $$$,$$$.99.                         ACCTSREC
00084   006090     02 FILLER         PICTURE X(4)  VALUE SPACES.                 ACCTSREC
00085   006100     02 AMT-PD-T-O     PICTURE $$,$$$,$$$.99.                      ACCTSREC
00086   006110     02 FILLER         PICTURE X(3)  VALUE ' **'.                  ACCTSREC
00087   007010 PROCEDURE DIVISION.                                              ACCTSREC
00088   007020 INIT. OPEN INPUT FILE-IN, OUTPUT FILE-OUT.                        ACCTSREC
00089   007030 PRT-HDG. WRITE PRINTOUT FROM HDG-1 AFTER ADVANCING SKIP-TO-ONE    ACCTSREC
00090   007040     LINES.                                                        ACCTSREC
00091   007050     WRITE PRINTOUT FROM HDG-2 AFTER ADVANCING 3 LINES.            ACCTSREC
00092   007060     MOVE SPACES TO PRINTOUT.                                      ACCTSREC
00093   007070     WRITE PRINTOUT AFTER ADVANCING 1 LINES.                       ACCTSREC
00094   007080 AGAIN. READ FILE-IN AT END GO TO FINISH.                          ACCTSREC
00095   007090     ADD DISCT-IN, AMT-PD-IN GIVING ACCT-REC-WS.                   ACCTSREC
00096   007100     ADD ACCT-REC-WS TO ACCT-REC-T-WS.                             ACCTSREC
00097   007110     ADD DISCT-IN TO DISCT-T-WS.                                   ACCTSREC
00098   007120     ADD AMT-PD-IN TO AMT-PD-T-WS.                                 ACCTSREC
00099   007130     MOVE CUST-NAME-IN TO CUST-NAME-O.                             ACCTSREC
00100   007140     MOVE CUST-NO-IN TO CUST-NO-O.                                 ACCTSREC
00101   007150     MOVE INV-NO-IN TO INV-NO-O.                                   ACCTSREC
00102   007160     MOVE ACCT-REC-WS TO ACCT-REC-O.                               ACCTSREC
00103   007170     MOVE DISCT-IN TO DISCT-O.                                     ACCTSREC
00104   007180     MOVE AMT-PD-IN TO AMT-PD-O.                                   ACCTSREC
00105   007190     WRITE PRINTOUT FROM DETAIL-LINE AFTER ADVANCING 1 LINES.      ACCTSREC
00106   007200     GO TO AGAIN.                                                  ACCTSREC
00107   007210 FINISH. MOVE ACCT-REC-T-WS TO ACCT-REC-T-O.                       ACCTSREC
00108   007220     MOVE DISCT-T-WS TO DISCT-T-O.                                 ACCTSREC
00109   007230     MOVE AMT-PD-T-WS TO AMT-PD-T-O.                               ACCTSREC
00110   007240     WRITE PRINTOUT FROM TOTAL-LINE AFTER ADVANCING 4 LINES.       ACCTSREC
00111   007250     CLOSE FILE-IN FILE-OUT.                                       ACCTSREC
00112   007260     STOP RUN.                                                     ACCTSREC
```

CUST. NO.	CUST. NAME	INV. NO.	ACCTS. REC.	DISCT. ALLOW.	AMT. PAID
67451	ACME MFG CO	345	$697.17	$13.67	$683.50
67452	AMERICAN STEEL CO	342	$1,398.93	$27.43	$1,371.50
67453	TAIYO CO LTD	447	$1,211.25	$23.75	$1,187.50
67454	ALLIS CHALMERS CO	451	$2,307.75	$45.25	$2,262.50
67455	XEROX CORP	435	$163.71	$3.21	$160.50
67456	GLOBE FORM CO	435	$229.50	$4.50	$225.00
67457	WATSON MFG CO	428	$113.73	$2.23	$111.50
67458	CALCOMP CORP	429	$165.75	$3.25	$162.50
67459	SHOP--RITE MARKETS	433	$168.30	$3.30	$165.00
67460	MICROSEAL CORP	440	$5.61	$.11	$5.50
67461	MITSUBISHI LTD	420	$2,305.20	$45.20	$2,260.00
67462	MARK KLEIN & SONS	431	$1,393.32	$27.32	$1,366.00
67463	HONEYWELL CORP	432	$11.73	$.23	$11.50
67464	SPERRY RAND CORP	449	$2,345.49	$45.99	$2,299.50
67465	WESTINGHOUSE CORP	460	$3,047.25	$59.75	$2,987.50
67466	GARRETT CORP	399	$184.62	$3.62	$181.00
67467	NANCY DOLL TOY CO	400	$22.95	$.45	$22.50
67468	RAMONAS FINE FOODS	430	$3,557.25	$69.75	$3,487.50
67469	EL CHOLOS	436	$1,795.71	$35.21	$1,760.50
67470	DATAMATION INC	437	$2,247.00	$374.50	$1,872.50
67471	MICROFICHE CORP	441	$2,555.10	$50.10	$2,505.00
67472	REALIST INC	389	$2,872.32	$56.32	$2,816.00
67473	EASTMAN KODAK CO	401	$2,311.32	$45.32	$2,266.00
67474	UNIVAC INC	410	$3,348.15	$65.65	$3,282.50
67475	AVCO CO	411	$5,015.85	$98.35	$4,917.50
67476	TRW SYSTEMS GROUP	412	$2,311.32	$45.32	$2,266.00
67477	BELL HELICOPTER CO	413	$2,878.95	$56.45	$2,822.50
67478	BOEING AEROSPACE CORP	414	$2,328.15	$45.65	$2,282.50
	TOTALS		$46,993.38	$1,251.88	$45,741.50 **

Exercises

Write your answers in the space provided.

1. The Data Division of a COBOL program describes the _____ of the information to be processed by the _____ program.
2. The manner in which data is _____ and _____ has a major effect upon the efficiency of the object program.
3. The categories of data to be processed are data in _____, data in _____ and _____ data.
4. Each Data Division entry must contain a _____, a _____ or _____ and a series of _____.
5. An item is considered a _____.
6. An item that is not divided into smaller units is known as a _____ item.
7. An item appearing in the Working-Storage Section that is not part of record or a record itself is known as a _____ item.
8. The _____ record is considered a group item comprising several related items.
9. A _____ is composed of a series of related data records.
10. Blocks of _____ records are referred to as the _____ record.
11. Once the relationship is established between _____ and _____ records, only the _____ records are made available to the program.

12. Label records are normally used for files that are stored on _____ or _____ devices.

13. The Data Division is divided into three fixed sections in the following sequence: _____, _____ and _____.

14. The _____ section defines the contents of data files stored on the external medium.

15. The _____ section describes records or noncontiguous data items which are not part of the data files.

16. For every file named in the _____ clause in the _____ Division, a file description entry must be written.

17. The file description entry describes the _____ of the file, how the data is _____, the size of the _____ and _____ in the file, information about _____ records, and the names of the _____ in the file.

18. The file description entry always begins with the level indicator _____ _____, followed by the _____ name and a series of _____.

19. The Block Contains clause specifies the number of _____ or _____ in a block.

20. The Record Contains clause is a _____ clause that specifies the size of the _____ records within a _____.

21. The IBM 360 or 370 computer has the following recording formats _____ length, _____ length, _____ length and _____.

22. The Label Records clause is _____ in every file description entry and specifies whether the labels are present or _____.

23. The _____ clause informs the compiler what the record(s) in the file are.

24. The Report clause is used in conjunction with the _____ feature.

25. A record description entry specifies the _____ of each item in the data record.

26. Each record description entry consists of a _____, a _____ _____ or _____ and a series of _____ clauses.

27. The level number _____ is used for the record itself.

28. In subdividing a level, level numbers need not be _____.

29. Group items consist of all items under it until a level number _____ _____ or _____ than the group level number is reached.

30. Indenting of items is _____ required.

31. Level numbers _____ through _____ are used for subdivisions of group items.

32. Separate entries are written for each _____.
33. The _____ permits the programmer to refer to items individually in procedure statements.
34. The highest qualifier of a data-name permitted is a _____.
35. Filler does not always represent a _____ area.
36. The Usage clause describes the form that _____ is stored in _____.
37. If the Usage clause is written at a _____ level, it applies to each elementary item in the group.
38. The type of Usage clauses permitted in the IBM 360 or 370 computer are _____, _____, _____, _____ and _____.
39. The Picture clause specifies the general _____ and the _____ descriptions for a _____ item.
40. The Picture clause is forbidden at the _____ level.
41. The categories of data that can be described with a Picture clause are _____, _____, _____, _____, and _____.
42. An _____ item may only contain the letters of the alphabet and a space.
43. An _____ item may contain any combination of characters in the COBOL character set.
44. A non edited Picture clause may contain a combination of the following characters: _____, _____, _____, _____, and _____.
45. The character _____ is used to represent an assumed decimal point.
46. The character _____ indicates that the position contains a decimal digit.
47. An _____ Picture clause is used to describe items to be out put on a printer.
48. When zero suppression is used, a _____ character may not follow a _____ character.
49. A floating string must begin with _____ consecutive characters.
50. The character _____ represents an actual decimal point to be inserted in the output.
51. The DB character symbols may appear only at the _____ end of a Picture clause and will print only if the item is _____.
52. _____ are a continuous string of characters and inserted immediately to the _____ of the digit position indicated.
53. The usage of an item must be compatible with the _____ clause.
54. The _____ clause may be used to assign an initial value to data in the _____ section.

55. A _____ is a name assigned by the programmer to a particular value that may be assumed by a data item.

56. To use the same area to contain different data items, a _____ clause is used.

57. In the absence of the Justified clause, when an item is moved to a location larger than itself, numeric data will be _____ justified after decimal alignment with any unused positions being filled with _____ while non numeric data will be _____ justified with unused positions being filled with _____.

58. The Occurs clause is used to _____ tables and other _____ sets of data whose elements can be referred to by _____ and _____.

59. The _____ clause is used to specify alignment of an elementary item in the natural boundaries of the computer memory.

60. _____ provides the facility to refer to data items in a list or a table that has been assigned individual values.

61. A _____ must always have a positive _____ integral value whose value determines which item is being _____ in the table or list.

62. The Working-Storage Section contains descriptions of records which are developed and processed _____. It is also used for _____ work areas and for _____ to be used in the program.

63. _____ items in the Working-Storage Section must precede record items.

Answers

1. CHARACTERISTICS, OBJECT
2. ORGANIZED, STORED
3. FILES, WORKING AREAS, CONSTANT
4. LEVEL INDICATOR, DATA NAME, OTHER NAME, CLAUSES
5. FIELD
6. ELEMENTARY
7. INDEPENDENT
8. DATA
9. FILE
10. LOGICAL, PHYSICAL
11. LOGICAL, PHYSICAL, LOGICAL
12. MAGNETIC TAPE, DIRECT ACCESS
13. FILE, WORKING-STORAGE, REPORT
14. FILE
15. WORKING-STORAGE
16. SELECT, ENVIRONMENT
17. NAME, RECORDED, BLOCKS, RECORDS, LABEL, RECORDS
18. FD, FILE, CLAUSES
19. RECORDS, CHARACTERS
20. OPTIONAL, LOGICAL, FILE
21. FIXED, VARIABLE, UNDEFINED, SPANNED
22. REQUIRED, OMITTED

23. DATA RECORDS
24. REPORT WRITER
25. CHARACTERISTICS
26. LEVEL NUMBER, DATA
    NAME, FILLER, INDEPENDENT
27. 01
28. CONSECUTIVE
29. EQUAL TO, LESS THAN
30. NOT
31. 02, 49
32. LEVEL NUMBER
33. DATA-NAME
34. FILE NAME
35. BLANK
36. DATA, MAIN STORAGE
37. GROUP
38. DISPLAY, COMPUTATIONAL,
    COMPUTATIONAL-1,
    COMPUTATIONAL-2,
    COMPUTATIONAL-3
39. CHARACTERISTICS, DETAIL,
    ELEMENTARY
40. GROUP
41. ALPHABETIC, NUMERIC,
    ALPHANUMERIC, ALPHA-
    NUMERIC EDITED, NUMERIC
    EDITED

42. ALPHABETIC
43. ALPHANUMERIC
44. 9, X, V, P, S, A
45. V
46. 9
47. EDITED
48. Z, 9
49. TWO
50. .
51. RIGHT, NEGATIVE
52. FLOATING STRINGS, LEFT
53. PICTURE
54. VALUE, WORKING-STORAGE
55. CONDITION-NAME
56. REDEFINES
57. RIGHT, ZEROS, LEFT,
    SPACES
58. DEFINE, HOMOGENOUS,
    SUBSCRIPTING, INDEXING
59. SYNCHRONIZED
60. SUBSCRIPTING
61. SUBSCRIPT, NONZERO,
    REFERENCED
62. INTERNALLY, INTERMEDIATE,
    CONSTANTS
63. INDEPENDENT

Questions for Review

1. Why is it important that data be stored properly?
2. What must each entry contain?
3. What is the relationship between an item, elementary item, group item and independent item?
4. What is the relationship between a data record, file and block?
5. What is the function of the File Section?
6. What does the file description entry describe?
7. Briefly differentiate between the types of recording modes used in a system 360 or 370 computer.
8. When is the Block Contains clause used?
9. What clauses are required in the file description entry?
10. Why are the items indented in the record description entries?

11. How are the various level numbers used?
12. How is 'FILLER' used and does it always represent a blank area?
13. What are the rules governing the use of the Usage clauses? Explain the various types of Usage clauses in the System 360 or 370 computer.
14. Describe the use of a Picture clause.
15. Describe the relationship between the Picture and Usage clauses.
16. What is the Value clause and how is it used?
17. What is the Occurs clause and how is it used?
18. What is the purpose of the Redefines clause?
19. What is the Blank When Zero clause used for?
20. What is the purpose of Editing Picture clauses?
21. What are Floating Strings and what is their purpose?
22. How does the COBOL compiler perform automatic justification?
23. How is the Synchronized clause used?
24. What is a condition-name and how is it used?
25. What are the principal uses of the Working-Storage Section?
26. What is subscripting and how is it used?

Problems

1. *Match each item with its proper description.*

_____ 1. Group Item
_____ 2. Data Record
_____ 3. Item
_____ 4. Block
_____ 5. Independent Item

_____ 6. File
_____ 7. Elementary Item

A. Series of related data records.
B. Named sequence of one or more elementary items.
C. Physical record.
D. Smallest item available.
E. Item appearing in Working-Storage Section that is not a record or part of a record.
F. Field.
G. Logical record.

2. *Match each clause with its proper description.*

_____ 1. Recording Mode
_____ 2. Record Contains
_____ 3. Block Contains
_____ 4. Label Records
_____ 5. Value Of
_____ 6. Data Records
_____ 7. Report

A. Presence or absence of labels.
B. Format of logical record.
C. Particularizes description of item in Label Records clause.
D. Size of logical record.
E. Used with Report Writer feature.
F. Number of records or characters in block.
G. Name of record(s) in file.

3. *Match each level number group with its proper classification.*

_____ 1. 01
_____ 2. 02–49
_____ 3. 66
_____ 4. 77
_____ 5. 88

A. Subdivisions of group record items.
B. Condition entry.
C. Designates item as a record.
D. Used with RENAMES clause.
E. Independent elementary item in Working-Storage Section.

4. *Match each USAGE clause with its proper description.*

_____ 1. Display
_____ 2. Computational
_____ 3. Computational-1
_____ 4. Computational-2
_____ 5. Computational-3

A. Short precision internal floating point format.
B. Packed decimal format.
C. One character per byte.
D. Binary data items.
E. Long precision internal floating point format.

5. *Match each category of data with its proper description.*

_____ 1. Alphabetic	A. Numerals.
_____ 2. Numeric	B. Combination of numerals and editing characters.
_____ 3. Alphanumeric	C. Letters and space.
_____ 4. Alphanumeric Edited	D. Any combination of characters in COBOL character set.
_____ 5. Numeric Edited	E. Combination of any character plus the characters B or O.

6. *Match each non-editing character with its proper description.*

_____ 1. 9	A. Assumed decimal point.
_____ 2. X	B. One decimal digit.
_____ 3. V	C. Operational sign.
_____ 4. P	D. Letter or space.
_____ 5. S	E. Any type of character in the COBOL character set.
_____ 6. A	F. Assumed zero.

7. *Match each editing character with its proper description.*

_____ 1. Z	A. Credit symbol.
_____ 2. .	B. Digit position.
_____ 3. *	C. Credit symbol.
_____ 4. CR	D. Actual decimal point.
_____ 5. DB	E. Check protection.

8. *Which of the following is a floating strings or insertion character? Use F for floating strings and I for insertion characters.*

_____ $

_____ B

_____ —

_____ 0

_____ +

_____ ,

9. *Match each clause with its proper description.*

_____ 1. Picture

_____ 2. Value

_____ 3. Condition-Name

_____ 4. Redefines

_____ 5. Blank When Zero

_____ 6. Justified

_____ 7. Synchronized

_____ 8. Occurs

A. Same area to contain different data items.

B. Item to be filled with spaces when value is zero.

C. Alignment of item on natural boundaries of computer memory.

D. Initial value of an item.

E. Override normal positioning of alphabetic data when moved to a larger area.

F. Particular value that may be assigned by a data item.

G. General characteristics and description of an item.

H. Define tables and other homogenous sets of data.

10. *List the group and elementary items in the following.*

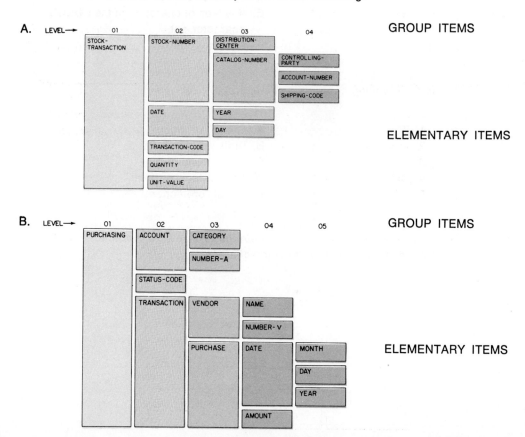

11. *Write the file description entry for a file whose name is EXPENSE-FILE. The file is on magnetic tape, has standard label records and one type of data record called EXPENSE-RECORD. All records are fixed length and each record is preceded by a record length control field. There are twenty records per block.*

12. *Write the record description entry for the following record. We are not concerned with the USAGE and PICTURE clauses of these items, just the level numbers, data-names or FILLER.*

13. *Write the complete record description entry for the following input record including level numbers, data-names or FILLER, together with all necessary PICTURE and VALUE clauses.*

14. *In the Working-Storage Section, write the entries to set up the following:*

    a. A work area large enough to hold 25 alphanumeric characters.

    b. An independent item called DIFFERENCE to contain a sign, five digits, and stored in packed decimal format.

    c. A constant called LIMIT, whose value is 600 and is stored in a binary format.

    d. An alphanumeric constant which is to serve as a title of a report. The contents of the item are to be DEPRECIATION SCHEDULE and the item is to be named TITLE.

    e. A record to be called ADDRESS composed of STREET (20 alphanumeric characters), CITY (20 alphanumeric characters), STATE (5 Alphanumeric characters) and ZIPCODE (5 digits).

15. *Write the necessary entries in the Working-Storage Section for the following headings:*

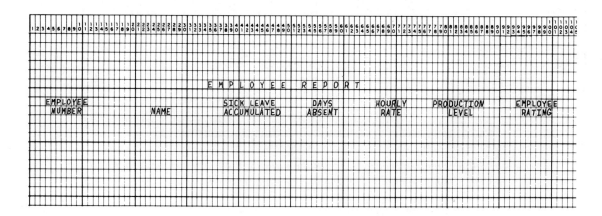

16. *Set up the Working-Storage Section for the following:*

    a. A percentage value of 25% to be used as the multiplier in a multiplication operation.

    b. A 4-digit counter containing an initial value of 1000.

    c. A 5-position field to be used as a temporary storage area.

    d. A 3-digit page number which will be incremented for each new page printed. The initial value equals 001.

    e. A record containing six fields of 15 characters each with the initial values equal to the names of the six New England States (Connecticut, Massachusetts, Maine, New Hampshire, Rhode Island and Vermont).

    f. Headings for a report as described in the following:

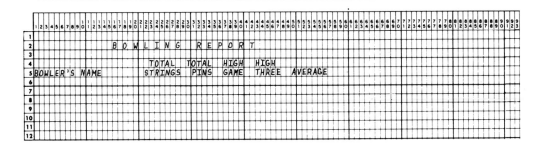

17. *How will the following source data be interpreted?*

	Source Data	Picture	Interpretation
a.	123	9V99	
b.	132̄	S999	
c.	15671	999V999	
d.	4071629	9(5)V99	
e.	9263	V999	
f.	6⁺1	S99	

18. *Specify the actions that will take place when the source area data is moved to the corresponding receiving area.*

	Source Area		Receiving Area	
	Picture	Data Value	Picture	Data Value Interpretation
a.	9999	1234	9(6)	
b.	99V99	1234	999V99	
c.	99V99	1234	99V999	
d.	99V99	1234	9(4)V9(4)	
e.	9(4)	1234	999	
f.	999V9	1234	99V99	
g.	999V9	1234	999	
h.	999V999	123456	99V99	
i.	99V999	12345	9(4)V99	
j.	999V99	12345	99V999	

19. *Specify the actions that will take place when the source area data is moved to the corresponding receiving area.*

	Source Area		Receiving Area	
	Picture	**Data Value**	**Picture**	**Edited Data**
a.	999V9	1234	999.9	
b.	9(5)V99	0001234	9(5).99	
c.	9(5)V99	0001234	Z(5).99	
d.	9(5)V99	0000123	ZZZ99.99	
e.	9(5)V99	0123456	99,999.99	
f.	9(5)V99	0123456	ZZ,999.99	
g.	9(5)V99	0000000	ZZ,ZZZ.ZZ	
h.	9(5)V99	1234567	$99,999.99	
i.	S9(6)	+123456	+9(6)	
j.	S999	−123	−999	
k.	S9(4)	+0012	ZZZ9+	
l.	S99V99	−1234	99.99CR	
m.	S99V99	−1234	99.99DB	
n.	S99V99	+1234	99.99DB	
o.	9(5)V99	0234567	$$$,$$9.99	
p.	9(6)V99	00001234	***,***.99	
q.	S9999	+0123	++++9	
r.	S9999	−0123	++++9	
s.	S9999	+0001	−−−−9	
t.	9(9)	123456789	999B99B9999	

20. *Write the Identification, Environment and Data divisions for the following:*

Problem Statement

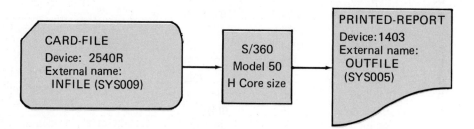

The system flowchart above shows the files and equipment to be used in this program. The forms of records in CARD-FILE and PRINTED-REPORT are illustrated on the following page.

CARD-RECORD

MARKER (5 digits)	DEPARTMENT (3 characters)	NAME (25 letters)	DEPENDENTS (2 digits)	FILLER (45 blanks)

```
                                      EMPLOYEE ROSTER
     NUMBER          NAME          [                              DEPARTMENT  DEPENDENTS
     X----X          X------------------------------X            XXX         XX
```

The file PRINTED-REPORT is to consist of a title and headings followed by a list-
ing of the records in CARD-FILE with the data items rearranged as shown in the
Printer Spacing Chart. Use the variables CARD-RECORD, PRINT-RECORD,
WORK-RECORD-1, WORK-RECORD-2, and WORK-RECORD-3.

21. *Write the Identification, Environment and Data divisions for the following:*

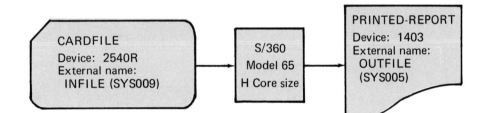

CUSTOMER-RECORD (input area for CARDFILE)

NAME (20 characters)	STREET (15 characters)	CITY-STATE (25 characters)		FILLER (18 characters)

YEAR-OPENED
(2 characters)

PRINT-RECORD (output area for PRINTED-REPORT)

```
  NAME                        ADDRESS              CITY-STATE                              YEAR-OPENED
  X-----------X           X------------X      X----------------X                      XX
```

DETAIL-RECORD in Working Storage
HEADING-RECORD in Working Storage

22. *Write the Identification, Environment and Data divisions for the following:*

Hardware
   Computer — IBM 370   Model 155 with H Core size
   Input   — Magnetic Tape Unit Model 2400
                   External name   RECBLES (SYS012).
   Output   — Printer   Model 1403
                   External name ACCTLIST (SYS005).
Input File—RECEIVABLE

There are 50 records per block and there are standard labels.

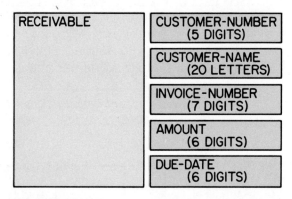

Output File—ACCOUNT

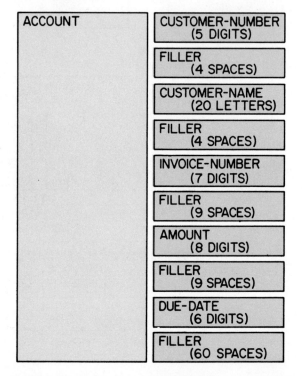

23. *Write the Identification, Environment and Data divisions for the following:*

Companies have master files of information that require changes and constant updating. Such a change may be the deletion of discontinued items from the master file and the subsequent listing of the deleted items. In order to make these changes, a maintenance program should be written.

The following processing is involved in writing the maintenance program.

1. *Card-to-tape-conversion*—Read a deck of delete cards and write the deleted items on a transaction file tape.
2. *File update*—Update the master file by passing the transaction file tape against the old master file deleting items according to the item number.
3. *Print*—Print those items which are deleted from the master file.

Hardware—
    Computer—IBM 370   Model 155 H Core size
    4 Magnetic Tape Units   Model 2400 (Tape-I-1, Tape-I-2,
                                Tape-O-1, Tape-O-2).
    1 Card Reader   Model 2540 (SYS009).
    1 Printer   Model 1403 (SYS005).

The following systems flowchart illustrates the two phases of the program.

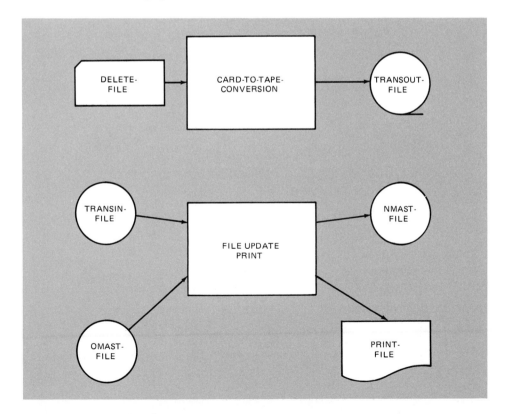

Data Division
  File Section

| DELETE-FILE | Read from Card Reader | Record name is DELETE-RECORD |

Field Name	**Card Columns**	**Field Class**
Item number	1–5	Numeric
Delete date	6–11	Numeric
Description	12–24	Alphabetic

	Tape Unit	*Record name is*
TRANSOUT-FILE	SYS012	TRANSOUT-RECORD

FORMAT SAME AS DELETE-FILE

| TRANSIN-FILE | *Tape Unit* SYS013 | *Record name is* TRANSIN-RECORD |

FORMAT SAME AS TRANSOUT-FILE

	Tape Unit	*Record name is*
OMAST-FILE	SYS014	OMAST-RECORD

Field Name	**Card Columns**	**Field Class**
Item number	1–5	Numeric
Item description	6–18	Alphabetic
Quantity	19–22	Numeric
Balance	23–28	Numeric XXXX.XX

	Tape Unit	*Record name is*
NMAST-FILE	SYS015	NMAST-RECORD

FORMAT SAME AS OMAST-FILE

ALL TAPE RECORDS IN BLOCKS OF 4 RECORDS AND HAVE STANDARD LABELS.

| PRINT-FILE | LISTED REPORT 'DELETED ITEMS REPORT' | Record name is PRINT-RECORD |

Field Name	**Print Positions**	**Field Class**
Delete Date	4–9	Numeric
Item number	14–18	Numeric
Item description	23–35	Alphabetic
Quantity	40–43	Numeric
Balance	49–56	Numeric Edited ($9999.99)

Working-Storage Section

Field Name	Size	Field Class
TOTAL	7	Numeric XXXXX.XX

Header Information

Constant Value	Print Positions
DATE	5–8
ITEM-NO	13–19
DESCRIPTION	24–34
QUANTITY	39–46
BALANCE	50–56

8

Procedure Division

INTRODUCTION

The Procedure Division of a source program specifies the actions necessary to solve a given problem. These steps (input/output, logical decisions, computations, etc.) are required to process the data and to control the sequence in which these actions are to be carried out. Statements similar to English are used to denote the processing to be performed. *A statement is a syntactical valid combination of words and symbols beginning with a COBOL verb.* Verbs are used in statements in a source program to specify the steps the object program is to perform.

```
Format    PROCEDURE DIVISION.
          procedure-name .
             sentence . . .
          [procedure-name .
             sentence . . .] . . .
```

Figure 8–1. Format—Procedure Division.

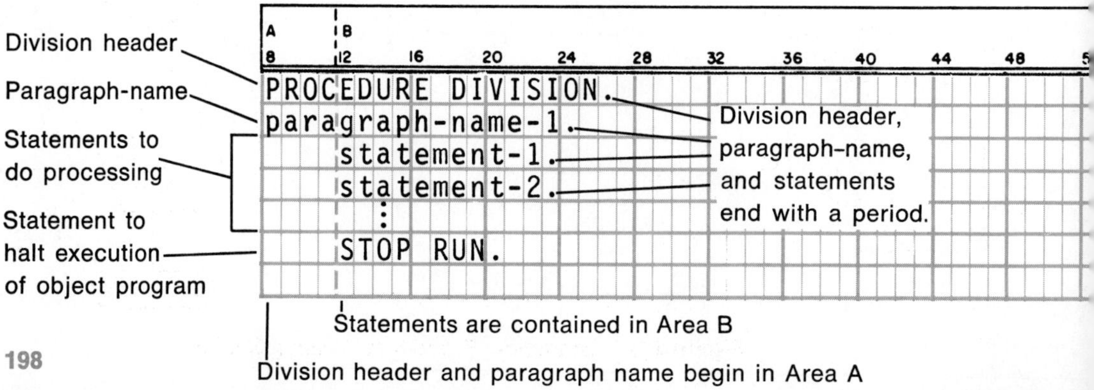

A
B
8
12
16
20
24
28
32
36
40
44
48
Division header
Paragraph-name
Statements to do processing
Statement to halt execution of object program
PROCEDURE DIVISION.
paragraph-name-1.
statement-1.
statement-2.
STOP RUN.
Division header, paragraph-name, and statements end with a period.
Statements are contained in Area B
Division header and paragraph name begin in Area A

Figure 8–2. Guide for Coding Procedure Division Entries.

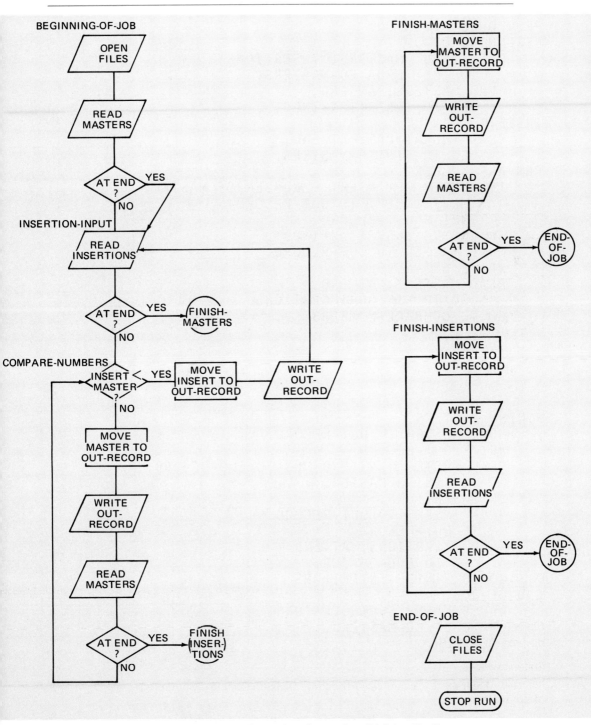

Figure 8–3. Example—Procedure Division Coding.

```
PROCEDURE DIVISION.
BEGINNING-OF-JOB.
    OPEN INPUT MASTERS, INSERTIONS;
        OUTPUT UPDATED-MASTERS.
    READ MASTERS; AT END,
        GO TO INSERTION-INPUT.
INSERTION-INPUT.
    READ INSERTIONS; AT END,
        GO TO FINISH-MASTERS.
COMPARE-NUMBERS.
    IF NUMBER OF INSERT < NUMBER OF MASTER,
        MOVE INSERT TO OUT-RECORD,
        WRITE OUT-RECORD,
        GO TO INSERTION-INPUT.
    MOVE MASTER TO OUT-RECORD.
    WRITE OUT-RECORD.
    READ MASTERS; AT END,
        GO TO FINISH-INSERTIONS.
    GO TO COMPARE-NUMBERS.
```

```
FINISH-MASTERS.
    MOVE MASTER TO OUT-RECORD.
    WRITE OUT-RECORD.
    READ MASTERS; AT END, GO TO END-OF-JOB.
    GO TO FINISH-MASTERS.
FINISH-INSERTIONS.
    MOVE INSERT TO OUT-RECORD.
    WRITE OUT-RECORD.
    READ INSERTIONS; AT END,
        GO TO END-OF-JOB.
    GO TO FINISH-INSERTIONS.
END-OF-JOB.
    CLOSE MASTERS, INSERTIONS,
        UPDATED-MASTERS.
    STOP RUN.
```

Figure 8–3.   Example—Procedure Division Coding—Continued.

The following are units of expressions that constitute the Procedure Division. These units may be combined to form larger units.

Statement

The statement is the basic unit of the Procedure Division. A statement consists of a COBOL verb or the words IF or ON followed by the appropriate operands (file-names, literals, data-names, etc.) and other COBOL words that are essential to the completion of the statement. COBOL statements may be compared to clauses in the English language. The statement may be of three types: imperative, conditional, or compiler-directing.

Imperative

An imperative statement consists of one or more unconditional "commands" to be performed by the object program. A simple imperative statement consists of one COBOL verb and its associated operands, excluding compiler-directing statements and conditional statements. An imperative statement may also consist of a series of imperative statements.

Imperative statements direct the computer to perform certain specified actions. These actions are specified and unequivocal, and the computer does not have the option of not performing them. An example of an imperative statement: SUBTRACT DEDUCTIONS FROM GROSS GIVING NET-PAY.

```
MOVE CATALOG-NUMBER TO CONTROL-ITEM.
```

Figure 8–4.   Example—Imperative Statements.

Conditional

A conditional statement is a statement that is to be tested, and the evaluation of the conditional expression will determine which of the alternate paths the program will follow. The modification of an imperative statement permits the computer to perform an operation under certain conditions. If the programmer attaches one or more conditional statements to an imperative statement, then the entire statement becomes a conditional statement.

In a conditional statement, the stated action is performed only if the specified conditions are present. Some examples of conditional statements are found in a READ statement, an arithmetic statement with the ON SIZE ER-ROR option, and IF statements. These and other statements involving conditions will be discussed later in the chapter. An example of a conditional statement: IF AGE IS LESS THAN 21 GO TO MINOR.

```
          IF A EQUALS B, MOVE A TO J
          OTHERWISE MOVE A TO M.
   ADD C, D; ON SIZE ERROR GO TO PARA-3.
   READ EMPLOYEE-FILE AT END GO TO END-ROUTINE.
```

Figure 8–5. Example—Conditional Statements.

Compiler-Directing

A compiler-directing statement directs the computer to take certain action at compiler time. The statement contains one of the compiler-directing verbs (COPY, ENTER, NOTE) and its associated operands. These statements will be discussed in greater detail later in the chapter.

```
                ENTER PARA-A
```

Figure 8–6. Example—Compiler Directing Statements.

Sentence

A sentence is composed of one or more statements specifying action to be taken terminated by a period and followed by a space. Commas, semicolons, or the word THEN may be used as separators between statements. When sepa-

```
The following are imperative sentences:

MOVE COMPUTED-PAY TO NET-PAY.
ADD EARNINGS OVERTIME GIVING WAGES.
MOVE TAX TO REPORT.

The following are conditional sentences:

IF CODE 1 IS EQUAL TO 4 GO TO PROCESS-PATH.
MOVE COMPUTED-PAY TO NET-PAY IF OVERTIME THEN MULTIPLY
      HOURS BY RATE GIVING O-T-RATE.
```

Figure 8–7. Examples—Imperative and Conditional Sentences.

rators are used, they must be followed by a space. Separators improve readability, but their absence or presence has no effect upon the compilation of the object program. An example of a sentence: ADD EARNINGS TO GROSS, GO TO FICA-PROC.

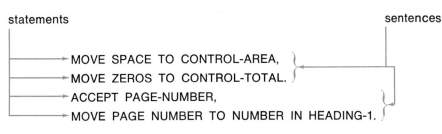

Figure 8–8. Difference—Statement and Sentence.

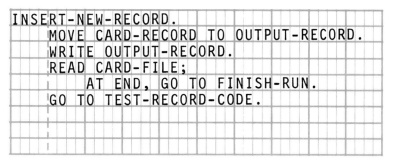

Figure 8–9. Example—Paragraph.

Paragraph

COBOL sentences may be combined into a logical entity called a paragraph. *A paragraph may be composed of one or more successive sentences.*

1. Each paragraph must begin with a procedure-name. Statements may be written on the same line as the procedure-name.
2. A procedure-name must not be duplicated within the same section.
3. Procedure-names follow the same rules as data-names with the exception that a procedure-name may be made up entirely of numerals.
4. A paragraph ends immediately before the next procedure-name or section-name, or at the end of the Procedure Division. If declaratives are used, the key words END DECLARATIVES will terminate the paragraph.

Sections

The section is the largest unit in a COBOL program to which a procedure-name may be assigned.

1. A section is composed of one or more successive paragraphs.
2. A section must begin with a section header (a procedure-name) followed by a space and the word SECTION followed by a period. The section header must appear on a line by itself, except in the DECLARATIVES portion of the Procedure Division, where it may be followed after an intervening space by a USE statement.
3. The Procedure Division need not be broken down into sections. Section usage is at the discretion of the programmer.
4. A section ends immediately before the next section name or at the end of the Procedure Division. If declaratives are used, the key words END DECLARATIVES will terminate the section.

Figure 8–10. Procedure Division Structure.

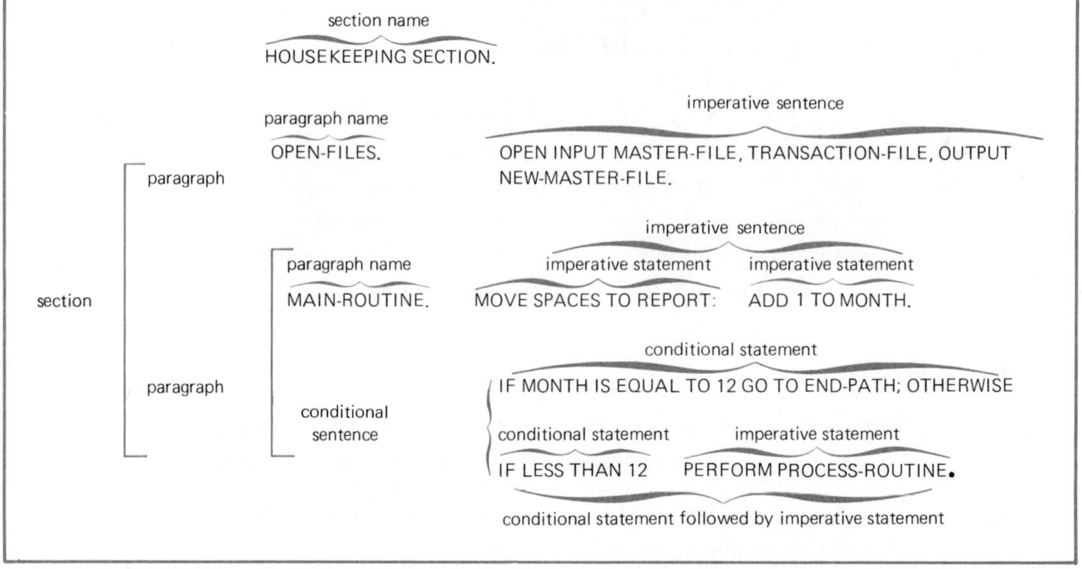

ORGANIZATION

The Procedure Division consists of instructions that are written in statement form which may be combined to form sentences. Groups of sentences form paragraphs.

The Procedure Division generally consists of a series of paragraphs which may be optionally grouped into programmer-created sections. Each paragraph has a data-name and may consist of a varying number of entries.

The Procedure Division may contain both declaratives and procedures.

The *Declaratives Section* must be grouped at the beginning of the Procedure Division, preceded by the key word DECLARATIVES, and followed by a period or space. Declarative sections are concluded by the key words END DECLARATIVES and followed by a period and a space. For a complete discussion, including examples and uses of declarative statements, see the section "Declaratives" later in the text.

Procedures are composed of paragraphs, groups of successive paragraphs, a section, or a group of successive sections within the Procedure Division. Paragraphs need not be grouped into sections. Execution begins with the first statement of the Procedure Division, *excluding the declaratives*. Statements are then executed in the sequence in which they are written, unless altered by the program.

The end of the Procedure Division is the physical end of a COBOL program after which no further procedures may appear.

Figure 8–11. Declaratives Format.

```
PROCEDURE DIVISION.
DECLARATIVES.
{section-name SECTION. USE sentence.
{paragraph-name. {sentence}... }... }...
END DECLARATIVES.
```

```
PROCEDURE DIVISION.
BEGIN-ROUTINE.
    OPEN INPUT CUSTOMER-FILE  OUTPUT PRINT-FILE.
HEADING-LINE.
    MOVE HEADINGS TO PRINT-RECORD.
    WRITE PRINT-RECORD AFTER POSITIONING 0 LINES.
SIGNAL-OPERATOR.
    DISPLAY 'PRINTOUT HAS BEGUN'.
LISTING-ROUTINE.
    READ CUSTOMER-FILE AT END GO TO FINISH.
    MOVE CORRESPONDING CUSTOMER TO LIST-RECORD.
    WRITE PRINT-RECORD FROM LIST-RECORD AFTER POSITIONING 1 LINES
        AT EOP GO TO HEADING-LINE.
    GO TO LISTING-ROUTINE.
FINISH.
    CLOSE CUSTOMER-FILE  PRINT-FILE.
    STOP RUN.
```

Figure 8–12. Example—Procedures.

COBOL VERBS

COBOL Verbs are the basis of the Procedure Division of a source program. The organization of the division is based on the following classification of COBOL verbs (other COBOL verbs will be discussed later in the text).

Input/Output	
	MULTIPLY
OPEN	DIVIDE
READ	COMPUTE
WRITE	
CLOSE	**Sequence Control**
ACCEPT	
DISPLAY	GO TO
	ALTER
	PERFORM
Data Manipulation	STOP
	EXIT
MOVE	
EXAMINE	
	Compiler-Directing
Arithmetic	
	COPY
ADD	ENTER
SUBTRACT	NOTE

Each of the verbs causes some event to take place either at compile time or at program-execution time.

Input/Output Verbs

In data processing operations, the flow of data through a system is governed by an input/output system. The COBOL statements discussed in this section are used to initiate the flow of data that is stored on an external media, such as punched cards or magnetic tape, and to govern the flow of low-volume information that is to be obtained from or sent to an input/output device, such as a console typewriter.

The programmer is concerned only with the use of individual records. The input/output system provides for operations such as the movement of data into buffers and/or internal storage, validity checking, and unblocking and blocking of physical records.

One of the important advantages of COBOL programming is the use of pretested input and output statements to get data into and out of data process-

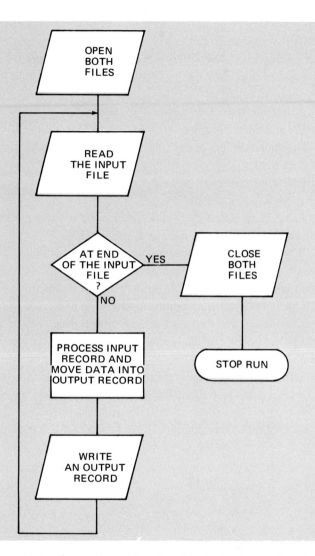

Figure 8–13. Overall Logic Input and Output (Sequential Files).

ing systems. The COBOL input and output verbs provide the means of storing data on an external device (magnetic tape, disk units, as well as card readers, punches, and printers) and extracting such data from these external devices.

Four verbs, OPEN, READ, WRITE, and CLOSE are used to specify the flow of data to and from files stored in an external media. ACCEPT and DIS-PLAY are used in conjunction with low-volume data that has to be obtained or sent to a card reader, console typewriter, or printer.

Open

The OPEN statement makes one or more input or output files ready for reading or writing, checks or writes labels if needed, and prepares the storage areas to receive or send data.

Rules Governing the Use of the Open Statement

1. An OPEN statement must be specified for all files used in a COBOL program. The file must be designated as either INPUT, OUTPUT, or I-O (mass storage files).
2. An OPEN statement must be executed prior to any other input or output statement for a particular file.
3. If the file has been closed during the processing, a second OPEN statement must be executed before the file can be used again.
4. The OPEN statement does not make input records available for processing nor release output records to their respective devices. A READ or WRITE statement respectively is required to perform these functions.
5. When a file is opened, such actions as checking and creating beginning file labels are done automatically for those files requiring such action.
6. An OPEN statement can name one or all the files to be processed by the program.
7. Each file that has been opened must be defined in the file description entry in the Data Division as well as the SELECT entry in the Environment Division.
8. At least one of the three optional clauses (INPUT, OUTPUT, or I-O) must be written.

Figure 8–14. Format—Open Statement.

```
OPEN [INPUT {file-name   ┌ REVERSED       ┐          }...]
                         │ WITH NO REWIND │
                         └                ┘
     [OUTPUT {file-name [WITH NO REWIND] }...]
     [I-O {file-name}...]
```

```
OPEN INPUT MASTER-FILE.
OPEN OUTPUT ERROR-LISTING.
OPEN INPUT MASTER-FILE, TRANSACTIONS-FILE.
OPEN INPUT MASTER-FILE, TRANSACTIONS-FILE,
OUTPUT NEW-MASTER-FILE, DELETIONS, ADDITIONS.
```

Figure 8–15. Examples—Open Statement.

9. The I-O option permits the opening of a mass storage file for both input and output operations. Since this option implies the existence of a file, it cannot be used if the mass storage file is being initially created.

Read

The READ statement makes a data record from a sequential input file (magnetic tape and card files) available for processing and allows the performance of one or more specified statements when the end of the file is detected.

The READ statement may also make a specific record from a mass storage available for random file processing and give control to a specified imperative statement if the contents of the associated ACTUAL KEY data item are found to be invalid.

READ file-name   RECORD [INTO identifier]

$$\left\{ \begin{array}{l} \text{AT END} \\ \text{INVALID KEY} \end{array} \right\} \text{imperative-statement}$$

Figure 8–16. Format—Read Statement.

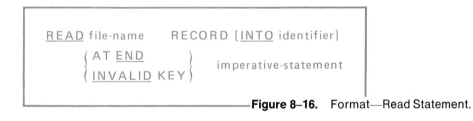

```
READ FORECAST-FILE;
     AT END, CLOSE FORECAST-FILE,
          STOP RUN.
```

Figure 8–17. Examples—Read Statement.

Rules Governing the Use of the Read Statement

1. The data records are made available in the input block one at a time. The record is available in the input until the next READ or a CLOSE statement is executed.
2. If the file contains more than one type of record for a file being executed, the next record is made available regardless of type. If more than one record description is specified in the FD entry, it is the programmers responsibility to recognize which record is in the input block at any one time, since these records automatically share the same storage area, one that is equivalent to an implicit redefinition of the area. The programmer cannot specify the type of record to be read because the format of the READ statement requires the name of a file, not a record.

3. The file must be opened before it can be read.

4. When the end of a volume is reached for multivolume files, such as tape files, volumes are automatically switched, the tape is rewound, and the next reel is read. All normal header and trailer labels are checked.

5. The INTO option converts the READ statement into a READ and MOVE statement. The identifier must be the name of a Working-Storage Section entry or a previously opened output record. The current record is now available in the input area as well as the area specified by the identifier. If the format of the INTO area is different than the input area, the data is moved into that area in accordance with the rules for the MOVE statement *without* the CORRESPONDING option.

(*Note:* The largest record may be described in any 01 level entry rather than it be the first level 01 entry. Using the INTO option, data is moved using the size of the largest record specified in the file description (FD) entry as the sending field size.)

```
READ MASTER-FILE RECORD INTO MASTER-WORK AT END
     GO TO END-DATA-MASTER.
```

Figure 8–18.   Example Read Statement—Into Option.

6. An AT END clause must be included in all READ statements for sequential input files. The statements following the records AT END up to the period are taken to be the end of file conditions. When the AT END clause is encountered, the last data record of the file has already been read.

7. Once the imperative statements in the AT END clause have been executed for a file, any later referral to the file will constitute an error unless subsequent CLOSE and OPEN statements for that file are executed.

8. The INVALID KEY option must be specified for mass storage files in the random access mode. Control of the program will be processed according to the imperative statements following the INVALID KEY when the contents of the ACTUAL KEY are invalid.

Write

The WRITE statement releases a data record for insertion in an output file. Format-1 is used for standard sequential files. Format-2 is used for processing mass storage files. See chapter 12.

Figure 8-19.   Format—Write Statement—Advancing Option.

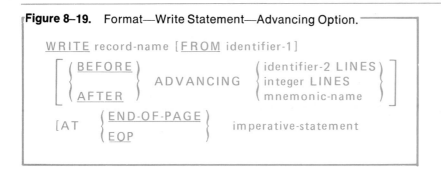

WRITE record-name [FROM identifier-1]

$$\left[\left\{ \begin{matrix} \text{BEFORE} \\ \text{AFTER} \end{matrix} \right\} \text{ADVANCING} \left\{ \begin{matrix} \text{identifier-2 LINES} \\ \text{integer LINES} \\ \text{mnemonic-name} \end{matrix} \right\} \right]$$

$$\left[\text{AT} \left\{ \begin{matrix} \text{END-OF-PAGE} \\ \text{EOP} \end{matrix} \right\} \text{imperative-statement} \right]$$

```
WRITE INVENTORY.
WRITE ERROR-RECORD FROM CHANGE-RECORD.
WRITE STATUS-REPORT BEFORE ADVANCING 2 LINES.
```
This will cause the report to be double spaced.

Figure 8-20.   Examples—Write Statement.

Rules Governing the Use of the Write Statement

1. If the records are blocked, the actual transfer of the data to the output block may not occur until later in the processing cycle when the output block is filled with the number of records specified in the file description entry in the Data Division.

2. When an end of volume is reached for multivolume files, such as magnetic tape files, volumes are switched, the tape is rewound, and the next reel is written. All normal standard header and trailer labels are written.

3. An OPEN statement must be executed prior to the execution of the first WRITE statement.

4. After the record has been released, the logical record named by the record-name is no longer available for processing. All necessary processing of a record must be done prior to the WRITE statement.

5. The file associated with the record-name must be defined in the FD entry in the Data Division of the program. When a WRITE statement is executed, the record-name record is released to the output device.

6. The format requires a *record-name* rather than a file-name.

7. When the FROM option is used, Identifier-1 must not be the name of an item in the file containing the record-name. The FROM option converts the WRITE statement into a MOVE and WRITE statement. Identifier-1 must be the name of an item defined in the Working-Storage Section or

in another FD. Moving takes place according to the rules specified for the MOVE statement without the CORRESPONDING option. After the execution of the WRITE statement with the FROM option, the information is still available in Identifier-1 although it is no longer available in the record-name area.

8. The ADVANCING options allow control of the vertical position of each record on a printed page of a report.

   a. If the ADVANCING option is used with a WRITE statement, every WRITE statement for records associated with the same file must also contain one of these options. Automatic spacing is overriden by the ADVANCING option.

   b. If the ADVANCING option is not used, automatic advancing will be provided by the implementor so as to cause single spacing.

   c. When the ADVANCING option is used, the first character in each logical record of a file must be reserved by the user for control characters. In a printed report, if 132 characters are to be printed, PICTURE X(133) should be specified to allow for the control character. The compiler will generate instructions to insert the appropriate control character as the first character of a record. If the records are to be punched, the first character is used for pocket selection. PICTURE X(81) should be specified for punched output. It is the users responsibility to see that the proper carriage-control tape is mounted on the printer prior to the execution of the program.

9. *ADVANCING option*

   Identifier-2. If the Identifier-2 option is specified, the printer page is advanced the number of lines equal to the current value of Identifier-2. If the identifier is used, it must be the name of a nonnegative numeric elementary item (less than 100) described as an integer.

   Integer. If the Integer option is specified, the printer page is advanced the number of lines equal to the value of the integer. The integer must be a nonnegative amount less than 100.

Action Taken for Function-names—ADVANCING Option

Function-name	Action Taken
CSP	Suppress spacing.
C01 through C09	Skip to channel 1 through 9, respectively.
C10 through C12	Skip to channel 10, 11, and 12, respectively.
S01, S02	Pocket select 1 or 2 on the IBM 1442, and P1 or P2 on the IBM 2540.

Figure 8–21. Advancing Option—Function-Names.

Mnemonic-Name. If the Mnemonic-Name option is specified, the printer page is advanced according to the rules specified by the implementor for that hardware device. The mnemonic-name must be defined as function-name in the SPECIAL-NAMES paragraph of the Environment Division. It is used to skip to channels 1–12 and to suppress spacing. It is also used for pocket selection for punched-card output files.

Before Advancing. If the BEFORE ADVANCING option is used, the record is written *before* the printer page is advanced according to the preceding rules.

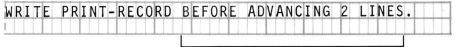

WRITE record-name

   BEFORE ADVANCING integer LINES

            Option

Figure 8–22. Before Advancing Option.

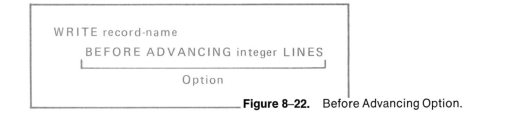

WRITE PRINT-RECORD BEFORE ADVANCING 2 LINES.

                    Option

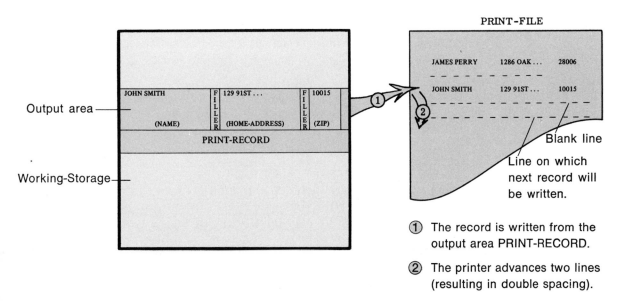

① The record is written from the output area PRINT-RECORD.

② The printer advances two lines (resulting in double spacing).

Figure 8–23. Execution of Write Statement—Before Advancing Option.

After Advancing. If the AFTER ADVANCING option is used, the record is written *after* the printer page is advanced according to the preceding rules.

```
WRITE record-name
      AFTER ADVANCING integer LINES.
```
Option

Figure 8-24. After Advancing Option.

```
WRITE OUTPUT-RECORD
      AFTER ADVANCING 3 LINES.
```

Figure 8-25. Example—After Advancing Option.

10. *END-OF-PAGE.* The END-OF-PAGE option can be used to test for channel 12 on an on-line printer. When the end of a page is reached, the imperative statement following END-OF-PAGE or EOP is executed. The writing and spacing operations are completed before the END-OF-PAGE imperative is executed. If the ADVANCING and END-OF-PAGE options are used together, the page is advanced before the END-OF-PAGE test.

11. The INVALID KEY phrase must be specified for a file that resides on a mass storage device. The imperative statement is executed when the mass storage file is specified as in sequential-access mode, the last segment of the file has been reached, and an attempt is made to execute a WRITE statement.

    Control is passed to the imperative statement if the access is random and a record is not found. See chapter 12 for an example.

```
WRITE OUTPUT-RECORD
      AFTER ADVANCING 1 LINE
      AT END-OF-PAGE
          GO TO HEADING-SEQUENCE.
```

(END-OF-PAGE may be abbreviated EOP.)

Figure 8-26. Example—End-of-Page Option.

```
ENVIRONMENT DIVISION.
CONFIGURATION SECTION.
SOURCE-COMPUTER. IBM-36Ø-H65.
OBJECT-COMPUTER. IBM-36Ø-H65.
SPECIAL-NAMES.
    CØ1 IS TO-FIRST-LINE.
```

Figure 8–27. Example—
Writing Record after
Skipping to Next Page.

```
WRITE OUTPUT-RECORD
         AFTER ADVANCING TO-FIRST-LINE.
```

12. *AFTER POSITIONING* (used with IBM/360-IBM/370 computers). In the AFTER POSITIONING option, Identifier-2 must be described as a one-character alphanumeric item, that is, with PICTURE X. The table shows the valid values that Identifier-2 may assume and their interpretations. If the integer option is used, the integer must be unsigned, and it must be the value 0, 1, 2, or 3. The values assume the meanings as shown in the table.

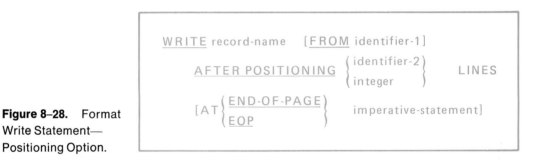

Figure 8–28. Format
Write Statement—
Positioning Option.

Value of Identifier-2	Interpretation
b (blank)	Single-spacing
0	Double-spacing
—	Triple-spacing
+	Suppress spacing
1 - 9	Skip to channel 1 - 9, respectively
A, B, C	Skip to channel 10, 11, 12, respectively
V, W	Pocket select 1 or 2, respectively, on the IBM 1442, and P1 or P2 on the IBM 2540.

Figure 8–29. Positioning Option-Values of Identifier-2 and Interpretation.

Value of Integer	Interpretation
0	Skip to channel 1 of next page (carriage control "eject")
1	Single-spacing
2	Double-spacing
3	Triple-spacing

Figure 8–30.   Positioning Option-Values of Integer and Interpretation.

```
PROCEDURE DIVISION.
PREPARATION-ROUTINE.
    OPEN INPUT CARDFILE
        OUTPUT PRINTED-REPORT.
HEADING-ROUTINE.
    MOVE HEADING-RECORD-1
        TO PRINT-RECORD.
    WRITE PRINT-RECORD
        AFTER POSITIONING Ø.
    MOVE HEADING-RECORD-2
        TO PRINT-RECORD.
    WRITE PRINT-RECORD
        AFTER POSITIONING 2.
MAIN-SEQUENCE.
    READ CARDFILE
        AT END GO TO FINISH.
    MOVE CORRESPONDING STUDENT-RECORD
        TO DETAIL-RECORD.
    MOVE DETAIL-RECORD TO PRINT-RECORD.
    WRITE PRINT-RECORD
        AFTER POSITIONING 2
        AT END-OF-PAGE
            GO TO HEADING-ROUTINE.
    GO TO MAIN-SEQUENCE.
FINISH.
    CLOSE CARDFILE PRINTED-REPORT.
    STOP RUN.
```
(Remember that you cannot mix ADVANCING and
POSITIONING options within a program.)

Figure 8–31.   Example—Positioning Option.

Close

The CLOSE statement terminates the processing of one or more data files, releases areas that serve as buffers, and optionally reverses and/or lock tape files where applicable.

Rules Governing the Use of the Close Statement

1. A CLOSE statement may be executed only for files that have been previously opened.
2. The file-name is the name of a file upon which the CLOSE statement is to operate. The file-name must be defined by a FD entry in the Data Division.
3. The REEL and WITH NO REWIND options apply only to files stored on magnetic tape devices and other devices to which these terms are applicable.
4. The UNIT option is applicable to mass storage devices in the sequential-access mode.
5. The LOCK option insures that the file cannot be opened during the execution of the object program.
6. The optional clauses (INPUT and OUTPUT) are not written for files closed.

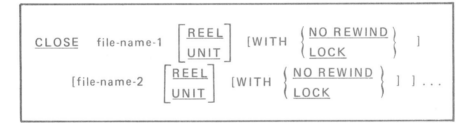

Figure 8–32.   Format—Close Statement.

CLOSE PAYROLL-MASTER.

CLOSE PAYROLL-MASTER, INCOMING-CHANGES, AND ERROR-PRINT.

This will close all three files as specified under the CLOSE file-name-1 statement.

CLOSE INVENTORY WITH NO REWIND.

CLOSE INVENTORY WITH NO REWIND, AND INVENTORY-CHANGES.

CLOSE NEW-INVENTORY-MASTER WITH LOCK, INVENTORY-MASTER WITH NO REWIND, AND INVENTORY-CHANGES.

Figure 8–33.   Examples—Close Statement.

INPUT-RECORD			
NAME		HOME-ADDRESS	
SUR (12 characters)	GIVEN (8 characters)	(40 characters)	(blank) (20 characters)

OUTPUT-RECORD	
LAST-NAME	ADDRESS-O
(12 characters)	(40 characters)

The program flowchart shows the order of operations for the Procedure Division.

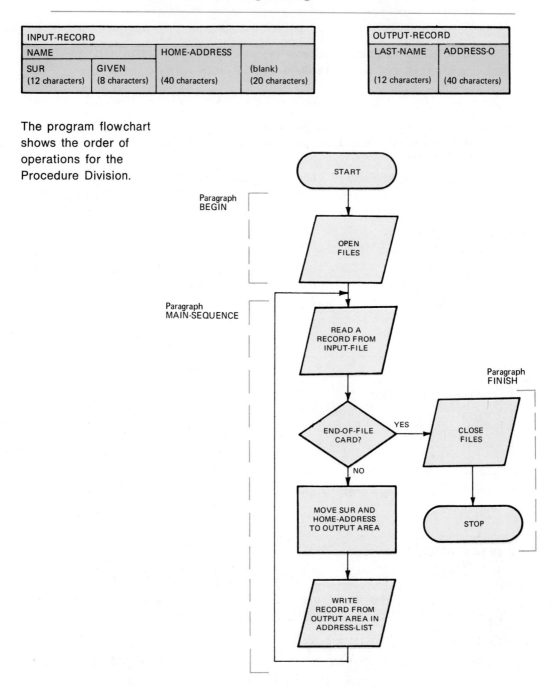

Figure 8–34. Example—Read and Write Statements.

Links file name to equipment
to be used for the file

Specifies whether file contains
records used to label the file

Defines an input area and
associates it with a file name

Prepares file for processing
and specifies its use as input

Reads a record from the file
into the input area associated
with the file in the File Section

Terminates processing
of the file

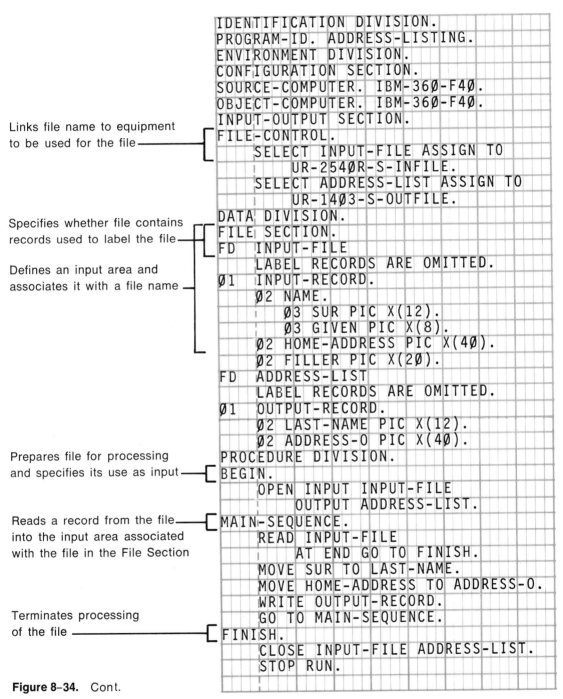

```
IDENTIFICATION DIVISION.
PROGRAM-ID. ADDRESS-LISTING.
ENVIRONMENT DIVISION.
CONFIGURATION SECTION.
SOURCE-COMPUTER. IBM-360-F40.
OBJECT-COMPUTER. IBM-360-F40.
INPUT-OUTPUT SECTION.
FILE-CONTROL.
        SELECT INPUT-FILE ASSIGN TO
            UR-2540R-S-INFILE.
        SELECT ADDRESS-LIST ASSIGN TO
            UR-1403-S-OUTFILE.
DATA DIVISION.
FILE SECTION.
FD  INPUT-FILE
        LABEL RECORDS ARE OMITTED.
01  INPUT-RECORD.
        02 NAME.
            03 SUR PIC X(12).
            03 GIVEN PIC X(8).
        02 HOME-ADDRESS PIC X(40).
        02 FILLER PIC X(20).
FD  ADDRESS-LIST
        LABEL RECORDS ARE OMITTED.
01  OUTPUT-RECORD.
        02 LAST-NAME PIC X(12).
        02 ADDRESS-O PIC X(40).
PROCEDURE DIVISION.
BEGIN.
        OPEN INPUT INPUT-FILE
            OUTPUT ADDRESS-LIST.
MAIN-SEQUENCE.
        READ INPUT-FILE
            AT END GO TO FINISH.
        MOVE SUR TO LAST-NAME.
        MOVE HOME-ADDRESS TO ADDRESS-O.
        WRITE OUTPUT-RECORD.
        GO TO MAIN-SEQUENCE.
FINISH.
        CLOSE INPUT-FILE ADDRESS-LIST.
        STOP RUN.
```

Figure 8-34. Cont.

$$\text{ACCEPT identifier } [\underline{FROM} \begin{Bmatrix} \underline{CONSOLE} \\ mnemonic\text{-}name \end{Bmatrix}]$$

Figure 8–35. Format—Accept Statement.

Accept

The ACCEPT statement obtains low-volume data from the systems logical input device or from the console.

Rules Governing the Use of the Accept Statement
1. If the same input/output device is specified for the READ and ACCEPT statements, the results may be unpredictable.
2. The identifier will be described in the Working-Storage Section of the Data Division. The ACCEPT statement will cause the transfer of data from the hardware device specified to the area specified by the identifier. This data replaces the previous contents of the area.
3. The *mnemonic-name* must be specified in the SPECIAL-NAMES paragraph of the Environment Division. The mnemonic-name may be either the system logical input device, a card reader with an assumed input record size of 80 characters or the CONSOLE which must not exceed 255 characters. If the FROM option is not specified, the systems logical input device is assumed.

EMPLOYEE-RECORD		
NAME (20 characters)	HOME-ADDRESS (30 characters)	EMPLOYEE-NUMBER (5 characters)

```
DATA DIVISION.
WORKING-STORAGE SECTION.
Ø1  EMPLOYEE-RECORD.
    Ø2 NAME PICTURE X(2Ø).
    Ø2 HOME-ADDRESS PICTURE X(3Ø).
    Ø2 EMPLOYEE-NUMBER PICTURE X(5).
```

```
    ACCEPT EMPLOYEE-RECORD FROM CONSOLE.
```

This statement will allow values of elementary variables in EMPLOYEE-REC-ORD to be entered into Working-Storage through the console typewriter.

Figure 8–36. Example—Accept Statement—Console Option.

CUSTOMER-RECORD		
NAME (25 characters)	HOME-ADDRESS (30 characters)	BALANCE (5 characters)

```
DATA DIVISION.
WORKING-STORAGE SECTION.
Ø1  CUSTOMER-RECORD.
    Ø2 NAME PICTURE X(25).
    Ø2 HOME-ADDRESS PICTURE X(3Ø).
    Ø2 BALANCE PICTURE X(5).

PROCEDURE DIVISION.
SEQUENCE-1.
    ACCEPT CUSTOMER-RECORD FROM CONSOLE.
    STOP RUN.
```

```
    ACCEPT CUSTOMER-RECORD FROM SYSIN.
```

The ACCEPT statement may be used for low-volume input from a card reader as well as from a console typewriter. The card reader, when it is the system logical input device, is referred to in a COBOL statement as SYSIN. The statement would transmit values to a Working-Storage variable from a punched card through a card reader.

Figure 8–37.   Example—Accept Statement—Mnemonic Name Option.

4. When the FROM CONSOLE option is used.

   a. A message code is automatically displayed followed by the literal "AWAITING REPLY." The operation is suspended until the operator types the same message code and the necessary information for the continuance of the program. The message code serves as a key in the control program to correlate the console input with the proper program.

   b. As many records as necessary are read to exhaust the operand, up to 255 characters.

5. If the hardware device specified is capable of transferring data of the same size as the receiving area, the transferred data is stored in the receiving data item. If the hardware device is not capable of transferring data of the same size as the receiving area item, then the following takes place:

a. If the size of receiving area is greater than the transferred data, the transferred data is stored in the left portion of the receiving area, and additional data is requested.

b. If the size of the receiving area is less than the transferred data, only the leftmost characters will be moved until the area is filled, with the excess character positions at the right being truncated.

6. If the mnemonic-name is associated with the logical input device, up to 80 characters can be obtained. The data to be moved will come from the leftmost positions of the input block. The data must be punched into a card and entered together with the job-control cards at the time the object program is to be executed.

Display

The DISPLAY statement causes the writing of low-volume data on an output device.

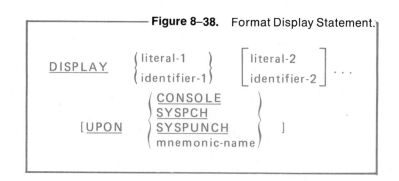

Figure 8–38. Format Display Statement.

```
 DISPLAY 'ENTER PROGRAM-NAME.'
     UPON CONSOLE.
```

The message ENTER PROGRAM-NAME will be written on the console typewriter.

```
 DISPLAY PROGRAM-NAME UPON CONSOLE.
```

The value of the variable PROGRAM-NAME will be written on the console typewriter.

Figure 8–39. Examples—Display Statement.

Rules Governing the Use of the Display Statement

1. A maximum logical record is assumed for each hardware device.

   a. Systems logical printing device—120 characters.
   b. Systems logical console device—100 characters.
   c. Systems logical punch device—72 characters with columns 73–80 reserved for identification purposes. If fewer than 72 characters are required, the remaining positions up to column 73 are filled with spaces.

2. If the same input/output device is used with both the WRITE and DISPLAY statement, the output resulting from the statements may not be in the sequence in which the statements were encountered.

3. The mnemonic-name is associated with a hardware device in the SPECIAL-NAMES paragraph in the Environment Division.

4. The identifier may be either an elementary or group item.

5. When a DISPLAY statement contains more than one operand, the size of the sending item is the sum of the sizes associated with the operands, and the value of the operands are transferred in the sequence in which the operands are encountered.

6. Numeric or nonnumeric literals may be used.

7. Figurative constants, except ALL, may be used in DISPLAY statements. If a figurative constant is used as one of the operands, only a single occurrence of the figurative constant is displayed.

```
A   B
8   12   16   20   24   28   32   36   40   44   48
PROCEDURE DIVISION.
SEQUENCE-1.
    DISPLAY
    'ENTER NUMBER OF LOAN-ACCOUNTS DUE.'
        UPON CONSOLE.
    ACCEPT LOAN-ACCOUNTS FROM CONSOLE.
    DISPLAY LOAN-ACCOUNTS UPON CONSOLE.
    STOP RUN.
```

The above entries will cause the following:

1. Write the message ENTER NUMBER OF LOAN-ACCOUNTS DUE on the console typewriter.
2. Allow the number of loan accounts that are due to be keyed into LOAN-ACCOUNTS.
3. Write the value of LOAN-ACCOUNTS on the console typewriter.
4. The STOP RUN statement will halt execution of the program.

Figure 8–40. Examples—Display and Accept Statements.

8. Any number of identifiers, literals, and figurative constants may be combined into one statement, but they must not exceed the specified maximum limit size. When more than one item is displayed, any spaces desired between multiple operands must be explicitly specified, either with designated spaces included in the literal or the figurative constant SPACE between operands.

9. If the hardware device is capable of receiving the data of the same size being transferred, then the data is moved; otherwise, the following applies:

   a. If the size of the data item being transferred exceeds the size of the data that the hardware device is capable of receiving in a single transfer, the data, beginning with the leftmost character, is stored aligned to the left in the receiving hardware device, and additional data is requested.

   b. If the size of the data item that the hardware device is capable of receiving exceeds the size of the data being transferred, the transferred data is stored aligned to the left in the receiving hardware device.

10. If the UPON option is not used, the systems logical display device is assumed.

Data-Manipulation Verbs

The data-manipulation verbs move data from one storage area to another within the computer, and the inspection of the data is explicit in the functioning of several of the COBOL words. The MOVE verb has as its primary function the transmission of information from one storage area to another, while the EXAMINE verb inspects the data with or without the movement of data.

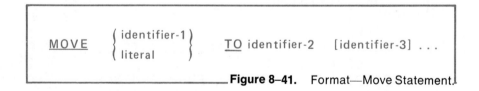

$$\underline{MOVE} \quad \left\{ \begin{array}{l} \text{identifier-1} \\ \text{literal} \end{array} \right\} \quad \underline{TO} \text{ identifier-2} \quad [\text{identifier-3}] \ldots$$

Figure 8–41. Format—Move Statement.

Move

The MOVE statement is used to move data from one area in main storage to one or more areas within the computer.

Rules Governing the Use of the Move Statement

1. Source data can be transferred to any number of receiving items.
2. When a group item is involved in a move, the data is moved without any

regard for the level structure of the group items involved, and without editing. Thus, when a group item is present, the data being moved is treated as
simply as a sequence of alphanumeric characters and is placed in the receiving area in accordance with the rules for moving elementary nonnumeric items. If the size of the group item differs, the compiler will produce a warning message when the statement is encountered. Normally,
when a group item is involved in a move, it is a group transfer, and the
description of the two items are the same.

3. When both the source and receiving areas are elementary items, editing appropriate to the format of the receiving area takes place automatically after
the MOVE instruction is executed. The type of editing depends upon
whether the item is numeric or nonnumeric.

4. Numeric literals and the figurative constant ZERO belong to the numeric
category. Nonnumeric literals and the figurative constant SPACE belong to
the nonnumeric category.

Sending variable \ Receiving variable	Group	Alpha-betic	Alpha-numeric	External decimal	Packed decimal	Edit
Group	A	A	A	AU	AU	I
Alphabetic	A	A	A	I	I	I
Alphanumeric	A	A	A	N*	N*	E*
External decimal	AU	I	A*	N	N	E
Packed decimal	AU	I	A*	N	N	E
Edit	A	I	A	I	I	I

A	Alphanumeric move
E	Edit move
AU	Alphanumeric move (value of receiving field is unpredictable)
N	Numeric move
*	Integers only
I	Invalid

Figure 8–42. Types of Moves.

Type of move	Receiving item	Compiler action during move	Alignment	Padding if necessary	Truncation if necessary
Alphanumeric	Group	none	at left of value	on right with spaces	on right
	Alphabetic or alphanumeric	any necessary conversion	at left of value	on right with spaces	on right
Numeric	External decimal or packed decimal	any necessary conversion	at decimal point	on left and right with zeros	on left and right
Edit	Edited	editing and any necessary conversion	at decimal point	on left and right with zeros (unless suppressed)	on left and right

Figure 8–43.   Effects of Types of Moves.

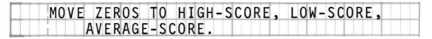

MOVE ZEROS TO HIGH-SCORE, LOW-SCORE, AVERAGE-SCORE.

The above statement will fill the entire area of
HIGH-SCORE, LOW-SCORE, and AVERAGE-SCORE with zeros.

Figure 8–44.   Example—Move Statement.

Source Field		Receiving Field		
PICTURE	Value	PICTURE	Value before MOVE	Value after MOVE
99V99	1234	99V99	9876	1234
99V99	1234	99V9	987	123
9V9	12	99V999	98765	01200
XXX	A2B	XXXXX	Y9X8W	A2Bbb
9V99	123	99.99	87.65	01.23
AAAAAA	REPORT	AAA	JKL	REP

Figure 8–45.   Example—Data Movement.

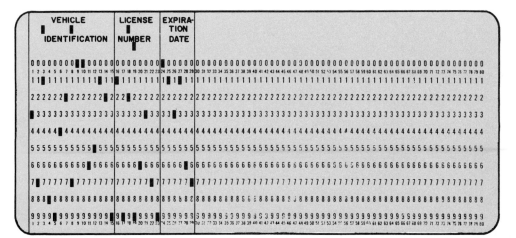

```
DATA DIVISION.
WORKING-STORAGE SECTION.
01   CARD-DATA.
     02   VEHICLE, PICTURE X(15).
     02   LICENSE, PICTURE X(8).
     02   EXPIRATION, PICTURE 9(6).
01   OUTPUT-LINE.
     02   AREA1, PICTURE X(15).
     02   FILLER, PICTURE X(5), VALUE SPACES.
     02   AREA2, PICTURE X(8).
     02   FILLER, PICTURE X(5), VALUE SPACES.
     02   AREA3, PICTURE 9(6).
```

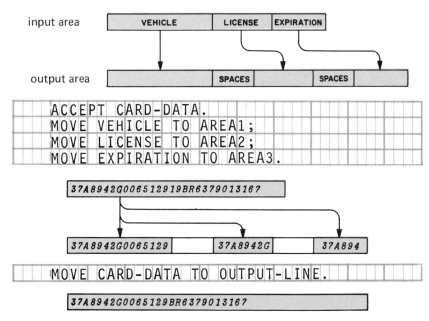

```
     ACCEPT CARD-DATA.
     MOVE VEHICLE TO AREA1;
     MOVE LICENSE TO AREA2;
     MOVE EXPIRATION TO AREA3.
```

Figure 8–46. Example—Individual Move and Group Move.

Numeric Data

1. The data from the source area is aligned with respect to the decimal point (assumed or actual) in the receiving area. This alignment may result in the loss of leading or low-order digits (or both) if the source area is larger than the receiving area. Excess positions in the receiving area at either end will be filled with zeros.
2. If the USAGE clause of both the source and receiving fields differ, conversion to the representation specified in the receiving area takes place.
3. If the receiving area specifies editing, zero suppression, insertion of dollar signs, commas, decimal points, etc., and decimal point alignment, all will take place in the receiving area.
4. If no decimal point is specified, and the receiving area is larger than the sending area, right justification will take place with the blank left positions being filled with zeros.

MOVE FIELD TO FIELD-1, FIELD-2, AND FIELD-3.

The data in FIELD is: [2|3|4|5|6|7|8|9]

The data in FIELD-1, FIELD-2, and FIELD-3 after the MOVE is executed is:

FIELD-1   [6|7|8|9|0|0]

FIELD-2   [2|3|4|5|6]

FIELD-3   [0|2|3|4|5|6|7|8]

∧ Indicates Assumed Decimal Point

Figure 8–47.   Example—Move Statement—Numeric Data.

Nonnumeric Data

1. The data from the source area is placed in the receiving area beginning at the left and continuing to the right, unless the field is specified as JUSTIFIED RIGHT, in which case the source data is placed in the right positions of the receiving area.
2. If the receiving area is not completely filled with data, the remaining positions are filled with spaces at the right or left for justified right items.
3. If the source field is longer than the receiving field, the move is terminated as soon as the receiving area is filled. Excess characters are truncated when the receiving area is filled.

MOVE NAME TO FIELD-A AND FIELD-B.

Data in NAME | J | O | H | N | B | R | O | W | N | 1 | 5 | 0 | 2 |

Data in FIELD-A and FIELD-B after the MOVE is executed.

FIELD-A | J | O | H | N | FIELD-B | J | O | H | N | B | R | O | W | N |

Figure 8–48.   Example—Move Statement—Nonnumeric Data.

MOVE NAME TO NAME-1.

The data in NAME is: | J | O | H | N |

The data in NAME-1 after the MOVE is executed is: | J | O | H | N | | |

Figure 8–49.   Example—Move Statement—Nonnumeric Data.

Rules Governing Elementary Items Move Statements

1. A numeric edited, alphanumeric edited, the figurative constant SPACE, or any alphabetic data item must not be moved to a numeric edited data item.
2. A numeric literal, the figurative constant ZERO, a numeric data item, or a numeric edited data item must not be moved to an alphabetic item.
3. A numeric literal or a numeric data item whose implicit decimal point is not immediately to the right of the least significant digit must not be moved to an alphanumeric or alphanumeric edited item.
4. All other elementary moves are legal and are performed in accordance with the rules mentioned previously.

Move Corresponding

When a MOVE CORRESPONDING statement is executed at object time, selected items within the source area are moved with any required editing to selected areas within the receiving area.

Figure 8–50.   Format—Move Corresponding Statement.

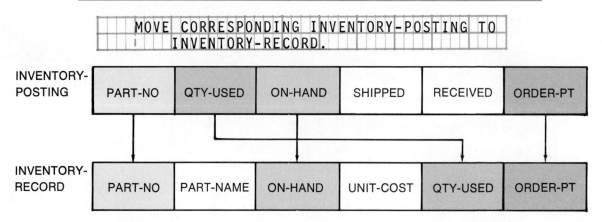

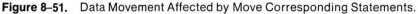

Figure 8–51. Data Movement Affected by Move Corresponding Statements.

Rules Governing the Use of the Move Corresponding Statement

1. Only corresponding data items having the same name and qualification of Identifier-1 and Identifier-2 are moved.
2. At least one of the items of the pair of matching items must be an elementary item.
3. The effect of a **MOVE CORRESPONDING** statement is equivalent to a series of simple **MOVE** statements.
4. Identifier-1 and Identifier-2 must be group items.
5. An item subordinate to Identifier-1 or Identifier-2 is not considered corresponding if:

   a. It is an item identified by the word FILLER and any items subordinate to it, or

   b. An item identified by a REDEFINES, OCCURS, RENAMES, or USAGE IS INDEX clauses and any items subordinate to it.

6. Either identifier may have REDEFINES or OCCURS clauses in its description or may be subordinate to a data item described with these clauses. If either identifier is described with an OCCURS clause, then the items must be subscripted; each data item that corresponds will also have to be subscripted by the computer.
7. Data-names with level number 66, 77, or 88 (RENAMES clause, independent item clause, or condition-names) cannot be referenced by Identifier-1 or Identifier-2.
8. Each matched source item is moved in conformity with the description of the receiving item.

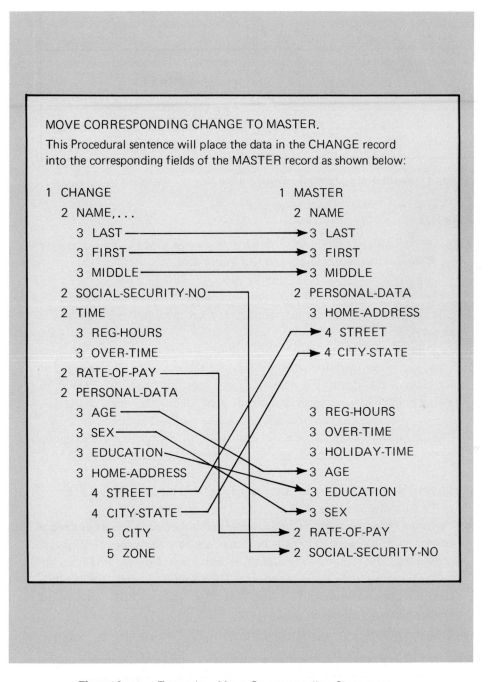

Figure 8–52. Example—Move Corresponding Statement.

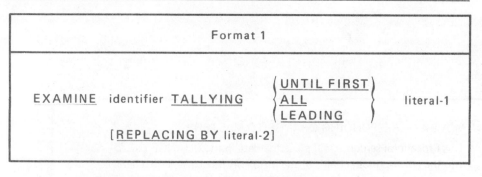

Figure 8–53. Format—Examine Statement Format 1.

Examine

The EXAMINE statement is used to replace a given character and/or to count the number of times it appears in a data item.

Rules Governing the Use of the Examine Statement

1. The EXAMINE statement may be only applied to an item whose USAGE IS DISPLAY.
2. Any literal used in the EXAMINE statement must be a number of characters associated with the class specified for the identifier. For example, if the class of the identifier is numeric, each literal in the statement must be numeric and may possess an operational sign. All must be single characters.
3. Nonnumeric literals must be single characters enclosed in quotation marks.
4. The examination of the data item begins with the first (leftmost) character of the data set and proceeds to the right. If the data item is numeric, any operational sign associated with it will be ignored.
5. Figurative constants may be used in place of Literal-2, with the exception of the figurative constant ALL.
6. *Tallying Option.* A count is made of the number of occurrences of certain characters in the identifier, and the count replaces the value of a special register called TALLY, whose length is five decimal digits. TALLY may be used in other procedural statements. The COBOL compiler sets up this special register. The count in TALLY at object time depends upon which of the following options is used.

   a. *UNTIL FIRST.* If the UNTIL FIRST option is specified, the TALLY count represents the number of characters other than LITERAL-1 encountered prior to the first occurrence of Literal-1.
   b. *ALL.* If the ALL option is specified, all occurrences of Literal-1 are counted and accumulated in the TALLY register.

EXAMINE ACCOUNT TALLYING UNTIL FIRST "A".

Data in ACCOUNT before EXAMINE	Data in ACCOUNT after EXAMINE	Contents of TALLY after EXAMINE
1 2 9 6 A A 1 0	no change	0 0 0 0 0 4
A A 1 2 3 4 5 6		0 0 0 0 0 0
∅ ∅ ∅ A 1 2 3	in	0 0 0 0 0 3
F R T S 9 8 7 1 2 3		0 0 0 0 1 0
+ A 1 2 3 4	data	0 0 0 0 0 1

EXAMINE ACCOUNT TALLYING UNTIL FIRST "A" REPLACING BY "Z".

Data in ACCOUNT before EXAMINE	Data in ACCOUNT after EXAMINE	Contents of TALLY after EXAMINE
0 9 8 7 6 A B @	Z Z Z Z Z A B @	0 0 0 0 0 5
A 8 7 6 1 A W E	A 8 7 6 1 A W E	0 0 0 0 0 0
J O H N 0 1 Z F F F	Z Z Z Z Z Z Z Z Z Z	0 0 0 0 1 0

Figure 8–54. Example—Examine Statement Format 1.

EXAMINE GROUP TALLYING ALL 9.

Data in GROUP before EXAMINE	Data in GROUP after EXAMINE	Contents of TALLY after EXAMINE
A B C 9 0 9 8 7 1 9	no change	0 0 0 0 0 3
* * * * 9 9 9 9 . 5 6 7 1 2	in	0 0 0 0 0 4
1 2 3 4 5 6 7 8 8 8	data	0 0 0 0 0 0

EXAMINE GROUP TALLYING ALL 9 REPLACING BY "*".

Data in GROUP before EXAMINE	Data in GROUP after EXAMINE	Contents of TALLY after EXAMINE
9 8 7 6 1 2 3 4 5	* 8 7 6 1 2 3 4 5	0 0 0 0 0 1
9 9 9 9 9 9 9	* * * * * * *	0 0 0 0 0 7
9 0 9 0 9 0 9 0	* 0 * 0 * 0 * 0	0 0 0 0 0 4

Figure 8–55. Example—Examine Statement Format 1.

EXAMINE PART-NUMBER TALLYING LEADING "Z".

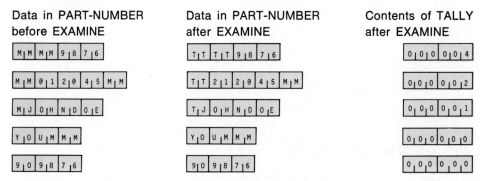

Data in PART-NUMBER before EXAMINE	Data in PART-NUMBER after EXAMINE	Contents of TALLY after EXAMINE
Z Z Z Z 9 0 9 8 2	no change	0 0 0 0 0 4
Z Z 1 2 3 @ Z Z		0 0 0 0 0 2
Z J O H N D O E	in	0 0 0 0 0 1
Y O U Z Z Z Z Z Q		0 0 0 0 0 0
1 2 3 4 5	data	0 0 0 0 0 0

Figure 8–56.   Example—Examine Statement Format 1.

EXAMINE PART-NUMBER TALLYING LEADING "M" REPLACING BY "T".

Data in PART-NUMBER before EXAMINE	Data in PART-NUMBER after EXAMINE	Contents of TALLY after EXAMINE
M M M M 9 8 7 6	T T T T 9 8 7 6	0 0 0 0 0 4
M M @ 1 2 @ 4 5 M M	T T 2 1 2 @ 4 5 M M	0 0 0 0 0 2
M J O H N D O E	T J O H N D O E	0 0 0 0 0 1
Y O U M M M	Y O U M M M	0 0 0 0 0 0
9 0 9 8 7 6	9 0 9 8 7 6	0 0 0 0 0 0

Figure 8–57.   Example—Examine Statement Format 1.

```
                              Format 2

    EXAMINE  identifier  REPLACING    ⎧ ALL        ⎫
                                      ⎪ LEADING    ⎪  literal-1
                                      ⎨ FIRST      ⎬
                                      ⎩ UNTIL FIRST ⎭

                 BY   literal-2
```

Figure 8–58.   Format—Examine Statement Format 2.

EXAMINE LOCATION REPLACING FIRST "E" BY ",".

Data in LOCATION before EXAMINE	Data in LOCATION after EXAMINE	TALLY after EXAMINE

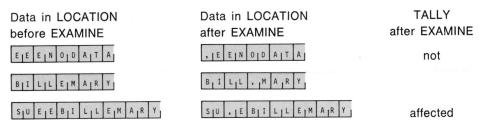

not

affected

Figure 8-59. Example—Examine Statement Format 2.

   c. *LEADING.* If the LEADING option is specified, the TALLY count represents the number of occurrences of Literal-1 prior to encountering other than Literal-1 data.

7. *Replacing Option.* The REPLACING option may be used with or without the TALLYING option. The replacement of characters depends upon which of the options is employed.

   a. *ALL.* If the ALL option is specified, Literal-2 is substituted for all occurrences of Literal-1.

   b. *LEADING.* If the LEADING option is specified, Literal-2 is substituted for Literal-1. The substitution is terminated either when a character other than Literal-1 is encountered or when the right-hand boundary of the data item is reached.

   c. *FIRST.* If the FIRST option is specified, only the first occurrence of Literal-1 is replaced by Literal-2.

   d. *UNTIL FIRST.* If the UNTIL FIRST option is specified, the substitution of Literal-2 terminates as soon as the first Literal-1 is encountered or until the right-hand boundary of the data item is reached.

Arithmetic Statements

Five arithmetic verbs are provided for in COBOL to perform the necessary arithmetic functions: ADD, SUBTRACT, MULTIPLY, DIVIDE, and COMPUTE. ADD, SUBTRACT, MULTIPLY, and DIVIDE are arithmetic verbs used to perform individual arithmetic operations. The fifth verb COMPUTE permits the programmer to combine arithmetic operations into arithmetic expressions in a formula type using the various arithmetic operators.

Arithmetic expressions can be composed of an identifier of a numeric elementary item, a numeric literal, those identifiers and literals separated by arithmetic operators, or an arithmetic expression enclosed in parenthesis.

Rules Governing the Use of Arithmetic Statements

1. All identifiers used in arithmetic statements must represent elementary numeric items that are defined in the Data Division.
2. The identifier that follows GIVING may contain editing symbols if it is not itself involved in the computation.
3. All literals used in arithmetic statements must be numeric.
4. The maximum size of a numeric literal or identifier is 18 decimal digits.
5. The maximum size of a result of a computation is 18 decimal digits after decimal alignment.
6. Decimal alignment is supplied automatically throughout the computation in accordance with individual PICTURE clauses of the results and operands.
7. The GIVING option applies to all arithmetic statements except the COMPUTE statement.

Giving

If the GIVING option is used, the value of the identifier following the word GIVING will be made equal to the calculated value of the arithmetic expression. This identifier may be an edited numeric item but must not be involved in the computation. *If the GIVING option is not used, the replaced operand in the arithmetic calculation must not be a literal.*

```
ADD A, B, C, D, GIVING R.
SUBTRACT A, B, C, FROM D, GIVING R.
MULTIPLY A BY B, GIVING R.
DIVIDE A INTO B, GIVING R.
```

Figure 8-60. Example—Giving Option.

Rounded

The ROUNDED option is used when the number of places in the calculated result exceeds the number of places allocated for the sum, difference, product, quotient, or computed result.

Rules Governing the Use of the Rounded Statement

1. Truncation (dropping of excess digits) is determined by the identifier associated with the result.
2. The least significant digit in the result is increased by 1 if the most significant digit of the excess is greater than or equal to 5.

3. If the option is not specified, truncation occurs without rounding after decimal alignment.
4. Rounding of a computed negative result occurs by rounding the absolute value of the computed result and making the final result negative.

```
MULTIPLY QUANTITY BY PRICE,
       GIVING AMOUNT, ROUNDED.
```

Figure 8–61. Example—Rounded Option.

Figure 8–62. Rounding or Truncation of Calculations.

	Item to Receive Calculated Result		
Calculated Result	PICTURE	Value After Rounding	Value After Truncating
-12.36	S99V9	-12.4	-12.3
8.432	9V9	8.4	8.4
35.6	99V9	35.6	35.6
65.6	99V	66	65
.0055	V999	.006	.005

Size Error

The SIZE ERROR option is used where the computed result after decimal alignment exceeds the number of integral places in the format of the identifier associated with the result.

Rules Governing the Use of the Size Error Statement
1. If the ROUNDED option is specified, rounding takes place before checking for size error.
2. If the SIZE ERROR option is not specified, and a size error condition arises, the result is unpredictable.

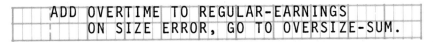
```
ADD OVERTIME TO REGULAR-EARNINGS
      ON SIZE ERROR, GO TO OVERSIZE-SUM.
```
Figure 8–63. Examples—On Size Error Option.

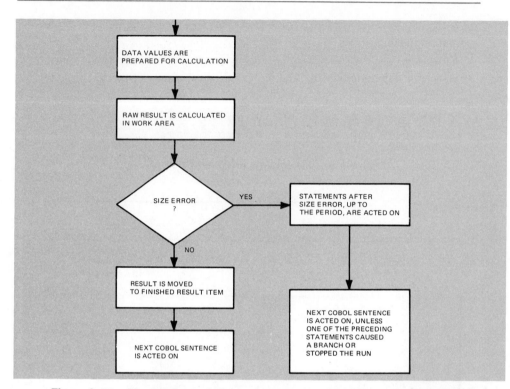

Figure 8–64. Flow of Control Through Arithmetic Statements That Control On Size Error.

3. If the SIZE ERROR option is specified, and a size error condition does arise, the value of the result is not altered, and a series of imperative statements specified for the condition will be executed.
4. An arithmetic statement written with the SIZE ERROR option becomes a conditional statement and is prohibited in context where only imperative statements are allowed.
5. Division by zero always causes a size error condition.
6. The SIZE ERROR option applies only to final results, and no assumption of an answer can be made if the size error condition arises in an intermediate result.

Corresponding

The CORRESPONDING option allows the user to perform computations on elementary items of the same name simply by specifying the group item to which they belong. This option can be used with the ADD or SUBTRACT verb whereby elementary data items within are added to or subtracted from elementary items of the same name in another group. (See Figure 8–69.)

The rules for MOVE CORRESPONDING apply to the ADD and SUB-TRACT CORRESPONDING statements. When the SIZE ERROR option is used with the CORRESPONDING option, the size error test is made after the completion of all add or subtract operations. If any of the additions or subtractions produce a size error condition, the resultant field remains unchanged for that particular item, and the imperative statement specified in the SIZE ERROR option is executed.

Add

The ADD statement is used to specify the addition of the numeric values of two or more items and to substitute the sum for the current value of an item.

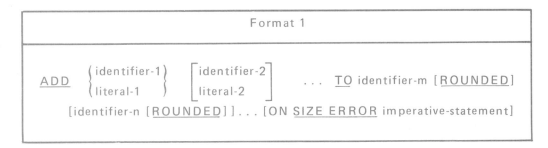

Figure 8–65. Format—Add Statement Format 1.

ADD 5 TO FIELD-A.

The data in FIELD-A before the ADD is executed: 0 0 1 5 0 5

The data in FIELD-A after the ADD has been executed: 0 0 1 5 5 5

ADD 125.25, FIELD-B, TO FIELD-C.
Data in the fields before the ADD is executed:

FIELD-B   6 8 5

FIELD-C   0 1 0 0 0 0

Data in the fields after the ADD has been executed:

FIELD-B   Unchanged

FIELD-C   0 2 9 3 7 5

Figure 8–66. Examples—Add Statement Format 1.

Rules Governing the Use of the Add Statement

1. An ADD statement must contain at least two addends (Elementary numeric items).
2. When the TO option is used, the values of the operands (literals and identifiers) preceding the word TO are added together. The sum is then added to the current value in each Identifier-m, Identifier-n, etc., and the resultant sum replaces the current values of Identifier-m, Identifier-n, etc.

Format 2
ADD $\begin{Bmatrix} \text{identifier-1} \\ \text{literal-1} \end{Bmatrix}$ $\begin{Bmatrix} \text{identifier-2} \\ \text{literal-2} \end{Bmatrix}$ $\begin{bmatrix} \text{identifier-3} \\ \text{literal-3} \end{bmatrix}$ . . .   GIVING identifier-m [ROUNDED]   [ON SIZE ERROR imperative-statement]

Figure 8–67. Format—Add Statement Format 2—Giving Option.

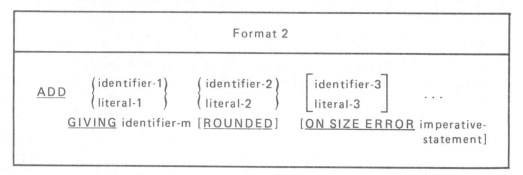

ADD FIELD-E, 5, FIELD-F GIVING FIELD-G.

Data in the fields before the ADD is executed:

FIELD-E   `0 0 0 2̬5 0`

FIELD-F   `1̬0 0`

FIELD-G   `- 0 0 5 0 0`

Data in the fields after the ADD has been executed:

FIELD-E   Unchanged

FIELD-F   Unchanged

FIELD-G   `0 0 0 6 0 0`

Figure 8–68. Examples—Add Statement Format 2.

3. The resultant sums are not edited with the TO option.
4. The word GIVING may not be written in the same statement as TO.
5. When the GIVING option is used, there must be at least two operands (literals and/or identifiers) preceding the word GIVING. The sum may be edited according to the items PICTURE and may be either an elementary numeric item or an elementary numeric edited item.
6. Decimal points are aligned in all ADD operations.
7. When the CORRESPONDING option is used, elementary data items within Identifier-1 are added to and stored in the corresponding data items in Identifier-2. Identifier-1 and Identifier-2 must be group items.
8. When the SIZE ERROR option is specified for CORRESPONDING option items, the test is made after the completion of all add operations. If any of the additions produce a size error condition, the resultant field for that addition remains unchanged, and the imperative statement specified in the SIZE ERROR option is executed.

```
ADD  AMOUNT, DISCOUNT, SUB-TOTAL GIVING  GRAND-TOTAL
ROUNDED, ON SIZE ERROR GO TO ERROR-ROUTINE.
```

Data in the fields before the ADD is executed:

AMOUNT	0 5 . 9 5 4
DISCOUNT	- 0 . 5 9
SUB-TOTAL	1 0 2 . 0 0 1
GRAND-TOTAL	0 0 5 . 0 0 6

Data in the fields after the ADD has been executed:

AMOUNT	Unchanged
DISCOUNT	Unchanged
SUB-TOTAL	Unchanged
GRAND-TOTAL	0 1 0 . 7 9 0

Figure 8–68. Continued.

Figure 8-69. Format Add Statement Format 3—Corresponding Option.

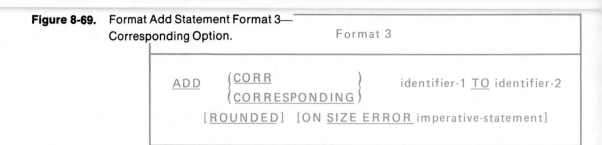

Format 3

```
ADD    (CORR          )    identifier-1 TO identifier-2
       (CORRESPONDING )
       [ROUNDED]   [ON SIZE ERROR imperative-statement]
```

```
ADD CORRESPONDING EMPLOYEE-RECORD TO PAYROLL-CHECK.
    01  EMPLOYEE-RECORD              01  PAYROLL-CHECK
        02  EMPLOYEE-NUMBER              02  EMPLOYEE-NUMBER
            03  PLANT-LOCATION               03  CLOCK-NUMBER
            03  CLOCK-NUMBER                 03  FILLER
                04  SHIFT-CODE           02  DEDUCTIONS
                04  CONTROL-NUMBER           03  FICA-RATE
        02  INCOME                           03  WITHHOLDING-TAX
            03  HOURS-WORKED                 03  PERSONAL-LOANS
            03  PAY-RATE                 02  INCOME
        02  FICA-RATE                        03  HOURS-WORKED
        02  DEDUCTIONS                       03  PAY-RATE
                                         02  NET-PAY
                                         02  EMPLOYEE- NAME
                                             03  SHIFT-CODE
```

According to the ADD CORRESPONDING rules, the following operations would take place:

1. HOURS-WORKED of INCOME.
2. PAY-RATE of INCOME.

The following items would not be added for the reasons stated:

1. EMPLOYEE-NUMBER (Item is not elementary in both groups.)
2. PLANT-LOCATION of EMPLOYEE-NUMBER (Name does not appear in PAYROLL-CHECK.)
3. CLOCK-NUMBER of EMPLOYEE-NUMBER (Item is not elementary in one group.)
4. SHIFT-CODE of CLOCK-NUMBER of EMPLOYEE-NUMBER of EMPLOYEE-RECORD (Qualification is not identical in PAYROLL-CHECK.)
5. CONTROL-NUMBER of CLOCK-NUMBER of EMPLOYEE-NUMBER of EM-PLOYEE-RECORD (Name does not appear in PAYROLL-CHECK.)
6. INCOME (Item is not elementary in both groups.)
7. FICA-RATE of EMPLOYEE-RECORD (Qualification is not identical in PAY-ROLL-CHECK.)
8. DEDUCTIONS (Item is not elementary in both groups.)

Figure 8–70. Example—Add Statement Format 3—Corresponding Option.

Subtract

The SUBTRACT statement is used to specify the subtraction of one or more numeric values from one or more specified items and to set the values of one or more items equal to the results.

Rules Governing the Use of the Subtract Statement
1. All operands (literals and identifiers) must be elementary numeric items.
2. All values of the operands (literals and identifiers) preceding the word FROM are added together, and this total is subtracted from the value of the Identifier or Literals-m, -n, etc., and the difference replaces the value of Identifier-m or Identifier-n, etc., if GIVING option is used.
3. Each identifier must refer to an elementary numeric item, except the identifier following the word GIVING, which may be a numeric edited item.
4. When the CORRESPONDING option is used, elementary data items within Identifier-1 are subtracted from corresponding data items in Identifier-2, and the differences are stored in the corresponding Identifier-2 data items.
5. When the CORRESPONDING option is used in conjunction with the SIZE ERROR option and a size error condition arises, the result for SUBTRACT is analogous to that of ADD.

Figure 8–71. Format Subtract Statement Format 1.

Format 1

$$\underline{\text{SUBTRACT}} \quad \begin{Bmatrix} \text{identifier-1} \\ \text{literal-1} \end{Bmatrix} \quad \begin{bmatrix} \text{identifier-2} \\ \text{literal-2} \end{bmatrix} \quad \cdots$$

$$\underline{\text{FROM}} \text{ identifier-m} \quad [\underline{\text{ROUNDED}}]$$

$$[\text{identifier-n} \quad [\underline{\text{ROUNDED}}]] \cdots [\text{ON SIZE ERROR imperative-statement}]$$

SUBTRACT −5.5 FROM INCREMENT.

	Before SUBTRACT	After SUBTRACT
INCREMENT	1 0 0	1 0 5

SUBTRACT −5.5 FROM INCREMENT ROUNDED.

	Before SUBTRACT	After SUBTRACT
INCREMENT	1 0 0	1 0 6

Figure 8–72. Example—Subtract Statement Format 1.

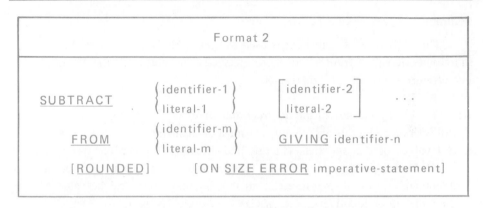

Figure 8–73. Format Subtract Statement Format 2—Giving Option.

SUBTRACT TOTAL-DEDUCTIONS FROM GROSS-PAY GIVING NET-PAY.

	Before SUBTRACT	After SUBTRACT
TOTAL-DEDUCTIONS	0 2 1 2 2	Unchanged
GROSS-PAY	0 1 1 4 7 6	Unchanged
NET-PAY	– 8 9 4 0 0	0 0 9 3 5 4

Figure 8–74. Example—Subtract Statement Format 2—Giving Option.

```
                              Format 3

SUBTRACT     ⎧ CORR          ⎫     identifier-1 FROM identifier-2
             ⎨ CORRESPONDING ⎬
             ⎩               ⎭
     [ROUNDED]    [ON SIZE ERROR imperative-statement]
```

Figure 8–75. Format Subtract Statement Format 3—Corresponding Option.

Multiply

The MULTIPLY statement is used to specify the multiplication of two numeric values and to substitute the resulting product for the current value of an item.

Figure 8–76. Format Multiply Statement Format 1.

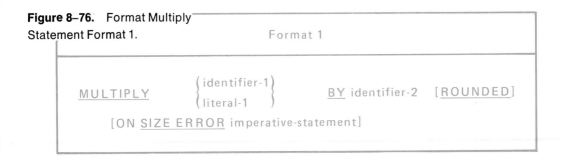

Format 1

MULTIPLY ⎰ identifier-1 ⎱ BY identifier-2 [ROUNDED]
         ⎱ literal-1   ⎰

[ON SIZE ERROR imperative-statement]

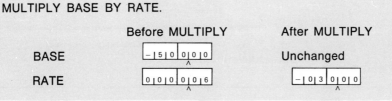

MULTIPLY BASE BY RATE.

	Before MULTIPLY	After MULTIPLY
BASE	– 5 0 0 0 0	Unchanged
RATE	0 0 0 0 0 6	– 0 3 0 0 0

Figure 8–77. Example—Multiply Statement Format 1.

Figure 8–78. Format Multiply Statement Format 2—Giving Option.

Format 2

MULTIPLY ⎰ identifier-1 ⎱ BY ⎰ identifier-2 ⎱ GIVING identifier-3
         ⎱ literal-1   ⎰   ⎱ literal-2   ⎰

[ROUNDED]   [ON SIZE ERROR imperative-statement]

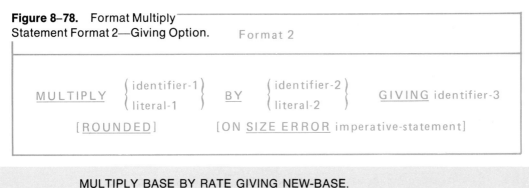

MULTIPLY BASE BY RATE GIVING NEW-BASE.

	Before MULTIPLY	After MULTIPLY
BASE	– 5 0 0 0 0	Unchanged
RATE	0 0 0 0 0 6	Unchanged
NEW-BASE	– 7 0 0 0 0	– 0 3 0 0 0

Figure 8–79. Example Multiply Statement Format 2—Giving Option.

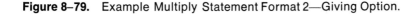

Rules Governing the Use of the Multiply Statement
1. All operands (literals and identifiers) must be elementary numeric items.
2. The value of Identifier-1 or Literal-1 is multiplied by the value of Identifier-2 or Literal-2. The value of Identifier-2 is replaced by the product.
3. Each identifier must refer to an elementary numeric item, except the identifier following the word GIVING, which may be a numeric edited item.

Divide

The DIVIDE statement specifies the division of one numeric data item by another and uses the result to replace the value of an item.

Format 1
DIVIDE $\left\{\begin{array}{l}\text{identifier-1}\\\text{literal-1}\end{array}\right\}$ INTO identifier-2 [ROUNDED] [ON SIZE ERROR imperative-statement]

Figure 8–80. Format Divide Statement Format 1.

DIVIDE 10 INTO QUANTITY.

	Before DIVIDE	After DIVIDE
QUANTITY	1 2 1 5	0 1 2 1

DIVIDE 10 INTO QUANTITY ROUNDED.

	Before DIVIDE	After DIVIDE
QUANTITY	1 2 1 5	0 1 2 2

Figure 8–81. Example—Divide Statement Format 1.

Rules Governing the Use of the Divide Statement

1. All operands (literals and identifiers) must represent elementary numeric items.
2. When the INTO option is used without the GIVING option, the value of Identifier-1 (or Literal-1) is divided into the value of Identifier-2. The value of the dividend (Identifier-2) is replaced by the quotient.
3. When the BY or INTO option is used in conjunction with the GIVING and REMAINDER options, the value of Identifier-1 or Literal-1 is divided into or by Identifier-2 or Literal-2, and the quotient is stored in Identifier-3, with the remainder being optionally stored in Identifier-4. A remainder is the result of subtracting the product of the quotient and the divisor from the dividend. If the ROUNDED option is specified, the quotient is rounded after the remainder is determined.

4. Each identifier must refer to an elementary numeric item, except the identifier following the word GIVING, which may be a numeric edited item.
5. A division by zero will always result in a size error condition.

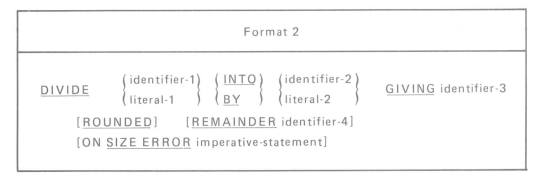

Figure 8-82. Format Divide Statement Format 2—Giving Option.

Figure 8-83. Example—Divide Statement Format 2—Giving Option.

In all four arithmetic statements, if the word GIVING is not used, the last operand (one replaced by the result) must not be a literal.

Compute

The COMPUTE statement specifies the use of an arithmetic expression, an identifier, or a numeric literal for a series of arithmetic operations.

Figure 8-84. Format Compute Statement.

COMPUTE Statement

COMPUTE identifier-1 [ROUNDED] = $\left\{ \begin{array}{l} arithmetic\text{-}expression \\ identifier\text{-}2 \\ literal\text{-}1 \end{array} \right\}$

[ON SIZE ERROR imperative-statement]

```
 COMPUTE CAPACITY = (UTILITY * SPAN) /
        (RANGE + CONSUMPTION * EFFICIENCY).
```

multiplication   *division*

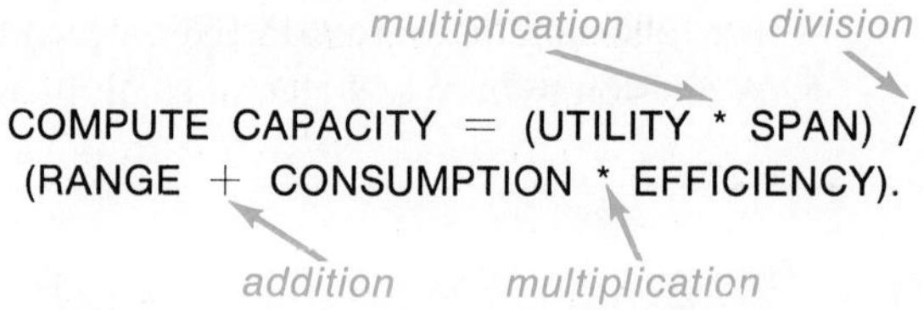

Figure 8–85. Example—
Compute Statement.

COMPUTE CAPACITY = (UTILITY * SPAN) /
(RANGE + CONSUMPTION * EFFICIENCY).

addition   *multiplication*

COMPUTE YEARS = MONTHS / 12.

	Before execution	After execution
MONTHS	$1\ 0\ 0\ 3$	Unchanged
YEARS	$0\ 1\ 2$	$0\ 8\ 3$

COMPUTE YEARS ROUNDED = MONTHS / 12.

MONTHS	$1\ 0\ 0\ 3$	Unchanged
YEARS	$0\ 0\ 1$	$0\ 8\ 4$

Figure 8–86. Example—Compute Statement.

Rules Governing the Use of the Compute Statement

1. The arithmetic expression option permits the use of a meaningful combination of identifier, numeric literal, figurative constant ZERO, joined by the following operators.

Operator	Function
+	Addition
−	Subtraction
*	Multiplication
/	Division
**	Exponentiation

This permits the user to combine arithmetic operations without the restrictions imposed by the arithmetic statements ADD, SUBTRACT, MULTIPLY, and DIVIDE.

2. Operators must be preceded and followed by one or more spaces.
3. If exponentiation is desired, the COMPUTE statement must be used.
4. When the Identifier-2 or Literal-1 option is used, the result is the same as a MOVE operation. The value of Identifier-1 is made equal to the value of Identifier-2 or Literal-1.
5. The value of the result of the calculation must be written to the left of the equal sign as the item represented by Identifier-1.

6. Identifier-1 must be an elementary numeric item or an elementary numeric edited data item. The calculated value is placed here and is edited according to the Identifier-1 item picture.
7. The ROUNDED and SIZE ERROR options apply also to the COMPUTE statement.

   The COMPUTE statement permits most arithmetic operations in much the same manner as specifying arithmetic verbs.

Rules for the Sequence of Calculation of Arithmetic Expressions Containing A Combination of Operators
1. Parenthetical arithmetic expressions are calculated first.
2. All exponentiations are performed next.
3. Multiplication and division operations are calculated next, from left to right.
4. Addition and subtraction operations are performed last, from left to right.

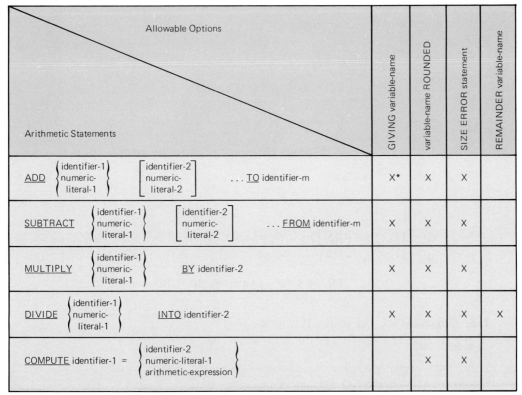

Arithmetic Statements / Allowable Options	GIVING variable-name	variable-name ROUNDED	SIZE ERROR statement	REMAINDER variable-name
ADD {identifier-1 / numeric-literal-1} [identifier-2 / numeric-literal-2] ... TO identifier-m	X*	X	X	
SUBTRACT {identifier-1 / numeric-literal-1} [identifier-2 / numeric-literal-2] ... FROM identifier-m	X	X	X	
MULTIPLY {identifier-1 / numeric-literal-1} BY identifier-2	X	X	X	
DIVIDE {identifier-1 / numeric-literal-1} INTO identifier-2	X	X	X	X
COMPUTE identifier-1 = {identifier-2 / numeric-literal-1 / arithmetic-expression}		X	X	

*The reserved word TO is omitted when the GIVING option is specified.

Figure 8–87. Summary of Arithmetic Statements and Their Options.

Sequence Control Statements

The SEQUENCE CONTROL statements are designed to specify the sequence in which the various source program instructions are to be executed. Statements, sentences, and paragraphs of the Procedure Division are executed normally in the sequence in which they are written, except when one of these sequence control verbs is encountered. Five verbs are used for procedure branching operations. The GO TO and PERFORM verbs interrupt the normal sequence and transfer control to another point in the program. The ALTER verb is used in conjunction with the GO TO verb to modify a branch instruction. The EXIT verb is used with the PERFORM verb in conditional exits from paragraphs. The STOP verb is used to halt execution of the program.

Go To

The GO TO statement provides a means of transferring control conditionally or unconditionally from one part of the program to another. The PERFORM statement also causes a branch out of normal sequence, but in addition provides a return back to the program.

```
Format 1

GO TO procedure-name-1
```

Figure 8–88. Format Go To Statement Format 1.

```
GO TO DETERMINE-TYPE-RECORD.
GO TO DEV-MR.
```

Figure 8–89. Examples Go To Statement Format 1.

Rules Governing the Use of Go To Statements

Unconditional

1. A procedure-name (name of paragraph or section) in the Procedure Division must follow the GO TO statement.
2. If the procedure-name is omitted, a paragraph-name must be assigned. The

paragraph-name must be the only name in a paragraph, and must be modified by an ALTER statement prior to the execution of the GO TO statement.

3. If the procedure-name is omitted, and the GO TO sentence is not preset by an ALTER statement prior to its execution, erroneous processing will occur.

4. The GO TO statement can only be used as the final sentence in the sequence in which it appears.

5. A procedure-name may be the name of the procedure that the GO TO statement is part of. It is permissable to branch from a point in the paragraph back to the beginning of the procedure.

Depending On (Conditional Go To)

The DEPENDING ON option permits the multiple-branch type of operations according to the value of the current value of the identifier.

1. The identifier must have a positive integral value.

2. Control is passed to the 1st, 2nd.............nth procedure-name as the value name of the identifier is 1, 2.............

Format 2
GO TO procedure-name-1 [procedure-name-2] ...   DEPENDING ON identifier

Figure 8–90. Format Go To Statement Format 2 Depending On Option.

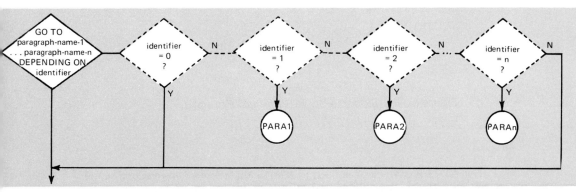

Figure 8–91. Flow of Logic Go To Statement Format 2 Depending On Option.

3. The value of the identifier must have a range of values starting at 1 and continuing successively upward.
4. If the value of the identifier is outside of the range of 1 through n, no branch occurs, and control passes to the next statement after the GO TO statement.

In a branching operation, after the transfer to the particular point in the program is executed, normal flow of control is resumed at the beginning of the particular procedure.

GO TO RECEIPTS, SHIPMENTS, CUSTOMER-ORDERS, DEPENDING ON TRANSACTION-CODE;

In the object program, if TRANSACTION-CODE contains the value 3, control will be transferred to CUSTOMER-ORDERS (the third procedure name in the series).

Figure 8–92. Example—Go To Statement Format 2 Depending On Option.

Format 3

GO TO.

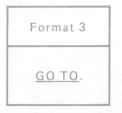

Figure 8–93. Format Go To Statement Format 3.

```
MODIFIER-GO. GO TO.
```

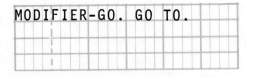

Figure 8–94. Example Go To Statement Format 3.

Alter

The ALTER statement is used to modify the effect of the unconditional GO TO statement elsewhere in the program thus changing the sequence of operations to be performed.

ALTER procedure-name-1 TO [PROCEED TO] procedure-name-2

[procedure-name-3 TO [PROCEED TO] procedure-name-4] . . .

Figure 8–95.   Format Alter Statement.

```
PARAGRAPH-1.
    GO TO BYPASS-PARAGRAPH.
PARAGRAPH-1A.

BYPASS-PARAGRAPH.

    ALTER PARAGRAPH-1 TO PROCEED TO PARAGRAPH-2.

PARAGRAPH-2.
```

Before the ALTER statement is executed, when control reaches PARAGRAPH-1, the GO TO statement transfers control to BYPASS-PARAGRAPH. After execution of the ALTER statement, however, when control reaches PARAGRAPH-1, the GO TO statement transfers control to PARAGRAPH-2.

Figure 8–96.   Example—Alter Statement.

Rules Governing the Use of the Alter Statement

1. A GO TO statement to be altered must be written as a single paragraph consisting solely of the unconditional GO TO statement preceded by a paragraph-name.
2. The ALTER statement replaces the procedure-name specified in the GO TO statement (if any) by the procedure-name specified in the ALTER statement.

Perform

The PERFORM statement provides a method of temporarily transferring control from the normal sequence of procedure execution in order to execute some other procedure a specified number of times or until a specified condition is satisfied. At the conclusion of the execution of the procedures, control is transferred back to the statement immediately following the point from which the transfer was made.

PERFORM has several different formats which vary in complexity. In the simplest form, the procedure referred to is executed once each time the PERFORM is encountered. Other formats provide repetitive execution using one or more optional controls to control the "looping."

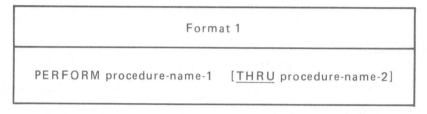

Format 1
PERFORM procedure-name-1   [THRU procedure-name-2]

Figure 8-97.   Format Perform Statement Format 1 Thru Option.

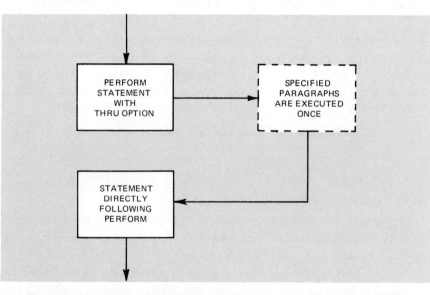

Figure 8-98.   Flow of Logic Perform Statement Format 1 Thru Option.

Rules Governing the Use of the Perform Statement

1. When a procedure is performed, the PERFORM statement transfers the sequence control to the first statement in procedure name-1 and also provides for the return of the control. The point at which the control is returned to the main program depends on the structure of the procedure being executed.

2. If procedure-name-1 is a paragraph-name, and procedure-name-2 is not

PERFORM COMPUTE-FICA

The paragraph COMPUTE-FICA will be executed; that is, PERFORMed and control will then pass to the statement following the PERFORM verb.

PERFORM COMPUTE-FICA THRU COMMON-CHECK-PRINT

    .   .

    .   .

    .   .

COMPUTE-FICA. . . .

COMPUTE-NET-PAY. . . .

COMMON-CHECK-PRINT. . . .

The range of procedures specified above is executed and control is passed to the statement following the PERFORM.

Figure 8–99.   Example—Perform Statement Format 1 Thru Option.

specified, control is returned after the execution of the last statement of procedure-name-1 paragraph.

3. If procedure-name-1 is the name of a section, and procedure-name-2 is not specified, control is returned after the last statement of the last paragraph in procedure-name-1 section.

4. If procedure-name-2 is specified, control is transferred after the last statement of the procedure-name-2 paragraph.

5. If procedure-name-2 is specified and is a section, control is transferred after the last statement of the procedure-name-2 section.

6. When procedure-name-2 is specified, the relationship between procedure-name-1 and procedure-name-2 must exist. Execution must proceed from procedure-name-1 throughout the last statement of procedure-name-2. GO TO and PERFORM statements are permitted between procedure-name-1 and the last statement in procedure-name-2 providing that the sequence ultimately returns prior to the final statement in procedure-name-2.

7. The last statement referred to must not contain an unconditional GO TO statement. If the logic of the procedure requires a conditional exit prior to the last sentence, the EXIT verb is used to satisfy the requirement. An EXIT statement consists solely of a paragraph-name and the word EXIT (see exit statement).

8. The procedure-name may be either a paragraph or section-name. The word SECTION is not required.
9. The procedure-name must not be the name of a procedure of which the PERFORM statement is a part.
10. A procedure-name can be referenced by more than one PERFORM statement.
11. Procedures to be performed can be outside the main program or can be part of the main routine so that they can be executed in line.
12. A referenced procedure may itself contain other PERFORM statements.
13. All procedures must be arranged in the order in which they are to be performed.

Simple Perform

In a simple PERFORM statement, the procedure referenced is executed once, and control then passes to the next statement after the PERFORM statement. All statements in paragraphs or sections named in procedure-name-1 (through procedure-name-2) constitute the range and are executed before control is returned.

Times

The TIMES option provides a means for performing a procedure, or section a repetitive number of times and for then returning control back to the next statement after PERFORM.

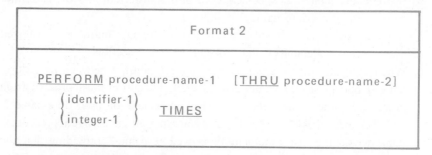

Format 2

PERFORM procedure-name-1   [THRU procedure-name-2]
$\begin{Bmatrix} \text{identifier-1} \\ \text{integer-1} \end{Bmatrix}$ TIMES

Figure 8–100. Format Perform Statement Format 2 Times Option.

Rules Governing the Use of the Times Option
1. The number of times the procedure is to be performed is specified as a number or identifier.
2. If an identifier is used, it must have an integral value.
3. The identifier or the number must have a positive value. If the value of the

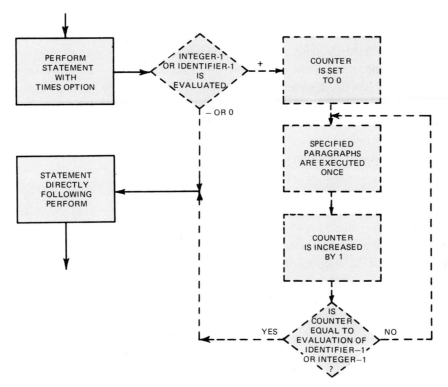

Figure 8–101. Flow of Logic Perform Statement Format 2 Times Option.

PERFORM ITERATION Q-NUMBER TIMES.

The procedure ITERATION will be performed exactly the number of times as specified by the numeric quantity in the field Q-NUMBER, each time the PERFORM verb is executed. If the numeric quantity in the field Q-NUMBER is zero, then the procedure is not executed. Keep in mind that the numeric quantity in the field Q-NUMBER can be changed from time to time.

PERFORM A THROUGH E DETERMINED-NUMBER-OF TIMES.

The entire series of procedures beginning with A and ending with E will be executed exactly the number of times as specified by the numeric quantity in the field DETERMINED-NUMBER-OF, each time the PERFORM verb is executed.

PERFORM ITERATION 3 TIMES.

The procedure ITERATION will be executed exactly 3 times each time the PERFORM verb is executed.

Figure 8–102. Example—Perform Statement Format 2 Times Option.

identifier is zero or negative, control is transferred immediately to the next statement following the PERFORM statement.

4. When the TIMES option is used, a counter is set up, and this counter is tested against the specified number of execution (times) before control is transferred to procedure-name-1. The counter is incremented by one after each execution, and the process is repeated until the value of the counter is equal to the number of times specified. At that point, control is passed to the next statement following the PERFORM statement. An initial value of zero will cause no execution of procedure-name-1.

Until

The UNTIL option operates in the same manner as the TIMES option, with the exception that no counting takes place and the PERFORM causes an evaluation of a specified test condition instead of testing the value of a counter against a specified number of executions.

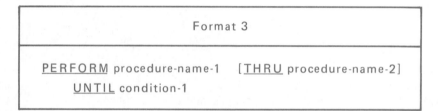

Figure 8–103. Format Perform Statement Format 3 Until Option.

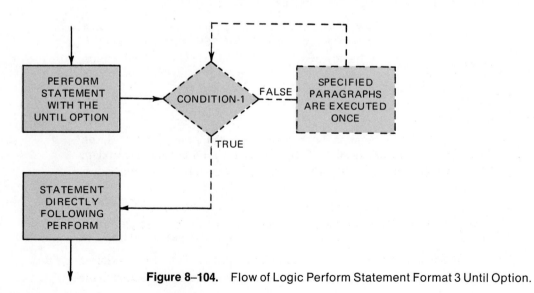

Figure 8–104. Flow of Logic Perform Statement Format 3 Until Option.

Rules Governing the Use of the Until Option
1. Condition-1 may be a simple or compound expression.
2. Condition-1 is evaluated before the specified procedures are executed.
3. If condition-1 is true, control passes to the next statement after the PER-FORM statement. The specified procedure is not executed.
4. If condition-1 is not true, control transfers to procedure-name-1.
5. The process is repeated until condition-1 is detected to be true.

```
PERFORM EDIT-ROUTINE UNTIL CODE IS EQUAL TO '5'.
```

The procedure EDIT-ROUTINE will be executed until the data in the field CODE compares equal to 5.

```
PERFORM EDIT-ROUTINE UNTIL TRANSACTION-NUMBER IS GREATER
    THAN '12345' OR IS EQUAL TO KEY-NUMBER.
```

The procedure EDIT-ROUTINE will be executed until the data in the field TRANSACTION-NUMBER compares greater than 12345 or until the data compares equal to the data in the field KEY-NUMBER.

```
PERFORM A THROUGH G UNTIL V IS EQUAL TO M OR EQUAL TO N
    OR EQUAL TO P.
```

Figure 8–105. Example—Perform Statement Format 3 Until Option.

Varying

The VARYING option is used to PERFORM a procedure repetitively, increasing or decreasing the value of one or more identifiers or index names once for each repetition until a specified condition is satisfied.

Rules Governing the Use of the Varying Option
1. The option may be used to increase or decrease the value of one or more identifiers or index names depending upon whether the **BY** value is positive or negative.
2. The specified test condition may be a simple or compound expression.
3. The identifier, index name, or literal is set to the specified initial value (FROM) when commencing the PERFORM statement. Then condition-1 is evaluated (UNTIL).
4. If condition-1 is true, control passes to the next statement immediately following the PERFORM statement, and no execution of the procedures take place.

    If the statement is false, the procedure specified in procedure-name-1 through procedure-name-2 is executed once. The BY value is added to the

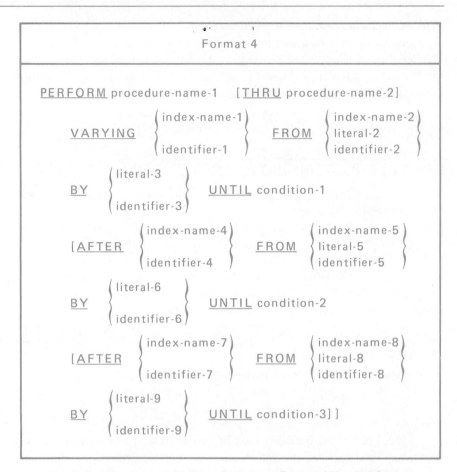

Figure 8–106. Format Perform Statement Format 4 Varying Option.

index name or identifier and again causes condition-1 to be evaluated. This process continues until the conditional expression is found to be true, whereupon control passes to the next statement after the PERFORM statement.

5. The items used in the BY and FROM must represent numeric value but need not be integers; such values may be positive, negative, or zero.

6. When more than one identifier is varied, the value of each identifier goes through the complete cycle (FROM, BY, UNTIL) each time that Identifier-1 is altered by its BY value.

7. Regardless of the number of identifiers being varied, as soon as test condition-1 is satisfied, control is transferred to the next statement after the PERFORM statement.

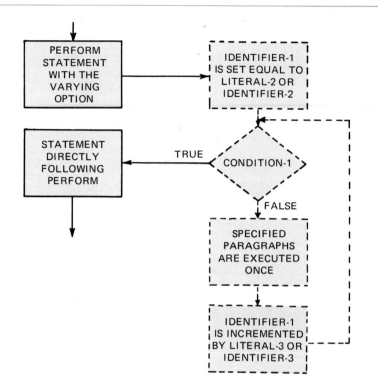

Figure 8–107. Flow of Logic Perform Statement Format 4 Varying Option.

PERFORM ☐1 VARYING ☐2 FROM ☐3 BY ☐4 UNTIL ☐5

☐1. the name of the procedure that is to be performed

☐2. the name of the base item

☐3. the initial value of the base item—either the literal value, or the name of the data item that contains the value

☐4. the amount by which the base item is to be increased each time the procedure is performed—either the literal amount, or the name of data item that contains the amount

☐5. a condition which is tested to determine when to stop performing the procedure

Figure 8–108. Using Perform Statement Format 4 Varying Option.

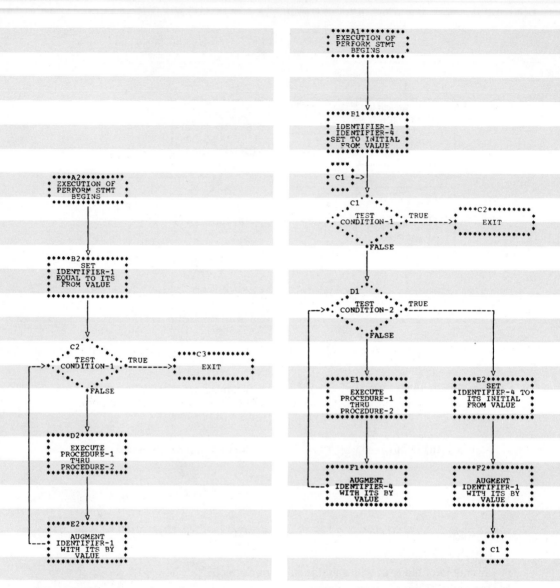

Figure 8-109. Logical Flow Perform
Statement Format 4 Varying 1 Identifier.

Figure 8–110. Logical Flow Perform
Statement Format 4 Varying 2 Identifiers.

```
PERFORM COMPUTE-FICA THRU CHECK-PRINT VARYING EMPLOYEE-
      COUNT FROM 0 BY 1 UNTIL EMPLOYEE-COUNT IS EQUAL TO
      TOTAL-EMPLOYEE.
```

The previous example illustrates an item (EMPLOYEE-COUNT) that is set to
0 and incremented by 1 each time procedures COMPUTE-FICA through
CHECK-PRINT are PERFORMed. If the item TOTAL-EMPLOYEE value is "5",
the procedures are PERFORMed five times; that is, until EMPLOYEE-COUNT
is incremented to 5.

Figure 8–111. Example—Perform Statement Format Varying Option.

Figure 8–112. Format Stop Statement.

Stop

The STOP statement permits the programmer to specify a temporary or permanent halt to the program.

Stop Run

Rules Governing the Use of the Stop Run Statement

1. The STOP RUN statement terminates the execution of a program.
2. Because of its terminal effect, the STOP RUN statement can be only used as a final statement in the sequence in which it appears; otherwise, the succeeding statements will never be executed.
3. All files should be closed before a STOP RUN statement is issued.
4. The actions following the execution of a STOP RUN statement depend upon the particular installation and/or a particular computer.

```
      STOP RUN.
```

Figure 8–113. Example—Stop Run Statement.

Stop 'Literal'

Rules Governing the Use of the Stop 'Literal' Statement

1. The STOP 'LITERAL' statement is used by the programmer to specify a temporary halt to the program.
2. When this statement is used, the specified literal will be displayed on the console at the time the stop occurs.
3. The program may be resumed only by operator intervention. A reply must be keyed in on the console to resume execution of the program.
4. Following the execution of the STOP 'LITERAL' statement, continuation of the object program begins with the next sentence in sequence.
5. The literal may be numeric or nonnumeric, or it may be a figurative constant except ALL.

```
      STOP 'HALT 350 -- CONSULT RUN BOOK'.
```

Figure 8–114. Example—Stop Literal Statement.

Exit

The EXIT statement is used when it is necessary to provide a common end point for a series of procedures. The EXIT statement is used when it is necessary to provide an ending point for a procedure that is executed by a PERFORM statement that may have one or more conditional exits prior to the last sentence. The EXIT verb serves as an ending point common to all paths.

```
paragraph-name. EXIT.
```

Figure 8–115. Format Exit Statement.

```
. . . PERFORM ANALYSIS-ROUTINE

                .

                .

                .

ANALYSIS-ROUTINE. COMPUTE RETURNS-RATIO = RETURNS / (ORDERS-
     FILLED + BACK-ORDERS  − RETURNS). IF RETURNS-RATIO IS LESS
     THAN .20 GO TO FINISH-ANALYSIS. IF RETURNS-RATIO IS LESS THAN
     .33 ADD 1 to HIGH-RATIO-COUNTER GO TO FINISH-ANALYSIS. PER-
     FORM  HIGH-RATIO-REPORT.
FINISH-ANALYSIS. EXIT.
```

Figure 8–116. Example—Exit Statement.

Rules Governing the Use of the Exit Statement
1. The statement must appear in a source program as a one-word paragraph preceded by a paragraph-name.
2. In a PERFORM statement, the EXIT paragraph-name may be given as the object of the THRU option.
3. If the THRU option is used for the EXIT paragraph, a statement in the range of the PERFORM being executed may transfer to an EXIT paragraph, bypassing the remainder of the statements in the PERFORM range.
4. If the control reaches an EXIT paragraph and no associated PERFORM statement is used, control passes through the exit point to the first sentence of the next paragraph.

Compiler-Directing Statements

Compiler-directing statements are special instructions for the COBOL compiler. They cause the compiler to take certain specific action at compile time. The compiler-directing statements are COPY, ENTER, and NOTE.

Copy

The COPY statement is used to include prewritten source program entries in a COBOL program at compile time. Thus, an installation can utilize standard file descriptions, record descriptions, or procedures, without having to repeat programming them. These entries and procedures are contained in user-created libraries. They are included in a source program by means of a COPY statement.

The use of the COPY statement together with its formats, functions, and examples are explained later in the text.

Enter

The ENTER statement enables the programmer to use other programming languages in the same COBOL source program. The ENTER statement serves as documentation and is intended to provide a means of allowing the use of more than one source language in the same source program.

```
ENTER language-name    [routine-name].
```

Figure 8–117. Format Enter Statement.

Figure 8–118. Example—Enter Statement.

Rules Governing the Use of the Enter Statement
1. The language-name informs the compiler as to what other language is desired at this point in the program. The publication for the various compilers will specify what languages may be entered.
2. The language entered must be written in a series of statements immediately following the ENTER statement.

3. If the statements in the entered language cannot be written in line, a routine-name is given to identify the portion of the other language coding to be executed at this point in the procedure sequence. A routine-name is a COBOL word, and it may be referenced to only in an ENTER statement.

4. If the other language statements can be written in line, the routine-name option is not used.

5. An ENTER COBOL statement must follow the last other language statement in order to indicate to the compiler the point where a return to COBOL source language takes place.

6. Each ENTER statement constitutes a separate paragraph in the source program.

7. The other language statements between the ENTER statement of the language and the following ENTER COBOL statement are executed in the object program as if they had been compiled in the object program following the ENTER statement. These other language statements must conform to the rules of the particular named language.

8. Implementors will specify all details on how the other languages are to be written for their compilers.

Note

The NOTE statement permits the programmer to insert comments and statements into the source program to explain or annotate the procedures being defined.

Figure 8–119. Format— Note Statement.

```
NOTE    any words, numbers, or symbols .
          [any sentence . . . ]
```

Rules Governing the Use of the Note Statement

1. A NOTE statement will be printed in the source program listing but will not be compiled into an object instruction.

2. Any combination of COBOL characters can follow the word NOTE.

3. If NOTE is the first word of a paragraph, the entire paragraph must be devoted to note(s). The paragraph must be named and must follow the format rules for paragraph structure.

4. If a NOTE sentence appears as other than the first sentence of a paragraph, the commentary must be terminated by a period followed by a space.

```
NOTE -- CONTROL AREA IS FILLED WITH
       9'S AFTER LAST RECORD OF MASTER
       FILE HAS BEEN READ.
```

Figure 8-120. Example—Note Statement Sentence.

```
COMMENT-6.
       NOTE THAT JUST THE FIRST 3 DIGITS OF
THE CLASSIFICATION CODE ARE
ANALYZED. THIS IS DONE IN ORDER TO
CHOOSE AMONG 8 SPECIALIZED SUB-
ROUTINES WHICH ANALYZE THE REMAINING
DIGITS. IF THE FIRST 3 DIGITS ARE
ILLEGAL, THE RECORD IS DUMPED OUT ON
THE CHECKPOINT TAPE AND THE NEXT
RECORD IS READ.
```

Figure 8-121. Example—Note Statement Paragraph.

CONDITIONAL EXPRESSIONS

A conditional expression is an expression containing one or more variables whose value may change during the course of the program. The conditional expression can be reduced to a single value that can be tested to determine which of the alternate paths the program flow is to be taken. A test condition is an expression that, taken as a whole, may be either true or false, depending on the circumstances existing when the expression is evaluated. Although IF is not a verb in the grammatical sense, it is regarded as such in COBOL. IF statements are used to evaluate test conditions. There are four types of test conditions. Relation Conditions, Class Conditions, Sign Conditions, and Condition-Name Conditions.

When the test condition is evaluated, the following action will take place.

1. If the condition is true, the statements immediately following the conditional expression are executed. Control then passes to the next sentence.
2. If the condition is false, the statements immediately following ELSE or OTHERWISE are executed, or the next sentence, if the ELSE or OTHERWISE clause is omitted.
3. An IF statement must be terminated by a period and a space.
4. Any number of statements may follow the test condition. These statements

are acted upon if the condition exists and skipped over if the condition does not exist or to the statements following ELSE or OTHERWISE.

5. In a series of imperative statements executed when the condition is true, only the last statement may be an unconditional GO TO or STOP RUN statement; otherwise, the series of statements would contain statements into which control cannot flow. It is the programmers responsibility to write the program steps in a logical sequence for execution.

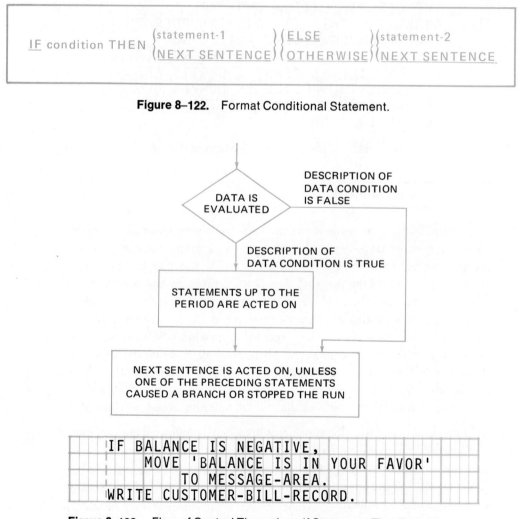

$$\text{IF condition THEN} \begin{Bmatrix} \text{statement-1} \\ \underline{\text{NEXT SENTENCE}} \end{Bmatrix} \begin{Bmatrix} \underline{\text{ELSE}} \\ \underline{\text{OTHERWISE}} \end{Bmatrix} \begin{Bmatrix} \text{statement-2} \\ \underline{\text{NEXT SENTENCE}} \end{Bmatrix}$$

Figure 8–122. Format Conditional Statement.

DATA IS EVALUATED

DESCRIPTION OF DATA CONDITION IS FALSE

DESCRIPTION OF DATA CONDITION IS TRUE

STATEMENTS UP TO THE PERIOD ARE ACTED ON

NEXT SENTENCE IS ACTED ON, UNLESS ONE OF THE PRECEDING STATEMENTS CAUSED A BRANCH OR STOPPED THE RUN

```
IF BALANCE IS NEGATIVE,
     MOVE 'BALANCE IS IN YOUR FAVOR'
          TO MESSAGE-AREA.
WRITE CUSTOMER-BILL-RECORD.
```

Figure 8–123. Flow of Control Through an If Statement That Does Not Contain an Else or Otherwise Statement.

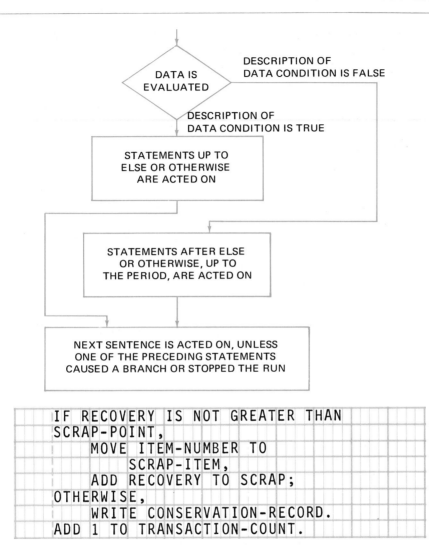

Figure 8–124. Flow of Control Through an If Statement That Contains an Else or Otherwise Statement.

Relation Condition

A Relation Condition test involves the comparison of two data values, either of which may be an identifier, a literal, or an arithmetic expression. Either the relational operator symbol or relational operator may be used in the test. If the symbols are used, they must be preceded and followed by a space. NOT is used to specify the opposite of the expression.

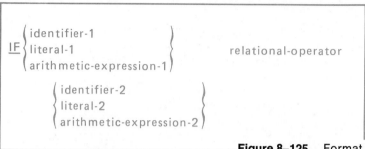

Figure 8–125. Format Relation Condition.

Relational-operator	Meaning
IS [NOT] GREATER THAN IS [NOT] >	Greater than or not greater than
IS [NOT] LESS THAN IS [NOT] <	Less than or not less than
IS [NOT] EQUAL TO IS [NOT] =	Equal to or not equal to

Figure 8–126. Relational Operators and Their Meanings.

Rules Governing Relation Condition Tests
1. The first operand is called the subject of the condition; the second operand is called the object of the condition. The subject and object may not be both literals.
2. Both operands must have the same USAGE, except when two numeric operands are involved.

Numeric Items Comparison Tests

1. The test determines that the value of one of the items is GREATER THAN, LESS THAN, or EQUAL TO the other item, regardless of the length of the operands.
2. The items are compared algebraically after decimal point alignment.
3. Zero is considered a unique value regardless of its length, sign, or implied decimal-point location.
4. Numeric operands that do not have signs are considered positive values for purposes of comparison.
5. Comparison of numeric operands is permitted regardless of the manner in which their USAGE is described.

Second Operand / First Operand		Group	Elementary			
			Alphanumeric	Alphabetic	Numeric	Literal
Group		C	C	C	C	C
Elementary	Alphanumeric	C	C	C	C	C
	Alphabetic	C	C	C	I	C
	Numeric	C	C	I	N	C
	Literal	C	C	C	C	I

C — Compared logically (one character at a time, according to collating sequence of a particular computer)

N — Compared algebraically (numeric values are compared)

I — Invalid comparison

Example:

IF TOTAL GREATER THAN MAXIMUM GO TO MESSAGE.

first operand   operator   second operand

condition

Explanation:

To use this chart find the data type (determined by the picture) of the first operand in the column headed First Operand. Then find the data type of the second operand across the top of the figure opposite Second Operand. Extend imaginary lines into the figure from the data types of the first and second operands. In the block where these two lines intersect is a letter that tells you how the values are compared.

Figure 8–127. Types of Valid Comparisons.

Nonnumeric Comparison Tests

1. The test determines that one item is GREATER THAN, LESS THAN, or EQUAL TO the other item with respect to the specified collating sequence of characters for the particular computer. (In the IBM collating sequence, the numerals are in the highest category, followed by alphabetic characters, with the special characters the lowest of the group.)

2. Numeric and nonnumeric operands may be compared only if both items have the same USAGE, implicitly or explicitly.

3. The size of the operand is the total number of characters in the operand. All group items are considered in the nonnumeric operand group.

4. If both operands are of equal length in a nonnumeric comparison, the test proceeds from left (high-order position) to right (low-order position), and each character is compared to the corresponding character of the other item. The comparison of characters continues until an unequal condition is noted.

   If each individual character compared results in an equality, and the two items consist of the same number of characters, the items are considered equal.

5. If the operands are of differing lengths, the comparison proceeds as though the shorter item was filled with spaces until it is of the same length as the other operands.

```
IF AMOUNT IS LESS THAN BALANCE
      MOVE SHIPMENT TO WORKSTORE.
```

Note: The MOVE is not executed on an "equal" or "greater" condition.

```
IF DATE OF MASTER IS EQUAL TO TODAYS-DATE
      PERFORM REVIEW OTHERWISE GO TO NEXT-DETAIL.
```

Note: On a "less" or "greater" condition the program transfers to NEXT-DETAIL.

Figure 8–128. Example—Relational Condition.

Class Condition

The Class Condition test is used to determine whether the data is numeric or alphabetic.

Numeric data consists entirely of the numerals 0–9 with or without an operational sign. If the PICTURE clause of the record description of the identifier being tested does not contain an operational sign, the identifier is determined to be numeric only if the contents are numeric and an operational sign is not present.

A numeric test cannot be used with an item whose data descriptions describes items as alphabetic.

Alphabetic data consists of the characters A through Z plus the space character.

An alphabetic test cannot be used with an item whose record description is numeric.

```
IF identifier is [NOT]    { NUMERIC   }
                          { ALPHABETIC }
```

Figure 8–129.   Format Class Condition.

Type of Identifier	Valid Forms of the Class Test	
Alphabetic	ALPHABETIC	NOT ALPHABETIC
Alphanumeric	ALPHABETIC NUMERIC	NOT ALPHABETIC NOT NUMERIC
External-Decimal	NUMERIC	NOT NUMERIC

Figure 8-130.   Valid Forms of Class Tests.

```
IF ACTIVITY-RATING IS ALPHABETIC,
    GO TO HIGH-ACTIVITY-ANALYSIS.
```

Figure 8–131.   Example—Class Test.

Sign Condition

The Sign Condition test is used to determine whether the algebraical value of a numeric item is less than zero (NEGATIVE), greater than zero (POSITIVE), or zero (ZERO).

1. The value of zero is considered neither positive or negative.
2. If an identifier appears in a Sign Condition test, it must represent a numeric value. If the value is unsigned and not equal to zero, it is considered to be positive.

```
IF { identifier            }  IS [NOT]  { POSITIVE }
   { arithmetic-expression }            { NEGATIVE }
                                        { ZERO     }
```

Figure 8–132.   Format Sign Condition.

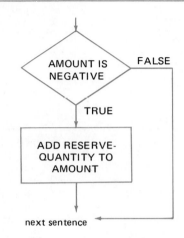

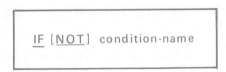

Figure 8–133. Example—Sign Test.

Condition-Name Condition

A Condition-Name Condition test is used to test a condition variable to determine whether or not its value is equal to one of the values assumed with its condition-name.

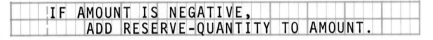

Figure 8–134. Format Condition-Name Test.

1. The condition-name must be defined in a level 88 entry in the Data Division associated with the condition-name.
2. The Condition-Name Condition test is an alternative way of expressing certain conditions that could be expressed by a simple relational condition. The rules for comparing condition variable with a condition-name value are the same as those specified for relation conditions.
3. The test is true if the value corresponding to the condition-name equals the value of its associated condition variables.

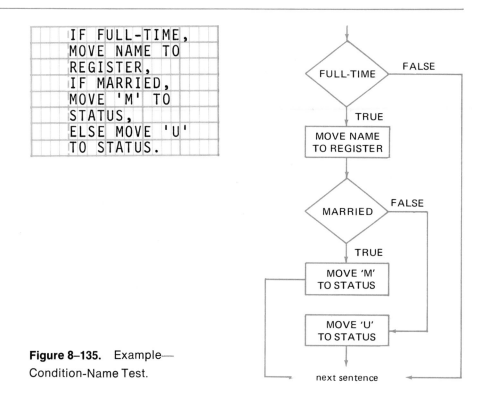

```
IF FULL-TIME,
MOVE NAME TO
REGISTER,
IF MARRIED,
MOVE 'M' TO
STATUS,
ELSE MOVE 'U'
TO STATUS.
```

Figure 8–135. Example—
Condition-Name Test.

COMPOUND CONDITIONAL EXPRESSIONS

A Compound Conditional Expression consists of two or more simple conditions combined with the logical operators AND and OR. These conditions are linked by AND and OR in any sequence which would produce the overall desired result.

The logical operators must be preceded by a space and followed by a space.

Logical Operator	Meaning
OR	Logical inclusive (either or both are true)
AND	Logical conjunction (both are true)
NOT	Logical negation (not true)

Type of Operation	Operator (operation symbol)	Operation
Relational	IS <u>GREATER</u> THAN (>)	is greater than
	IS <u>LESS</u> THAN (<)	is less than
	IS <u>EQUAL TO</u> (=)	is equal to
Logical	<u>OR</u>	logical inclusive OR (either or both are true)
	<u>AND</u>	logical conjunction (both are true)
	<u>NOT</u>	logical negation

Figure 8–136. Relational and Logical Operators.

Rules for the Formation of Compound Conditional Expressions

1. Two or more simple conditions combined by AND/OR make up a compound condition.
2. The word OR is used to mean either or both. Thus the expression A OR B is true if A is true or B is true or both A and B are true.
3. The word AND is used to mean that both expressions must be true. Thus the expression A AND B is true only if both A and B are true.
4. The word NOT may be used to specify the opposite of the compound expression. Thus NOT A AND B is true if both A and B are false, A is false, or if B is false.
5. Parentheses may be used to specify the sequence in which the conditions are to be evaluated. Parentheses must always appear in a pair. Logical evaluation begins with the innermost pair and proceeds to the outermost pairs of parentheses.
6. If the sequence of evaluation is not specified by parentheses, the expression is evaluated in the following manner.
   a. Arithmetic expressions.
   b. Relational operators.
   c. [NOT] conditions.
   d. Conditions surrounding all ANDs are evaluated first, starting at left and proceeding to the right.
   e. OR and its surrounding conditions are then evaluated, also proceeding from left to right.

Thus the expression A IS GREATER THAN B OR A IS EQUAL
TO C AND D IS POSITIVE would be evaluated as if it were parenthisized
as follows.

(A IS GREATER THAN B) OR (A IS EQUAL TO C) AND (D
IS POSITIVE).

```
IF SCORE IS GREATER THAN 84 AND SCORE IS LESS
THAN 93, MOVE 'B' TO GRADE.
```

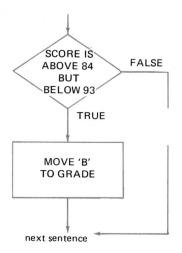

Figure 8–137.   Example—Compound Conditional Statements.

NESTED CONDITIONAL EXPRESSIONS

If a conditional statement appears as Statement-1 or as part of State-
ment-1, it is said to be nested. Nesting a statement is like specifying a subordinate arithmetic expression enclosed in parenthesis combined in a larger arithmetic expression. IF statements contained within are considered paired, IF and
ELSE or OTHERWISE combinations proceeding from left to right. Thus any
ELSE or OTHERWISE statement encountered must be considered to apply
to the immediately preceding IF test has not already been paired with an ELSE
or OTHERWISE.

Certain compilers may place some restrictions on the number and types
of conditionals that can be nested.

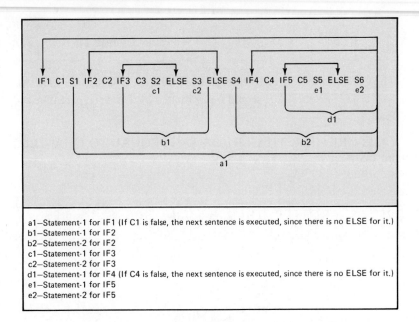

a1—Statement-1 for IF1 (If C1 is false, the next sentence is executed, since there is no ELSE for it.)
b1—Statement-1 for IF2
b2—Statement-2 for IF2
c1—Statement-1 for IF3
c2—Statement-2 for IF3
d1—Statement-1 for IF4 (If C4 is false, the next sentence is executed, since there is no ELSE for it.)
e1—Statement-1 for IF5
e2—Statement-2 for IF5

Figure 8–138. Conditional Statements with Nested IF Statements.

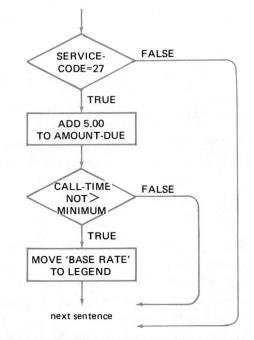

```
IF SERVICE-CODE IS EQUAL TO 27,
    ADD 5.00 TO AMOUNT DUE
IF CALL-TIME IS NOT GREATER THAN
    MINIMUM, MOVE 'BASE RATE' TO
    LEGEND.
```

Figure 8–139. Examples—Nested IF Statements.

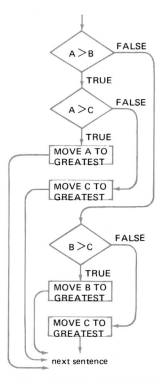

```
IF A IS GREATER THAN B,
IF A IS GREATER THAN C   MOVE A TO GREATEST
                   ELSE MOVE C TO GREATEST
ELSE IF B IS GREATER THAN C
                        MOVE B TO GREATEST
                   ELSE MOVE C TO GREATEST.
```

Figure 8–139. Examples—Nested IF Statements Cont.

IMPLIED SUBJECT

Many times a conditional expression will contain several simple relational conditions. These conditions may have the same subject. For example, IF A IS GREATER THAN B AND LESS THAN C, the second occurrence of A is implied.

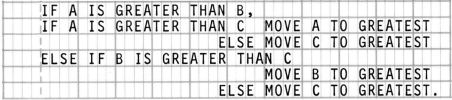

Figure 8–140. Format Implied Subject.

Rules Governing the Use of Implied Subjects

1. Only conditional expressions written as simple relational conditions may have implied subjects. SIGN and CLASS condition tests can never have implied subjects.

2. The first series of simple relational conditions must always consist of a subject, operator, and operation, all of which must be explicitly stated.

3. The subject may be implied only in a series of simple relational conditions connected by the logical operators AND and/or OR.

4. When the subject of a simple relational condition is implied, the subject used is the first subject to the left which is explicitly stated. For example, IF A = B OR =C OR D= E AND = F, A is the implied subject for C and D, while D is the implied subject of F since D is the first subject to the left of F.

5. When NOT is used in conjunction with a relational operator and an implied subject, the NOT is treated as a logical operator. For example, A IS GREATER THAN B AND NOT EQUAL TO C AND D is equivalent to A IS GREATER THAN B AND NOT A IS EQUAL TO C AND A IS EQUAL TO D.

A = B OR NOT > C	(The subject, A, is implied.)
A = B OR NOT A > C	(The subject, A, is explicit.)

Figure 8–141. Example Implied Subject.

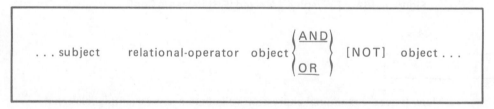

Figure 8–142. Format Implied Subject and Operator.

IMPLIED OPERATORS

Relational operators may be implied in a series of consecutive simple relational conditions in much the same way in which the subject can be implied. For example, IF A IS GREATER THAN B AND C OR D, GO TO X. Not only is the subject implied (A), but also the relational operator (GREATER THAN).

Rules Governing the Use of Implied Operators

1. A relational operator may be implied only in a simple relational condition when the subject is implied. SIGN and CLASS conditions can never be implied (do not have operators).
2. When an operator is implied, it is assumed to be the operator of the nearest completed stated simple condition to the left.

A = B AND C	(Subject and relational-operator, A = , are implied.)
A = B AND A = C	(Subject and relational-operator, A = , are explicit.)

Figure 8-143. Example—Implied Subject and Operator.

A > B AND NOT < C AND D	(Subject, A, is implied in the second condition. Subject, A, and relational-operator, <, are implied in the third condition.)
A > B AND NOT A < C AND A < D	(Subject, A, and relational-operator, <, are explicit.)

Figure 8-144. Example—Implied Subject and Subject and Operator.

PAYROLL REGISTER PROBLEM

INPUT

Field	Card Columns	
Department	14–16	
Serial	17–21	
Gross Earnings	57–61	XXX.XX
Insurance	62–65	XX.XX
Withholding Tax	69–72	XX.XX
State UCI Tax	73–75	X.XX
Miscellaneous Deductions	76–79	XX.XX
Code (Letter E)	80	

CALCULATIONS TO BE PERFORMED

1. FICA TAX = Gross Earnings X .052 (Rounded to 2 decimal places).
2. NET EARNINGS = Gross Earnings — Insurance — FICA Tax — Withholding Tax — State UCI — Miscellaneous Deductions.
3. Department Earnings value is the sum of the Net Earnings for each employee.

4. The Total Net Earnings is the sum of the Net Earnings for each department.

OUTPUT

Print a report as follows:

WEEKLY PAYROLL REGISTER

| Employee No. | | Gross | | FICA | With-hold-ing | State | Misc. | Net |
| Dept. | Serial | Earnings | Insurance | Tax | Tax | UCI | Ded. | Amount |

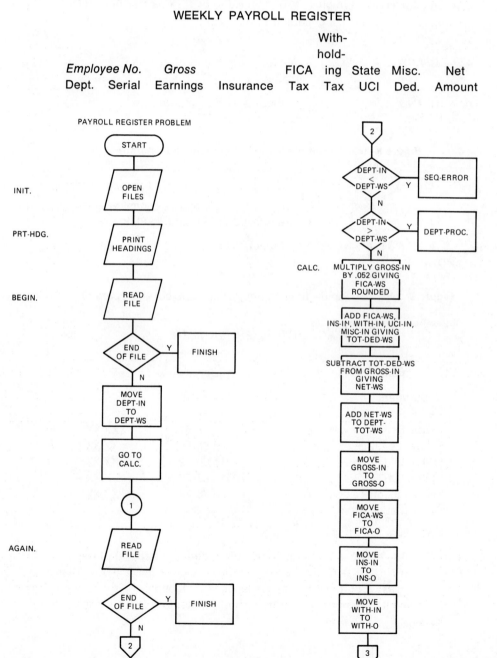

PAYROLL REGISTER PROBLEM

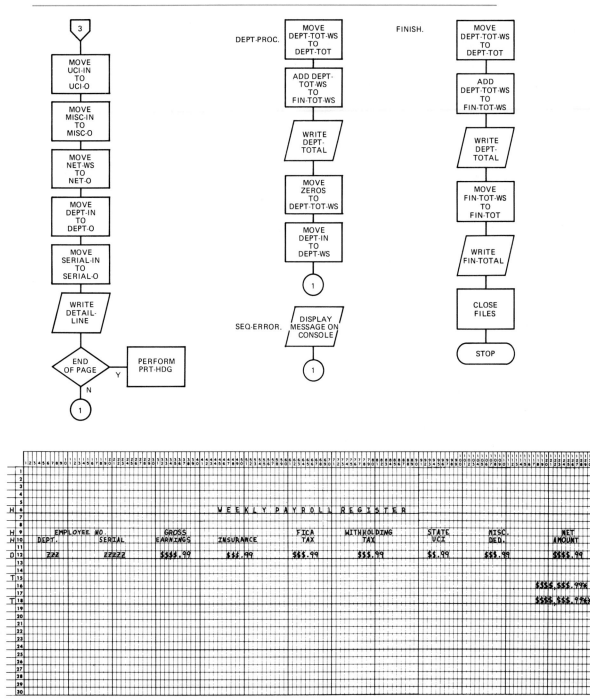

```
00001   001010 IDENTIFICATION DIVISION.                                      PAYREGIS
00002   001020 PROGRAM-ID. PAYROLL-REGISTER.                                 PAYREGIS
00003   001030 AUTHOR. C FEINGOLD.                                           PAYREGIS
00004   001040 DATE-WRITTEN. JUNE 14 1972.                                   PAYREGIS
00005   001045 DATE-COMPILED. 10/27/72                                       PAYREGIS
00006   001050 REMARKS. THIS IS A WEEKLY PAYROLL REGISTER.                   PAYREGIS
00007   001060 ENVIRONMENT DIVISION.                                         PAYREGIS
00008   001070 CONFIGURATION SECTION.                                        PAYREGIS
00009   001080 SOURCE-COMPUTER. IBM-360-H50.                                 PAYREGIS
00010   001090 OBJECT-COMPUTER. IBM-360-H50.                                 PAYREGIS
00011   001100 INPUT-OUTPUT SECTION.                                         PAYREGIS
00012   001110 FILE-CONTROL.                                                 PAYREGIS
00013   001120     SELECT FILE-IN ASSIGN TO SYS009-UR-2540R-S.              PAYREGIS
00014   001130     SELECT FILE-OUT ASSIGN TO SYS005-UR-1403-S.              PAYREGIS
00015   001131         RESERVE NO ALTERNATE AREA.                            PAYREGIS
00016   002010 DATA DIVISION.                                                PAYREGIS
00017   002020 FILE SECTION.                                                 PAYREGIS
00018   002030 FD  FILE-IN                                                   PAYREGIS
00019   002040     RECORDING MODE F                                          PAYREGIS
00020   002050     LABEL RECORDS OMITTED                                     PAYREGIS
00021   002060     DATA RECORD IS CARD-IN.                                   PAYREGIS
00022   002070 01  CARD-IN.                                                  PAYREGIS
00023   002080     02 FILLER       PICTURE X(13).                           PAYREGIS
00024   002090     02 DEPT-IN      PICTURE 999.                             PAYREGIS
00025   002100     02 SERIAL-IN    PICTURE 9(5).                            PAYREGIS
00026   002110     02 FILLER       PICTURE X(35).                           PAYREGIS
00027   002120     02 GROSS-IN     PICTURE 9(3)V99.                         PAYREGIS
00028   002130     02 INS-IN       PICTURE 99V99.                           PAYREGIS
00029   002140     02 FILLER       PICTURE X(3).                            PAYREGIS
00030   002150     02 WITH-IN      PICTURE 99V99.                           PAYREGIS
00031   002160     02 UCI-IN       PICTURE 9V99.                            PAYREGIS
00032   002170     02 MISC-IN      PICTURE 99V99.                           PAYREGIS
00033   002180     02 KODE-IN      PICTURE X.                               PAYREGIS
00034   003010 FD  FILE-OUT                                                  PAYREGIS
00035   003020     RECORDING MODE F                                          PAYREGIS
00036   003030     LABEL RECORDS OMITTED                                     PAYREGIS
00037   003040     DATA RECORD IS PRINTOUT.                                  PAYREGIS
00038   003050 01  PRINTOUT        PICTURE X(133).                          PAYREGIS
00039   003060 WORKING-STORAGE SECTION.                                      PAYREGIS
```

2

```
00040   003070 77  DEPT-WS         PICTURE 999 VALUE ZEROS.                 PAYREGIS
00041   003080 77  FICA-WS         PICTURE 99V99 VALUE ZEROS.               PAYREGIS
00042   003090 77  TOT-DED-WS      PICTURE 999V99 VALUE ZEROS.              PAYREGIS
00043   003090 77  NET-WS          PICTURE 999V99 VALUE ZEROS.              PAYREGIS
00044   003100 77  DEPT-TOT-WS     PICTURE 9(4)V99 VALUE ZEROS.             PAYREGIS
00045   003110 77  FIN-TOT-WS      PICTURE 9(6)V99 VALUE ZEROS.             PAYREGIS
00046   003130 01  HDG-1.                                                    PAYREGIS
00047   003140     02 FILLER       PICTURE X(45) VALUE SPACES.              PAYREGIS
00048   003150     02 FILLER       PICTURE X(43) VALUE 'W E E K L Y   P A Y R O L PAYREGIS
00049   003160-    'L   R E G I S T E R'.                                    PAYREGIS
00050   003170 01  HDG-2.                                                    PAYREGIS
00051   003180     02 FILLER       PICTURE X(8) VALUE SPACES.               PAYREGIS
00052   003190     02 FILLER       PICTURE X(119) VALUE 'EMPLOYEE NO.      PAYREGIS
00053   003200-    ' GROSS                         FICA        WITHHOLDING  PAYREGIS
00054   003210-    ' STATE          MISC.          NET'.                     PAYREGIS
00055   004010 01  HDG-3.                                                    PAYREGIS
00056   004020     02 FILLER       PICTURE X(4) VALUE SPACES.               PAYREGIS
00057   004030     02 FILLER       PICTURE X(60) VALUE 'DEPT.       SERIAL  PAYREGIS
00058   004040-    ' EARNINGS     INSURANCE       '.                        PAYREGIS
00059   004050     02 FILLER       PICTURE X(64) VALUE 'TAX           TAX   PAYREGIS
00060   004055-    '  UCI          DED.            AMOUNT'.                   PAYREGIS
00061   004060 01  DETAIL-LINE.                                              PAYREGIS
00062   004070     02 FILLER       PICTURE X(6) VALUE SPACES.               PAYREGIS
00063   004080     02 DEPT-O       PICTURE ZZZ.                             PAYREGIS
00064   004090     02 FILLER       PICTURE X(10) VALUE SPACES.              PAYREGIS
00065   004100     02 SERIAL-O     PICTURE Z(5).                            PAYREGIS
00066   004110     02 FILLER       PICTURE X(8) VALUE SPACES.               PAYREGIS
00067   004120     02 GROSS-O      PICTURE $$$$.99.                         PAYREGIS
00068   004130     02 FILLER       PICTURE X(8) VALUE SPACES.               PAYREGIS
00069   004140     02 INS-O        PICTURE $$$.99.                          PAYREGIS
00070   004150     02 FILLER       PICTURE X(9) VALUE SPACES.               PAYREGIS
00071   004160     02 FICA-O       PICTURE $$$.99.                          PAYREGIS
00072   004170     02 FILLER       PICTURE X(9) VALUE SPACES.               PAYREGIS
00073   004180     02 WITH-O       PICTURE $$$.99.                          PAYREGIS
00074   004190     02 FILLER       PICTURE X(9) VALUE SPACES.               PAYREGIS
00075   004200     02 UCI-O        PICTURE $$.99.                           PAYREGIS
00076   005010     02 FILLER       PICTURE X(9) VALUE SPACES.               PAYREGIS
00077   005020     02 MISC-O       PICTURE $$$.99.                          PAYREGIS
00078   005030     02 FILLER       PICTURE X(10) VALUE SPACES.              PAYREGIS
```

00079	005040	02 NET-O	PICTURE $$$$.99.		PAYREGIS
00080	005050	01 DEPT-TOTAL.			PAYREGIS
00081	005060	02 FILLER	PICTURE X(118) VALUE SPACES.		PAYREGIS
00082	005070	02 DEPT-TOT	PICTURE $$$$,$$$.99.		PAYREGIS
00083	005080	02 FILLER	PICTURE X VALUE '*'.		PAYREGIS
00084	005090	01 FIN-TOTAL.			PAYREGIS
00085	005100	02 FILLER	PICTURE X(118) VALUE SPACES.		PAYREGIS
00086	005110	02 FIN-TOT	PICTURE $$$$,$$$.99.		PAYREGIS
00087	005120	02 FILLER	PICTURE XX VALUE '**'.		PAYREGIS
00088	006010	PROCEDURE DIVISION.			PAYREGIS
00089	006020	INIT. OPEN INPUT FILE-IN OUTPUT FILE-OUT.			PAYREGIS
00090	006030	PRT-HDG. WRITE PRINTOUT FROM HDG-1 AFTER POSITIONING 0 LINES.			PAYREGIS
00091	006040	WRITE PRINTOUT FROM HDG-2 AFTER POSITIONING 3 LINES.			PAYREGIS
00092	006050	WRITE PRINTOUT FROM HDG-3 AFTER POSITIONING 1 LINES.			PAYREGIS
00093	006051	BEGIN. READ FILE-IN AT END GO TO FINISH.			PAYREGIS
00094	006052	MOVE DEPT-IN TO DEPT-WS.			PAYREGIS
00095	006053	GO TO CALC.			PAYREGIS
00096	006060	AGAIN. READ FILE-IN AT END GO TO FINISH.			PAYREGIS
00097	006070	IF DEPT-IN < DEPT-WS GO TO SEQ-ERROR.			PAYREGIS
00098	006080	IF DEPT-IN > DEPT-WS GO TO DEPT-PROC.			PAYREGIS
00099	006090	CALC. MULTIPLY GROSS-IN BY .052 GIVING FICA-WS ROUNDED.			PAYREGIS
00100	006100	ADD FICA-WS, INS-IN, WITH-IN, UCI-IN, MISC-IN,			PAYREGIS
00101	006105	GIVING TOT-DED-WS.			PAYREGIS
00102	006110	SUBTRACT TOT-DED-WS FROM GROSS-IN GIVING NET-WS.			PAYREGIS
00103	006120	ADD NET-WS TO DEPT-TOT-WS.			PAYREGIS
00104	006130	MOVE GROSS-IN TO GROSS-O.			PAYREGIS
00105	006140	MOVE FICA-WS TO FICA-O.			PAYREGIS
00106	006150	MOVE INS-IN TO INS-O.			PAYREGIS
00107	006160	MOVE WITH-IN TO WITH-O.			PAYREGIS
00108	006170	MOVE UCI-IN TO UCI-O.			PAYREGIS
00109	006180	MOVE MISC-IN TO MISC-O.			PAYREGIS
00110	006190	MOVE NET-WS TO NET-O.			PAYREGIS
00111	006200	MOVE DEPT-IN TO DEPT-O.			PAYREGIS
00112	006210	MOVE SERIAL-IN TO SERIAL-O.			PAYREGIS
00113	006230	WRITE PRINTOUT FROM DETAIL-LINE AFTER POSITIONING 2 LINES			PAYREGIS
00114	006235	AT END-OF-PAGE PERFORM PRT-HDG.			PAYREGIS
00115	006240	GO TO AGAIN.			PAYREGIS
00116	007010	DEPT-PROC. MOVE DEPT-TOT-WS TO DEPT-TOT.			PAYREGIS
00117	007015	ADD DEPT-TOT-WS TO FIN-TOT-WS.			PAYREGIS

00118	007020	WRITE PRINTOUT FROM DEPT-TOTAL AFTER POSITIONING 3 LINES.	PAYREGIS
00119	007030	MOVE ZEROS TO DEPT-TOT-WS.	PAYREGIS
00120	007035	MOVE DEPT-IN TO DEPT-WS.	PAYREGIS
00121	007040	GO TO CALC.	PAYREGIS
00122	007050	SEQ-ERROR. DISPLAY 'EMPLOYEE NUMBER ' DEPT-IN SERIAL-IN 'IS OUT O	PAYREGIS
00123	007060-	'F SEQUENCE' UPON CONSOLE.	PAYREGIS
00124	007070	GO TO AGAIN.	PAYREGIS
00125	007071	FINISH. MOVE DEPT-TOT-WS TO DEPT-TOT.	PAYREGIS
00126	007072	ADD DEPT-TOT-WS TO FIN-TOT-WS.	PAYREGIS
00127	007073	WRITE PRINTOUT FROM DEPT-TOTAL AFTER POSITIONING 3 LINES	PAYREGIS
00128	007074	MOVE FIN-TOT-WS TO FIN-TOT.	PAYREGIS
00129	007090	WRITE PRINTOUT FROM FIN-TOTAL AFTER POSITIONING 3 LINES.	PAYREGIS
00130	007100	CLOSE FILE-IN FILE-OUT. STOP RUN.	PAYREGIS

W E E K L Y   P A Y R O L L   R E G I S T E R

EMPLOYEE NO. DEPT.	SERIAL	GROSS EARNINGS	INSURANCE	FICA TAX	WITHHOLDING TAX	STATE UCI	MISC. DED.	NET AMOUNT
9	1217	$84.17	$.00	$4.38	$8.90	$.84	$.00	$70.05
9	1218	$100.65	$1.00	$5.23	$16.02	$1.19	$1.75	$75.46
9	1219	$116.40	$3.00	$6.05	$12.57	$1.34	$.00	$93.44
								$238.95*
10	374	$156.80	$2.00	$8.15	$18.90	$1.85	$2.00	$123.90
10	375	$186.57	$2.00	$9.70	$22.46	$2.02	$.00	$150.39
10	940	$67.20	$.00	$3.49	$4.80	$.60	$.75	$57.56
10	992	$75.38	$1.25	$3.92	$9.75	$.78	$.00	$59.68
								$391.53*
19	1217	$84.17	$.00	$4.38	$8.90	$.84	$.00	$70.05
19	1218	$100.65	$1.00	$5.23	$16.02	$1.19	$1.75	$75.46
19	1219	$116.40	$3.00	$6.05	$12.57	$1.34	$.00	$93.44
								$238.95*
20	374	$156.80	$2.00	$8.15	$18.90	$1.85	$2.00	$123.90
20	375	$186.57	$2.00	$9.70	$22.46	$2.02	$.00	$150.39
20	940	$67.20	$.00	$3.49	$4.80	$.60	$.75	$57.56
20	992	$75.38	$1.25	$3.92	$9.75	$.78	$.00	$59.68

W E E K L Y   P A Y R O L L   R E G I S T E R

EMPLOYEE NO. DEPT.	SERIAL	GROSS EARNINGS	INSURANCE	FICA TAX	WITHHOLDING TAX	STATE UCI	MISC. DED.	NET AMOUNT
								$391.53*
29	1217	$84.17	$.00	$4.38	$8.90	$.84	$.00	$70.05
29	1218	$100.65	$1.00	$5.23	$16.02	$1.19	$1.75	$75.46
29	1219	$116.40	$3.00	$6.05	$12.57	$1.34	$.00	$93.44
								$238.95*
30	374	$156.80	$2.00	$8.15	$18.90	$1.85	$2.00	$123.90
30	375	$186.57	$2.00	$9.70	$22.46	$2.02	$.00	$150.39
30	940	$67.20	$.00	$3.49	$4.80	$.60	$.75	$57.56
30	992	$75.38	$1.25	$3.92	$9.75	$.78	$.00	$59.68
								$391.53*
39	1217	$84.17	$.00	$4.38	$8.90	$.84	$.00	$70.05
39	1218	$100.65	$1.00	$5.23	$16.02	$1.19	$1.75	$75.46
39	1219	$116.40	$3.00	$6.05	$12.57	$1.34	$.00	$93.44
								$238.95*
								$2,130.39**

DISTRICT SALES REPORT PROBLEM

INPUT

Field	Card Columns
Product Number	1–2
Sales Amount	3–7
Salesman Number	8–9
District Number	10

CALCULATIONS TO BE PERFORMED

Accumulate totals for sales amount as follows:

a. Minor Control—Salesman Number
b. Intermediate Control—District
c. Final Total—Monthly

OUTPUT

Prepare a salesman report per the following output format:

DISTRICT SALES REPORT

| SALESMAN NUMBER   SALES | DISTRICT NUMBER   SALES | MONTHLY TOTAL SALES |

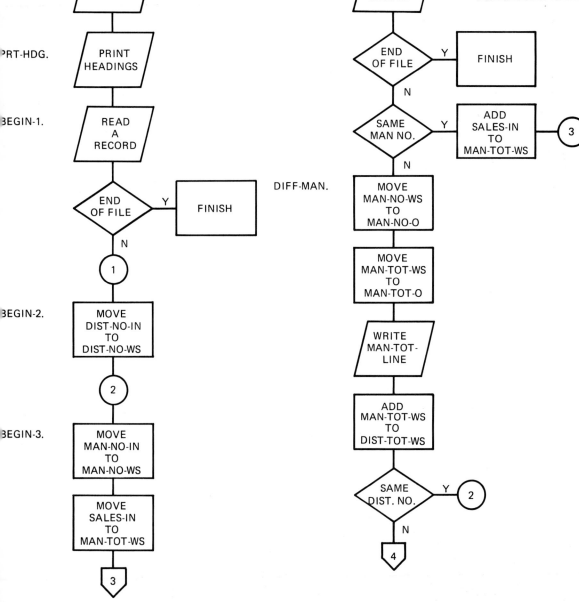

DIFF-DIST.

FINISH.

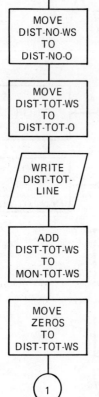

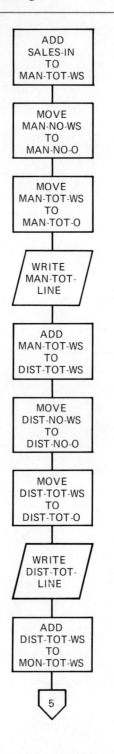

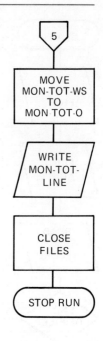

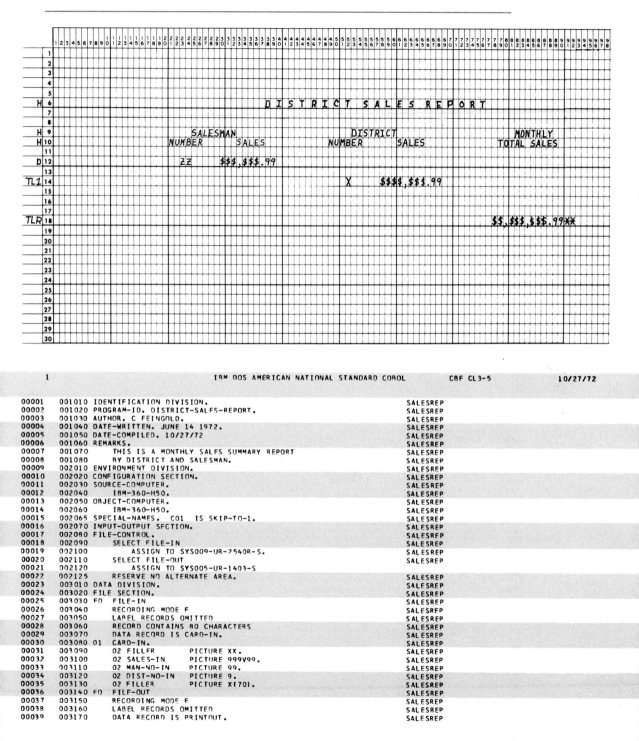

The coding form shows the report layout:

	SALESMAN		DISTRICT		MONTHLY
	NUMBER	SALES	NUMBER	SALES	TOTAL SALES

DISTRICT SALES REPORT

- H 6: DISTRICT SALES REPORT
- H 9 / H 10: SALESMAN NUMBER / SALES — DISTRICT NUMBER / SALES — MONTHLY TOTAL SALES
- D 12: ZZ $$$,$$$.99
- TL1 14: X $$$$,$$$.99
- TLR 18: $$,$$$,$$$.99**

```
   1                    IBM DOS AMERICAN NATIONAL STANDARD COBOL        CBF CL3-5            10/27/72

00001   001010 IDENTIFICATION DIVISION.                                 SALESREP
00002   001020 PROGRAM-ID. DISTRICT-SALES-REPORT.                       SALESREP
00003   001030 AUTHOR. C FEINGOLD.                                      SALESREP
00004   001040 DATE-WRITTEN. JUNE 14 1972.                              SALESREP
00005   001050 DATE-COMPILED. 10/27/72                                  SALESREP
00006   001060 REMARKS.                                                 SALESREP
00007   001070     THIS IS A MONTHLY SALES SUMMARY REPORT               SALESREP
00008   001080     BY DISTRICT AND SALESMAN.                            SALESREP
00009   002010 ENVIRONMENT DIVISION.                                    SALESREP
00010   002020 CONFIGURATION SECTION.                                   SALESREP
00011   002030 SOURCE-COMPUTER.                                         SALESREP
00012   002040     IBM-360-H50.                                         SALESREP
00013   002050 OBJECT-COMPUTER.                                         SALESREP
00014   002060     IBM-360-H50.                                         SALESREP
00015   002065 SPECIAL-NAMES.  C01  IS SKIP-TO-1.                       SALESREP
00016   002070 INPUT-OUTPUT SECTION.                                    SALESREP
00017   002080 FILE-CONTROL.                                            SALESREP
00018   002090     SELECT FILE-IN                                       SALESREP
00019   002100         ASSIGN TO SYS009-UR-2540R-S.                     SALESREP
00020   002110     SELECT FILE-OUT                                      SALESREP
00021   002120         ASSIGN TO SYS005-UR-1403-S                       SALESREP
00022   002125         RESERVE NO ALTERNATE AREA.                       SALESREP
00023   003010 DATA DIVISION.                                           SALESREP
00024   003020 FILE SECTION.                                            SALESREP
00025   003030 FD  FILE-IN                                              SALESREP
00026   003040     RECORDING MODE F                                     SALESREP
00027   003050     LABEL RECORDS OMITTED                                SALESREP
00028   003060     RECORD CONTAINS 80 CHARACTERS                        SALESREP
00029   003070     DATA RECORD IS CARD-IN.                              SALESREP
00030   003080 01  CARD-IN.                                             SALESREP
00031   003090     02 FILLER      PICTURE XX.                           SALESREP
00032   003100     02 SALES-IN    PICTURE 999V99.                       SALESREP
00033   003110     02 MAN-NO-IN   PICTURE 99.                           SALESREP
00034   003120     02 DIST-NO-IN  PICTURE 9.                            SALESREP
00035   003130     02 FILLER      PICTURE X(70).                        SALESREP
00036   003140 FD  FILE-OUT                                             SALESREP
00037   003150     RECORDING MODE F                                     SALESREP
00038   003160     LABEL RECORDS OMITTED                                SALESREP
00039   003170     DATA RECORD IS PRINTOUT.                             SALESREP
```

```
00040    003180 01  PRINTOUT PICTURE X(133).                               SALESREP
00041    004010 WORKING-STORAGE SECTION.                                   SALESREP
00042    004020 77  DIST-NO-WS      PICTURE 9.                             SALESREP
00043    004030 77  MAN-NO-WS       PICTURE 99.                            SALESREP
00044    004050 77  MAN-TOT-WS      PICTURE 9(5)V99.                       SALESREP
00045    004055 77  DIST-TOT-WS     PICTURE 9(6)V99 VALUE ZEROS.           SALESREP
00046    004060 77  MON-TOT-WS      PICTURE 9(7)V99 VALUE ZEROS.           SALESREP
00047    004070 01  HDG-1.                                                 SALESREP
00048    004080 02  FILLER          PICTURE X(38) VALUE SPACES.            SALESREP
00049    004090 02  FILLER          PICTURE X(39)                         SALESREP
00050    004100     VALUE 'D I S T R I C T   S A L E S   R E P O R T'.     SALESREP
00051    004110 01  HDG-2.                                                 SALESREP
00052    004120 02  FILLER          PICTURE X(25) VALUE SPACES.            SALESREP
00053    004130 02  FILLER          PICTURE X(8)  VALUE 'SALESMAN'.        SALESREP
00054    004140 02  FILLER          PICTURE X(20) VALUE SPACES.            SALESREP
00055    004150 02  FILLER          PICTURE X(8)  VALUE 'DISTRICT'.        SALESREP
00056    004160 02  FILLER          PICTURE X(21) VALUE SPACES.            SALESREP
00057    004170 02  FILLER          PICTURE X(7)  VALUE 'MONTHLY'.         SALESREP
00058    004180 01  HDG-3.                                                 SALESREP
00059    004190 02  FILLER          PICTURE X(20) VALUE SPACES.            SALESREP
00060    004200 02  FILLER          PICTURE X(19) VALUE 'NUMBER      SALES'. SALESREP
00061    004210 02  FILLER          PICTURE X(11) VALUE SPACES.            SALESREP
00062    004215 02  FILLER          PICTURE X(18) VALUE 'NUMBER      SALES'. SALESREP
00063    004225 02  FILLER          PICTURE X(11) VALUE SPACES.            SALESREP
00064  **004220 02  FILLER          PICTURE X(11) VALUE 'TOTAL SALES'.     SALESREP
00065    005010 01  MAN-TOT-LINE.                                          SALESREP
00066    005020 02  FILLER          PICTURE X(23)   VALUE SPACES.          SALESREP
00067    005030 02  MAN-NO-O        PICTURE ZZ.                            SALESREP
00068    005040 02  FILLER          PICTURE X(5)    VALUE SPACES.          SALESREP
00069    005050 02  MAN-TOT-O       PICTURE $$$,$$$.99.                    SALESREP
00070    005060 01  DIST-TOT-LINE.                                         SALESREP
00071    005070 02  FILLER          PICTURE X(52)   VALUE SPACES.          SALESREP
00072    005080 02  DIST-NO-O       PICTURE 9.                             SALESREP
00073    005090 02  FILLER          PICTURE X(5)    VALUE SPACES.          SALESREP
00074    005100 02  DIST-TOT-O      PICTURE $$$$,$$$.99.                   SALESREP
00075    005110 01  MON-TOT-LINE.                                          SALESREP
00076    005120 02  FILLER          PICTURE X(78)   VALUE SPACES.          SALESREP
00077    005130 02  MON-TOT-O       PICTURE $$,$$$,$$$.99.                 SALESREP
00078    005140 02  FILLER          PICTURE X(3)    VALUE ' **'.           SALESREP
```

3

```
00079    006005 PROCEDURE DIVISION.                                       SALESREP
00080    006010 INIT. OPEN INPUT FILE-IN OUTPUT FILE-OUT.                  SALESREP
00081    006020 PRT-HDG. WRITE PRINTOUT FROM HDG-1 AFTER ADVANCING        SALESREP
00082    006030     SKIP-TO-1 LINES.                                      SALESREP
00083    006040     WRITE PRINTOUT FROM HDG-2 AFTER ADVANCING 3 LINES.    SALESREP
00084    006045     WRITE PRINTOUT FROM HDG-3 AFTER ADVANCING 1 LINES.    SALESREP
00085    006050     MOVE SPACES TO PRINTOUT.                              SALESREP
00086    006060     WRITE PRINTOUT AFTER ADVANCING 1 LINES.               SALESREP
00087    006070 BEGIN-1. READ FILE-IN AT END GO TO FINISH.                SALESREP
00088    006080 BEGIN-2. MOVE DIST-NO-IN TO DIST-NO-WS.                   SALESREP
00089    006090 BEGIN-3. MOVE MAN-NO-IN TO MAN-NO-WS.                     SALESREP
00090    006100     MOVE SALES-IN TO MAN-TOT-WS.                          SALESREP
00091    006110 AGAIN.  READ FILE-IN AT END GO TO FINISH.                 SALESREP
00092    006120     IF MAN-NO-IN IS NOT EQUAL TO MAN-NO-WS GO TO DIFF-MAN. SALESREP
00093    006130     ADD SALES-IN TO MAN-TOT-WS.                           SALESREP
00094    006140     GO TO AGAIN.                                          SALESREP
00095    006150 DIFF-MAN. MOVE MAN-NO-WS TO MAN-NO-O.                     SALESREP
00096    006160     MOVE MAN-TOT-WS TO MAN-TOT-O.                         SALESREP
00097    006170     WRITE PRINTOUT FROM MAN-TOT-LINE AFTER ADVANCING 1 LINES SALESREP
00098    006175     AT END-OF-PAGE PERFORM PRT-HDG.                       SALESREP
00099    006180     ADD MAN-TOT-WS TO DIST-TOT-WS.                        SALESREP
00100    006190     IF DIST-NO-IN IS NOT EQUAL TO DIST-NO-WS GO TO DIFF-DIST. SALESREP
00101    006200     GO TO BEGIN-3.                                        SALESREP
00102    007010 DIFF-DIST. MOVE DIST-NO-WS TO DIST-NO-O.                  SALESREP
00103    007020   /  MOVE DIST-TOT-WS TO DIST-TOT-O.                      SALESREP
00104    007030     WRITE PRINTOUT FROM DIST-TOT-LINE AFTER ADVANCING 2 LINES. SALESREP
00105    007040     ADD DIST-TOT-WS TO MON-TOT-WS.                        SALESREP
00106    007050     MOVE ZEROS TO DIST-TOT-WS.                            SALESREP
00107    007060     GO TO BEGIN-2.                                        SALESREP
00108    007070 FINISH.  ADD SALES-IN TO MAN-TOT-WS.                      SALESREP
00109    007080     MOVE MAN-NO-WS TO MAN-NO-O.                           SALESREP
00110    007090     MOVE MAN-TOT-WS TO MAN-TOT-O.                         SALESREP
00111    007100     WRITE PRINTOUT FROM MAN-TOT-LINE AFTER ADVANCING 1 LINES SALESREP
00112    007110     AT END-OF-PAGE PERFORM PRT-HDG.                       SALESREP
00113    007120     ADD MAN-TOT-WS TO DIST-TOT-WS.                        SALESREP
00114    007130     MOVE DIST-NO-WS TO DIST-NO-O.                         SALESREP
00115    007135     MOVE DIST-TOT-WS TO DIST-TOT-O.                       SALESREP
00116    007140     WRITE PRINTOUT FROM DIST-TOT-LINE AFTER ADVANCING 2 LINES SALESREP
00117    007150     ADD DIST-TOT-WS TO MON-TOT-WS.                        SALESREP
```

```
00118   007160   MOVE MON-TOT-WS TO MON-TOT-O.                              SALESREP
00119   007165   WRITE PRINTOUT FROM MON-TOT-LINE AFTER ADVANCING 3 LINES.  SALESREP
00120   007170   CLOSE FILE-IN, FILE-OUT.                                   SALESREP
00121   007180   STOP RUN.                                                  SALESREP
```

DISTRICT SALES REPORT

SALESMAN		DISTRICT		MONTHLY
NUMBER	SALES	NUMBER	SALES	TOTAL SALES
10	$241.80			
20	$148.08			
		1	$389.88	
6	$117.40			
41	$457.50			
		2	$574.90	
31	$145.60			
32	$404.48			
61	$189.12			
		3	$739.20	
10	$241.80			
20	$148.08			
		1	$389.88	
6	$117.40			
41	$457.50			
		2	$574.90	
31	$145.60			
32	$404.48			
61	$189.12			
		3	$739.20	
10	$241.80			
20	$148.08			
		1	$389.88	
6	$117.40			
41	$457.50			
		2	$574.90	
31	$86.99			
32	$256.83			

DISTRICT SALES REPORT

SALESMAN		DISTRICT		MONTHLY
NUMBER	SALES	NUMBER	SALES	TOTAL SALES
61	$189.12			
		3	$532.94	
10	$94.22			
20	$15.92			
		1	$110.14	
6	$36.74			
41	$105.72			
		2	$142.46	
31	$49.05			
32	$147.65			
61	$78.47			
		3	$275.17	
10	$15.75			
20	$15.92			
		1	$31.67	
6	$36.74			
41	$105.72			
		2	$142.46	
31	$49.05			
32	$147.65			
61	$156.94			
		3	$353.64	
				$5,961.22 **

Exercises

Write your answers in the space provided.

1. The Procedure Division specifies the _____ necessary to solve a given problem.
2. A statement is a syntactical valid combination of _____ and _____ beginning with a COBOL _____.
3. COBOL statements may be compared to _____ in the English language.
4. The imperative statement consists of one or more _____ commands to be performed by the object program.
5. A conditional statement is a statement that is to be _____ and the _____ of the conditional expression will determine which of the _____ paths the program will follow.
6. A _____ statement directs the computer to perform some action at compile time.
7. A sentence is composed of one or more _____ specifying action to be taken and is terminated by a _____ and a _____.
8. Separators when used must be followed by at least one _____.
9. COBOL sentences may be combined into a logical entity called a _____ _____.
10. A procedure-name must not be _____ within the same section.
11. A _____ is composed of one or more successive paragraphs.
12. The Procedure Division generally consists of a series of _____ which may be optionally grouped by the programmer into _____.
13. The Declaratives Section must be grouped at the _____ of the Procedure Division.
14. Statements are executed in the sequence in which they are written unless altered by the _____.
15. COBOL _____ are the basis of the Procedure Division.
16. The programmer is concerned only with the use of _____ records.
17. In data processing operations, the flow of data through a system is governed by the _____ system.
18. The four verbs used to specify the flow of data to or from files stored on an external media are _____, _____, _____ and _____.
19. _____ and _____ verbs are used in conjunction with low volume data.
20. The _____ statement makes one or more input/output files ready for reading or writing.
21. An _____ statement must be specified for all _____

in a COBOL program and must be executed prior to any other input/output statement for that file.

22. Each file that has been opened must be defined in the _____ entry in the Data Division as well as in the _____ clause in the Environment Division.

23. The _____ statement makes a data record ready for processing.

24. The file must be _____ before it is read.

25. The INTO option converts the READ statement into a _____ and _____ statement.

26. An _____ clause must be included in all READ statements for sequential files.

27. The _____ option must be specified for mass storage files in the random access mode.

28. The WRITE statement releases a _____ for insertion in an _____ file.

29. The format for a WRITE statement requires a _____ rather than a file name.

30. The _____ option is used with the WRITE statement to allow vertical positioning up to 99 lines.

31. The _____ option can be used to test for channel 12 on an on-line printer.

32. The CLOSE statement _____ the processing of one or more files and must be written for all files that have previously _____.

33. The ACCEPT statement obtains _____ data from the systems logical _____ device or from the _____.

34. The DISPLAY statement causes the _____ of low volume data on an _____ device.

35. The MOVE statement transmits data from _____ storage area to _____ or more _____ area within the computer.

36. When a group item is involved in a move, the data is moved without any regard to the _____ of the group item.

37. When both the sending and receiving areas are elementary items, appropriate _____ to the format of the _____ area takes place.

38. The figurative constant _____ belongs to the numeric category of data while the figurative constant _____ belongs to the non-numeric category.

39. In a numeric data MOVE statement, the source area is aligned with regard to the _____ in the receiving area and any necessary _____ will take place.

40. Nonnumeric data from a source area is placed in the receiving area beginning at the _____ and continuing to the _____ unless the field is specified as _____.

41. In a MOVE CORRESPONDING statement execution, selected items within the _____ area are moved with required _____ to the selected _____ area.

42. At least one of selected items in a MOVE CORRESPONDING statement must be an _____ item.

43. The EXAMINE statement is used to replace a given _____ and/ or to _____ the number of times it appears in the data item.

44. All identifiers used in arithmetic statements must represent elementary _____ items.

45. The identifier that follows GIVING may contain _____ characters.

46. The literals used in arithmetic statements must be _____.

47. Decimal alignment is performed automatically throughout the computation in accordance with the _____ clause of the _____ and _____.

48. The _____ option is used to half adjust the result of an arithmetic operation.

49. The _____ option is used when the computed result after _____ alignment _____ the number of positions identified with the result.

50. The CORRESPONDING option of the ADD and SUBTRACT verbs allows the user to perform _____ on elementary items by simply specifying the _____ to which they belong.

51. The ADD statement must contain at least _____ operands.

52. The _____ must not be written in the same ADD statement as TO.

53. In a SUBTRACT statement, all values of operands preceding the word _____ are added together and this total is subtracted from the value of the _____.

54. The _____ statement specifies the use of an arithmetic expression.

55. All operators used in a _____ statement must be _____ and _____ by one or more spaces.

56. If exponentiation is desired, the _____ statement must be used.

57. In an arithmetic expression, all _____ expressions are performed first.

58. The GO TO statement provides a means of transferring control _____ or _____ from one part of a program to another.

59. The GO TO statement can only be used as the _____ sentence in the sequence in which it appears.

60. If the DEPENDING ON option of the _____ statement is used,

the value of the identifier must have a range starting at _____ and continuing successively upward.

61. The _____ statement is used to modify the effect of a GO TO statement.

62. The PERFORM statement permits a _____ transfer of sequence control and a _____ back at the conclusion of the execution of a specified condition.

63. In its simplest form, the PERFORM statement provides control back to the _____ statement after the PERFORM statement.

64. The last statement in a referenced procedure of a PERFORM statement must not contain an unconditional _____ statement.

65. The _____ statement is used to halt execution of a program.

66. The EXIT verb is used with the _____ verb in _____ exits from a paragraph.

67. The _____ statements cause the compiler to take specific action at _____ time.

68. The _____ statement enables the programmer to use other programming languages in a COBOL source program.

69. The NOTE statement is used to insert _____ in the source program.

70. If NOTE is the first word of a paragraph, the paragraph must be devoted to _____.

71. A conditional expression is an expression containing one or more _____ _____ whose _____ may change during the course of the program.

72. If a test condition is _____, the statements immediately following the _____ expression are executed.

73. A _____ condition test involves the comparison of two data values.

74. A Class Condition test is used to determine whether an item is _____ _____ or _____.

75. The Condition-Name Condition test is an alternate way of expressing certain conditions that could be expressed in a simple _____ condition.

76. In a compound conditional expression, if either or both are true, the logical operator _____ is used.

77. Nesting a conditional expression is like specifying a _____ arithmetic expression enclosed in _____ enclosed in a larger arithmetic expression.

78. If the operator is implied, then the _____ must also be implied.

79. _____ and _____ conditions can never have implied subjects.

80. A Relational Operator may be implied only in a _____ relational condition.

Answers

1. ACTIONS
2. WORDS, SYMBOLS, VERB
3. CLAUSES
4. UNCONDITIONAL
5. TESTED, EXPLANATION, ALTERNATE
6. COMPILER-DIRECTING
7. STATEMENTS, PERIOD, SPACE
8. SPACE
9. PARAGRAPH
10. DUPLICATED
11. SECTION
12. PARAGRAPHS, SECTIONS
13. BEGINNING
14. PROGRAM
15. VERBS
16. INDIVIDUAL
17. INPUT/OUTPUT
18. OPEN, READ, WRITE, CLOSE
19. ACCEPT, DISPLAY
20. OPEN
21. OPEN, FILES
22. FILE DESCRIPTION, SELECT
23. READ
24. OPENED
25. READ, MOVE
26. AT END
27. INVALID KEY
28. RECORD, OUTPUT
29. RECORD NAME
30. ADVANCING
31. END-OF-PAGE
32. TERMINATES, OPENED
33. LOW VOLUME, INPUT, CONSOLE
34. WRITING, OUTPUT
35. ONE, ONE, STORAGE
36. LEVEL STRUCTURE
37. EDITING, RECEIVING
38. ZERO, SPACE
39. DECIMAL POINT, EDITING
40. LEFT, RIGHT, JUSTIFIED RIGHT
41. SOURCE, EDITING, RECEIVING
42. ELEMENTARY
43. CHARACTER, COUNT
44. NUMERIC
45. EDITING
46. NUMERIC
47. PICTURE, OPERANDS, RESULTS
48. ROUNDED
49. SIZE ERROR, DECIMAL, EXCEEDS
50. COMPUTATION, GROUP
51. TWO
52. GIVING OPTION
53. FROM, IDENTIFIER
54. COMPUTE
55. COMPUTE, PRECEDED, FOLLOWED
56. COMPUTE
57. PARENTHETICAL
58. CONDITIONALLY, UNCONDITIONALLY
59. FINAL
60. GO TO, ONE
61. ALTER
62. TEMPORARY, RETURN
63. NEXT
64. GO TO
65. STOP
66. PERFORM, CONDITIONAL
67. COMPILER-DIRECTING, COMPILE
68. ENTER
69. COMMENTS
70. NOTES
71. VARIABLES, VALUES

72. TRUE, CONDITIONAL
73. RELATION
74. ALPHABETIC, NUMERIC
75. RELATIONAL
76. OR

77. SUBORDINATE, PAREN-
    THESIS
78. SUBJECT
79. SIGN, CLASS
80. SIMPLE

Questions for Review

1. Define a statement and explain the three types of statements used in the Procedure Division.
2. Define a sentence, paragraph and section.
3. How is the Procedure Division organized?
4. What are the main functions of input and output verbs? Give examples.
5. What are the main functions of the OPEN and READ statements and how are they related to each other?
6. What are the main functions of the WRITE and CLOSE statement?
7. Explain the use of the ADVANCING, POSITIONING and END-OF-PAGE options of the WRITE statement.
8. What are the functions of the ACCEPT and DISPLAY statements?
9. What are data manipulation verbs? Give purposes and examples of usage of each type of verb.
10. Explain the movement of numeric and nonnumeric data.
11. What is the function of a MOVE CORRESPONDING verb? What are the advantages and disadvantages of using this verb?
12. What is meant by "Rounding" and how is it used in arithmetic statements?
13. How is the ON SIZE ERROR option used in arithmetic statements?
14. Explain the use of the CORRESPONDING option of the ADD and SUB-TRACT statements.
15. How is the COMPUTE statement used?
16. What are rules for the sequence of arithmetic expression concerning a number of operators?
17. What are the purposes of sequence control verbs. Give function and examples of each type of verb.
18. What are the functions of the compiler-directing verbs? Give functions and examples of each type of verb.
19. What is a conditional expression. Explain the functions of the four test condition statements.
20. What is a compound conditional expression?
21. What is a nested conditional statement?
22. What is an implied subject? An implied operator?

Problems

1. *Match each term with its proper description.*

_____ 1. Statement   A. One or more successive sentences.

_____ 2. Sentence   B. Unconditional command.

_____ 3. Paragraph   C. Largest unit within the Procedure Division.

_____ 4. Section   D. Basic unit of the Procedure Division.

_____ 5. Procedures   E. Tested and evaluation.

_____ 6. Imperative   F. One or more statements.

_____ 7. Conditional   G. Groups of successive paragraphs.

2. *Match each verb with its proper description.*

_____ 1. Open   A. Terminates processing of files.

_____ 2. Read   B. Causes writing of low volume data.

_____ 3. Write   C. Makes record available for processing.

_____ 4. Close   D. Obtains low volume data.

_____ 5. Accept   E. Prepares an input or output file for reading or writing.

_____ 6. Display   F. Releases record for insertion in output file.

3. *Match each verb with its proper description.*

_____ 1. Move   A. Product of two numeric items.

_____ 2. Examine   B. Specifies accumulation of numeric values.

_____ 3. Add   C. Requires use of an arithmetic expression.

_____ 4. Subtract   D. Replace and/or tally the occurrences of a given character.

_____ 5 Multiply   E. Difference between two numeric values.

_____ 6. Divide   F. Shift data to another area.

_____ 7. Compute   G. Division of one numeric value by another.

4. *Match each verb with its proper description.*

_____ 1. Go To   A. Causes transfer of control from normal execution and returns control back.

_____ 2. Alter   B. Common end point for set of procedures.

_____ 3. Perform   C. Temporary or permanent halt to the program.

_____ 4. Stop

_____ 5. Exit

_____ 6. Copy

_____ 7. Enter

_____ 8. Note

D. Include other programming languages in a COBOL program.

E. Include prewritten procedures at compile time.

F. Transfers control conditionally or unconditionally to another point in the program.

G. Insert comments into a source program listing.

H. Modify the effect of an unconditional Go To statement.

5. _Match each statement at left with its proper category at right._

_____ 1. ADD X, Y; ON SIZE
ERROR GO TO
SPEC-ROUTINE.

A. Imperative.

_____ 2. STOP RUN

B. Conditional.

_____ 3. GO TO ROUTINE-1.

C. Compiler-directing.

_____ 4. NOTE THE FOL-
LOWING ROUTINE....

_____ 5. READ FILE-IN; AT
END GO TO FINISH.

_____ 6. CLOSE FILE-IN, FILE-OUT.

6. _The hierarchy of entries in the Procedure Division beginning with the largest unit are:_

1. _____.
2. _____.
3. _____.
4. _____.

7. _Write Procedure Division statements for the following:_
   a. Prepare a READ statement for a card file named CARD-INPUT with a record named CARD-REC-DATA. The termination paragraph is named LAST-RECORD.
   b. Prepare a WRITE statement for a printed report with a file name of PRINT-LIST and a record name of PRINT-IT, where each line is to be separated by two blank lines.
   c. Type on the console typewriter, the literal VALUE EXCEEDS BALANCE and the field defined in the Working-Storage Section as REMAINING-BALANCE.
   d. Prepare a CLOSE statement for the file named, INPUT-FILE, OUTPUT-FILE and PRINT-FILE.

8. *Write the necessary WRITE statement with the ADVANCING or POSITIONING option to accomplish the following:*

   a. Advance the form three lines before a record is written.
   b. Advance the form three lines after a record is written.
   c. Double spacing.
   d. Triple spacing.
   e. Skipping to the first printing line of a new page before the line is printed.
   f. Branching at the bottom of a page.

9. *Write the necessary Procedure Division entries for the following:*
   a. Allow a value of CODE-DATA to be entered into Working-Storage through the console typewriter.
   b. Write the value of CODE-DATA on the console typewriter.

10. *Match the result with the correct statement.*

Statement	Result
_____ 1. DISPLAY DATE UPON CONSOLE.	A. The word DATE will be written on the console typewriter.
_____ 2. DISPLAY 'DATE' UPON CONSOLE.	B. The word 'DATE' will be written on the console typewriter.
	C. The value of the variable DATE will be written on the console typewriter.

11. *Write the necessary Data Division and Procedure Division entries for the following:*

    a. In the paragraph INIT, the following message is to be written out on the console typewriter ENTER OPERATION-CODE.
    b. A value of OPERATION-CODE is to be entered into storage through the console keyboard. Values of OPERATION-CODE have a form such as 107B, 509X, or 879G.
    c. The value of OPERATION-CODE is to be written on the console typewriter.

12.   02 TRANSACTION-FLD.
            03 TRANS-CODE   PICTURE X   OCCURS 20 TIMES.

    Write an instruction to clear data from the fifth TRANS-CODE item in the TRANSACTION-FLD.

13. *Using the partial Data Division entry that follows, write the necessary coding for the MOVE problem.*

```
01  RECORD-1                      01  RECORD-2
    03  STOCK-NUMBER                  03  STOCK-NUMBER
    03  UNITS                         03  DATA-MESSAGE
    03  VALUE                         03  QUANTITY
    03  WEIGHT                        03  UNITS
```

a. Transfer UNITS from RECORD-1 to RECORD-2.
b. Transfer all like named fields from RECORD-1 to RECORD-2.
c. Clear a field in Working-Storage Section called DATA-MESSAGE of previous field, move information to area above in RECORD-2.

14. *A name has been defined in the input record as follows:*

```
02  NAME.
    03  LAST-NAME         PICTURE  A(20).
    03  FIRST-INITIAL     PICTURE  A.
    03  SECOND-INITIAL    PICTURE  A.
```

a. Write the necessary entries to define a Working-Storage record called EDITED-NAME, with INITIAL-1 in the first position, followed by a period and space; then INITIAL-2 in the fourth position, another period and space; finally 20 positions called SURNAME.
b. Write the MOVE statement to put each part of the name into their proper places in the Working-Storage record.
c. Write a MOVE statement to transfer EDITED-NAME to CUSTOMER-NAME (Assume that CUSTOMER-NAME is a 26 position alphanumeric item in the output record which has been previously defined).

15. *Imagine you are preparing a customer invoice, at the bottom of which you want to print three lines that look like*

```
GROSS AMOUNT        $205.30
    DISCOUNT        $   4.11
  NET AMOUNT        $201.19
```

Set up the data division entry for the item AMOUNT-ID to store the literals and appropriate MOVE statements to accomplish the above,

a. Use the JUSTIFIED RIGHT clause.
b. Without the use of the JUSTIFIED RIGHT clause.

16. *Given the following data record.*

I-RECORD	W-RECORD
EMPLOYEE-NO	EMPLOYEE-NO
EMPLOYEE-NAME	FILLER
RATE	EMPLOYEE-NAME
	FILLER
	RATE
	FILLER

Write the necessary procedural statements to move the I-RECORD items to the appropriate W-RECORD fields. Use two different methods.

17. *Indicate the RECEIVED DATA in the following:*

	Source Data	Source Picture	Receiving Picture	Received Data
1.	8736	9999	9999	
2.	8736	9999P	P9999	
3.	8736	99V99	99V99	
4.	8736	99V99	99.99	
5.	8736	P9999	99.99	
6.	8736	9999P	99.99	
7.	8736	P9999	99V99	
8.	8736	9999P	99V99	
9.	8736	9999	$99.99	
10.	8736	99V99	$99.999	
11.	8736	9999P	99999.99	
12.	ERROR	XXXXX	XXXXX	
13.	ERROR	AAAAA	AAAAA	
14.	ERROR	AAAAA	AAAAAAAA	

18. *For each of the following, fill in TALLY.*

a. EXAMINE FLD-A TALLYING UNTIL FIRST ZERO.

FLD-A `1 0 3 5 0 0 1`   TALLY `       `

b. EXAMINE FLD-B TALLYING ALL ZEROS.

FLD-B `1 0 3 5 0 0 1`   TALLY `       `

c. EXAMINE FLD-C TALLYING LEADING SPACES.

FLD-C `          * * * *` TALLY `       `

For each of the following, fill in the resulting data.

d. EXAMINE FLD-D REPLACING ALL ZEROS BY QUOTES.

FLD-D | 0 | 0 | 0 | 3 | 4 | 5 | 0 | FLD-D | | | | | | | |

e. EXAMINE FLD-E REPLACING FIRST "0" BY "—".

FLD-E | 5 | 7 | 3 | 0 | 5 | 1 | 4 | FLD-E | | | | | | | |

f. EXAMINE FLD-F TALLYING LEADING ZEROS REPLACING
   BY SPACES.   FLD-F | | | | | | | |

FLD-F | 0 | 0 | 0 | 0 | 6 | 7 | 0 | TALLY | | | | | |

19. *ARITHMETIC PROBLEMS*

Data-Name	Picture	Data Values Before Execution	Data Values After Execution
FLD-A	S999V99	+10000	
FLD-B	S999V999	+045550	
FLD-C	S999V99	−12345	
FLD-D	S9999	1234	
FLD-E	S99V9999	+123456	
FLD-F	S999V99	+90000	
FLD-G	S999V9	+12345	
FLD-H	S9V9	−45	
FLD-I	S999V99	−32045	
FLD-J	S99V99	+0475	
FLD-K	S9999V9999	+46250000	
FLD-L	S999V9	+4259	
FLD-M	S999V99	−32007	
FLD-N	S999V99	00000	
FLD-O	S9999	4567	
FLD-P	S9999V99	+123456	

Arithmetic Statements

1. ADD FLD-A, FLD-B GIVING FLD-C.
2. ADD FLD-A, FLD-B, FLD-H, FLD-I, FLD-J TO FLD-K.
3. SUBTRACT FLD-M FROM FLD-I ROUNDED.
4. MULTIPLY FLD-A BY FLD-B GIVING FLD-D ROUNDED.
5. DIVIDE FLD-A INTO FLD-B GIVING FLD-E ON SIZE ERROR GO TO ERROR-RT.
6. MULTIPLY FLD-A BY FLD-F GIVING FLD-G ROUNDED ON SIZE ERROR GO TO FIX-IT.
7. DIVIDE FLD-N INTO FLD-A GIVING FLD-P.
8. ADD FLD-O TO FLD-O.

Required: In the DATA VALUES AFTER EXECUTION column, write the results of the arithmetic statements shown above.

20. *Show the contents of each field after the calculation in the After Execution area.*

a. ADD FLD-A TO FLD-B.

Data-Name	Picture	Before Execution	After Execution
FLD-A	S99V99	+ 1234	
FLD-B	S99V99	− 1200	

b. SUBTRACT FLD-A, FLD-B FROM FLD-C.

Data-Name	Picture	Before Execution	After Execution
FLD-A	S99V99	+ 1234	
FLD-B	S9999V99	− 987654	
FLD-C	S9999V99	+ 123456	

c. MULTIPLY FLD-A BY FLD-B GIVING FLD-C.

Data-Name	Picture	Before Execution	After Execution
FLD-A	S99V99	+ 1234	
FLD-B	S9999V99	+ 98765	
FLD-C	S9(7)V9999	+ 1234567890	

d. DIVIDE FLD-A INTO FLD-B ROUNDED.

Data-Name	Picture	Before Execution	After Execution
FLD-A	S99V99	+1234	
FLD-B	S999V9	+9879	

e. ADD FLD-A, FLD-B TO FLD-C ON SIZE ERROR GO TO ERROR-ROUTINE.

Data-Name	Picture	Before Execution	After Execution
FLD-A	S99V99	+1234	
FLD-B	S99V99	+9876	
FLD-C	S999V99	+98765	

21. *Prepare the following arithmetic statements.*

a. Add the fields of GIANT and CONTAINER and place the result in CONTAINER.
b. Add the fields TOOL, TOTAL-NUMB, and NUMB, placing the result in TOTAL-NUMB.
c. Add the fields DATA-IN, PROD, ROYALTY and place the result in GRAND-SUM.
d. Subtract the field QUANTITY from TOTAL-BALANCE and place the result in TOTAL-BALANCE.
e. Subtract the fields DATA-GIVEN, HOLD-DATA, CON-HOLD from TOTAL-HOLD and place the result in TOTAL-HOLD.
f. Subtract the field BALANCE-B from CON-NUMB and place the result in NEW-NUMB.

22. *To permanently change the sequence of execution of instructions in the Procedure Division, you use the _____ verb. To change the sequence temporarily, you use the _____.*

23. *Prepare the following procedural statements using the GO TO verb.*

a. A statement to transfer control to a paragraph called COMPUTE-PROCESS.
b. A statement for the true condition of an equality comparison. The fields BALANCE and TOTAL are compared for equality. When the condition is true, control is transferred to COMPUTE-ROUTINE.
c. A statement to transfer the program to PROC-1, PROC-2, PROC-3 or PROC-4 if the CLASS-CODE is 1, 2, 3 or 4. If the CLASS-CODE is out of this range, the program should branch to a paragraph called ERROR-ROUTINE.

24. *Assume that a numeric item has been defined and that it meets the requirements of the GO TO statement with the DEPENDING ON option. This series
of IF statements is based on testing that item. Write the GO TO statements
with the DEPENDING ON option which will cause the same branches as
the series of IFs.*

a. IF JOB = 1 GO TO MANAGER.
   IF JOB = 2 GO TO ANALYST.
   IF JOB = 3 GO TO PROGRAMMER.
   IF JOB = 4 GO TO OPERATOR.

b.

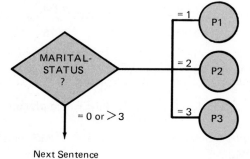

Next Sentence

The diagram above shows the paragraph to which control is to be
passed depending on the value of MARITAL-STATUS. Write the procedural
statements to transfer control as specified in the diagram.

25. FIX. GO TO IN-STATE.
   a. ALTER FIX TO PROCEED TO OUT-STATE.
   b. ALTER IN-STATE TO PROCEED TO OUT-STATE.
   c. ALTER FIX TO PROCEED TO IN-STATE.

   Which of the above ALTER statements could alter the GO TO statement
   above so that the execution of the paragraph FIX would cause control to be
   transferred to paragraph OUT-STATE.

26. SWITCH-PARAGRAGH. GO TO PENALTY.
   ALTER-PARAGRAPH.

   Write a statement that will cause execution of SWITCH-PARAGRAPH
   to transfer control to DISCOUNT.

27. You are writing the Procedure Division for PROGRAM-1. In the Data Division, there is a two character alphanumeric field called CDE. At various
   times during the execution of the program, CDE can contain a value ranging from 01 through 05 and from AA through AE.

   Using the PERFORM statement, write the necessary entries to execute
   the following three separate points in the program depending upon the
   contents of CDE.

CDE Value	Action
01	ADD AMT-01 TO GRAND-TOTAL. MOVE A TO WORK-AREA.
02	ADD AMT-02 TO GRAND-TOTAL. MOVE B TO WORK-AREA.
.	
.	
.	
AA	ADD AMT-AA TO GRAND-TOTAL. MOVE F TO WORK-AREA.
.	
.	
AE	ADD AMT-AE TO GRAND-TOTAL. MOVE H TO WORK-AREA.

28. *Using the PERFORM verb, write the necessary procedural statements for the following print routine.*

   a. Print a header line (HDG-1) at the top of each page.
   b. Print a maximum of 40 detail lines (PRINTOUT) per page.
   c. Before processing a new department (compare DEPT-NO with PREV-DEPT, which is set up in Working-Storage) print a total header line (DEPT-TOTAL-HDG) followed by a department total (DEPT-TOTAL-LINE). Skip to a new page and print HDG-1 before continuing.

29. *A program contains the following:*

```
TAX-DEDUCTION SECTION.
    TAX-PARA-1.
    TAX-PARA-2.
    TAX-PARA-3.
FICA-DEDUCTION SECTION.
    FICA-PARA-1.
    FICA-PARA-2.
    FICA-PARA-3.
TOTAL-DEDUCTIONS SECTION.
    TOTAL-PARA-1.
    TOTAL-PARA-2.
```

In the following PERFORM statement indicate after the *last Statement of which paragraph,* will control be transferred to the next statement after PERFORM.

   a. PERFORM TAX-PARA-2, SUBTRACT TAX-FIGURED FROM TOTAL-TAX.
   b. PERFORM TAX-DEDUCTION, SUBTRACT TAX-FIGURED FROM TO-TAL-TAX.
   c. PERFORM TAX-DEDUCTION THRU FICA-PARA-2, ADD TAX-FIG-URED, FICA-FIGURED GIVING TAX-DEDUCTIONS.
   d. PERFORM TAX-DEDUCTION THRU TOTAL-DEDUCTIONS.

30. *Which of the following COPY entries are correctly written?*
    a. INPUT-OUTPUT SECTION.
       COPY IN-OUT-SECT.
    b. SELECT COPY FILES.
    c. FD   CARD-FILE
          COPY FILE-DESCRIPTION-ENTRY.
    d. 01   COPY CARD-RECORD.
    e. 77   SAVE-NUMBER COPY LIBRARY-1.
    f. BEGIN. COPY OPEN-PARAGRAPH.

31. *In the following NOTE statements indicate what will appear on the compilation output listing.*

    a. EXPLANATION.
          NOTE WHEN THE FIELD LOW-QUANTITY CONTAINS 150 IT IS
          TIME TO REORDER. IF THIS IS A DISCONTINUED ITEM, A "D"
          WILL BE IN THE STATUS FIELD.
    b. MOVE ORDER TO MASTER-LIST. NOTE THIS CUSTOMER IS EN-
       TITLED TO A 2% DISCOUNT ON THIS ITEM. COMPUTE TOTAL-COST
       = (NO-ITEMS * COST-PER-ITEM) * .98.

32.

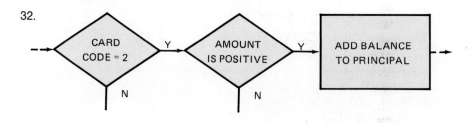

Select the proper coding for the procedures above.

    a. IF CARD-CODE IS EQUAL TO 2 OR AMOUNT IS POSITIVE, ADD BAL-
       ANCE TO PRINCIPAL.
    b. IF CARD-CODE IS EQUAL TO 2 AND AMOUNT IS POSITIVE, ADD BAL-
       ANCE TO PRINCIPAL.

33. *Write the conditional statements for the following:*

    a. When the account number MAST-ACCT of the master file is not equal
       to the transaction account number, TRANS-ACCT, display 'SEQUENCE
       ERROR' TRANS-ACCT, on the console typewriter, otherwise continue
       regular processing.

b. When the stock of parts, TOTAL-UNITS, is below the minimum RE-ORDER-POINT, transfer the stock number PART-NO to the reorder report, REORDER-NUMBER; otherwise continue processing.

c. When the line counter, LINE-COUNT, exceeds the specified number of lines per page, LINE-CONSTANT, control is passed to a page change routine, PAGE-CHANGE; otherwise a "1" (ONE-CONSTANT) is added to the line counter, LINE-COUNT.

34. *For a given application, it is necessary to select all records that contain an item number equal to 41571, 58001 through 59720 or 64225.*

Write the necessary procedural statements to accomplish the above.

35. *A percentage of sales is offered to each salesman as a commission. The percentage differs if the item sold is class A, B, C or D. If the item sold is not class A, B, C or D, no commission is calculated and the program proceeds to the NO-COMM-ROUTINE.*

Compute the sales commission based on the following rates.

CLASS A — equal to or less than 1,000, the commission is 6%.
        — greater than 1,000 but less than 2,000, the commission is 7%.
        — 2,000 or greater, the commission is 10%.
CLASS B — less than 1,000, the commission is 4%.
        — 1,000 or greater, the commission is 6%.
CLASS C — all amounts, the commission is 4½%.
CLASS D — all amounts, the commission is 5%.

The result of the computation is stored in COMMISSION.
Upon completion of the computation, proceed to NEXT-ROUTINE.

Write the necessary procedural statements for the above.

36. *Using the following data values, solve the conditional statement by determining whether the tested condition is true or false.*

| A1 = 5 | B1 = 3 | C1 = 8 | D1 = 15 |
| A2 = 4 | B2 = 3 | C2 = 4 | D2 = 15 |

Statement:

IF A1 = B1 OR (C1 IS LESS THAN D1 AND (B2 = C2 OR A1 IS GREATER THAN A2) AND A2 = C2) OR C1 is GREATER THAN D2 and D1 is EQUAL TO D2.

37.

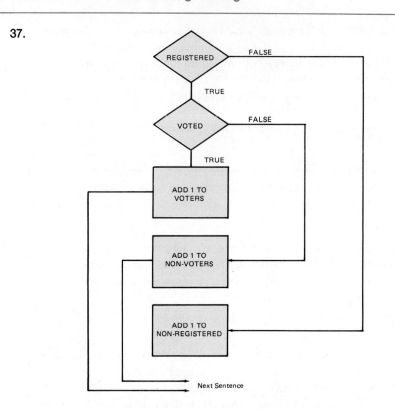

Write the single IF sentence that corresponds to the flowchart above. (Assume that all names have been defined. The decisions are condition-name tests.)

38. *Write the necessary procedural statements to accomplish the following:*

a.

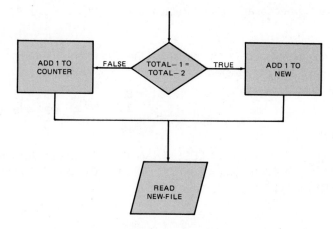

b.

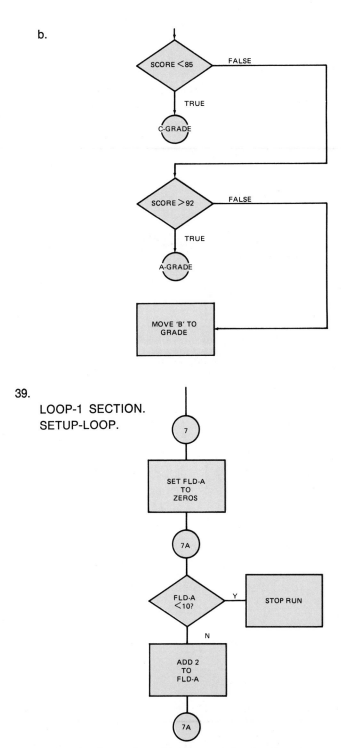

39.

LOOP-1 SECTION.
SETUP-LOOP.

Write the Procedure Division entries for the above.

40. *LARGEST NUMBER PROBLEM*

There are three unequal numbers labeled NUM-A, NUM-B and NUM-C. Write the IF and MOVE statements necessary to move the largest number of the three to FLD-1, the next largest number to FLD-2 and the smallest number to FLD-3 and proceed to ROUT-X.

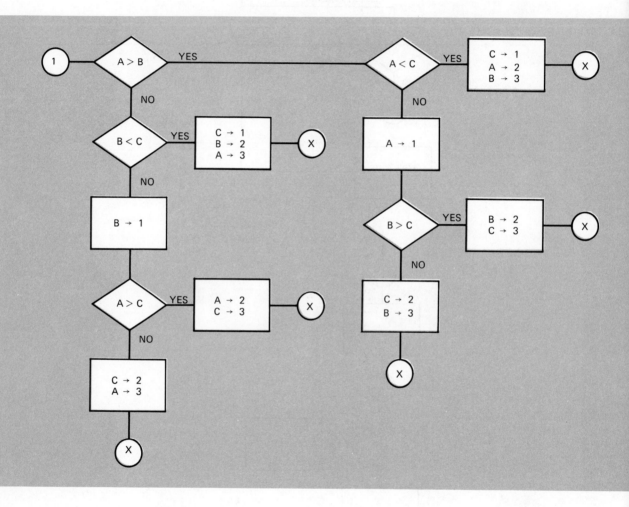

41. *LISTING*

This is a simple program whereby each card is read and a line printed for each card.

INPUT	*File-name*	FILE-IN	*Record-name*	RECORD-IN
OUTPUT	*File-name*	FILE-OUT	*Record-name*	RECORD-OUT

Write the procedural statements to accomplish the following:

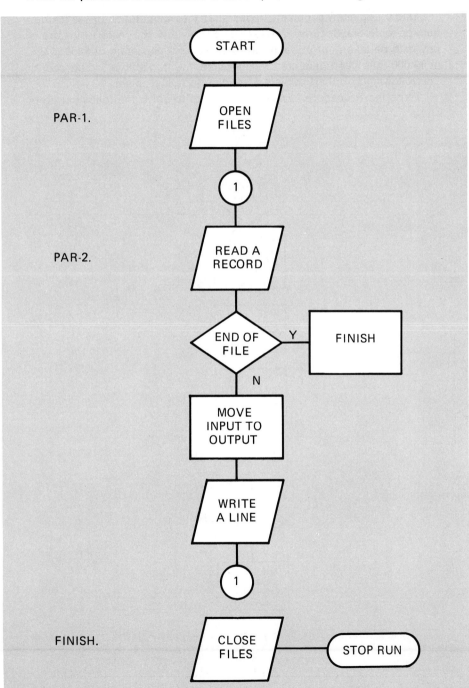

42. *PAYROLL PROBLEM*

One of the many problems in payroll is the computation of the tax deduction for Social Security. The law (for 1972) states that 5.2% of the gross pay is to be taken out of each pay check until a maximum of $468 (5.2% of $9,000) has been deducted. At this time, the deductions would cease. The following flowchart depicts a solution to this problem.

Write the Procedure Division statements to solve the following flowchart.

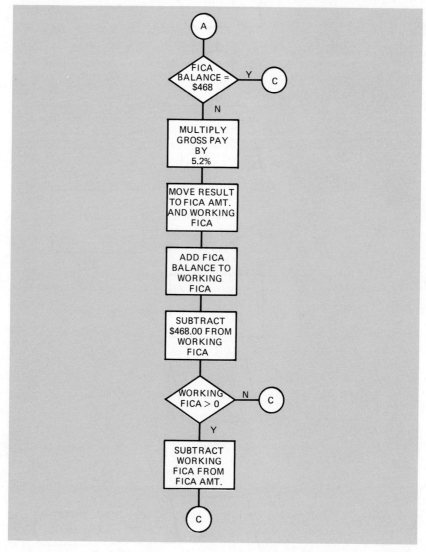

43.

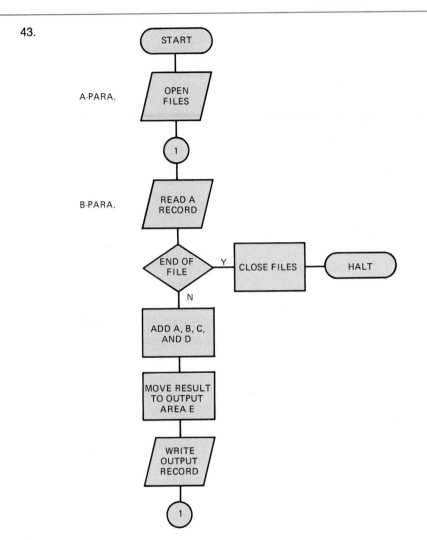

Below you are given the COBOL Procedure Division statements necessary to code the above flowchart. Rearrange them in their correct sequence and enter them on a COBOL coding form.

STOP RUN.
READ FILE-IN;
OPEN INPUT FILE-IN;
OUTPUT FILE-OUT.
AFTER ADVANCING 2 LINES.
A-PARA.

B-PARA.
GO TO B-PARA.
AT END CLOSE FILE-IN, FILE-OUT;
WRITE E-RECORD,
PROCEDURE DIVISION.
ADD A, B, C, D, GIVING E.

9

Table Handling

INTRODUCTION

The Table Handling Feature enables the COBOL programmer to process tables or lists of repeated data conveniently. A table may be set up with three dimensions; for example, three levels of subscripting or indexing can be handled. This Table Handling module provides a capability for defining tables of contiguous data items and for accessing an item relative to its position in the table. Language facility is provided for specifying how many times an item can be repeated. Each item may be identified through the use of a subscript or an index-name. Such a case exists when a group item described with an OCCURS clause contains another group item with an OCCURS clause, which in turn contains another group with an OCCURS clause. To make reference to any element within such a table, each level must be subscripted or indexed.

The Table Handling Feature provides a capability for accessing items in three-dimensional variable-length tables. The feature also provides the additional facilities for specifying ascending or descending keys, and permits searching of a table for an item satisfying a specified condition.

SUBSCRIPTING

Subscripts are used only to refer to an individual element within a list or table of elements that have not been assigned individual data-names (see "Subscripting" in Data Division).

```
data-name (subscript[, subscript] [, subscript] )
```

Figure 9–1. Format Subscripting.

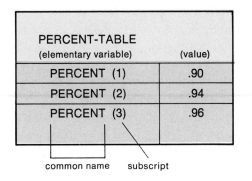

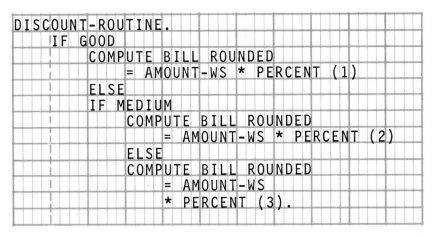

Figure 9–2. Example—Subscripting.

INDEXING

References can be made to individual elements within a table of elements by specifying indexing or that reference. The INDEXED BY option allows both direct and relative referencing of tables of repeated data in a more efficient manner than subscripting.

An index is assigned to a given level of a table by using an INDEXED BY clause in the definition of the table. A name given in the INDEXED BY clause is known as an index-name and is used to refer to the assigned index. An index-name must be initialized by a SET statement before it can be used in a table reference. An index may be modified only by a SET, SEARCH, or PERFORM statement. Data items described by the USAGE IS INDEX clause permit storage of the values of index-names as data without conversion. Such data items are called index-data items.

Direct Indexing is specified by using an index-name in the form of a subscript; for example, ELEMENT (PRIME-INDEX).

Relative Indexing is specified when the terminal space of the data-name is followed by a parenthesized group of items: the index-name, followed by a space, followed by one of the operators + or --, followed by another space, followed by an unsigned integral numeric literal; for example, ELEMENT (PRIME -- INDEX + 5).

Qualification may be used in conjunction with indexing, in which case OF or IN follows the data-name being indexed.

$$\text{data-name} \left\{ \begin{array}{c} \underline{OF} \\ \underline{IN} \end{array} \right\} \text{data-name-1} \left[\left\{ \begin{array}{c} \underline{OF} \\ \underline{IN} \end{array} \right\} \text{data-name-2} \right] \ldots$$

$$(\text{index-name} \left[\left\{ \begin{array}{c} + \\ - \end{array} \right\} \text{integer} \right] \left[, \text{index-name} \left[\left\{ \begin{array}{c} + \\ - \end{array} \right\} \text{integer} \right] \right]$$

$$\left[, \text{index-name} \left[\left\{ \begin{array}{c} + \\ - \end{array} \right\} \text{integer} \right] \right])$$

Figure 9–3. Format Qualification with Indexing.

Rules Governing Subscripting, Indexing, and Qualification

Tables may have one, two, or three dimensions; therefore, reference to an element in a table may require up to three subscripts or indexes.

1. A data-name must not be subscripted or indexed when the data-name is itself being used as an index, subscript, or qualifier.
2. When subscripting, indexing, or qualification are required for a given data item, the indexes or subscripts are specified after all necessary qualifications are given.
3. Subscripting and indexing must not be used together in a single reference.
4. Whenever subscripting is not permitted, indexing is not permitted.
5. The commas shown in the format for indexing and subscripting are required.

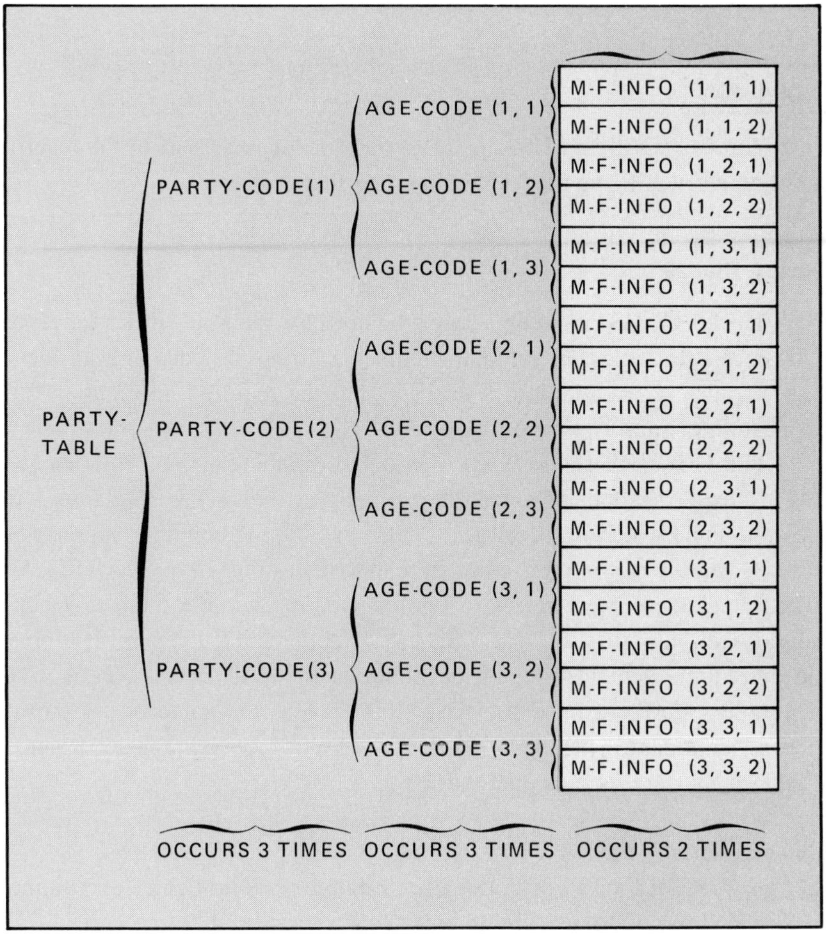

Figure 9–4. Storage Layout for PARTY-TABLE.

```
01    PARTY-TABLE REDEFINES TABLE.
    05    PARTY-CODE OCCURS 3 TIMES INDEXED BY PARTY.
        10    AGE-CODE OCCURS 3 TIMES INDEXED BY AGE.
            15    M-F-INFO OCCURS 2 TIMES INDEXED BY M-F
                  PICTURE 9(7)V9 USAGE DISPLAY.
```

PARTY-TABLE contains three levels of indexing. Reference to elementary items within PARTY-TABLE is made by use of a name that is subscripted or indexed. A typical Procedure Division statement might be:

```
MOVE M-F-INFO (PARTY, AGE, M-F) TO M-F-RECORD.
```

Figure 9–5. Example—Subscripting and Indexing.

DATA DIVISION

The OCCURS and USAGE clause are included as part of the record description entry utilizing the Table Handling Feature.

Occurs Clause

The OCCURS clause eliminates the need for separate entries for repeated data since it indicates the number of times a series of items with an identical form is repeated. In addition, it also supplies the required information for the application of subscripts and indexes.

The OCCURS clause is used in defining tables and other homogenous sets of repeated sets of repeated data. Whenever the OCCURS clause is used, the data-name which is the subject of this entry must be either subscripted or indexed whenever it is referred to in a statement other than SEARCH. When subscripted, the subject refers to one occurrence within the table. When not subscripted (permitted only in a SEARCH statement), the subject represents the entire table element. (A table element consists of all occurrences of one level of a table.) Further, if the subject of this entry is the name of a group item, then all data-names belonging to the group must be subscripted or indexed whenever they are used as operands.

Rules Governing the Use of the Occurs Clause

1. The OCCURS clause is optional in a data description entry and cannot be specified in a data description entry that

   a. Has an 01 or 77 level number.
   b. Describes an item whose size is variable. The size of an item is variable if the data description of any subordinate item contains an OCCURS clause with a DEPENDING ON option.

2. A record description entry that contains an OCCURS clause may not also contain a VALUE clause except for condition-name entries.

3. Integer-1 and Integer-2 must be positive integers. Where both are used, the value of Integer-1 must be less than the value of Integer-2. The value of Integer-1 may be zero, but Integer-2 may not be zero.

4. Data-name-1, data-name-2 and data-name-3 may not be qualified.

5. In Format-1, the value of Integer-2 represents the exact number of occurrences. In Format-2, the value of Integer-2 represents the maximum number occurrences.

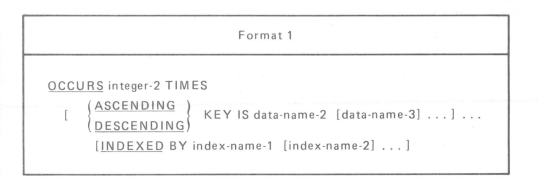

Format 1

OCCURS integer-2 TIMES

[$\begin{Bmatrix} \underline{ASCENDING} \\ \underline{DESCENDING} \end{Bmatrix}$ KEY IS data-name-2 [data-name-3] ...] ...

[INDEXED BY index-name-1 [index-name-2] ...]

Format 2

OCCURS integer-1 TO integer-2TIMES [DEPENDING ON data-name-1]

[$\begin{Bmatrix} \underline{ASCENDING} \\ \underline{DESCENDING} \end{Bmatrix}$ KEY IS data-name-2 [data-name-3] ...] ...

[INDEXED BY index-name-1 [index-name-2] ...]

Format 3

OCCURS integer-2TIMES [DEPENDING ON data-name-1]

[$\begin{Bmatrix} \underline{ASCENDING} \\ \underline{DESCENDING} \end{Bmatrix}$ KEY IS data-name-2 [data-name-3] ...] ...

[INDEXED BY index-name-1 [index-name-2] ...]

Figure 9–6. Occurs Clause Formats.

Depending On Option

The DEPENDING ON option is used in Format-2. This option is only required when the end of the occurrences cannot otherwise be determined. This indicates that the subject has a variable number of occurrences. This does not mean that the subject is variable but rather that the number of times that the subject may be repeated is variable. The number of times is being controlled by the value of data-name-1 at object time.

Integer-1 represents the minimum number of occurrences while Integer-2 represents the maximum number of occurrences.

Data-name-1 is the object of the DEPENDING ON option.

1. Must be described as a positive integer,
2. Must not exceed Integer-2 in value,
3. May be qualified when necessary,
4. Must not be subscripted (that is, itself the subject of or an entry within a table), and
5. Must, if it appears in the same record as the table it controls, appear before the variable portion of the record.

Key Option

The KEY option is used in conjunction with the INDEXED BY option in the execution of a SEARCH ALL statement. The option is used to indicate that the repeated data is arranged in ASCENDING or DESCENDING order according to the values contained in data-name-2, data-name-3, etc. The data-names are listed in descending order of significance.

If data-name-2 is the subject of the table entry, it is the only key that may be specified for the table otherwise

1. All of the items identified by the data-name in the KEY IS phrase must be within the group item which is the subject of this entry.
2. None of the items identified by the data-name in KEY IS phrase can be described by an entry which either contains an OCCURS clause or is subordinate to an entry which contains an OCCURS clause.

Indexed By Option

The INDEXED BY option is required if the subject of this entry (the data name described by the OCCURS clause, or an item within this data-name, if it is a group item) is to be referred to by indexing. The index-name(s) identified by this clause is not defined elsewhere in the program since its allocation and format are dependent upon the system, and not being data, cannot be associated with any data hierarchy.

Rules Governing the Use of Index-Names

1. The number of index-names for a Data Division entry must not exceed 12.
2. An index-name must be initialized through a SET statement before it can be used.

SALE-TABLE		
SALE-ITEM	(1)	A21033
SALE-ITEM	(2)	A21455
SALE-ITEM	(3)	A22223
SALE-ITEM	(4)	A23762
SALE-ITEM	(5)	A24689
SALE-ITEM	(6)	A24643
SALE-ITEM	(7)	A29567
SALE-ITEM	(8)	J33468
SALE-ITEM	(9)	J24788
SALE-ITEM	(10)	J67011

```
1 WORKING-STORAGE SECTION.
  77  TABLE-SIZE PIC 99.
  77  TABLE-VALUE PIC X(6).
  77  SUBSCRIPT PIC 99.
  Ø1  SALE-TABLE.
      Ø2 SALE-ITEM
         OCCURS 1Ø TIMES
         DEPENDING ON TABLE-SIZE
         PIC X(6).
```

```
2 PROCEDURE DIVISION.
  INITIAL-ROUTINE.
      ACCEPT TABLE-SIZE FROM SYSIN.
      PERFORM ACCEPT-TABLE-VALUE
         VARYING SUBSCRIPT
         FROM 1 BY 1
         UNTIL SUBSCRIPT GREATER THAN
            TABLE-SIZE
               .
               :
               .
  ACCEPT-TABLE-VALUE.
      ACCEPT TABLE-VALUE FROM SYSIN.
      MOVE TABLE-VALUE
         TO SALE-ITEM (SUBSCRIPT).
```

1. Working-Storage Section entries to define the variable:

    TABLE-SIZE which is to contain the number of sale items,

    TABLE-VALUE to which a table value will be transmitted prior to being moved to a specific table element,

    SUBSCRIPT to be used as a subscript in referring to table elements.

    SALE-TABLE whose size is to be determined by TABLE-SIZE, and

2. Procedure Division entries to accept the table size and the table values.

Figure 9–7. Example—Subscripting.

3. Each index-name contains a binary value that represents an actual displacement from the beginning of the table that corresponds to an occurrence number in the table. The value is calculated as the occurrence number minus one, multiplied by the length of the entry that is indexed by the index-name.

Usage Is Index Clause

The USAGE IS INDEX clause is used to specify the format of a data item in the computer storage. The clause permits the programmer to specify index-data items.

Rules Governing the Use of the Usage Is Index Clause

1. The USAGE clause may be written at any level. If the USAGE clause is written at a group level, it applies to each elementary item in the group. The USAGE clause at an elementary level cannot contradict the USAGE clause of a group to which the item belongs, unless the group USAGE clause is not stated.

2. An elementary item described with the USAGE IS INDEX clause is called an index-data item. An index-data item is an elementary item (not necessarily connected with any table) that can be used to save index-name values for future reference. An index-data item must be assigned an index-name (i.e., [occurrence number-1] * entry length) through the SET statement. Such a value corresponds to an occurrence number in a table.

3. An index-data item can be referred to directly only in a SEARCH or SET statement or in a relation condition. An index-data item can be part of a group which is referred to in a MOVE or I/O statement, in which case no conversion will take place.

PROCEDURE DIVISION

The SEARCH and SET statements may be used to facilitate table handling. In addition, there are special rules involving Table-Handling elements when they are used in relation conditions.

Relation Conditions

Comparisons involving index-names and/or index-data items conform to the following rules.

1. The comparison of two index-names is actually the comparison of the corresponding occurrence numbers.
2. In the comparison of an index-name with a data item (other than an index-data item), or in the comparison of an index-name with a literal, the occurrence number that corresponds to the value of the index-name is compared with the data item or literal.
3. In the comparison of an index-data item with an index-name or another index-data item, the actual values are compared without conversion.

Search Statement

The SEARCH statement is used to search a table from a table-element that satisfies the specified condition and to adjust the value of the associated index-item to the occurrence number corresponding to the table-element.

Rules Governing the Use of the Search Statement
1. Identifier-1 must not be subscripted or indexed, but its description must contain an OCCURS clause and AN INDEXED BY clause.
2. Identifier-2, when specified, must be described as USAGE IS INDEX or as a numeric elementary item without any positions to the right of the assumed decimal point. Identifier-2 is incremented by the same amount as, and at the same time as, the occurrence number.

Procedure of Search Statement—Format 1

1. Upon execution of a SEARCH statement, a serial search takes place, starting with the current index setting.
2. If at the start of the search the value of the index-name associated with Identifier-1 is not greater than the highest possible occurrence number for Identifier-1, the following action takes place.

   a. The conditions in the WHEN option are evaluated in the order that they are written.
   b. If none of the conditions is satisfied, the index-number for Identifier-1 is incremented to reference the next table-element, and the search is repeated.
   c. If upon evaluation, one of the WHEN conditions is satisfied, the search terminates immediately, and the imperative statement associated with that condition is executed. The index-name points to the table-element that satisfied the condition.

d. If the end of the table is reached without the WHEN condition being satisfied, the search is terminated immediately, and if the AT END option is specified, the imperative statement is executed. If the AT END option is omitted, control passes to the next sentence.

Condition-1 or Condition-2 may be any condition as follows: a relation condition, class condition, condition-name condition, or sign condition.

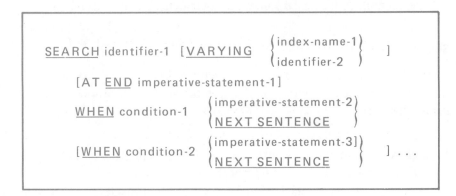

Figure 9–8.   Format Search Statement Format 1.

```
Ø1   SALE-TABLE.
     Ø2 SALE-ITEM
         OCCURS 1Ø TIMES
         DEPENDING ON TABLE-SIZE
         INDEXED BY S PIC X(6).
```

```
     SET S TO 1.
     SEARCH SALE-ITEM
         WHEN ORDER-ITEM
         EQUAL TO SALE-ITEM (S)
         COMPUTE PRICE-WS ROUNDED
             = PRICE-WS * NINETY.
     COMPUTE AMOUNT
         = PRICE-WS * QUANTITY-WS.
```

Figure 9–9.   Example—Search Statement.

Simple SEARCH Sentence

Format

SEARCH identifier WHEN condition imperative-statement.

Explanation

Beginning with the table element whose occurrence number corresponds to the current value of the index defined for identifier, table elements with the common name identifier are tested serially by index until an element that satisfies condition is found. The imperative statement is then executed and control moves either to the sentence directly following the SEARCH sentence or the paragraph specified in a GO TO statement within the imperative statement.

Flow of logic

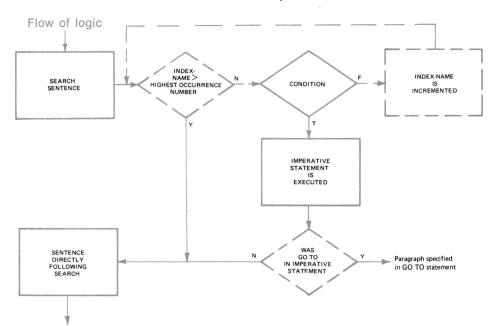

Rules

1. Identifier must be the common name of the table elements for which the OCCURS clause with the INDEXED BY option is specified.
2. Identifier must not be a level 01 variable.
3. Index-name (not specified in the SEARCH sentence but necessary for its execution) must be defined by the INDEXED BY option of the OCCURS clause in the data de-description entry for identifier.

(The dashed lines indicate logic that is done automatically by the compiler.)

Figure 9–10. Example—Simple Search Statement.

Varying Option

When the VARYING option is specified, one of the following applies:

1. If index-name-1 is one of the indexes for Identifier-1, index-name-1 is used for the search; otherwise, the first (or only) index-name is used for Identifier-1.

2. If index-name-1 is an index for another table entry, then when the index-name for Identifier-1 is incremented to represent the next occurrence of the table, index-name-1 is simultaneously incremented to represent the next occurrence of the table it indexes.

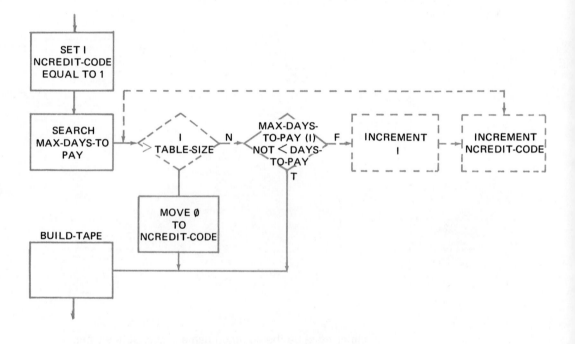

```
      SET I NCREDIT-CODE TO 1.
      SEARCH MAX-DAYS-TO-PAY
          VARYING NCREDIT-CODE
          AT END MOVE Ø TO NCREDIT-CODE
          WHEN MAX-DAYS-TO-PAY (I)
              NOT LESS THAN DAYS-TO-PAY
          NEXT SENTENCE.
BUILD-TAPE.
```

Figure 9–11.   Example—Search Statement Varying Option.

Format

SEARCH identifier-1 $\left[$ VARYING $\begin{Bmatrix} \text{index-name-1} \\ \text{identifier-2} \end{Bmatrix}\right]$ WHEN condition $\begin{Bmatrix} \text{imperative-statement} \\ \text{NEXT SENTENCE} \end{Bmatrix}$

Explanation Beginning with the table element whose occurrence number corresponds to the current value of the index defined for identifier-1, table elements with the common name identifier-1 are tested serially by index until an element that satisfies condition is found. Beginning with its value at the time the SEARCH sentence is executed the variable specified in the VARYING option is incremented each time the index defined for identifier-1 is incremented. When a table element satisfying condition is found, if NEXT SENTENCE is specified in the WHEN option, control moves to the sentence directly following the SEARCH sentence. Otherwise, the imperative statement is executed and control moves either to the sentence directly following the SEARCH sentence or the paragraph specified in a GO TO statement within the imperative statement.

Flow of Logic

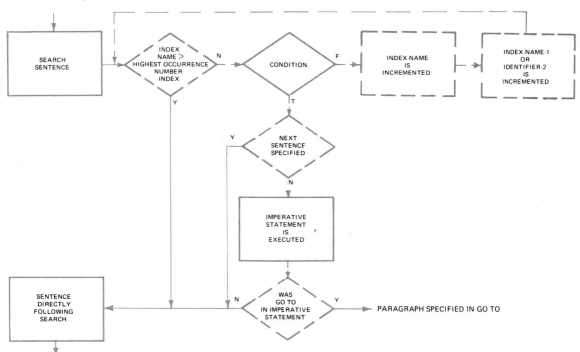

Rules

1. Identifier-1 must be the common name of the table elements for which the OCCURS clause with the INDEXED BY option is specified.
2. Identifier-1 must not be a level 01 variable.
3. Index-name (not specified in the SEARCH sentence but necessary for its execution) must be defined by the IN-DEXED BY option of the OCCURS clause in the data description entry for identifier-1.
4. Index-name-1 may be the index defined for identifier-1 or for another identifier.
5. Identifier-2 may be a variable defined with the USAGE IS INDEX clause or an elementary variable that will have integer values.

(The dashed lines indicate logic that is done automatically by the compiler.)

Figure 9–12. Example—Search Statement Varying Option.

Format

SEARCH identifier $\left[\text{AT } \underline{\text{END}} \left\{ \begin{array}{l} \text{imperative-statement-1} \\ \underline{\text{NEXT SENTENCE}} \end{array} \right\} \right]$ $\underline{\text{WHEN}}$ condition imperative-statement-2.

Explanation   Beginning with the table element whose occurrence number corresponds to the current value of the index defined for identifier, table elements are tested serially by index until an element that satisfies condition is found. Imperative-statement-2 is then executed and control moves either to the sentence directly following the SEARCH sentence or the paragraph specified in a GO TO statement within imperative-statement-2. If no table element satisfies condition, imperative-statement-1 is executed and control moves either to the sentence directly following the SEARCH sentence or the paragraph specified in a GO TO statement within imperative-statement-1.

Flow of logic

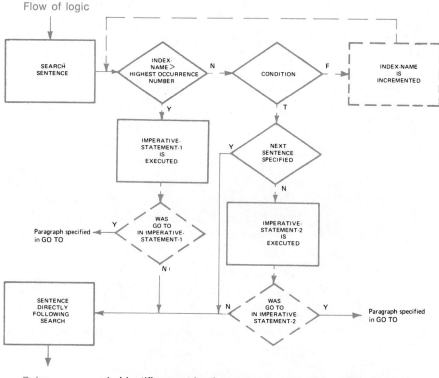

Rules

1. Identifier must be the common name of the table elements for which the OCCURS clause with the INDEXED BY option is specified.
2. Identifier must not be a level 01 variable.
3. Index-name (not specified in the SEARCH sentence but necessary for its execution) must be defined by the IN-DEXED BY option of the OCCURS clause in the data description entry for identifier.

(The dashed lines indicate logic that is done automatically by the compiler.)

Figure 9–13. Example—Search Statement at End Option.

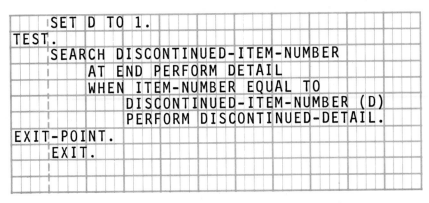

```
        SET D TO 1.
TEST.
        SEARCH DISCONTINUED-ITEM-NUMBER
           AT END PERFORM DETAIL
           WHEN ITEM-NUMBER EQUAL TO
                DISCONTINUED-ITEM-NUMBER (D)
                PERFORM DISCONTINUED-DETAIL.
EXIT-POINT.
        EXIT.
```

Figure 9–14. Example—Search Statement at End Option.

Procedure for Search Statement—Format-2

1. A nonserial type of search operation takes place. When this occurs, the initial setting of the index-name for Identifier-1 is ignored, and its setting is varied during the search. At no time is it less than the value that corresponds to the first element of the table, nor is it ever greater than the value that corresponds to the last element of the table.

   a. If condition-1 cannot be satisfied for any setting of the index within the permitted range, control is passed to imperative statement-1 when the AT END option appears, or to the next sentence when this clause does not appear. In either case, the final setting of the index is unpredictable.

   b. If the index indicates an occurrence that allows condition-1 to be satisfied, control passes to imperative statement-2.

2. The first index-name assigned to Identifier-1 will be used for the search.

3. The description of Identifier-1 must contain the KEY option in its OCCURS clause.

SEARCH ALL identifier-1 [AT END imperative-statement-1]

WHEN condition-1 $\begin{Bmatrix} \text{imperative-statement-2} \\ \text{NEXT SENTENCE} \end{Bmatrix}$

Figure 9–15. Format Search Statement Format 2.

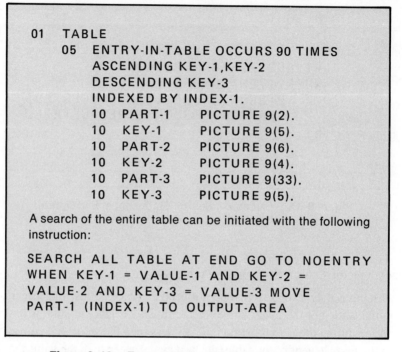

```
01   TABLE
     05   ENTRY-IN-TABLE OCCURS 90 TIMES
          ASCENDING KEY-1,KEY-2
          DESCENDING KEY-3
          INDEXED BY INDEX-1.
          10   PART-1      PICTURE 9(2).
          10   KEY-1       PICTURE 9(5).
          10   PART-2      PICTURE 9(6).
          10   KEY-2       PICTURE 9(4).
          10   PART-3      PICTURE 9(33).
          10   KEY-3       PICTURE 9(5).
```

A search of the entire table can be initiated with the following instruction:

```
SEARCH ALL TABLE AT END GO TO NOENTRY
WHEN KEY-1 = VALUE-1 AND KEY-2 =
VALUE-2 AND KEY-3 = VALUE-3 MOVE
PART-1 (INDEX-1) TO OUTPUT-AREA
```

Figure 9–16. Example—Search Statement Format 2.

Condition-1 must consist of one of the following:

1. *Relation Condition*—One of the data-names must appear in the KEY clause.
2. *Condition-name Condition*—the conditional variable associated with condition-name must be one of the names that appear in the KEY clause of Identifier-1.
3. A compound condition from simple conditions of the types described above, with AND as the only connector.

Any data-name that appears in the KEY clause of Identifier-1 may be tested in condition-1. However, all data-names in the KEY clause preceding the one to be tested must also be tested on condition-1. No other tests can be made on condition-1.

Set Statement

The SET statement establishes reference points for table-handling operations by setting index-names associated with table-elements. The SET state-

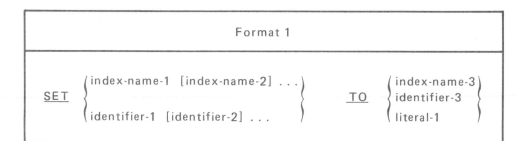

Figure 9–17. Format Set Statements.

ment must be used when initializing index-name values before execution of a SEARCH statement. It may also be used to transfer values between index-names and other elementary data items.

Rules Governing the Use of the Set Statement
1. All identifiers must name either index-data items or elementary items described as integers, except that Identifier-4 must not name an index-data item. When a literal is used, it must be a positive integer. Index-names are considered related to a given table through the INDEXED BY option.

Format-1

When the SET statement is executed, one of the following actions takes place.
1. Index-name-1 is set to a value that corresponds to the same table-element to which either index-name-3, Identifier-3, or literal-1 corresponds. If Identifier-3 is an index-data item, or if index-name-3 is related to the same table as index-name-1, no conversion takes place.
2. If Identifier-1 is an index-data item, it may be set to equal either the contents of index-name-3 or Identifier-3 where Identifier-3 is also an index-data item. Literal-1 cannot be used in this case.

3. If Identifier-1 is not an index-data item, it may be set only to an occurrence number that corresponds to the value of index-name-3. Neither Identifier-3 or literal-1 can be used in this case.

Format-2

When the SET statement is executed, the content of index-number-4 (index-name-5, etc.), if present, are incremented (UP BY) or decremented (DOWN BY) a value that corresponds to the number of occurrence represented by the value of literal-2 or Identifier-4.

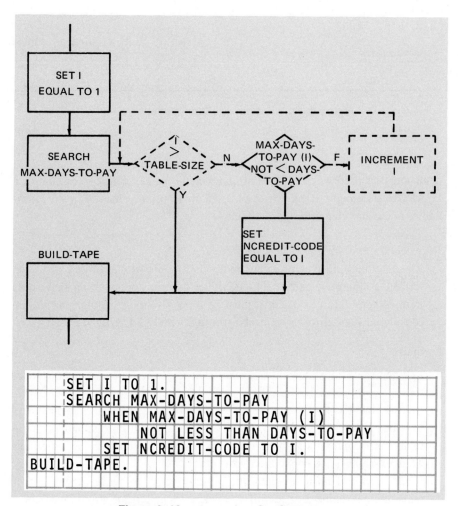

Figure 9–18.   Example—Set Statement.

```
IDENTIFICATION DIVISION.
PROGRAM-ID. TABLES.
ENVIRONMENT DIVISION.
CONFIGURATION SECTION.
SOURCE-COMPUTER. IBM-360-H50.
OBJECT-COMPUTER. IBM-360-H50.
SPECIAL-NAMES. CONSOLE IS TYPEWRITER.
INPUT-OUTPUT SECTION.
FILE-CONTROL.
     SELECT INFILE ASSIGN TO UT-2400-S-INTAPE.
     SELECT OUTFILE ASSIGN TO UR-S-PRTOUT.
     SELECT INCARDS ASSIGN TO UR-S-ICARDS.
DATA DIVISION.
FILE SECTION.
FD   INFILE LABEL RECORDS ARE OMITTED.
01   TABLE PIC X(28200).
01   TABLE-2 PIC X(1800).
FD   OUTFILE LABEL RECORDS ARE OMITTED.
01   PRTLINE PIC X(133).
FD   INCARDS LABEL RECORDS ARE OMITTED.
01   CARDS.
     05   STATE-NAME   PIC X(4).
     05   SEXCODE      PIC 9.
     05   YEARCODE     PIC 9(4).
     05   FILLER       PIC X(71).
WORKING-STORAGE SECTION.
01   PRTAREA-20.
     05   FILLER       PIC X VALUE SPACES.
     05   YEARS-20     PIC 9(4).
     05   FILLER       PIC X(3) VALUE SPACES.
     05   BIRTHS-20    PIC 9(7).
     05   FILLER       PIC X(3) VALUE SPACES.
     05   DEATHS-20    PIC 9(7).
     05   FILLER       PIC X(108) VALUE SPACES.

01   PRTAREA.
     05   FILLER       PIC X.
     05   YEAR         PIC 9(4).
     05   FILLER       PIC X(3) VALUE SPACES.
     05   BIRTHS       PIC 9(5).
     05   FILLER       PIC X(3) VALUE SPACES.
     05   DEATHS       PIC 9(5).
     05   FILLER       PIC X(112) VALUE SPACES.
01   CENSUS-STATISTICS-TABLE.
     05   STATE-TABLE OCCURS 50 TIMES INDEXED BY ST.
          10   STATE-ABBREV    PIC X(4).
          10   SEX OCCURS 2 TIMES INDEXED BY SE.
               15   STATISTICS OCCURS 20 TIMES ASCENDING KEY IS YEAR
                    INDEXED BY YR.
                    20   YEAR      PIC 9(4).
                    20   BIRTHS    PIC 9(5).
                    20   DEATHS    PIC 9(5).
```

Figure 9–19. Sample Table Handling Program.

```
01   STATISTICS-LAST-20-YRS.
     05   SEX-20 OCCURS 2 TIMES INDEXED BY SE-20.
          10   STATE-20 OCCURS 50 TIMES INDEXED BY ST-20.
               15   YEARS-20      PIC 9(4).
               15   BIRTHS-20     PIC 9(7).
               15   DEATHS-20     PIC 9(7).

PROCEDURE DIVISION.
OPEN-FILES.
     OPEN INPUT INFILE INCARDS OUTPUT OUTFILE.
READ-TABLE.
     READ INFILE INTO CENSUS-STATISTICS-TABLE
          AT END GO TO READ-CARDS.
     READ INFILE INTO STATISTICS-LAST-20-YRS
          AT END GO TO READ-CARDS.
READ-CARDS.
     READ INCARDS
          AT END GO TO EOJ.
DETERMINE-ST.
     SET ST ST-20 TO 1.
     SEARCH STATE-TABLE VARYING ST-20 AT END GO TO ERROR-MSG-1
          WHEN STATE-NAME = STATE-ABBREV (ST) NEXT SENTENCE.
DETERMINE-SE.
     SET SE SE-20 TO SEXCODE.
DETERMINE-YR.
     SEARCH ALL STATISTICS AT END GO TO ERROR-MSG-2
          WHEN YEAR OF STATISTICS (ST, SE, YR) = YEARCODE
               GO TO WRITE-RECORD.
ERROR-MSG-1.
     DISPLAY "INCORRECT STATE" STATE-NAME UPON TYPEWRITER.
     GO TO READ-CARDS.
ERROR-MSG-2.
     DISPLAY "INCORRECT YEAR"  YEARCODE UPON TYPEWRITER.
     GO TO READ-CARDS.
WRITE-RECORD.
     MOVE CORRESPONDING STATISTICS (ST, SE, YR) TO PRTAREA.
     WRITE PRTLINE FROM PRTAREA AFTER ADVANCING 3.
     MOVE CORRESPONDING STATE-20 (SE-20, ST-20) TO PRTAREA-20.
     WRITE PRTLINE FROM PRTAREA-20 AFTER ADVANCING 1.
     GO TO READ-CARDS.
EOJ.
     CLOSE INFILE INCARDS OUTFILE.
     STOP RUN.
```

The census bureau uses the program to compare:

1. The number of births and deaths that occurred in any one of the 50 states in any one of the past 20 years with

2. The total number of births and deaths that occurred in the same state over the entire 20-year period

Figure 9–19. Sample Table Handling Program—Continued.

The input file, INCARDS, contains the specific information upon which the search of the table is to be conducted. INCARDS is formatted as follows:

STATE-NAME   a 4-character alphabetic abbreviation of the state name

SEXCODE   1 = male; 2 = female

YEARCODE   a 4-digit field in the range 1950 through 1969

A typical run might determine the number of females born in New York in 1953 as compared with the total number of females born in New York in the past 20 years.

Figure 9–19.   Sample Table Handling Program—Continued.

SUBSCRIPT PROBLEM

INPUT

Field	Card Columns	
Customer Number	2–5	
Item Number	6–10	
Item Cost	21–24	XX.XX
Department	30	
Customer Name	32–50	

CALCULATIONS TO BE PERFORMED

Calculate the total bill for each customer by applying the appropriate discount for the department, that is, multiply the item cost by the discount factor for the department to arrive at the charge price.

OUTPUT

Print reports as follows:

1.   DISCOUNT TABLE

Department   Discount

2.   CUSTOMER REPORT

CUST. NO.   CUST. NAME   DEPT.   ITEM NO.   ITEM COST   DISCT. PER.   DISCT. AMT.   CHARGE

SUBSCRIPT PROBLEM

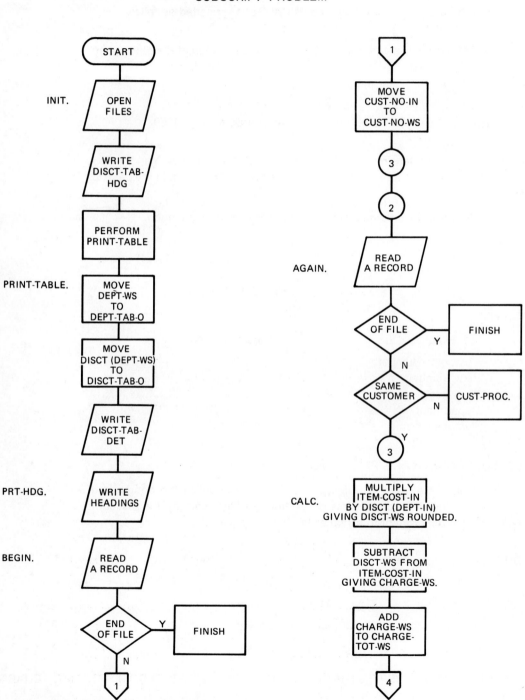

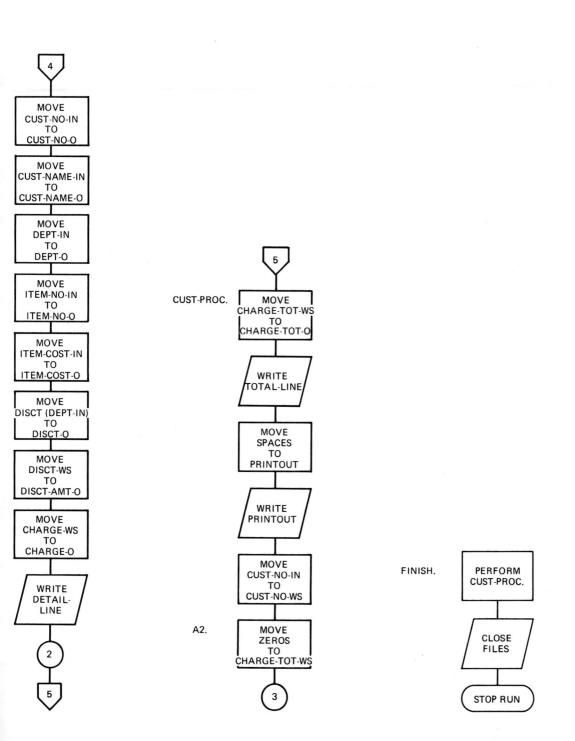

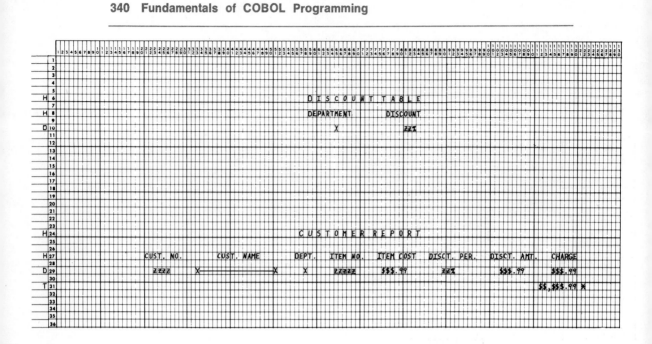

```
00001    001010 IDENTIFICATION DIVISION.                                      SUBSCRIP
00002    001020 PROGRAM-ID. SUBSCRIPT.                                        SUBSCRIP
00003    001030 DATE-WRITTEN.  JUNE 14 1972.                                  SUBSCRIP
00004    001040 DATE-COMPILED. 10/27/72                                       SUBSCRIP
00005    001050  REMARKS.                                                     SUBSCRIP
00006    001060      THIS IS A PROGRAM TO CALCULATE THE TOTAL BILL FOR        SUBSCRIP
00007    001070      EACH CUSTOMER.                                           SUBSCRIP
00008    002010 ENVIRONMENT DIVISION.                                         SUBSCRIP
00009    002020 CONFIGURATION SECTION.                                        SUBSCRIP
00010    002030 SOURCE-COMPUTER.                                              SUBSCRIP
00011    002040      IBM-360-H50.                                             SUBSCRIP
00012    002050 OBJECT-COMPUTER.                                              SUBSCRIP
00013    002060      IBM-360-H50.                                             SUBSCRIP
00014    002070 SPECIAL-NAMES. C01 IS SKIP-TO-1.                              SUBSCRIP
00015    002080 INPUT-OUTPUT SECTION.                                         SUBSCRIP
00016    002090 FILE-CONTROL.                                                 SUBSCRIP
00017    002100      SELECT FILE-IN                                           SUBSCRIP
00018    002110          ASSIGN TO SYS009-UR-2540R-S.                         SUBSCRIP
00019    002120      SELECT FILE-OUT                                          SUBSCRIP
00020    002130          ASSIGN TO SYS005-UR-1403-S                           SUBSCRIP
00021    002140          RESERVE NO ALTERNATE AREA.                           SUBSCRIP
00022    003010 DATA DIVISION.                                                SUBSCRIP
00023    003020 FILE SECTION.                                                 SUBSCRIP
00024    003030 FD  FILE-IN                                                   SUBSCRIP
00025    003040      RECORDING MODE F                                         SUBSCRIP
00026    003050      LABEL RECORDS OMITTED                                    SUBSCRIP
00027    003060      RECORD CONTAINS 80 CHARACTERS                            SUBSCRIP
00028    003070      DATA RECORD IS CARD-IN.                                  SUBSCRIP
00029    003080 01  CARD-IN.                                                  SUBSCRIP
00030    003090      02  FILLER        PICTURE X.                             SUBSCRIP
00031    003100      02  CUST-NO-IN    PICTURE 9(4).                          SUBSCRIP
00032    003110      02  ITEM-NO-IN    PICTURE 9(5).                          SUBSCRIP
00033    003120      02  FILLER        PICTURE X(10).                         SUBSCRIP
00034    003130      02  ITEM-COST-IN  PICTURE 99V99.                         SUBSCRIP
00035    003140      02  FILLER        PICTURE X(5).                          SUBSCRIP
00036    003150      02  DEPT-IN       PICTURE 9.                             SUBSCRIP
00037    003160      02  FILLER        PICTURE X.                             SUBSCRIP
00038    003170      02  CUST-NAME-IN  PICTURE X(19).                         SUBSCRIP
00039    003180      02  FILLER        PICTURE X(30).                         SUBSCRIP
```

```
                                                                              2

00040    003190 FD  FILE-OUT                                          SUBSCRIP
00041    003200     RECORDING MODE F                                 SUBSCRIP
00042    003210     LABEL RECORDS OMITTED                            SUBSCRIP
00043    003220     DATA RECORD IS PRINTOUT.                         SUBSCRIP
00044    003230 01  PRINTOUT           PICTURE X(133).               SUBSCRIP
00045    004010 WORKING-STORAGE SECTION.                             SUBSCRIP
00046    004020 77  DEPT-WS         PICTURE 99        VALUE 01.       SUBSCRIP
00047    004030 77  CUST-NO-WS      PICTURE 9(4).                    SUBSCRIP
00048    004040 77  DISCT-WS        PICTURE 99V99.                   SUBSCRIP
00049    004050 77  CHARGE-WS       PICTURE 99V99.                   SUBSCRIP
00050    004055 77  CHARGE-TOT-WS   PICTURE 9999V99   VALUE ZEROS.   SUBSCRIP
00051    004060 01  FILLER.                                          SUBSCRIP
00052    004070     02  DISCT-TAB.                                   SUBSCRIP
00053    004080         03  FILLER       PICTURE V99       VALUE  .05.   SUBSCRIP
00054    004090         03  FILLER       PICTURE V99       VALUE  .07.   SUBSCRIP
00055    004100         03  FILLER       PICTURE V99       VALUE  .10.   SUBSCRIP
00056    004110         03  FILLER       PICTURE V99       VALUE  .15.   SUBSCRIP
00057    004120         03  FILLER       PICTURE V99       VALUE  .06.   SUBSCRIP
00058    004130         03  FILLER       PICTURE V99       VALUE  .22.   SUBSCRIP
00059    004140         03  FILLER       PICTURE V99       VALUE  .12.   SUBSCRIP
00060    004150         03  FILLER       PICTURE V99       VALUE  .09.   SUBSCRIP
00061    004160         03  FILLER       PICTURE V99       VALUE  .20.   SUBSCRIP
00062    004170     02  DISCT-TABLE REDEFINES DISCT-TAB.             SUBSCRIP
00063    004180         03  DISCT        PICTURE V99       OCCURS 9 TIMES.   SUBSCRIP
00064    004190 01  DISCT-TAB-HDG-1.                                 SUBSCRIP
00065    004200     02  FILLER           PICTURE X(59)     VALUE     SPACES.   SUBSCRIP
00066    004210     02  FILLER           PICTURE X(26)               SUBSCRIP
00067    004220         VALUE   'D I S C O U N T   T A B L E'.       SUBSCRIP
00068    005010 01  DISCT-TAB-HDG-2.                                 SUBSCRIB
00069    005020     02  FILLER           PICTURE X(59)     VALUE     SPACES.   SUBSCRIB
00070    005030     02  FILLER           PICTURE X(26)               SUBSCRIB
00071    005040         VALUE   'DEPARTMENT        DISCOUNT'.        SUBSCRIB
00072    005050 01  DISCT-TAB-DET.                                   SUBSCRIB
00073    005060     02  FILLER           PICTURE X(64)     VALUE     SPACES.   SUBSCRIB
00074    005070     02  DEPT-TAB-O       PICTURE ZZ.                 SUBSCRIB
00075    005080     02  FILLER           PICTURE X(15)     VALUE     SPACES.   SUBSCRIB
00076    005090     02  DISCT-TAB-O      PICTURE VZZ.                SUBSCRIB
00077    005100     02  FILLER           PICTURE X         VALUE '%'.   SUBSCRIB
00078    005110 01  HDG-1.                                           SUBSCRIP
```

```
                                                                              3

00079    005120     02  FILLER           PICTURE X(57)  VALUE     SPACES.   SUBSCRIB
00080    005130     02  FILLER           PICTURE X(28)               SUBSCRIB
00081    005140         VALUE   'C U S T O M E R   R E P O R T'.     SUBSCRIB
00082    005150 01  HDG-2.                                           SUBSCRIB
00083    005160     02  FILLER           PICTURE X(21)     VALUE SPACES.   SUBSCRIB
00084    005170     02  FILLER           PICTURE X(9)      VALUE 'CUST. NO.'.   SUBSCRIB
00085    005180     02  FILLER           PICTURE X(8)      VALUE SPACES.   SUBSCRIB
00086    005190     02  FILLER           PICTURE X(10)     VALUE 'CUST. NAME'.   SUBSCRIB
00087    005200     02  FILLER           PICTURE X(8)      VALUE SPACES.   SUBSCRIB
00088    005210     02  FILLER           PICTURE X(5)      VALUE 'DEPT.'.   SUBSCRIB
00089    005220     02  FILLER           PICTURE X(3)      VALUE SPACES.   SUBSCRIB
00090    005230     02  FILLER           PICTURE X(8)      VALUE 'ITEM NO.'.   SUBSCRIB
00091    006010     02  FILLER           PICTURE X(3)      VALUE SPACES.   SUBSCRIP
00092    006020     02  FILLER           PICTURE X(9)      VALUE 'ITEM COST'.   SUBSCRIP
00093    006030     02  FILLER           PICTURE X(3)      VALUE SPACES.   SUBSCRIP
00094    006040     02  FILLER           PICTURE X(11)     VALUE 'DISCT. PER.'.   SUBSCRIP
00095    006050     02  FILLER           PICTURE X(3)      VALUE SPACES.   SUBSCRIP
00096    006060     02  FILLER           PICTURE X(11)     VALUE 'DISCT.AMT.'.   SUBSCRIP
00097    006070     02  FILLER           PICTURE X(3)      VALUE SPACES.   SUBSCRIP
00098    006080     02  FILLER           PICTURE X(6)      VALUE 'CHARGE'.   SUBSCRIP
00099    006090 01  DETAIL-LINE.                                     SUBSCRIP
00100    006100     02  FILLER           PICTURE X(23)     VALUE SPACES.   SUBSCRIP
00101    006110     02  CUST-NO-O        PICTURE Z(4).               SUBSCRIP
00102    006120     02  FILLER           PICTURE X(6)      VALUE SPACES.   SUBSCRIP
00103    006130     02  CUST-NAME-O      PICTURE X(19).              SUBSCRIP
00104    006140     02  FILLER           PICTURE X(6)      VALUE SPACES.   SUBSCRIP
00105    006150     02  DEPT-O           PICTURE 9.                  SUBSCRIP
00106    006160     02  FILLER           PICTURE X(6)      VALUE SPACES.   SUBSCRIP
00107    006170     02  ITEM-NO-O        PICTURE Z(5).               SUBSCRIP
00108    006180     02  FILLER           PICTURE X(6)      VALUE SPACES.   SUBSCRIP
00109    006190     02  ITEM-COST-O      PICTURE $$$.99.             SUBSCRIP
00110    006200     02  FILLER           PICTURE X(8)      VALUE SPACES.   SUBSCRIP
00111    006210     02  DISCT-O          PICTURE VZZ.                SUBSCRIP
00112    006220     02  FILLER           PICTURE X         VALUE '%'.   SUBSCRIP
00113    006230     02  FILLER           PICTURE X(10)     VALUE SPACES.   SUBSCRIP
00114    007010     02  DISCT-AMT-O      PICTURE $$$.99.             SUBSCRIP
00115    007020     02  FILLER           PICTURE X(6)      VALUE SPACES.   SUBSCRIP
00116    007030     02  CHARGE-O         PICTURE $$$.99.             SUBSCRIP
00117    007040 01  TOTAL-LINE.                                      SUBSCRIP
```

```
                4

00118   007050     02  FILLER          PICTURE X(112) VALUE SPACES.        SUBSCRIP
00119   007060     02  CHARGE-TOT-O    PICTURE $$,$$$.99.                   SUBSCRIP
00120   007070     02  FILLER          PICTURE XX       VALUE ' *'.         SUBSCRIP
00121   008010 PROCEDURE DIVISION.                                         SUBSCRIP
00122   008020 INIT. OPEN INPUT FILE-IN OUTPUT FILE-OUT.                   SUBSCRIP
00123   008030     WRITE PRINTOUT FROM DISCT-TAB-HDG-1 AFTER ADVANCING     SUBSCRIP
00124   008040     SKIP-TO-1 LINES.                                        SUBSCRIP
00125   008050     WRITE PRINTOUT FROM DISCT-TAB-HDG-2 AFTER ADVANCING 3 LINES.  SUBSCRIP
00126   008060     PERFORM PRINT-TABLE VARYING DEPT-WS FROM 1 BY 1 UNTIL DEPT-WSSUBSCRIP
00127   008070     IS GREATER THAN 9. GO TO PRT-HDG.                       SUBSCRIP
00128   008080 PRINT-TABLE.  MOVE DEPT-WS TO DEPT-TAB-O.                    SUBSCRIP
00129   008090     MOVE DISCT (DEPT-WS) TO DISCT-TAB-O.                     SUBSCRIP
00130   008100     WRITE PRINTOUT FROM DISCT-TAB-DET AFTER ADVANCING 2 LINES.  SUBSCRIP
00131   008110 PRT-HDG.  WRITE PRINTOUT FROM HDG-1 AFTER ADVANCING SKIP-TO-1 SUBSCRIP
00132   008120     LINES.                                                  SUBSCRIP
00133   008130     WRITE PRINTOUT FROM HDG-2 AFTER ADVANCING 3 LINES.      SUBSCRIP
00134   008140     MOVE SPACES TO PRINTOUT.                                SUBSCRIP
00135   008150     WRITE PRINTOUT AFTER ADVANCING 1 LINES.                 SUBSCRIP
00136   008160 BEGIN.  READ FILE-IN AT END GO TO FINISH.                   SUBSCRIP
00137   008170     MOVE CUST-NO-IN TO CUST-NO-WS.                          SUBSCRIP
00138   008180     GO TO CALC.                                             SUBSCRIP
00139   008190 AGAIN.  READ FILE-IN AT END GO TO FINISH.                   SUBSCRIP
00140   008200     IF CUST-NO-IN IS GREATER THAN CUST-NO-WS GO TO CUST-PROC.  SUBSCRIP
00141   008210 CALC.  MULTIPLY ITEM-COST-IN BY DISCT (DEPT-IN) GIVING DISCT-WS  SUBSCRIP
00142   008220     ROUNDED.                                                SUBSCRIP
00143   008230     SUBTRACT DISCT-WS FROM ITEM-COST-IN GIVING CHARGE-WS.   SUBSCRIP
00144   008240     ADD CHARGE-WS TO CHARGE-TOT-WS.                         SUBSCRIP
00145   009010     MOVE CUST-NO-IN TO CUST-NO-O.                           SUBSCRIP
00146   009020     MOVE CUST-NAME-IN TO CUST-NAME-O.                       SUBSCRIP
00147   009030     MOVE DEPT-IN TO DEPT-O.                                 SUBSCRIP
00148   009040     MOVE ITEM-NO-IN TO ITEM-NO-O.                           SUBSCRIP
00149   009050     MOVE ITEM-COST-IN TO ITEM-COST-O.                       SUBSCRIP
00150   009060     MOVE DISCT (DEPT-IN) TO DISCT-O.                        SUBSCRIP
00151   009070     MOVE DISCT-WS TO DISCT-AMT-O.                           SUBSCRIP
00152   009080     MOVE CHARGE-WS TO CHARGE-O.                             SUBSCRIP
00153   009090     WRITE PRINTOUT FROM DETAIL-LINE AFTER ADVANCING 1 LINES  SUBSCRIP
00154   009100     AT EOP PERFORM PRT-HDG.                                 SUBSCRIP
00155   009110     GO TO AGAIN.                                            SUBSCRIP
00156   009120 CUST-PROC. MOVE CHARGE-TOT-WS TO CHARGE-TOT-O.              SUBSCRIP


                5

00157   009130     WRITE PRINTOUT FROM TOTAL-LINE AFTER ADVANCING 1 LINES.  SUBSCRIP
00158   009131     MOVE SPACES TO PRINTOUT.                                SUBSCRIP
00159   009132     WRITE PRINTOUT AFTER ADVANCING 1 LINES.                 SUBSCRIP
00160   009133     MOVE CUST-NO-IN TO CUST-NO-WS.                          SUBSCRIP
00161   009140 A2. MOVE ZEROS TO CHARGE-TOT-WS.                            SUBSCRIP
00162   009150     GO TO CALC.                                             SUBSCRIP
00163   009160 FINISH. PERFORM CUST-PROC.                                  SUBSCRIP
00164   009170     CLOSE FILE-IN FILE-OUT.                                 SUBSCRIP
00165   009180     STOP RUN.                                               SUBSCRIP
```

DISCOUNT TABLE

DEPARTMENT	DISCOUNT
1	05%
2	07%
3	10%
4	15%
5	06%
6	22%
7	12%
8	09%
9	20%

C U S T O M E R   R E P O R T

CUST. NO.	CUST. NAME	DEPT.	ITEM NO.	ITEM COST	DISCT. PER.	DISCT. AMT.	CHARGE
152	J. LANGDON	1	17410	$2.51	05%	$.13	$2.38
152	J. LANGDON	4	41915	$13.70	15%	$2.06	$11.64
152	J. LANGDON	6	64025	$9.45	22%	$2.08	$7.37
152	J. LANGDON	8	87653	$24.75	09%	$2.23	$22.52
							$43.91 *
2468	L. MORRISEY	1	18520	$3.75	05%	$.19	$3.56
2468	L. MORRISEY	2	20012	$4.20	07%	$.29	$3.91
2468	L. MORRISEY	3	31572	$10.15	10%	$1.02	$9.13
2468	L. MORRISEY	4	48792	$37.50	15%	$5.63	$31.87
2468	L. MORRISEY	5	50407	$15.15	06%	$.91	$14.24
2468	L. MORRISEY	6	61575	$20.10	22%	$4.42	$15.68
2468	L. MORRISEY	7	79204	$51.70	12%	$6.20	$45.50
2468	L. MORRISEY	8	85075	$37.84	09%	$3.41	$34.43
2468	L. MORRISEY	9	98476	$87.94	20%	$17.59	$70.35
							$228.67 *
3451	M. JACKSON	3	37847	$27.90	10%	$2.79	$25.11
3451	M. JACKSON	5	58492	$68.50	06%	$4.11	$64.39
3451	M. JACKSON	6	60010	$20.40	22%	$4.49	$15.91
3451	M. JACKSON	8	85260	$78.52	09%	$7.07	$71.45
3451	M. JACKSON	9	90520	$27.52	20%	$5.50	$22.02
							$198.88 *
4512	S. LEVITT	2	24680	$30.50	07%	$2.14	$28.36
4512	S. LEVITT	5	56784	$52.53	06%	$3.15	$49.38
4512	S. LEVITT	6	60410	$12.15	22%	$2.67	$9.48
4512	S. LEVITT	7	78952	$89.25	12%	$10.71	$78.54
4512	S. LEVITT	8	85278	$49.75	09%	$4.48	$45.27
4512	S. LEVITT	9	87492	$64.25	09%	$5.78	$58.47
4512	S. LEVITT	9	97204	$84.75	20%	$16.95	$67.80
							$337.30 *
5417	K. CONKLIN	1	13579	$35.72	05%	$1.79	$33.93
5417	K. CONKLIN	2	24615	$18.75	07%	$1.31	$17.44
5417	K. CONKLIN	2	29718	$98.52	07%	$6.90	$91.62
5417	K. CONKLIN	3	34928	$37.45	10%	$3.75	$33.70

C U S T O M E R   R E P O R T

CUST. NO.	CUST. NAME	DEPT.	ITEM NO.	ITEM COST	DISCT. PER.	DISCT. AMT.	CHARGE
5417	K. CONKLIN	4	48527	$87.50	15%	$13.13	$74.37
5417	K. CONKLIN	5	50150	$18.95	06%	$1.14	$17.81
5417	K. CONKLIN	5	54652	$38.92	06%	$2.34	$36.58
5417	K. CONKLIN	5	59765	$98.95	06%	$5.94	$93.01
5417	K. CONKLIN	7	71572	$18.95	12%	$2.27	$16.68
5417	K. CONKLIN	8	85175	$80.10	09%	$7.21	$72.89
5417	K. CONKLIN	9	90275	$4.60	20%	$.92	$3.68
5417	K. CONKLIN	9	91572	$18.57	20%	$3.71	$14.86
5417	K. CONKLIN	9	97576	$84.95	20%	$16.99	$67.96
							$574.53 *
6213	Z. HAMPTON	1	15792	$64.25	05%	$3.21	$61.04
6213	Z. HAMPTON	1	19975	$98.75	05%	$4.94	$93.81
6213	Z. HAMPTON	3	34576	$51.15	10%	$5.12	$46.03
6213	Z. HAMPTON	4	49512	$85.20	15%	$12.78	$72.42
							$273.30 *
7545	M. LARSON	1	14676	$38.45	05%	$1.92	$36.53
7545	M. LARSON	1	18592	$82.51	05%	$4.13	$78.38
7545	M. LARSON	1	19994	$98.98	05%	$4.95	$94.03
7545	M. LARSON	2	21214	$15.15	07%	$1.06	$14.09
7545	M. LARSON	3	37515	$82.12	10%	$8.21	$73.91
7545	M. LARSON	3	38592	$96.15	10%	$9.62	$86.53
7545	M. LARSON	4	48485	$87.14	15%	$13.07	$74.07
7545	M. LARSON	5	52762	$37.92	06%	$2.28	$35.64
7545	M. LARSON	5	57684	$80.15	06%	$4.81	$75.34
7545	M. LARSON	7	79015	$96.25	12%	$11.55	$84.70
7545	M. LARSON	8	80123	$5.60	09%	$.50	$5.10
7545	M. LARSON	8	82462	$20.15	09%	$1.81	$18.34
7545	M. LARSON	9	91520	$18.15	20%	$3.63	$14.52
7545	M. LARSON	9	93715	$40.15	20%	$8.03	$32.12
							$723.30 *

Exercises

Write your answers in the space provided.

1. The Table Handling feature enables the COBOL program to process _____ or _____ of _____ data.

2. _____ levels of subscripting are permitted in a COBOL source program.

3. Through the use of a _____ or _____, a data item may be accessed _____ to its position in a file rather than its individual name.

4. The _____ option allows both direct and relative referencing of data.

5. An index is assigned to a given table through the use of the _____ clause in the definition of the table.

6. An index-name must be initialized by a _____ statement before it can be used as a table reference.

7. Direct Indexing is specified by using an _____ in the form of a subscript.

8. Subscripting and _____ must not be used together in a single reference.

9. An _____ clause eliminates the need for separate entries for repeated data and indicates the number of times an identical form item is repeated.

10. When the _____ clause is used, the data-name which is the subject of the entry must be either subscripted or indexed whenever it is referred to.

11. A _____ consists of all occurrences of one level of a table.

12. The _____ option of the OCCURS clause is used when the end of the occurrences cannot be determined.

13. The KEY option is used in conjunction with the _____ option in the execution of a _____ statement.

14. The _____ clause permits the programmer to specify index data items.

15. In the Procedure Division, the _____ and _____ statements may be used to facilitate table handling elements.

16. The SEARCH statement is used to search a table from a _____ that satisfies the specific condition and to adjust the value of the associated _____ to the occurrence number corresponding to the Table Element.

17. Upon execution of a SEARCH statement, a serial search takes place starting with the _____ setting.

18. The search through a table file continues until one of the _____ conditions is satisfied.

19. If the end of the search is reached without the condition being satisfied, the _____ statement is executed.
20. The SET statement must be used when initializing an _____ value before the execution _____ statement.

Answers

1. LISTS, TABLES, REPEATED
2. THREE
3. SUBSCRIPTED, INDEX-NAME, RELATIVE
4. INDEXED BY
5. INDEXED BY
6. SET
7. INDEX-NAME
8. INDEXING
9. OCCURS
10. OCCURS
11. TABLE ELEMENT
12. DEPENDING ON
13. INDEXED BY, SEARCH ALL
14. USAGE IS INDEX
15. SEARCH, SET
16. TABLE ELEMENT, INDEX-ITEM
17. CURRENT INDEX
18. AT END
19. AT END
20. INDEX-NAME, SEARCH

Questions for Review

1. What are the principal functions of the Table Handling feature?
2. What are subscripts?
3. Explain the use of indexing. How is it more effective than subscripting?
4. What is the function of the OCCURS clause? Explain the use of the DEPENDING ON, KEY, and INDEXED BY options.
5. What is the function of the USAGE IS INDEX clause?
6. What is the purpose of the SEARCH statement? Explain the procedures of the SEARCH statement in locating a data item in a file serially and locating an item in a non serial manner.
7. What is the purpose of the SET statement and how is it used in table handling operations?

Problems

1. *Match each term with its proper description.*

    ____ 1. Subscripting   A. Number of times the identical item is repeated.

    ____ 2. Indexing   B. Table element that satisfies specified condition.

    ____ 3. Occurs   C. Refer to an item within a table without the use of data-names.

    ____ 4. Search   D. Initializing index-names.

    ____ 5. Set   E. Direct or relative referencing of tables.

2. *A typical tax table*

Dependents	Rate
1	.175
2	.164
3	.159
4	.153
5	.147
6	.141
7	.121

In the Working-Storage Section,

a. Set up table.

b. Redefine the table describing it as one value entry repeated a certain number of times.

c. Write the procedural statement using subscripts to multiply GROSS by the fourth element in the table to arrive at TAXAMT.

3. *In the following insurance table, (the entries for ages are 1 to 65), (Premium XXX.XX)*

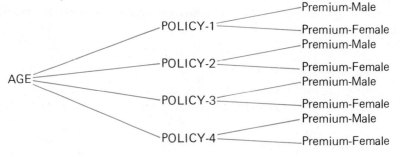

It is necessary to reference the premium for a female, age 64 for policy 2. Write the necessary Data and Procedure Divisions entries to accomplish above.

4. *A deck of sales cards (in random sequence) is read and the total from each card is accumulated in the appropriate counter depending upon the value (01–50) punched in the STATE-CODE field of the card. At the end of the file, the totals of each of the 50 cards is to be printed along with the state code.*

Write the necessary Data and Procedure Division entries to accomplish the following:

a. Set up a table for 50 items. Each item is to contain eight positions to represent a sales total counter for each of the 50 states.
b. Print a report indicating the state number and total.

FLOWCHART

Input File
    State sales cards in
    random sequence.

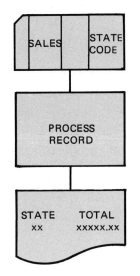

Output Record

5. 02 A OCCURS 5 TIMES.

      03 B OCCURS 4 TIMES.
          04 C PICTURE 99.

It is necessary to reference C in the 4th B in the 5th A.
Which of the following entries are correct? (There is more than one correct answer.)

a. C IN B IN A (5, 4)
b. C (5, 4) IN B IN A
c. C IN B (5, 4)
d. C IN A (5, 4)
e. C (4) IN A (5)

6. *A common method used for encoding a date punched in a card is as follows:*

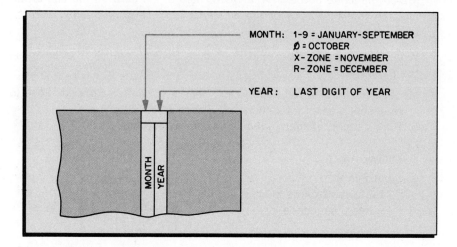

MONTH: 1-9 = JANUARY-SEPTEMBER
0 = OCTOBER
X-ZONE = NOVEMBER
R-ZONE = DECEMBER

YEAR: LAST DIGIT OF YEAR

Write the necessary Data and Procedure Division entries to translate this code into a readable format for printing purposes: For example,

22 = FEBRUARY 1972

7. *Assume you wish to print a header line as follows:*

```
01   HEADING-1.
     02  H1            PICTURE X(8) VALUE IS 'ITEM-NO.'.
     02  FILLER        PICTURE X(5).
     02  DESC          PICTURE X(8).
     02  FILLER        PICTURE X(5).
     02  H2            PICTURE X(6) VALUE IS 'TOTAL.'.
     02  FILLER        PICTURE X(5).
     02  DATE.
         03  MONTH     PICTURE X(9).
         03  FILLER    PICTURE X(3).
         03  DAY       PICTURE 99.
         03  FILLER    PICTURE XX.
         03  YEAR      PICTURE 99.
```

In another work area, you have the following record:

```
01   WORK-AREA.
     02  ITEM-NO       PICTURE 99.
     02  MONTH-CODE    PICTURE 99.
     02  DAY-CODE      PICTURE 99.
     02  YEAR-CODE     PICTURE 99.
```

Write the necessary procedural entries to fill in the header-line as follows:

1. ITEM-NO can vary from 01 through 10. Depending upon its contents, DESC is set to one of the following:

   01 — PENCIL #2   04 — PAINTSET   07 — STAPLES   10 — MISC.
   02 — PENCIL #3   05 — BNDPAPERS   08 — CARBONS
   03 — PENCIL #4   06 — STAPLERS   09 — ERASERS

2. MONTH is to be set depending upon the contents of MONTH-CODE:

   01 — JANUARY   04 — APRIL   07 — JULY   10 — OCTOBER
   02 — FEBRUARY 05 — MAY   08 — AUGUST   11 — NOVEMBER
   03 — MARCH   06 — JUNE   09 — SEPTEMBER 12 — DECEMBER

3. DAY-CODE and YEAR-CODE are to be inserted into DAY and YEAR.

8. *In an insurance premium run, the monthly rates are determined by the risk class. Here, we have a situation where there is a wide and irregular gap between the argument assigned to one table value and the argument assigned to the table value which follows. This means that the risk class code could not be used directly as a subscript.*

Write the necessary Data and Procedure Division entries to

1. Set up the table in the Working-Storage Section and
2. Step-by-step search to locate the appropriate premium rate.

Risk Class	Premium Rate
210	17.50
273	15.50
370	12.30
420	11.95
465	14.60
481	15.25
900	19.45
950	20.01
988	18.10
1030	8.55
1245	14.03
1366	19.99
1505	20.33
1666	12.22
1899	10.00

9. *Write the necessary entries for the Data and Procedure Divisions for the following:*

1. Define the input and output areas with data description entries for each of the values shown in the employee master record diagram.
2. Code the Working-Storage Section with the following:

   a. A variable to be used in the computation of the new pay rate.
   b. A table to allow the percent factor of one plus the percent increase shown in the diagram to be processed as a table.
   c. A variable to be used as a subscript.
   d. A work area to store the variable to which a percent factor of one plus the percent increase may be transmitted from the card reader.

3. The Procedure Division entries to accept the table values that have been punched into cards as follows: 103, 103, 103, 105, 105, 108, 108, 108, 110 and 110; then update the employee master records.

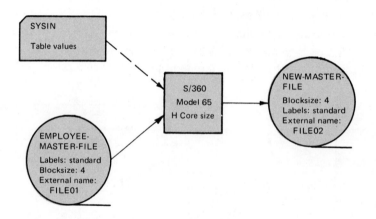

Records in EMPLOYEE-MASTER-FILE (EMPLOYEE-MASTER-RECORD)
and NEW-MASTER-FILE (NEW-MASTER-RECORD)

EMPLOYEE-NUMBER	EMPLOYEE-NAME	SOCIAL-SECURITY			PAYRATE	MEDICAL	LIFE	RETIRE-MENT	
6 digits	21 letters	9 digits			4 digits 2 decimal places	4 digits 2 decimal places	4 digits 2 decimal places	4 digits 2 decimal places	

GRADE
2 digits

DEPENDENTS
2 digits

MARITAL-STATUS
1 letter

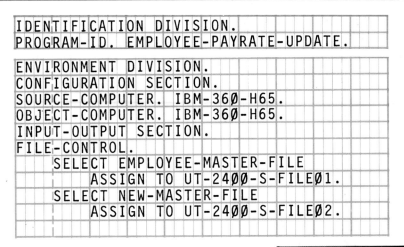

```
IDENTIFICATION DIVISION.
PROGRAM-ID. EMPLOYEE-PAYRATE-UPDATE.

ENVIRONMENT DIVISION.
CONFIGURATION SECTION.
SOURCE-COMPUTER. IBM-360-H65.
OBJECT-COMPUTER. IBM-360-H65.
INPUT-OUTPUT SECTION.
FILE-CONTROL.
     SELECT EMPLOYEE-MASTER-FILE
         ASSIGN TO UT-2400-S-FILE01.
     SELECT NEW-MASTER-FILE
         ASSIGN TO UT-2400-S-FILE02.
```

Employees of a manufacturing company have been assigned a grade of 1 through 10 according to the skills and knowledge required by their jobs. Recently the company has approved pay rate increases for all employees. The increases vary with employee grade as shown in the table to the right. A program is to be written to update the pay rate portion of each employee master record. The system flowchart, a diagram of the employee master record, and the first two divisions of the program are shown.

GRADE	INCREASE
1	3%
2	3%
3	3%
4	5%
5	5%
6	8%
7	8%
8	8%
9	10%
10	10%

10. *Given the following information:*

```
01  TRANS-RECORD.
    02  CITY-ITEM  OCCURS 2 TIMES.
        03  STORE-ITEM  OCCURS 4 TIMES.
            04  DEPT-NO  PICTURE X(5).
            04  DAILY-SALES  PICTURE 9999V99  OCCURS 3 TIMES.
77  DAY     PICTURE 99.
77  DEPT    PICTURE 99.
77  STORE   PICTURE 99.
```

REQUIRED:

a. Write the procedural statements to add DAILY-SALES to TOTAL-SALES for each item using STORE, DEPT and DAY as subscripts.

b. Using the INDEXED BY option, write the necessary Data and Procedure Division entries to add DAILY-SALES to TOTAL-SALES for each item using STORE-INDEX, DEPT-INDEX and DAY-INDEX as indexes.

11. *Given the following information:*

```
02  PRODUCT-NO        PICTURE 9999.
02  WAREHOUSE-DATA    OCCURS 3 TIMES
                      ASCENDING KEY IS QTY-ON-HAND
                      INDEXED BY WAREHOUSE-ITEM.
    03  LOCATION      PICTURE 99.
    03  BIN-NO        PICTURE 999.
    03  QTY-ON-HAND   PICTURE 9(5).
```

Write the necessary procedural statements to search the above to locate QTY-ON-HAND equal to 100. If the item is found, the program is to branch to FOUND-ITEM where the quantity will be moved to an output area (OUTPUT-FIELD). If the item is not found, the program is to branch to NOT-IN-TABLE-ROUTINE.

12. *Orders for merchandise are received and punched into cards as follows:*

ORDER-ITEM

Field	Card Columns	
Code	1	
Stock Number	2–7	
Date	8–13	
Customer Number	14–19	
Customer Name	20–35	
Quantity	36–39	
Price	40–44	XXX.XX
Blank	45–80	

Set up a table for DISCOUNT-TABLE which can be used for items subject to discount. The stock number and discount rate are punched into cards and are treated as values of the DISCOUNT-TABLE as follows:

DISCOUNT-TABLE

DISCOUNT-ITEM (1)	.87
DISCOUNT-ITEM (2)	.79
DISCOUNT-ITEM (3)	.85
.	.
.	.
.	.
DISCOUNT-ITEM (15)	.69

The total number of discount items for each month will be punched into a card to determine the size of the DISCOUNT-TABLE for that month. The maximum number of discount items for one months is 15.

a. In the Working-Storage Section, write the entries to define the variables, TABLE-MAXIMUM—which is to contain the number of discount items. TABLE-VALUE—to which a table value will be transmitted prior to being moved to a specific table element. DISCOUNT-TABLE—whose size is determined by the TABLE-MAXIMUM. DISCOUNT—to be used as a subscript in referring to table elements.

b. Write the necessary Procedure Division entries to accept the TABLE-MAXIMUM and the DISCOUNT-TABLE.

13. *Using the information in problem 12,*

a. Code the record description for DISCOUNT-TABLE so that a SEARCH statement can be used for the text of discount items. (Specify an index for the table. Use D as an index.)

b. Using the SET statement at one, search the DISCOUNT-TABLE until you find a stock number equal to a discount item number, multiply the quantity of the equal stock number by the price and the discount percentage to arrive at a charge price. If an equal stock number is not found in the search, multiply the quantity by the price to arrive at the charge price.

Write the necessary procedural entries to accomplish the above.

10

Report Writer Feature

The Report Writer Feature provides the facility for producing reports by specifying the physical appearance of a report rather than requiring specification of the detailed procedures necessary to produce that report. The programmer can specify the format of the printed report in the Data Division, thereby minimizing the amount of Procedure Division coding he would have to write to create the report.

A hierarchy is used in defining that logical organization of the report. Each report is divided into report groups, which in turn are divided into sequence of items. Such a hierarchical structure permits explicit reference to a report group with implicit reference to other levels in the hierarchy. A report group contains one or more items to be presented on one or more lines.

The specification for the format of the printed output together with any necessary control totals and control headings can be written into the program. The detailed report group items are the basic elements of this report. The necessary data for the detail group items can be supplied from sources outside of the report or by the summation of data items within the report. This summation is the process of adding either the individual data items or other control totals.

Additional information in the form of control headings and control totals can be printed with the detail group items. Control totals and control headings occur automatically when the machine senses a control break. When the value of a specified item used for control purposes changes, a control break occurs.

Report headings at the beginning of the report, as well as totals at the end of the report, can be printed as the report is being prepared. Individual page headings at the top of each page, and totals at the bottom of each sheet, may also be printed concurrently. As the program is being executed, line and page counters are incremented automatically and are used by the program to print the various headings, as well as to control the skipping and spacing of the printed items. Data is added, and the totals are printed automatically.

The Report Writer option can print the report as the information is being processed and can also put the data into intermediate storage where it may be used for subsequent off-line printing in a specified format.

A printed report consists of the information reported in the format in which it is printed. Several reports may be printed from the same program. A special single-character identification is necessary to specify each individual report.

At program execution time the report is put in the specified format, the data to be accumulated is added, the necessary totals are printed, counters are incremented and reset, and each line and page is printed. Thus the programmer need not concern himself with any of the details of the operations.

In the Data Division, the programmer provides the necessary data-names and describes the formats of the reports he wishes to produce. In the Procedure Division he writes the necessary statements that provide the desired reports.

DATA DIVISION

The Report Writer Feature allows the programmer to describe his report pictorially in the Data Division thereby minimizing the amount of Procedure Division coding necessary. The programmer must write in the File Section of the Data Division a description of all names and formats of the reports he wishes to produce. In addition, a complete file and record description of the input data must also be written in this section. A Report Section must be added at the end of the Data Division to define the format of each finished report. A report may be written in two files at the same time.

File Description

The file description entry furnishes the necessary information concerning the identification, physical structure, and record-names pertaining to the file. A detailed discussion of the clauses, with the exception of the Report clause, will be found in the Data Division.

Report Clause

A Report clause is required in the FD entry to list the name of the report to be produced. The name or names of each report to be produced appears here.

```
FD   file-name
     [BLOCK CONTAINS Clause]
     [RECORD CONTAINS Clause]
     [RECORDING MODE Clause]
     LABEL RECORDS Clause
     [VALUE OF Clause]
     [DATA RECORDS Clause]
     REPORT Clause.
```

Figure 10–1. Format File Description Entry.

Figure 10–2. Format Report Clause.

```
ENVIRONMENT DIVISION.
     SELECT FILE-1     ASSIGN UR-1403-S-PRTOUT.
     SELECT FILE-2     ASSIGN UT-2400-S-SYSUT
     .
     .
     .
DATA DIVISION.
FD   FILE-1   RECORDING MODE F
              RECORD CONTAINS 121 CHARACTERS
              REPORT IS REPORT-A.
FD   FILE-2   RECORDING MODE V
              RECORD CONTAINS 101 CHARACTERS
              REPORT IS REPORT-A.
```

For each GENERATE in the Procedure Division, the records for REPORT-A will be written on FILE-1 and FILE-2, respectively. The records on FILE-2 will not contain columns 102 through 121 of the corresponding records on FILE-1.

Figure 10–3. Example—Report Clause.

The sequence of the names is not important, and these reports may be of different sizes, formats, etc., The Report Name(s) must be the same name as appears in the Report Section since the Report clause references the description entries with their associated file description entry.

Report Section

The Report Section must begin on a separate line by itself with the Report Section header. The specification for each report is written here. The physical layout of the report, as well as the users logical organization, are stipulated in this section. These entries should include:

1. The maximum number of lines to be printed on each page.
2. The format and contents of the headings and when and where they are to appear.
3. The source and format of the data and where it is to appear in a report.
4. The data items that are to act as control factors during the presentation of the report.
5. The format of the totals to be printed and accumulated and when and where they are to appear.

Structure

The Report Section consists of two types of entries for each report: one describes the physical aspects of the report format, while the other describes the conceptual characteristics of the items that make up the report and their relation to the report format. These entries are:

1. Report Description Entry-RD.
2. Report Group Description Entries.

Report Description Entry—RD

The Report Section must contain at least one report description entry. This entry contains information pertaining to the overall format of a report named in the File Section and is uniquely identified by the level indicator RD. The characteristics of the report page are provided by describing the number of physical lines per page and the limits for presenting the specified headings, footings, and details within a page structure. RD is the reserved word for the level indicator, and each report named in a FD entry in the File Section must be defined by an RD entry.

```
REPORT SECTION.

RD  report-name
      [CODE Clause]
      [CONTROL Clause]
      [PAGE LIMIT Clause].
```

Figure 10–4. Format Report Description Entry.

Report-Name

Report-Name is the unique name of the report and must be specified in the Report clause of the file description entry for the file in which the report is to be written.

Code Clause

The CODE clause is used to specify an identifying character added at the beginning of each line produced. This is an identifying one-character code that is added to the beginning of each line when there is more than one report to be written for the file. The identifying character is appended to the beginning of the line preceding the carriage-control line-spacing character. This clause must not be specified if the report is printed on-line.

Mnemonic-Name. This name must be associated with a single character in the SPECIAL-NAMES paragraph in the Environment Division.

```
WITH CODE mnemonic-name
```

Figure 10–5. Format Code Clause.

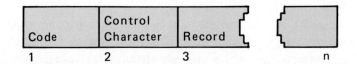

Code	Control Character	Record		
1	2	3		n

When the programmer wishes to write a report from a file, he needs merely to read a record, check the first character for the desired code, and have it printed if the desired code is found. The record should be printed starting from the third character.

Figure 10–6. Format of a Report Record with the Code Clause Specified.

```
ENVIRONMENT DIVISION.
   .
   .

   .
SPECIAL-NAMES.    'A' IS CHR-A.
                  'B' IS CHR-B.
   .

   .

   .
DATA DIVISION.
FILE SECTION.
FD  RPT-OUT- FILE
          RECORDS CONTAIN 122 CHARACTERS
          LABEL RECORDS ARE STANDARD
          REPORTS ARE REP-FILE-A REP-FILE-B.
   .

   .

   .
REPORT SECTION.
RD  REP-FILE-A       CODE CHR-A. . .
   .

   .

   .
RD  REP-FILE-B       CODE CHR-B. . .
   .

   .

   .
```

Figure 10–7. How to Create and
Print a Report with a Code of A.

Control Clause

The CONTROL clause is used to specify the different levels of controls to be applied to the report. *A control is a data item that is tested each time a detail group is generated.* Controls govern the basic format of the report. When a control break occurs, special actions will be taken before the next line of the report is printed. Controls are listed in hierarchical proceeding from the most important down to the least important. Thus, by specifying HEADING and FOOTING controls, the programmer is able to instruct the Report Writer to produce the report in the desired sequence and format.

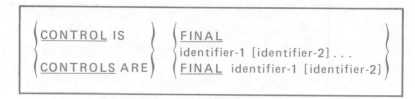

Figure 10–8. Format Control Clause.

RD...CONTROLS ARE YEAR MONTH WEEK DAY

Figure 10–9. Example—Control Clause.

Rules Governing the Use of the Control Clause
1. A control is a data item whose value is tested each time a detail group item is to be printed.
2. If the test indicates a change in the value of the data item, a control break occurs, and special action is taken before the detail line is printed.
3. The special action to be taken depends upon what the programmer has stipulated. When controls are tested, the highest control level specified is tested first, then the second-highest level, etc. When a control break is indicated for a higher level, an implied lower control break occurs as well. A control heading or control totals or neither may be defined for each control break by the programmer.
4. The control footing and headings that are defined are printed prior to printing the original referenced data. They are printed in the following sequence: lowest-level control footing, next-higher-level footing, etc. up to and including the control footing for the level at which the control break occurred; then the control heading for that level, then the next-lower control heading, etc. down to and including the minor control heading; then the detail line is printed.

   If in the course of printing control headings and footing, an end-of-page condition is detected, the current page is ejected, and a new page is begun. If the associated report groups are given, a page footing and/or a page heading is also printed.
5. The levels of control are indicated by the order in which they are written. The identifiers specify the hierarchy of controls. Identifier-1 is the major

control, Identifier-2 is the intermediate control, Identifier-3 is the minor control, etc.

6. FINAL is the exception to the rule that controls the data items. It is the highest control level possible. A control break by FINAL occurs at the beginning and at the end of the report only. All implied lower-level control breaks are taken at the same time as FINAL.

7. All level totals are printed in the sequence in which they are written with the exception of the FINAL total.

8. The CONTROL clause is required when CONTROL FOOTING or CONTROL HEADING is specified.

Page Limit Clause

The PAGE LIMIT clause is used to describe the physical format of a page of the report. The clause specifies the specific line control to be maintained within the logical presentation of a page. If there is no PAGE LIMIT clause specified, the PAGE-COUNTER and LINE-COUNTER special registers are not generated, and line control is not performed. The PAGE LIMIT clause is required when the page format is to be controlled by the Report Writer.

The fixed data-names, PAGE-COUNTER and LINE-COUNTER are numeric counters automatically generated by the Report Writer based on the presence of specific entries, and they do not require any data description clauses. The description of these two counters is included here to explain their resultant effect on the overall report format.

$$
\underline{PAGE} \quad \begin{bmatrix} \underline{LIMIT} \ IS \\ \underline{LIMITS} \ ARE \end{bmatrix} \quad integer\text{-}1 \quad \begin{Bmatrix} \underline{LINE} \\ \underline{LINES} \end{Bmatrix}
$$

$$
[\underline{HEADING} \ integer\text{-}2]
$$
$$
[\underline{FIRST \ DETAIL} \ integer\text{-}3]
$$
$$
[\underline{LAST \ DETAIL} \ integer\text{-}4]
$$
$$
[\underline{FOOTING} \ integer\text{-}5]
$$

Figure 10–10. Format Page Limit Clause.

PAGE-COUNTER

A numeric counter that may be used as a source data item in order to present the page number on a report. The maximum size of a PAGE-COUNTER is based on the size specified in the PICTURE clause associated with the elementary item whose SOURCE is PAGE-COUNTER. This counter may be referred to in any Procedure Division statement. *A PAGE-COUNTER is generated for a report by the Report Writer only if the PAGE LIMIT clause is specified.*

Rules Governing the Use of the Page-Counter Clause

1. The numeric counter is generated automatically by the Report Writer to be used as a SOURCE item in order to automatically present consecutive page numbers.
2. One counter is supplied for each report described in the Report Section. The size of the counter is based on the size specified in the PICTURE clause associated with the elementary SOURCE data item description.
3. If more than one counter is given as a SOURCE data item within a given report, the number of numeric characters indicated by the PICTURE clause must be identical. The size must indicate sufficient numeric character positions to prevent overflow.
4. If more than one report description entry exists in the Report Section, the user must qualify PAGE-COUNTER by the Report Name. The PAGE-COUNTER may be referred to by Data Division clauses and Procedure Division statements.
5. The counter is automatically set to 1 initially by the Report Writer (INITI-ATE statement); if a starting value for the PAGE-COUNTER is to be other than 1, the programmer may change the contents of the counter by a Procedure Division statement after an INITIATE statement has been executed.
6. The counter is automatically incremented by 1 each time a page break is recognized by the Report Writer, after the production of any PAGE FOOT-ING report group but before the production of any PAGE HEADING report group.

LINE-COUNTER

A numeric counter used by the Report Writer to determine when a PAGE HEADING and/or a PAGE FOOTING report group is to be printed. If a PAGE LIMIT clause is written in the report description entry, a LINE-COUNTER is supplied for that report. The maximum value of the counter is based on the number of lines per page as specified in the PAGE LIMIT clause.

Rules Governing the Use of the Line-Counter Clause

1. One line counter is supplied for each report with a PAGE LIMIT clause written in the report description entry.

2. If more than one report description entry exists in the Report Section, the user must qualify LINE-COUNTER by the report name. LINE-COUNTER may be referred to in Data Division clauses or by Procedure Division statements.

3. Changing the LINE-COUNTER by Procedure Division statements may cause the page format control to become unpredictable in the Report Writer.

4. The counter is automatically tested and incremented by the Report Writer based on control specification in the PAGE LIMIT clause and values specified in the LINE NUMBER and NEXT GROUP clauses.

5. The counter is automatically set to zero initially by the Report Writer (INITIATE statement); likewise, the counter is automatically set to zero when PAGE LIMIT Integer-1 LINES entry is exceeded during the execution.

6. If a relative LINE NUMBER indication or relative NEXT GROUP indication exceeds the LAST DETAIL PAGE LIMIT specification during object time, that is, a page break, the counter is set to zero. No additional setting based on the relative LINE NUMBER indication or NEXT GROUP indication that forced the page break takes place.

7. If an absolute LINE NUMBER indication or an absolute NEXT GROUP indication is equal to, or less than, the contents of the counter during object time, the LINE-COUNTER is set to the absolute LINE NUMBER indication following the implicit generation of any specified report groups.

8. The value of the counter during any Procedure Division test statement represents the number of the last line used by the previous report group or represents the number of the last line skipped to by the previous NEXT GROUP specification.

9. The Report Writer LINE-COUNTER control prohibits the printing of successive report lines or report groups on the same line of the same page.

The format of the PAGE LIMIT clause is as follows:

LIMIT(S). LIMIT IS and LIMITS ARE are optional words and need not be included in the clause.

Integer-1. The Integer-1 LINE(S) clause is required to specify the depth of the report page; the depth of the report page may or may not be equal to the physical perforated continuous form often associated in a report with the page length. The size of the fixed data-name LINE-COUNTER is the maximum numeric size based on Integer-1 LINE(S) required for counter to prevent overflow.

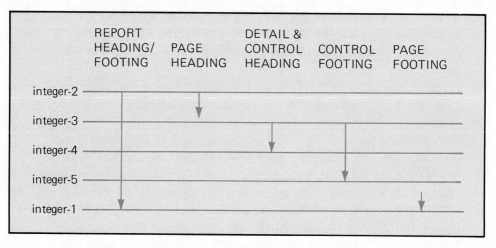

Figure 10–11. Page Format When the Page Limit Clause Is Specified.

HEADING Integer-2. The first line number of the first heading print group. No print group will start preceding Integer-2. Integer-2 is the first line upon which anything is printed.

FIRST DETAIL Integer-3. The first line number of the first normal print group, that is body; no DETAIL print group will start before Integer-3.

LAST DETAIL Integer-4. The last line number of the last normal print group, that is body; no DETAIL print group will extend beyond Integer-4.

FOOTING Integer-5. The last line number of the last CONTROL FOOT-ING print group is specified by Integer-5. No CONTROL FOOTING print group will extend beyond Integer-5. PAGE FOOTING print groups will follow Integer-5.

Note:

The following implicit control is assumed for omitted specifications.

1. If HEADING Integer-2 is omitted, Integer-2 is considered to be equivalent to the value 1, that is, LINE NUMBER one.
2. If FIRST DETAIL Integer-3 is omitted, Integer-3 is considered to be equivalent to the value of Integer-2.
3. If LAST DETAIL Integer-4 is omitted, Integer-4 is considered to be equivalent to the value of Integer-5.
4. If FOOTING Integer-5 is omitted, Integer-5 is considered to be equivalent to the value of Integer-4. If both LAST DETAIL Integer-4 and FOOTING Integer-5 are omitted, Integer-4 and Integer-5 are both considered to be equivalent to the value of Integer-1.

Report Group Description Entry

The Report Group Description entry specifies the characteristics of a particular report group and of the individual data-names within a report group. A report group may comprise one or more report groups. Each report group is described by a hierarchy of entries similar to the description of the data record. There are three types of report groups: heading, detail, and footing. The relative placement of a particular report group within the hierarchy of report groups, the format of all items, and any control factors associated with the group are defined in this entry.

A report group is considered to be one unit of the report consisting of a line or a series of lines that are printed (or not printed) under certain conditions.

```
01    [data-name-1]
      [LINE Clause]
      [NEXT GROUP Clause]
      TYPE Clause
      [USAGE Clause].
```

Figure 10–12. Format Report Group Description Entry Format 1.

```
level-number [data-name-1]
      [BLANK WHEN ZERO Clause]
      [COLUMN Clause]
      [GROUP Clause]
      [JUSTIFIED Clause]
      [LINE Clause]
      [NEXT GROUP Clause]
      PICTURE Clause
      [RESET Clause]
      ⎧ SOURCE ⎫
      ⎨ SUM     ⎬   Clause
      ⎩ VALUE  ⎭
      TYPE Clause
      [USAGE Clause].
```

Figure 10–13. Format Report Group Description Entry Format 2.

Rules Governing the Use of the Report Group Description Entry

1. Except for the data-name clause (which, when present, must immediately follow the level number) the clauses may be written in any order.
2. In order for a report group to be referred to by a Procedure Division statement, it must have a data-name.
3. If a COLUMN clause is present in the data description of an item, the data description must also contain a PICTURE clause in addition to one of the clauses, SOURCE, SUM, or VALUE.
4. In Format 2, the level numbers may be any number from 1 through 49.
5. If Format 1 is used to indicate a report group, a report group must contain

a report group entry (level 01), and it must be the first entry. A report group extends from this entry either to the next group level 01 or to the end of the next group description.

6. Format 2 is used to indicate an elementary item or a group item within a report group. If a report group is an elementary item, Format 2 may include the TYPE or NEXT GROUP clause to specify the report group and elementary item in the same entry.

7. When the LINE clause is specified in Format 1, the entries for the first report line within the report group are presented on the specified line. When the LINE clause is specified in Format 2, sequential entries with the same level number in the report group are implicitly presented on the same line. A LINE NUMBER at a subordinate level must not contradict a LINE NUMBER at a group level.

8. The NEXT GROUP clause, when specified, refers to the spacing at object time between the last line of this report group and the first line of the next report group.

Data-Name-1

Report group names are required in the following cases:

1. When the data-name represents a DETAIL report group referred to by a GENERATE statement in the Procedure Division.

2. When the data-name represents a HEADING or FOOTING report group referred to by a USE statement in the Procedure Division.

3. When a reference is made in the Report Section to a DETAIL report group by a SUM UPON clause.

Line Clause

The LINE clause indicates the absolute or relative line number of this entry in reference to the page or previous entry.

Rules Governing the Use of the Line Clause

1. Integer-1 and Integer-2 must be positive integers. Integer-1 must be within the range specified in the PAGE LIMIT(S) clause in the report description entry.

2. The LINE clause must be given for each report line of a report group. For the first line of a report group, the LINE clause must be given either at the report group level or prior to or for the first elementary item in the line. For report lines other than the first in a report group, it must be given prior to the first elementary item in the line.

$$\text{LINE} \quad \left\{ \begin{array}{l} \text{integer-1} \\ \underline{\text{PLUS}} \text{ integer-2} \\ \underline{\text{NEXT PAGE}} \end{array} \right\}$$

Figure 10–14.   Format Line Clause.

3. When a LINE clause is encountered, subsequent entries following the entry with the LINE clause are implicitly presented on the same line until either another LINE clause or the end of the report group is encountered.
4. Absolute LINE NUMBER entries must be indicated in ascending order, and an absolute LINE NUMBER cannot be preceded by a relative LINE NUMBER.

Integer-1 indicates an absolute line number which sets the LINE-COUNTER to this value for printing the item in this and following entries within the report group until a different value for the LINE-COUNTER is specified. It indicates the fixed line of the page in which the line is to be printed.

Integer-2 indicates a relative line number that specifies the number of lines to be skipped before printing the line. The line is relative to the previous line printed or skipped. The LINE-COUNTER is incremented by the value of Integer-2 and is used for printing the items in this and following entries until a different value for LINE-COUNTER is specified.

NEXT PAGE phrase may be used to indicate an automatic skip to the next page before presenting the first line of the next report group. Appropriate TYPE PAGE FOOTINGS, TYPE PAGE HEADINGS will be produced as specified. This LINE clause may appear only in a report group entry or may be the LINE clause of the first line of a report group.

Next Group Clause

The NEXT GROUP clause is used to define the line control following the printing of the current report group being processed.

Rules Governing the Use of the Next Group Clause
1. The same rules apply for Integer-1, Integer-2, and NEXT PAGE options as enumerated previously for the LINE clause.
2. The NEXT GROUP clause must appear only at the 01 level which defines the report group. When specified for a CONTROL FOOTING/HEADING report group, the NEXT GROUP clause results in automatic line spacing

Figure 10–15. Format Next Group Clause.

$$\text{NEXT GROUP} \quad \begin{Bmatrix} \text{integer-1} \\ \underline{\text{PLUS}} \text{ integer-2} \\ \underline{\text{NEXT PAGE}} \end{Bmatrix}$$

Figure 10–16. Example—Next Group Clause.

```
RD  EXPENSE-REPORT CONTROLS ARE FINAL,
    MONTH, DAY
            .
            .
            .
01  TYPE CONTROL FOOTING DAY
    LINE PLUS 1 NEXT GROUP NEXT PAGE
            .
            .
            .
01  TYPE CONTROL FOOTING MONTH
    LINE PLUS 1 NEXT GROUP
    NEXT PAGE.
            .

            .
(Execution Output)

EXPENSE REPORT
        .
        .
        .
January 31 . . . . . . . . . . . . 29.30
    (Output for CF DAY)

January total  . . . . . . . . .131.40
    (Output for CF MONTH)

Note:  The NEXT GROUP NEXT PAGE clause
for the control footing DAY is not activated.
```

only when a control break occurs on the level for which that control is specified.

Integer-1 indicates an absolute line number which sets the LINE-COUNTER to the value after printing the last line of the report group.

Integer-2 indicates a relative number which increments the LINE-COUNTER by the Integer-2 value after printing the last line of the report group.

NEXT PAGE phrase may be used to indicate an automatic skip to the next page before printing the first line of the next group.

Type Clause

The TYPE clause specifies the particular type of report group that is described in this entry and indicates the time at which the report group is to be generated. Abbreviations may be used in the TYPE clause.

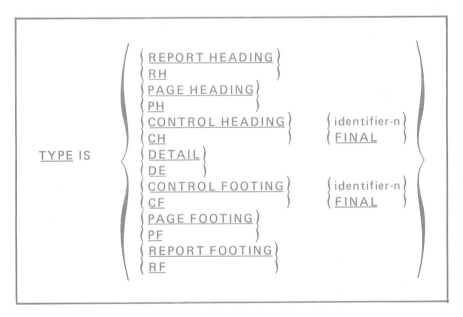

Figure 10–17. Format Type Clause.

Rules Governing the Use of the Type Clause
1. The level number 01 identifies a particular report group to be generated as output and the TYPE clause indicates the time for the generation of this report group.

2. If the report group is described other than TYPE DETAIL, its generation is an automatic Report Writer function.

3. If the report group is described with the TYPE DETAIL clause, the Procedure Division statement—GENERATE data-name—directs the Report Writer to produce the named report group.

4. Nothing precedes a REPORT HEADING entry and nothing follows a REPORT FOOTING entry within a report.

5. A FINAL type control break may be designated only once for CONTROL HEADING or CONTROL FOOTING entries within a particular report group.

6. CONTROL HEADING report groups appear with the current values of any indicated SOURCE data items before the DETAIL report groups of the CONTROL group are produced.

7. CONTROL FOOTING report groups appear with the previous value of any indicated CONTROL SOURCE data items just after the DETAIL report groups of the CONTROL groups have been produced.

8. The USE procedure specified for a CONTROL FOOTING report group refers to:

   a. Source data items specified in the CONTROL clause affect the previous value of the data item.

   b. Source data items not specified in the CONTROL clause affect the current value of the item.

   These report groups appear whenever a control break is noted.

9. LINE NUMBER determines the absolute or relative position of the CONTROL report group exclusive of the other HEADING and FOOTING report group.

Report Heading (RH). The REPORT HEADING entry indicates a report group that is produced only once at the beginning of the report during the execution of the first GENERATE statement. Only one REPORT HEADING is permitted in a report. SOURCE clauses used in REPORT HEADING report group items refer to the value of data items at the time the first GENERATE statement is executed.

Page Heading (PH). The PAGE HEADING entry indicates a report group that is automatically produced at the beginning of each page of the report. Only one page heading is permitted for each report. The page heading is printed on the first page after the REPORT HEADING is specified.

Control Heading (CH). The CONTROL HEADING entry indicates a report group that is printed at the beginning of a control group for a designated

```
REPORT HEADING      (one occurrence only)
PAGE HEADING
       .
       .
       .
CONTROL HEADING
DETAIL
CONTROL FOOTING
       .
       .
       .
PAGE FOOTING
REPORT FOOTING      (one occurrence only)
```

Figure 10–18. Heading or Footing Report Groups Sequence.

```
Final Control Heading     (one occurrence only)
Major Control Heading
       .
       .                          .
       .
Minor Control Heading
```

Figure 10–19. Control Heading Report Groups Sequence.

identifier, or, in the case of FINAL, is produced once before the first control at the initiation of a report during the execution of the first GENERATE statement. There can be only one report group of this type for each identifier and for the FINAL specified in a report. In order to produce any CONTROL HEADING report groups, a control break must occur. SOURCE clauses used in TYPE CONTROL HEADING FINAL report groups refer to the value of the items at the time the first GENERATE statement is executed.

Identifier-n as well as FINAL, must be one of the identifiers described in the CONTROL clause in the report description entry.

Detail (DE). The DETAIL entry indicates a report group that is produced for each GENERATE statement in the Procedure Division. (The data-name specified in the 01 level is referred to by the GENERATE statement. This name must be unique.) There is no limit to the number of DETAIL report groups that may be included in a report.

Control Footing (CF). The CONTROL FOOTING entry indicates a report group that is produced at the end of a control group for a designated identifier or one that is produced once at the termination of a report ending in a FINAL control group. There can be only one report group for each identifier and for the FINAL entry specified in a report. In order to produce any CONTROL FOOTING report group, a control break must occur. SOURCE clauses used in TYPE CONTROL FOOTING FINAL report groups refer to the values of the items at the time the TERMINATE statement is executed.

Minor Control Footing

.

.

.

Major Control Footing
Final Control Footing   (one occurrence only)

Figure 10-20. Control Footing Report Groups Sequence.

Page Footing (PF). The PAGE FOOTING entry indicates a report group that is automatically produced at the bottom of each page of the report. There can be only one report group of this type in a report.

Report Footing (RF). The REPORT FOOTING entry indicates a report group that is produced only once at the termination of a report. There can be only one report group of this type in a report. SOURCE clauses used in TYPE REPORT FOOTING report groups refer to the value of the items at the time the TERMINATE statement is executed.

Usage Clause

DISPLAY is the only option that may be specified for elementary or group items in a report group description entry. (See "USAGE" clause in Data Division.)

Column Clause

The COLUMN clause indicates the absolute column number in the printed page of the high-order (leftmost) character of an elementary item. Integer-1 must be a positive integer. The clause can only be given at the elementary level within a report group.

The COLUMN clause indicates that the *leftmost* character of the elementary item is placed in the position specified by the integer. If the column number is not indicated, the elementary item, though included in the description of the report group, is suppressed when the report group is produced at object time.

Figure 10–21.   Format Column Clause.

Group Indicate Clause

The GROUP INDICATE clause specifies that the elementary item is to be produced only on the first occurrence of the item after any CONTROL or PAGE break. The clause must be specified only at the elementary level within a DETAIL report group.

The elementary item is not only group indicated on the first DETAIL report group containing the item after a control break, but is also indicated on the first DETAIL report group containing the item on a new page, even though a control break did not occur.

Figure 10–22.   Format Group Indicate Clause.

```
REPORT SECTION.
        .
        .
        .

01   DETAIL-LINE TYPE IS DETAIL LINE
     NUMBER IS PLUS 1.
     05   COLUMN IS 2 GROUP INDICATE
          PICTURE IS A(9) SOURCE IS
          MONTHNAME OF RECORD-AREA (MONTH).
        .
        .
        .

          (Execution Output)

        .
        .
        .
```

JANUARY   15   A00 . . .
                 A02 . . .

PURCHASES AND COST . . .

JANUARY   21   A03 . . .
                 A03 . . .

GROUP INDICATE items are printed after page and control breaks.

Figure 10–23. Sample Showing Group Indicate Clause and Resultant Execution Output.

Justified Clause

The same rules are applicable to the use of the JUSTIFIED clause in a report group description as discussed in the Data Division. (See "Justified" clause in Data Division.)

Picture Clause

The same rules are applicable to the use of the PICTURE clause in a report group description as discussed in the Data Division. (See "Picture" clause in Data Division.)

Reset Clause

The RESET clause indicates the CONTROL identifier that causes the SUM counter in the elementary item entry to be reset to zero on a control break.

After presentation of the TYPE CONTROL FOOTING report group, the counters associated with the report are reset automatically to zero unless an explicit RESET clause is given specifying reseting based on a higher-level control than the associated control for the report group.

The RESET clause may be used for programming totaling of identifiers where subtotals of identifiers may be desired without automatic resetting upon printing the report group.

The RESET clause may only be used in conjunction with a SUM clause at the elementary level.

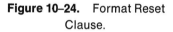

Figure 10–24. Format Reset Clause.

Identifier-1 must be one of the identifiers described in the CONTROL clause in the report description entry. Identifier-1 must be a higher-level CONTROL identifier than the CONTROL identifier associated with the CONTROL FOOTING report group in which the SUM and RESET clause appear.

Blank When Zero Clause

The same rules are applicable to the use of the BLANK WHEN ZERO clause in a report group description as described in the Data Division. (See "blank when zero" clause in Data Division.)

Source Clause

The SOURCE clause indicates a data item to be used as the source for this report item. The item is presented according to the PICTURE clause and the COLUMN clause in this elementary item entry.

SOURCE IS identifier-1

Figure 10–25. Format Source Clause.

The SOURCE clause has two functions:

1. To specify a data item that is to be printed.
2. To specify a data item that is to be summed in a CONTROL FOOTING report group.

Sum Clause

The SUM clause is used to cause automatic summation of data and may appear only in an elementary item entry of a CONTROL FOOTING report group.

$$\underline{SUM} \qquad identifier\text{-}2 \quad identifier\text{-}3 \quad \ldots \; [\,\underline{UPON} \; data\text{-}name\,]$$

Figure 10–26. Format Sum Clause.

Rules Governing the Use of the Sum Clause
1. A SUM clause may appear only in a TYPE CONTROL FOOTING report group.
2. If a SUM counter is referred to by a Procedure Division statement or Report Section entry, a data-name must be specified with the SUM clause entry. The data-name then represents the summation counter automatically generated by the Report Writer to total the operands immediately following the SUM. If a summation counter is never referred to, the counter need not be named explicitly by a data-name entry. A SUM counter is only algebraically incremented just before the presentation of the TYPE DETAIL report group in which the item being summed appears as a source item.
3. Whether the SUM clause names the summation counter or not, the PICTURE clause must be specified for each SUM counter. Editing characters or editing clauses may be included in the description of a SUM counter. Editing of a SUM counter only occurs upon presentation of that SUM counter. At all other times, the SUM counter is treated as a numeric data item. The SUM counter must be large enough to accommodate the summed quantity without truncating of integral digits.
4. An operand of a SUM clause must be an elementary numeric data item that appears in the File, Working-Storage Sections, or one that is the name of a SUM counter.

RD . . . CONTROLS ARE YEAR MONTH WEEK DAY

Method 1:

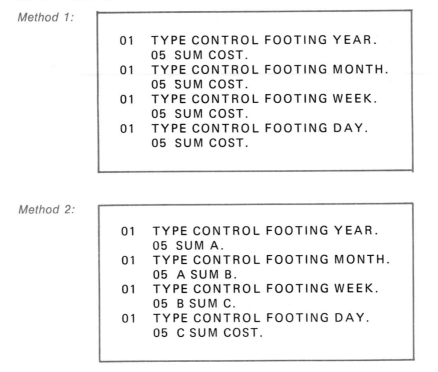

```
01    TYPE CONTROL FOOTING YEAR.
      05 SUM COST.
01    TYPE CONTROL FOOTING MONTH.
      05 SUM COST.
01    TYPE CONTROL FOOTING WEEK.
      05 SUM COST.
01    TYPE CONTROL FOOTING DAY.
      05 SUM COST.
```

Method 2:

```
01    TYPE CONTROL FOOTING YEAR.
      05 SUM A.
01    TYPE CONTROL FOOTING MONTH.
      05  A SUM B.
01    TYPE CONTROL FOOTING WEEK.
      05  B SUM C.
01    TYPE CONTROL FOOTING DAY.
      05  C SUM COST.
```

Method 2 will execute faster. One addition will be performed for each day, one more for each week, and one for each month. In Method 1, four additions will be performed for each day.

Figure 10–27. Example—Sum Clause.

5. Each item being summed—that is, Identifier-2, Identifier-3, etc., must appear as a SOURCE item in a TYPE DETAIL report group or be the name of a SUM counter in a TYPE CONTROL FOOTING report group at an equal or lower position in the control hierarchy. Although the items must be explicitly written in a TYPE DETAIL report group, they may be actually suppressed at presentation time. In this manner, direct association without ambiguity can be made from the current data available by a GENERATE statement to the data items to be presented within the Report Section.

6. If higher-level report groups are indicated in the control hierarchy, counter updating (commonly called "rolling counter" forward) procedures take place prior to the reset operation.

7. The summation of data items defined as SUM counter in the TYPE CON-
   TROL FOOTING report groups is accomplished explicitly or implicitly with
   the Report Writer automatically handling the updating function. If a sum
   control of a data item is not desired for presentation at a higher level, the
   lower-level SUM specification may be omitted. In this case the same results
   are obtained as if the lower-level SUM were specified.

8. The *UPON data-name* is required to obtain selective summation for a particular data item which is named as a SOURCE item in two or more TYPE
   DETAIL report groups. Identifier-2 and Identifier-3 must be source data
   items in data-names. Data-name must be the name of a TYPE DETAIL
   report group. If the UPON data-name option is not used, Identifier-2 and
   Identifier-3, etc. respectively, are added to the SUM counter at each execution of a GENERATE statement. This statement generates a TYPE DE-
   TAIL report group that contains the SUM operands at the elementary level.

Value Clause

The VALUE clause causes the report data item to assign the specified
value each time its report group is presented only if the elementary item entry
does not contain a GROUP INDICATE clause. If the GROUP INDICATE
clause is present, and a given object time condition exists, the item will assume
the specified value. (See "group Indicate" rules.)

VALUE IS literal-1

Figure 10–28.   Format Value Clause.

PROCEDURE DIVISION

To produce a report using the Report Writer Feature, the INITIATE,
GENERATE, and TERMINATE statements must be specified in the Procedure Division.

A USE BEFORE REPORTING declarative statement may be written
in the Declarative Section of the Procedure Division if the programmer wishes
to alter or manipulate the data before it is presented in the report.

Initiate Statement

The INITIATE statement begins the processing of a report.

INITIATE report-name-1 [report-name-2] . . .

Figure 10-29. Format Initiate Statement.

Rules Governing the Use of Initiate Statement

1. Each report name must be defined by a report description entry in the Report Section of the Data Division.
2. The INITIATE statement resets all data-name entries that contain SUM clauses associated with the report. The Report Writer controls for all the TYPE report groups that are associated with the report are set up in their respective order.
3. The PAGE-COUNTER, if specified, is set to 1 prior to or during the execution of the INITIATE statement. If a different starting value for the PAGE-COUNTER other than 1 is desired, the programmer may reset this counter with a statement in the Procedure Division following the INITIATE statement.
4. The LINE-COUNTER, if specified, is set to zero prior to or during the execution of the INITIATE statement.
5. The INITIATE statement does not open the file with which the report is associated. An OPEN statement for the file must be specified. The INITIATE statement performs Report Writer functions for individually described programs analogous to the input-output functions that the OPEN statement performs for individually described files.
6. A second INITIATE statement for a particular report-name may not be executed unless a TERMINATE statement has been executed for that report-name subsequent to the first INITIATE statement.

Generate Statement

The GENERATE statement is used to produce a report. It links the Procedure Division to the Report Writer described in the Report Section of the Data Division at process time.

Figure 10–30.   Format Generate
Statement.

Rules Governing the Use of the Generate Statement

1. Identifier represents a TYPE DETAIL report group or an RD (report description) entry.

2. If the identifier is the name of a TYPE DETAIL report group, the GENERATE statement performs all the automatic operations of the Report Writer and produces an actual output detail report group in the output. This is called *detail reporting*.

3. If the identifier is the name of a RD entry, the GENERATE statement does all the automatic operations of the Report Writer and updates the footing report group(s) within a particular report group without producing an actual detail report group associated with the report. In this case, all SUM counters associated with the report descriptions are algebraically incremented each time a GENERATE statement is executed. This is called *summary reporting*. If more than one TYPE DETAIL group is specified, all SUM counters are algebraically incremented each time a GENERATE statement is executed.

4. The GENERATE statement, implicit in both detail and summary reporting, produces the following automatic operations (if defined).

    a. Steps and tests the LINE-COUNTER and/or PAGE-COUNTER to produce appropriate PAGE-FOOTING and/or PAGE HEADING report groups.

    b. Recognizes any specified control breaks to produce appropriate CONTROL FOOTING and/or CONTROL HEADING report groups.

    c. Accumulates into the SUM counters all specified INDENTIFIERS. Resets the SUM counters on an associated control break. Performs an updating procedure between control break levels for each set of SUM counters.

    d. Executes any specified routines defined by a USE statement before generation of the associated report groups.

5. During the execution of the first GENERATE statement, the following report groups associated with the report, if specified, are produced in the following order:

    a. REPORT HEADING report group.

    b. PAGE HEADING report group.

    c. All CONTROL HEADING report groups in this order: FINAL, major to minor.

    d. The DETAIL report group, if specified, in the GENERATE statement.

6. If a control break is recognized at the time of the execution of a GENERATE statement (other than the first that is executed for the report), all CONTROL FOOTING report groups specified for the report are produced from the minor group up to and including the report group specified for the identifier which cause the control break. Then the CONTROL HEADING report group(s) specified for the report, from the report group specified for the identifier that causes the control breakdown to the minor report group, are produced in that order. The DETAIL report group specified in the GENERATE statement is then produced.

7. Data is moved to the data item in the report group description entry of the Report Section and is edited under control of the Report Writer according to the same rules for movement and editing as described for the MOVE statement. (See "move" statement in the Procedure Division.)

Terminate Statement

    The TERMINATE statement is used to terminate the processing of a report.

```
TERMINATE report-name-1 [report-name-2] . . .
```

Figure 10–31. Format Terminate Statement.

Rules Governing the Use of the Terminate Statement

1. Each report-name given in a TERMINATE statement must be defined by an RD entry in the Data Division.

2. The TERMINATE statement produces all the control footings associated with this report, as if a control break had just occurred at the highest level, and completes the Report Writer functions for the named report. The TERMINATE statement also produces the last page footings and report footing report groups associated with this report.

3. Appropriate PAGE HEADING or FOOTING report groups are prepared in their respective order for the report description.

4. A second TERMINATE statement for a particular file may not be executed unless a second INITIATE statement has been executed for the report-name. If a TERMINATE statement has been executed for a report, a GENERATE statement for that report must not be executed unless an intervening INITIATE statement for that report is executed.

5. The TERMINATE statement does not close the file with which the report is associated. A CLOSE statement for the file must be given by the user. The TERMINATE statement performs Report Writer functions for individually described report programs analogous to the input-output functions that the CLOSE statement performs for individual described files.

6. SOURCE clauses used in TYPE CONTROL FOOTING FINAL or TYPE REPORT FOOTING report groups refer to the values of the items during the execution of the TERMINATE statement.

Use Statement

The USE statement specifies Procedure Division statements that are executed just before a report group named in the Report Section of the Data Division is produced.

```
USE BEFORE REPORTING data-name.
```

Figure 10–32. Format Use before Reporting Declarative.

Rules Governing the Use of a Use Statement

1. A USE statement, when present, must immediately follow a section header in the Declaratives portion of the Procedure Division and must be followed by a period and a space. The remainder of the section must consist of one or more procedural paragraphs that define the procedures to be processed.

2. Data-name represents a report group named in the Report Section of the Data Division. The data-name must not be used in more than one USE statement. The data-name must be qualified by the report-name if not unique.

3. No Report Writer statement (INITIATE, GENERATE or TERMINATE) may be written in a procedural paragraph or a paragraph following the USE sentence in the Declaratives Section.

4. The USE statement itself is never executed; rather, it defines the conditions calling for the execution of the USE procedures.

5. The designated procedures are executed by the **Report Writer** just before the named report is produced, regardless of page or control breaks associated with report groups. The report group may be any type except DETAIL.
6. Within a USE procedure, there must not be any reference to any nondeclarative procedure. Conversely, in the nondeclarative portion, there must be no reference to procedure-names that appear in the Declaratives portion, except that PERFORM statements may refer to USE declaratives or to procedures associated with USE declaratives.

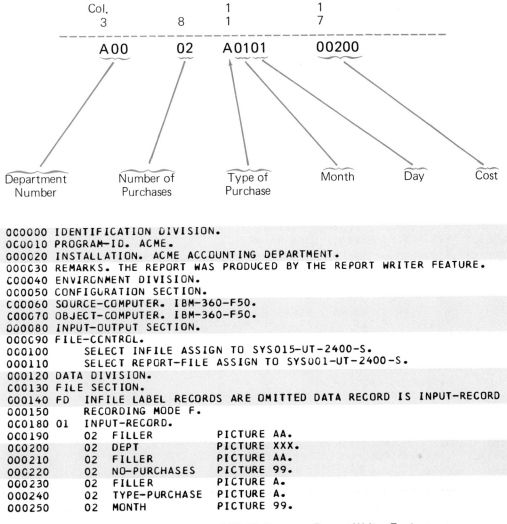

```
0C0000 IDENTIFICATION DIVISION.
0C0010 PROGRAM-ID. ACME.
000020 INSTALLATION. ACME ACCOUNTING DEPARTMENT.
000C30 REMARKS. THE REPORT WAS PRODUCED BY THE REPORT WRITER FEATURE.
C00040 ENVIRONMENT DIVISION.
0C0050 CONFIGURATION SECTION.
C00060 SOURCE-COMPUTER. IBM-360-F50.
C00C70 OBJECT-COMPUTER. IBM-360-F50.
000080 INPUT-OUTPUT SECTION.
000C90 FILE-CCNTROL.
0C0100     SELECT INFILE ASSIGN TO SYS015-UT-2400-S.
000110     SELECT REPORT-FILE ASSIGN TO SYS001-UT-2400-S.
000120 DATA DIVISION.
C00130 FILE SECTION.
C00140 FD  INFILE LABEL RECORDS ARE OMITTED DATA RECORD IS INPUT-RECORD
000150     RECORDING MODE F.
0C0180 01  INPUT-RECORD.
0C0190     02  FILLER         PICTURE AA.
0C0200     02  DEPT           PICTURE XXX.
000210     02  FILLER         PICTURE AA.
000220     02  NO-PURCHASES   PICTURE 99.
000230     02  FILLER         PICTURE A.
000240     02  TYPE-PURCHASE  PICTURE A.
000250     02  MONTH          PICTURE 99.
```

Figure 10-33. Example—COBOL Program Report Writer Feature.

```
C00260        02  DAY           PICTURE 99.
000270        02  FILLER        PICTURE A.
C00280        02  COST          PICTURE 999V99.
000281        02  FILLER PICTURE X(59).
000290 FD  REPORT-FILE, REPORT IS EXPENSE-REPORT
000300        LABEL RECORDS ARE STANDARD.
000310 WORKING-STORAGE SECTION.
0C0320 77  SAVED-MONTH PICTURE 99 VALUE 1.
0C0330 77  SAVED-DAY   PICTURE 99 VALUE O.
0C0340 77  CONTINUED   PICTURE X(11) VALUE SPACE.
C00380 01  FILLER.
0C0390        02  RECORD-MONTH.
0C0400            03  FILLER PICTURE A(9) VALUE IS 'JANUARY  '.
0C0410            03  FILLER PICTURE A(9) VALUE IS 'FEBRUARY '.
0C0420            03  FILLER PICTURE A(9) VALUE IS 'MARCH    '.
000430            03  FILLER PICTURE A(9) VALUE IS 'APRIL    '.
000440            03  FILLER PICTURE A(9) VALUE IS 'MAY      '.
000450            03  FILLER PICTURE A(9) VALUE IS 'JUNE     '.
000460            03  FILLER PICTURE A(9) VALUE IS 'JULY     '.
000470            03  FILLER PICTURE A(9) VALUE IS 'AUGUST   '.
C00480            03  FILLER PICTURE A(9) VALUE IS 'SEPTEMBER'.
CC0490            03  FILLER PICTURE A(9) VALUE IS 'OCTOBER  '.
000500            03  FILLER PICTURE A(9) VALUE IS 'NOVEMBER '.
000510            03  FILLER PICTURE A(9) VALUE IS 'DECEMBER '.
000520        02  RECORD-AREA REDEFINES RECORD-MONTH OCCURS 12 TIMES.
000530            03  MONTHNAME PICTURE A(9).
CC0540 REPORT SECTION.
0C0550 RD  EXPENSE-REPORT CONTROLS ARE FINAL, MONTH, DAY
000560        PAGE 59 LINES HEADING 1 FIRST DETAIL 9 LAST DETAIL 48
CC0570        FOOTING 52.
000580 01  TYPE REPORT HEADING.
000590        02  LINE 1 COLUMN 27 PICTURE A(26) VALUE IS
000600        'ACME MANUFACTURING COMPANY'.
000610        02  LINE 3 COLUMN 26 PICTURE A(29) VALUE IS
000620        'QUARTERLY EXPENDITURES REPORT'.
000630 01  PAGE-HEAD TYPE PAGE HEADING LINE 5.
000640        02  COLUMN 30 PICTURE A(9) SOURCE MONTHNAME OF
C00650        RECORD-AREA (MONTH).
0C0660        02  COLUMN 39 PICTURE A(12) VALUE IS 'EXPENDITURES'.
C00661        02  COLUMN 52 PICTURE X(11) SOURCE CONTINUED.
000670        02  LINE 7 COLUMN 2 PICTURE X(35) VALUE IS
0C0680        'MONTH    DAY    DEPT NO-PURCHASES'.
000690        02  COLUMN 40 PICTURE X(33) VALUE IS
0C0700        'TYPE     COST   CUMULATIVE-COST'.
000710 01  DETAIL-LINE TYPE DETAIL LINE PLUS 1.
000720        02  COLUMN 2 GROUP INDICATE PICTURE A(9)  SOURCE MONTHNAME
0C0730        OF RECORD-AREA (MONTH).
0C0740        02  COLUMN 13 GROUP INDICATE PICTURE 99 SOURCE DAY.
000750        02  COLUMN 19 PICTURE XXX SOURCE DEPT.
CC0760        02  COLUMN 31 PICTURE Z9 SOURCE NO-PURCHASES.
000770        02  COLUMN 42 PICTURE A SOURCE TYPE-PURCHASE.
000780        02  COLUMN 50 PICTURE ZZ9.99 SOURCE COST.
000790 01  TYPE CONTROL FOOTING DAY LINE PLUS 2.
000800        02  COLUMN 2 PICTURE X(22) VALUE IS 'PURCHASES AND COST FOR'.
000810        02  COLUMN 24 PICTURE Z9 SOURCE SAVED-MONTH.
0C0820        02  COLUMN 26 PICTURE X VALUE IS '-'.
0C0830        02  COLUMN 27 PICTURE 99 SOURCE SAVED-DAY.
```

Figure 10-33.   Example—COBOL Program Report Writer Feature—Continued.

```
000840       02   COLUMN 30 PICTURE ZZ9 SUM NO-PURCHASES.
000850       02   MIN COLUMN 49 PICTURE $$$9.99 SUM COST.
000860       02   COLUMN 65 PICTURE $$$$9.99 SUM COST RESET ON FINAL.
000870       02   LINE PLUS 1 COLUMN 2 PICTURE X(70) VALUE ALL '*'.
000880 01    TYPE CONTROL FOOTING MONTH LINE PLUS 1 NEXT GROUP NEXT PAGE.
000890       02   COLUMN 16 PICTURE A(14) VALUE IS 'TOTAL COST FOR'.
000900       02   COLUMN 31 PICTURE A(9) SOURCE MONTHNAME OF RECORD-AREA
000910            (SAVED-MONTH).
000920       02   COLUMN 40 PICTURE AAA VALUE 'WAS'.
000930       02   INT COLUMN 46 PICTURE $$$9.99 SUM MIN.
000940 01    TYPE CONTROL FOOTING FINAL LINE PLUS 1.
000950       02   COLUMN 16 PICTURE A(26) VALUE IS
000960       'TOTAL COST FOR QUARTER WAS'.
000970       02   COLUMN 45 PICTURE $$$$9.99 SUM INT.
000980 01    TYPE PAGE FOOTING LINE 55.
001000       02   LINE 57 COLUMN 59 PICTURE X(12) VALUE IS, 'REPORT-PAGE-'.
001010       02   COLUMN 71 PICTURE 99 SOURCE PAGE-COUNTER.
001020 01    TYPE REPORT FOOTING.
001030       02   LINE PLUS 1 COLUMN 32 PICTURE A(13) VALUE IS
001040       'END OF REPORT'.
001050 PROCEDURE DIVISION.
001060 DECLARATIVES.
001070 PAGE-HEAD-RTN SECTION. USE BEFORE REPORTING PAGE-HEAD.
001080    PAGE-HEAD-RTN-SWITCH. GO TO PAGE-HEAD-RTN-TEST.
001090    PAGE-HEAD-RTN-TEST. IF MONTH = SAVED-MONTH MOVE '(CONTINUED)'
001100       TO CONTINUED ELSE MOVE SPACES TO CONTINUED
001101       MOVE MONTH TO SAVED-MONTH.
001102    GO TO PAGE-HEAD-RTN-EXIT.
001103    PAGE-HEAD-RTN-SUPPRESS. MOVE 1 TO PRINT-SWITCH.
001104    PAGE-HEAD-RTN-EXIT. EXIT.
001110 END DECLARATIVES.
001120       OPEN INPUT INFILE, OUTPUT REPORT-FILE.
001121          READ INFILE AT END GO TO COMPLETE.
001130          INITIATE EXPENSE-REPORT.
001140 READATA. GENERATE DETAIL-LINE MOVE DAY TO SAVED-DAY
001141              READ INFILE AT END GO TO
001150                  COMPLETE. GO TO READATA.
001160 COMPLETE. ALTER PAGE-HEAD-RTN-SWITCH TO PROCEED TO
001161              PAGE-HEAD-RTN-SUPPRESS, TERMINATE EXPENSE-REPORT
001170       CLOSE INFILE, REPORT-FILE. STOP RUN.
  A00  02 A0101 00200
  A02  01 A0101 00100
  A02  02 C0101 01600
  A01  02 B0102 00200
  A04  10 A0102 01000
  A04  10 C0102 08000
  A01  02 B0105 00200
  A01  10 A0108 01000
  A01  08 B0108 01248
  A01  20 D0108 03840

        .
        .
        .

  A01  06 C0329 04800
  A03  20 E0331 06000
  A03  10 G0331 05000
```

Figure 10–33.   Example—COBOL Program Report Writer Feature—Continued.

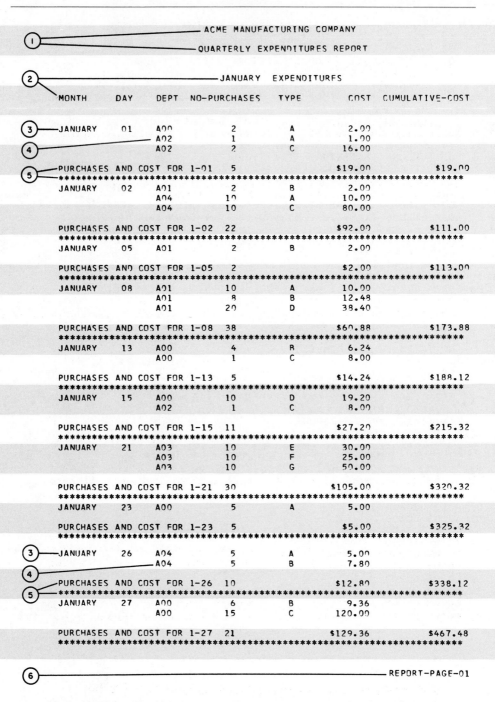

```
                              ACME MANUFACTURING COMPANY
    (1)
                              QUARTERLY EXPENDITURES REPORT


    (2)                            JANUARY  EXPENDITURES

       MONTH      DAY    DEPT  NO-PURCHASES    TYPE       COST  CUMULATIVE-COST


    (3)  JANUARY    01    A00        2          A         2.00
         (4)              A02        1          A         1.00
                          A02        2          C        16.00

    (5)  PURCHASES  AND COST FOR  1-01   5                $19.00           $19.00
         ***********************************************************************
         JANUARY    02    A01        2          B         2.00
                          A04       10          A        10.00
                          A04       10          C        80.00

         PURCHASES  AND COST FOR  1-02   22               $92.00          $111.00
         ***********************************************************************
         JANUARY    05    A01        2          B         2.00

         PURCHASES  AND COST FOR  1-05   2                 $2.00          $113.00
         ***********************************************************************
         JANUARY    08    A01       10          A        10.00
                          A01        8          B        12.48
                          A01       20          D        38.40

         PURCHASES  AND COST FOR  1-08   38               $60.88          $173.88
         ***********************************************************************
         JANUARY    13    A00        4          B         6.24
                          A00        1          C         8.00

         PURCHASES  AND COST FOR  1-13   5                $14.24          $188.12
         ***********************************************************************
         JANUARY    15    A00       10          D        19.20
                          A02        1          C         8.00

         PURCHASES  AND COST FOR  1-15   11               $27.20          $215.32
         ***********************************************************************
         JANUARY    21    A03       10          E        30.00
                          A03       10          F        25.00
                          A03       10          G        50.00

         PURCHASES  AND COST FOR  1-21   30              $105.00          $320.32
         ***********************************************************************
         JANUARY    23    A00        5          A         5.00

         PURCHASES  AND COST FOR  1-23   5                 $5.00          $325.32
         ***********************************************************************
    (3)  JANUARY    26    A04        5          A         5.00
         (4)              A04        5          B         7.80

         PURCHASES  AND COST FOR  1-26   10               $12.80          $338.12
    (5)  ***********************************************************************
         JANUARY    27    A00        6          B         9.36
                          A00       15          C       120.00

         PURCHASES  AND COST FOR  1-27   21              $129.36          $467.48
         ***********************************************************************


    (6)                                                       REPORT-PAGE-01
```

Figure 10–34.   Example—Report Produced by the Report Writer Feature.

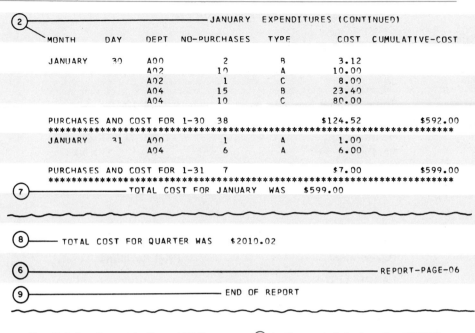

Key Relating Report to Report Writer Source Program

① is the report heading resulting from source lines 00580–00620.

② is the page heading resulting from source lines 00630–00700.

③ is the detail line resulting from source lines 00710–00780 (note that since it is the first detail line after a control break, the fields defined with 'group indicate', lines 00720–00740, appear).

④ is a detail line resulting from the same source lines as 3. In this case, however, the fields described as 'group indicate' do not appear (since the control break did not immediately precede the detail line).

⑤ is the control footing (for DAY) resulting from source lines 00790–00870.

⑥ is the page footing resulting from source lines 00980–01010.

⑦ is the control footing (for MONTH) resulting from source lines 00880–00930.

⑧ is the control footing (for FINAL) resulting from source lines 00940–00970.

⑨ is the report footing resulting from source lines 01020–01040.

Lines 01070–01104 of the example illustrate a use of 'USE BEFORE REPORTING'. The effect of the source is that each time a new page is started, a test is made to determine if the new page is being started because a change in MONTH has been recognized (the definition for the control footing for MONTH specifies 'NEXT GROUP NEXT PAGE') or because the physical limits of the page were exhausted. The calculation involved sets up a fixed ('PAGE GROUP') which is referenced by a SOURCE clause in the PAGE FOOTING description. Consequently, two page counters can be maintained: one indicating physical pages and one indicating logical pages.

Figure 10–34. Example—Report Produced by the Report Writer Feature—Continued.

REPORT WRITER PROBLEM

INPUT

Field	Card Columns	
Department	1–3	
Serial Number	4–10	
Name	14–32	
Hours	38–40	XX.X
Net Pay	41–47	XXX.XX

OUTPUT

Headings

Report Headings

Description	Print Positions
LABOR LISTING	18–30

Page Headings

Line 1

Description	Print Positions
SERIAL	12–17
HOURS	44–48

Line 2

Description	Print Positions
DEPT.	5–9
NUMBER	12–17
N A M E	27–33
WORKED	43–48
NET PAY	54–60

Detail

Description	Print Positions	
Department	6–8	
Serial Number	11–17	
Name	20–38	
Hours Worked	44–47	XX.X
Net Pay	51–60	$$$,$$$.99

Control Footing   MINOR—Department   FINAL

Description		Print Positions	
HEADING—TOTAL FOR DEPARTMENT (Dept. No.)		25–47	
MINOR	Net Pay	50–60	$$$$,$$$.99
		61	*
FINAL	Net Pay	49–60	$$$$$,$$$.99
		61–62	**

		1234567890	1111111111 2	2222222222 3	3333333333 4	4444444444 5	5555555555 6	66666666
	1							
	2							
	3							
	4							
	5							
H	6	LABOR LISTING						
	7							
H	8	SERIAL			HOURS			
H	9	DEPT. NUMBER	N A M E		WORKED	NET PAY		
	10							
D	11	ZZZ ZZZZZZZ	A————————A		ZZ.9	$$$,$$$.99		
TL1	12		TOTAL FOR DEPARTMENT ZZ $$$$,$$$.99X					
	13							
	14							
TLR	15					$$$$$,$$$.99XX		
	16							
	17							
	18							

```
00001   001010 IDENTIFICATION DIVISION.                                          LIBLISTG
00002   001020 PROGRAM-ID.         REPORT-WRITER.                                LIBLISTG
00003   001030 AUTHOR.             C FEINGOLD.                                   LIBLISTG
00004   001040 INSTALLATION.       DISTRICT OFFICE.                              LIBLISTG
00005   001050 DATE-WRITTEN.       JUNE 14 1972.                                 LIBLISTG
00006   001060 DATE-COMPILED. 10/27/72                                           LIBLISTG
00007   001070 REMARKS.            THIS IS A PROGRAM TO PREPARE A LABOR LISTING. LIBLISTG
00008   002010 ENVIRONMENT DIVISION.                                            LIBLISTG
00009   002020 CONFIGURATION SECTION.                                           LIBLISTG
00010   002030 SOURCE-COMPUTER.                                                 LIBLISTG
00011   002040     IBM-360-H50.                                                 LIBLISTG
00012   002050 OBJECT-COMPUTER.                                                 LIBLISTG
00013   002060     IBM-360-H50.                                                 LIBLISTG
00014   002070 INPUT-OUTPUT SECTION.                                            LIBLISTG
00015   002080 FILE-CONTROL.                                                    LIBLISTG
00016   002090     SELECT FILE-IN                                               LIBLISTG
00017   002100        ASSIGN TO SYS009-UR-2540R-S.                              LIBLISTG
00018   002110     SELECT FILE-OUT                                              LIBLISTG
00019   002120        ASSIGN TO SYS005-UR-1403-S.                               LIBLISTG
00020   003010 DATA DIVISION.                                                   LIBLISTG
00021   003020 FILE SECTION.                                                    LIBLISTG
00022   003030 FD  FILE-IN                                                      LIBLISTG
00023   003040     RECORDING MODE F                                            LIBLISTG
00024   003050     LABEL RECORDS OMITTED                                       LIBLISTG
00025   003060     RECORD CONTAINS 80 CHARACTERS                               LIBLISTG
00026   003070     DATA RECORD IS CARD-IN.                                     LIBLISTG
00027   003080 01  CARD-IN.                                                    LIBLISTG
00028   003090     02  DEPT-IN        PICTURE 999.                             LIBLISTG
00029   003100     02  SERIAL-IN      PICTURE 9(7).                            LIBLISTG
00030   003110     02  FILLER         PICTURE X(3).                            LIBLISTG
00031   003120     02  NAME-IN        PICTURE A(19).                           LIBLISTG
00032   003130     02  FILLER         PICTURE X(5).                            LIBLISTG
00033   003140     02  HOURS-IN       PICTURE 99V9.                            LIBLISTG
00034   003150     02  NET-IN         PICTURE 9(5)V99.                         LIBLISTG
00035   003160     02  FILLER         PICTURE X(33).                           LIBLISTG
00036   003170 FD  FILE-OUT                                                    LIBLISTG
00037   003180     LABEL RECORDS OMITTED                                       LIBLISTG
00038   003190     REPORT IS LABOR-LIST.                                       LIBLISTG
00039   004010 REPORT SECTION.                                                 LIBLISTG
```

```
2
```

```
00040   004020 RD  LABOR-LIST                                                  LIBLISTG
00041   004030     CONTROLS ARE FINAL, DEPT-IN                                 LIBLISTG
00042   004040     PAGE             59 LINES                                   LIBLISTG
00043   004050     HEADING          1                                         LIBLISTG
00044   004060     FIRST DETAIL     6                                         LIBLISTG
00045   004070     LAST DETAIL     46                                         LIBLISTG
00046   004080     FOOTING         52.                                       LIBLISTG
00047   004090 01  TYPE REPORT HEADING.                                       LIBLISTG
00048   004100     02  LINE 1  COLUMN 18 PICTURE X(13)                        LIBLISTG
00049   004110         VALUE IS 'LABOR LISTING'.                              LIBLISTG
00050   004120 01  TYPE PAGE HEADING LINE 3.                                  LIBLISTG
00051   004130     02  COLUMN 12  PICTURE X(6)                                LIBLISTG
00052   004140         VALUE IS 'SERIAL'.                                     LIBLISTG
00053   004150     02  COLUMN 44  PICTURE X(5)                                LIBLISTG
00054   004160         VALUE IS 'HOURS'.                                      LIBLISTG
00055   004170     02  LINE 4  COLUMN 5  PICTURE X(5)                         LIBLISTG
00056   004180         VALUE IS 'DEPT.'.                                      LIBLISTG
00057   004190     02  COLUMN 12  PICTURE X(6)                                LIBLISTG
00058   004200         VALUE IS 'NUMBER'.                                     LIBLISTG
00059   004210     02  COLUMN 27  PICTURE X(7)                                LIBLISTG
00060   004220         VALUE IS 'N A M E'.                                    LIBLISTG
00061   004230     02  COLUMN 43  PICTURE X(16)                               LIBLISTG
00062   004240         VALUE IS 'WORKED'.                                     LIBLISTG
00063   005010     02  COLUMN 54  PICTURE X(7)                                LIBLISTG
00064   005020         VALUE IS 'NET PAY'.                                    LIBLISTG
00065   005030 01  DETAIL-LINE  TYPE DETAIL LINE PLUS 1.                      LIBLISTG
00066   005040     02  COLUMN 6  GROUP INDICATE  PICTURE ZZZ SOURCE DEPT-IN.  LIBLISTG
00067   005050     02  COLUMN 11  PICTURE Z(7)  SOURCE SERIAL-IN.             LIBLISTG
00068   005060     02  COLUMN 20  PICTURE A(19) SOURCE NAME-IN.               LIBLISTG
00069   005070     02  COLUMN 44  PICTURE ZZ.9  SOURCE HOURS-IN.              LIBLISTG
00070   005080     02 COLUMN 51    PICTURE $$$,$$$.99    SOURCE NET-IN.        LIBLISTG
00071   005090 01  TYPE CONTROL FOOTING DEPT-IN LINE PLUS 1                   LIBLISTG
00072   005095     NEXT GROUP PLUS 1.                                         LIBLISTG
00073   005100     02  COLUMN 25  PICTURE X(20)                               LIBLISTG
00074   005110         VALUE IS 'TOTAL FOR DEPARTMENT'.                       LIBLISTG
00075   005120     02  COLUMN 45  PICTURE ZZZ  SOURCE  DEPT-IN.               LIBLISTG
00076   005130     02  MIN COLUMN 50 PICTURE $$$$,$$$.99 SUM NET-IN.          LIBLISTG
00077   005140     02  COLUMN 61  PICTURE X  VALUE IS '*'.                    LIBLISTG
00078   005150 01  TYPE CONTROL FOOTING FINAL  LINE PLUS 3.                   LIBLISTG
```

```
00079   005160    02  COLUMN 49  PICTURE $$$$$,$$$.99 SUM MIN.           LIBLISTG
00080   005170    02  COLUMN 61  PICTURF XX VALUE IS '**'.               LIBLISTG
00097   006010 PROCEDURE DIVISION.                                       LIBLISTG
00098   006020 INIT.    OPEN INPUT FILE-IN  OUTPUT FILE-OUT.             LIBLISTG
00099   006030         INITIATE LABOR-LIST.                              LIBLISTG
00100   006040 AGAIN.  READ FILE-IN AT END GO TO FINISH.                 LIBLISTG
00101   006050         GENERATE DETAIL-LINE.                             LIBLISTG
00102   006060         GO TO AGAIN.                                      LIBLISTG
00103   006070 FINISH. TERMINATE LABOR-LIST.                            LIBLISTG
00104   006080         CLOSE FILE-IN, FILE-OUT.                          LIBLISTG
00105   006090         STOP RUN.                                         LIBLISTG
```

                              LABOR LISTING

DEPT.	SERIAL NUMBER	NAME	HOURS WORKED	NET PAY
1	1475176	P ACKLEY	42.1	$215.67
	2497561	A BECKER	47.1	$462.54
	3948252	N CHAPMAN	34.1	$276.84
	4987124	E FELS	43.0	$424.31
	8526941	H KUBO	31.9	$315.20
	9247617	G WITT	51.4	$610.40
		TOTAL FOR DEPARTMENT 1		$2,304.96*
2	1472481	B ANCHETA	35.2	$324.21
	2759415	D BLACK	41.5	$410.51
	4107151	S CHOW	48.2	$574.27
	4326415	M EISNER	37.6	$242.50
	6929412	F SACKS	31.8	$204.60
		TOTAL FOR DEPARTMENT 2		$1,756.09*
3	2468015	T BARRET	41.8	$412.60
	3461915	M KARL	42.7	$432.75
	4671421	Y LERNER	31.5	$261.72
	5176234	J MCFADDEN	48.9	$515.72
	8349512	R STERNBERG	52.5	$672.42
	9567415	H WALKER	41.2	$412.62
		TOTAL FOR DEPARTMENT 3		$2,707.83*
1	1475176	P ACKLEY	42.1	$215.67
	2497561	A BECKER	47.1	$462.54
	3948252	N CHAPMAN	34.1	$276.84
	4987124	E FELS	43.0	$424.31
	8526941	H KUBO	31.9	$315.20
	9247617	G WITT	51.4	$610.40
		TOTAL FOR DEPARTMENT 1		$2,304.96*
2	1472481	B ANCHETA	35.2	$324.21
	2759415	D BLACK	41.5	$410.51
	4107151	S CHOW	48.2	$574.27
	4326415	M EISNER	37.6	$242.50
	6929412	F SACKS	31.8	$204.60
		TOTAL FOR DEPARTMENT 2		$1,756.09*
3	2468015	T BARRET	41.8	$412.60
	3461915	M KARL	42.7	$432.75
	4671421	Y LERNER	31.5	$261.72

DEPT.	SERIAL NUMBER	NAME	HOURS WORKED	NET PAY
3	5176234	J MCFADDEN	48.9	$515.72
	8349512	R STERNBERG	52.5	$672.42
	9567415	H WALKER	41.2	$412.62
		TOTAL FOR DEPARTMENT 3		$2,707.83*
1	1475176	P ACKLEY	42.1	$215.67
	2497561	A BECKER	47.1	$462.54
	3948252	N CHAPMAN	34.1	$276.84
	4987124	E FELS	43.0	$424.31
	8526941	H KUBO	31.9	$315.20
	9247617	G WITT	51.4	$610.40
		TOTAL FOR DEPARTMENT 1		$2,304.96*
2	1472481	B ANCHETA	35.2	$324.21
	2759415	D BLACK	41.5	$410.51
	4107151	S CHOW	48.2	$574.27
	4326415	M EISNER	37.6	$242.50
	6929412	F SACKS	31.8	$204.60
		TOTAL FOR DEPARTMENT 2		$1,756.09*
3	2468015	T BARRET	41.8	$412.60
	3461915	M KARL	42.7	$432.75
	4671421	Y LERNER	31.5	$261.72
	5176234	J MCFADDEN	48.9	$515.72
	8349512	R STERNBERG	52.5	$672.42
	9567415	H WALKER	41.2	$412.62
		TOTAL FOR DEPARTMENT 3		$2,707.83*

                                        $20,306.64**

Exercises

1. The Report Writer feature provides the facility for producing reports by specifying the _____ appearance of a report rather than requiring the specifications for the detailed _____ necessary to produce the report.

2. A _____ of levels is used in defining the logical organization of the report.

3. Each report is divided into _____ groups which in turn are divided into a sequence of _____.

4. The _____ report group items are the basic element of the report.

5. Control _____ and _____ occur automatically when the machine senses a control break.

6. _____ headings at the beginning of the report as well as _____ at the end of the report can be printed as the report is being prepared.

7. _____ and _____ counters are incremented automatically as the report is being prepared.

8. The Report Writer feature can place data into _____ storage where it may be used for subsequent _____ printing in a specified format.

9. The Report Writer feature allows the programmer to describe the report _____.

10. A _____ section must be added at the end of the Data Division to define the format of each finished report.

11. The _____ clause is required in every FD entry to list the name of the report to be produced.

12. The Report Section must begin on a _____ line by itself.

13. The Report Section describes the _____ aspects of the report format and the _____ characteristics of the items of the report.

14. The report description entry contains information pertaining to the _____ format of the report.

15. The _____ must be specified in the Report clause of the file description entry.

16. The Code clause is used when _____ than one report is written for the file.

17. A _____ is a data item that is tested each time a detail group is to be written.

18. All level totals are printed in _____ in which they are written with the exception of the _____ total.

19. The _____ clause describes the physical format of a page of the report.

20. The _____ and _____ are numeric counters generated automatically by the Report Writer feature.
21. The Page-Counter clause may be referred to by _____ clauses and _____ statements.
22. The Page-Counter clause is set to _____ initially by the _____ statement in the Procedure Division.
23. The Line-Counter is automatically set to _____ initially by the Initiate statement in the Procedure Division.
24. The value of a Line Counter during any Procedure Division test represents the number of the _____ line used by the previous group.
25. The report group description entry specifies the _____ of a particular report group of the individual _____ within a report group.
26. The Line clause indicates the _____ or _____ line number of this entry in reference to the page or previous entry.
27. Absolute line number entries must be indicated in _____ order and cannot be preceded by a _____ line number.
28. The _____ clause is used to indicate an automatic skip to the next page before the _____ of the next group.
29. The Next Group clause is used to define the line control _____ the printing of the current group being processed.
30. Any report group other than _____ is automatically generated by the Report Writer feature.
31. Nothing precedes a _____ entry and nothing follows a _____ entry within a report.
32. A Final total control break can be designated only once for _____ or _____ entries within a report.
33. The _____ entry is produced only once at the beginning of the report during the execution of the first _____ statement.
34. The _____ entry indicates that the report group is to be produced for each Generate statement.
35. _____ is the only Usage option that can be specified for an elementary or group item in a report group description entry.
36. The Column clause indicates the _____ character of the printing position.
37. The Group Indicate clause specifies that the elementary item is to be printed only on the _____ occurrence of the item after any _____ or _____ break.
38. The Reset clause causes the _____ counter in the elementary item to be reset to _____ on a _____.
39. The Source clause specifies a data item to be _____ or to be _____.

40. The Sum clause is used to cause automatic _____ of data and may appear only in an _____ item entry of a _____ report group.

41. A _____ declarative may be written in the Declaratives section of the Procedure Division if the programmer wishes to _____ or manipulate the data in any manner before it is printed on a report.

42. The _____ statement begins processing of a report.

43. The Initiate statement does not _____ the file with which the report is associated.

44. The Generate statement is used to _____ a report and link the _____ to the Report Writer described in the _____ of the Data Division at process time.

45. The Generate statement does all the _____ operations of the Report Writer feature.

46. The identifier of a Generate statement must be a _____ report group to produce detailed reporting.

47. If the identifier of a Generate statement is a Report entry, a _____ report is produced without any detailed printing of the items.

48. The Terminate statement is used to terminate the processing of a _____ _____ and to produce all _____ associated with the report.

49. A Terminate statement does not _____ the files.

50. The _____ statement specifies Procedure Division statements that are executed just before the named report group is processed.

51. The _____ statement, when present, must immediately follow a section header in the _____ portion of the Procedure Division.

Answers

1. PHYSICAL, PROCEDURES
2. HIERARCHY
3. REPORT, ITEMS
4. DETAIL
5. TOTALS, HEADINGS
6. REPORT, TOTALS
7. LINE, PAGE
8. INTERMEDIATE, OFF-LINE
9. PICTORIALLY
10. REPORT
11. REPORT
12. SEPARATE
13. PHYSICAL, CONCEPTUAL
14. OVERALL
15. REPORT NAME
16. MORE
17. CONTROL
18. SEQUENCE, FINAL
19. PAGE LIMIT
20. PAGE-COUNTER, LINE-COUNTER
21. DATA DIVISION, PROCEDURE DIVISION
22. ONE, INITIATE
23. ZERO
24. LAST
25. CHARACTERISTICS, DATA NAMES

26. ABSOLUTE, RELATIVE
27. ASCENDING, RELATIVE
28. NEXT PAGE, FIRST LINE
29. FOLLOWING
30. TYPE DETAIL
31. REPORT HEADING, REPORT FOOTING
32. CONTROL HEADING, CONTROL FOOTING
33. REPORT HEADING, GENERATE
34. DETAIL
35. DISPLAY
36. LEFTMOST
37. FIRST, CONTROL, PAGE
38. SUM, ZERO, CONTROL BREAK
39. PRINTED, SUMMED
40. SUMMATION, ELEMENTARY, CONTROL FOOTING
41. USE BEFORE REPORTING, ALTER
42. INITIATE
43. OPEN
44. PRODUCE, PROCEDURE DIVISION, REPORT SECTION
45. AUTOMATIC SUMMATION
46. DETAIL
47. SUMMARY
48. REPORT, CONTROL FOOTINGS
49. CLOSE
50. USE
51. USE, DECLARATIVES

Questions for Review

1. What is the purpose of the Report Writer feature?
2. Describe the principal features of the Report Writer.
3. What is meant by a control break?
4. What is the purpose of the Report clause?
5. What should the entries include in the Report Section?
6. Explain the structure of the Report Section.
7. What is the Code clause used for?
8. How is the Control clause used in the Report Writer feature?
9. What is the importance of the Page Limit clause?
10. Describe the operation of the Page Counter and the Line Counter.
11. What is a Report Group? What are the three types of Report Groups?
12. Explain the use of the Line clause and how it operates.
13. What is the Type clause? Briefly describe the different types of Type clauses.
14. Explain the uses of the following clauses: Column, Group Indicate, Reset, Source.
15. What is the purpose of the Sum clause? How does it operate on data?
16. Explain the purpose and use of the Initiate, Generate and Terminate statements.
17. What are the uses of the Use Before Reporting declarative?

Problems

1. *Match each item with its proper description.*

    _____ 1. Report Section   A. Begins processing of a report.

    _____ 2. Report Descrip-   B. Stops processing of a report.
             tion Entry

    _____ 3. Report Group De-   C. Specification for each report.
             scription Entry

    _____ 4. Initiate Statement   D. Characteristics of particular report group.

    _____ 5. Generate Statement   E. Information pertaining to overall format of a report.

    _____ 6. Terminate Statement   F. Statements executed before report group.

    _____ 7. Use Statement   G. Produces a report.

2. *Match each clause with its proper description.*

    _____ 1. Report   A. Physical format of a page.

    _____ 2. Code   B. Line control following current report group.

    _____ 3. Control   C. First occurrence after control or page break.

    _____ 4. Page Limit   D. Name of report to be produced.

    _____ 5. Line   E. Automatic summation of data.

    _____ 6. Next Group   F. Value to be tested.

    _____ 7. Type   G. More than one report from a file.

    _____ 8. Group Indicate   H. Time that report group is to be generated.

    _____ 9. Source   I. Absolute or relative number.

    _____ 10. Sum   J. Item to be used for report item.

3. *Prepare the Report Writer entries for the following:*

INPUT

OUTPUT

DEPT.	SERIAL NUMBER	N A M E		HOURS WORKED	NET PAY
1	1234560	SMITH	JW	40.1	285.15
1	1892750	JONES	RA	39.6	152.16
1	8929016	MAUS	JB	62.5	182.55
					619.86
2	0238648	GOLDMAN	H	31.7	100.25
2	0333367	WOLFE	DJ	9.5	26.60
					126.85

4. *Prepare the Report Writer entries for the following:*

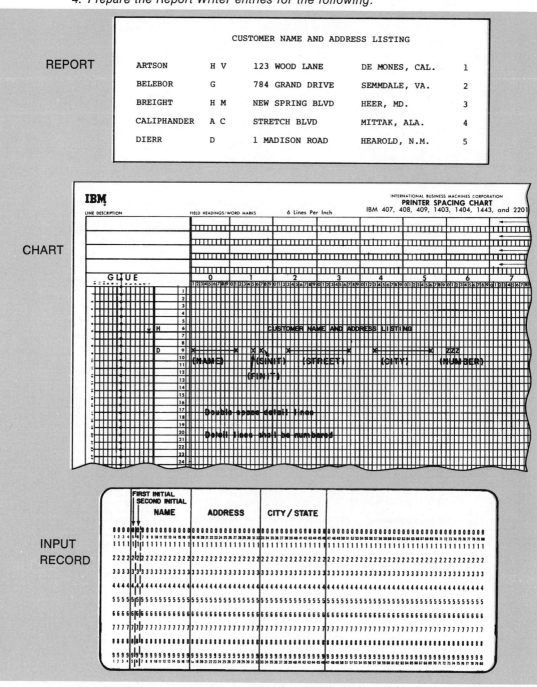

5. *Prepare the Report Writer entries for the following:*

INPUT

Field	Card Columns	
Date	1–6	
Location	7–9	
Department	10–13	
Employee Number	14–17	
Employee Name	18–32	First Initial, second initial, name.
Group Insurance	33–36	XX.XX
Union Dues	37–40	XX.XX
Bonds	41–44	XX.XX
United Fund	45–48	XX.XX
Pension	49–52	XX.XX
Major Medical	53–56	XX.XX
Other	57–60	XX.XX
Total Deductions	61–65	XXX.XX

CALCULATIONS: Cards are in sequence by departments within locations.

    a. Totals by departments for Group Insurance, Union Dues, Bonds, United Fund, Pension, Major Medical, Other and Total Deductions.

    b. Totals by location for Group Insurance, Union Dues, Bonds, United Fund, Pension, Major Medical, Other and Total Deductions.

OUTPUT

6. *Prepare the Report Writer entries for the following:*

INPUT

Field	Card Columns
Date	1–6
Customer Number	7–10
Old Balance	11–15
Purchases	16–20
Payments	21–25
New Balance	26–30

CALCULATIONS:

a. Totals by customer number for Old Balance, Purchases, Payments and New Balance.

b. Final totals for Old Balance, Purchases, Payments and New Balance.

11

Sort Feature

The Sort Feature provides the COBOL programmer with a convenient access to the sorting capacity of the Sort/Merge program by including a COBOL SORT statement and specifying other necessary elements of the Sort Feature in his program. The Sort Feature provides the capability for sorting a file of records according to a set of user-specified keys within each record. Sorting operations for fixed or variable records of varying modes of data representation can be specified by the programmer. Optionally, the programmer may apply some special processing which may consist of addition, deletion, creation, alteration, editing, or other modification of individual records by input or output procedures. This special processing allows the programmer to summarize, delete, shorten, or otherwise alter the records being sorted during the initial or final phases of the sort.

BASIC ELEMENTS OF THE SORT FEATURE

To use the Sort Feature, the COBOL programmer must provide additional information in the Environment, Data, and Procedure Divisions of the source program. The basic elements of the Sort Feature are the SORT statement in the Procedure Division and the Sort-File-Description (SD) entry, with its associated record description entries in the Data Division.

1. The programmer must name in the Environment Division, with SELECT sentences for all files to be used as input to and output from Sort-file.
2. In the Data Division, the programmer must write file description entries (FD) for all files that are to provide input and output to the sort program. In addition, a Sort-File-Description entry (SD) must be written describing the records to be sorted, including the sorting-key fields. The record de-

scription entry associated with the Sort-File-Description may be considered as redefining the records being sorted.

3. The programmer must specify the records being sorted, the sort-key names to be sorted on, and whether the sort is to be in ascending or descending sequence or a mixture of both—that is, sort-keys may be specified as ascending or descending, independent of one another and the sequence of the records will conform to the mixture specified, and whether the records are to be processed before and/or after the sort. The programmer writes a SORT statement in the Procedure Division specifying all of the aforementioned options.

4. The sort-work files are provided by the Sort/Merge program to serve as intermediate work files during the sorting process.

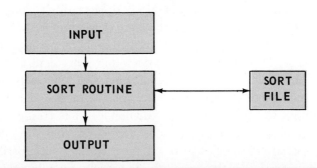

In this illustration the execution of the SORT statement performs the following functions:

1. Opens the input, sort, and output files.

2. Transcribes all of the input file to the sort file.

3. Sorts the file according to the prescribed specifications.

4. Merges the output of the sort to the output file.

5. Closes the input, sort, and output files.

Figure 11–1. Example—Sort with No Input or Output Procedure.

The SORT statement in the Procedure Division is the primary element of a source program that performs one or more sorting operations. A sorting operation is based on the sort-keys named in the SORT statement. A sort-key specifies the fields within a record on which the file is sorted. Sort-keys are defined in the record description clauses associated with the Sort-File-Description

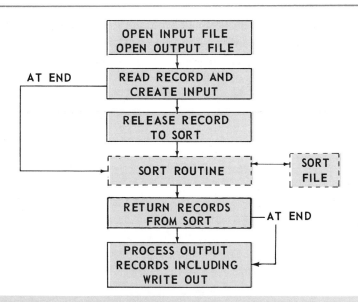

In this operation the following functions are performed:

1. When a SORT statement is executed, control is transferred to the input procedures.

2. In the input procedures, the programmer opens the input file(s) to the sort. Records are read, created, and released to the sort. When the input data is exhausted, the file is to be closed.

3. The sort is performed when all records to be sorted have been passed to the sort by the RELEASE verb and the last logical instruction of the INPUT procedure has been executed.

4. On the final merge pass of the sort, control is given to the programmer to perform output procedures in which the output file is opened, sorted records are processed, and the output file is closed.

5. The sort terminates when all records have been sorted and passed by the RETURN verb to the OUTPUT procedures and the last logical instruction of the OUTPUT procedures have been executed.

Figure 11–2.   Example—Sort with Input and Output Procedures.

(SD) entry. The term sorting operation means not only the manipulation of the Sort Program of sort-work files on the basis of sort-keys designated by the COBOL program, but it also includes the method of making available to, and returning records from, these sort-work files. A *sort-work file* is a collection of records that is involved in the sorting operation as it exists in intermediate device(s). Records are made available to the Sort/Merge program by the USING or INPUT PROCEDURE options of the Sort Statement. Sorted records are returned from the Sort/Merge program by either the GIVING or OUTPUT PROCEDURE options of the SORT statement.

ENVIRONMENT DIVISION

Input-Output Section

File-Control Paragraph

The File-Control paragraph of the Input-Output Section names each file, identifies the file medium, and allows particular hardware assignments. SELECT entries must be written in the File-Control paragraph of the Input-Output Section for all files used within input and output procedures and files specified in the USING or GIVING options of the SORT statement in the Procedure Division. The SELECT clause may be specified for the sort-file. The file-name identifies the sort-file to the compiler.

The presence of the OR clause means the file-name emerging from the sorting operation is either on the assigned hardware units preceding the key word OR, or on the hardware units following the key word OR. At the conclusion of the sorting operation, an indication will be given of which hardware units contain the file. The proper hardware units are addressed when this file is opened for input.

The RESERVE clause may be used in conjunction with the above format. The RESERVE clause is applicable as described in the Environment Division. (See "Reserve" clause in Environment Division.)

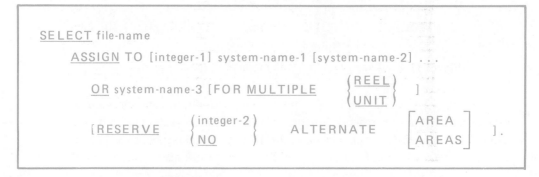

Figure 11–3. Format Select Clause.

SE LECT sort-file-name

    ASSIGN TO [integer-1] system-name-1 [system-name-2] . . .

Figure 11–4. Format Select Clause for Sort File.

I-O-Control Paragraph

    The I-O-Control paragraph of the Input-Output Section specifies the memory areas to be shared by different files.

    Same Record/Sort Area Clause. When the RECORD option is used, the clause specifies that two or more named files are to use the same memory for processing of the current logical record. All of the files may be opened at the same time; however, the logical record of only one of the files can exist in the record area at one time.

    If the SAME SORT AREA clause is used, at least one of the file-names must represent a sort-file. Files that do not represent sort-files may also be named in this clause. This clause specifies that storage is shared as follows:

SAME ${RECORD \atop SORT}$ AREA FOR file-name-1 {file-name-2}. . .

Figure 11–5. Format Same Record/Sort Area Clause.

1. The SAME SORT AREA clause specifies a memory area which will be made available for use in sorting each sort-file named. Thus, any memory area allocated for the sorting of a sort-file is available for reuse in sorting any of the other sort-files.
2. In addition, storage areas assigned to files that do not represent sort-files may be allocated as needed for sorting the sort-files named in the SAME SORT AREA clause. The extent of such allocation will be specified by the implementor.
3. Files other than sort-files do not share the same storage area with each other. If the user wishes these files to share the same storage area with each other,

he must also include in the program a SAME SORT AREA or SAME RECORD AREA naming these files.

4. During the execution of a SORT statement that refers to a sort-file named in this clause, any non-sort-file named in this clause must not be opened.

In the IBM System/360 or 370 computer, the function of the SORT option is to optimize the assignment of storage areas to a given SORT statement. The system handles storage assignments automatically; hence, the SORT option, if given, is treated as a comment.

DATA DIVISION

In the Data Division, the programmer must include file description entries for files to be sorted, sort-file description entries for sort-work files, and record description entries for each.

File Section

The File Section of a program which contains a sorting operation must furnish information concerning the physical structure, identification, and record-names of the records to be sorted. This is provided in the Sort-File-Description only.

Sort-File-Description Entry

The Sort-File-Description entry describes the records to be processed by the Sort Feature. The entry must appear in the File Section for every file named as the first operand of a SORT statement.

SD

A COBOL reserved word that must appear at the A margin. The level indicator SD identifies the beginning of the Sort-File-Description and must precede the file-name.

Sort-File Name

A programmer supplied name that is used in the Sort Feature. The SORT statement in the Procedure Division specifies this name. All rules for data-names apply, and it must not be qualified or subscripted.

```
SD sort-file-name
   [RECORDING MODE IS mode]
   [RECORD CONTAINS [integer-1 TO]
   integer-2 CHARACTERS]
   DATA  {RECORD IS   } record-name ...
         {RECORDS ARE }
```

Figure 11–6. Format Sort-File-Description Entry.

Data Record and Record Contains Clauses

These clauses follow the same rules prescribed for File Section entries in the Data Division. (See "Data Record and Record Contains" entries in the Data Division.)

Record Description Entry

The format of the Record Description entry will vary according to the type of item being described. All rules for Record Description entries in the Data Division apply to this entry. (See "Record Description Entry" in the Data Division.)

Sort Keys

Sort-Keys are identified by data-names assigned to each field involved in the sorting operation.

Rules Governing the Use of Sort-Keys
1. The keys must be physically located in the same position and must have the same data format in every logical record of the sort-file.
2. Key items must not contain an OCCURS clause or be subordinate to entries that contain an OCCURS clause.
3. A maximum of 12 keys may be specified. The total length of all the keys must not exceed 256 bytes.
4. All keys must be at a fixed displacement from the beginning of a record; that is, they cannot be located after a variable table in a record.
5. All key fields must be located within the first 4,092 bytes of a logical record.
6. The data-names describing the keys may be qualified.

PROCEDURE DIVISION

The Procedure Division must contain a SORT statement to describe the sorting operation and, optionally, any necessary input and output procedures. The procedure-names constituting the input and output procedures are specified in the SORT statements.

The Procedure Division may contain more than one SORT statement appearing anywhere except in the Declaratives portion or in the input or output procedures associated with the SORT statement.

Sort Statement

The SORT statement provides the information necessary to execute the SORT feature.

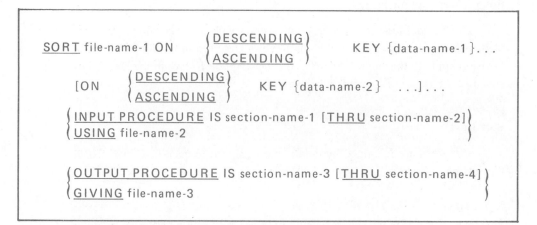

Figure 11–7.   Format Sort Statement.

Functions of the SORT Statement
1. Directs the sorting operation to obtain the necessary records to be sorted either from an INPUT PROCEDURE or the USING file.
2. The records are then sorted on a set of specified keys.
3. After the last sort is completed, the sorted records are made available to either an OUTPUT PROCEDURE or to the GIVING file.

```
SORT    SALES-RECORDS    ON    ASCENDING    KEY
    CUSTOMER-NUMBER, DESCENDING KEY DATE,

        USING FN-1,
        GIVING FN-2.
```

Figure 11–8. Example—Sort Statement.

File-name-1

The name given in a Sort-File-Description entry in the Data Division that describes the records to be sorted.

Ascending or Descending

One of these clauses must be included (both may be included) to specify the sequence of records to be sorted. The sequence is applicable to all sort-keys immediately following the clause. More than one data-name may be specified for sorting after the ASCENDING or DESCENDING word. Every data-name used must have been described in a clause associated with the Sort-File-Description entry. Sort-keys are always listed from left to right in order of decreasing significance regardless of whether they are ASCENDING or DESCENDING. The sort-keys must be specified in the logical sequence that the records are to be sorted.

When ASCENDING clause is used, the sorted sequence is from the lowest value of the key to the highest value, according to the collating sequence for the COBOL character set.

When DESCENDING clause is used, the sorting sequence is from the highest value of the key to lowest value, according to the collating sequence for the COBOL character set.

Data-Name

This is the data-name assigned to each sort-key; it is required in every statement.

Rules Governing the Use of Data-Names
1. More than one data-name may be specified after the ASCENDING or DESCENDING options.

2. The same data-name must not be used twice in the same SORT statement.
3. Every data-name must have been defined in a Record Description entry associated with the Sort Description entry.
4. The sort-keys are specified in the desired order of sorting.

Input Procedure

The presence of an INPUT PROCEDURE indicates that the programmer has written an input procedure to process the records before they are sorted. This procedure is included in the Procedure Division in one or more sections. This procedure passes one record at a time to the Sort Feature after it has completed its processing.

Section-name-1 is the name of the first or only section in the main program that contains the input procedures. This section is required if the INPUT PROCEDURE is used.

Section-name-2 is the name of the last section and is required if the procedure terminates in a section other than that in which it was started.

The INPUT PROCEDURE consists of one or more sections that are written into a source program.

Rules Governing the Use of Input Procedures
1. The INPUT PROCEDURE can include any statements needed to select, create, or modify records.
2. Control must not be passed on to an INPUT PROCEDURE unless the related SORT statement is executed, because the RELEASE statement in the INPUT PROCEDURE has no meaning unless it is controlled by a SORT statement.
3. The INPUT PROCEDURE must not include any SORT statements.
4. Any files used as sort-work files may not be opened or referred to by an INPUT PROCEDURE.
5. The INPUT PROCEDURE must build the records to be sorted one at a time. The record must have been described and assigned a data-name in the record description entry associated with the Sort Description entry.
6. The INPUT PROCEDURE must make the record available to the sorting operation after it has been processed. A RELEASE statement is used for this purpose.
7. After all the records have been released to the sorting operation, the INPUT PROCEDURE must transfer control to the last statement in the INPUT PROCEDURE to terminate the procedure.

8. The INPUT PROCEDURE must not contain any transfers of control to points outside the INPUT PROCEDURE.

9. The remainder of the Procedure Division must not contain any transfer of control to points inside the INPUT PROCEDURES (with the exception of the return of control from a Declarative section).

If an INPUT PROCEDURE is specified, control is passed to the INPUT PROCEDURE when the SORT program input phase is ready to receive the first record. The compiler inserts a return mechanism at the end of the last section of the INPUT PROCEDURE, and when control passes the last statement in the INPUT PROCEDURE, the records that have been released to file-name-1 are sorted. The RELEASE statement transfers records from the INPUT PROCEDURE to the input phase of the sort operation. (See "Release" statement.)

Using

The USING option indicates that the records to be sorted are all in one file and are to be passed to the sorting operation as one unit when the SORT statement is executed. If the option is used, all records to be sorted must be in the same files.

If this option is used, all the records in file-name-2 are transferred automatically to file-name-1. At the time of the execution of the SORT statement, file-name-2 must not be open. File-name-2 must be a standard sequential file. For the USING option, the compiler will automatically OPEN, READ, RELEASE, and CLOSE file-name-2 without the programmer specifying these functions.

Output Procedure

This procedure indicates that the programmer has written an OUTPUT PROCEDURE to process the sorted records. This procedure is included in the Procedure Division in the form of one or more sections. The procedure returns records one at a time from the Sort Feature after they have been sorted.

Section-name-3 is the name of the first or only section in the main program that contains the OUTPUT PROCEDURE. This section is required if the output procedures are used.

Section-name-4 is the name of the last section that contains output procedures and is required if the procedure terminates in a section other than the one in which it started.

The OUTPUT PROCEDURE consists of one or more sections that are written into a source program.

Rules Governing the Use of Output Procedures

1. The OUTPUT PROCEDURE can include any statement necessary to select, modify, or copy the sorted records being returned one at a time in sorted order from the sort-file.
2. Control must not be passed to the OUTPUT PROCEDURE, except when a related SORT statement is being executed, because RETURN statements in the OUTPUT PROCEDURE have no meaning unless they are controlled by the SORT statement.
3. The OUTPUT PROCEDURE must not contain any SORT statements.
4. Any files used as sort-files may not be opened or referred to by the OUTPUT PROCEDURE.
5. Records must be obtained one at a time from Sort/Merge program over the RETURN statement. Once a record is returned, the previously returned record is no longer available.
6. The OUTPUT PROCEDURE must manipulate the returned sorted record by referring to the data record that has been described and assigned a data-name in the record description entry. If the records are to be written on an output file, the programmer must provide the appropriate OPEN statement prior to the execution of the SORT statement or the OUTPUT PROCE-DURE itself.
7. The OUTPUT PROCEDURE must not contain any transfer of control out-side the OUTPUT PROCEDURE.
8. The remainder of the Procedure Division must not contain any transfers of control to points inside the OUTPUT PROCEDURE (with the exception of the return of control from a Declaratives section).
9. After all the records have been returned by the Sort Feature, and the OUT-PUT PROCEDURE attempts to execute another RETURN statement, the AT END clause of the RETURN statement will be executed. The AT END clause should direct control of the program to the last statement of the OUTPUT PROCEDURE to terminate the OUTPUT PROCEDURE.

If an OUTPUT PROCEDURE is specified, control passes to it after file-name-1 has been placed in sequence by the SORT statement. The compiler inserts a return mechanism at the end of the last section of the OUTPUT PRO-CEDURE. When control passes the last statement in the OUTPUT PROCE-DURE, the return mechanism provides for the termination of the sort and then passes control to the next statement after the SORT statement.

When all records are sorted, control is passed to the OUTPUT PROCE-DURE. The RETURN statement in the OUTPUT PROCEDURE is a request for the next record. (See "Return" statement.)

Giving

The GIVING option indicates where the records are to be placed after sorting. If this option is used, all sorted records will be placed in one file. If this option is used, all sorted records in file-name-1 are automatically transferred to file-name-3. At the time of execution of the SORT statement, file-name-3 must not be open. File-name-3 must name a standard sequential file. For the GIVING option, the compiler will OPEN, RETURN, WRITE, and CLOSE file-name-3 without the programmer specifying these functions.

(*Note:* The SORT statements and INPUT and OUTPUT PROCE-DURES are permitted anywhere in the Procedure Division except in the Declaratives Section.)

Release Statement

The RELEASE statement transfers records from the INPUT PROCE-DURE to the input phase of the sort operation.

RELEASE sort-record-name [FROM identifier]

Figure 11–9.   Format Release Statement.

RELEASE INPUT-RECORD.

RELEASE RECORD-ONE.

Figure 11–10.   Example—Release Statement.

Rules Governing the Use of the Release Statement
1. A RELEASE statement may only be used within the range of an INPUT PROCEDURE.
2. If the INPUT PROCEDURE option is specified, the RELEASE statement must be included within the given set of procedures.
3. Sort-record-name must be the name of a logical record in the associated sort-file-description entry and may be qualified.

4. If FROM option is used, the contents of the identifier data area are moved to the record-name, then the contents of sort-record-name are released to the sort-file. Moving takes place according to the rules of the MOVE statement with the CORRESPONDING option. The information in the record area is no longer available, but the information in the data area associated with identifier is available.

5. After the RELEASE statement is executed, the logical record is no longer available. When control passes from the INPUT PROCEDURE, the file consists of all those records that were placed in it by the execution of the RELEASE statement.

6. Sort-record-name and identifier must not refer to the same storage area.

Return Statement

The RETURN statement causes individual records to be obtained from the sorting operation after the records have been sorted and indicates what action is to be taken with each sorted record.

<u>RETURN</u> sort-file-name RECORD [<u>INTO</u> identifier]

    AT <u>END</u> imperative-statement

Figure 11–11. Format Return Statement.

```
RETURN FILE-ONE AT END GO TO END-PROGRAM.

RETURN FILE-SORT AT END GO TO LAST.
```

Figure 11–12. Example—Return Statement.

Rules Governing the Use of the Return Statement

1. Sort-file-name must be described by a Sort File Description entry in the Data Division.

2. A RETURN statement may only be used within the range of an OUTPUT PROCEDURE associated with a SORT statement for a file-name.

3. The INTO option may only be used when the input file contains just one type of record. The storage area associated with identifier and the storage area which is the record area associated with file-name must not be the same storage area.

4. The identifier must be the names of a Working-Storage area or an output record area. Use of the INTO option has the same affect as the MOVE statement for alphanumeric items.

5. The imperative statement in the AT END phrase specifies the action to be taken when all the sorted records have been obtained for the sorting operation.

6. When a file consists of more than one type of logical record, these records automatically share the storage area. This is equivalent to saying that there exists an implicit redefinition of the area, and only the information that is present in the current record is available.

7. After the execution of the imperative statement in the AT END phrase, no RETURN statement may be executed within the OUTPUT PROCEDURE.

CONTROL OF INPUT AND OUTPUT PROCEDURES

The INPUT and OUTPUT PROCEDURES function in a manner similar to option 1 of the PERFORM statement; for example, naming a section in an INPUT PROCEDURE clause causes execution of that section during the sorting operation to proceed as though that section had been the subject of a PERFORM statement. As with the PERFORM statement, the execution of the section is terminated after execution of its last statement.

Return is back to the next statement after the INPUT or OUTPUT PROCEDURES have been executed. The EXIT verb may be used as a common exit point for conditional exits from INPUT or OUTPUT PROCEDURES. If the EXIT verb is used, it must appear as the last paragraph of the INPUT or OUTPUT PROCEDURES (see "Exit" statement).

```
000005    IDENTIFICATION DIVISION.
000010    PROGRAM-ID. CONTEST.
000015    ENVIRONMENT DIVISION.
000016    CONFIGURATION SECTION.
000017    SOURCE-COMPUTER.  IBM-360-H50.
000018    OBJECT-COMPUTER.  IBM-360-H50.
000019    SPECIAL-NAMES. SYSOUT IS PRINTER.
000020    INPUT-OUTPUT SECTION.
000025    FILE-CONTROL.
000030        SELECT NET-FILE-IN ASSIGN TO UT-2400-S-INFILE.
000035        SELECT NET-FILE-OUT ASSIGN TO UT-2400-S-SORTOUT.
000040        SELECT NET-FILE ASSIGN TO UT-2400-S-NETFILE.
```

Figure 11–13. Sample Program Using Sort Feature.

```
000050    DATA DIVISION.
000055    FILE SECTION.
000060    SD  NET-FILE
000065        DATA RECORD IS SALES-RECORD.
000070    01  SALES-RECORD.
000075        05  EMPL-NO          PICTURE 9(6).
000080        05  DEPT             PCITURE 9(2).
000085        05  NET-SALES        PICTURE 9(7)V99.
000090        05  NAME-ADDR        PICTURE X(55).
000095    FD  NET-FILE-IN
000096        LABEL RECORDS ARE OMITTED
000100        DATA RECORD IS NET-CARD-IN.
000105    01  NET-CARD-IN.
000110        05  EMPL-NO-IN       PICTURE 9(6).
000115        05  DEPT-IN          PICTURE 9(2).
000120        05  NET-SALES-IN     PICTURE 9(7)V99.
000125        05  NAME-ADDR-IN     PICTURE X(55).
000130    FD  NET-FILE-OUT
000131        LABEL RECORDS ARE OMITTED
000135        DATA RECORD IS NET-CARD-OUT.
000140    01  NET-CARD-OUT.
000145        05  EMPL-NO-OUT      PICTURE 9(6).
000150        05  DEPT-OUT         PICTURE 9(2).
000155        05  NET-SALES-OUT    PICTURE 9(7)V99.
000160        05  NAME-ADDR-OUT    PICTURE X(55).
000165    PROCEDURE DIVISION.
000170    ELIM-DEPT-7-9-NO-PRINTOUT.
000175        SORT NET-FILE
000180            ASCENDING KEY DEPT, DESCENDING KEY NET-SALES
000185            INPUT PROCEDURE SCREEN-DEPT
000190            GIVING NET-FILE-OUT.
000200    CHECK-RESULTS SECTION.
000205    C-R-1.
000210        OPEN INPUT NET-FILE-OUT.
000215    C-R-2.
000220        READ NET-FILE-OUT AT END GO TO C-R-FINAL.
000225        DISPLAY EMPL-NO-OUT DEPT-OUT NET-SALES-OUT
000230            NAME-ADDR-OUT UPON PRINTER.
000235    C-R-3.
000240        GO TO C-R-2.
000245    C-R-FINAL
000250        CLOSE NET-FILE-OUT.
000255        STOP RUN.
000260    SCREEN-DEPT SECTION.
000265    S-D-1.
000270        OPEN INPUT NET-FILE-IN.
000275    S-D-2.
000280        READ NET-FILE-IN AT END GO TO S-D-FINAL.
000285        DISPLAY EMPL-NO-IN DEPT-IN NET-SALES-IN
000290            NAME-ADDR-IN UPON PRINTER.
000295    S-D-3.
```

Figure 11–13. Continued.

```
000300        IF DEPT-IN IS EQUAL TO 7 OR 9 GO TO S-D-2
000305            ELSE
000310                MOVE NET-CARD-IN TO SALES-RECORD
000315                RELEASE SALES-RECORD
000320                GO TO S-D-2.
000325    S-D-FINAL.
000330        CLOSE NET-FILE-IN.
000335    S-D-END.
000340        EXIT.
```

Figure 11–13 illustrates a sort based on a sales contest. The records to be sorted contain data on salesmen: name and address, employee number, department number, and pre-calculated net sales for the contest period.

The salesman with the highest net sales in each department wins a prize, and smaller prizes are awarded for second highest sales, third highest, etc. The order of the SORT is (1) by department, the lowest numbered first (ASCENDING KEY DEPT); and (2) by net sales within each department, the highest net sales first (DESCENDING KEY NET-SALES).

The records for the employees of departments 7 and 9 are eliminated in an input procedure (SCREEN-DEPT) before sorting begins. The remaining records are then sorted, and the output is placed on another file for use in a later job step.

Figure 11–13.   Continued.

Exercises

Write your answers in the space provided.
1. The Sort feature provides the COBOL programmer a convenient access to the _____ of the _____ program.
2. A file of records are sorted according to a set of user-supplied _____ _____ within each record.
3. A programmer may _____, _____, _____ or otherwise alter the records during the _____ or _____ phases of the sort.
4. The basic element of the Sort feature are the _____ statement in the Procedure Division and the _____ entry in the Data Division.
5. In the Environment Division, the programmer must name with _____ _____ sentences for all files to be used as input to or output from Sort-file.
6. In the Data Division, _____ entries must be written for all files that provide input to the Sort procedure.

7. The programmer must specify the _____ being sorted, the _____ names to be sorted, whether the sort is to be in _____ _____ or _____ sequence or mixture of both and whether the records are to be processed _____ and/or _____ _____ the sort.

8. A sorting operation is based on the _____ named in the _____ _____ statement.

9. A _____ is a collection of records that is involved in the sorting operation as it exists in intermediate devices.

10. Records are made available to the Sort/Merge program by the _____ _____ or _____ option of the Sort statement.

11. Sorted records returned from the Sort/Merge program may be written with the _____ or _____ options of the Sort statement.

12. Select entries in the Environment Division must be written for files used with _____ and _____ procedures and files specified in the _____ or _____ options of the Sort statement in the Procedure Division.

13. When two or more files are to use the same area for processing of the current logical record, the _____ clause in the I-O-Control paragraph is used.

14. All sort keys must be physically located in the _____ position and have the _____ data formats in every logical record.

15. A maximum of _____ sort keys may be specified.

16. The Sort statement provides the necessary information to _____ the Sort feature.

17. Either _____ or _____ clause or both must be included to specify the sequence of records to be sorted.

18. A _____ must be assigned to each sort key.

19. The sort keys are specified in the _____ order of sorting.

20. The Input Procedure indicates a procedure to process records _____ _____ they are sorted.

21. The Input Procedure passes _____ record at a time to the Sort feature.

22. The Input Procedure can include any statements to _____, _____, or _____ records.

23. An Input Procedure must not include any _____ statements.

24. The Using option indicates that all records are in _____ file.

25. For the Using option, the compiler will automatically _____, _____, _____ and _____ the file without the programmer having to specify these operations.

26. The Output Procedure is used to process the _____ records.

27. The _____ option indicates where records are to be placed after sorting.

28. The Sort statements and Input and Output Procedures are permitted anywhere in the Procedure Division except in the _____.

29. The Release statement transfers records from the _____ to the _____ phase of the sort operation.

30. A Release statement must be included and may only be used within the range of _____.

31. The Return statement causes individual records to be obtained from the sorting operation after they have been _____ and indicate what _____ are to be taken with each sorted record.

32. A Return statement must be included and may only be used within the range of _____.

33. When a file contains more than one type of logical record, these records automatically share the _____ storage area.

34. The Input and Output Procedure functions in the same manner as the _____ statement.

35. An _____ verb may be used as a common exit point for the Input or Output procedures.

Answers

1. SORTING CAPACITY, SORT/MERGE
2. KEYS
3. SUMMARIZE, DELETE, SHORTEN, INITIAL, FINAL
4. SORT, SORT-FILE-DESCRIPTION
5. SELECT
6. FILE DESCRIPTION
7. RECORD, SORT KEY, ASCENDING, DESCENDING, BEFORE, AFTER
8. SORT KEYS, SORT
9. SORT WORK FILE
10. USING, INPUT PROCEDURE
11. GIVING, OUTPUT PROCEDURE
12. INPUT, OUTPUT, USING, GIVING
13. SAME RECORD
14. SAME, SAME
15. 12
16. EXECUTE
17. ASCENDING, DESCENDING
18. DATA-NAME
19. DESIRED
20. BEFORE
21. ONE
22. SELECT, CREATE, MODIFY
23. SORT
24. ONE
25. OPEN, READ, RELEASE, CLOSE
26. SORTED
27. GIVING
28. DECLARATIVES SECTION
29. INPUT PROCEDURE, INPUT
30. INPUT PROCEDURE
31. SORTED, ACTIONS
32. OUTPUT PROCEDURE
33. SAME
34. PERFORM
35. EXIT

Questions for Review

1. What is the purpose of the Sort feature?
2. What are the basic elements of the Sort feature?
3. What is the purpose of the Sort Description entry and how it differs from a File Description entry?
4. What are the sort keys and how are they used in the Sort feature?
5. What is a Sort statement and what are its main functions?
6. When is the Using option used?
7. What is an Input Procedure and how does it operate with the Sort feature?
8. What is the function of the Release statement?
9. What is an Output Procedure and how does it operate with the Sort feature?
10. What is the function of the Return statement?
11. In what manner are Input and Output Procedures and Perform statements alike?

Problems

1. *Match the item with its proper description.*

_____ 1. Using
_____ 2. Sort Keys
_____ 3. Output Procedure
_____ 4. Return Statement

_____ 5. Select Entry
_____ 6. Input Procedure

_____ 7. Giving

_____ 8. Release Statement
_____ 9. Sort Description Entry

_____ 10. Sort Statement

A. Process records before sorting.
B. Execute the Sort feature.
C. Specify files in Sort statement.
D. Causes records to be transferred to sort.
E. Describes the records to be sorted.
F. Where records are to be placed after sort.
G. Causes records to be obtained from sort.
H. Process sorted records.
I. Data-names assigned to fields in sort.
J. Records in one file.

2. *Given the following information:*

APE FORMAT:

IRG	Dept. No.	Clock No.	Name	SS#	YTD gross	YTD W/T	YTD fica	IRG
	2 pos.	3 pos.	20 pos.	9 pos.	7 pos.	6 pos.	5 pos.	

52 character logical record, fixed length
10 logical records/block

Write a program to

a. Input the tape record.
b. Sort the record on Social Security Number sequence.
c. Output the tape record in the some format as the input record.

3. *Given the following information:*

CARD FORMAT

Dept. No.	Clock No.		Name		Soc. Sec. No.		Current gross	Current W/T	Current fica	code
1-2	3-5	6	7	26	27-35		62-68	69-74	75-79	80

TAPE FORMAT

IRG	Dept. No.	Clock No.	Name	Soc. Sec. No.	Gross	W/T	Fica	IRG
	2 pos.	3 pos.	20 pos.	9 pos.	7 pos.	6 pos.	5 pos.	

52 characters per logical record, fixed length
5 records per block

Write the program to accomplish the following:

a. Input the card record.
b. Sort record to Department Number and Clock Number sequence.
c. Write card record on tape output.

4. *Given the following information:*

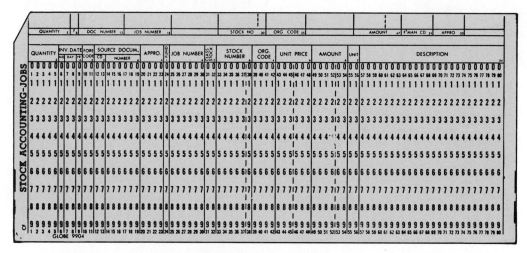

Write the necessary program to accomplish the following:

a. Read in the input records.
b. Multiply quantity by unit price giving amount.
c. Sorting the records into stock number sequence.
d. Out put a report on the printer as follows:

Record Positions	Field	Print Positions	
31–32	Class Stock	3–4	
33–38	Stock Number	6–11	
55–56	Unit	13–14	
57–80	Description	16–39	
1–5	Quantity	41–46	XX,XXX
43–48	Unit Price	48–55	$XXX.XXX
49–54	Amount	58–66	$X,XXX.XX

Final total of all amounts.

5. *Using the following information, write a program to accomplish the following:*

a. Read the input record.
b. Calculate the net pay by multiplying hours by the rate.
c. Sort records into Department and Serial Number sequence.
d. Punch card using the same format as the input record: including net pay.
e. Write report per format using the Report Writer Feature.

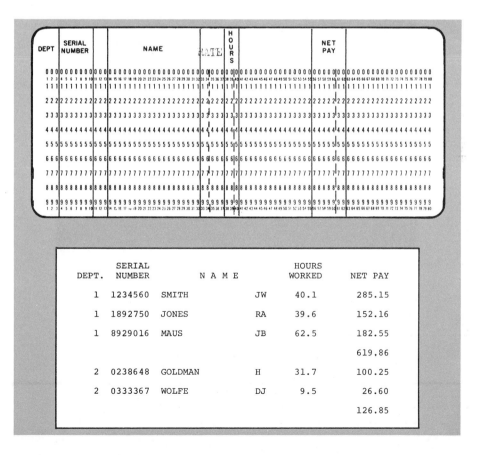

DEPT.	SERIAL NUMBER	N A M E		HOURS WORKED	NET PAY
1	1234560	SMITH	JW	40.1	285.15
1	1892750	JONES	RA	39.6	152.16
1	8929016	MAUS	JB	62.5	182.55
					619.86
2	0238648	GOLDMAN	H	31.7	100.25
2	0333367	WOLFE	DJ	9.5	26.60
					126.85

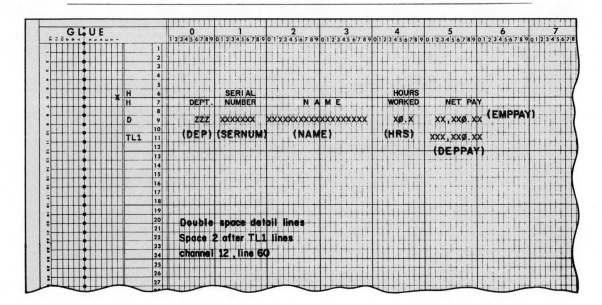

12

Mass Storage Devices (Direct Access)

INTRODUCTION

"In-Line" processing denotes the ability of the data processing system to process data as soon as it becomes available. This implies that the input data does not have to be sorted in any manner, manipulated, or edited before it can be entered into a system, whether the input consists of transactions of a single application or of many applications.

Mass storage direct-access devices have made in-line processing feasible for many applications. While sorting transactions are still advantageous before certain processing runs, in most instances the necessity for presorting has been eliminated. The ability to process data "in-line" provides solutions to problems which heretofore were thought impractical.

Mass direct-access storage enables the user to maintain current records of diversified applications and to process nonsequential and intermixed data for multiple application areas. The term "direct access" implies access at random by multiple users of data (files, programs, subroutines, programming aids) involving mass storage devices. These storage devices differ in physical appearance, capacity, and speed, but functionally they are similar in terms of data recording, checking, and programming. The direct-access devices used for mass memory storage are disk storage, drum, and data cells. The disk storage is the most popular of the mass storage devices in use today.

PROCESSING TECHNIQUES

Sequential Processing

In sequential processing, input transactions are grouped together and sorted into a predetermined sequence and processed against a master file. When

IBM 2311 Disk Storage Drive.

Removable Disk.

IBM 2302 Disk Storage—Non-Removable Disks.

Figure 12–1. Disk Storage Devices.

information is recorded in magnetic tape or punched cards, the most efficient method of processing is sequential. Mass storage devices are also efficient sequential processors, especially when the percentage of activity against the master file is high.

SEQUENTIAL ACCESS: RANDOM ACCESS:

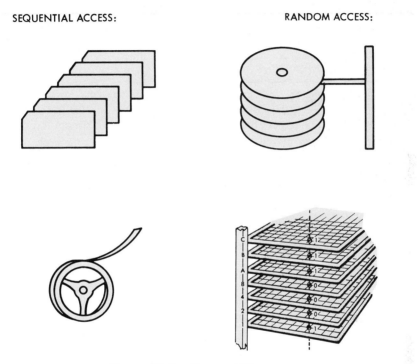

Figure 12–2.   Types of Storage

Random Processing

The processing of detail transactions against a master file regardless of the sequence of the input documents is called random processing. With mass storage devices it can be very efficient, especially if the files are organized in such a manner that each record can be located quickly. It is possible to process input transactions against more than one file in a single run. This saves time both in setup and sorting, and minimizes the control problems, since the transactions are handled less frequently.

The use of mass storage devices makes it possible to select the best processing technique to suit the application. Thus, some applications may be processed sequentially, while those in which the time required to sort, or the delay with the batching process is a material factor, can be processed randomly. Real savings in overall processing time for a job can be made by combining runs in which the same input data affects several files. The detail items can be processed sequentially against a primary file and randomly against the secondary file, all in one run. This is the basis of "in-line" processing.

DATA FILE ORGANIZATIONS

The data file organizations refer to the physical arrangement of data records within a file. To give the programmer maximum flexibility in reading and writing data sets from mass storage devices, the following methods of data organization are most commonly used for disk operations. Sequential (Standard), Indexed Sequential, and Direct (Random).

Sequential Organization

In a sequential file, records are organized solely on the basis of their successive physical locations in the file. The records are written one after the other—track by track, cylinder by cylinder—at successively higher locations. The records are usually, but not necessarily, in sequence according to their keys (control numbers). The records are usually read or updated in the same sequence in which they appear.

Updating a sequential file that is located on a mass storage device is more efficient than updating a file located on a magnetic tape or punched cards. After the file is opened, the record can be read, updated, and written back in the same location in the file without creating a new file. Thus the file can be used for both input and output activities without the necessity for opening and closing files between operations.

A file on a mass storage device may have the same standard sequential data file organization just as any of the unit record or magnetic tape files. The

RECORD 1	RECORD 2	RECORD 3	RECORD 4	RECORD 5

Figure 12–3. Sequentially Organized Data Set.

mass storage file, however, may be differently organized so that any record may be accessed merely by specifying the "key" or unique field that tells the system where the desired record is located. This differs from standard sequential organization in that the desired records can be accessed at random without accessing all previous records.

Creating a Standard Sequential Disk File

ENVIRONMENT DIVISION. In order to specify that a file will be on a mass storage device, certain entries must be specified in the SELECT clause.

Select Clause. A file-name (programmer supplied) specified for the file. The SELECT clause for a sequential disk file should contain the following.

Assign Clause. The file assigned to a particular mass storage device.

Class Indicator (UT). A two-character field that specifies the device class. A class indicator for a file on a mass storage device may be either DA (Direct Access) or UT (Utility). Since sequential disk files are used in the same manner as magnetic tape files, the class indicator ordinarily used for sequential disk files would be UT.

Device Number (2311). A four- or five-character field used to specify a particular device within a device class. This device number specifies that the file is to be located on a model 2311 disk unit.

Organization (S). A one-character field that indicates the file organization. The organization symbol "S" indicates that the file will have sequential organization.

Name. A one- to eight-character field specifying the external name by which the file is known to the system. If the name is not specified, the symbolic name (SYSnn) is used as the external name. This name (SYSnn) may be used as the first name in the system name, in which case this would represent the symbolic unit to which the file is assigned.

```
      SELECT DISK-SEQ
            ASSIGN TO UT-2311-S-SEQUEND.

FD  DISK-SEQ
      LABEL RECORDS ARE STANDARD
      BLOCK CONTAINS 4 RECORDS.
```

Figure 12–4.   Example—Environment and Data Division Entries for a Sequential Disk File.

DATA DIVISION. The Data Division entries required for sequential disk files are as follows.

FD—File-name of disk file.

Block Contains—This clause is required if records are blocked.

Label Records Are Standard—All files in direct-access devices must have standard labels.

PROCEDURE DIVISION. To create a sequential file, you must use an output file and a WRITE statement.

Write Statement. The INVALID option of the WRITE statement must be used when a sequential disk file is being created. The statement following the reserved word INVALID is activated when an attempt is made to write beyond the limit of space reserved for the file. An appropriate action to be specified in an INVALID option might be a branch to a routine that will display a message on the console to indicate that the area is filled. The amount of space reserved for a file is usually specified on job-control cards according to the operating system in a particular installation.

Updating a Standard Sequential Disk File

After a sequential disk file has been created, it may be maintained by updating the records and placing them back on the file. This can be accomplished only if the file has been opened with the I-O option. The I-O option must be used if the sequential file is used for both input and output operations.

The I-O option may be specified only for files that are stored on direct-access devices. The INVALID option of the WRITE statement is unnecessary when the sequential file has been opened as I-O because there is no

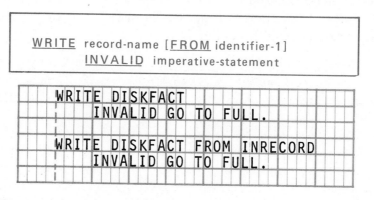

```
WRITE record-name [FROM identifier-1]
      INVALID imperative-statement
```

```
WRITE DISKFACT
      INVALID GO TO FULL.

WRITE DISKFACT FROM INRECORD
      INVALID GO TO FULL.
```

Figure 12–5. Format Write Statement with Invalid Option—Examples Write Statement with Invalid Option.

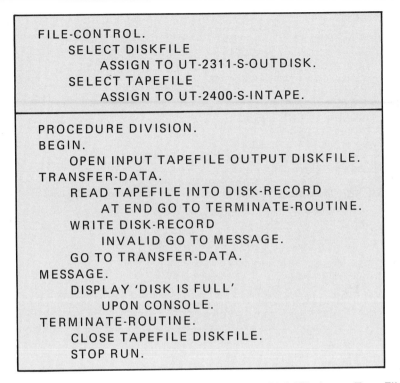

```
FILE-CONTROL.
     SELECT DISKFILE
          ASSIGN TO UT-2311-S-OUTDISK.
     SELECT TAPEFILE
          ASSIGN TO UT-2400-S-INTAPE.

PROCEDURE DIVISION.
BEGIN.
     OPEN INPUT TAPEFILE OUTPUT DISKFILE.
TRANSFER-DATA.
     READ TAPEFILE INTO DISK-RECORD
          AT END GO TO TERMINATE-ROUTINE.
     WRITE DISK-RECORD
          INVALID GO TO MESSAGE.
     GO TO TRANSFER-DATA.
MESSAGE.
     DISPLAY 'DISK IS FULL'
          UPON CONSOLE.
TERMINATE-ROUTINE.
     CLOSE TAPEFILE DISKFILE.
     STOP RUN.
```

Figure 12–6.   Program for Creating a Sequential Disk File from a Tape File

possibility of overfilling the file, since each record is replaced in the same position from which it was accessed.

Indexed Sequential Organization

An indexed sequential organization file is a sequential file with indexes that permit rapid access to individual records as well as rapid sequential processing. The indexes are created and written by the system as the file is created or organized. A key provided by the user precedes each block of data and is used to provide the index. An index sequential file is similar to a sequential file; however, by referring to the indexes maintained with the file, it is possible to quickly locate individual records for random processing. Moreover, a separate area can be set aside for additions making it unnecessary to rewrite the entire file, a process that would be required for sequential processing. Although the records are not maintained in key sequence, the indexes are referred to in order to re-

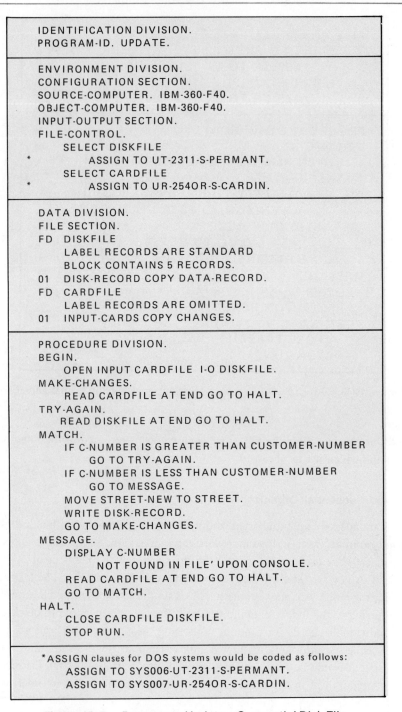

```
        IDENTIFICATION DIVISION.
        PROGRAM-ID. UPDATE.

        ENVIRONMENT DIVISION.
        CONFIGURATION SECTION.
        SOURCE-COMPUTER. IBM-360-F40.
        OBJECT-COMPUTER. IBM-360-F40.
        INPUT-OUTPUT SECTION.
        FILE-CONTROL.
            SELECT DISKFILE
 *              ASSIGN TO UT-2311-S-PERMANT.
            SELECT CARDFILE
 *              ASSIGN TO UR-2540R-S-CARDIN.

        DATA DIVISION.
        FILE SECTION.
        FD  DISKFILE
            LABEL RECORDS ARE STANDARD
            BLOCK CONTAINS 5 RECORDS.
        01  DISK-RECORD COPY DATA-RECORD.
        FD  CARDFILE
            LABEL RECORDS ARE OMITTED.
        01  INPUT-CARDS COPY CHANGES.

        PROCEDURE DIVISION.
        BEGIN.
            OPEN INPUT CARDFILE  I-O DISKFILE.
        MAKE-CHANGES.
            READ CARDFILE AT END GO TO HALT.
        TRY-AGAIN.
           READ DISKFILE AT END GO TO HALT.
        MATCH.
            IF C-NUMBER IS GREATER THAN CUSTOMER-NUMBER
                GO TO TRY-AGAIN.
            IF C-NUMBER IS LESS THAN CUSTOMER-NUMBER
                GO TO MESSAGE.
            MOVE STREET-NEW TO STREET.
            WRITE DISK-RECORD.
            GO TO MAKE-CHANGES.
        MESSAGE.
            DISPLAY C-NUMBER
                NOT FOUND IN FILE' UPON CONSOLE.
            READ CARDFILE AT END GO TO HALT.
            GO TO MATCH.
        HALT.
            CLOSE CARDFILE DISKFILE.
            STOP RUN.

        *ASSIGN clauses for DOS systems would be coded as follows:
            ASSIGN TO SYS006-UT-2311-S-PERMANT.
            ASSIGN TO SYS007-UR-2540R-S-CARDIN.
```

Figure 12–7. Program to Update a Sequential Disk File.

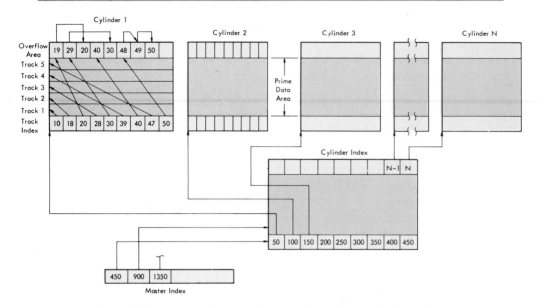

Figure 12–8. Index Structure for an Indexed Sequential Data Set.

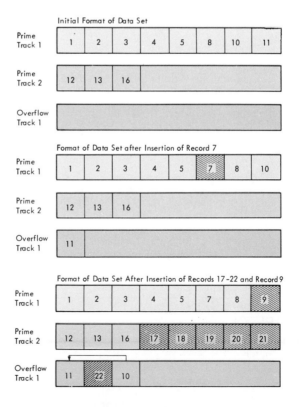

Figure 12–9. Addition of Records to an Indexed Sequential Data Set.

trieve the added records in key sequence, thus making rapid sequential processing possible.

The programming system has control over the location of the individual records in this method of organization. The user need do very little input or output programming—the programming system does most of it since the characteristics of the file are known.

Indexed sequential organization gives the programmer greater flexibility in the operations he can perform on the data file. He has the ability to read or write records in a manner similar to that for sequential organization. He can also read or write individual records whose keys may be in any order, and can add logical records with new keys. The system locates the proper position in the data file for the new record and makes all the necessary adjustments to the indexes.

The indexed sequential file must be stored on a direct-access device. Just as with standard sequential files, the indexed sequential files must be created sequentially. Identify-data in the control field of the record, called "keys," must be in ascending sequence in succeeding records. As the records are written into the file, the system creates indexes based on the key, or control field, in each record to make possible quick location of any record in the file. Thus any record in an indexed sequential file may be accessed by specifying the appropriate key.

In addition to quick access of any record, an advantage of indexed sequential file is that records may be added to any part of the file after it has been created, and the system will keep all records in logical sequence, although some records may technically be in a special "overflow" area. In accessing the file sequentially, the system will access records in logical sequence by key rather than in physical sequence by position on the device.

Creating an Indexed Sequential Disk File

ENVIRONMENT DIVISION. In order to specify that a file will be on a mass storage device, certain entries must be specified in the SELECT clause.

Select Clause. A file-name (programmer supplied) for the file. The SELECT clause for an indexed sequential disk file should contain the following.

```
SELECT PAYROLL-REGISTER
    ASSIGN TO DA-2311-I-PAYFILE
    RECORD KEY IS SOCIAL-SECURITY-NO.
```

Figure 12–10. Example—Select Clause for an Indexed Sequential File.

Class Indicator (DA). The class indicator must be direct-access. All indexed storage files must be stored on a direct-access device.

Device Number (2311). This device number specifies that the file is to be located on a model 2311 disk unit.

Organization (I). This organization symbol indicates that the file has an indexed sequential organization.

Name. The name identifies the external name by which the file is known to the system. If the name is not specified, the symbolic name (SYSnn) is used as the actual external name. This name (SYSnn) may be used as the first name in system-name, in which case this would represent the symbolic unit to which the file is assigned.

Access Mode Clause. The ACCESS MODE clause defines the manner in which the records or a file are to be accessed. If the clause is not specified, ACCESS IS SEQUENTIAL is assumed and records are placed or obtained sequentially. The next logical record is made available from the file when the READ statement is executed, or the next logical record is placed into the file when a WRITE statement is executed. ACCESS IS SEQUENTIAL may be applied to files assigned to magnetic tape, unit record, or direct-access devices.

When the ACCESS IS RANDOM option is used, storage and retrieval are based on an ACTUAL KEY or NOMINAL KEY associated with each record. When the RANDOM option is used, the file must be assigned to a direct-access device.

In creating an indexed sequential disk file, the clause ACCESS IS SEQUENTIAL is optional.

Record Key Clause. The RECORD KEY clause is used to access an indexed sequential file. It specifies the elementary variable within the file record

```
01  WAGE-RECORD.
    02  EMPLOYEE-NUMBER        PICTURE 9(5).
    02  HOURS.
        03  REGULAR            PICTURE 9(3).
        03  OVERTIME           PICTURE 9(3).
    02  WAGES.
        03  REGULAR            PICTURE 9(3).
        03  OVERTIME           PICTURE 9(3).
    02  FILLER                 PICTURE X(61).

SELECT WAGE-FILE
    ASSIGN TO DA-2311-I-WAGESOUT
    RECORD KEY IS EMPLOYEE-NUMBER.
```

Figure 12–11. Example— Record Key Clause.

that identifies the record and is required for all records stored in indexed sequential files.

Any unique elementary variable in the record associated with the indexed sequential file can be specified as the RECORD KEY.

DATA DIVISION. The Data Division entries required for indexed sequential disk files are as follows.

FD—Name of disk file.

Block Contains—This clause required of all records that are blocked.

Label Records Are Standard—All files on direct-access devices must have standard labels.

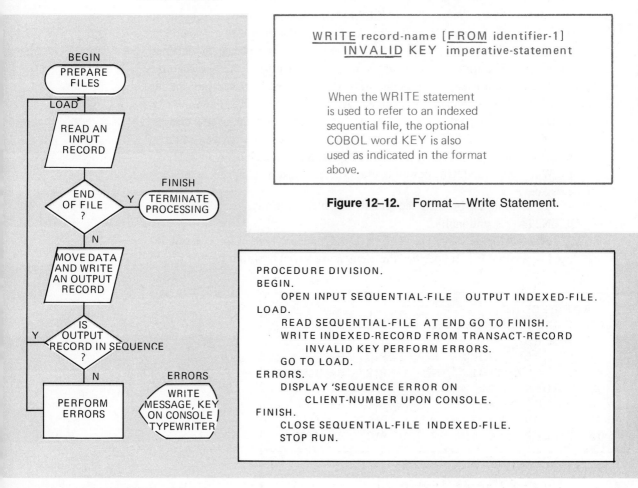

WRITE record-name [FROM identifier-1]
        INVALID KEY imperative-statement

When the WRITE statement
is used to refer to an indexed
sequential file, the optional
COBOL word KEY is also
used as indicated in the format
above.

Figure 12–12.   Format—Write Statement.

```
PROCEDURE DIVISION.
BEGIN.
      OPEN INPUT SEQUENTIAL-FILE   OUTPUT INDEXED-FILE.
LOAD.
      READ SEQUENTIAL-FILE AT END GO TO FINISH.
      WRITE INDEXED-RECORD FROM TRANSACT-RECORD
            INVALID KEY PERFORM ERRORS.
      GO TO LOAD.
ERRORS.
      DISPLAY 'SEQUENCE ERROR ON
            CLIENT-NUMBER UPON CONSOLE.
FINISH.
      CLOSE SEQUENTIAL-FILE  INDEXED-FILE.
      STOP RUN.
```

Figure 12–13.   Example—
Creation of Indexed Sequential File.

PROCEDURE DIVISION. To create an indexed sequential file, you must use an output file and the INVALID KEY option in any WRITE statement.

Write Statement. When the WRITE statement is being used to refer to an indexed sequential file, the optional word KEY must be used. The INVALID KEY option is activated if the key field of the record being written does not

```
IDENTIFICATION DIVISION.
PROGRAM-ID.  CREATEIS.

ENVIRONMENT DIVISION.
CONFIGURATION SECTION.
SOURCE-COMPUTER.  IBM-360-H65.
OBJECT-COMPUTER.  IBM-360-H65.
INPUT-OUTPUT SECTION.
FILE-CONTROL.
     SELECT DISKFILE ASSIGN TO UT-2311-S-INDISK.
     SELECT IND-SEQ ASSIGN TO DA-2311-I-OUTDISK
     RECORD KEY IS RECORD-ID.

DATA DIVISION.
FILE SECTION.
FD  DISKFILE
     LABEL RECORDS ARE STANDARD
     BLOCK CONTAINS 5 RECORDS.
01   DISK-RECORD COPY DATA-RECORD.
FD  IND-SEQ
     LABEL RECORDS ARE STANDARD
     BLOCK CONTAINS 5 RECORDS.
01   IS-RECORD COPY OUT-RECORD.

PROCEDURE DIVISION.
BEGIN.
     OPEN INPUT DISKFILE  OUTPUT IND SEQ.
TRANSFER.
     READ DISKFILE AT END GO TO END-JOB.
     MOVE NAME TO IS-NAME.
     MOVE CUSTOMER-NUMBER TO IS-RECORD-ID.
     MOVE STREET TO IS-STREET.
     MOVE CITYSTATE TO IS-CITYSTATE.
     MOVE PAYRECORD TO IS-PAYRECORD.
     WRITE IS-RECORD INVALID KEY GO TO ERRORS.
     GO TO TRANSFER.
ERRORS.
     DISPLAY 'RECORD NOT WRITTEN ' RECORD-ID
          UPON CONSOLE.
     GO TO TRANSFER
END-JOB.
     DISPLAY 'INDEXED-FILE CREATED ' UPON CONSOLE.
     CLOSE DISKFILE  IND-SEQ.
     STOP RUN.
```

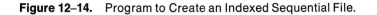

Figure 12–14. Program to Create an Indexed Sequential File.

contain a greater value than the key field of the record just written—that is, a key out of sequence or a duplicate key may generate an INVALID KEY option. An imperative statement after the word INVALID KEY directs the program to an error procedure.

When the WRITE statement with the INVALID KEY option is executed, the key of the record is checked for correct sequence before the record is written. If the INVALID KEY option is activated in an attempt to write a record into an indexed sequential file, that record is not placed into the indexed sequential file. Subsequent records, however, may still be placed into the file. The record with the INVALID KEY may be placed into a sequential file, if desired, for subsequent individual checking of the key. The imperative statement following the words INVALID KEY could direct the program to the proper routine to accomplish this.

Accessing Records From an Indexed Sequential File

It is frequently necessary to access records from an indexed sequential file sequentially. These records may be accessed sequentially, record by record, until the file is closed. This program would be similar to a program for accessing a standard sequential file, with the exception of the File-Control paragraph entries describing file as indexed sequential.

Records in an indexed sequential file may be accessed at a record that is not the first record in a file, continuing until the file is closed. This is not possible in a standard sequential file, but this can be accomplished in an indexed sequential file by specifying the desired beginning key and positioning the file at that desired key prior to the accessing of the record.

Accessing an Indexed Sequential File Sequentially

ENVIRONMENT DIVISION. The Environment Division entries for an indexed sequential file from which all records will be accessed sequentially are identical to the entries required when an indexed sequential file is to be created.

DATA DIVISION. The Data Division entries for an indexed sequential file from which all records will be accessed sequentially are similar to entries previously described for standard and indexed sequential programs.

PROCEDURE DIVISION. The Procedure Division coding is similar to standard sequential accessing of records.

Whenever sequential access of records from an indexed sequential file will begin at some other record than the beginning of the file, the NOMINAL KEY clause must be specified in addition to the RECORD KEY clause in the File-Control paragraph of the Environment Division.

```
FILE-CONTROL.
    SELECT STUDENT-FILE ASSIGN TO DA-2311-I-PERM
        RECORD KEY IS STUDENT-NUMBER.
    SELECT PRINTOUT ASSIGN TO UR-1403-S-PRINT.

PROCEDURE DIVISION.
BEGIN.
    OPEN INPUT STUDENTFILE OUTPUT PRINTOUT.
PROCESSING.
    READ STUDENTFILE AT END GO TO FINAL.
    MOVE STUDENT-NUMBER TO S-NUMBER.
    MOVE CORRESPONDING STUDENT-DATA TO PRINTDATA.
    WRITE PRINTDATA.
    GO TO PROCESSING.
FINAL.
    CLOSE STUDENTFILE PRINTOUT.
    STOP RUN.
```

Figure 12–15. Accessing Records Sequentially in an Indexed Sequential File

Nominal Key Clause. A NOMINAL KEY clause is used with indexed sequential files and specifies an elementary variable described in the Working-Storage Section of the program.

In order to access sequentially the records in an indexed sequential file beginning at some record other than the first record of a file, the value of the NOMINAL KEY variable must be set equal to the RECORD KEY of the record at which the sequential access is to begin. Since the NOMINAL KEY variable must be given a value before accessing of records begins, a value must be set in Working-Storage through the execution of a MOVE, ACCEPT, or VALUE clause.

After the NOMINAL KEY variable has been set to the value of the RECORD KEY variable of the record at which accessing of records is to begin, the indexed sequential file must be positioned so that a READ statement will access the desired record. A START statement is used to position the file. The absence of START statement causes the searching of a file to start at the first record.

Start Statement. The START statement initiates the processing of a segment of a sequentially indexed sequential file at a specified key.

File-name is the name of the indexed sequential file to be processed. The

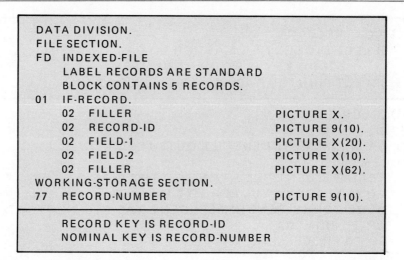

```
DATA DIVISION.
FILE SECTION.
FD  INDEXED-FILE
        LABEL RECORDS ARE STANDARD
        BLOCK CONTAINS 5 RECORDS.
01  IF-RECORD.
        02   FILLER                        PICTURE X.
        02   RECORD-ID                     PICTURE 9(10).
        02   FIELD-1                        PICTURE X(20).
        02   FIELD-2                        PICTURE X(10).
        02   FILLER                         PICTURE X(62).
WORKING-STORAGE SECTION.
77  RECORD-NUMBER                        PICTURE 9(10).

    RECORD KEY IS RECORD-ID
    NOMINAL KEY IS RECORD-NUMBER
```

Figure 12–16.   Example—Record Key and Nominal Key Clauses.

value must be stored in the data-name specified in the NOMINAL KEY clause before executing the START statement.

INVALID KEY option is executed when the value of the NOMINAL KEY at the time the START statement is executed is not equal to some RECORD KEY variable in the file.

A START statement must be executed after the OPEN statement but before the first READ statement. Processing will continue sequentially until a START statement or a CLOSE statement or until the end of file is reached.

If processing is to begin at the first record, a START statement is unnecessary before the first READ statement.

The START statement will be used only to position the file, and the READ statement will access the subsequent records in the file.

```
START file-name   INVALID KEY imperative-statement
```

```
    NOMINAL KEY IS PATIENT-NUMBER
77  PATIENT-NUMBER                    PICTURE X(7).
    MOVE 'A208787' TO PATIENT-NUMBER.
    START PATIENT-FILE INVALID KEY GO TO END-ROUTINE.
```

Figure 12–17.   Format Start Statement and to Position File before Accessing an Indexed Sequential File Sequentially.

A large department store wishes to send a special brochure to selected sample of customers. The manager has decided to make a preliminary listing of some customers. The first fifty customers in the file will be checked and then fifty customers will be checked starting at a key that the operator will key in at the appropriate time. Of those 100 customers, only addresses of those who have had charge accounts for longer time than three years will be listed.

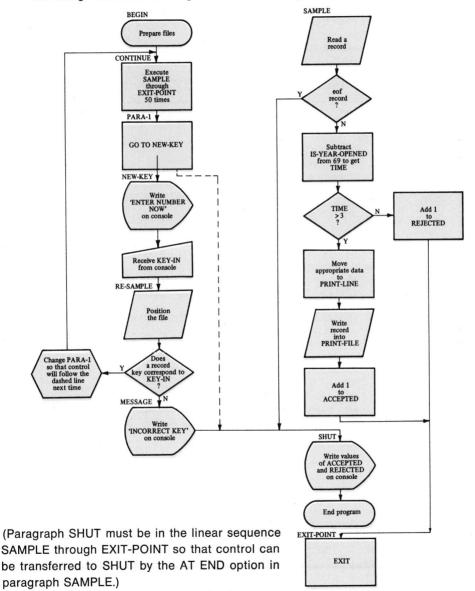

(Paragraph SHUT must be in the linear sequence SAMPLE through EXIT-POINT so that control can be transferred to SHUT by the AT END option in paragraph SAMPLE.)

Figure 12–18.   Example—Program Accessing Records Sequentially from an Indexed Sequential File Starting at Any Point.

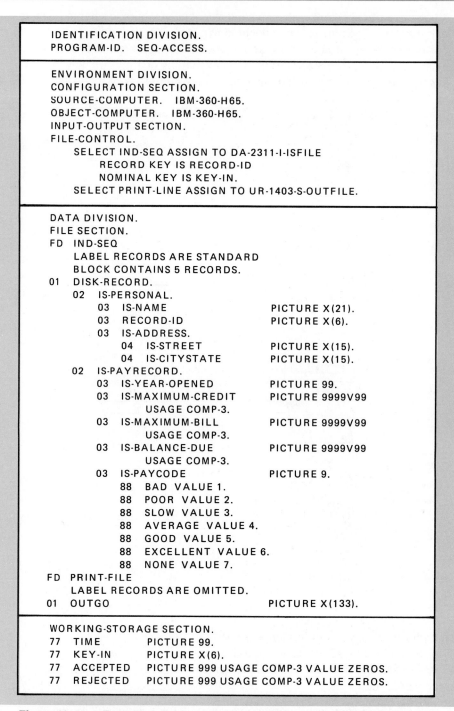

```
IDENTIFICATION DIVISION.
PROGRAM-ID.   SEQ-ACCESS.

ENVIRONMENT DIVISION.
CONFIGURATION SECTION.
SOURCE-COMPUTER.   IBM-360-H65.
OBJECT-COMPUTER.   IBM-360-H65.
INPUT-OUTPUT SECTION.
FILE-CONTROL.
     SELECT IND-SEQ ASSIGN TO DA-2311-I-ISFILE
          RECORD KEY IS RECORD-ID
          NOMINAL KEY IS KEY-IN.
     SELECT PRINT-LINE ASSIGN TO UR-1403-S-OUTFILE.

DATA DIVISION.
FILE SECTION.
FD   IND-SEQ
     LABEL RECORDS ARE STANDARD
     BLOCK CONTAINS 5 RECORDS.
01   DISK-RECORD.
     02   IS-PERSONAL.
          03   IS-NAME                PICTURE X(21).
          03   RECORD-ID              PICTURE X(6).
          03   IS-ADDRESS.
               04   IS-STREET         PICTURE X(15).
               04   IS-CITYSTATE      PICTURE X(15).
     02   IS-PAYRECORD.
          03   IS-YEAR-OPENED         PICTURE 99.
          03   IS-MAXIMUM-CREDIT      PICTURE 9999V99
                    USAGE COMP-3.
          03   IS-MAXIMUM-BILL        PICTURE 9999V99
                    USAGE COMP-3.
          03   IS-BALANCE-DUE         PICTURE 9999V99
                    USAGE COMP-3.
          03   IS-PAYCODE             PICTURE 9.
               88   BAD  VALUE 1.
               88   POOR  VALUE 2.
               88   SLOW  VALUE 3.
               88   AVERAGE  VALUE 4.
               88   GOOD  VALUE 5.
               88   EXCELLENT  VALUE 6.
               88   NONE VALUE 7.
FD   PRINT-FILE
     LABEL RECORDS ARE OMITTED.
01   OUTGO                            PICTURE X(133).

WORKING-STORAGE SECTION.
77   TIME       PICTURE 99.
77   KEY-IN     PICTURE X(6).
77   ACCEPTED   PICTURE 999 USAGE COMP-3 VALUE ZEROS.
77   REJECTED   PICTURE 999 USAGE COMP-3 VALUE ZEROS.
```

Figure 12–18.   Example—Program Accessing Records Sequentially from an
                     Indexed Sequential File Starting at Any Point—Continued.

```
01   PRINT-LINE.
     02  FILLER  PICTURE X(9)   VALUE SPACES.
     02  FILLER  PICTURE XX     VALUE '19'.
     02  YEARS   PICTURE 99.
     02  FILLER  PICTURE X(10)  VALUE SPACES.
     02  IDENT   PICTURE X(6).
     02  FILLER  PICTURE X(10)  VALUE SPACES.
     02  CUSTOMER   PICTURE X(20).
     02  FILLER  PICTURE X(15)  VALUE SPACES.
     02  O-STREET    PICTURE X(15).
     02  FILLER  PICTURE X(10)  VALUE SPACES.
     02  O-CITYSTATE   PICTURE X(15).
     02  FILLER  PICTURE X(18)  VALUE SPACES.
```

```
PROCEDURE DIVISION.
BEGIN.
     OPEN INPUT IND-SEQ OUTPUT PRINT-FILE.
CONTINUE.
     PERFORM SAMPLE THRU EXIT-POINT 50 TIMES.
PARA-1.
     GO TO NEW-KEY.
NEW-KEY.
     DISPLAY 'ENTER NUMBER NOW' UPON CONSOLE.
     ACCEPT KEY-IN FROM CONSOLE.

RE-SAMPLE.
     START IND-SEQ INVALID KEY GO TO MESSAGE.
     ALTER PARA-1 TO PROCEED TO SHUT.
     GO TO CONTINUE.
MESSAGE.
     DISPLAY 'INCORRECT KEY' UPON CONSOLE.
     GO TO SHUT.
SAMPLE.
     READ IND-SEQ AT END GO TO SHUT.
     SUBTRACT IS-YEAR-OPENED FROM 69 GIVING TIME.
     IF TIME IS GREATER THAN 3
          MOVE IS-YEAR-OPENED TO YEARS.
          MOVE RECORD-ID TO IDENT
          MOVE IS-NAME TO CUSTOMER
          MOVE IS-STREET TO O-STREET
          MOVE IS-CITYSTATE TO O-CITYSTATE
          WRITE OUTGO FROM PRINT-LINE
          ADD 1 TO ACCEPTED
     ELSE ADD 1 TO REJECTED.
     GO TO EXIT-POINT.
SHUT.
     DISPLAY ACCEPTED REJECTED UPON CONSOLE.
     CLOSE IND-SEA PRINT FILE.
     STOP RUN.
EXIT-POINT.
     EXIT.
```

Figure 12-18. Example—Program Accessing Records Sequentially from an Indexed Sequential File Starting at Any Point—Continued.

Accessing an Indexed Sequential File Randomly

ENVIRONMENT DIVISION. The SELECT, ASSIGN, RECORD KEY, and NOMINAL KEY clauses are used in the same manner as accessing an indexed sequential file sequentially.

ACCESS IS RANDOM option is required for random access of records from a file. Storage and retrieval are based on the ACTUAL KEY or NOMINAL KEY associated with each record. The RECORD KEY must be specified in the File-Control paragraph when sequential access is to begin at some record other than the first record of the file or when the ACCESS IS RANDOM option is specified.

When the records are accessed randomly, the NOMINAL KEY field must be set to the value of the RECORD KEY field of the desired record before a READ statement is executed for the file. The NOMINAL KEY in Working-Storage will contain the key of the desired record.

Any READ statement that refers to a randomly accessed indexed sequential file must include the INVALID KEY option. The end-of-file record is not checked when a file is accessed randomly. The INVALID KEY option of a READ statement is activated when no record with a control field equal to the value of the NOMINAL KEY variable can be found in the file.

READ file-name [INTO record-name] INVALID KEY imperative-
statement

```
SELECT RANDOM-FILE
    ASSIGN TO DA-2311-I-RANDACC
    RECORD KEY IS ID-FIELD
    NOMINAL KEY IS W-S-ID
    ACCESS IS RANDOM.

READ RANDOM-FILE INVALID KEY PERFORM SPECIAL-CASES.
```

Figure 12–19. Format Read Statements and Necessary Entries to Access a Record Randomly from an Indexed Sequential File.

Adding Records to an Indexed Sequential File Randomly

When adding records to an indexed sequential file, it is not necessary to recreate an indexed sequential file as it was with standard sequential files. Any record with a RECORD KEY that is not currently in the indexed sequential file may be added to it.

```
SELECT STUDENT-MASTER ASSIGN TO DA-2311-I-PERM
    RECORD KEY IS STUDENT-NUM
    NOMINAL KEY IS KEY-NUMBER
    ACCESS IS RANDOM.
SELECT UPDATE-DATA ASSIGN TO UR-2540R-S-CARDS.
```

```
PROCEDURE DIVISION.
BEGIN.
    OPEN INPUT UPDATE-DATA I-O STUDENT-MASTER.
GET-CARD.
    READ UPDATE-DATA AT END GO TO SHUT.
    MOVE CARD-NUMBER TO KEY-NUMBER.
ADD-THE-RECORD.
    WRITE STUDENT-DATA FROM TRANSFER INVALID KEY PERFORM BAD-KEY.
    GO TO GET-CARD.
BAD-KEY.
    DISPLAY KEY-NUMBER 'DUPLICATE KEY' UPON CONSOLE.
SHUT.
    CLOSE UPDATE-DATA STUDENT-MASTER.
    STOP RUN.
```

Figure 12–20. Example—Adding Records Randomly to an Indexed Sequential File.

ENVIRONMENT DIVISION. SELECT, ASSIGN, RECORD KEY, NOMINAL KEY, and ACCESS IS RANDOM clauses similar to those clauses used in indexed sequential file accessing randomly are required.

DATA DIVISION. Similar entries for indexed sequential files accessed randomly.

PROCEDURE DIVISION. When records are to be added to an indexed sequential file, the file must have random access and be opened as I-O file. The INVALID KEY option of the WRITE statement is activated if the NOMINAL KEY field associated with the record duplicates the RECORD KEY field of a record already in the file.

Updating and Replacing Records in an Indexed Sequential File Randomly

ENVIRONMENT DIVISION. Same entries as *adding* records to an indexed sequential file randomly.

DATA DIVISION. Same entries as *adding* records to an indexed sequential file randomly.

PROCEDURE DIVISION. Every *READ* statement that refers to a randomly accessed indexed sequential file must have the INVALID KEY option. The INVALID KEY option of a READ statement refers to a randomly accessed indexed sequential file opened as I-O is activated under the same circumstances as the INVALID KEY option of a READ statement that refers to randomly accessed files opened as INPUT. The INVALID KEY option is activated when no RECORD KEY equal to the current value of the NOMINAL KEY variable can be located in the file.

Before a READ statement can be executed for a randomly accessed indexed sequential file, the NOMINAL KEY variable must be set to the desired value, and the file must be opened as I-O or INPUT.

After a READ statement is executed for an indexed sequential file opened as I-O, the accessed record may be updated and placed back in the same position in the file. An updated record is placed back into an indexed sequential file with a REWRITE statement. The next input or output statement for an indexed sequential file opened as I-O after a READ statement may be a statement to place the record back into the file with a REWRITE statement. The key fields should not be altered between a READ and a REWRITE statement.

The READ statement and its associated REWRITE statement may be separated by any number of statements as long as they are not separated by any other input or output statements that refer to the indexed sequential file.

Rewrite Statement. The function of the REWRITE statement is to place a logical record on a direct-access device with a specified record, if the contents of the associated ACTUAL KEY or NOMINAL KEY are found to be valid.

The READ statement for a file must be executed before a REWRITE statement for the file can be executed. A REWRITE statement can be executed only for direct or indexed sequential files opened as I-O. If the ACCESS IS RANDOM option is specified for the file, the ACTUAL or NOMINAL KEY must be set to the desired value prior to the execution of the REWRITE statement. The record name-is the name of the logical record in the Data Division.

The record-name must be associated with an indexed sequential file that was opened as I-O. The record that is placed back into the file is the last record accessed by the READ statement referring to that file.

If the INVALID KEY option of a READ statement is activated, no record has been accessed. The next input or output statement for an indexed sequential file after the INVALID KEY of a READ statement is activated could be another READ statement to access a different record.

REWRITE record-name [FROM identifier]
  INVALID KEY imperative-statement

NOTE: The INVALID KEY option must be used for the IBM DOS 360/370 compilers. The INVALID KEY option is optional for the IBM OS 360/370 compiler.

Figure 12–21. Format Rewrite Statement.

The Toluca Community College has a problem with students who move frequently and needs a program to update addresses in its indexed master file.

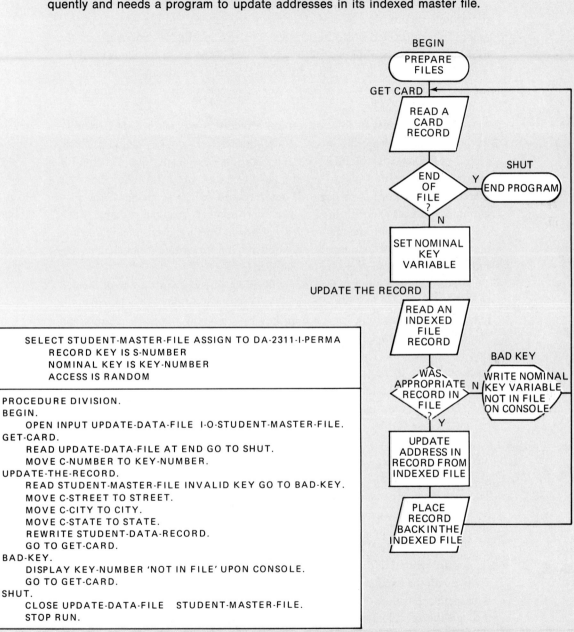

```
SELECT STUDENT-MASTER-FILE ASSIGN TO DA-2311-I-PERMA
       RECORD KEY IS S-NUMBER
       NOMINAL KEY IS KEY-NUMBER
       ACCESS IS RANDOM

PROCEDURE DIVISION.
BEGIN.
    OPEN INPUT UPDATE-DATA-FILE I-O-STUDENT-MASTER-FILE.
GET-CARD.
    READ UPDATE-DATA-FILE AT END GO TO SHUT.
    MOVE C-NUMBER TO KEY-NUMBER.
UPDATE-THE-RECORD.
    READ STUDENT-MASTER-FILE INVALID KEY GO TO BAD-KEY.
    MOVE C-STREET TO STREET.
    MOVE C-CITY TO CITY.
    MOVE C-STATE TO STATE.
    REWRITE STUDENT-DATA-RECORD.
    GO TO GET-CARD.
BAD-KEY.
    DISPLAY KEY-NUMBER 'NOT IN FILE' UPON CONSOLE.
    GO TO GET-CARD.
SHUT.
    CLOSE UPDATE-DATA-FILE   STUDENT-MASTER-FILE.
    STOP RUN.
```

Figure 12–22.   Program to Add and Change Records Randomly in an Indexed Sequential File.

Direct (Random) Organization

A file organized in a Direct (random) manner is characterized by some predictable relationship between the key of the record and the address of that record in a direct-access storage device. The relationship is established by the user and permits the rapid access to any record of the file if the file is carefully organized. The records will probably be distributed nonsequentially throughout the file. If so, processing the record in key sequence requires a preliminary sort or the use of a finder file.

When a request to store or retrieve a record is made, an address relative to the beginning of the file or an actual address (i.e., device, cylinder, track, record position) must be furnished. This address can be specified as being the address of the desired record or as a starting point within the file where the search for the record is to begin. When a record search is specified, the programmer must also furnish the key (i.e., part number, customer number, etc.) that is associated with the record. With direct addressing, every possible key in the file converts to a unique address, thus making it possible to locate any record in the file with one search and one read.

The user has complete freedom in deciding where records are to be located in a direct organized file. When creating or making additions to the file, the user may specify the location for a record key by supplying the track address and identifier or just simply the track address while letting the system find the location for the record. The record is written in the first available location on the track specified. If the specified track is full, the system continues to search successive tracks until a location is found.

Direct organization is generally used for files whose characteristics do not permit the use of sequential or indexed sequential files, or for where the time required to locate individual records must be kept at a minimum. This method has considerable flexibility, but it has a serious disadvantage in that the programming system must provide the routines to read a file of direct organization. The user is largely responsibile for the logic and programming requirements to locate records since he establishes the relationship between the key of the record and the addresses in the direct-access storage device.

ENVIRONMENT DIVISION. The SELECT, ASSIGN, and ACCESS clauses are written in the same manner as *indexed sequential files accessed randomly,* with the exception of *NOMINAL KEY.* When direct data organization is used, the position of the logical records in a file is controlled by the user through the specifications of an ACTUAL KEY defined in the Environment Division. The ACTUAL KEY has two components. The first is the track identifier, which identifies the relative or actual track at which a record is to be placed or at which the search for a record is to begin. The second component is a record identifier, which serves as a unique logical identifier for a specific record on the track. Files with direct organization must be assigned to direct-access devices.

DATA DIVISION. Same entries as *indexed sequential files accessed randomly*.

Procedure Division

Read Statement. The INVALID KEY option must be specified for files in the random-access mode. The imperative statements following INVALID KEY is executed when the contents of the ACTUAL KEY field are invalid. Only the track specified in ACTUAL KEY is searched for records being read.

The contents of the ACTUAL KEY must be set to the desired value before the READ statement. The READ statement implicitly performs the functions of the SEEK statement, unless a SEEK statement for the file has been executed prior to the READ statement.

Seek Statement. The SEEK statement serves only as documentation, and it is meant to initiate the accessing of a mass storage data record for subsequent reading or writing. The file-name must be defined by a file description entry in the Data Division.

A SEEK statement pertains only to direct files in the random-access mode and may be executed prior to the execution of a READ or WRITE statement.

The SEEK statement uses the contents of the data-name in the ACTUAL KEY clause for the location of the record to be accessed. If the key is invalid, when the next READ or WRITE statement for the associated file is executed, control will be passed to the imperative statement following the INVALID KEY option.

```
SEEK file-name RECORD
```

Figure 12–23. Format Seek Statement.

Write Statement. The INVALID KEY phrase must be specified for a file that resides on a direct-access device. The INVALID KEY option is executed when the file is opened as I-O or OUTPUT and where the track address specified in the ACTUAL KEY is outside the limits of the file, or if a direct file is opened as I-O, or when a record is not found, or where the track number is outside the limits of the file.

For randomly accessed files the WRITE statement performs the functions of the SEEK statement, unless the SEEK statement for this record is executed prior to the WRITE statement. A WRITE statement executed for a direct file in the random-access mode assumes the meaning of a REWRITE statement when the file is opened as I-O and the WRITE statement is the next output operation following a READ for a record with the same key.

This program creates a file with direct organization through the use of an ACTUAL KEY. The ACTUAL KEY consists of a relative track address and a unique record indentifier. In the program, a field in the input record (CD-ITEM-CODE) is converted to a track address (TRACK-ID) through the use of a simple remainder randomizing technique. This technique consists of dividing the value in the field of the input record (CD-ITEM-CODE) by 19, and using the resulting remainder (TRACK-ID) as the relative track address.

```
IDENTIFICATION DIVISION.
PROGRAM-ID.   CREATEDF.
REMARKS.  ILLUSTRATE CREATION OF A DIRECT FILE.
ENVIRONMENT DIVISION.
CONFIGURATION SECTION.
SOURCE-COMPUTER.   IBM-360-H50.
OBJECT-COMPUTER.   IBM-360-H50.
INPUT-OUTPUT SECTION.
FILE-CONTROL.
     SELECT DA-FILE ASSIGN TO DA-2311-D-MASTER
          ACCESS IS RANDOM
          ACTUAL KEY IS FILEKEY.
     SELECT CARD-FILE ASSIGN TO UR-1442R-S-INFILE
          RESERVE 3 ALTERNATE AREAS.
DATA DIVISION.
FILE SECTION.
FD   DA-FILE
     DATA RECORD IS DISK
     LABEL RECORDS ARE STANDARD.
01   DISK.
     05   DISK-ITEM-CODE            PICTURE X(3).
     05   DISK-ITEM-NAME            PICTURE X(29).
     05   DISK-STOCK-ON-HAND        PICTURE X9(6)        USAGE COMP SYNC.
     05   DISK-UNIT-PRICE           PICTURE S999V99      USAGE COMP SYNC.
     05   DISK-STOCK-VALUE          PICTURE S9(9)V99     USAGE COMP SYNC.
     05   DISK-ORDER-POINT          PICTURE S9(3)        USAGE COMP SYNC.
FD   CARD-FILE
     LABEL RECORDS ARE OMITTED
     DATA RECORD IS CARDS.
```

Figure 12-24.   Creation of a Direct File.

```
01   CARDS.
      05   CD-ITEM-CODE              PICTURE X(3).
      05   CD-ITEM-NAME              PICTURE X(29).
      05   CD-STOCK-ON-HAND          PICTURE S9(6).
      05   CD-UNIT-PRICE             PICTURE S999V99.
      05   CD-STOCK-VALUE            PICTURE S9(9)V99.
      05   CD-ORDER-POINT            PICTURE S9(3).
      05   FILLER                    PICTURE X(23).
WORKING-STORAGE SECTION.
77   SAVE                           PICTURE S9(5)    USAGE COMP SYNC RIGHT.
77   QUOTIENT                       PICTURE S9(4)    USAGE COMP SYNC RIGHT.
77   PRODUCT                        PICTURE S9(4)    USAGE COMP SYNC RIGHT.
01   FILEKEY.
      05   TRACK-ID                 PICTURE S9(5)    USAGE COMP SYNC RIGHT.
      05   RECORD-ID                PICTURE X(29).
PROCEDURE DIVISION.
BEGIN.
      OPEN INPUT CARD-FILE.
      OPEN OUTPUT DA-FILE.
PARA-1.
      READ CARD-FILE AT END GO TO END-JOB.
      MOVE CD-ITEM-CODE TO SAVE.
      DIVIDE 19 INTO SAVE GIVING QUOTIENT
            REMAINDER TRACK-ID.
      MOVE CD-ITEM-NAME TO RECORD-ID.
      MOVE CD-ITEM-CODE TO DISK-ITEM-CODE.
      MOVE CD-ITEM-NAME TO DISK-ITEM-NAME.
      MOVE CD-STOCK-ON-HAND TO DISK-STOCK-ON-HAND.
      MOVE CD-UNIT-PRICE TO DISK-UNIT-PRICE.
      MOVE CD-STOCK-VALUE TO DISK-STOCK-VALUE.
      MOVE CD-ORDER-POINT TO DISK-ORDER-POINT.
WR.
      WRITE DISK INVALID KEY GO TO ERROR-ROUTINE.
      GO TO PARA-1.
END-JOB.
      CLOSE CARD-FILE DA-FILE.
      DISPLAY "END OF JOB".
      STOP RUN.
ERROR-ROUTINE.
      DISPLAY "UNABLE TO WRITE RECORD".
      DISPLAY TRACK-ID.
      GO TO PARA-1.
```

Figure 12–24.   Creation of a Direct File—Continued.

This program creates an indexed file. These records are presented in ascending sequence by RECORD KEY. The APPLY clause builds the master index.

```
IDENTIFICATION DIVISION.
PROGRAM-ID.   CREATEIS.
REMARKS.   ILLUSTRATE CREATION OF INDEXED SEQUENTIAL FILE.
ENVIRONMENT DIVISION.
CONFIGURATION SECTION.
SOURCE-COMPUTER'  IBM-360-F50.
OBJECT-COMPUTER.   IBM-360-F50.
INPUT-OUTPUT SECTION.
FILE-CONTROL.
     SELECT IS-FILE ASSIGN TO SYS016-DA-2311-I-MASTER
          ACCESS IS SEQUENTIAL
          RECORD KEY IS REC-ID.
     SELECT CARD-FILE ASSIGN TO SYS007-UR-2540R-S
          RESERVE 1 ALTERNATE AREA.
I-O-CONTROL.
     APPLY MASTER-INDEX TO 2311 ON IS-FILE.
DATA DIVISION.
FILE SECTION.
FD  IS-FILE
     BLOCK CONTAINS 5 RECORDS
     RECORDING MODE IS F
     LABEL RECORDS ARE STANDARD
     DATA RECORD IS DISK.
01   DISK.
     05   DELETE-CODE    PICTURE X.
     05   REC-ID         PICTURE 9(10).
     05   DISK-FLD1      PICTURE X(10).
     05   DISK-NAME      PICTURE X(20).
     05   DISK-BAL       PICTURE 99999V99.
     05   FILLER         PICTURE X(52).
FD  CARD-FILE
     RECORDING MODE IS F
     LABEL RECORDS ARE OMITTED
     DATA RECORD IS CARDS.
01   CARDS.
     05   KEY-ID         PICTURE 9(10).
     05   CD-NAME        PICTURE X(20).
     05   CD-BAL         PICTURE 99999V99.
     05   FILLER         PICTURE X(43).
PROCEDURE DIVISION.
BEGIN.
     OPEN INPUT CARD-FILE.
     OPEN OUTPUT IS-FILE.
PARA-1.
     READ CARD-FILE AT END GO TO END-JOB.
     MOVE LOW-VALUE TO DELETE-CODE.
     MOVE KEY-ID TO REC-ID.
     MOVE CD-NAME TO DISK-NAME.
     MOVE CD-BAL TO DISK-BAL.
     WRITE DISK INVALID KEY GO TO ERR.
     GO TO PARA-1.
ERR.
     DISPLAY "DUPLICATE OR SEQ-ERR" UPON CONSOLE.
     DISPLAY KEY-ID UPON CONSOLE.
     GO TO PARA-1.
END-JOB.
     CLOSE CARD-FILE IS-FILE.
     DISPLAY "END OF JOB" UPON CONSOLE.
     STOP RUN.
```

Figure 12–25.   Creation of an Indexed Sequential File.

This program randomly updates an existing indexed file. The READ IS-FILE statement causes a search of indexes for an equal compare between the NOMINAL KEY obtained from the input record and the RECORD KEY of the I-O file. If an equal compare occurs, the record is updated, and the details of this update are printed. If a matching record is not found, the invalid key branch is taken.

```
IDENTIFICATION DIVISION.
PROGRAM-ID. RANDOMIS.
REMARKS. ILLUSTRATE RANDOM RETRIEVAL FROM IS-FILE.
ENVIRONMENT DIVISION.
CONFIGURATION SECTION.
SOURCE-COMPUTER. IBM-360-H50.
OBJECT-COMPUTER. IBM-360-H50.
INPUT-OUTPUT SECTION.
FILE-CONTROL.
    SELECT IS-FILE ASSIGN TO DA-2311-I-MASTER
        ACCESS IS RANDOM
        NOMINAL KEY IS KEY-ID
        RECORD KEY IS REC-ID.
    SELECT CARD-FILE ASSIGN TO UR-1442R-S-INFILE
        RESERVE 10 ALTERNATE AREAS.
    SELECT PRINT-FILE ASSIGN TO UT-2400-S-PROUT
        RESERVE NO ALTERNATE AREAS.
I-O-CONTROL.
    RERUN ON UT-2400-S-CKPT EVERY 10000 RECORDS OF IS-FILE.
DATA DIVISION.
FILE SECTION.
FD  IS-FILE
    BLOCK CONTAINS 5 RECORDS
    RECORD CONTAINS 100 CHARACTERS
    LABEL RECORDS ARE STANDARD
    RECORDING MODE IS F
    DATA RECORD IS DISK.
01  DISK.
    05   DELETE-CODE       PICTURE X.
    05   REC-ID            PICTURE 9(10).
    05   DISK-FLD1         PICTURE X(10).
    05   DISK-NAME         PICTURE X(20).
    05   DISK-BAL          PICTURE 99999V99.
    05   FILLER            PICTURE X(52).
FD  CARD-FILE
    RECORDING MODE IS F
    LABEL RECORDS ARE OMITTED
    DATA RECORD IS CARDS.
01  CARDS.
    05   KEY-IDA           PICTURE 9(10).
    05   CD-NAME           PICTURE X(20).
    05   CD-AMT            PICTURE 99999V99.
    05   FILLER            PICTURE X(43).
FD  PRINT-FILE
    RECORDING MODE IS F
    LABEL RECORDS ARE STANDARD
    DATA RECORD IS PRINTER.
```

Figure 12–26.   Random Retrieval and Updating of an Indexed Sequential File.

```
01   PRINTER.
     05   FORMSC              PICTURE X.
     05   PRINT-ID            PICTURE X(10).
     05   FILLER              PICTURE X(10).
     05   PRINT-NAME          PICTURE X(20).
     05   FILLER              PICTURE X(10).
     05   PRINT-BAL           PICTURE $ZZZ,999.99-.
     05   FILLER              PICTURE X(10).
     05   PRINT-AMT           PICTURE $ZZZ,ZZZ.99-.
     05   FILLER              PICTURE X(10).
     05   PRINT-NEW-BAL       PICTURE $ZZZ,ZZZ.99-.
WORKING-STORAGE SECTION.
77   KEY-ID                  PICTURE 9(10).
PROCEDURE DIVISION.
BEGIN.
     OPEN INPUT CARD-FILE.
     OPEN OUTPUT PRINT-FILE.
     OPEN I-O IS-FILE.
PARA-1.
     MOVE SPACES TO PRINTER.
     READ CARD-FILE AT END GO TO END-JOB.
     MOVE KEY-IDA TO KEY-ID.
     READ IS-FILE INVALID KEY GO TO NO-RECORD.
     MOVE REC-ID TO PRINT-ID.
     MOVE DISK-NAME TO PRINT-NAME.
     MOVE DISK-BAL TO PRINT-BAL.
     MOVE CD-AMT TO PRINT-AMT.
     ADD CD-AMT TO DISK-BAL.
     MOVE DISK-BAL TO PRINT-NEW-BAL.
     REWRITE DISK INVALID KEY GO TO NO-RECORD.
     WRITE PRINTER AFTER POSITIONING 2 LINES.
     GO TO PARA-1.
NO-RECORD.
     DISPLAY 'NO RECORD FOUND' UPON CONSOLE.
     DISPLAY KEY-ID UPON CONSOLE.
     GO TO PARA-1.
END-JOB.
     CLOSE CARD-FILE PRINT-FILE IS-FILE.
     DISPLAY 'EDN OF JOB' UPON CONSOLE.
     STOP RUN.
```

Figure 12–26. Random Retrieval and Updating of an Indexed Sequential File—Continued.

Exercises

Write your answers in the space provided.

1. _____ processing denotes the ability of the system to process data as soon as it becomes available.

2. Mass direct access storage enables the user to maintain _____ records of diversified applications and also to process _____ data for multiple application areas.

3. The direct access storage devices used for mass memory storage are
   _____, _____, and _____.
4. In sequential processing, input transactions are grouped together and
   sorted into a _____ sequence.
5. Mass storage devices are efficient sequential processors when the percentage of activity against the master file is _____.
6. Random processing is the processing of all transactions against a master
   file regardless of the _____ of the documents.
7. The data file organization refers to the _____ of data records
   within a file.
8. In sequential organization, the data records are organized solely in their
   _____ physical locations.
9. After a sequential file is opened, the record can be _____,
   _____ and _____ in the same location without
   _____ a new file.
10. A sequential file can be used for both input and output activities without
    the necessity for _____ and _____ files between op-
    erations.
11. In creating a standard sequential file, the file must be assigned to a par-
    ticular _____ device.
12. To create a sequential file, the procedural statements must use an _____
    _____ file, and a _____ statement.
13. The _____ option of the Write statement must be used when a
    sequential disk file is being created.
14. The statements following _____ is activated when an attempt
    is made to write beyond the spaces reserved for the file.
15. After a sequential disk file has been created, it may be maintained by
    _____ the records and placing them back in the file.
16. The _____ option of the Write statement may be used if the
    sequential file is to be used for both input and output operations.
17. An indexed sequential file is a _____ file with _____
    that permit rapid access to records.
18. A _____ provided by the user precedes each _____
    of data and is used to provide the index.
19. In an indexed sequential file, the _____ has control over the lo-
    cation of the individual records.
20. The _____ is an indexed sequential file are created and writ-
    ten by the system as the file is created or organized.
21. In an indexed sequential file, the system will access records sequentially
    by _____ written rather than by the physical sequence in the file.
22. The Access Mode clause defines the manner in which the _____
    of a file are to be _____.
23. If the Access Mode clause is not specified _____ is assumed.

24. When the Access Is Random clause is used, the storage and retrieval of records are based on an _____ or _____ key associated with each record.

25. The _____ clause is used to access an indexed sequential file.

26. Records in an ascending sequential file may be accessed at a record that is not the _____ record In a file and continued until the file is _____.

27. A Nominal Key is used with indexed sequential file to specify an elementary _____ defined in the _____ of the program.

28. A Start statement is used to _____ a file.

29. The Start statement _____ the processing of a segment of a _____ indexed sequential file at a specified _____.

30. A Start statement must be executed after the _____ statement but before the _____ statement.

31. When accessing an indexed sequential file randomly, the _____ field must be set to the _____ field of the desired record before a _____ statement is executed for the file.

32. When adding records to an indexed sequential file, it is not necessary to _____ a file.

33. An updated record is placed back in a disk file with a _____ statement.

34. A Read statement for a file must be executed before a _____ statement for the file can be executed.

35. A Direct organized file is characterized by some predictable relationship between the _____ of the record and the _____ of that record in a direct access-storage device.

36. The relationship in a Direct organized file is established by the _____ _____ and permits access to records in a file.

37. Direct file organization is usually for files where the time required to _____ individual records must be kept at a _____ _____.

38. The Seek statement serves only as _____.

39. The Seek statement pertains only to a _____ file in the _____ mode.

40. A Seek statement uses the contents of the data in the _____ clause for the _____ of the record to be accessed.

Answers

1. IN-LINE
2. CURRENT, NON SEQUENTIAL

3. DISK STORAGE, DRUM, DATA CELLS

4. PREDETERMINED
5. HIGH
6. SEQUENCE
7. PHYSICAL ARRANGEMENT
8. SUCCESSIVE
9. OPENED, UPDATED, WRITTEN BACK, CREATING
10. OPENING, CLOSING
11. MASS STORAGE
12. OUTPUT, WRITE
13. INVALID
14. INVALID
15. UPDATING
16. I-O
17. SEQUENTIAL, INDEXES
18. KEY, BLOCK
19. PROGRAMMING SYSTEM
20. INDEXES
21. KEYS
22. RECORDS, ACCESSED
23. ACCESS IS SEQUENTIAL
24. ACTUAL, NOMINAL
25. RECORD KEY
26. FIRST, CLOSED
27. VARIABLE, WORKING-STOR- AGE SECTION
28. POSITION
29. INITIATES, SEQUENTIALLY, KEY
30. OPEN, READ
31. NOMINAL KEY, RECORD KEY, READ
32. RELOCATE
33. REWRITE
34. REWRITE
35. KEY, ADDRESS
36. USER
37. LOCATE, MINIMUM
38. DOCUMENTATION
39. DIRECT, RANDOM ACCESS
40. ACTUAL KEY, LOCATION

Questions for Review

1. Explain the "in line" processing technique and how it is used with mass storage devices.
2. What is sequential processing and how does it differ from random processing?
3. How is a file organized in a sequential organization manner?
4. What are the necessary entries in the Environment, Data and Procedure divisions to create a sequential disk file?
5. How is a standard sequential file updated?
6. Explain the operations of a standard sequential organized file.
7. What is an indexed sequential file organization?
8. What are the important advantages of an indexed sequential file?
9. What are the necessary entries in the Environment, Data and Procedure divisions to create an indexed sequential file?
10. How are the records accessed in an indexed sequential file?
11. What is the purpose of the Start statement and how is it used in processing records in an indexed sequential file?
12. How are records added to an indexed sequential file randomly?

13. What is the function of the Rewrite statement and how is it used with mass storage devices?
14. What is a Direct organization?
15. Explain the operation of a Direct organization file.
16. What are the necessary entries in the Environment, Data and Procedure divisions to create a Direct organization file?
17. What is the Seek statement used for?

Problems

1. *Match each item with its proper description.*

_____ 1. In Line	A. Process predetermined sequence transactions.
_____ 2. Sequential Processing	B. Organized in successive physical locations.
_____ 3. Random Processing	C. Beyond limit of space reserved for file.
_____ 4. Sequential Organization	D. Process data as soon as possible.
_____ 5. Invalid Key	E. Processes documents regardless of sequence.
_____ 6. Indexed Sequential Org.	F. Sequential files accessed through indexes.

2. *Match each item with its proper description.*

_____ 1. Access Mode	A. Variable described in Working-Storage Section.
_____ 2. Record Key	B. Place logical record on a Direct-Access file.
_____ 3. Nominal Key	C. Manner of records accessed.
_____ 4. Start	D. Initiate accessing of mass storage records for subsequent reading or writing.
_____ 5. Rewrite	E. Variable required for accessing indexed sequential file records.
_____ 6. Direct Organization	F. Initiates processing of sequential indexed sequential file records at a specified record.
_____ 7. Seek	G. Relationship between key and address of record.

3. *The Johnson Corporation is converting its master tape file for sales to a master sequential disk file with the same organization.*

The file-name for the tape is SALES-TAPE and the record–name is TAPE-RECORD. The record lengths are fixed at 100 characters and recorded in blocks of five with standard labels.

The disk file name is SALES-DISK and the record-name is DISK-RECORD with the same organization as the tape file.

Write the program to create the disk file. Assume following device numbers.

(In all subsequent problems, if the device numbers are not mentioned, the following will be assumed.)

Computer	— IBM 370 Model H155.
Tape Unit	— Model 2400.
Disk Unit	— Model 2311.
Printer	— Model 1403.
Card Reader	— Model 2540.
Card Punch	— Model 2540.

4. *The Acme Manufacturing Company wishes to create a sequential disk file* from a set of cards.

   a. Write the necessary entries for the Environment and Data Divisions based on the following information:

   Computer to be used   IBM 370   Model H155.
   Input — File-name   FILE-IN   Record-name   CARD-IN.
   Output — File-name   DISK-SEQ   Record-name   DISK-IN
              Record Size 80 characters.
      All records on the disk are in blocks of five and are of a fixed length.
   Output Device — Disk Model 2311.

   b. Write the necessary procedural statements to create the disk file by transferring the input data to the output file. Assume both records are of the same size. The program should branch to a routine called FULL-DISK when the disk is full and display a message on the console to that effect.

5. *The Bryan Tool Corporation is converting its present master tape file to a disk with the same organization. You are asked to write a program based on the following:*

   a. Write the necessary entries for the Environment and Data Division based on the following:

   Computer to be used — IBM 370   Model H155.
   Input — File-name   TAPE-FILE   Record-name   TAPE-IN
             Record Size 100 characters.
      All records on the tape are in blocks of five and are of a fixed length.
      All label records are standard.
   Output — File-name   DISK-SEQ   Record-name   DISK-IN
              Record Size 100 characters.

   b. Write the necessary procedural statements to create the disk file by transferring the input data to the output file. The program should branch to a routine called FULLDISK when the disk is full and display a message on the console to that effect.

6. *Write a program to update the Bryan Tool Corporation sequential disk file (Problem 5) for new addresses. The following information is provided:*

Disk Record Record name RECORD-IN has the following format.

Field	Record Positions
Date	1–6
Customer Number	7–12
Customer Name	13–27
Address—Street	28–42
—City and State	43–57
Balance	58–64
Credit Limit	65–71
Unused in this program	72–100

Changes Card File-name CHANGES Record-name CHANGE-CARD

Field	Record Positions
Date	1–6
Customer Number	7–12
Street	13–27
City and State	28–42
Unused	43–80

If a customer number is not in the disk file, the program should branch to a routine called NOT-IN-FILE where the appropriate message together with the customer number will be displayed on console.

7. *Using the same information in Problem 5, Byran Tool Corporation, create an indexed sequential file from its present master tape file. The Record Key will be the customer number.*

If the record is not written for any reason, the program should branch to ERROR-ROUTINE where the proper message will be displayed.

When the program is complete, display INDEXED FILE FOR CUSTOMER ACCOUNTS CREATED on console.

8. *Given the following information:*

An indexed sequential file contains the following records:
DISK-RECORD

Field	Record Position
Balance	1–6
Date	7–12
Cumulative Disbursements	13–20
Cumulative Receipts	21–28
Minimum Balance	29–36

Class of Stock	37–40
Stock Number	41–47
Unit Price	48–53 XXX.XXX
Amount	54–61 XXXXXX.XX
Unit	62–65
Description	66–95
Unused	96–100

Write the necessary entries for

a. The File-Control paragraph. The file name is DISK-FILE and the record name is DISK-RECORD. The disk device is a model 2311. The elementary variable stock-number contains the identifier for each record.

b. The File Section entry. The records in the file are blocked in groups of five.

c. The procedural statements to access all records sequentially and list them on a model 1403 printer in the same format as the input record leaving two spaces between each field. Appropriate headings for each field should be printed and totals of the balance and amount should be accumulated and printed at end of report.

9. *Using the same record as Problem 8, the outside auditors wish to sample check our inventory as follows:*

    A listing of the accounts in the same print format as Problem 8 for the following groups of accounts.

    Five accounts starting with stock-number 1456845, 5152467, and 8759415.

    Write the necessary entries for

    a. The File-Control paragraph for above.

    b. The procedural statements to access the specified records and print them.

10. *Using the disk record described in Problem 8, you wish to add records to the indexed sequential disk file without having to recreate the file. Write the necessary entries for the File-Control paragraph and Procedure Division to accomplish this.*

11. *Using the same record as Problem 8, you wish to access randomly to print selected critical inventory items.*

    The finder cards will contain the following information:

File-name	FINDER-FILE	Record-name	FINDER-CARD
Field		**Card Columns**	
Date		1–6	
Stock Number		7–13	

The card reader is model 2540.

Write the necessary entries for

a. The File-Control paragraph.
b. The procedural statements to access the records and print the selected records in the same format as Problem 8. If record is not found, display a message on the console to that effect and proceed to the next record.

12. *Using the same record as Problem 8, write a program to update the records in the disk randomly.*

   The format for the transaction card is as follows: (The card will be read on a model 2540 card reader).

   File-name TRANSACTION-FILE   Record-name TRANSACTION-CARD

Field	**Card Columns**
Date	1–6
Stock Number	7–13
Transaction Code	14
Receipts—1	
Disbursements—2	
Quantity	15–19
Amount	20–26
Unused	27–80

   Write the necessary entries for the

   a. File-Control paragraph.
   b. The procedural entries for the following:

   1. *Receipts Card.*
      Add Quantity to Balance.
      Add Quantity to Cumulative Receipts.
      Add Amount to Amount in Disk Record.
   2. *Disbursement Card.*
      Subtract Quantity from Balance.
      Add Quantity to Cumulative Disbursements.
      Subtract Amount from Amount in Disk Record.
   3. If Stock Number not found in Disk Record, branch to ERROR-ROUTINE and display appropriate message and read another transaction record.
   4. Compute new Unit Price by dividing Balance into Amount.
   5. Print TRANSACTION REGISTER as follows: Same print format as Problem 8.
      List the old balance, then the transaction record and finally the new balance.
   6. Write new record back on disk file.

13

Declaratives and Linkage Sections

DECLARATIVES SECTION

The Declaratives Section is written in the Procedure Division to specify any special circumstance under which a procedure is to be executed in the object program. Although the COBOL compiler provides error recovery routines in the case of input/output errors, the programmer may wish to specify additional procedures of his own to supplement those supplied by the compiler. The system automatically handles checking and creation of labels in tape files, but the programmer may wish to use his own tape table-handling procedures. The Report Writer feature may also use declarative sections.

Since these procedures can be executed only at a time when an error occurs in the reading or writing of records, or when the labels of a file are to be processed, or before a report group is to be produced, they cannot appear in the regular sequence of procedural statements. The procedures are invoked non-synchronously, that is, they are not executed as part of the sequential coding written by the programmer, but rather when a condition occurs which cannot normally be tested by the program.

The Declaratives Section is written as a subdivision at the beginning of the Procedure Division prior to the execution of the first procedure. A group of declarative procedures constitutes a declarative section. Although the declarative sections are located at the beginning of the Procedure Division, execution of the object program actually starts with the first procedure following the termination of the declarative section.

The declarative section subdivision of the Procedure Division must begin with the key word DECLARATIVES at the A margin followed by a period

```
PROCEDURE DIVISION.
DECLARATIVES.
{section-name SECTION.   USE-sentence.
{paragraph-name.      sentence ...   .} ... } ..
END DECLARATIVES.
```

Figure 13–1. Format Declaratives Section.

and a space. The declaratives section is terminated by the key words END DECLARATIVES followed by a period and a space. Both DECLARATIVES and END DECLARATIVES must appear on a separate line by themselves with no other coding permissable on the same line. Every declarative section is terminated by the occurrence of another declaratives section or the words END DECLARATIVES.

A declarative section consists of

1. A section-name followed by the key word SECTION written at the A margin.
2. A USE statement must follow the section header on the same line after an intervening space or spaces and terminated by a period.

Use Statement

The USE statement specifies procedures to be performed for each type of declarative which are in addition to the standard procedures provided by the compiler. The USE statement is itself never executed; rather, it defines the conditions calling for the execution of the USE procedures. The remainder of the section must consist of one or more procedural paragraphs that specify the procedures to be performed.

Within a USE procedure, there must be no reference to any nondeclarative procedure. Conversely, in the nondeclaratives portion, there must be no reference to procedure names that appear in the declarative section, except that the PERFORM statement may refer to a USE declarative handling label and error procedures associated with a USE statement.

The following types of procedures are associated with the USE statement.

1. Input/output label-handling procedures.
2. Input/output error-handling procedures.
3. Report-writing procedures.

Label-Processing Declaratives

The statements in these declaratives are used to handle user-created header labels. Nonstandard labels can be specified only for tape files. These procedures are in addition to the standard procedures provided by the input/output system.

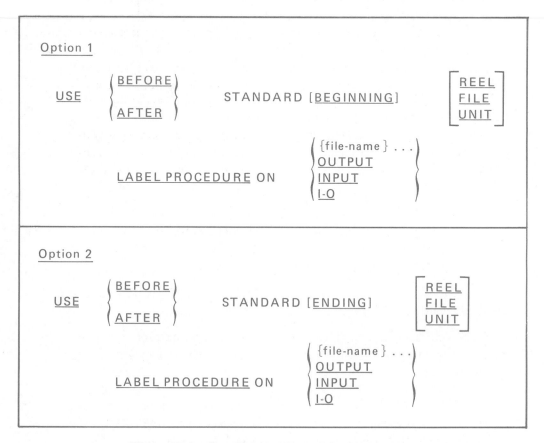

Figure 13–2. Format Label Processing Declaratives.

Rules Governing the Use of Label-Processing Declaratives

1. An OPEN statement in the Procedure Division causes the execution of the USE statement associated with the BEGINNING label.
2. A CLOSE statement in the Procedure Division causes the execution of the USE statement associated with the ENDING label.
3. The word BEGINNING refers to the user's header labels and the word ENDING refers to any trailer labels. If neither is specified, both header and trailer labels are processed.

4. The labels must be listed as data-names in the LABEL RECORDS clause in the file description entry for the file and must be described as level 01 data item subordinate to the file entry.

5. If neither UNIT, REEL, nor FILE is included, the designated procedures are executed for both REEL or UNIT, whichever is appropriate and FILE labels. The REEL option is not applicable to direct-access (mass storage) files. The UNIT option is not applicable to random-access mode since only FILE labels are processed in this mode.

6. The same file-name can appear in a different specific arrangement of a format. However, appearance of a file-name in a USE statement must not cause the execution or the simultaneous request for execution of more than one USE declarative. No file may request a sort-file.

7. The file-name option must not be used with a LABEL RECORDS ARE OMITTED clause.

The designated procedures of a USE statement are executed as follows. The OUTPUT, INPUT, or I-O options are specified, when

a. The OUTPUT is specified only for files opened as OUTPUT.
b. The INPUT is specified only for files opened as INPUT.
c. The I-O is specified only for files opened as I-O.

If the OUTPUT, INPUT, or I-O option is specified, the USE procedure does not apply respectively to OUTPUT, INPUT, or I-O files that are described with the LABEL RECORDS ARE OMITTED clause.

The following program creates a file with user labels. To create the labels, the program contains a DECLARATIVES section, with USE procedures for creating both header and trailer labels.

The program illustrates the following items:

1. For the file requiring the creation of user labels, the LABEL RECORDS clause uses the data-name option.

2. The USE *AFTER* BEGINNING/ENDING LABEL option is specified to create user labels.

3. The program creates two user header labels, utilizing the special exit GO TO MORE LABELS to create the second label.

4. The information to be inserted in the user labels comes from input file records. Therefore, records containing the information must be read and stored before the output file is opened, and the header label procedures are invoked.

Figure 13–3. Sample Label Declarative Program.

```
IDENTIFICATION DIVISION.
PROGRAM-ID.  LABELPGM.
ENVIRONMENT DIVISION.
CONFIGURATION SECTION.
SOURCE-COMPUTER.   IBM-360-F50.
OBJECT-COMPUTER.   IBM-360-F50.
INPUT-OUTPUT SECTION.
FILE-CONTROL.
     SELECT NO-LBL ASSIGN TO UT-2400-S-INFILE.
     SELECT USER ASSIGN TO UT-2400-S-USRFILE.
DATA DIVISION.
FILE SECTION.
FD  NO-LBL
     RECORD CONTAINS 80 CHARACTERS
     LABEL RECORD IS OMITTED.
01  IN-REC.
     05   TYPEN PIC X(4).
     05   DEPT-ID PIC X(11).
     05   BIL-PERIOD PIC X(5).
     05   NAME PIC X(20).
     05   AMOUNT PIC 9(6).
     05   FILLER PIC X(15).
     05   SECUR-CODE PIC XX.
     05   FILLER PIC 9.
     05   ACCT-NUM PIC 9(10).
     05   FILLER PIC 9(6).
01  IN-LBL-HIST REDEFINES IN-REC.
     05   FILLER PIC X(4).
     05   FILE-HISTORY PIC X(76).
FD  USER
     RECORD CONTAINS 80 CHARACTERS
     BLOCK CONTAINS 5 RECORDS
     LABEL RECORDS ARE USR-LBL USR-LBL-HIST.
01  USR-LBL.
     05   USR-HDR PIC X(4).
     05   DEPT-ID PIC X(11).
     05   USR-REC-CNT PIC 9(8)  COMP-3.
     05   BIL-PERIOD PIC X(5).
     05   FILLER PIC X(50).
     05   SECUR-CODE PIC XX.
01  USR-LBL-HIST REDEFINES USR-LBL.
     05   FILLER PIC X(4).
     05   LBL-HISTORY PIC X(76).
01  USR-REC.
     05   TYPEN PIC X(4).
     05   FILLER PIC X(5).
     05   NAME PIC X(20).
     05   FILLER PIC X(4).
     05   ACCT-NUM PIC 9(10).
     05   AMOUNT PIC 9(6)  COMP-3.
     05   FILLER PIC X(23).
     05   U-SEQ-NUMB PIC 9(8).
```

Figure 13–3.   Sample Label Declarative Program—Continued.

```
WORKING-STORAGE SECTION
77   U-REC-NUMB PIC 9(8) VALUE ZERO.
77   SAV-DEPT-ID PIC X(11).
77   LBL-SWITCH PIC 9 VALUE ZERO.
77   USER-SWITCH PIC 9 VALUE ZERO.
01   STOR-REC.
     05   DEPT-ID PIC X(11).
     05   BIL-PERIOD PIC X(5).
     05   SECUR-CODE PIC XX.
PROCEDURE DIVISION


DECLARATIVES.
USR-HDR-LBL SECTION.  USE AFTER BEGINNING FILE
     LABEL PROCEDURE ON USER.


A.   IF LBL-SWITCH = 0
          MOVE SPACES TO USR-LBL
          MOVE ZEROES TO USR-REC-CNT
          MOVE 'UHL1' TO USR-HDR
          MOVE CORRESPONDING STOR-REC TO USR-LBL
          ADD 1 TO LBL-SWITCH GO TO MORE-LABELS
               'ELSE MOVE 'UHL2' TO USR-HDR
                    MOVE FILE-HISTORY TO LBL-HISTORY.
USR-TRLR-LBL SECTION.  USE AFTER ENDING FILE
     LABEL PROCEDURE ON USER.
B.   MOVE SPACES TO USR-LBL.
     MOVE 'UTL1' TO USR- HDR.
     MOVE SAV-DEPT-ID TO DEPT-ID IN USR-LBL.
     MOVE U-REC-NUMB TO USR-REC-CNT.
END DECLARATIVES.
NON-DECLARATIVES SECTION.
     OPEN INPUT NO-LBL.
READ-IN.
     READ NO-LBL AT END GO TO END-JOB.
A.   IF USER-SWITCH = 1 NEXT SENTENCE
          ELSE ADD 1 TO USER-SWITCH
               MOVE CORRESPONDING IN-REC TO STOR-REC
               MOVE DEPT-ID OF IN-REC TO SAV-DEPT-ID
     PERFORM READ-IN
          OPEN OUTPUT USER
          GO TO READ-IN.
     MOVE SPACES TO USR-REC
     ADD 1 TO U-REC-NUMB
     MOVE CORRESPONDING IN-REC TO USR-REC
     MOVE U-REC-NUMB TO U-SEQ-NUMB
     WRITE USR-REC
     GO TO READ-IN.
END-JOB.
     CLOSE NO-LBL USER
     STOP RUN.
```

Figure 13–3.   Sample Label Declarative Program—Continued.

Within the procedures of a USE declarative in which the USE statement specifies an option other than file-name-1 option, reference to common label items need not be qualified by a file-name. A common label is an elementary data item that appears in every label record of the program but does not appear in any data record of the program. Such items must have the same name, description, and relative position in every label record.

The exit from the declarative section is inserted following the last statement of the section. All logical program paths within the section must lead to the exit point.

Input-Output Error-Processing Declaratives

These declaratives are used to specify procedures to be followed if an input/output error occurs during the processing. This option provides the users input/output correction procedures in addition to those specified by the compiler.

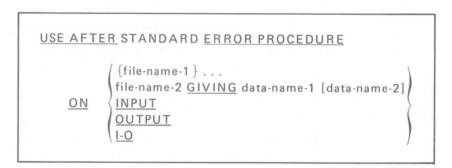

Figure 13–4. Format Input-Output Processing Declarative.

Rules Governing the Use of Input-Output Error-Processing Declaratives

1. The error-handling procedures are activated when an input/output error occurs during the execution of a READ, WRITE, REWRITE, or START statement.
2. Automatic system error routines are executed before user-specified procedures.
3. When the file-name is used, error-handling procedures are executed for input/output errors occuring for that file(s) only.
4. A file-name must not be referenced, implicitly or explicitly, by more than one USE statement.

5. User handling procedures are executed for invalid key conditions if the INVALID KEY option is not specified in the statement causing the condition.
6. Within the error procedures, the allowable executable statements depend on the organization and the access specified for the file in error.
7. The user error-handling procedures are executed when the INPUT, OUTPUT, or I-O option is as follows:

   a. If the INPUT option is specified and input/output error occurs, only the files opened as INPUT will be affected.
   b. If the OUTPUT option is specified, and input/output error occurs, only the files opened as OUTPUT will be affected.
   c. When the I-O option is specified, and input/output error occurs, only the files opened as I-O will be affected.

An exit form of this type of declarative can be affected by executing the last statement in the section (normal return) or by means of a GO TO statement. This is the normal return from an error declarative to the statement following the input/output statement that causes the error.

To gain access to error information, the GIVING option must be used. Error-processing statements must be coded in the COBOL program or in a subprogram to analyze the contents of data-name-1, or data-name-1 and data-name-2.

When an uncorrectable input/output error occurs, the declarative is entered. Data-name-1 will contain information indicating the condition. Data-name-2 is an area large enough to hold the largest physical block that exists on or can be written on file-name, and will contain the block in error when the error occurs during the READ operation.

Continued Processing of a File

The continued processing of a file is permitted under the following conditions.

1. An error-processing procedure exists in the declarative section.
2. The detection of the error results in an automatic transfer to the error-processing procedure which permits the programmer to examine the error condition before entering the process.
3. At the conclusion of the processing of the error, it is the programmer's responsibility to update the parameters normally returned by the Input/Output Control System.

Report Writer Declaratives

The USE BEFORE REPORTING sentence specifies Procedure Division statements that are to be executed just before a report group named in the Report Section of the Data Division is produced.

```
USE BEFORE REPORTING data-name.
```

Figure 13–5.   Format Report Writer Declarative.

Rules Governing the Use of Report Writer Declaratives

1. Data-name represents a report group named in the Report Section of the Data Division and must not appear in more than one USE statement. Data-name must be qualified if not unique.
2. No Report Writer statement (INITIATE, GENERATE, or TERMINATE) may be written in any procedural paragraph(s) following the USE statement in the declaratives.
3. The designated procedures are executed by the Report Writer just before the named report is produced, regardless of page or control breaks associated with the report group. The report group may be of any type except DETAIL.
4. There must not be any reference to any nondeclarative procedure. Conversely, in the nondeclarative portion, there must be no reference of procedure-names that appear in the declarative portion, except that PERFORM statements may refer to a USE declarative or to procedures associated with the USE declarative.

Note:

When the user wishes to suppress the printing of a specified report group, the statement MOVE 1 TO PRINT-SWITCH is used in the USE BEFORE REPORTING declarative section. When this statement is encountered, only the specified report group is not printed. The statement must be written for each report group whose printing is to be suppressed.

The use of PRINT-SWITCH to suppress printing of a report group implies that:

1. Nothing is to be printed.
2. The LINE-COUNTER is not changed.
3. The function of the NEXT GROUP clause, if one appears in the report group, is nullified.

LINKAGE SECTION

The Linkage Section is written in the Data Division to describe data from another program. The data item description entries and record description entries in the Linkage Section provide names and descriptions, but storage within the program is not reserved since the data area exists elsewhere. Any data description clause may be used to describe items in the Linkage Section, with one exception: the VALUE clause may not be specified for other than level 88 items.

```
LINKAGE SECTION.
[data item description entry] . . .
[record description entry] . . .
```

Figure 13–6.   Format Linkage Section.

Subprogram Linkage Statements

Subprogram linkage statements are special statements permitting communication between object programs. These statements are CALL, ENTRY, GOBACK, and **EXIT PROGRAM.**

Calling and Called Programs

A COBOL program can refer to and pass control to other COBOL programs, or to programs written in other languages. A program in another language can refer to and pass control to a COBOL program. A program that

1. A is considered a calling program by B

2. B is considered a called program by A

3. B is considered a calling program by C

4. C is considered a called program by B

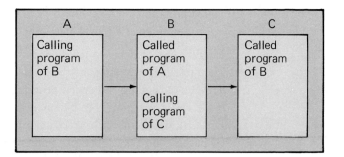

Figure 13–7.   Example—Calling and Called Programs.

refers to another program is a *calling program*. A program that is referred to is a *called program*. Control is returned from the called program to the first instruction following the calling sequence in the calling program.

A called program can also be a calling program, that is, a called program can in turn call another program.

Specifying Linkage

Whenever a program calls another program, linkage must be established between the two. The calling program must state the entry point of the called program and must specify any arguments to be passed. The called program must have an entry point and must be able to accept the arguments. Further, the called program must establish the linkage for the return of control to the calling program.

A calling COBOL program must contain the following statement at the point where another program is to be called.

Call Statement

The CALL statement permits the communication between the COBOL object program and one or more subprograms or other language subprograms.

```
CALL literal    [USING identifier-1    [identifier-2]  ...  ]
```

Figure 13–8.   Format Call Statement.

Rules Governing the Use of the Call Statement

1. The CALL statement appears in the calling program. It may not appear in the called program.
2. *Literal* is a nonnumeric literal and is the name of the program being called.

   a. Literal must conform to rules for the formation of a program-name.
   b. The first eight characters of the literal are used to make correspondence between the calling and called program.
   c. If the called program is to be entered at the beginning of the Procedure Division, the literal must specify the program-name in the PROGRAM-ID paragraph of the called program.

3. If there is a USING clause in the CALL statement that invoked it, the called program must have a USING clause as part of its Procedure Division header.

4. When the called program is to be entered at entry points other than the beginning of the Procedure Division, these alternate entry points are identified by an ENTRY statement and a USING option corresponding to the USING option of the invoking CALL statement. In the case of a CALL statement with a corresponding ENTRY, literal must be a name other than the program-name but must follow the same rules as those for the formation of a program-name.

5. The *identifier* specified in the USING option of the CALL statement indicates those data items available to a calling program that may be referred to in the called program. When the called subprogram is a COBOL program, each of the USING options of the calling program must be identified as a data item in the File Section, Working-Storage Section, or Linkage Section. If the called subprogram is in a language other than COBOL, the operands may either be a file-name or a procedure-name.

6. Names in the USING lists (that of CALL in the main program and that of the Procedure Division header or the ENTRY statement in the subprogram) are paired on one-for-one correspondence, even though there is no necessary relationship between the actual names for the paired items; but the data-names must be equivalent.

7. The USING option is used only if there is a USING option in the called entry point either at the beginning of the Procedure Division of the called program or included in an ENTRY statement of the called program. The number of operands in the USING option of the CALL statement should be the same as the number of operands in the USING option of the Procedure Division header, or an ENTRY statement.

Linkage in a Called Program

A called program must contain two sets of statements.

1. One of the following statements must appear at the point where the program is entered. If the called program is entered as the first instruction in the Procedure Division, the program is called, and arguments are passed by using the Procedure Division header with the USING option.

    If the entry point of the called program is not the first statement of the Procedure Division, then the ENTRY statement is used.

ENTRY literal   [USING identifier-1   [identifier-2] ...]

Figure 13–9.   Format Using Option—Calling and Called Programs.

Entry Statement

The ENTRY statement establishes an entry point in a COBOL subprogram.

Rules Governing the Use of Entry Statement

a. Control is transferred to the ENTRY point by a CALL statement in an invoking program.

b. Literal must not be the name of the called program but is formed according to the same rules followed for program-name. Literal must not be the name of any other entry point or specified in the CALL statement that invoked it.

c. A called program, once invoked, is entered at that ENTRY statement literal.

Format 1 (Within a Calling Program)

CALL literal-1   [USING identifier-1   [identifier-2] ...]

Format 2 (Within a Called Program)

Option 1
    ENTRY literal-1   [USING identifier-1   [identifier-2] ...]

Option 2
    PROCEDURE DIVISION   [USING identifier-1   [identifier-2] ...].

Figure 13–10.   Example—Using Options—Calling and Called Programs.

2. Either of the following statement must be inserted where control is to be returned to calling program: GOBACK and EXIT PROGRAM.

 Both the GOBACK and EXIT PROGRAM statements cause the restoration of the necessary registers and the return of control to the point in the calling program immediately following the calling sequence.

Goback Statement

 The GOBACK statement marks the logical end of a called program.

GOBACK.

Figure 13–11.   Format Goback Statement.

Rules Governing the Use of the Goback Statement
1. A GOBACK statement must appear as the only statement or as the last of a series of imperative statements in a sentence.
2. If control reaches a GOBACK statement while operating under the control of a CALL statement, control returns to the point in the calling program immediately following the CALL statement.
3. If control reaches a GOBACK statement and there is no CALL statement active, there will be an abnormal termination of the job.

Exit Program Statement

 This form of the EXIT statement marks the logical end of a called program. The statement is used in the same manner and performs as other EXIT statements.

paragraph-name.   EXIT PROGRAM.

Figure 13–12.   Format Exit Program
Statement.

Rules Governing the Use of the Exit Program Statement
1. The statement must be preceded by a paragraph-name and must be the only statement in a paragraph.
2. If the control reaches an EXIT PROGRAM statement while operation is under the control of a CALL statement, control returns to the point in the calling program immediately following the CALL statement.

3. If control reaches an **EXIT PROGRAM** statement and no **CALL** statement is active, control passes through the exit point to the first sentence of the next paragraph.

OPERATION OF CALLING AND CALLED PROGRAMS

The execution of a CALL statement causes control to pass to the called program. The first time a called program is entered, its state is that of fresh copy of the program. Each subsequent time a called program is entered, the state is as it was upon the last exit from that program. The reinitiation of items in the called program is the responsibility of the programmer.

```
IDENTIFICATION DIVISION.                IDENTIFICATION DIVISION.
PROGRAM-ID. CALLPROG.                   PROGRAM-ID. USBPROG.
        .                                       .
        .                                       .
        .                                       .
DATA DIVISION.                          DATA DIVISION.
        .                                       .
        .                                       .
        .                                       .
WORKING-STORAGE SECTION.                LINKAGE SECTION.
01   RECORD-1.                          01   PAYREC.
     10   SALARY     PICTURE S9(5)V99.       05   PAY          PICTURE S9(5)V99.
     10   RATE       PICTURE S9V99.          05   HOURLY-RATE  PICTURE S9V99.
     10   HOURS      PICTURE S99V9.          05   HOURS        PICTURE S99V9.
        .                                       .
        .                                       .
        .                                       .
PROCEDURE DIVISION.                     PROCEDURE DIVISION USING PAYREC.
        .                                       .
        .                                       .
     CALL "SUBPROG" USING RECORD-1.         GOBACK.
        .                                   ENTRY "PAYMASTR" USING PAYREC.
        .                                       .
        .                                       .
     CALL "PAYMASTR" USING RECORD-1.           .
        .                                   GOBACK.
        .
        .                                   CALLED PROGRAM
     STOP RUN.

     CALLING PROGRAM
```

Figure 13–13. Example—Calling and Called Programs.

When a called program has a USING option in its Procedure Division header and linkage was affected by a CALL statement where literal is the name of the called program, execution of the called program begins with the first instruction in the Procedure Division after the Declaratives Section.

When linkage to a called subprogram is affected by a CALL statement when literal is the name of an entry point specified in the ENTRY statement of the called program, that execution of the called program begins with the first statement following the ENTRY statement.

When the USING option is present, the object program operates as though each occurrence of Identifier-1, Identifier-2, etc. in the Procedure Division had been replaced by the corresponding identifier for the USING option of the CALL statement of the calling program—that is, corresponding identifiers refer to a single set of data which is available to the calling program. The correspondence is positional, not nominal.

When control reaches the GOBACK or EXIT PROGRAM statement in the called program, control returns to the point in the calling program immediately following the CALL statement.

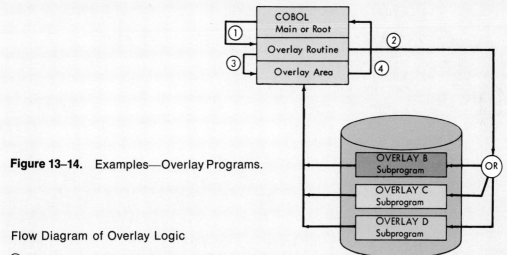

Figure 13–14. Examples—Overlay Programs.

Flow Diagram of Overlay Logic

① The main program calls the overlay routine.

② The overlay routine fetches the particular COBOL subprogram and places it in the overlay area.

③ The overlay routine transfers control to the first instruction of the called program.

④ The called program returns to the COBOL calling program (*not* to the assembler language overlay routine).

COBOL Program Main (Root or Main Program)

```
IDENTIFICATION DIVISION.
PROGRAM-ID. MAINLINE.
  .
  .
  .

ENVIRONMENT DIVISION.
  .
  .
  .

DATA DIVISION.
  .
  .
  .

WORKING-STORAGE SECTION.
77   PROCESS-LABEL PICTURE IS X(8) VALUE IS "OVERLAYB".
77   PARAM-1 PICTURE IS X.
77   PARAM-2 PICTURE IS XX.
77   COMPUTE-TAX PICTURE IS X(8) VALUE IS "OVERLAYC".

01   NAMET.
     02   EMPLY-NUMB PICTURE IS 9(5).
     02   SALARY PICTURE IS 9(4)V99.
     02   RATE PICTURE IS 9(3)V99.
     02   HOURS-REG PICTURE IS 9(3)V99.
     02   HOURS-OT PICTURE IS 9(2)V99.
01   COMPUTE-SALARY PICTURE IS X(8) VALUE IS "OVERLAYD".
01   NAMES.
     02   RATES PICTURE IS 9(6).
     02   HOURS PICTURE IS 9(3)V99.
     02   SALARYX PICTURE IS 9(2)V99.
  .
  .
  .

PROCEDURE DIVISION.
  .
  .
  .

    CALL "OVRLAY" USING PROCESS-LABEL' PARAM-1, PARAM-2.
  .
  .

    CALL "OVRLAY" USING COMPUTE-TAX, NAMET.
  .
  .
  .

    CALL "OVRLAY" USING COMPUTE-SALARY, NAMES.
  .
  .
  .
```

Figure 13–14. Examples—Overlay Programs—Continued.

COBOL Subprogram B

```
IDENTIFICATION DIVISION.
PROGRAM-ID. OVERLAY1.
.
.
.
ENVIRONMENT DIVISION.
.
.
.
DATA DIVISION.
.
.
LINKAGE SECTION.

01   PARAM-10  PICTURE X.
01   PARAM-20  PICTURE XX.
.
.

PROCEDURE DIVISION.
PARA-NAME.  ENTRY "OVRLAY1" USING PARAM-10, PARAM-20.
.
.

            GOBACK.
```

COBOL Subprogram C

```
IDENTIFICATION DIVISION.
PROGRAM-ID. OVERLAY2.
.
.
ENVIRONMENT DIVISION.
.
.
.
DATA DIVISION.
.
.
LINKAGE SECTION.

01   NAMEX.
     02   EMPLY-NUMBX PICTURE IS 9(5).
     02   SALARYX PICTURE IS 9(4) V99.
     02   RATEX PICTURE IS 9(3)V99.
     02   HOURS-REGX   PICTURE IS 9(3)V99.
     02   HOURS-OTX PICTURE IS 9(2)V99.

PROCEDURE DIVISION.
PARA-NAME.  ENTRY "OVRLAY2" USING NAMEX.
.
.

            GOBACK.
```

Figure 13–14. Examples—Overlay Programs—Continued.

```
COBOL Subprogram D

IDENTIFICATION DIVISION.
PROGRAM-ID. OVERLAY3.
    .
    .
    .
ENVIRONMENT DIVISION.
    .
    .

DATA DIVISION.
    .
    .
LINKAGE SECTION
01  NAMES.
    02   RATES PICTURE IS 9(6).
    02   HOURS PICTURE IS 9(3)V99.
    02   SALARYX PICTURE IS 9(†)V99.
    .
PROCEDURE DIVISION.
PARA-NAME.  ENTRY "OVRLAY3" USING NAMES.
    .
    .
    .
                    GOBACK.
```

Figure 13–14. Examples—Overlay Programs—Continued.

Exercises

Write your answers in the space provided.

1. The Declaratives Section is written in the _____ Division to specify any special circumstance under which a _____ is to be executed in the _____ program.

2. The programmer may wish to supply additional _____ of his own to supplement those supplied by the _____.

3. The declaratives cannot appear in the _____ sequence of procedural statements.

4. A declarative procedure is invoked _____, not part of the _____ coding of the program but when a condition arises that cannot normally be _____ by the program.

5. The Declaratives Section is written at the _____ of the Procedure Division prior to the execution of the _____ procedure.

6. The Declaratives Section must begin with the key word _____ at the _____ margin followed by a _____ and a _____.

7. The Declaratives Section is terminated by the key words _____.

8. A Use statement specifies the _____ to be performed for each _____ of declarative.

9. A Use statement is never itself _____ but defines conditions calling for the _____ of the _____ procedure.

10. The type of procedures associated with the Use statement are _____ _____, _____, and _____ procedures.

11. Label Processing declaratives are used to handle _____ header labels.

12. An Open statement in the Procedure Division causes the execution of the Use statement, associated with the _____ labels which refers to the users _____ labels.

13. A Close statement in the Procedure Division causes the execution of the Use statement associated with the _____ labels which refers to the users _____ labels.

14. The labels in a Label Processing declarative must be listed as _____ _____ in the _____ clause for the file description entry.

15. Error Processing declaratives are used to specify procedures if an _____ _____ error occurs during the processing and provides input/output _____ procedures in addition to those specified by the _____.

16. The error-handling procedures are activated when an error occurs during the execution of a _____, _____, _____ or _____ statement.

17. Automatic _____ routines are executed before _____ procedures.

18. The continued processing of a file is permitted if an _____ procedure exists in the _____ section.

19. A Report Writer declarative specifies Procedure Division statements that are to be executed before a _____ name in the _____ Section of the Data Division is produced.

20. When the user wishes to suppress the printing of a specified report group, he writes the statement _____ in the _____ declarative section.

21. The Linkage Section is written in the _____ Division to describe _____ from _____ program.

22. The entries in the Linkage Section provides name and descriptions but _____ storage areas are reserved.

23. _____ linkage statements permit communication between object programs.

24. A COBOL program can _____ and _____ to other COBOL programs or to programs written in _____ languages.

25. A program that refers to another program is called a _____ program.

26. A program that is referred to is a _____ program.
27. Control is returned from the _____ program to the first instruction following the _____ sequence in the _____ program.
28. Whenever the program calls another program, _____ must be established between the two programs.
29. The calling program must state the _____ point of the called program and must specify the _____ to be passed.
30. The called program must have an _____ point and must be able to accept the _____.
31. The called program must establish the _____ for return of _____ to the _____ program.
32. The Call statement permits communication between the _____ program and one or more _____ or other _____.
33. The Call statement appears in the _____ program and may not appear in the _____ program.
34. A called program must contain a statement where the program is to be _____.
35. The Entry statement establishes an entry in a COBOL _____ of a _____ program.
36. If the called program is entered as the first instruction in the Procedure Division, the _____ option is used.
37. If the entry point of a called program is other than the first statement of the Procedure Division, the _____ statement is used.
38. Either the _____ or _____ statement must be used to return control to the calling program.
39. The Goback statement marks the _____ end of a called program.
40. The Exit Program statement is used in the same manner as other _____ _____ statements.

Answers

1. PROCEDURE, PROCEDURE, OBJECT
2. PROCEDURES, COMPILER
3. REGULAR
4. NONSYNCHRONOUSLY, SEQUENTIAL, TESTED
5. BEGINNING, FIRST
6. DECLARATIVES, A, PERIOD, SPACE
7. END DECLARATIVES
8. PROCEDURES, TYPE
9. EXECUTED, EXECUTION, USE
10. LABEL-HANDLING, ERROR-HANDLING, REPORT WRITING
11. USER CREATED
12. BEGINNING, HEADER
13. ENDING, TRAILER
14. DATA-NAMES, LABEL RECORDS

15. INPUT/OUTPUT, CORREC-
    TION, COMPILER
16. READ, WRITE, REWRITE,
    START
17. SYSTEM ERRORS, USER
    SPECIFIED
18. ERROR-PROCESSING,
    DECLARATIVES
19. REPORT GROUP, REPORT
20. MOVE 1 TO PRINT-SWITCH,
    USE BEFORE REPORTING
21. DATA, DATA, ANOTHER
22. NO
23. SUBPROGRAM
24. REFER TO, PASS CONTROL,
    OTHER
25. CALLING
26. CALLED
27. CALLED, CALLING, CALLING
28. LINKAGE
29. ENTRY, ARGUMENTS
30. ENTRY, ARGUMENTS
31. LINKAGE, CONTROL, CALLING
32. OBJECT, SUBPROGRAM,
    LINKAGE SUBPROGRAMS
33. CALLING, CALLED
34. ENTERED
35. SUBPROGRAM, CALLED
36. USING
37. ENTRY
38. GOBACK, EXIT PROGRAM
39. LOGICAL
40. EXIT

Questions for Review

1. Why is a Declarative Section written? Give the steps necessary to write the section.
2. What is the primary function of the Use statement? List the types of procedures associated with the Use statement.
3. What are Label Processing Declaratives? What are their purposes and uses?
4. What are Error Processing Declaratives? What are their purposes and uses?
5. Under what conditions is the continued processing of a file containing errors permitted?
6. When is the Use Before Reporting option used? What is its purpose and how is it used?
7. How can the printing of a report group in the Report Writer be suppressed?
8. What is the function of the Linkage Section?
9. What are Subprogram Linkage statements? Give examples.
10. Differentiate between a calling and called program.
11. How is linkage specified in calling and called programs?
12. What is the function of the Call statement and how is it used in a calling program?
13. What is the function of the Entry statement and how is it used in a called program?
14. What is the function of the Goback and Exit Program and when is each used in a called program?
15. Explain the operation of a calling and called program.

Problems

1. *Match each item with its proper description.*

    _____ 1. Declaratives Section   A. Correction procedures.

    _____ 2. Label-Processing   B. Execution of statements just before
            Declarative   the report group named.

    _____ 3. Error-Processing   C. Handle user created labels.
            Declarative

    _____ 4. Report Writer   D. Special circumstance under which a
            Declarative   procedure is to be executed.

    _____ 5. Linkage Section   E. Describes data from another program.

2. *Match each item with its proper description.*

    _____ 1. Called Program   A. Permits communication between object program and subprogram.

    _____ 2. Calling Program   B. Entry point in a subprogram.

    _____ 3. Call Statement   C. A program that refers to another program.

    _____ 4. Entry Statement   D. Logical end of a called program.

    _____ 5. Goback Statement   E. Operates in same manner as Exit statement.

    _____ 6. Exit Program   F. A program that is referred to.
            Statement

3. *The following is the Procedure Division of a program to create a Direct file organization.*

```
PROCEDURE DIVISION.
DECLARATIVES.
ERROR-PROCEDURE SECTION. USE AFTER STANDARD ERROR PROCEDURE
    ON D-FILE GIVING ERROR-COND.
ERROR-ROUTINE.
    EXHIBIT NAMED ERROR-COND.
    IF ERR = 1 GO TO SYNONYM-ROUTINE    ELSE
        DISPLAY 'CTHER STANDARD ERROR ' REC-ID
        GO TO EOJ.
SYNONYM-ROUTINE.
    IF CC = 84 AND HD = 9  DISPLAY 'OVERFLCW AREA FULL'
        GO TO EOJ.
    IF CC = 84 ADD 1 TO HD  GO TO ADJUST-HD.
    IF HH = 9 GO TO END-CYLINDER.
    ADD 1 TO HH.
    GO TO WRITES.
ENC-CYLINDER.
    MOVE 84 TO CC.
ADJUST-HD.
    MOVE HD TO HH.
    GO TO WRITES.
END DECLARATIVES.
FILE-CREATION SECTION.
    OPEN INPUT C-FILE
        OUTPUT D-FILE.
```

```
READS.
    READ C-FILE AT END GO TO EOJ.
    MOVE CORRESPONDING C-REC TO D-REC.
    MOVE PART-NUM OF C-REC TO REC-ID SAVE.
    DIVIDE SAVE BY 829 GIVING QUOTIENT REMAINDER TRACK-1.
    ADD 10 TO TRACK-1.
    MOVE CYL TO CC.
    MOVE HEAD TO HH.
WRITES.
    EXHIBIT NAMED TRACK-ID  C-REC   CC   HH.
    WRITE D-REC INVALID KEY GO TO INVALID-KEY.
    GO TO READS.
INVALID-KEY.
    DISPLAY 'INVALID KEY '   REC-ID.
EOJ.
    CLOSE C-FILE D-FILE.
    STOP RUN.
```

Explain the function of the Error-Processing declarative.

4.

PROCEDURE DIVISION.

DECLARATIVES.

RW-1 SECTION. USE BEFORE REPORTING PAGE-HED.

RW-2. IF CBL-CTR IS LESS THAN 1 OR EQUAL TO 1
    MOVE 'BEGIN' TO BEGIN-FIELD-FOR-PH
    MOVE SPACES TO CONTINUED-FIELD-FOR-PH
    ELSE MOVE SPACES TO BEGIN-FIELD-FOR-PH
    MOVE 'CONTINUED' TO CONTINUED-FIELD-FOR-PH.

RW-3 SECTION. USE BEFORE REPORTING PAGE-FOOT.

RW-4. IF CBL-CTR IS GREATER THAN 1
    MOVE MONTHNAME (MONTH) TO MONTH-FOR-PF
    MOVE 'CONTINUED ON NEXT PAGE' TO TEXT-FOR-PF
    ELSE MOVE SPACES TO MONTH-FOR-PF
    MOVE SPACES TO TEXT-FOR-PF.

END DECLARATIVES.

In the above declarative procedural statements, what is the main purpose of each. Give examples to illustrate your point.

5. *Write the Report Writer declarative to suppress printing for a footing group (FOOT-LINE) for job numbers 15–20.*

6. *Write a Label Processing declarative to process the user header labels on an input file, FILE-IN. The condition to be tested is as follows:*

If the LAB-ID is greater than ALLOWABLE-DATE, stop the run and display the message "File-In Is Incorrect; Label Error, Mount Proper Reel" on the console and wait for a reply. Branch back to recheck the labels after correction.

If the LAB-ID is not greater than ALLOWABLE-DATE, display "Label Is OK" upon console and proceed to the procedural statements to execute the program.

7. *Given the following information:*

```
IDENTIFICATION DIVISION.
PROGRAM-ID.  INVENTORY.
      .
      .
      .
DATA DIVISION.
      .
      .
      .
WORKING-STORAGE SECTION.
01  TRANS-RECORD.
      02  QUANTITY        PICTURE 9(5).
      02  UNIT-PRICE      PICTURE 999V99.
      02  AMOUNT          PICTURE 9(5)V99.
      .
      .
      .
PROCEDURE DIVISION.
      .
      .
      .
      CALL 'INVENTORYSUB' USING TRANS-RECORD.
      .
      .
      .
      CALL 'INVUPDATE' USING TRANS-RECORD.
      .
      .
      .
IDENTIFICATION DIVISION.
PROGRAM-ID.  INVENTORYSUB.
      .
      .
      .
DATA DIVISION.
      .
      .
      .
LINKAGE SECTION.
01  INVREC.
      02  UNITS           PICTURE 9(5).
      02  PRICE           PICTURE 999V99.
      02  INV-BALANCE     PICTURE 9(5)V99.
      .
      .
PROCEDURE DIVISION USING INVREC.
      .
      .
      GOBACK.
      ENTRY 'INVUPDATE' USING INVREC.
      .
      .
      GOBACK.
```

In the above programs, explain the processing routines between the calling and called programs. How are the different values handled in each program by what data name? What happens with each execution of the Call statement?

14

Additional and Optional Features

Configuration Section—Special-Names Paragraph

The SPECIAL-NAMES paragraph is used to equate special function-names with user-specified mnemonic-names. The entire paragraph may be omitted if no user mnemonic-names are specified in the Procedure Division.

Rules Governing the Use of Special-Names Paragraph
1. In ACCEPT and DISPLAY statements, associated mnemonic-names **may** be used to identify the function-names identified with the input or output

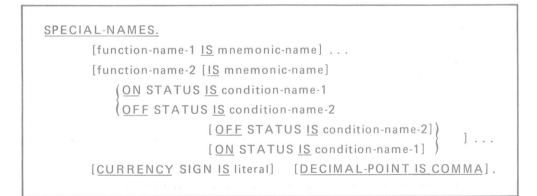

```
SPECIAL-NAMES.
      [function-name-1 IS mnemonic-name] . . .
      [function-name-2 [IS mnemonic-name]
          ( ON STATUS IS condition-name-1
          ( OFF STATUS IS condition-name-2
                      [OFF STATUS IS condition-name-2])
                      [ON STATUS IS condition-name-1] )    ] . . .
      [CURRENCY SIGN IS literal]    [DECIMAL-POINT IS COMMA].
```

Figure 14–1. Format Special–Names Paragraph.

489

device. The function-name may only be chosen from the following list.

SYSIN
SYSOUT
SYSPUNCH
CONSOLE

2. When the mnemonic-name option is used in a WRITE statement with the ADVANCING option, the mnemonic-name must be defined as a function-name in the SPECIAL-NAMES paragraph. It is used to skip to channel 1–12 and to suppress spacing if desired. It may also be used for pocket selection for a card punch file.

Function-Name	Action Taken
CSP	Suppress spacing
C01-C12	Skip to channel 1 to 12 respectively
S01-S02	Pocket selection

3. Mnemonic-names with a single character enclosed in quotation marks are used in the CODE clause in the report description entry of the Report Writer Feature to identify output where more than one type of output is desired from a single input. (See "Report Writer.")
4. Mnemonic-names may not be used in a source program except in the verb format which permits their usage.
5. The literal that appears in the CURRENCY SIGN IS clause is used in the PICTURE clause to represent the currency symbol. The literal is limited to a single character, must be a nonnumeric, and must not be any of the following:

   a. Digits 0–9.
   b. Alphabetic characters A–Z and space.
   c. Special characters * − , . ; ( ) + " or '

   If the CURRENCY SIGN clause is not used, only the $ can be used as the currency symbol in the PICTURE clause.
6. The clause DECIMAL-POINT IS COMMA means that the function of the comma and the period are exchanged in the PICTURE character string and in numeric literals. When the clause is used, the user must use a comma to represent a decimal point when required in numeric literals or in a PICTURE clause. The period is used for all functions ordinarily served by the comma.

Input-Output Section—File-Control Paragraph

Reserve Clause

The RESERVE clause is used to reserve additional input or output areas in addition to the buffers allocated by the compiler.

Rules Governing the Use of the Reserve Clause

1. The clause specifies the number of buffers represented by the integer to be reserved for standard sequential or an indexed sequential file that is accessed sequentially in addition to the one buffer which is reserved automatically.
2. The clause must not be specified for direct files. If specified, the clause is ignored, and only one buffer is reserved.
3. If NO is written, no additional areas are assigned besides the minimum of one.

Figure 14–2. Format Reserve Clause.

File-Limit Clause

The FILE-LIMIT clause is used to specify the logical beginning and logical end of a file on a mass storage (direct-access) device. The logical beginning of a mass storage file is the address specified in the first operand of the clause, and the logical end is the address specified in the last operand of the clause.

Because file boundaries are determined by the operating system job-control card, no allocation is made by this clause, and the entire clause is treated as comments, serving only as documentation for the program.

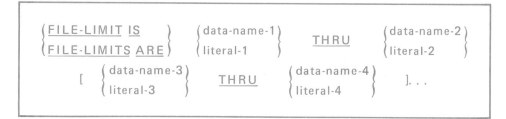

Figure 14–3. Format File-Limit Clause.

Track-Area Clause

The TRACK-AREA clause is used to specify a required area where records are to be added to a random-access device with indexed sequential organization. The size of the track must be at least the size of an entire track plus one logical record.

Rules Governing the Use of the Track-Area Clause

1. The clause is required when variable-length records are added to the file. Efficiency can be improved in adding a record when the TRACK-AREA clause is specified.
2. If an integer is specified, an area equal to the number specified is obtained by the system when the file is opened. When the file is closed, the assigned area is released to the system.
3. If a record is added to an indexed sequential file and the TRACK-AREA clause is not used for the file, the contents of the NOMINAL KEY field are unpredictable after a WRITE statement is executed.

```
TRACK-AREA IS integer CHARACTERS
```

Figure 14–4.   Format Track-Area Clause.

Input-Output Section—I-O-Control Paragraph

Rerun Clause

The RERUN clause is used to establish any rerun or restart procedures. This clause specifies that checkpoint areas are to be written on the actual device at the time of the checkpoint, and that they can be read back into core storage to restart the program from that point. A checkpoint record is the recording of the status of the problem program and main storage resources at desired intervals. The presence of this clause specifies that checkpoint records are to be taken. Checkpoint records are read sequentially and must be assigned to tape or mass storage devices.

I-O-CONTROL
    [RERUN Clause] . . .
    [SAME AREA Clause] . . .
    [MULTIPLE FILE TAPE Clause] . . .
    [APPLY Clause] . . .

Figure 14–5. Format Environment Division—I-O-Control Paragraph.

RERUN ON system-name
        EVERY integer RECORDS OF file-name

Figure 14–6. Format Rerun Clause.

System-name specifies the external medium for the checkpoint file, the file upon which the checkpoint records are written. It must not be the same as the system-name used in the File-Control ASSIGN clause, but it follows the same rules of formation. System-name must specify a tape or mass storage device.

File-name represents the file for which checkpoint records are to be written. It must be described with a file description entry in the Data Division.

Multiple File Tape Clause

The MULTIPLE FILE TAPE clause is used for documentation purposes and indicates that two or more files are sharing the same physical reel of tape.

Apply Write-Only

This option is used to make optimum use of buffers and device space when creating a file whose recording mode is V. Normally a buffer is truncated when there is not enough space remaining to accommodate the maximum size record. The use of this option will cause the buffer to be truncated only when the next record does not fit in the unused remainder of the buffer. This option is meaningful only when the file is opened as OUTPUT.

The files named in this option must be standard sequential.

Every WRITE statement associated with this option must use WRITE RECORD NAME FROM identifier option.

• To write single checkpoint records using tape:

```
//CHECKPT    DD    DSNAME=CHECK1,              X
//                 VOLUME=SER=ND003,           X
//                 UNIT=2400,DISP=(NEW,KEEP),  X
//                 LABEL=(,NL)
                       .
                       .
                       .
           ENVIRONMENT DIVISION.
                       .
                       .
                       .
           RERUN ON UT-2400-S-CHECKPT EVERY
           5000 RECORDS OF ACCT-FILE.
```

• To write single checkpoint records using disk (note that more than one data set may share the same external-name):

```
//CHEK       DD    DSNAME=CHECK2,              X
//                 VOLUME=(PRIVATE,RETAIN,     X
//                    SER=DB030,               X
//                 UNIT=2314,DISP=(NEW,KEEP),  X
//                 SPACE=(TRK,300)
                       .
                       .
                       .
           ENVIRONMENT DIVISION.
                       .
                       .
                       .
           RERUN ON UT-2314-S-CHEK EVERY
           20000 RECORDS OF PAYCODE.
           RERUN ON UT-2314-S-CHEK EVERY
           30000 RECORD OF IN-FILE.
```

• To write multiple contiguous checkpoint records (on tape):

```
//CHEKPT     DD    DSNAME=CHECK3,              X
//                 VOLUME=SER=111111,          X
//                 UNIT=2400,DISP=(MOD,PASS),  X
//                 LABEL=(,NL)
                       .
                       .
                       .
           ENVIRONMENT DIVISION.
                       .
                       .
                       .
           RERUN ON UT-2400-S-CHEKPT EVERY
           10000 RECORDS OF PAY-FILE.
```

Figure 14–7.   Examples—Rerun and Checkpoint Procedures—IBM.

MULTIPLE FILE TAPE CONTAINS file-name-1

    [POSITION integer-1]   [file-name-2   [POSITION integer-2]] ...

Figure 14–8. Format Multiple File Tape Clause.

APPLY WRITE-ONLY ON file-name-1   [file-name-2] ...

Figure 14–9. Format Apply Write-Only Clause.

Apply Core-Index on Clause

This option may be specified only for an indexed sequential file whose access mode is random. It is used to specify the highest-level index to be processed in core. The area will be obtained at open time and released at close time.

APPLY CORE-INDEX TO data-name ON file-name-1 [file-name-2] ...

Figure 14–10. Format Apply Core-Index Clause.

APPLY RECORD-OVERFLOW ON file-name-1 [file-name-2] ...

Figure 14–11. Format Apply Record-Overflow on Clause.

Apply Record-Overflow on Clause

If the record-overflow feature is available for mass storage devices being specified, the amount of unused space on a volume may be reduced by specifying this option for files on that volume. If the option is used, a block that does not fit on this track is partially written on that track and continued on the next available track.

This option may only be specified for a standard sequential file (with F, U, or V recording mode records) assigned to a mass storage device, or a direct file with fixed-length records.

DATA DIVISION

Renames Clause

The RENAMES clause permits possible overlapping and groupings of elementary data.

---

66 data-name-1 <u>RENAMES</u> data-name-2 [<u>THRU</u> data-name-3]

Figure 14–12.   Format Renames Clause.

Rules Governing the Use of the Renames Clause
1. Level number 66 must be used with RENAMES clause.
2. All logical entries associated with a given logical record must immediately follow its last data description entry.
3. Data-name-2 and data-name-3 must be the name of elementary items or groupings of elementary items in the associated logical record and cannot be the same data-name.
4. Data-name-3 cannot be subordinate to data-name-2.
5. A level 66 cannot rename another level 66 entry nor can it rename a level 77, 88, or 01 entry.
6. Data-name-1 cannot be used as a qualifier and can be qualified only by level 01 or FD entries.
7. Data-name-2 and data-name-3 may be qualified.
8. An OCCURS clause may not appear in data-name-2, data-name-3, or any item subordinate to it.
9. Data-name-2 must precede data-name-3 in the record description entry.

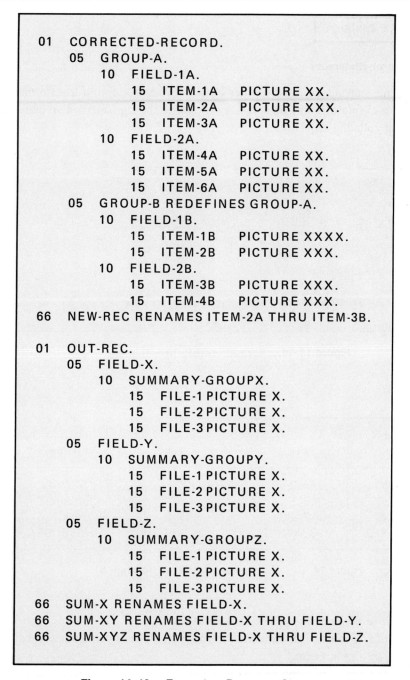

```
01   CORRECTED-RECORD.
     05   GROUP-A.
          10   FIELD-1A.
               15   ITEM-1A   PICTURE XX.
               15   ITEM-2A   PICTURE XXX.
               15   ITEM-3A   PICTURE XX.
          10   FIELD-2A.
               15   ITEM-4A   PICTURE XX.
               15   ITEM-5A   PICTURE XX.
               15   ITEM-6A   PICTURE XX.
     05   GROUP-B REDEFINES GROUP-A.
          10   FIELD-1B.
               15   ITEM-1B   PICTURE XXXX.
               15   ITEM-2B   PICTURE XXX.
          10   FIELD-2B.
               15   ITEM-3B   PICTURE XXX.
               15   ITEM-4B   PICTURE XXX.
66   NEW-REC RENAMES ITEM-2A THRU ITEM-3B.

01   OUT-REC.
     05   FIELD-X.
          10   SUMMARY-GROUPX.
               15   FILE-1 PICTURE X.
               15   FILE-2 PICTURE X.
               15   FILE-3 PICTURE X.
     05   FIELD-Y.
          10   SUMMARY-GROUPY.
               15   FILE-1 PICTURE X.
               15   FILE-2 PICTURE X.
               15   FILE-3 PICTURE X.
     05   FIELD-Z.
          10   SUMMARY-GROUPZ.
               15   FILE-1 PICTURE X.
               15   FILE-2 PICTURE X.
               15   FILE-3 PICTURE X.
66   SUM-X RENAMES FIELD-X.
66   SUM-XY RENAMES FIELD-X THRU FIELD-Y.
66   SUM-XYZ RENAMES FIELD-X THRU FIELD-Z.
```

Figure 14–13.   Example—Renames Clause.

PROCEDURE DIVISION

Transform Statement

This statement is used to alter characters according to a transformation rule. For example, it may be necessary to change the characters in an item to a different collating sequence.

TRANSFORM identifier-3 CHARACTERS FROM
$$\begin{Bmatrix} \text{figurative-constant-1} \\ \text{nonnumeric-literal-1} \\ \text{identifier-1} \end{Bmatrix}$$

TO
$$\begin{Bmatrix} \text{figurative-constant-2} \\ \text{nonnumeric-literal-2} \\ \text{identifier-2} \end{Bmatrix}$$

Figure 14–14. Format Transform Statement.

Identifier-3 (Before)	FROM	TO	Identifier-3 (After)
1b7bbABC	SPACE	QUOTE	1"7" "ABC
1b7bbABC	"17CB"	"QRST"	QbRbbATS
1b7bbABC	b17ABC	CBA71b	BCACC71b
1234WXY89	98YXW4321	ABCKEFGHI	IHGFEDCBA

Figure 14–15. Examples—Data Transformation.

Rules Governing the Use of the Transform Statement

1. Identifier-3 must be an elementary alphabetic, alphanumeric, numeric edited item, or a group item.
2. The combination of the FROM and TO options determine what the transformation rule is to be.
3. Nonnumeric literals require enclosing quotation marks.

Operands	Transformation Rule
FROM figurative-constant-1 TO figurative-constant-2	All characters in the data item represented by identifier-3 equal to the single character figurative-constant-1 are replaced by the single character figurative-constant-2.
FROM figurative-constant-1 TO nonnumeric-literal-2	All characters in the data item represented by identifier-3 equal to the single character figurative-constant-1 are replaced by the single character nonnumeric-literal-2.
FROM figurative-constant-1 TO identifier-2	All characters in the data item represented by identifier-3 equal to the single character figurative-constant-1 are replaced by the single character represented by identifier-2.
FROM nonnumeric-literal-1 TO figurative-constant-2	All characters in the data item represented by identifier-3 that are equal to any character in nonnumeric-literal-1 are replaced by the single character figurative-constant-2.
FROM nonnumeric-literal-1 TO nonnumeric-literal-2	Nonnumeric-literal-1 and nonnumeric-literal-2 must be equal in length or nonnumeric-literal-2 must be a single character. If the nonnumeric-literals are equal in length, any character in the data item represented by identifier-3 equal to a character in nonnumeric-literal-1 is replaced by the character in the corresponding position of nonnumeric-literal-2. If the length of nonnumeric-literal-2 is one, all characters in the data item represented by identifier-3 that are equal to any character appearing in nonnumeric-literal-1 are replaced by the single character given in nonnumeric-literal-2.

Figure 14–16.   Transform Statement Rules.

Figure 14–16. Transform Statement Rules—Continued.

Operands	Transformation Rule
FROM nonnumeric-literal-1 TO identifier-2	Nonnumeric-literal-1 and the data item represented by identifier-2 must be equal in length or identifier-2 must represent a single character item.
	If nonnumeric-literal-1 and identifier-2 are equal in length, any character represented by identifier-3 equal to a character in nonnumeric-literal-1 is replaced by the character in the corresponding position of the item represented by identifier-2.
	If the length of the data item represented by identifier-2 is one, all characters represented by identifier-3 that are equal to any character appearing in nonnumeric literal-1 are replaced by the single character represented by identifier-2.
FROM identifier-1 TO figurative-constant-2	All characters represented by identifier-3 that are equal to any character in the data item represented by identifier-1 are replaced by the single character figurative-constant-2.
FROM identifier-1 TO nonnumeric-literal-2	The data item represented by identifier-1 and nonnumeric-literal-2 must be of equal length or nonnumeric-literal-2 must be one character.
	If identifier-1 and nonnumeric-literal-2 are equal in length, any character in identifier-3 equal to a character in identifier-1 is replaced by the character in the corresponding position of nonnumeric-literal-2.
	If the length of nonnumeric-literal-3 is one, all characters represented by identifier-3 that are equal to any character represented by identifier-1 are replaced by the single character given in nonnumeric-literal-2.
FROM identifier-1 TO identifier-2	Any character in the data item represented by identifier-3 equal to a character in the data item represented by identifier-1 is replaced by the character in the corresponding position of the data item represented by identifier-2. Identifier-1 and identifier-2 can be one or more characters, but must be equal in length.

4. Identifier-1 and Identifier-2 must be elementary alphabetic or alphanumeric items or any fixed-length group items not to exceed 255 characters in length.
5. A character may not be repeated in a nonnumeric-literal-1 or in the area defined by Identifier-1. If a character is repeated, the results will be unpredictable.
6. The allowable figurative constants are ZERO, ZEROS, ZEROES, SPACE, SPACES, QUOTE, QUOTES, HIGH-VALUE, HIGH-VALUES, LOW-VALUE, and LOW-VALUES.
7. When either Identifier-1 or Identifier-2 appears as an operand of the specific transformation, the user can change the transformation rule at object time.

SOURCE PROGRAM LIBRARY FACILITY

The library module provides a capability for specifying text that is to be copied from a library. The COBOL library contains text that is available to a source program at compile time. Prewritten source program entries can be included in a source program at compile time. Thus an installation can use standard file descriptions, record descriptions, or procedures without recoding them. The effect of the compilation of the library text is the same as if the text were actually written as part of the source program.

The COBOL library contains text that is available to a source program at compile time. These entries and procedures are contained in these user-created libraries; they are included in a source program by means of a COPY statement.

COBOL library text is placed in the COBOL library as a function independent of the COBOL program and according to implementor defined techniques. An entry in the COBOL library may contain source program texts for the Environment, Data, or Procedure Divisions, or any combination thereof.

Copy Statement

The COPY statement permits the inclusion of prewritten Environment, Data, and Procedure Division entries at compile time in the source program.

Library-name is the name of a member of a partitioned data set contained in the user's library; it identifies the library subroutine to the control program. Library-name must follow the rules for the formation of a program-name. The first eight characters are used to identify the name.

Option 1 (within the Configuration Section):

> SOURCE-COMPUTER. COPY statement.
> OBJECT-COMPUTER. COPY statement.
> SPECIAL-NAMES. COPY statement.

Option 2 (within the Input-Output Section):

> FILE-CONTROL. COPY statement.
> I-O-CONTROL. COPY statement.

Option 3 (within the FILE-CONTROL Paragraph):

> SELECT file-name COPY statement.

Option 4 (within the File Section):

> FD file-name COPY statement.
> SD sort-file-name COPY statement.

Option 5 (within the Report Section):

> FD report-name COPY statement.
> RD report-name [WITH CODE mnemonic-name] COPY statement.

Option 6 (within a File or Sort description entry, or within the Working-Storage Section or the Linkage Section):

> 01 data-name COPY statement.

Option 7 (with a Report Group):

> 01 [data-name] COPY statement.

Option 8 (within the Working-Storage Section or the Linkage Section):

> 77 data-name COPY statement.

Option 9 (within the Procedure Division):

> section-name SECTION [priority-number]. COPY statement.
> paragraph-name. COPY statement.

Figure 14–17. Format Copy Statement.

Rules Governing the Use of Copy Statement

1. The COPY statement may appears as follows:
    a. In any of the paragraphs of the Environment Division.
    b. In any of the level indicators entries or any 01 level entry in the Data Division.
    c. In a Section or a paragraph in the Procedure Division.

2. No other statement may appear in the same entry as the COPY statement.

3. The library text is copied from the library and the result of the compilation is the same as if the text were actually a part of the source program. The words COPY *Library-name* are replaced by the information by library-name. This information comprises the sentences or clauses which are necessary to complete the paragraph, sentence, or entry containing the COPY statement.

4. The copying process is terminated by the end of the library text itself.

5. The text in the library must not contain a COPY statement.

6. If the REPLACING option is used, each word specified in the format is replaced by the stipulated word, identifier, or literal which is associated with it in the format. The use of the REPLACING option does not alter the material as it appears in the library.

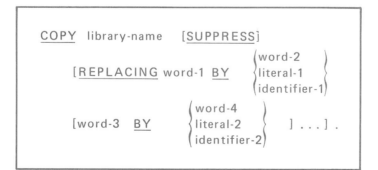

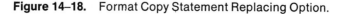

Figure 14–18. Format Copy Statement Replacing Option.

If the library entry PAYLIB consists of the following Data Division record:

```
01   A.
     05     B     PICTURE S99.
     05     C     PICTURE S9(5)V99.
     05     D     PICTURE S9999 OCCURS 0 TO 52 TIMES
                  DEPENDING ON B OF A.
```

the programmer can use the COPY statement in the Data Division of his program as follows:

```
01   PAYROLL COPY PAYLIB.
```

In this program, the library entry is then copied and appears in the source listing as follows:

```
01   PAYROLL.
     05     B     PICTURE S99.
     05     C     PICTURE S9(5)V99.
     05     D     PICTURE S9999 OCCURS 0 TO 52 TIMES
                  DEPENDING ON B OF A.
```

Note that the data-name A has not been change in the DEPENDING ON option. To change some (or all) of the names within the library entry to names he wishes to reference in his program, the programmer can use the REPLACING option:

```
01   PAYROLL COPY PAYLIB REPLACING A BY PAYROLL
     B BY PAY-CODE C BY GROSSPAY.
```

In this program the library entry is copied and appears in the source listing as follows:

```
01   PAYROLL.
     05   PAY-CODE     PICTURE S99.
     05   GROSSPAY     PICTURE S9(5)V99.
     05   D     PICTURE S9999 OCCURS 0 TO 52 TIMES
               DEPENDING ON PAY-CODE OF PAYROLL.
```

The entry as it appears in the library remains unchanged.

Figure 14–19. Example —Copy Statement.

Exercises

Write your answers in the space provided.

1. The Special-Names paragraph is used to equate special _____ names with _____ mnemonic names.

2. The Special-Names paragraph is written only if the user specifies a _____ name in the _____ Division.

3. When the _____ option is used in a Write statement with the Advancing option, the _____ name must be defined as a _____ _____ name in the Special-Names paragraph.

4. Mnemonic names with a single character enclosed in quote marks is used in the _____ clause of the report description entry.

5. If the Currency Sign clause is not used, only the _____ can be used as the currency Symbol in the Picture clause.

6. If the function of commas and periods are to be exchanged in the Picture clause or in a numeric literal, the clause _____ is used.

7. The Reserve clause is used to reserve additional _____ or _____ areas in addition to the buffer allocated by the _____.

8. The Reserve clause must not be specified for _____ files.

9. If no additional input/output areas aside from the minimum of one are needed, the _____ option is used.

10. The File-Limit clause is used for the logical _____ and logical _____ of a file on a _____ device.

11. The Multiple-File Tape clause indicates that two or more tape files share the same _____ reel of tape.

12. The Track-Area clause may be used when records are to be added to an _____ file in the _____ access mode.

13. The Apply Write-Only On clause is used to make optimum use of _____ _____ and _____ space when creating a file whose recording mode is _____.

14. The Apply Core-Index On option is used with _____ files whose access mode is _____ and is used to specify the highest level _____ to be processed in core storage.

15. The Apply Record-Overflow On clause is used to reduce the amount of _____ space in disk storage.

16. The Rerun clause is used to check the status for a _____ of a problem program at _____ intervals.

17. The Renames clause permits possible _____ and _____ of elementary data.

18. Level number _____ must be used with the Renames clause.

19. The Transform statement is used to _____ characters according to a _____ rule.

20. The library module contains _____ that is available to a _____ program at _____ time.
21. _____ source items can be included at _____ time.
22. The Copy statement permits the inclusion of prewritten _____, _____ and Procedure Division entries at _____ time in a _____ program.
23. The words Copy _____ are replaced by the prewritten library entries.
24. The text in a library must not contain a _____ statement.
25. If the Replacing option is used each word is replaced by the stipulated _____, _____ or _____ which is associated with it in the format.

Answers

1. FUNCTION, USER SPECIFIED
2. MNEMONIC, PROCEDURE
3. MNEMONIC NAME, MNEMONIC, FUNCTION
4. CODE
5. $
6. DECIMAL POINT IS COMMA
7. INPUT, OUTPUT, COMPILER
8. DIRECT
9. NO
10. BEGINNING, END, MASS STORAGE
11. PHYSICAL
12. INDEXED, RANDOM
13. BUFFER, DEVICE, V
14. INDEXED, RANDOM, INDEX
15. UNUSED
16. RECORD, DESIRED
17. OVERLAPPING, GROUPINGS
18. 66
19. ALTER, TRANSFORMATION
20. TEXT, SOURCE, COMPILE
21. PREWRITTEN, COMPILE
22. ENVIRONMENT, DATA, COMPILE, SOURCE
23. LIBRARY-NAME
24. LIBRARY
25. WORD, IDENTIFIER, LITERAL

Questions for Review

1. What is the purpose of the Special-Names paragraph?
2. How is the Special-Names paragraph used with the Advancing option of the Write statement? Give an example.
3. What are the main uses of the Reserve clause?
4. How is the File-Limit clause used with mass storage devices.
5. What are the main purposes of the Multiple-File Tape clause?
6. Give the main uses of the following Apply clauses: Apply Write-Only On, Apply Core-Index On, Apply Record-Overflow On.
7. What is the main function of the Rerun clause? Explain the operation of the Rerun clause.

8. What is the purpose of the Renames clause?
9. How is a Transform statement used? Give an example.
10. What purposes does the Copy statement serve? Give examples of its use.
11. What are libraries and how are they used in COBOL programs?
12. How are standardized library texts included in the users program?

Problems

1. *Match each item with its proper description.*

_____ 1. Special-Names   A. User specified name.

_____ 2. Mnemonic Name   B. Additional input/output areas.

_____ 3. Function Name   C. Equate function name with user specified mnemonic name.

_____ 4. Reserve   D. Two files sharing the same physical reel of tape.

_____ 5. File-Limit   E. Name of device or action taken.

_____ 6. Multiple-File Tape   F. Logical beginning and ending of a mass storage file.

2. *Match each item with its proper description.*

_____ 1. Track-Area   A. Optimum use of buffer and device space.

_____ 2. Apply Write-Only   B. Reduce amount of unused space on a volume.

_____ 3. Apply Core-Index On   C. Checkpoint record.

_____ 4. Apply Record-Overflow On   D. Inclusion of prewritten library entries.

_____ 5. Rerun   E. Records added to indexed file in random access mode.

_____ 6. Renames   F. Highest level index in core storage.

_____ 7. Copy   G. Overlapping and grouping of elementary data items.

3. *You are using an IBM 370 Model H155 computer, write the necessary entries to accomplish the following:*

   a. The Configuration Section of the Environment Division entries including the Special-Names paragraph to define the mnemonic name FIRST-LINE as the first line of the form.

   b. The procedural Write statement with the After Advancing option to write the output record RECORD-OUT after skipping to the first line of the next form after reaching the last line of the form.

4. *A file called CUSTOMER-FILE with a record name of CUSTOMER-RECORD is to be outputted on a printer in the same format as the input record.*

   Using the following hardware devices:

Device	Model Number
Card Reader	2540
Printer	1403

Write the necessary entries to accomplish the following:

a. Configuration Section including the Special-Names paragraph.
b. File-Control paragraph including the Reserve clause.
c. The procedural entries to move the input record to the output including end of page procedures.

5.

```
01   CORRECTED-RECORD.
     05   GROUP-A.
          10   FIELD-1A.
               15   ITEM-1A   PICTURE XX.
               15   ITEM-2A   PICTURE XXX.
               15   ITEM-3A   PICTURE XX.
          10   FIELD-2A.
               15   ITEM-4A   PICTURE XX.
               15   ITEM-5A   PICTURE XX.
               15   ITEM-6A   PICTURE XX.
     05   GROUP-B REDEFINES GROUP-A.
          10   FIELD-1B.
               15   ITEM-1B   PICTURE XXXX.
               15   ITEM-2B   PICTURE XXX.
          10   FIELD-2B.
               15   ITEM-3B   PICTURE XXX.
               15   ITEM-4B   PICTURE XXX.
```

In the above record it is necessary to group items ITEM-3A to ITEM-4B for future processing.

Write the necessary entry to accomplish the above using the Renames clause.

6. *Since we are using the same Configuration Section in all of our programs, write the Configuration Section using the following library names:*

Paragraph	Library Name
Source-Computer	S-COMPUTER
Object-Computer	O-COMPUTER
Special-Names	S-NAMES

7. *In many of our programs, we are using the same headiings and detail line formats. We have decided to put these formats in our library as follows:*

Library Name	Function
SALES-HEAD	Name of report.
COLUMN-HEAD	Column headings of report.
DETAIL-RECORD	Detail line of the report.

Write the necessary entries for

Working-Storage items for headings and detail using the COPY clause for the report heading (HDG-1), column headings (HDG-2), and detail line (DETAIL-LINE).

8. *Most of our programs contain the same routine for printing headings on the first page and each overflow. We have decided to put these procedures in our library. Assume that the library name of the routine is HEADING-ROUTINE, write the Procedure Division entry using the COPY clause for the paragraph called PRT-HDG.*

9.

	Identifier-3 (Before)	From	To	Identifier-3 (After)
1.	149b07b9965	SPACE	'_'	
2.	JONES	'SNOEJ'	'HIMTS'	
3.	2b49b7512	'b729514'	'7586931'	
4.	12345658	'5386142'	'OSLBACN'	

In the above, fill in identifier-3 after the data transformation.

Note: b denotes blank character.

15

COBOL Programming Techniques

The writing of a computer program is a difficult and tedious task. Many times a program rapidly solves a particular problem without any regard for the efficiency of the program itself. In the writing of COBOL programs, this problem is more serious than in other programming languages. As mentioned earlier, COBOL does not produce a program as efficient as one written in the basic language of the particular computer. Thus it is imperative that the programmer adopt techniques that will increase the efficiency of the COBOL program.

Prior to the writing of the program, the problem should be properly defined, and the appropriate flowcharts, source document formats, and output formats should be available to the programmer.

The writing of the COBOL program can be simplified and the efficiency increased if the following programming techniques are applied. All four divisions of the COBOL program must be completed before the source program can be compiled and executed.

IDENTIFICATION DIVISION

This is the simplest division of the four. It contains the information that identifies the program and is intended to provide information to the reader of the program. The name of the program must be stated, and other information about the program may optionally be mentioned.

Entries That Should Appear in the Identification Division

1. The name of the division-Division Header.
2. The name of the program.
3. The name of the programmer.
4. When the program was written.
5. Remarks that will explain the data processing job from which the program was written.
6. Any other optional information.

Only items (1) and (2) are necessary for the proper execution of the program. Additional information is desirable for adequate documentation of the program. The reader of the program would be interested in the REMARKS paragraph where the intent of the program is mentioned. The pertinent information contained therein should provide the reader with a better understanding of the program. Therefore, it is essential that the REMARKS paragraph be as thorough as possible.

```
REMARKS.
      OUTPUT OF THIS PROGRAM IS A REPORT OF
      ALL PURCHASES FOR THE PREVIOUS MONTH.
      THE REPORT IS REQUIRED BY THE 5TH DAY
      OF EACH MONTH, AND IS DISTRIBUTED TO
      ALL PURCHASING REPRESENTATIVES. INPUT
      IS THE PURCHASING RECORDS CARD FILE,
      SORTED BY PURCHASE DATE WITHIN COMMODITY.
```

Figure 15–1. Example—Identification Division Remarks Paragraph.

ENVIRONMENT DIVISION

The Environment Division is the only division in the COBOL program that is machine oriented. The division contains information about the equipment to be used when the object program is compiled and executed. Most importantly, it links the devices of the computer system and the data files to be processed.

Entries That Should Appear in the Environment Division

1. The name of the division-Division Header.
2. Configuration Section—Source and Object Computer Paragraphs.
3. Input-Output Section—File-Control and I-O-Control Paragraphs.

The external device names in the File-Control paragraph should be checked with the system programmers since they will vary with each data processing unit.

All files mentioned in the File-Control paragraph should be properly defined in the Data Division, and opened and closed in the Procedure Division.

All device numbers used in the File-Control paragraph should be verified.

Any special input/output techniques should be defined in the I-O-Control paragraph.

DATA DIVISION

The Data Division describes the information to be processed by the object program. Each file mentioned in the Environment Division must be described in the Data Division. In addition, each data item within these files must be described. All data items that comprise the Working-Storage Section, such as constants and work areas, must also be described.

The Data Division should be written using copies of the source document formats and output formats as guides for writing the file description entries and the record description entries.

Entries That Should Appear in the Data Division

1. The name of the division-Division Header.
2. File Section-file description entries and record description entries.
3. Working-Storage Section record description entries for constants and work areas.
4. Linkage Section-record description entries used for subprograms.
5. Report Section-report description entries for the Report Writer Feature.

File Section

The File Section specifies the characteristics of the file.

File Description Entries

FD File-name is required and must agree with the name specified in the Environment Division.

Recording Mode Clause is optional but should be included if records are fixed variable or undefined; otherwise, the compiler will generate an algorithm that does not always give V.

Block Contains clause must be included when the records are blocked (e.g., when records are blocked on a tape). If the records vary in size, the character option should be used instead of records to specify the total number of characters in each block. When there is only one record per block, the clause may be omitted.

Record Contains clause is used when variable size records are used. The clause should specify the length of the shortest and longest record in the file. This clause may be omitted since the compiler determines the record size from the record description entries.

A good programming practice is to include this clause in every FD entry for the following reasons:

1. The compiler will check the agreement of the record count in the record description entry with the RECORD CONTAINS clause in the FD entry. This will assure that no data fields were erroneously omitted in the record description entry. Otherwise, the compiler will assume the count in the record description entries as being the correct record length.
2. It provides the programmer and reader of the program with the size of the record without the necessity of counting all field lengths stated in the record description entries.

Label Records clause must be included in every record description entry even if the files are located in cards where the OMITTED option is used.

Data Records clause is optional, and each record-name should be written in sequence as it appears in the record description entries. The record description entries must appear immediately after the file description entries.

Record Description Entries

Level Numbers are required for each entry. Each level is a given number, always beginning with 01 for the data record itself. Each succeeding level is given a larger number to indicate a further breakdown of the data item. These larger numbers need not be in sequence. This may provide the programmer with more flexibility in assigning numbers. All level numbers may be written at the A margin, although only the 01 and 77 level numbers are required to be written at the A margin. However, indentation should be used, as this improves the readability of the program.

Data-names may be unique or otherwise qualified. The highest qualifier must be a unique name. In the File Section, the highest qualifier is the file-name; thus it is possible for two records to have the same name.

Names of independent items in the Working-Storage Section must be unique since they cannot be qualified. The highest qualifier in the Working-Storage Section is the record-name.

A recommended programming procedure for writing Data Division entries for output files for the printer is to describe the formats of the output file in the Working-Storage section and to use the WRITE verb with the FROM option referring to the Working-Storage item. This technique provides the programmer with

1. The ability to define heading with appropriate VALUE clauses (forbidden in the File Section) in the Working-Storage Section. Areas in the output can be blanked where necessary.
2. The ability to use one record description entry to define the output for both headings and detail listings.

Picture clause tells the number of characters to be stored and what type they will be. Picture clauses are only found in the descriptions of elementary items. Picture and usage clauses must be compatible. For example, an alphabetic item cannot have a usage clause of computational.

Value clause is used to assign initial values. The Value clause is not permitted in the File section, except Level 88 (Condition-name) entries. The Value clause must agree with its picture. For example,

77 Discount Picture SV99, Value + .02.

77 Total-Identification, Picture A(15), Value "Pay This Amount".

Usage clause is allowed at both the group and elementary levels. If the clause is omitted, the items usage is assumed to be display.

If a data item field is to be used in a series of arithmetic operations, it would be advisable to define an area in Working-Storage Section in the computational mode. The data item would be moved from the input area to the Working-Storage area. After all the computations are completed, the computed item would be returned to the output area in the display mode.

This technique would save processing time of the compiler in changing the item from display to computational mode and back to display mode for each arithmetic operation.

Suffixes

To make it easier for programmers to locate items in a program listing, especially during the debugging stage, a good practice is to attach a suffix to a data-name to indicate where the item is to be found in the program. For example, if a QUANTITY item appears in the input and output records as well as in a Working-Storage area, the data-names may be assigned as follows:

Input item	— QUANTITY-IN
Output item	— QUANTITY-OUT
Working-Storage item	— QUANTITY-WS

The same principle may be applied to all items that appear in these areas in order to make it simpler for the reader to know which fields are logically part of the same record or area.

Move Corresponding

The MOVE CORRESPONDING statement can save time in writing many MOVE statements of identical items, usually from an input to an output record. However, this technique involves qualification whenever an identical item is involved in a Procedure Division statement. To eliminate excessive qualifying, a REDEFINES or RENAMES statement may be used with the corresponding items. For example,

```
01   PAY-RECORD-IN.
     05   SAME-NAMES.   (**)
          10   SAME-LAST-NAME        PICTURE........
          10   SAME-FIRST-NAME       PICTURE........
          10   SAME-PAYROLL          PICTURE........
     05   DIFF-NAMES REDEFINES SAME-NAMES.
          10   DIFF-LAST-NAME        PICTURE........
          10   DIFF-FIRST-NAME       PICTURE........
          10   DIFF-PAYROLL          PICTURE........
          .
          .
          .

01   PAY-RECORD-OUT.
     05   SAME-NAMES.   (**)
          10   SAME-PAYROLL          PICTURE........
          10   FILLER                PICTURE........
```

```
10  SAME-FIRST-NAME        PICTURE........
10  FILLER                 PICTURE........
10  SAME-LAST-NAME         PICTURE........
 .
 .
 .
```

PROCEDURE DIVISION.
   .
   .
   .
   .

IF DIFF-PAYROLL IS EQUAL TO PAYROLL-WS AND DIFF-LAST-NAME IS NOT EQUAL TO LAST-NAME-WS MOVE CORRESPONDING PAY-RECORD-IN TO PAY-RECORD-OUT.

(NOTE: Fields marked with a double asterisk (**) in the foregoing listing must have exactly the same names for their subordinate fields in order to be considered corresponding. The same names must not be the redefining ones, or they will not be considered to correspond.)

Level Numbers

The programmer should use widely incremented level numbers (i.e., 01, 05, 10, 15, etc., instead of 01, 02, 03, 04, etc.) in order to allow room for future insertions of group levels. For readability, indent level numbers. Use level-88 numbers for codes. Then, if the codes must be changed, the Procedure Division coding for these tests need not be changed.

INCREASING EFFICIENCY OF DATA DIVISION ENTRIES

Conserving Core Storage

When writing Data Division statements, the COBOL programmer need not concern himself with data problems such as decimal alignment and mixed format: the compiler generates extra instructions to perform the necessary adjustments. Entries in the Data Division can significantly affect the amount of core storage required by a program.

Decimal Alignment

Procedure Division operations are most efficient when the decimal positions of the data items involved are aligned. If they are not, the compiler generates instructions to align the decimal positions before any operations involving the data items can be executed.

In a typical source program, the frequency of the most common verbs written in the Procedure Division of a COBOL program averaged over a number of programs is:

```
Moves — 50%
Go to — 20%
If     — 15%
```

Miscellaneous (Arithmetic, Calculations, Input/Output, Perform) 15%.

An example of a pair of fields:

```
77 A  Picture 99V9     Computational-3.  (Sending Field).
77 B  Picture 999V99   Computational-3.  (Receiving Field).
MOVE A TO B.
```

Because the receiving field is one decimal position larger than the sending field, decimal alignment must be performed. Each time the move is executed, 2250 bytes of storage are used. Adding one additional decimal position in the data sending or receiving field is small in cost compared to the savings possible in the Procedure Division.

Unequal-Length Fields

An intermediate operation may be required when handling fields of unequal length. For example, zeros may have to be inserted in numeric fields and blanks in the alphabetic or alphanumeric fields in order to pad out to the proper length. The compiler will have to generate instructions to perform these insertions.

To avoid these operations, the number of digits should be equal. Any increase in data fields is more than compensated by the savings in the generated object program. For example,

```
SENDFIELD            Picture S999
RECFIELD             Picture S99999
Change SENDFIELD to  Picture S99999
```

Mixed Data Formats

When fields are used together in move, arithmetic, or relational statements, they should be in the same format whenever possible. Conversions require additional storage and longer execution time. Operations involving mixed data formats require one of the items to be converted to a matching data format before the operation is executed.

For maximum efficiency, avoid mixed data formats or use a one-time conversion; that is, move the data to a work area, thus converting it to the matching format. By referencing the work area in procedural statements, the data is converted only once instead of each operation.

The following examples show what must logically be done before indicated operations can be performed when working with mixed data fields.

Display to Computational-3

To execute a move. No additional code is required (if proper alignment exists) because one instruction can both move and convert the data.

To execute a compare. Before a Compare is executed, Display data must be converted to Computational-3 format.

To perform arithmetic calculations. Before arithmetics are performed, Display data is converted to Computational-3 format.

Computational-3 to Display

To execute a move. Before a Move is executed, Computational-3 data is converted to Display data format.

To execute a compare. Before a compare is executed, Display data is converted to Computational-3 data format.

To perform arithmetic calculations. Before arithmetic calculations are performed, Display data is converted to Computational-3 data format. The result is generated in a Computational-3 work area, which is then converted and moved to Display result field.

Display to Display

To perform arithmetic calculations. Before arithmetic calculations are performed, Display data is converted to Computational-3 format. The result is generated in Computational-3 work area, which is then converted and moved to the Display result field.

Sign Control

The absence or presence of a plus or minus sign in the description of an arithmetic field can affect the efficiency of a program. For numeric fields specified, the compiler attempts to insure that a positive is present so that the values are treated as absolute.

The use of unsigned numeric fields increases the possibility of error (an unintentional negative sign could cause invalid results) and requires additional generated code to control the sign. The use of unsigned fields should be limited to fields treated as absolute values.

For example, if data is defined as

```
A Picture 999
B Picture S999
C Picture S999,
```

the following moves are made: MOVE B TO A. MOVE B TO C. Moving B to A causes four more bytes to be used than moving B to C because A is an absolute value.

Conditional Statements

Computing arithmetic values separately and then comparing them may produce more accurate results than including arithmetic statements in conditional statements. The final result of an expression included in a conditional statement is *limited to an accuracy of six decimal places.* The following example shows how separating computations from conditional statements can improve the accuracy.

The data is defined as

```
77 A  Picture S9V9999     Computational-3
77 B  Picture S9V9999     Computational-3
77 C  Picture S999V9(8)   Computational-3
```

and the following conditional statement is written.

If A * B = C, GO TO EQUAL-X.

the final result will be 99V9(6). Although the receiving field for the final result (C) specifies eight decimal positions, the final result actually obtained in the example specifies six decimal places. For increased accuracy, define the final result field as desired, perform the computation, and then make the desired comparison as follows:

```
77  X   Picture  S999V9(8)          Computational-3
COMPUTE X = A * B.
IF X = C, GO TO EQUAL-X.
```

Summary-Basic Principles of Effective Coding

1. Match decimal places in related fields (decimal point alignment).
2. Match integer places in related fields (unequal length fields).
3. Do not mix usage of data formats (mixed data formats).
4. Include an S (sign) in all numeric pictures (sign control).
5. Keep arithmetic expressions out of conditionals (conditional statements).

Reusing Data Areas

The main storage area can be used more efficiently by writing different data descriptions for the same data area. For example, the coding that follows shows how the same area can be used as a work area for records of several input files that are not processed concurrently.

Working-Storage Section

```
01  Work-Area-File-1       (Largest record description for File-1.)
01  Work-Area-File-2       Redefines Work-Area-File-2
                           (Largest record description for File-2.)
```

Alternate Groupings and Descriptions

Program data can be described more efficiently by providing alternate groupings or data descriptions for the same data. As an example of alternate groupings, suppose a program makes references to both a field and its subfields where it could be more efficient to describe the subfields with different usages.

This can be done with the Redefines clause, as follows:

```
01  Payroll-Record.
    02  Employee-Record    Picture  X(28).
    02  Employee-Field Redefines Employee-Record.
        03  Name       Picture  X(24).
        03  Number     Picture  S9(4)    Computational-3.
    02  Date-Record    Picture  X(10).
```

An example of different data descriptions specified for the same data, the following example illustrates how a table can be utilized.

```
02  Value-A.
    03 A1    Picture S9(9)   Computational-3   Value is Zeroes.
    03 A2    Picture S9(9)   Computational-3   Value is 1.
02  Table-A Redefines Value-A    Picture S9(9)    Computational-3
                                                  Occurs 100 times.
```

Data Formats in Computer

The following examples illustrate how various COBOL data formats appear in the System 360/370 computer in Extended Binary Coded-Decimal Interchange Code (EBCDIC) format.

Numeric Display (External Decimal)

The value of an item is -1234.

Picture 9(4) Display	F1 F2 F3 F4
	Byte
Picture S9(4). Display	F1 F2 F3 D4

Hexadecimal F is treated arithmetically as a plus in the low-order byte. The hexadecimal D represents a negative sign.

COMPUTATIONAL-3   (INTERNAL DECIMAL)

The value of an item is $+1234$.

Picture 9(4)	Computational-3	01 23 4F
		Byte
Picture S9(4)	Computational-3	01 23 4C

Hexadecimal F is treated arithmetically as plus.
Hexadecimal C represents a positive sign.

COMPUTATIONAL (BINARY)

The value of an item is 1234.

Picture S9(4)   Computational   0 000 0000 0000 0100 1101 0010
                                Sign   Byte

An 0 bit in the sign position means the number is positive. Negative numbers appear in the 2s complement form with a 1 in the sign position.

Redundant Coding

To avoid redundant coding of usage designations, use computational at the group level (this does not affect the object program).

For example,

Instead of

```
02  Fuller.
    03 A  Computational-3  Picture 99V9.
    03 B  Computational-3  Picture 99V9.
    03 C  Computational-3  Picture 99V9.
```

write

```
02  Fuller    Computational-3.
    03 A  Picture 99V9.
    03 B  Picture 99V9.
    03 C  Picture 99V9.
```

PROCEDURE DIVISION

The Procedure Division should be written using the Data Division as a guide to file, data-names, constants, and work areas used. The programmer actually writes the COBOL program using the program flowchart as a guide for the procedure entries.

The Procedure Division specifies the action, such as input/output, data movement, and arithmetic operations that are required to process the data. A series of English-like statements are written in the sequence of the program flowchart.

Entries That Appear In the Procedure Division

1. The name of the division-Division Header.
2. Any optional sections.
3. A series of procedural paragraphs specifying the actions to be performed.

The OPEN and READ statement must reference a file assigned in the Environment Division and described in the Data Division.

The CLOSE statement must be written for each file opened.

The WRITE statement references a record-name.

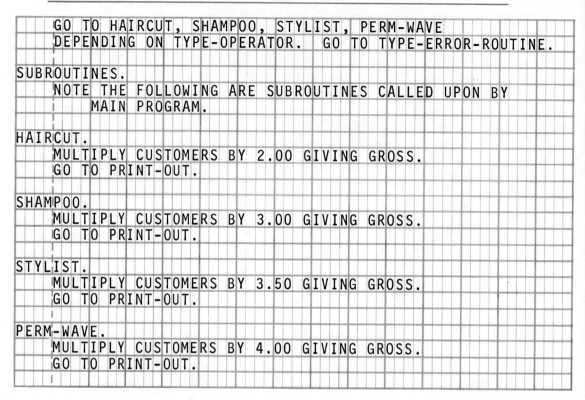

```
      GO TO HAIRCUT, SHAMPOO, STYLIST, PERM-WAVE
      DEPENDING ON TYPE-OPERATOR.   GO TO TYPE-ERROR-ROUTINE.

SUBROUTINES.
      NOTE THE FOLLOWING ARE SUBROUTINES CALLED UPON BY
          MAIN PROGRAM.

HAIRCUT.
      MULTIPLY CUSTOMERS BY 2.00 GIVING GROSS.
      GO TO PRINT-OUT.

SHAMPOO.
      MULTIPLY CUSTOMERS BY 3.00 GIVING GROSS.
      GO TO PRINT-OUT.

STYLIST.
      MULTIPLY CUSTOMERS BY 3.50 GIVING GROSS.
      GO TO PRINT-OUT.

PERM-WAVE.
      MULTIPLY CUSTOMERS BY 4.00 GIVING GROSS.
      GO TO PRINT-OUT.
```

Figure 15–2.   Example—Subroutines.

The Procedure Division can be written as a series of subroutine paragraphs. This technique will permit the programmer to write procedures in any sequence he wishes. Each procedure will be referenced by a procedure name, thus allowing the programmer more flexibility in the writing of the program. A GO TO statement at the end of each paragraph directs control of the program.

The disadvantage of using this approach is that these paragraphs cannot be referred to by a PERFORM statement since each statement ends with a GO TO statement which is invalid for the PERFORM statement. This disadvantage can be overcome through the use of an EXIT paragraph at the end of each procedural series of paragraphs or by simply omitting the GO TO statement and performing the routine.

Since the last statement in the Procedure Division denotes the end of the source program, it is imperative that all divisions remain in the proper sequence. If the sequence is disturbed, many diagnostic errors will be generated unnecessarily.

INCREASING THE EFFICIENCY OF PROCEDURE DIVISION ENTRIES

A program can be made more efficient in the Procedure Division with some of the techniques described below.

Intermediate Results

The compiler treats arithmetic statements as a succession of operations and sets up intermediate result fields to contain the results of these operations. The compiler can process complicated statements, but not always with the same efficiency of storage utilization as the source program. Because truncation may occur during compilation, unexpected intermediate results may occur.

Binary Data

If an operation involving binary operand requires an intermediate result greater than 18 digits, the compiler converts the operands to internal decimal before performing the operation. If the result field is binary, the result will be converted from internal decimal to binary.

If an intermediate result will not be greater than nine digits, the operation is performed most efficiently as binary data fields.

COBOL Library Subroutines

If a decimal multiplication operation requires an intermediate result greater than 30 digits, a COBOL library subroutine is used to perform the multiplication. The result of this multiplication is truncated to 30 digits.

A COBOL library subroutine is used to perform division if (1) the divisor is equal to or greater than 15 digits, (2) the length of the divisor plus the length of the dividend is greater than 16 bytes, or (3) the scaled dividend is greater than 30 digits (a scaled dividend is a number that has been multiplied by a power of 10 in order to obtain the desired number of decimal places in the quotient).

Intermediate Result Greater than 30 Digits

When the number of digits in a decimal intermediate result field is greater than 30, the field is truncated to 30. A warning message will be generated at compilation time, but the program flow will not be interrupted at execution time. This truncation may cause the result to be invalid.

On Size Error

The ON SIZE ERROR option applies only to the final tabulated results, not to intermediate result fields.

A method of avoiding unexpected intermediate results is to make critical computations by assigning maximum (or minimum) values to all fields and analyzing the results by testing the critical computations for results expected.

Because of concealed intermediate results, the final result is not always obvious.

The necessity of computing the worst case (or best case) results can be eliminated by keeping statements simple. This can be accomplished by splitting up the statement and controlling the intermediate results to be sure unexpected final results are not obtained.

For example,

```
COMPUTE B = (A + 3) / C + 27.600.
```

First define adequate intermediate result fields, i.e.,

```
02  INTERMEDIATE-RESULT-A    PICTURE  S9(6)V999.

02  INTERMEDIATE-RESULT-B    PICTURE  S9(6)V999.
```

Then split up the expression as follows:

```
ADD A, 3 GIVING INTERMEDIATE-RESULT-A.
```

Then write:

```
DIVIDE  C  INTO  INTERMEDIATE-RESULT-A  GIVING  INTERMEDIATE-
RESULT-B.
```

Then compute the final results by writing:
```
ADD INTERMEDIATE-RESULT-B, 27.600 GIVING B.
```

Arithmetic Fields

Initialize arithmetic fields before using them in computation. Failure to do so may result in invalid results, or the job might terminate abnormally.

Comparison Fields

Numeric comparisons are usually done in Computational-3 format; therefore, Computational-3 is the most efficient data format.

Because the compiler inserts slack bytes which can contain meaningless data, group comparisons should not be attempted when slack bytes are within the group unless the programmer knows the contents of the slack bytes.

Open and Close Statements

Each opening or closing of a file requires the use of main storage that is directly proportional to the number of files being opened. Opening or closing more than one file with the same statement is faster than using a separate statement for each file. Separate statements, however, require less storage area.

For example,

one statement OPEN INPUT FILE-A, FILE-B, FILE-C. rather than

```
OPEN INPUT FILE-A.
OPEN INPUT FILE-B.
OPEN INPUT FILE-C.
```

Accept Verb

The Accept verb does not provide for the recognition of the last card being read from the card reader. When COBOL detects /* card, it drops through to the next statement. Because no indication of this is given by COBOL, the end-of-file detection requires special treatment. Thus the programmer must provide his own end card (some card other than /*) which he can test to detect an end-of-file condition.

Paragraph-Names

Paragraph-names use storage when the PERFORM verb is used in the program. Use of paragraph-names for comments requires more storage than the use of a Note or a blank card. Use Note and/or a blank card for identifying in-line procedures where paragraph-names are not required.

For example, avoid writing the following:

```
MOVE A TO B.
PERFORM JOES-ROUTINE.


JOES-ROUTINE. COMPUTE A = D + C * F.
```

Recommended Coding

```
MOVE A TO B.
PERFORM ROUTINE.
NOTE JOES-ROUTINE.
ROUTINE. COMPUTE A = D + C * F.
```

COMPUTE Statement

The use of the COMPUTE statement generates more efficient coding than does the use of individual arithmetic statements because the compiler can keep track of internal work areas and does not have to store the results of intermediate calculations. It is the user's responsibility, however, to insure that the data is defined with the level of significance required in the answer.

IF Statement

Nested and computed IF statements should be avoided, as the logic is difficult to debug. Performing an IF operation for an item greater than 256 bytes in length requires the generation of more instructions than are required for that of an IF operation of an item of 256 bytes or less.

MOVE Statement

Performing a MOVE operation for an item greater than 256 bytes in length requires the generation of more instructions than is required for that of a MOVE statement for an item of 256 bytes or less.

When a MOVE statement with CORRESPONDING option is executed, data items are considered CORRESPONDING only if their respective data-names are the same, including all implied qualifications, up to but not including the data-names used in the MOVE statement itself.

NOTE Statement

An asterisk (*) should be used in place of the NOTE statement because there is the possibility that when NOTE is the first sentence in a paragraph, it will inadvertently cause the whole paragraph to be treated as part of the NOTE.

PERFORM Verb

PERFORM is a useful verb if the programmer adheres to the following rules.

1. Always execute at the last statement of a series of routines being operated on by a PERFORM statement. When branching out of the routine, make sure control will eventually return to the last statement of the routine. This statement should be an EXIT statement. Although no code is generated, the EXIT statement allows a programmer to immediately recognize the extent of a series of routines within the range of a PERFORM statement.

2. Always either PERFORM routine-name THRU routine name-exit or PERFORM a section name. A PERFORM paragraph-name can cause trouble for the programmer trying to maintain the program. For example, if a paragraph must be broken into two paragraphs, the programmer must examine every statement to determine whether or not this paragraph is within the range of the PERFORM statement. Then all statements referencing the paragraph-name must be changed to PERFORM THRU statements.

Read Into and Write From Options

Use READ INTO and WRITE FROM to do all the processing in the Working-Storage Section. This is suggested for two reasons.

1. Debugging is much simpler. Working-Storage areas are easier to locate in a dump and so are buffer areas. And, if files are locked, it is much easier to determine which record in a block was being processed when the abnormal termination occurred.

2. Trying to access a record area after the AT END condition has occurred (for example, AT END MOVE HIGH-VALUE TO INPUT-RECORD) can cause problems if the record area is only in the File Section.

(*Note:* The programmer should be aware that additional time is used to execute the move operations involved in each READ INTO or WRITE FROM instruction.)

Some of the programming techniques that will aid the programmer in preparing efficient programs have been explained and illustrated. Additional programming techniques will be found in the reference manuals of the computer manufacturers. It is hoped that as the programmer becomes more proficient in COBOL programming, he will develop his own programming techniques.

Exercises

Write your answers in the space provided.

1. COBOL does not produce a program as _____ as one written in the _____ language of a particular computer.

2. Prior to the writing of the program, the program should be properly _____ and the appropriate _____, _____ formats and _____ formats be available to the programmer.

3. The Identification Division is the _____ of the four and provides information that _____ the program and provides _____ to the reader relative to the program.

4. The required entries in the Identification Division are the name of the _____ and _____.

5. The Remarks paragraph provides the reader with information regarding the _____ of the program.

6. The Environment Division is the only COBOL division that is _____ _____ oriented.

7. The Environment Division contains information about the _____ to be used, the computer upon which the program will be _____ and _____ and links the _____ to the computer system and the _____ to be processed.

8. The external device names should be checked with the _____ programmer.

9. All files mentioned in the File-Control paragraph should be properly _____ in the Data Division and _____ and _____ in the Procedure Division.

10. All device numbers used in the File-Control paragragh should be _____ _____.

11. The Data Division describes information to be _____ by the _____ program.

12. Each file mentioned in the _____ Division should be _____ _____ in the Data Division.

13. The Working-Storage Section is used for _____ and _____ _____.

14. The Data Division should be written using copies of the _____ formats and _____ formats as guides before writing the _____ entries and _____ entries.

15. The File Section contains _____ entries and _____ entries.

16. The Linkage Section contains record description entries for _____ _____.

17. The Report Section contains entries related to the _____ feature.

18. The Record Contains clause should be included in the FD entry because the compiler will check the agreement of the _____ entry with the _____ clause and it provides the reader with the _____ _____ of the record to be processed without the necessity of _____ all field positions.

19. When variable records are used, the Record Contains clause should specify the length of the _____ and _____ record in the file.

20. Record description entries must immediately follow _____ entries.

21. The data record must begin with a _____ level number.

22. The highest qualifier of a data-name permitted in the File Section is a _____.

23. Value clauses, outside of condition-name entries, are forbidden in the _____ Section.

24. If a data item is to be used in a series of arithmetic operations, it would be advisable to define an area in the _____ Section with the _____ mode.

25. When writing Data Division statements, the programmer is not concerned with _____ alignment and _____ formats as the _____ generates _____ instructions to perform the necessary _____.

26. Procedure Division operations are most efficient when the decimal positions of the data involved are _____.

27. The most used verb in the Procedure Division is the _____ verb.

28. When fields are used together in move, arithmetic or relational statements, they should be in the same _____ whenever possible.

29. The absence or presence of a _____ or _____ sign in the description of an arithmetic field can effect the _____ of a program.

30. Computing arithmetic values _____ and then comparing them may produce more _____ results than including _____ statements in _____ statements as the final result of a conditional statement is limited to an accuracy of _____ decimal places.

31. The main storage area can be used more efficiently by writing different _____ for the _____ data area.

32. Program data can be described more efficiently by providing _____ _____ groupings or _____ descriptions for the same data.

33. In the IBM 360/370 computer, the hexadecimal _____ is treated arithmetically as a plus sign in the _____ order byte.

34. The usage designation of _____ at the _____ level can avoid redundant coding.

35. The Procedure Division should be written using the Data Division as a guide to _____, _____, _____, and _____.

36. _____ flowchart acts as a guide for procedure entries and a series of _____ statements are written in the _____ specified in the flowchart.

37. The _____ and _____ statement must reference a file assigned in the _____ Division.

38. The _____ statement must be written for each file opened.

39. The Procedure Division can be written as a series of _____ programs which will permit the programmer to write _____ in any _____ he wishes.

40. The _____ statement in the Procedure Division signals the end of the source program.

41. The computer cannot process complicated statements with the same efficiency of _____ utilization as the _____ program.

42. If an intermediate result will not be greater than nine digits, the operation is performed more efficiently as _____ data file.

43. If a decimal multiplication requires an intermediate result greater than 30 digits, a COBOL _____ subroutine is used for the multiplication and the result is truncated to _____ digits.

44. The On Size Error option applies only to the _____ tabulated result.

45. A good practice is to _____ arithmetic fields before using them in a computation.

46. Numeric comparisons are more efficient when the data is in the _____ _____ mode.

47. _____ and _____ more than one file with one statement is faster than any separate statement for each file.

48. The _____ verb does not provide for the recognition of the _____ card being read from the card reader.

49. Use of paragraph-name for comments requires more storage than the use of a _____ statement or a _____ card.

50. The use of the Compute statement generates more efficient coding than does the use of individual _____ statements.

51. _____ and _____ IF statements should be avoided as the logic is difficult to debug.

52. Performing a move operation for an item greater than _____ bytes in length requires the generation of more instructions than that required for one with less.

53. An _____ should be used in place of a Note statement if it is the first statement of a paragraph.

54. A Perform statement can be used if the _____ of the flow of data is returned to the _____ statement of the routine referred.

55. A Read Into and Write From option can make debugging simpler because _____ and _____ areas are easier to locate in a dump.

Answers

1. EFFICIENT, BASIC
2. DEFINED, FLOWCHARTS, SOURCE DOCUMENTS, OUTPUT
3. SIMPLEST, IDENTIFIES, INFORMATION
4. DIVISION, PROGRAM
5. INTENT
6. MACHINE
7. EQUIPMENT, COMPILED, EXECUTED, DEVICES, DATA FILES
8. SYSTEMS
9. DEFINED, OPENED, CLOSED
10. VERIFIED
11. PROCESSED, OBJECT
12. ENVIRONMENT, DESCRIBED
13. CONSTANTS, WORK AREAS
14. SOURCE DOCUMENT, OUTPUT, FILE DESCRIPTION, RECORD DESCRIPTION
15. FILE DESCRIPTION, RECORD DESCRIPTION
16. SUBPROGRAMS
17. REPORT WRITER
18. RECORD DESCRIPTION, RECORD CONTAINS, SIZE, COUNTING
19. SHORTEST, LONGEST
20. FILE DESCRIPTION
21. 01
22. FILE NAME
23. FILE
24. WORKING-STORAGE, COMPUTATIONAL-3
25. DECIMAL, MIXED, COMPILER, EXTRA, ADJUSTMENT
26. ALIGNED
27. MOVE
28. FORMAT
29. PLUS, MINUS, EFFICIENCY
30. SEPARATELY, ACCURATE, ARITHMETIC, COMPUTATIONAL, SIX
31. DATA DESCRIPTION, SAME
32. ALTERNATE, DATA
33. F, LOW
34. COMPUTATIONAL, GROUP
35. FILE, DATA-NAMES, CONSTANTS, WORK AREAS USED
36. PROGRAM, ENGLISH-LIKE, SEQUENCE
37. OPEN, READ, ENVIRONMENT
38. CLOSE
39. SUBROUTINE, PROCEDURES, SEQUENCE
40. LAST
41. STORAGE, SOURCE
42. BINARY
43. LIBRARY, 30
44. FINAL
45. INITIALIZE
46. COMPUTATIONAL-3
47. OPENING, CLOSING
48. ACCEPT, LAST
49. NOTE, BLANK
50. ARITHMETIC
51. NESTED, COMPUTED
52. 256
53. ASTERISK
54. CONTROL, LAST
55. WORKING-STORAGE, BUFFER

Questions for Review

1. Why is it so important to write an efficient COBOL program?

2. What additional information should be included in the Identification Division?

3. What precautions should be taken in writing the Environment Division?

4. Why should the Records Contains clause be included in every file description entry in the Data Division?

5. Why is it desirable to write Data Division entries for output files in the Working-Storage Section?

6. When should the computational mode be used with data items?

7. How could storage be conserved in decimal alignment?

8. How does the compiler align fields of unequal length?

9. What problem is caused by operations involving data items of mixed data format? How can this be overcome?

10. Explain the operation of sign control in the efficiency of a program.

11. Why is it possible to have an inaccurate answer as a result of an arithmetic statement in a conditional statement?

12. List the basic principles of effective coding.

13. How may alternate groupings provide a more efficient program?

14. How may the Procedure Division be written more efficiently?

15. What is the danger of intermediate results in arithmetic operations?

16. What is the problem involved in using an Accept statement?

17. Why is it more efficient to use a Compute statement rather than a series of arithmetic statements?

18. Why should nested and computed IF statements be avoided?

19. Why is Perform a useful verb?

20. Why is the Read Into and Write From options suggested for input/output operations?

Problems

1. *Match each item with its proper description.*

_____ 1. Environment Division	A. Conversion to matched format.
_____ 2. Mixed Data Formats	B. Computational at group level.
_____ 3. Alternate Descriptions	C. Performs multiplications on intermediate results greater than 30 digits.
_____ 4. Redundant Coding	D. Machine oriented.
_____ 5. Intermediate Results	E. Redefine fields.
_____ 6. COBOL Library Subroutine	F. Limited to 30 digits.

2. *Write the minimum number of entries required for the following information for the Identification and Environment Divisions.*

   a. The program is to be written to process data on a IBM 370 computer model H155.
   b. The input/output devices to be used are the model 2540 card reader and a 2400 tape unit.

3. *In the following Compute statement, the accuracy of the result (X) will be affected by the number of integers and decimal digits returned in the various intermediate results.*

   Rewrite the statement into a series of Compute statements to assure that this does not occur. Assume all fields will not exceed eight digits.

   COMPUTE X = A + (B / C) + ((D ** E) * F) − G.

4. *A program references a field and its subfields, each with different usages. The fields are as follows:*

Field	Record Positions
Name	1–24
Number	25–28

   The number will be involved in numerous calculations. The entire field by itself will be used for display purposes.

   Write the record description entries for the above so that both the name and number fields can be referenced as well as each subfield with different Usage clauses.

5. *Set up Working-Storage areas for WORK-AREA-FILE1 and WORK-AREA-FILE2 so that the same area can be used as a work area for records of several input files that can not be processed concurrently.*

6. *A program contains the following instructions:*

```
77  FLD-A    PICTURE S9(5)V9999.
77  FLD-B    PICTURE S99V99.
     .
     .
     .
PROCEDURE DIVISION.
     .
     .
     .
     ADD FLD-A TO FLD-B.
```

What Picture clause must be changed to make the program correct and more efficient?
Write the correct Picture clause for the item to be changed.

7. *Which of the following Perform statements is incorrect.*

A. x PERFORM a THRU m

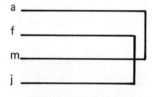

    d PERFORM f THRU j

C. x PERFORM a THRU m

    a
    d PERFORM f THRU j
    f
    j
    m

B. x PERFORM a THRU m

    a
    d PERFORM f THRU j
    f
    m
    j

D. x PERFORM a THRU m

    a
    d PERFORM f THRU j
    h
    m
    f
    j

Appendix **A**

Debugging COBOL Programs

Diagnostic messages are generated by the compiler and listed on the systems printer when errors are found in the source program. A complete listing of diagnostic messages will be found in the programmers guide reference manual for that particular computer.

Debugging Diagnostic Messages

1. Approach each diagnostic message in sequence as it appears in the compilation source listing. It is possible to get compound diagnostic messages as frequently as an earlier diagnostic message indicates the reason for a later diagnostic message. For example, a missing quotation mark for a nonnumeric literal could involve the inclusion of some clauses not intended for that particular literal. This could cause an apparently valid clause to be diagnosed as invalid because it is not complete, or because it is in conflict with something that preceded it.
2. Check for missing or superfluous punctuation or errors of this type.
3. Frequently, a seemingly meaningless message is clarified when the invalid syntax or format of the clause or statement in question is referenced.

Diagnostic Messages

The diagnostic messages associated with the compilation are always listed. The format of the diagnostic message is:

CARD	ERROR MESSAGE	
7	ILA1100I-W	1 SEQUENCE ERROR IN SOURCE PROGRAM.
12	ILA1095I-W	WORD 'SECTION' OR 'DIVISION' MISSING. ASSUMED PRESENT.
13	ILA1132I-E	INVALID SYSTEM-NAME. SKIPPING TO NEXT CLAUSE.
19	ILA1132I-E	INVALID SYSTEM-NAME. SKIPPING TO NEXT CLAUSE.
35	ILA1056I-E	FILE-NAME NOT DEFINED IN A SELECT. DESCRIPTION IGNORED.
46	ILA1056I-E	FILE-NAME NOT DEFINED IN A SELECT. DESCRIPTION IGNORED.
50	ILA1077I-C	ALPHANUMERIC LIT CONTINUES IN A-MARGIN. ASSUME B-MARGIN.
51	ILA1077I-C	ALPHANUMERIC LIT CONTINUES IN A-MARGIN. ASSUME B-MARGIN.
55	ILA1077I-C	ALPHANUMERIC LIT CONTINUES IN A-MARGIN. ASSUME B-MARGIN.
56	ILA1077I-C	ALPHANUMERIC LIT CONTINUES IN A-MARGIN. ASSUME B-MARGIN.
56	ILA1076I-C	ALPHANUMERIC LIT EXCEEDS 120 CHARACTERS. TRUNCATED TO 120.
79	ILA1037I-E	* INVALID IN DATA DESCRIPTION. SKIPPING TO NEXT CLAUSE.
79	ILA2039I-C	PICTURE CONFIGURATION ILLEGAL. PICTURE CHANGED TO 9 UNLESS USAGE IS 'DISPLAY-ST', THEN L(6)BDZ9BDZ9.
83	ILA1037I-E	** INVALID IN DATA DESCRIPTION. SKIPPING TO NEXT CLAUSE.
83	ILA2039I-C	PICTURE CONFIGURATION ILLEGAL. PICTURE CHANGED TO 9 UNLESS USAGE IS 'DISPLAY-ST', THEN L(6)BDZ9BDZ9.
85	ILA3001I-E	FILE-IN NOT DEFINED. DELETING TILL LEGAL ELEMENT FOUND.
85	ILA3001I-E	FILE-OUT NOT DEFINED. DELETING TILL LEGAL ELEMENT FOUND.
85	ILA4002I-E	OPEN STATEMENT INCOMPLETE. STATEMENT DISCARDED.
86	ILA4050I-E	SYNTAX REQUIRES RECORD-NAME . FOUND DNM=1-337 . STATEMENT DISCARDED.
86	ILA3001I-E	HDG-1 NOT DEFINED.
86	ILA3001I-E	O NOT DEFINED.
87	ILA4050I-E	SYNTAX REQUIRES RECORD-NAME . FOUND DNM=1-337 . STATEMENT DISCARDED.
88	ILA4050I-E	SYNTAX REQUIRES RECORD-NAME . FOUND DNM=1-337 . STATEMENT DISCARDED.
89	ILA3001I-E	FILE-IN NOT DEFINED. STATEMENT DISCARDED.
94	ILA3001I-E	TOT-DED-WS NOT DEFINED. SUBSTITUTING TALLY.
105	ILA4091I-E	SYNTAX REQUIRES OPERAND. FOUND END OF PAGE . TEST DISCARDED.
106	ILA4050I-E	SYNTAX REQUIRES RECORD-NAME . FOUND DNM=1-337 . STATEMENT DISCARDED.
108	ILA5011I-W	HIGH ORDER TRUNCATION MIGHT OCCUR.
110	ILA4050I-E	SYNTAX REQUIRES RECORD-NAME . FOUND DNM=1-337 . STATEMENT DISCARDED.
114	ILA1077I-C	ALPHANUMERIC LIT CONTINUES IN A-MARGIN. ASSUME B-MARGIN.
113	ILA4003I-E	EXPECTING NEW STATEMENT. FOUND TO . DELETING TILL NEXT VERB OR PROCEDURE NAME.
116	ILA5011I-W	HIGH ORDER TRUNCATION MIGHT OCCUR.
117	ILA4050I-E	SYNTAX REQUIRES RECORD-NAME . FOUND DNM=1-337 . STATEMENT DISCARDED.
117	ILA3001I-E	FINAL-TOTAL NOT DEFINED.

Figure A-1.   Diagnostic Messages.

5

1. *Compiler Generated Card Number.* This is the number of a line in the source program related to the error.
2. *Message Identifier.* Message identification for the system.
3. *The Severity Level.* There are four severity levels as follows:

   (W) WARNING. This level indicates that an error was made in the source program. However, it is not serious enough to interfere with the execution of the program.

   (C) CONDITIONAL. This level indicates that an error was made, but the compiler usually makes a corrective assumption. The statement containing the error is retained. Execution can be attempted.

   (E) ERROR. This level indicates that a serious error was made. Usually the compiler makes no corrective assumption. The statement or operand containing the error is dropped. Compilation is completed, but execution of the program should not be attempted.

   (D) DISASTER. This level indicates that a serious error was made. Compilation is not completed and results are unpredictable.

4. *Message Text.* The text identifies the condition that causes the error and indicates the actions taken by the compiler.

Execution Output

The output generated by the program execution (in addition to data written on output files) may include
1. Data displayed on the console or on the printer.
2. Messages to the operator.
3. System informative messages.
4. System diagnostic messages.
5. A system dump.

A dump and system diagnostic messages are generated automatically during the program execution only if the program contains errors that cause the abnormal termination of the program.

Operator Messages

The COBOL phase may issue operator messages. In the message, XX denotes a system-interated 2-character numeric file that is used to identify the program issuing the message.

C110A   STOP literal

Explanation: The programmer has issued a STOP literal statement in the American National Standard COBOL source program.

System Action: Awaits operator response.

Programmer Response: Not applicable.

Operator Response: Operator should respond with end-of-block, or with any character in order to proceed with the program.

C111A   AWAITING REPLY

Explanation: This message is issued in connection with the American National Standard COBOL ACCEPT statement.

System Action: Awaits operator response.

Programmer Response: Not applicable.

Operator Response: The operator should reply as specified by the programmer.

Figure A–2.   Object Time Messages—Console.

STOP Statement

The following message is generated by the STOP statement with the *literal* option:

     XX   C110A   STOP   'literal'

This message is issued at the programmer's discretion to indicate possible alternative action to be taken by the operator.

The operator responds according to the instructions given both by the message and on the job request form supplied by the programmer. If the job is to be resumed, the programmer presses the end-of-block key on the console.

ACCEPT Statement

The following message is generated by an ACCEPT statement with the FROM CONSOLE option:

     XX   C111A   "AWAITING REPLY"

This message is issued by the object program when operator intervention is required.

The operator responds by entering the reply and by pressing the end-of-block key on the console. (The contents of the text field should be supplied by the programmer on the job request form.)

System Output

Informative and diagnostic messages may appear in the listing during the execution of the object program.

Each of these messages contains an identification code in the first column of the message to indicate the portion of the operating system that generated the message.

Dump

If a serious error occurs during the execution of the problem program, the programmer can request a printout of storage through the use of the DUMP option in the job-control cards. The job would be abnormally terminated, any remaining steps bypassed, and a program phase dump is generated. The programmer can use the dump to checkout his program. In cases where a serious error occurs in other than the problem program (for example, in the control program), a dump is not produced. (*Note:* the program phase dump can be suppressed if the NODUMP option of the job-control card statement has been specified.)

How to Use a Dump

When a job is abnormally terminated due to a serious error in the problem program, a message is written on the system output device which indicates the following:

1. Type of interrupt (for example, program check).
2. The hexadecimal (IBM) address of the instruction that caused the interrupt.
3. Condition code.

The hexadecimal address of the instruction that caused the dump is subtracted from the load address of the module (which can be obtained from the map of main storage generated by the Linkage Editor) to obtain the relative instruction address as shown in the Procedure Division map. If the interrupt occurred within the COBOL program, the programmer can use the error address to locate the specific statement which caused a dump to be generated. Examination of the statement and fields associated with it may produce information as to the specific nature of the error.

Figure A–3 illustrates a sample Dump caused by a data exception. Invalid data (for example, data that did not correspond to its usage) was placed in the numeric field B as a result of redefinition. Letters identify the text corresponding to the letter in the program listing. (See pages 543–549.)

Errors That Can Cause the Dump

A dump may be caused by one of many different types of errors. Several of these errors may occur at the COBOL language level while others can occur at job-control levels.

The following are examples of COBOL language errors that can cause a dump.

1. *A* GO TO *statement with no procedure-name following it.* This statement may have been improperly initialized with an ALTER statement, and the execution of this statement will cause an invalid branch to be taken with unpredictable results.
2. *Moves of arithmetic calculations that have not been properly initialized.* For example, neglecting to initialize the object of an OCCURS clause with the DEPENDING ON option, referencing data fields prior to the first READ statement may cause a program interrupt or dump.
3. Invalid data placed in a numeric field as a result of redefinition.
4. Input/output errors that are nonrecoverable.
5. An input file contains invalid data, such as blanks or partially blank numeric fields or data incorrectly specified by its data description.

The compiler does not generate a test to check the sign position for a valid configuration before the item is used as operand. The programmer must test for valid data by means of the class test and by using either the EXAMINE or TRANSFORM statement to convert it to valid data.

For example, if the high-order positions of a numeric data field contains blanks and is to be involved in a calculation requiring a numeric PICTURE, the blank positions could be transformed to zeros through the use of the TRANSFORM or EXAMINE verbs, thus creating a valid numeric field.

```
// JOB DTACHK                                              05.00.19
// OPTION NODECK,LINK,LIST,LISTX,SYM,ERRS
// EXEC FCOBOL
```

```
    CBL QUOTE,SEQ
    00001    000010 IDENTIFICATION DIVISION.
    00002    000020 PROGRAM-ID. TESTRUN.
    00003    000030    AUTHOR. PROGRAMMER NAME.
    00004    000040    INSTALLATION. NEW YORK PROGRAMMING CENTER.
    00005    000050    DATE-WRITTEN.  FEBRUARY 4, 1971
    00006    000060 DATE-COMPILED. 04/24/71
    00007    000070    REMARKS. THIS PROGRAM HAS BEEN WRITTEN AS A SAMPLE PROGRAM FOR
    00008    000080    COBOL USERS. IT CREATES AN OUTPUT FILE AND READS IT BACK AS
    00009    000090    INPUT.
    00010    000100
    00011    000110 ENVIRONMENT DIVISION.
    00012    000120 CONFIGURATION SECTION.
    00013    000130 SOURCE-COMPUTER. IBM-360-H50.
    00014    000140 OBJECT-COMPUTER. IBM-360-H50.
    00015    000150 INPUT-OUTPUT SECTION.
    00016    000160 FILE-CONTROL.
    00017    000170    SELECT FILE-1 ASSIGN TO SYS008-UT-2400-S.
    00018    000180    SELECT FILE-2 ASSIGN TO SYS008-UT-2400-S.
    00019    000190
    00020    000200 DATA DIVISION.
    00021    000210 FILE SECTION.
    00022    000220 FD   FILE-1
    00023    000230    LABEL RECORDS ARE OMITTED
    00024    000240    BLOCK CONTAINS 5 RECORDS
    00025    000250    RECORDING MODE IS F
    00026    000255    RECORD CONTAINS 20 CHARACTERS
    00027    000260    DATA RECORD IS RECORD-1.
    00028    000270 01   RECORD-1.
    00029    000280    05 FIELD-A PIC X(20).
    00030    000290 FD   FILE-2
    00031    000300    LABEL RECORDS ARE OMITTED
    00032    000310    BLOCK CONTAINS 5 RECORDS
    00033    000320    RECORD CONTAINS 20 CHARACTERS
    00034    000330    RECORDING MODE IS F
    00035    000340    DATA RECORD IS RECORD-2.
    00036    000350 01   RECORD-2.
    00037    000360    05 FIELD-A PIC X(20).

    00038    000370 WORKING-STORAGE SECTION.
    00039    000380 01   FILLER.
    00040    000390    02 COUNT PIC S99 COMP SYNC.
    00041    000400    02 ALPHABET PIC X(26) VALUE IS "ABCDEFGHIJKLMNOPQRSTUVWXYZ".
    00042    000410    02 ALPHA REDEFINES ALPHABET PIC X OCCURS 26 TIMES.
    00043    000420    02 NUMBR PIC S99 COMP SYNC.
    00044    000430    02 DEPENDENTS PIC X(26) VALUE "01234012340123401234012340".
    00045    000440    02 DEPEND REDEFINES DEPENDENTS PIC X OCCURS 26 TIMES.
    00046    000450 01   WORK-RECORD.
    00047    000460    05 NAME-FIELD PIC X.
    00048    000470    05 FILLER PIC X.
    00049    000480    05 RECORD-NO PIC 9999.
    00050    000490    05 FILLER PIC X VALUE IS SPACE.
    00051    000500    05 LOCATION PIC AAA VALUE IS "NYC".
    00052    000510    05 FILLER PIC X VALUE IS SPACE.
    00053    000520    05 NO-OF-DEPENDENTS PIC XX.
    00054    000530    05 FILLER PIC X(7) VALUE IS SPACES.
```

(E)

Figure A–3.   Sample Dump Resulting from Abnormal Termination.

```
00055    000534 01  RECORDA.
00056    000535     02 A PICTURE S9(4) VALUE 1234.
00057    000536     02 B REDEFINES A PICTURE S9(7) COMPUTATIONAL-3.
00058    000540
00059    000550 PROCEDURE DIVISION.
00060    000560 BEGIN. READY TRACE.
00061    000570     NOTE THAT THE FOLLOWING OPENS THE OUTPUT FILE TO BE CREATED
00062    000580          AND INITIALIZES COUNTERS.
00063    000590 STEP-1. OPEN OUTPUT FILE-1. MOVE ZERO TO COUNT, NUMBR.
00064    000600     NOTE THAT THE FOLLOWING CREATES INTERNALLY THE RECORDS TO BE
00065    000610          CONTAINED IN THE FILE, WRITES THEM ON TAPE, AND DISPLAYS
00066    000620          THEM ON THE CONSOLE.
00067    000630 STEP-2. ADD 1 TO COUNT, NUMBR. MOVE ALPHA (COUNT) TO
00068    000640          NAME-FIELD.
00069    000645          COMPUTE B = B + 1.
00070    000650     MOVE DEPEND (COUNT) TO NO-OF-DEPENDENTS.
00071    000660     MOVE NUMBR TO RECORD-NO.
00072    000670 STEP-3. DISPLAY WORK-RECORD UPON CONSOLE. WRITE RECORD-1 FROM
00073    000680          WORK-RECORD.
00074    000690 STEP-4. PERFORM STEP-2 THRU STEP-3 UNTIL COUNT IS EQUAL TO 26.
00075    000700     NOTE THAT THE FOLLOWING CLOSES THE OUTPUT FILE AND REOPENS
00076    000710          IT AS INPUT.
00077    000720 STEP-5. CLOSE FILE-1. OPEN INPUT FILE-2.
00078    000730     NOTE THAT THE FOLLOWING READS BACK THE FILE AND SINGLES
00079    000740          OUT EMPLOYEES WITH NO DEPENDENTS.
00080    000750 STEP-6. READ FILE-2 RECORD INTO WORK-RECORD AT END GO TO STEP-8.
00081    000760 STEP-7. IF NO-OF-DEPENDENTS IS EQUAL TO "0" MOVE "Z" TO
00082    000770          NO-OF-DEPENDENTS. EXHIBIT NAMED WORK-RECORD. GO TO STEP-6.
00083    000780 STEP-8. CLOSE FILE-2.
00084    000790          STOP RUN.
```

At line 00069, an arrow points to the text with a circled **D**.

INTRNL NAME	LVL	SOURCE NAME	BASE	DISPL	INTRNL NAME	DEFINITION	USAGE	R	O	Q	M
DNM=1-148	FD	FILE-1	DTF=01		DNM=1-148		DTFMT				F
DNM=1-178	01	RECORD-1	BL=1	000	DNM=1-178	DS 0CL20	GROUP				
DNM=1-199	02	FIELD-A	BL=1	000	DNM=1-199	DS 20C	DISP				
DNM=1-216	FD	FILE-2	DTF=02		DNM=1-216		DTFMT				F
DNM=1-246	01	RECORD-2	BL=2	000	DNM=1-246	DS 0CL20	GROUP				
DNM=1-267	02	FIELD-A	BL=2	000	DNM=1-267	DS 20C	DISP				
DNM=1-287	01	FILLER	BL=3	000	DNM=1-287	DS 0CL56	GROUP				
DNM=1-306	02	COUNT	BL=3	000	DNM=1-306	DS 1H	COMP				
DNM=1-321	02	ALPHABET	BL=3	002	DNM=1-321	DS 26C	DISP				
DNM=1-339	02	ALPHA	BL=3	002	DNM=1-339	DS 1C	DISP	R	O		
DNM=1-357	02	NUMBR	BL=3	01C	DNM=1-357	DS 1H	COMP				
DNM=1-372	02	DEPENDENTS	BL=3	01E	DNM=1-372	DS 26C	DISP				
DNM=1-392	02	DEPEND	BL=3	01E	DNM=1-392	DS 1C	DISP	R	O		
DNM=1-408	01	WORK-RECORD	BL=3	038	DNM=1-408	DS 0CL20	GROUP				
DNM=1-432	02	NAME-FIELD	BL=3	038	DNM=1-432	DS 1C	DISP				
DNM=1-452	02	FILLER	BL=3	039	DNM=1-452	DS 1C	DISP				
DNM=1-471	02	RECORD-NO	BL=3	03A	DNM=1-471	DS 4C	DISP-NM				
DNM=1-490	02	FILLER	BL=3	03E	DNM=1-490	DS 1C	DISP				
DNM=2-000	02	LOCATION	BL=3	03F	DNM=2-000	DS 3C	DISP				
DNM=2-018	02	FILLER	BL=3	042	DNM=2-018	DS 1C	DISP				
DNM=2-037	02	NO-OF-DEPENDENTS	BL=3	043	DNM=2-037	DS 2C	DISP				
DNM=2-063	02	FILLER	BL=3	045	DNM=2-063	DS 7C	DISP				
DNM=2-082	01	RECORDA	BL=3	050	DNM=2-082	DS 0CL4	GROUP				
DNM=2-102	02	A	BL=3	050	DNM=2-102	DS 4C	DISP-NM				
DNM=2-113	02	B	BL=3	050	DNM=2-113	DS 4P	COMP-3	R			

At line DNM=2-113 (B), an arrow points to the row with a circled **J**.

Figure A–3. Sample Dump Resulting from Abnormal Termination
—Continued.

```
MEMORY MAP

      TGT                          003E8

      SAVE AREA                    003E8
      SWITCH                       00430
      TALLY                        00434
      SORT SAVE                    00438
      ENTRY-SAVE                   0043C
      SORT CORE SIZE               00440
      NSTD-REELS                   00444
      SORT RET                     00446
      WORKING CELLS                00448
      SORT FILE SIZE               00578
      SORT MODE SIZE               0057C
      PGT-VN TBL                   00580
      TGT-VN TBL                   00584
      SORTAB ADDRESS               00588
      LENGTH OF VN TBL             0058C
      LNGTH OF SORTAB              0058E
      PGM ID                       00590
      A(INIT1)                     00598
      UPSI SWITCHES                0059C
      OVERFLOW CELLS               005A4
      BL CELLS          (N)        005A4
      DTFADR CELLS                 005B0 ◄ (F)
      TEMP STORAGE                 005B8
      TEMP STORAGE-2               005C0
      TEMP STORAGE-3               005C0
      TEMP STORAGE-4               005C0
      BLL CELLS                    005C0
      VLC CELLS                    005C4
      SBL CELLS                    005C4
      INDEX CELLS                  005C4
      SUBADR CELLS                 005C4
      ONCTL CELLS                  005CC
      PFMCTL CELLS                 005CC
      PFMSAV CELLS                 005CC
      VN CELLS                     005D0
      SAVE AREA =2                 005D4
      XSASW CELLS                  005D4
      XSA CELLS                    005D4
      PARAM CELLS                  005D4
      RPTSAV AREA                  005D8
      CHECKPT CTR                  005D8
      IOPTR CELLS                  005D8
```

Figure A–3. Sample Dump Resulting from Abnormal Termination—Continued.

```
REGISTER ASSIGNMENT

  REG 6    BL =3   ◄ (K)
  REG 7    BL =1
  REG 8    BL =2
```

```
67   0006FC   41 40 6 002              LA    4,002(0,6)          DNM=1-339
     000700   48 20 6 000              LH    2,000(0,6)          DNM=1-306
     000704   4C 20 C 03A              MH    2,03A(0,12)         LIT+2
     000708   1A 42                    AR    4,2
     00070A   5B 40 C 038              S     4,038(0,12)         LIT+0
     00070E   50 40 D 1DC              ST    4,1DC(0,13)         SBS=1
     000712   58 E0 D 1DC              L     14,1DC(0,13)        SBS=1
69   000716   D2 00 6 038 E 000        MVC   038(1,6),000(14)    DNM=1-432      DNM=1-339
69   00071C   FA 30 6 050 C 03C  (C)►  AP    050(4,6),03C(1,12)  DNM=2-113      LIT+4
70   000722   41 40 6 01E              LA    4,01E(0,6)          DNM=1-392
     000726   48 20 6 000              LH    2,000(0,6)          DNM=1-306
     00072A   4C 20 C 03A              MH    2,03A(0,12)         LIT+2
     00072E   1A 42                    AR    4,2
     000730   5B 40 C 038              S     4,038(0,12)         LIT+0
     000734   50 40 D 1E0              ST    4,1E0(0,13)         SBS=2
     000738   58 E0 D 1E0              L     14,1E0(0,13)        SBS=2
     00073C   D2 00 6 043 E 000        MVC   043(1,6),000(14)    DNM=2-37       DNM=1-392
     000742   92 40 6 044              MVI   044(6),X'40'        DNM=2-37+1
```

```
// EXEC LNKEDT
```

PHASE	XFR-AD	LOCORE	HICORE	DSK-AD	ESD TYPE	LABEL	LOADED	REL-FR
PHASE***	0032A0	0032A0	004ADB	53 01 2	CSECT	TESTRUN	0032A0	0032A0	←Ⓑ
					CSECT	IJFFBZZN	003C50	003C50
					* ENTRY	IJFFZZZN	003C50
					* ENTRY	IJFFBZZZ	003C50
					* ENTRY	IJFFZZZZ	003C50
					CSECT	ILBDSAE0	0049F0	0049F0
					ENTRY	ILBDSAE1	004A06
					CSECT	ILBDMNS0	0049E8	0049E8
					CSECT	ILBDDSP0	0041B8	0041B8
					* ENTRY	ILBDDSP1	004708
					* ENTRY	ILBDDSP2	0047A0
					* ENTRY	ILBDDSP3	004958
					CSECT	ILBDIML0	004990	004990
					CSECT	IJJCPD1	003FC0	003FC0
					ENTRY	IJJCPD1N	003FC0
					* ENTRY	IJJCPD3	003FC0

```
// ASSGN SYS008,X'182'
// EXEC
```

```
0S03I PROGRAM CHECK INTERRUPTION – HEX LOCATION 00398C – CONDITION CODE 0 – DATA EXCEPTION    Ⓐ
0S00I JOB DTACHK    CANCELED
```

```
             DTACHK                                                      Ⓛ

GR 0-7   00003850 00003960 00000001 00000001    0000338A 50003C12 00003388 00003550
GR 8-F   000035B8 00003BE2 000032A0 000032A0    00003880 00003688 0000338A 000041B8
FP REG   00000000 00000000 00000000 00000000    00000000 00000000 00000000 00000000
COMREG   BG ADDR IS 000208


000000   00000000 00000000 00000000 00000000    00000000 00000208 FF050000 00000000
000020   FF050007 40002E06 FF150007 C00039C2    5B5BC2C5 D6D1F440 FF05000E 80002E00
000040   00002F28 08000000 00002F18 00000000    FCBF1CB3 015005E8 00040000 0F0014BA
000060   00040000 00000336 00040000 0000147A    00000000 00000BBC 00040000 000002D4
000080   00000000 00000000 00000000 00000003    00050003 06B006B0 06B041BB 00734570
0000A0   0146940F B47B41A0 C0544570 0B8418A8    41900156 4180B2CE 47F000DA 06B006B0
0000C0   06B006B0 06B006B0 06B041BB 001741BB    00504570 01464180 01569640 A0019120
0000E0   A00C4710 00EA9260 A00195E2 A0024780    0DC695C1 A0024780 0DC69561 A0024780
```

Figure A–3. Sample Dump Resulting from Abnormal Termination
—Continued.

```
000100   010E9104 A0004780 010E9203 008F9281     A0004BA0 0262487A C00049A0 027641AA
000120   C0440778 94F9703B D7017058 70589283     A0009680 A0014400 04080788 947FA001
000140   4570B218 07F842B0 00E748B0 02C847F0     BC704570 BC70D205 BEEEBEF5 DC05BEEE
000160   C0441BAA DD06BEEE 000C43A1 000742A0     023741AA C0444400 A0045890 A0044220
000180   A0009140 A0014710 BB64D207 01F09008     68009058 68209060 68409068 68609070
0001A0   4BA00262 41AAC000 D2010016 A0009898     90108200 01F04400 A0045890 A0049818
0001C0   9030989D 01F08200 00389284 C0A4D207     01F0BF50 9890BF58 820001F0 9680A000
0001E0   41100030 47F0B166 96030039 82000038     FF050007 40002E06 00001000 00002000
000200   00003000 80001048 F0F461F2 F461F7F1     32A03000 00000000 00000000 00000000
000220   C4E3C1C3 C8D24040 0007AFFF 00004ADB     00004ADB 00000010 0007FFFF F875ECD1
000240   A8A07CD0 00C62171 21782269 226A0000     25102514 25183CF0 F4F2F4F7 F1F1F1F4
000260   00002044 0000000C 22E21E4E 1EF41F04     1F140020 214C0010 5B5BC2D6 00130001
000280   01001F98 20000000 00000000 02080000     00000294 00000000 000025AC 00000044
0002A0   00001F2C 00000000 00000000 00000000     00000000 00000000 00000000 00000000
0002C0   0000289C 00003228 100020CE 00001DC8     00002A9C 923801C9 909D01F0 4190086C
0002E0   48A00236 4AA00262 9180A000 47100306     58B0A004 9018B030 48B002C8 41CBB000
000300   41DCB000 07F99601 A00048B0 02C841CB     B00041DC B00095FF A00F0789 90E0BF6C
000320   48E001C8 D207BF50 E00094FD BF51D213     BF5801F0 07F9909D 01F09220 01C94590
000340   02E04190 01B69500 00234780 03F49526     00234780 00BE4860 00221A66 487002CA
000360   48667000 07F6181F 1B664121 000F4570     BCAC4860 BE5C1B22 43201007 4130001F
000380   18234740 03904130 00151B23 47B00392     1A234220 04094320 100747F0 04584720
0003A0   00CA4230 04D94820 02364322 C0031A23     950B1007 47F00454 472000C8 96801002
0003C0   960C1004 07F91858 41430002 43540000     41455000 1A444A40 BE5495FF 40004770
0003E0   03CC4284 00007F9 95FF04B1 07891B00     5000BF74 95FF04B1 4780B238 48600236
000400   95600237 47800366 D502A005 02814770     04204111 00004910 BE3A47B0 04201B66
000420   4121000F 4570BCAC D5021009 02394780     00C61B33 43301007 95011006 4770039E
000440   92FF04D9 D200004D 4A00D123 00000500     1007A00E 47B000CA D4031002 C0B04182
000460   20004870 02544338 70004930 BE3847B0     03B88930 00034A30 024891F0 30044780
000480   B6OED501 0022BB2C 478088E4 D501BE4C     BE5A4720 04AE4930 BE744770 04AE950F
0004A0   00234780 04AE9110 30064780 B2384180     00014148 800014A4 4A40BE54 18584A50
0004C0   0274D200 04B14000 50104000 92FF4000     42205000 4260500C 92035018 91F03004
0004E0   4780B62E 47F004EC 5880BF8C 44000CB8     9560C09C 47700566 D20202CD 10095860
000500   02CC9507 60004770 0566D202 02CD6001     587002CC 1B444340 30054C40 BE485A40
000520   02D04144 0000D503 70014000 47800566     9120100C 47100560 91051002 47700560
000540   91406004 47800560 94BF6004 91101002     47800558 96401002 96141002 9601100C
000560   D2034000 700195FF 30024770 03C64280     30029198 30060779 43203000 4322C09D
000580   48603000 95003000 47800592 9F006000     07694060 05E29550 30044780 080C9504
0005A0   50184780 08409101 100C4710 05D0940F     06FF91F0 500C4780 05D0D300 C09C3004
0005C0   95035018 47D00634 9560C09C 4780067C     D2020049 1009940F 0703D300 0048500C
0005E0   9C00000E 477005F2 4032C0B4 96803006     07F94730 08C69106 00454770 0E9C913F
000600   00454770 060C91AF 00440789 D201003A     05E29550 30044770 06200202 00491009
000620   58600048 4A60BDDC 50600040 4032C0B4     47F0089A 95015018 4720065C 9560C09C
000640   47700654 45700B84 9120800F 47100094     47F0065C 91203006 47100094 9560C09C
000660   477005D0 45700B84 4B800262 4878C000     91407038 471005D0 96F006FF 95003003
```

DTACHK

```
0032E0   00005218 00000208 00000000 00000000     00000000 00000000 00000000 00000000
003300   00000000 --SAME--
003320   00000000 58C0F0C6 58E0C000 58D0F0CA     9500E000 4770F0A2 9610D048 92FFE000
003340   47F0F0AC 98CEF03A 90ECD00C 185D989F     F0BA9110 D0480719 07FF0700 00003BE2
003360   000032A0 000032A0 00003880 00003688     000038EC 00003BC8 C3D6C2C6 F0F0F0F1
003380   E3C5E2E3 D9E4D540 0001C1C2 C3C4C5C6     C7C8C9D1 D2D3D4D5 D6D7D8D9 E2E3E4E5
0033A0   E6E7E8E9 0001F0F1 F2F3F4F0 F1F2F3F4     F0F1F2F3 F4F0F1F2 F3F4F0F1 F2F3F4F0    (M)
0033C0   C1000000 000040D5 E8C34000 00404040 (H) 40404040 00000000 F1F2F3C4 00004C40    (M)
0033E0   01010014 00000000 00000000 00000000     0E000000 04000000 00009200 00000108
003400   00003430 00000000 10003C50 1160E2E8     E2F0F0F8 40400162 10000000 04000000
003420   00000000 86BCF018 41E0E001 58201044     010034E8 20000064 00003550 00003550
003440   00000014 000035B3 00640063 00000000     00000000 000049F0 01010014 00000000
003460   00000000 00000000 00000000 04000000     00008200 00001108 000034A8 00000000
003480   10003C50 1168E2E8 E2F0F0F8 40400272     00000000 20000000 00000000 86BCF018
0034A0   41E0E001 58201044 020035B8 00000064     00003620 00000000 00000014 00000000
0034C0   00640063 00000000 00004A06 000049F0     00000000 00000000 00000000 00000000
```

Figure A–3. Sample Dump Resulting from Abnormal Termination —Continued.

```
0034E0  00000000 00000000 00004770 30129261    10004110 100107F3 D20467CE 6017D201
003500  67D56274 C6C3D6C2 D6D3F8F0 F8F0F1F0    F1F2F1F1 F2F0F2F2 F2F1F3F0 F4F0F5F0
003520  F5F1F6F0 F6F1F7F0 0100DDA8 10006670    20006148 40005DC8 70004C40 41110004
003540  41110004 41110004 58110000 58F10010    45EF0018 41105342 07FB0000 000032B0
003560  000035A4 000035F8 00003DB4 000039B0    00003944 00004096 00003D0A 000032B0
003580  000062B8 00004478 00004C94 00005704    00005A4C 00005B68 0000373E 000035E4
0035A0  000036A6 060C40FF C4B2DE09 D2106276    D207601C D212F363 603B6276 96F06041
0035C0  4110601C 5840C65C 41200008 05301B24    47403018 95401000 47703012 92611000
0035E0  41101001 00000000 6276C494 58F0C340    077F9240 6820D206 00004218 000042B0
003600  00004348 000043E0 00006288 00004478    00004510 000045F8 D500627C 00000000
003620  000001FF 00003800 00003982 00003968    00003F2C 00003BAA 00003D60 00003C40
003640  000037DA 00003BAA 00003E6C 00003D60    00004090 00003DBE 00003B20 00003BC6
003660  00003BC6 00000203 02030001 04050104    00000203 00000105 00000404 00000104
003680  04040202 01030000 00202020 20210000    1C404040 40404000 00200000 00006148
0036A0  00180014 0F0F0000 000C1C0C 00000000    58F0C010 000036F4 10000006 0C000822
0036C0  00000000 00040D00 01E40267 00000003    7000004B 00000000 00000000 000038EC
0036E0  00000000 00000000 000033F8 00003550    000032A0 000033F8 50003C12 02AA1000
003700  00000C00 09EE0000 FFFFD201 6030C49A    4810C4A6 06104C10 C48C5010 D24C4810
003720  C4A60610 4C10C48C 5010D264 414062AE    5A40D24C F871D208 4000D205 00000000
003740  50D05362 41D053F6 5430536A 98675366    18809506 800041E0 568E58F0 52BA078F
003760  43680000 8C600004 89600002 8870001B    5BB6536E 91508000 477054D0 91A08000
003780  47E054D0 00003958 00003550 01005366    70003934 000041B8 00003850 00003960
0037A0  00003550 000032A0 000033F8 50003C12    00003388 00003550 000035B8 00003BE2
0037C0  000032A0 000032A0 00003880 00003960    000041B8 00003850 00004708 00003550
0037E0  00015540 00003958 58F10010 45EF0008  (G)180747F0 568ED703 532E532E 47F0568E
003800  49A053E2 58C053E6 078C91FF 53D14780    566845B0 55F445B0 00000000 00000000
003820  E000590C 478056AC 91FF53D0 47105686    41B05686 47F055F4 000032A0 91FF53D1
(N)003840  47105598 00003550 00003588 00003388  00033F8 00003470 00000000 0000001C
003860  00000000 0000338A 42F90000 88F00008    00003A3E 17671776 1767D201 60045366
003880  000049E8 000041B8 00004990 00003950    00003A3E 00003AE0 00003B2C 00003B88
0038A0  00003A5E 00003A72 00003826 00003B58    00003A3E 504088AE 00000001 1C00001A
0038C0  5B5BC2D6 D7C5D540 5B5BC2C3 D3D6E2C5    5B5BC2C6 C3D4E4D3 F0E90000 C0000000
0038E0  E6D6D9D2 60D9C5C3 D6D9C420 58F0C004    051F0001 4004F6F0 404040AA 9640D048
003900  58F0C004 051F0001 4004F6F3 40404010    4110C040 5800D1C8 184005F0 5000F008
003920  4500F00C 000033F8 0A024100 D1C858F0    C00805EF 5810D1C8 96101020 5020D1BC
003940  5870D1BC D2016000 C038D201 601CC038    58F0C004 051F0001 4004F6F7 404040F1
003960  4830C03A 4A306000 4E30D1D0 D705D1D0    D1D04F30 D1D64F30 D1D04030 60004830
003980  C03A4A30 601C4E30 D1D0D705 D1D0D1D0    940FD1D6 4F30D1D0 4030601C 41406002
0039A0  48206000 4C20C03A 1A425B40 C0385040    D1DC58E0 D1DCD200 6038E000 FA306050
0039C0  C03C4140 601E4820 60004C20 C03A1A42    5B40C038 5040D1E0 58E0D1E0 D2006043
0039E0  E0009240 60444830 601C4E30 D1D0F331    603AD1D6 96F0603D 58F0C004 051F0001
003A00  4004F7F2 4040404F 58F0C004 051F0002    00000014 0D0001C4 0038FFFF D2137000
```

Figure A–3 is a sample dump which was caused by a data exception. Invalid data (i.e., data which did not correspond to its usage) was placed in the numeric field B as a result of redefinition. The following notes illustrate the method of finding the specific statement in the program which caused the dump. Letters identifying the text correspond to letter in the program listing.

(A) The program interrupt occurred at HEX LOCATION 0039BC. This is indicated in the SYSLST message printed just before the dump.

(B) The linkage editor map indicates that the program was loaded into address 0032A0. This is determined by examining the load point of the control section TESTRUN. TESTRUN is the name assigned to the program module by the source coding:

PROGRAM-ID. TESTRUN.

(C) The specific instruction which caused the dump is located by subtracting the load address from the interrupt address (i.e., subtracting 32A0 from 39BC). The result, 71C, is the relative interrupt address and can be found in the object code listing. In this case the instruction in question is an AP (add decimal).

Figure A–3.   Sample Dump Resulting from Abnormal Termination
—Continued.

Ⓓ The left-hand column of the object code listing gives the compiler-generated card number associated with the instruction. It is card 69. As seen in the source listing, card 69 contains the COMPUTE statement.

Ⓔ The DTF for FILE-1 procedes the DTF for FILE-2.

Ⓕ DTFADR CELLS begin at relative location 5B0.

Ⓖ Since the relocation factor is 32A0, the DTRADR CELLS begin at location 3850 in the dump.

Ⓗ The DTF for FILE-1 begins at location 33F8, and the DTF for FILE-2 begins at location 3470.

Since the problem program in Figure A–3 interrupted because of a data exception, the programmer should locate the contents of field B at the time of the interruption. This can be done as follows?

Ⓙ Locate data-name B in the glossary. It appears under the column headed SOURCE-NAME. Source-Name B has been assigned to base locator 3 (i.e., BL = 3) with a displacement of 050. The sum of the value of base locator 3 and the displacement value 50 is the address of data-name B.

Ⓚ The Register Assignment table lists the registers assigned to each base locator. Register 6 has been assigned to BL = 3.

Ⓛ The contents of the 16 general registers at the time of the interrupt are displayed at the beginning of the dump. Register 6 contains the address 00003388.

Ⓜ The location of data-name B can now be determined by adding the contents of register 6 and the displacement value 50. The result, 33D8, is the address of the leftmost byte of the 4-byte field B.

Note: Field B contains F1F2F3C4. This is external decimal representation and does not correspond to the USAGE COMPUTATIONAL-3 defined in the source listing.

Ⓝ The location assigned to a given data-name may also be found by using the BL CELLS pointer in the TGT Memory Map. Figure 10 indicates that the BL cells begin at location 3844 (add 5A4 to the load point address, 32A0, of the object module). The first four bytes are the first BL cell, the second four bytes are the second BL cell, etc. Note that the third BL cell contains the value 3388. This is the same value as that contained in register 6.

Note: Some program errors may destroy the contents of the general registers or the BL cells. In such cases, alternate methods of locating the DTF's are useful.

Figure A–3. Sample Dump Resulting from Abnormal Termination
—Continued.

Locating Data in a Dump

The location assigned to a given data-name may be found by using the BL number and displacement given for that entry in the glossary and then locating the appropriate BL in the TGT. The hexadecimal sum of the glossary displacement and the contents of the cell should give the relative address of the desired area. This can be converted to an absolute address.

A programmer using the COBOL compiler has several methods available to him for testing his programs, debugging them, and revising them for increased efficiency in operation.

The COBOL debugging language can be used by itself or in conjunction with other COBOL statements. A dump can also be used for program checkout.

THE DEBUG LANGUAGE

The COBOL debugging language is designed to aid the COBOL programmer in producing an error-free program in the shortest possible time. The sections that follow discuss the use of the debug language and other methods of program checkout.

The three debug language statements are TRACE, ON, and EXHIBIT. Any one of these statements can be used as often as necessary. They can be interspersed throughout a COBOL source program, or they can be in a packet in the input stream to the compiler.

Program checkout may not be desired after testing is completed. A debug packet can be removed after testing. This allows elimination of the extra object program coding generated for the debug statements.

The output produced by the TRACE and EXHIBIT statements is listed on the system logical output device.

The following discussions describe ways to use the debug language.

Following the Flow of Control

The READY TRACE statement causes each section and paragraph-name (or number) to be listed on the system output unit when control passes to that point. The output appears as a list of unqualified procedure names.

To reduce the number of names that are generated and the time taken to generate them, a trace can be stopped with a RESET TRACE statement. The READY TRACE/RESET TRACE combination is helpful in examining a particular area of the program. The READY TRACE statement can be coded so that the trace begins before control passes to that area. The RESET TRACE statement can be coded so that the trace stops when the program has passed the area. The two TRACE statements can be used together where the flow of control is difficult to determine, e.g., with a series of PERFORM statements or with nested conditionals.

Trace Statement

The format of the TRACE statement is

$$\left. \begin{array}{l} READY \\ RESET \end{array} \right\} \quad TRACE$$

After a READY TRACE statement is executed, a message is written each time execution of a paragraph or section begins. The READY TRACE statement is placed where the trace is to begin.

The execution of a RESET TRACE statement terminates the functions of a previous READY TRACE statement. The RESET TRACE statement is placed in the location where the trace is to terminate.

Compile-Time Debugging Packet

Debugging statements for a given paragraph or section in a program may be grouped together into a debugging packet. These statements will be compiled with the source language program, and will be executed at object time. Each packet refers to a specified paragraph-name or section-name in the Procedure Division.

Each compile-time debug packet is headed by the control card DEBUG. The general form of this card is

Card Column 1	Card Column 8
DEBUG	location

where the parameters are described as follows:

Location

Location is the COBOL section-name or paragraph-name (qualified, if necessary) indicating the point in the program at which the packet is to be executed. Effectively, the statements in the packet are executed as if they were physically placed in the source program following the section-name or paragraph-name, but preceding the text associated with the name. The same *location* must not be used in more than one DEBUG control card. *Location* may not be a paragraph-name within the DEBUG packet itself.

(*Note:* Location can start anywhere within Margin A.)

A debug packet may consist of any procedural statements conforming to the requirements of COBOL. A GO TO, PERFORM, or ALTER statement in a debug packet may refer to a procedure-name in any debug packet or in the main body of the Procedure Division.

Another way to control the amount of tracing so that it is done conditionally is to use the ON statement with the TRACE statement. When the COBOL compiler encounters an ON statement, it sets up a mechanism, such as a counter which is incremented during execution whenever control passes through the ON statement. For example, if an error occurs when a specific record is processed, the ON statement can be used to isolate the problem record. The statement should be placed where control passes only once for each record that is read. When the contents of the counter equal the number of the record (as specified in the ON statement), a trace can be taken on that record.

ON (Count-Conditional Statement)

The ON statement is a conditional statement. It specifies when the statements it contains are to be executed. ELSE (or OTHERWISE) NEXT SENTENCE may be omitted if it immediately precedes the period for the sentence. All integers contained in the statement must be positive.

The count-condition (Integer-1 AND EVERY Integer-2 UNTIL Integer-3) is evaluated as follows:

Each ON statement has a compiler-generated counter associated with it. The counter is initialized in the object program with a value of zero.

Each time the path of program flow reaches the ON statement, the counter is advanced by 1. Where m is any positive integer, if the value of the counter is equal to Integer-1 + (m * Integer-2), but is less than Integer-3 (if specified), then the imperative statements (or NEXT SENTENCE) are executed. Otherwise, the statements after ELSE (or NEXT SENTENCE) are executed. If the ELSE option does not appear, the next sentence is executed.

If Integer-2 is not given, but Integer-3 is given, it is assumed that Integer-2 has a value of 1. If Integer-3 is not given, no upper limit is assumed for it.

If neither Integer-2 nor Integer-3 is specified, the imperative statements are executed only once.

Figure A–4.   Format on Statement.

Examples:

ON 2 AND EVERY 2 UNTIL 10 DISPLAY A ELSE DISPLAY B.

On the second, fourth, sixth, and eighth times, A is displayed. B is displayed at all other times.

ON 3 DISPLAY A.

On the third time through the count-conditional statement, A is displayed. No action is taken at any other time.

The following example shows a way in which the 200th record could be selected for a TRACE statement.

```
      Col.
      1       Area A
---------------------------------------------------------------
              RD-REC.
                .
                .
                .
      DEBUG   RD-REC
              PARA-NM-1.    ON 200 READY TRACE.
                            ON 201 RESET TRACE.
```

If the TRACE statement were used without the ON statement, every record would be traced.

An example of a common program error is failing to break a loop or unintentionally creating a loop in the program. If many iterations of the loop are required before it can be determined that there is a program error, the ON statement can be used to initiate a trace only after the expected number of iterations has been completed. (*Note:* If an error occurs in an ON statement, the diagnostic may refer to the previous statement number.)

Displaying Data Values During Execution

A programmer can display the value of a data item during program execution by using the EXHIBIT statement. The three forms of this statement display: (1) the names and values of the data-names listed in the EXHIBIT statement (EXHIBIT NAMED) whenever the statement is encountered during execution; (2) the values of the data-names listed in this statement only if the value has changed since the last execution (EXHIBIT CHANGED); and (3) the data-names listed in the statement and the value of the data-names only if the values have changed since the previous execution (EXHIBIT CHANGED NAMED).

Exhibit Statement

The execution of an EXHIBIT NAMED statement causes a formatted display of the data-names (or nonnumeric literals) listed in the statement. The format of the output for each data-name listed in the NAMED or CHANGED NAMED form of an EXHIBIT statement is:

> original data-name (including qualifiers, if written)
> blank
> equal sign
> blank
> value of data-name
> blank

Literals listed in the statement are preceded by a blank, when displayed.

The CHANGED form of the EXHIBIT statement provides for a display of items when they change value, compared to the value at the previous time the EXHIBIT CHANGED statement was executed. The initial time such a statement is executed, all values are considered changed; they are displayed and saved for purposes of comparison.

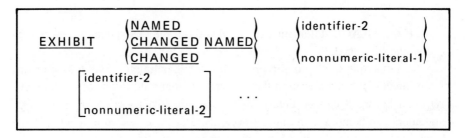

Figure A–5.   Format Exhibit Statement.

Data values can be used to check the accuracy of the program. For example, using EXHIBIT NAMED, the programmer can display specified fields from records, compute the calculations himself, and compare his calculations with the output from his program. The coding for a payroll problem might be:

```
Col.
1              Area A


              .
              .
              .
              GROSS-PAY-CALC.
                  COMPUTE GROSS-PAY =
                  RATE-PER-HOUR * (HRSWKD
                  + 1.5 * OVERTIMEHRS).
              NET-PAY-CALC.
                  .
                  .
                  .
DEBUG         NET-PAY-CALC
              SAMPLE-1. ON 10 AND
                  EVERY 10 EXHIBIT NAMED
                  RATE-PER-HOUR, HRSWKD,
                  OVERTIMEHRS, GROSS-PAY.
```

This coding will cause the values of the four fields to be listed for every tenth data record before net pay calculations are made. The output could appear as:

```
RATE-PER-HOUR = 4.00 HRSWKD = 40.0
    OVERTIMEHRS = 0.0 GROSS-PAY = 160.00



RATE-PER-HOUR = 4.10 HRSWKD = 40.0
    OVERTIMEHRS = 1.5 GROSS-PAY = 173.23



RATE-PER-HOUR = 3.35 HRSWKD = 40.0
    OVERTIMEHRS = 0.0 GROSS-PAY = 134.00
```

Note: Decimal points are included in this example for clarity, but actual printouts depend on the data description in the program.

Figure A–6.   Example—Exhibit Named Statement.

Note that if two distinct EXHIBIT CHANGED data-name statements appear in a program, changes in *data-name* are associated with the two separate statements. Depending on the path of program flow, the values of *data-name* saved for comparison may differ for the two statements.

If the list of operands in an EXHIBIT CHANGED statement includes literals, they are printed as remarks and are preceded by a blank. A check of any unusual conditions can be made by using various combinations of COBOL statements in the debug packet. For example:

IF OVERTIMEHRS GREATER THAN 2.0 EXHIBIT NAMED PAYRCDHRS.

In connection with the previous example, this statement could cause the entire pay record to be displayed whenever an unusual condition (overtime exceeding two hours) is encountered.

The EXHIBIT CHANGED statement also can be used to monitor conditions that do not occur at regular intervals. The values of data-names are listed only if the value has changed since the last execution of the statement. For example, suppose the program calculates postage rates to various cities. The flow of the program might be:

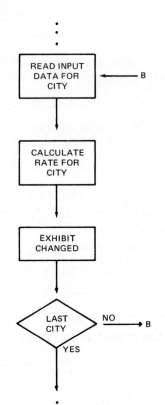

EXHIBIT CHANGED STATE CITY RATE

The output from the EXHIBIT statement with the CHANGED option could appear as:

```
01   01   10
     02   15
     03
     04   10
02   01
     02   20
     03   15
     04
03   01   10
      .
      .
      .
```

The first column contains the code for a state, the second column contains the code for a city, and the third column contains the code for the postage rate. The value of a data-name is listed only if it has changed since the previous execution. For example, since the postage rate to city 02 and city 03 in state 01 are the same, the rate is not printed for city 03.

Figure A–7. Example—Exhibit Changed Statement.

The EXHIBIT CHANGED NAMED statement lists the data-name and the value of that data-name if the value has changed. For example, the program might calculate the cost of various methods of shipping to different cities. After the calculations are made, the following statement could be in the program:

```
                EXHIBIT CHANGED NAMED STATE CITY RAIL
                    BUS TRUCK AIR

STATE = 01 CITY = 01 RAIL = 10 BUS = 14 TRUCK = 12 AIR = 20
CITY = 02
CITY = 03 BUS = 06 AIR = 15
CITY = 04 RAIL = 30 BUS = 25 TRUCK = 28 AIR = 34
STATE = 02 CITY = 01 TRUCK = 25
CITY = 02 TRUCK = 20 AIR = 30
    .
    .
    .
```

Figure A–8. Example—Exhibit Changed Named Statement.

Note that a data-name and its value are listed only if the value has changed since the previous execution.

Testing a Program Selectively

A debug packet allows the programmer to select a portion of the program for testing. The packet can include test data and can specify operations the programmer wants to be performed. When the testing is completed, the packet can be removed. The flow of control can be selectively altered by the inclusion of debug packets, as illustrated in the following example of selective testing of B:

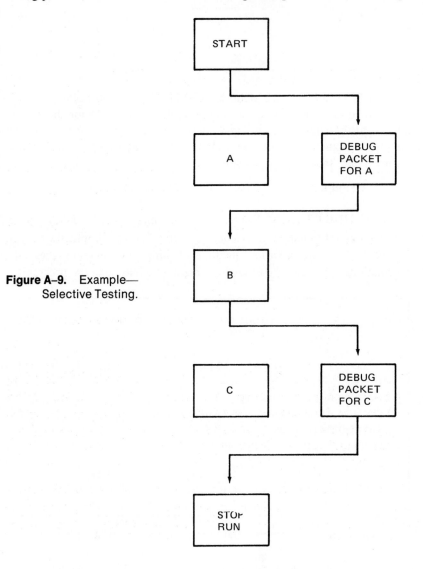

Figure A–9. Example— Selective Testing.

In this program, A creates data, B processes it, and C prints it. The debug packet for A simulates test data. It is first in the program to be executed. In the packet, the last statement is GO TO B, which permits A to be bypassed. After B is executed with the test data, control passes to the debug packet for C, which contains a GO TO statement that transfers control to the end of the program, bypassing C.

TESTING CHANGES AND ADDITIONS TO PROGRAMS

If a program runs correctly, but changes or additions can make it more efficient, a debug packet can be used to test changes without modifying the original source program.

If the changes to be incorporated are in the middle of a paragraph, the entire paragraph, with the changes included, must be written in the debug packet. The last statement in the packet should be a GO TO statement that transfers control to the next procedure to be executed.

There are usually several ways to perform an operation. Alternative methods can be tested by putting them in debug packets.

The source program library facility can be used for program checkout by placing a source program in a library (see "Libraries"). Changes or additions to the program can be tested by using the BASIS card and any number of INSERT and DELETE cards. Such changes or additions remain in effect only for the duration of the run.

A debug packet can also be used in conjunction with the BASIS card to debug a program or to test deletions or additions to it. The debug packet is inserted in the input stream immediately following the BASIS card and any INSERT or DELETE cards.

```
000730                    IF ANNUAL-PAY GREATER THAN 9000  GO TO PAY-WRITE.
000735                    IF ANNUAL-PAY GREATER THAN 9000 - BASE-PAY GO TO LAST-FICA.
000740    FICA-PAYR.  COMPUTE FICA-PAY = BASE-PAY * .052
000745                      MOVE FICA-PAY TO OUTPUT-FICA.
000750    PAY-WRITE.      MOVE BASE-PAY TO OUTPUT-BASE.
000755                    ADD BASE- PAY TO ANNUAL-PAY.
     .              .
     .              .
     .              .
000850              STOP RUN.
```

Sample Coding to Calculate FICA

```
// JOB PGM2
// OPTION LOG,DECK,LIST,LISTX,ERRS
// EXEC FCOBOL
 CBL QUOTE
BASIS PAYROLL
DELETE 000730, 000735
                IF OCCUPATION-CODE = "DR" PERFORM PAY-INCREASE THRU EX1.
INSERT 000850
        PAY-INCREASE.   MULTIPLY 1.05 BY BASE-PAY.
        EX1.            EXIT.
```

Altering a Program from the Source Statement Library Using INSERT and DELETE Cards

```
                IF OCCUPATION-CODE = "DR" PERFORM PAY-INCREASE THRU EX1.
000740    FICA-PAYR.  COMPUTE FICA-PAY = BASE-PAY * .052
000745              MOVE FICA-PAY TO OUTPUT-FICA.
000750    PAY-WRITE.  MOVE BASE-PAY TO OUTPUT-BASE.
000755              ADD BASE-PAY TO ANNUAL-PAY.
     .          .
     .          .
     .          .
000850              STOP RUN.
        PAY-INCREASE. MULTIPLY 1.05 BY BASE-PAY.
        EX1.            EXIT.
```

Effect of INSERT and DELETE Cards

Figure A–10.   Example—Insert and Delete Cards.

Appendix B

Job-Control Language

INTRODUCTION

Job-Control Cards (JCL) establish the communication link between the COBOL programmer and the control system of the computer. The control system consists of a number of processing programs and a control program. The processing programs will include the COBOL compiler, service programs, as well as any user-written programs.

The control program supervises the execution and loading of the processing programs; controls the location, storage, and retrieval of data; and schedules the jobs for continuous processing of problem programs.

EXECUTING A COBOL PROGRAM

The basic operations to be performed to execute a COBOL program are:

A. *Compilation.* The process of translating a COBOL source program into a series of instructions comprehensible to the computer. In computer terminology, the input (source program) to the compiler is called the *source module.* The output (compiled source program) from the compiler is called the *object module.*

B. *Linkage Editing.* The Linkage Editor is a source program that prepares object modules for execution. It can also be used to combine two or more separately compiled object modules into a format suitable for execution as a single program. The executed output of the Linkage Editor is called a *load module.* The Linkage Editor may also combine previously edited load

561

modules with or without one or more object modules to form one load module.

C. *Loading.* The loader is a service program that processes COBOL object and load modules, resolves any references to subprograms, and executes the loaded module. All these functions are specified in one step.

D. *Execution.* Actual execution is under the supervision of the control program, which obtains a load module, loads it into main storage, and initiates execution of the machine language instructions contained in the load module.

The JOB statement identifies the beginning of a job and the job to be performed. It may be also used by the installation's accounting routines.

The EXEC statement describes the job step and calls for execution.

Sample DOS JCL Statements

All JCL cards start in card column 1. Slashes in column 1 and 2 (//) identify the cards to the system as JCL, and not program or data cards. If commas are indicated in certain JCL statements, they must be included.

```
1.  // JOB EXAMPLE
2.  // OPTION LINK
3.  // EXEC FCOBOL
4.     Source Program Cards
5.  /*
6.  // EXEC LNKEDT
7.  // EXEC
8.     Data Cards
9.  /*
10. /&
```

Card 1. The JOB statement identifies the program to the system. There must be at least one space before and after JOB. Name is limited to eight characters or less and need not be related to the PROGRAM-ID.

Card 2. The OPTION LINK card may vary from installation to installation depending upon the needs and requirements of the programmer. For example, if the program is unexecutable, a dump of storage may be requested.

Card 3. The EXEC FCOBOL card is calling for the execution of the COBOL compiler to translate the source program into the object module.

Card 4. The punched source program cards would be inserted here.

Card 5. The delimiter (/*) signals the end of the source program and separates the source program from subsequent JCL statements.

Card 6. The execution of the EXEC LNKEDT statement will prepare the object module for execution.

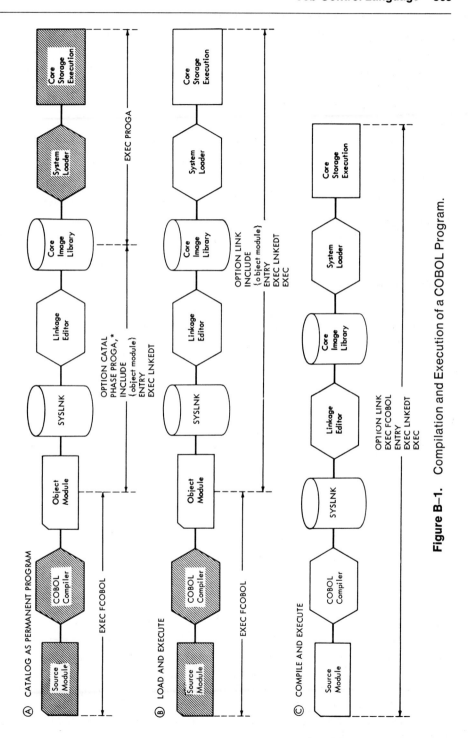

Figure B–1. Compilation and Execution of a COBOL Program.

Card 7. The EXEC statement controls the execution of the machine language instructions contained in the load module upon the data deck which follows.

Card 8. The data deck containing the source data to be processed.

Card 9. Another delimiter (/*) to signal the end of the data deck and separate the data from any subsequent JCL statements.

Card 10. The delimiter (/&) to signal the end of the program and to separate the executed program from any subsequent programs. An important note to remember is that the omission of this delimiter may cause two programs to be executed together.

It is beyond the scope of this text to discuss the various combinations of JCL cards permissable. There are many options available to the programmer, and they should be carefully studied in the programmer's guide reference manual for the particular computer. The above example is just a typical example of the use and purpose of JCL cards. Following is a brief explanation of the format, use, and purpose of IBM DOS JCL cards.

JOB-CONTROL LANGUAGE (DOS) (IBM)

Job-control statements prepare the system for the execution of COBOL programs.

Job Control Statements

Job control statements are designed for an eighty-column card format. The statements are punched into cards in essentially free form, but certain rules must be observed, as follows:

1. *Name*. Two slashes (//) identify the statement as a job-control statement. These punches must be in columns one and two of the card followed immediately by at least one blank.

   Exception: The end-of-job statement delimiter contains /& in columns one and two; the end-of-data statement delimiter contains /* in columns one and two, and the comments statement contains an * in column one and a blank in column two.

2. *Operation*. This identifies the operation to be performed. It can be up to eight characters long with at least one blank following its last character.

3. *Operand*. This may be a blank or may contain one or more entries separated by commas. The last term must be followed by a blank, unless its last character is in column 71.

4. *Comments.* Optional programmer comments must be separated from the operand by at least one space.

All JCL cards are read by the systems input device specified by the symbolic name SYSRDR.

Comment Statements

Comment statements (statements preceded by an asterisk in column one and followed by a blank) may be placed anywhere in the job deck. They may contain any character and are usually for communication with the operator; accordingly, they are written on the console printer keyboard as well as on the printer.

JOB DEFINITION

A *JOB* is a specified unit of work to be performed under the control of the operating system. A typical job might be the processing of a COBOL program—compiling the source program, editing the module to form a phase, and then executing the phase.

A *JOBSTEP* is exactly what the name implies—one step in the processing of the job. Thus, in the JOB mentioned above, one job step is the compilation of the source statements, another is the line editing of the module, and the other is the execution of the phase. A compilation requires the execution of the COBOL compiler, an editing process implies the execution of the Linkage Editor, and, finally, the execution phase is the execution of the problem program itself.

COMPILATION OF JOB STEPS

The compilation of a COBOL program may necessitate more than one job step (more than one execution of the COBOL compiler). In some cases, a COBOL program consists of a main program and one or more subprograms. To compile such a program, a separate job step must be specified for the main program and for each of the subprograms. Thus the COBOL compiler is executed once for the main program and once for each subprogram. Each execution produces a module. The separate modules can be then combined into one phase by a single job step—the execution of the Linkage Editor.

```
// JOB PROG1
    .
    .
    .
// EXEC FCOBOL
    {source deck - main program }
/*
    .
    .
    .
// EXEC FCOBOL
    {source deck - first subprogram }
/*
    .
    .
    .
// EXEC FCOBOL
    {source deck - second subprogram }
/*
    .
    .
    .
// EXEC LNKEDT
    .
    .
    .
// EXEC
```

Figure B–2.   Sample Structure of Job Deck for Compiling, Linkediting, and Executing a Main Program and Two Subprograms.

There are four job-control statements that are used for job definition: the JOB statement, the EXEC statement, end-of-data statement (/*), and the end-of-job statement (/&). These are optional job-control statements that may be used to specify specific JCL functions.

The *JOB* statement defines the start of a job. One JOB statement is required for every job; it must be the first statement in the job deck. The programmer must name his job on the JOB statement.

The *EXEC* statement request the execution of a program. Therefore, one EXEC statement is required for each job step within a job stream. The EXEC statement identifies the program that is to be executed (for example, the COBOL compiler, the Linkage Editor).

The end-of-data statement, also referred to as the slash asterisk (/*) statement, defines the end of a programmers input data. The slash asterisk statement immediately follows the input data. For example, COBOL source statements would be placed immediately after the EXEC statement for the COBOL compiler; a /* statement would follow the last COBOL source statement. If input data is kept separate, the /* immediately follows each set of input data.

The end-of-job statement, also referred to as slash ampersand (/&) statement, defines the end of the job. A /& statement must appear as the last statement in the job deck. If this statement is omitted, the preceding job would be combined with this job.

COMPILATION

Compilation is the execution of the COBOL compiler. The programmer requests compilation by placing in the job deck an EXEC statement specifying the name of the COBOL compiler. Input to the compiler is a set of COBOL source statements consisting of either a main program or a subprogram.

Output from the COBOL compiler is dependent upon the options specified. This output may include a listing of source statements exactly as they appear in the input deck. Separate data and/or Procedure Division maps, a symbolic cross-reference list, and diagnostic messages can also be produced. The format of the compiler output is described and illustrated in the "Debugging" section.

The programmer can override any of the compiler options specified when the system was generated or can include some not specified by specifying the OPTION control statement in the compiler job step.

EDITING

Editing is the execution of the Linkage Editor. The programmer requests editing by placing in the job deck an EXEC statement that contains the name LNKEDT, the name of the Linkage Editor.

Statement	Function
// ASSGN	Input/output assignments.
// CLOSE	Closes a logical unit assigned to magnetic tape.
// DATE	Provides a date for the Communication Region.
// DLAB	Disk file label information.
// DLBL	Disk file label information.
// EXEC	Execute program.
// EXTENT	Disk file extent.
// JOB	Beginning of control information for a job.
// LBLTYP	Reserves storage for label information.
// LISTIO	Lists input/output assignments.
//MTC	Controls operations on magnetic tape.
// OPTION	Specifies one or more job control options.
// PAUSE	Creates a pause for operator intervention.
// RESET	Resets input/output assignments to standard assignments.
// RSTRT	Restarts a checkpointed program.
// TLBL	Tape label information.
// TPLAB	Tape label information.
// UPSI	Sets user-program switches.
// VOL	Disk/tape label information.
// XTENT	Disk file extent.
/*	End-of-data-file or end-of-job-step.
/&	End-of-job.
*	Comments.

Figure B–3.   Job-Control Statements.

Output from the Linkage Editor consists of one or more phases. A phase may be an entire program or it may be part of an overlay structure (multiple phases).

A phase produced by the Linkage Editor can be executed immediately after it is produced (that is, in the job step immediately following the Linkage Editor), or it can be executed later, either in a subsequent job step of the same job or a subsequent job step.

PHASE EXECUTION

Phase execution is the execution of the problem program—for example, the program written by the COBOL programmer. If the program is an overlay structure (multiple phases), the execution job step actually involves the execution of all phases in the program.

The programmer requests the execution of a phase by placing in the job deck an EXEC statement that specifies the name of the phase. However, if the phase to be executed was produced in the immediately preceding job step, it is not necessary to specify its name in the EXEC statement.

SEQUENCE OF JOB-CONTROL STATEMENTS

The job deck for a specific job always begins with a JOB statement and ends with a /& (end-of-job) statement. A specific job consists of one or more job steps. The beginning of a job step is indicated by the appearance of an EXEC statement. When an EXEC statement is encountered, it initiates the execution of the job step, which includes all preceding control statements up to but not including a previous EXEC statement.

ASSGN Statements

The ASSGN control statement assigns a logical input/output unit to a physical device. An ASSGN control statement must be present in the job deck for each data file assigned to an external storage device in the COBOL program where these assignments differ from those established at system generation time. Data files are assigned to programmer logical units in COBOL by means of the source language ASSGN clause. The ASSGN control statement may also be used to change a system standard assignment for the duration of the job. Device assignments made by the ASSGN statement are considered temporary until another ASSGN statement appears.

Appendix C

Segmentation Feature

INTRODUCTION

The Segmentation Feature allows the problem programmer to communicate with the compiler to specify object program overlay requirements. Segmentation feature permits segmentation of procedures only. Segmentation will allow the programmer to divide the Procedure Division of the source program into sections. Through the use of a system of priority numbers, certain sections are designated as permanently resident in core storage and other sections as overlayable fixed segments and/or independent segments. Thus a large program can be executed in a defined area of core storage by limiting the number of segments in the program that are permanently resident in core.

Although COBOL segmentation deals only with segmentation of procedures, the Environment Division must be considered in determining the segmentation requirements for object programs.

ORGANIZATION

Program Segments

Although it is not mandatory, the Procedure Division for a source program is usually written as a consecutive group of sections, each of which is composed of a series of closely related operations that are designed to collectively perform a particular function. However, when segmentation is used, *the entire Procedure Division must be in sections.* In addition, each section must be classified as belonging either to the fixed portion or to one of the independent segments of the object program. Segmentation in no way affects the need for qualification of procedure-names to insure uniqueness.

section-name <u>SECTION</u> [priority-number] .

Figure C–1. Format Program Segmentation.

```
IDENTIFICATION DIVISION
PROGRAM-ID. SAVECORE.
.
.

ENVIRONMENT DIVISION.
OBJECT-COMPUTER. IBM-360-H50
        SEGMENT-LIMIT IS 15.
.

.

DATA DIVISION.
.

.

PROCEDURE DIVISION.
SECTION-1    SECTION 8.
.

.

SECTION-2    SECTION 8.
.

.

SECTION-3    SECTION 16.
.

.

SECTION-4    SECTION 8.
.

.

SECTION-5    SECTION 50.
.

.

SECTION-6    SECTION 16.
.

.

SECTION-7    SECTION 50.
.

.
```

Figure C–2. Example—Program Segmentation.

Fixed Portion

The fixed portion is defined as that part of the object program that is logically treated as if it were always in storage. This portion of the program is composed of two types of storage segments: permanent segments and overlayable fixed segments.

A permanent segment is a segment in the fixed portion which cannot be overlaid by any other part of the program.

An *overlayable segment* is a segment in the fixed portion which, although logically treated as if it were always in storage, can be overlaid (if necessary) by another segment to optimize storage utilization. However, such a segment, if called for by the program, is always available in the state it was when it was last used.

Depending on the availability of storage, the number of permanent segments in the fixed portion can be varied through the use of a special facility called SEGMENT-LIMIT. (See discussion of SEGMENT-LIMIT later in section.)

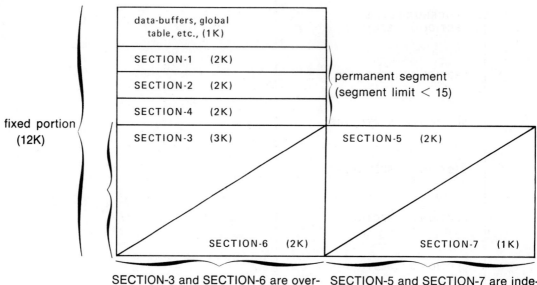

SECTION-3 and SECTION-6 are overlayable fixed segments (14 < segment limit < 50)

SECTION-5 and SECTION-7 are independent segments (49 < segment limit < 100)

Figure C–3. Example—Storage Layout for Segmented Program.

Independent Segments

An independent segment is defined as part of the object program which can overlay, and can be overlaid by another independent segment. An independent segment is effectively in its initial state each time the segment is made available to the program.

Segment Classification

Segments which are to be segmented are classified, using a system of priority numbers and the following criteria.

1. *Logic Requirements.* Sections that must be available for reference at all times, or which are referred to very frequently, are normally classified as belonging to one of the permanent segments; sections that are less frequently used are normally classified as belonging either to one of the overlayable fixed segments or to one of the independent segments, depending on logic requirements.
2. *Frequency of Use.* Generally, the more frequently a section is referred to, the lower its priority-number; the less frequently it is referred to, the higher its priority-number.
3. *Relationship to Other Sections.* Sections which frequently communicate with one another should be given equal priority-numbers. All sections with the same priority-number constitute a single program segment.

Segmentation Control

The logical sequence of a program is the same as the physical sequence except for specific transfers of control. A reordering of the object module will be necessary if a given segment has its sections scattered throughout the source program. However, the compiler will provide transfers to maintain the logic flow of the source program. The compiler will also insert instructions necessary to load and/or initialize a segment when necessary. Control may be transferred within a source program to any paragraph in a section; that is, it is not mandatory to transfer control to the beginning of a section.

Structure of Program Segments

Priority-Numbers. Section classification is accomplished by means of a system of priority-numbers. The priority-number is included in the section header.

Rules Governing the Use of Priority-Numbers

1. The priority-number must be an integer ranging in value from 0 through 99.
2. If the priority-number is omitted from the section header, the priority is assumed 0.
3. All sections which have the same priority-number must be together in the source program, and they constitute a program segment with that priority.
4. Segments with priority-number 0 through 49 belong to the fixed portion of the object program.
5. Segments with priority-numbers 50 through 99 are independent segments.
6. Sections in the declaratives portion of the Procedure Division must *not* contain priority-numbers in their section headers. They are treated as permanent segments with a priority-number of 0.

Segment-Limit

Ideally, all program segments having priority-numbers ranging from 0 through 49 are treated as permanent segments. However, when insufficient storage is available to contain all permanent segments plus the largest overlayable segment, it becomes necessary to decrease the number of permanent segments. The SEGMENT-LIMIT feature provides the user with a means by which he can reduce the number of permanent segments in his program, while these permanent segments still retain the logical properties of fixed portion segments (priority numbers 0 through 49).

[SEGMENT-LIMIT IS priority-number]

Figure C–4. Format Segment-Limit Clause.

Rules Governing the Use of the Segment-Limit Clause

1. The SEGMENT-LIMIT clause is coded in the OBJECT-COMPUTER paragraph in the Environment Division.
2. The priority-number must be an integer that ranges in value from 1 through 49.
3. When the SEGMENT-LIMIT clause is specified, only those segments having priority-numbers from 0 up to, but not including, the priority number designated as the segment limit are considered as permanent segments of the object program.

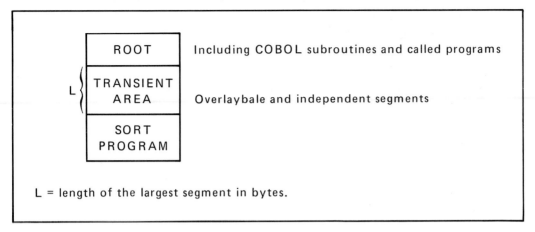

ROOT — Including COBOL subroutines and called programs

L { TRANSIENT AREA — Overlaybale and independent segments

SORT PROGRAM

L = length of the largest segment in bytes.

Figure C–5. Location of Sort Program in a Segmented Structure.

4. Those segments having priority numbers from the segment limit through 49 are considered as overlayable fixed segments.
5. When the SEGMENT-LIMIT clause is omitted, all segments having priority numbers from 0 through 49 are considered to be permanent segments of the object program.

Restrictions on Program Flow

When segmentation is used, the following restrictions are placed on the ALTER and PERFORM statements.

Alter Statement

1. A GO TO statement is a section whose priority-number is 50 or greater must not be referred to by an ALTER statement in a section with a different priority-number.
2. A GO TO statement in a section whose priority-number is lower than 50 may be referred to by an ALTER statement in any section, even if the GO TO statement to which the ALTER refers is in a segment of the program that has not been called for execution.

Perform Statement

1. A PERFORM statement that appears in a section whose priority-number is lower than SEGMENT-LIMIT can have within its range only the following:

    a. Sections with priority-numbers lower than 50.

    b. Sections wholly contained in a single segment whose priority-number is higher than 49.

2. A PERFORM statement that appears in a section whose priority-number is equal to or higher than the SEGMENT-LIMIT can have within its range only the following:

    a. Sections with the same priority-number as the section containing the PERFORM statement.

    b. Sections with priority-numbers that are lower than the SEGMENT-LIMIT.

Appendix D

COBOL Differences
COBOL D/E/F and American
National Standard COBOL

CONTENTS

C O B O L   D I F F E R E N C E S
IDENTIFICATION DIVISION

Language Element	D/E/F COBOL	ANS COBOL	Comments
PROGRAM-ID paragraph D E F	PROGRAM-ID. 'program-name.' Example: PROGRAM-ID. 'PROB1.'	PROGRAM-ID. program-name. Example: PROGRAM ID. PROB1.	Quotation marks are elimi- nated. Program-name must conform to rules for the for- mation of a procedure-name.
DATE-COMPILED paragraph D E	DATE-COMPILED. comment-entry. Example: DATE-COMPILED. MAY 15, 1972. (Unchanged by compilation on July 23, 1972.)	DATE-COMPILED. comment-entry. Example: DATE-COMPILED. MAY 15, 1972. (Changed to: DATE-COMPILED. JULY 23, 1972.)	The ANS compilation re- places the comment-entry with the actual compilation date.

C O B O L   D I F F E R E N C E S
ENVIRONMENT DIVISION

Language Element	D/E/F COBOL	ANS COBOL	Comments

SOURCE-COMPUTER paragraph
 	
(Configuration Section)
 	
D   E   F
	SOURCE-COMPUTER.
	    IBM-360 [model-number].
	
	Example:
	SOURCE-COMPUTER.
	    IBM-360 H50.
		SOURCE-COMPUTER.
		    IBM-360 [-model-number].
		
		Example:
		SOURCE-COMPUTER.
		    IBM-360-H50.
			A hyphen must be inserted before model-number.
			
			(The ANS standard requires that the computer name conform to the rules for a COBOL word.)

OBJECT-COMPUTER paragraph
 	
(Configuration Section)
 	
D   E   F
	OBJECT-COMPUTER.
	    IBM-360 [model-number].
	
	Example:
	OBJECT-COMPUTER.
	    IBM-360 H50.
		OBJECT-COMPUTER.
		    IBM-360 [-model-number].
		
		Example:
		OBJECT-COMPUTER.
		    IBM-360-H50.
			A hyphen must be inserted before model-number.
			
			(The ANS standard requires that the computer name conform to the rules for a COBOL word.)

SPECIAL-NAMES paragraph
 	
(Configuration Section)
 	
                 F
	a) DECIMAL-POINT IS COMMA
	
	b) Function-name IS
	       mnemonic-name
		a) DECIMAL-POINT IS COMMA
		
		b) Function-name IS
		       mnemonic-name
			IS must be added as a key word, if missing.

ASSIGN clause
 	
(File-Control paragraph)
 	
D   E   F
	ASSIGN TO external-name
	
	{ DIRECT-ACCESS
	  UTILITY
	  UNIT-RECORD }
	
	[device-number UNIT [S]]
	
	[ORGANIZATION IS { INDEXED
	                              DIRECT
	                              RELATIVE* }]
	
	Example (COBOL F):
	
	SELECT PAYROLL ASSIGN TO
	'SYSUT6' DIRECT-ACCESS 2314
	UNIT ORGANIZATION IS DIRECT.
	
	*Option not available in COBOL D.
		ASSIGN TO [integer]
		system-name
		
		Example (OS ANS):
		
		SELECT PAYROLL ASSIGN TO
		DA-2314-D-SYSUT6.
		
		(For an example of the DOS ANS system-name, see the RERUN entry.)
			The functions of the ASSIGN and ORGANIZATION clauses must be compressed into one COBOL word (system-name).

ACCESS clause
 	
(File-Control paragraph)
 	
D   E   F
	ACCESS IS { SEQUENTIAL
	                    RANDOM }
		ACCESS MODE IS { SEQUENTIAL
		                            RANDOM }
			IS must be added as a key word, if missing.

ACCESS clause (direct organization, opened as OUTPUT) (File-Control paragraph) D	A direct organization file can be opened as OUTPUT only if access is sequential.	A direct organization file can be opened as OUTPUT only if ACCESS IS RANDOM is specified.	If ACCESS IS SEQUENTIAL was specified, it must be replaced by ACCESS IS RANDOM; if no ACCESS clause was specified, ACCESS IS RANDOM must be added.

Language Element	D/E/F COBOL	ANS COBOL	Comments
KEY clauses (direct organization, and either random access, opened as INPUT or I-O, or sequential access, opened as OUTPUT) (File-Control paragraph)	ACTUAL KEY IS data-name (where data-name contains the track address) SYMBOLIC KEY IS data-name (where data-name contains the symbolic identity associated with a given record)	ACTUAL KEY IS data-name (where data-name is made up of two components: a. the track address, and b. the symbolic identity associated with the record)	The KEY clauses must be condensed into one ACTUAL KEY clause. The actual and symbolic keys can be made subordinate data items as in the OS ANS example. IS must be added as a key word, if missing. (The ANS standard requires that all information needed to access a record be contained in the actual key.)
	Example (COBOL E and F): SELECT PAYROLL ASSIGN TO 'SYSUT6' DIRECT-ACCESS ORGANIZATION IS DIRECT SYMBOLIC KEY SYM-KEY ACTUAL KEY ACT-KEY. . . . WORKING-STORAGE SECTION. 01 ACT-KEY PICTURE S9(5) USAGE COMPUTATIONAL. 01 SYM-KEY PICTURE 99. (For an example of an actual key in COBOL D, see the next "KEY Clauses" entry.)	Example (OS ANS): SELECT PAYROLL ASSIGN TO DA-2314-D-SYSUT6 ACTUAL KEY IS SALES-NO. . . . WORKING-STORAGE SECTION. 01 SALES-NO. 02 ACT-KEY PICTURE S9(5) USAGE COMPUTATIONAL. 02 SYM-KEY PICTURE 99. (For an example of an actual key in DOS ANS COBOL, see the next "KEY Clauses" entry.)	
KEY clauses (direct organization, sequential access, opened as INPUT) (File-Control paragraph)	Required for COBOL D: ACTUAL KEY IS data-name (where data-name contains the track address) Required for COBOL D, E, F: SYMBOLIC KEY IS data-name (The symbolic identity of the record is stored in the SYMBOLIC KEY data-name whenever a READ statement is executed for the file.) Example (COBOL D): SYMBOLIC KEY IS SYM-KEY ACTUAL KEY IS THE-ACT-KEY . . . WORKING-STORAGE SECTION. 01 ACT-KEY. 02 DISK-NUM USAGE COMPUTATIONAL PICTURE S999 VALUE 0. 02 CELL-NUM USAGE COMPUTATIONAL PICTURE S9 VALUE 0. 02 CYL-NUM USAGE COMPUTATIONAL PICTURE S999 VALUE 10. 02 HEAD-NUM USAGE COMPUTATIONAL PICTURE S9 VALUE 0. 02 REC-NUM PICTURE X VALUE LOW-VALUE. 01 KEY-REDEF REDEFINES ACT-KEY. 02 FILLER PICTURE X. 02 THE-ACT-KEY PICTURE X(8). 01 SYM-KEY PICTURE 99.	ACTUAL KEY IS data-name (where data-name is made up of two components: a. the track address, and b. the symbolic identity associated with the record) (The ACTUAL KEY clause is optional. The key associated with the record is placed in the field if the clause is specified.) Example (DOS ANS): ACTUAL KEY IS WHOLE-KEY . . . WORKING-STORAGE SECTION. 01 SALES-NO. 02 DISK-NUM USAGE COMPUTATIONAL PICTURE S999 VALUE 0. 02 CELL-NUM USAGE COMPUTATIONAL PICTURE S9 VALUE 0. 02 CYL-NUM USAGE COMPUTATIONAL PICTURE S999 VALUE 10. 02 HEAD-NUM USAGE COMPUTATIONAL PICTURE S9 VALUE 0. 02 REC-NUM PICTURE X VALUE LOW-VALUE. 02 SYM-KEY PICTURE 99. 01 KEY-REDEF REDEFINES SALES-NO. 02 FILLER PICTURE X. 02 WHOLE-KEY PICTURE X(10).	If the programmer needs either or both keys, the complete two-part ACTUAL KEY form must be used. Otherwise, no key need be specified. IS must be added as a key word, if missing. (The ANS standard requires that all the information needed to access a record be contained in the actual key.)

D   E   F

D   E   F

Language Element	D/E/F COBOL	ANS COBOL	Comments
SYMBOLIC KEY clause (relative or indexed organization) (File-Control paragraph) D E F	SYMBOLIC KEY IS data-name	NOMINAL KEY IS data-name	Replace SYMBOLIC with NOMINAL. (Under CODASYL specifications, SYMBOLIC has a different meaning from the COBOL D, E, and F usage.)
SYMBOLIC KEY clause (indexed organization, sequential access, opened as INPUT or I-O) (File-Control paragraph) D	OPEN {INPUT / I-O} file-name (Part of the coding that results from an OPEN statement consists of testing the data-name specified in the SYMBOLIC KEY clause. If it contains binary zeros, processing begins with the first record of the file. If its contents are other than binary zeros, processing begins with the specified key and progresses sequentially.) Example: SYMBOLIC KEY IS SERIAL . . . MOVE START-KEY TO SERIAL. OPEN INPUT PAYROLL. READ PAYROLL AT END GO TO PAYROLL-SUM.	OPEN {INPUT / I-O} file-name START file-name INVALID KEY (There is no test at OPEN time. The START statement must be used to begin at a record other than the first in the file.) Example: NOMINAL KEY IS SERIAL . . . OPEN INPUT PAYROLL. MOVE START-KEY TO SERIAL. START PAYROLL INVALID KEY GO TO PAYROLL-ERROR. READ PAYROLL AT END GO TO PAYROLL-SUM.	If the program is written to process the file starting with the first record, no change is required, except to change SYMBOLIC to NOMINAL. If the program is written to process the file starting with a record other than the first, a START statement must be included. (ANS COBOL provides a more flexible method of processing segments of files.)
FILE-LIMIT clause (File-Control paragraph) E F	FILE-LIMIT IS integer TRACKS	TRACK-LIMIT IS integer TRACKS	Replace FILE-LIMIT with TRACK-LIMIT. (Under the ANS standard, FILE-LIMIT has a different meaning.)

I-O-CONTROL paragraph
 	
D   E   F
	I-O-CONTROL.
	    [SAME-clause.]
	    [RERUN-clause.]
	    [APPLY-clause.]
		I-O-CONTROL.
		    [SAME-clause]
		    [RERUN-clause]
		    [MULTIPLE FILE-clause]
		    [APPLY-clause] .
			All periods embedded in the I-O-Control paragraph must be removed.
			
			(The ANS standard allows only one period—at the end of the section.)

RERUN clause (I-O-Control paragraph) D	RERUN ON 'external-name' [{DIRECT-ACCESS / UTILITY} [device-number UNIT[S]]] EVERY integer RECORDS OF file-name Example (COBOL D): RERUN ON 'SYS006' UTILITY 2400 UNITS EVERY 2000 RECORDS OF PAY-FILE.	RERUN ON system-name EVERY integer RECORDS OF file-name Example (DOS ANS): RERUN ON SYS006-UT-2400-S-PAYROLL EVERY 2000 RECORDS OF PAY-FILE	The system-name must be constructed as shown under the ASSIGN clause entry. (The ANS standard requires that the name conform to the rules for a COBOL word.)

Language Element	D/E/F COBOL	ANS COBOL	Comments
RERUN clause (I-O-Control paragraph) E F	RERUN ON 'external-name' EVERY integer RECORDS OF file-name	RERUN ON system-name EVERY integer RECORDS OF file-name	The system-name must be constructed as shown under the ASSIGN clause entry. (The ANS standard requires that the name conform to the rules for a COBOL word.)

APPLY RESTRICTED SEARCH clause
 	
(I-O-Control paragraph)
 	
D   E   F
	APPLY RESTRICTED SEARCH OF
	integer TRACKS ON file-name
	
	(The default option is a search of the entire cylinder for COBOL D, and the entire file for COBOL E and F.)
	
	Example:
	
	APPLY RESTRICTED SEARCH OF 1
	TRACKS ON PAYROLL
		OS ANS COBOL:
		
		The clause has been deleted from the language.
		
		DOS ANS COBOL:
		
		   APPLY EXTENDED-SEARCH ON
		   file-name
		
		(The default option in both OS ANS and DOS ANS COBOL is a search of one track.)
		
		Example:
		
		(no clause)
			COBOL E and COBOL F:
			Any search beyond one track must be activated through a DD card option. The APPLY RESTRICTED SEARCH clause must be deleted.
			
			COBOL D:
			If the APPLY RESTRICTED SEARCH clause is used in the current program, it must be deleted. If it is not used, the APPLY EXTENDED-SEARCH clause must be used.
			
			(The ANS standard default option is the search of one track.)

APPLY . . . FORM-OVERFLOW clause
 	
(I-O-Control paragraph)
 	
D   E   F
	APPLY overflow-name TO
	FORM-OVERFLOW ON file-name.
	
	Example:
	
	APPLY OVERFLOW-PRINTER-1 TO
	FORM-OVERFLOW ON REP-FILE.
	      .
	      .
	
	IF OVERFLOW-PRINTER-1 PERFORM
	PAGE-HEAD ELSE WRITE X AFTER
	ADVANCING 2 LINES.
		WRITE record-name AT
		   END-OF-PAGE
		   EOP
		imperative statement
		Example:
		
		WRITE X AT END-OF-PAGE
		PERFORM PAGE-HEAD.
			The APPLY overflow-name clause must be deleted, as well as any references to the overflow-name. Each WRITE directed to the file must be replaced by WRITE record-name AT END-OF-PAGE imperative statement.
			
			(Since there is now a CODASYL specification for an end-of-page, the overflow-name extension is no longer necessary.)

COPY clause D E F	COPY library-name. (Library-name is an external name.) Example: FILE-CONTROL. COPY 'PAYFC.'	COPY library-name. (Library-name must follow the rules for forming a program-name.) Example: FILE-CONTROL. COPY PAYFC.	Quotation marks must be deleted from library-name. If library-name is a reserved word, it must be changed.

COBOL Differences
Data Division
ANS COBOL New Features

ALPHANUMERIC ITEMS. The PICTURE clause of an alphanumeric item may contain the characters A and 9 as well as X. The character string is treated as if it were all Xs. For example, STOCK-NO PICTURE 99AAA99 would indicate that there are three alphabetic characters in the stock number.

ALPHANUMERIC EDITED ITEMS. Programmers can represent data as alphanumeric edited items. These items are described in the PICTURE clause by combinations of the characters A, X, 9, 0, and B. The editing consists of the insertion of zeros and blanks. For example, STOCK-NO PICTURE 99BAAAB99 would appear on an output listing as 34 JCH 54.

CONDITION-NAMES—Values in Series or Ranges. The VALUE clause can be used to define a condition-name as a series of values (VALUES ARE 1 56 234), as a range of values (VALUES ARE 1 THRU 58, 75 THRU 250). When the condition-name is cited, all its values are tested.

RENAMES CLAUSE. A level-66 entry contain a RENAMES clause permits alternate, possibly overlapping, grouping of elementary data items.

BOUNDARY ALIGNMENT—SYNCHRONIZED CLAUSE. The programmer can cause binary and internal floating-point items to be aligned (with slack bytes) or unaligned (without slack bytes). The compiler is directed to align an elementary item with the SYNCHRONIZED clause. If the clause is not used, the compiler does not attempt to align the item. All the elementary binary and internal floating-point items in a record can be aligned by using the SYNCHRONIZED clause in the definition at the 01 level.

ALL LITERAL. The literal may be up to 120 characters in length.

C O B O L   DIFFERENCES
DATA DIVISION

Language Element	D/E/F COBOL	ANS COBOL	Comments
RECORDING MODE clause (File or Sort File Description entry) D E F	RECORDING MODE IS mode (The default option is V.)	RECORDING MODE IS mode (The default option is determined by an algorithm that does not always give V.)	If the clause is missing, RECORDING MODE IS V must be added.

Language Element	D/E/F COBOL	ANS COBOL	Comments
BLOCK CONTAINS clause (format V files) (File Description entry) D E F	BLOCK CONTAINS integer CHARACTERS (Four-byte physical record count is not included.) Example: BLOCK CONTAINS 600 CHARACTERS RECORDING MODE IS V	BLOCK CONTAINS [integer-1 <u>TO</u>] integer-2 CHARACTERS (Integer-1 and integer-2 must include an additional four bytes for the physical record count.) Example: BLOCK CONTAINS 204 TO 604 CHARACTERS RECORDING MODE IS V	Integer-1 and integer-2 must include an additional four bytes for the physical record count. COBOL F: COBOL F programmers may disregard the above if using BLOCK CONTAINS 0 to allow specifying the block size in the DD card at object time.

LABEL RECORDS clause (user labels)
 	
(File Description entry)
 	
D
	LABEL {RECORD IS / RECORDS ARE} data-name
	
	(user labels)
	
	Example:
	
	LINKAGE SECTION.
	01 LABEL-RECORD.
	          02 DATE . . .
	               03 YEAR . . .
	               03 DAY . . .
		LABEL {RECORD IS / RECORDS ARE} data-name-1 [data-name-2] . . .
		(user or nonstandard labels)
		
		Example:
		
		FILE SECTION.
		FD MASTER-FILE
		          .
		          .
		          .
		     LABEL RECORD IS
		     LABEL-RECORD.
		     01 LABEL-RECORD.
		          02 DATE
		               03 YEAR . . .
		               03 DAY . . .
			Data-name must be defined in the File Section of the Data Division, where it must be associated with the appropriate FD entry.

SD entry
 	
(File Section)
 	
F
	Files with a sort description (SD) entry do not require a SELECT sentence in the File-Control paragraph.	Files with a sort description (SD) entry must have a SELECT sentence in the File-Control paragraph.
		
		Example:
		FILE-CONTROL.
		     SELECT SORT-FILE
		     ASSIGN TO UT-2400-S-INFILE.
		          .
		          .
		          .
		SD SORT-FILE
			Add a SELECT sentence for each sort file.

USAGE clause
 	
(Record Description entry)
 	
D   E   F
	USAGE IS {COMPUTATIONAL / COMPUTATIONAL-1 / COMPUTATIONAL-2}
	
	(The compiler automatically aligns the item at the next halfword or fullword boundary as appropriate.)
	
	Example:
	05 COMP-ITEM USAGE
	     COMPUTATIONAL PICTURE S999.
		USAGE IS {COMPUTATIONAL / COMP / COMPUTATIONAL-1 / COMP-1 / COMPUTATIONAL-2 / COMP-2}
		
		{SYNCHRONIZED / SYNC} [LEFT / RIGHT]
		
		(The compiler aligns the item at the next half-word or fullword boundary when the SYNCHRONIZED clause is used. LEFT and RIGHT are treated as comments; items are always synchronized right.)
		
		Example:
		05 COMP-ITEM USAGE
		     COMPUTATIONAL SYNCHRONIZED
		     RIGHT PICTURE S999.
			The SYNCHRONIZED clause must be added to the definition of all COMPUTATIONAL items that require alignment or to the level-01 descriptions that contain such items.

Language Element	D/E/F COBOL	ANS COBOL	Comments
COMPUTATIONAL item D E F	If an item specified as USAGE COMPUTATION-AL does not contain an S in its PICTURE clause, an S is assumed.	If an item specified as USAGE COMPUTATION-AL does not contain an S in its PICTURE clause, it is treated as an absolute value.	An S must be added, if missing, to the PICTURE of items specified as USAGE COMPUTATIONAL.

OCCURS clause
 	
(Level-77 item Description entry, Working-Storage Section)
 	
D   E   F
	OCCURS integer TIMES
	
	(The OCCURS clause can be specified for a level-77 entry.)
	
	Example:
	
	77 EMPLOYEE-TABLE OCCURS
	      1000 TIMES PICTURE 9(5).
		OCCURS integer TIMES
		
		(The OCCURS clause cannot be specified for a level-77 entry. The programmer can achieve the same effect by making the item containing the OCCURS clause a level-02 entry subordinate to a dummy level-01 entry.)
		
		Example:
		
		01 TABLE.
		    02 EMPLOYEE-TABLE
		        OCCURS 1000 TIMES
		        PICTURE 9(5).
			A level-77 entry containing an OCCURS clause must either be deleted or changed to a level-02 entry subordinate to a dummy level-01 entry.
			
			(The ANS standard does not permit a level-77 entry to contain an OCCURS clause.)

VALUE clause (Record Description entry) D E F	VALUE IS literal (When a VALUE clause containing an unsigned literal is specified for a signed internal or external decimal field, the plus sign generated is an F, rather than the standard C.) Example: An item defined as PICTURE S9 VALUE 1 would be generated as F1.	VALUE IS literal (When a VALUE clause containing an unsigned literal is specified for a signed internal or external decimal field, the plus sign generated is a C.) Example: An item defined as PICTURE S9 VALUE 1 would be generated as C1.	The display of a signed numeric field containing a positive number defined in a VALUE clause will be different under the ANS compilation.
COPY clause D E F	COPY library-name. (Library-name is an external name.) Example: FD MYLIB COPY 'PAYFILE.'	COPY library-name. (Library-name must follow the rules for forming a program-name.) Example: FD MYLIB COPY PAYFILE.	Quotation marks must be deleted from library-name. If library-name is a reserved word, it must be changed.

COPY clause
 	
(File or Sort Description entry, or Working-Storage or Linkage Section)
 	
D   E   F
	01 data-name COPY library-name
	
	(If the level-01 data-name in the library entry being copied is also used in that library entry as a qualifier of the object of an OCCURS DEPENDING ON clause, both the level-01 data-name and the qualifier will be replaced by the program data-name.)
	
	Example:
	01 A COPY LIBNAM.
	
	library entry LIBNAM
	01 B.
	    02 C PICTURE S99.
	    02 D PICTURE 9(5).
	    02 E OCCURS 5 TIMES
	        DEPENDING ON C OF B
	        PICTURE S99.
	
	(A will replace B in the level-01 entry and in the level-02 entry named E.)
		01 data-name COPY library-name
		[REPLACING word-1 BY
		$\left\{ \begin{array}{l} \text{word-2} \\ \text{literal-1} \\ \text{identifier-1} \end{array} \right\}$]
		
		(If the level-01 data-name in the library entry being copied is also used in that library entry as a qualifier of the object of an OCCURS DEPENDING ON cluase, the REPLACING option must be specified, so that the qualifier as well as the level-01 data-name will be replaced by the program data-name.)
		
		Example:
		01 A COPY LIBNAM REPLACING B BY A.
		
		library entry LIBNAM
		01 B.
		    02 C PICTURE S99.
		    02 D PICTURE 9(5).
		    02 E OCCURS 5 TIMES
		        DEPENDING ON C OF B
		        PICTURE S99.
		
		(A will replace B in the level-01 entry and in the level-02 entry named E.)
			Add the REPLACING option to the COPY clause if the level-01 data-name in the library entry being copied is also used in that library entry as a qualifier of the object of an OCCURS DEPENDING ON clause.

COBOL Differences
Procedure Division
ANS COBOL New Features

NONSTANDARD LABEL-HANDLING PROCEDURES. Programmers can code the USE BEFORE . . . LABEL PROCEDURE declarative to create and check nonstandard labels for their files.

CYLINDER OVERFLOW RECORDS. When creating or adding records to an indexed sequential file, the programmer can reserve a specific number of tracks on each cylinder as overflow records with the APPLY CYL-OVER-FLOW clause. When the clause is not specified, the compiler reserves 20% of each cylinder.

INPUT/OUTPUT ERROR BYTES. The GIVING option of the USE AFTER STANDARD ERROR PROCEDURE declarative statement can be used to determine the nature of the error condition on an input/output interrupt. The programmer can also specify a storage area to contain the block that is in error during a READ operation.

CONTROL OF INDEXES FOR INDEXED FILES. Programmers can use the COBOL language to control the creation and use of indexes for indexed files.

COBOL D programmers can use the APPLY MASTER-INDEX or CYL-INDEX clause to specify the highest-level index and the type of device on which it must reside. They can also use the APPLY CORE-INDEX clause to provide an area in core storage for the cylinder index of an indexed file being accessed randomly.

COBOL E and COBOL F programmers can use the APPLY CORE-INDEX clause to specify that the highest-level index will reside in core storage during the input/output operation.

MORE EFFICIENT USE OF MASS STORAGE. The amount of unused space in a volume on a mass storage device can be reduced with the APPLY RECORD-OVERFLOW clause. Any block that does not fit on a track is partially written on the track and then continued on the next available track.

Programmers can use this clause if the record-overflow feature is available on the device being used. It can be specified only for a sequential file on a mass storage device, or a direct file with fixed-length records.

Other Procedure Division Operations

CORRESPONDING OPTION. The ADD, SUBTRACT, and MOVE statements can be written with the CORRESPONDING option. Elementary data items within one group item are added to, subtracted from, or moved to, elementary items of the same name in another group item.

MULTIPLE RESULTS FOR ADD AND SUBTRACT STATEMENTS. In a single ADD or SUBTRACT statement, the first operand can be added to, or subtracted from, each of a series of operands. Each of the results can be rounded or not, as desired.

Input/Output Operations

BEFORE ADVANCING OPTION OF THE WRITE STATEMENT. A record can be printed before the printer page is advanced up to 99 lines by using the BEFORE ADVANCING option of the WRITE statement.

AFTER ADVANCING OPTION OF THE WRITE STATEMENT. A record can be printed after the printer page has been advanced up to 99 lines by using the AFTER ADVANCING option of the WRITE statement.

END-OF-PAGE OPTION OF THE WRITE STATEMENT. The END-OF-PAGE condition replaces the APPLY . . . FORM-OVERFLOW clause. It can be used to test for channel 12 on an on-line printer. When the end of the page is detected, the imperative statement specified in the END-OF-PAGE phrase is executed. If the ADVANCING and END-OF-PAGE options are used together, the page is advanced before the end-of-page test.

START STATEMENT. The programmer can begin processing a sequentially accessed, indexed sequential file at any record after the first by using the START statement before reading or writing. The key for the record at which processing is to begin is stored in the data-name specified in the NOMINAL KEY clause. A new START statement for the same file starts processing at a new record.

SEEK STATEMENT. The programmer can read and write mass-storage data records more efficiently if he initiates the accessing of the record first with a SEEK statement.

ACCEPT STATEMENT. A mnemonic-name can be defined in the Special-Names paragraph of the Environment Division to represent the system input device or the console. More data can be obtained by using the ACCEPT statement. If the system input device is used, as many records as are necessary to exhaust the operand are read. If the console is used, up to 255 characters can be transmitted.

DISPLAY AND EXHIBIT STATEMENTS. For the DISPLAY statement, a mnemonic-name can be defined in the Special-Names paragraph to represent the console, the system punch device, or the system output device. More data can be written using a DISPLAY or EXHIBIT statement: as many records as are necessary to exhaust the operand(s) are produced. The logical record length of the console has been increased to 100 characters.

USER LABEL-HANDLING PROCEDURES. COBOL E and COBOL F programmers can code the USE AFTER . . . LABEL PROCEDURE declarative to create and check user labels for their files. COBOL D programmers have more options to use the feature.

REMAINDER OPTION OF THE DIVIDE STATEMENT. The DIVIDE statement can be written with the REMAINDER option. The result of subtracting the product of the quotient and the divisor is stored in the REMAINDER operand.

COMPOUND CONDITIONS-IMPLIED SUBJECTS AND OPERATORS. In compound conditions, the first operand (subject) of a relation condition can be omitted, as well as its relational operator. Omitted subjects and operators are taken from the most recently stated subject or operator respectively, within the sentence.

C O B O L   DIFFERENCES
PROCEDURE DIVISION

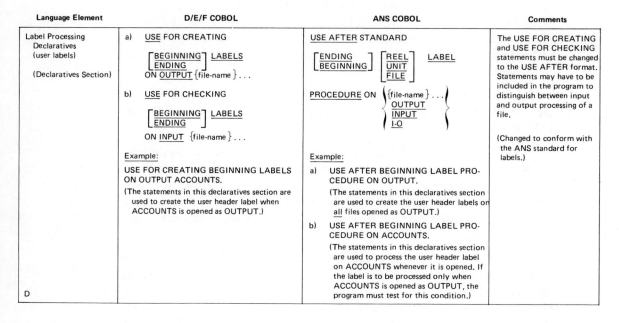

Language Element	D/E/F COBOL	ANS COBOL	Comments

Label Processing Declaratives (user labels)
 	
(Declaratives Section)
	a) USE FOR CREATING
	
	⌈BEGINNING⌉ LABELS
	⌊ENDING ⌋
	ON OUTPUT {file-name } . . .
	
	b) USE FOR CHECKING
	
	⌈BEGINNING⌉ LABELS
	⌊ENDING ⌋
	
	ON INPUT {file-name } . . .
	
	Example:
	
	USE FOR CREATING BEGINNING LABELS ON OUTPUT ACCOUNTS.
	(The statements in this declaratives section are used to create the user header label when ACCOUNTS is opened as OUTPUT.)
		USE AFTER STANDARD
		
		⌈ENDING ⌉ ⌈REEL⌉ LABEL
		⌊BEGINNING⌋ ⌊UNIT⌋
		         ⌊FILE⌋
		
		PROCEDURE ON {file-name } . . .
		              OUTPUT
		              INPUT
		              I-O
		
		Example:
		
		a) USE AFTER BEGINNING LABEL PROCEDURE ON OUTPUT.
		    (The statements in this declaratives section are used to create the user header labels on all files opened as OUTPUT.)
		
		b) USE AFTER BEGINNING LABEL PROCEDURE ON ACCOUNTS.
		    (The statements in this declaratives section are used to process the user header label on ACCOUNTS whenever it is opened. If the label is to be processed only when ACCOUNTS is opened as OUTPUT, the program must test for this condition.)
			The USE FOR CREATING and USE FOR CHECKING statements must be changed to the USE AFTER format. Statements may have to be included in the program to distinguish between input and output processing of a file.
			
			(Changed to conform with the ANS standard for labels.)

D

Language Element	D/E/F COBOL	ANS COBOL	Comments

Error Processing Declaratives
 	
(Declaratives Section)
 	
D   E   F
	USE AFTER STANDARD ERROR
	   PROCEDURE ON file-name
	
	COBOL D:
	(When an uncorrectable input/output error oc-curs, the declarative is entered. If a subpro-gram is called using file-name as a parameter, the address of the DTF table is passed. The user can take the desired action.)
	
	COBOL E:
	(When an uncorrectable input/output error oc-curs, the declarative is entered, and the con-tents of registers 14, 15, 0 and 1 are stored in the four words starting at the address of the DCB minus 20 bytes. If a subprogram is called using file-name as a parameter, the address of the DCB is passed, and the user can take the desired action.)
	
	COBOL F:
	(When an uncorrectable input/output error oc-curs the declarative is entered. If a subpro-gram is called using file-name as a parameter, the address of the DCB or DECB is passed, the contents of registers 0 and 1 can be deter-mined, and the user can take the desired action.)
		USE AFTER STANDARD ERROR
		   PROCEDURE ON file-name
		   GIVING data-name-1
		   [data-name-2]
		
		(When an uncorrectable input/output error oc-curs, the declarative is entered. Data-name-1 will contain information indicating the error condition. Data-name-2 is an area large enough to hold the largest physical block that exists on or can be written on file-name, and will con-tain the block in error when the error occurs during a READ operation.)
			To gain access to error in-formation, the GIVING op-tion of the USE AFTER ERROR statement must be used. Error processing state-ments must be coded in the COBOL program or in a subprogram to analyze the contents of data-name-1, or data-name-1 and data-name-2.

Error Processing Declaratives
 	
(Declaratives Section)
 	
D   E   F
	USE AFTER STANDARD ERROR
	   PROCEDURE ON file-name.
		USE AFTER STANDARD ERROR
		   PROCEDURE ON file-name.
			PROCEDURE must be added as a key word, if missing.

CLOSE statement (file with OPEN . . . REVERSED)
 	
E   F
	CLOSE file-name [WITH NO REWIND]
	
	(Rewind is associated with the logical beginning and ending of a file.)
	
	Example:
	   OPEN OUTPUT ACCOUNTS.
	         .
	         .
	         .
	   CLOSE ACCOUNTS NO REWIND.
	   OPEN INPUT ACCOUNTS
	   REVERSED. READ ACCOUNTS AT
	   END GO TO SUM-TOTAL.
	         .
	         .
	         .
	   SUM-TOTAL.
	   CLOSE ACCOUNTS.
	
	(After the second CLOSE, the tape unit is posi-tioned at the logical beginning of the file, which is the physical ending.)
		CLOSE file-name [WITH NO REWIND]
		
		(Rewind is associated with the physical beginning and ending of a file.)
		
		Example:
		   OPEN OUTPUT ACCOUNTS.
		         .
		         .
		         .
		   CLOSE ACCOUNTS NO REWIND.
		   OPEN INPUT ACCOUNTS
		   REVERSED. READ ACCOUNTS AT
		   END GO TO SUM-TOTAL.
		         .
		         .
		         .
		   SUM-TOTAL.
		   CLOSE ACCOUNTS.
		
		(After the second CLOSE, the tape unit is posi-tioned at the physical beginning of the tape.)
			This difference is shown for planning purposes only, since for the first release results are the same. In a subsequent release, results of a CLOSE after an OPEN . . . REVERSED will be different.

CLOSE statement (WITH LOCK specified) E F	CLOSE file-name WITH LOCK (The disposition of the file is determined by the DISP parameter of the DD card for the file.)	CLOSE file-name WITH DISP (The disposition of the file is determined by the DISP parameter of the DD card for the file.)	Change LOCK to DISP. (The ANS standard mean-ing of LOCK is different from COBOL E and F usage under the Operat-ing System.)

Language Element	D/E/F COBOL	ANS COBOL	Comments
CLOSE statement (REEL/UNIT specified)	COBOL E, F: a) CLOSE file-name {REEL}{UNIT} (When the file is OPEN . . . REVERSED, the implied rewind is to the logical beginning; i.e., the physical end of the file on each reel or unit.) COBOL F: b) CLOSE file-name {REEL}{UNIT} WITH NO REWIND (NO REWIND positions the device to the logical end of the file on each reel or unit.) c) CLOSE file-name {REEL}{UNIT} WITH LOCK (The positioning of each reel or unit is determined by the DD card DISP parameter.) Examples: a) OPEN INPUT ACCOUNTS REVERSED. . . . CLOSE ACCOUNTS REEL. . CLOSE ACCOUNTS. b) OPEN INPUT ACCOUNTS. . . . CLOSE ACCOUNTS REEL WITH NO REWIND. . . . CLOSE ACCOUNTS WITH NO REWIND. c) OPEN INPUT ACCOUNTS. . . . CLOSE ACCOUNTS REEL WITH LOCK. . . . CLOSE ACCOUNTS WITH LOCK. E F	OPEN {INPUT}{OUTPUT} file-name [REVERSED] {REREAD}{LEAVE}{DISP} CLOSE file-name {REEL}{UNIT} WITH POSITIONING (REREAD positions the device to the logical beginning of the file on each reel or unit; LEAVE positions it to the logical end of the file; and DISP positions the device as specified by the DISP parameter of the DD card. POSITIONING indicates that each reel or unit is to be positioned as specified in the OPEN statement.) Examples: a) OPEN INPUT ACCOUNTS REVERSED REREAD. . . . CLOSE ACCOUNTS REEL WITH POSITIONING. . CLOSE ACCOUNTS. b) OPEN INPUT ACCOUNTS LEAVE. . . CLOSE ACCOUNTS REEL WITH POSITIONING. . . . CLOSE ACCOUNTS WITH NO REWIND. c) OPEN INPUT ACCOUNTS DISP. . . . CLOSE ACCOUNTS REEL WITH POSITIONING. . . CLOSE ACCOUNTS WITH DISP.	Specify WITH POSITIONING in all CLOSE statements with the REEL/UNIT option. Add REREAD, LEAVE, or DISP to the OPEN statement. (The ANS standard meaning of rewind, NO REWIND and LOCK is different from COBOL E and F usage under the Operating System.)
INTO option (READ statement) D E	READ file-name RECORD [INTO data-name] (Data is moved using the size of the first record specified in the file description (FD) entry as the sending field size.)	READ file-name RECORD [INTO identifier] (Data is moved using the size of the largest record specified in the file description (FD) entry as the sending field size.)	Different results may be obtained when the first record of an FD is not the largest. (ANS COBOL permits the user to describe his largest record in any level-01 entry rather than requiring that it be the first level-01 entry.)

Language Element	D/E/F COBOL	ANS COBOL	Comments
INVALID KEY phrase (READ statements for mass storage files) D	READ file-name RECORD 　[INVALID KEY imperative statement] (The INVALID KEY phrase is optional.) (For an example of INVALID KEY use see the next "INVALID KEY phrase" entry.)	READ file-name RECORD 　INVALID KEY imperative statement (The INVALID KEY phrase is required.) (For an example of INVALID KEY use see the next "INVALID KEY phrase" entry.)	The INVALID KEY phrase must be used to process invalid key errors. The USE AFTER STANDARD ERROR declarative should be used for other error processing.
INVALID KEY phrase (WRITE statements for mass storage files) D	WRITE record-name [INVALID KEY imperative statement] (The INVALID KEY phrase is optional.) Example: DECLARATIVES. ERROR-PROCESS SECTION. 　USE AFTER STANDARD ERROR 　PROCEDURE ON ACCOUNTS. 　　　． 　　　． 　(coding to process invalid key errors) 　　　． 　(coding to process other errors) END DECLARATIVES. 　　　． 　　　． WRITE ACCOUNTS-RECORD.	WRITE record-name INVALID KEY imperative statement (The INVALID KEY phrase is required.) Example: DECLARATIVES. ERROR-PROCESS SECTION. 　USE AFTER STANDARD ERROR 　PROCEDURE ON ACCOUNTS. 　　　． 　　　． 　(coding to process errors other than invalid keys) END DECLARATIVES. 　　　． 　　　． WRITE ACCOUNTS-RECORD INVALID KEY GO TO I-K-P. 　　　． 　　　． I-K-P. (coding to process invalid key errors)	The INVALID KEY phrase must be used to process invalid key errors. The USE AFTER STANDARD ERROR declarative should be used for other error processing.
INVALID KEY condition (WRITE statement for direct files accessed randomly) D	WRITE record-name [INVALID KEY imperative statement] (If the required space for writing a record is not available, this is considered an INVALID KEY condition. If an INVALID KEY phrase is specified, the phrase is executed.)	WRITE record-name INVALID KEY imperative statement (If the required space for writing a record is not available, this is not considered an INVALID KEY condition. Instead, the USE AFTER STANDARD ERROR declarative is executed.)	When the required space for writing a record is not available, the USE AFTER STANDARD ERROR declarative will be entered.
AFTER ADVANCING phrase (WRITE statement) D　　E　　F	WRITE record-name AFTER ADVANCING {data-name / integer} LINES	WRITE record-name AFTER POSITIONING {identifier / integer} LINES	POSITIONING replaces ADVANCING. (IBM) (The ANS standard meaning for ADVANCING . . . LINES is different from COBOL D, E, and F usage.)
REWRITE statement (standard sequential file, opened as I-O) D　　E　　F	REWRITE record-name (The REWRITE verb is used when the file is being updated.) Example: OPEN I-O PAYFILE. 　　　． 　　　． READ PAYFILE AT END 　GO TO ENDFILE. 　　　． 　　　． REWRITE PAY-REC.	WRITE record-name INVALID KEY imperative statement (The WRITE verb is used when the file is being updated.) Example: OPEN I-O PAYFILE. 　　　． 　　　． READ PAYFILE AT END 　GO TO ENDFILE. 　　　． 　　　． WRITE PAY-REC INVALID KEY GO TO I-K-P.	Each REWRITE for the file must be replaced by WRITE. INVALID KEY must be supplied for the WRITE statement.

Language Element	D/E/F COBOL	ANS COBOL	Comments
TALLY register D E F	TALLY is a special register whose implicit description is that of a 5-digit signed computational item.	TALLY is a special register whose implicit description is that of a 5-digit unsigned computational item.	In the IBM ANS compilers, a move of a negative field to TALLY will produce different results than the COBOL D, E, and F compilers.
TALLY register (with Sort) F	TALLY contains the Sort return code at the end of a sorting operation. TALLY can be used as the operand of an ACCEPT, DISPLAY, or EXHIBIT statement. Example: SORT ACCOUNTS-X ASCENDING KEY SERIAL USING ACCOUNTS GIVING ACCOUNTS-Y. IF TALLY NOT = ZERO DISPLAY 'SORT UNSUCCESSFUL' UPON CONSOLE STOP RUN.	SORT-RETURN contains the Sort return code at the end of a sorting operation. SORT-RETURN cannot be used as the operand of an ACCEPT, DISPLAY, or EXHIBIT statement. Example: SORT ACCOUNTS-X ASCENDING KEY SERIAL USING ACCOUNTS GIVING ACCOUNTS-Y. IF SORT-RETURN NOT = ZERO DISPLAY 'SORT UNSUCCESSFUL' UPON CONSOLE STOP RUN.	SORT-RETURN replaces TALLY. SORT-RETURN cannot be used as the operand of an ACCEPT, DISPLAY, or EXHIBIT statement.

CALL statement
(Calling COBOL subprograms or assembler language routines)
 	
D   E   F
	Calling program:
	
	  ENTER LINKAGE.
	  CALL entry-name
	    [USING {argument} ...] .
	  ENTER COBOL.
	
	COBOL subprogram:
	
	  ENTER LINKAGE.
	  ENTRY entry-name
	    [USING {data-name} ...] .
	  ENTER COBOL.
	      .
	      .
	  ENTER LINKAGE.
	  RETURN.
	  ENTER COBOL.
	
	Example:
	
	ENTER LINKAGE. ⎫
	CALL 'SUBENTRY.' Calling
	ENTER COBOL. program
	    . ⎭
	    .
	ENTER LINKAGE. ⎫
	ENTRY 'SUBENTRY.'
	ENTER COBOL
	    . COBOL
	    . subprogram
	ENTER LINKAGE.
	RETURN.
	ENTER COBOL. ⎭
		Calling program:
		
		  CALL literal
		    [USING {identifier} ...] .
		
		COBOL subprogram:
		
		  ENTRY literal
		    [USING {identifier} ...] .
		      .
		      .
		      .
		  GOBACK.
		
		Example:
		
		CALL 'SUBENTRY.' ⎫
		    . Calling
		    . program
		ENTRY 'SUBENTRY.' ⎭
		    .
		    . COBOL
		    . subprogram
		GOBACK. ⎭
			ENTER LINKAGE and ENTER COBOL may be deleted; if included, they will be treated by ANS COBOL as comments. GOBACK replaces RETURN.
			
			(Changed to conform to the CODASYL specification for the CALL statement.)

CALL statement (Calling COBOL subprograms) F	Subprograms are serially reusable.	Subprograms remain in their last-used state.	Different results may be obtained if subprograms are reused that contain ALTER or PERFORM statements.
STOP RUN statement E F	STOP RUN. (The statement returns control to the operating system unless the program has been invoked by another program, in which case it returns control to the invoking program.)	GOBACK. (The statement returns control to the operating system unless the program has been invoked by another program, in which case it returns control to the invoking program. The ANS GOBACK statement is equivalent to the COBOL E and F STOP RUN statement.)	Replace STOP RUN statements with GOBACK statements. (The ANS standard specifies that the STOP RUN statement always returns control to the operating system.)

Language Element	D/E/F COBOL	ANS COBOL	Comments
INCLUDE statement D E F	section-name <u>SECTION</u>. INCLUDE library-name. paragraph-name. INCLUDE library-name. (Library-name is an external name.) Example: PAYROLL-CALCULATION. INCLUDE 'PAYCAL'.	section-name <u>SECTION</u>. COPY library-name. paragraph-name. COPY library-name. (Library-name must follow the rules for the formation of a program-name.) Example: PAYROLL-CALCULATION. COPY PAYCAL.	COPY must replace IN-CLUDE. Quotation marks must be deleted from library-name. If library-name is a reserved word, it must be changed.
ACCEPT statement D E F	An ACCEPT statement reads a single record.	If the system input device is used, an ACCEPT statement reads as many records as are necessary to exhaust the operand. If the console is used, an ACCEPT statement reads as many records as are necessary to exhaust the operand, up to a limit of 255 characters for DOS or 114 characters for OS.	If the identifier specified in an ACCEPT statement is larger than the input record, the next record will be read. (Changed to conform to the ANS standard.)

DISPLAY and EXHIBIT statements
 	
D   E   F
	a) <u>COBOL D, E:</u>
	    A DISPLAY or EXHIBIT statement writes a single record.
	
	b) <u>COBOL F:</u>
	    A DISPLAY or EXHIBIT statement writes as many records as are necessary to exhaust the operand(s). If multiple operands are specified, operands are not continued from one record to another. An operand that cannot be completely written on one record begins a new record.
		a) A DISPLAY or EXHIBIT statement writes as many records as are necessary to exhaust the operand(s).
		
		b) A DISPLAY or EXHIBIT statement writes as many records as are necessary to exhaust the operand(s). If multiple operands are specified, operands that can be partially written on one record will begin there and will continue on the next record.
			The format of the output may be different from that produced by COBOL F.
			
			(Changed to conform to the ANS standard.)

DISPLAY, EXHIBIT statements (COMPUTATIONAL-1 data items) D E F	All internal floating-point data items are printed with 16 digits. In the short form, the eight leading digits are filled with zeros.	Short-form internal floating-point data items are displayed with eight digits.	COMPUTATIONAL-1 data items will not be displayed with eight extra leading digits.
EXHIBIT NAMED statement (formatting of subscripted data-names) D E	Subscripted data-names in EXHIBIT NAMED statements are displayed without subscripts. Example: The statement EXHIBIT NAMED PAY (5) would result in the display of: PAY = 310.25	Subscripted data-names in EXHIBIT NAMED statements are displayed with subscripts. Example: The statement EXHIBIT NAMED PAY (5) would result in the display of: PAY (5) = 310.25	Subscripts will appear in the display of all subscripted data-names in EXHIBIT NAMED statements.

Language Element	D/E/F COBOL	ANS COBOL	Comments

Class Test (field defined as unsigned numeric or alpha-numeric, but contains signed value at testing)	data-name IS [NOT]
	
	NUMERIC
	ALPHABETIC
	
	(If the units position on an otherwise numeric field contains a digit with an operational sign, the field is considered numeric even though the data-name description does not contain an operational sign (S).)
	
	Example:
	05 NO-PURCHASES USAGE IS
	    DISPLAY PICTURE IS 999.
	05 NO-DIVIDENDS USAGE
	    IS DISPLAY PICTURE IS XXX.
	
	.
	.
	.
	
	IF NO-PURCHASES IS NUMERIC
	GO TO SALARY-PROC.
	IF NO-DIVIDENDS IS
	NUMERIC GO TO SALARY-PROC.
	
	(If NO-PURCHASES contains +123, it will test numeric. If NO-DIVIDENDS contains 12C, it will test numeric.)
	
	D E F
		identifier IS [NOT]
		
		NUMERIC
		ALPHABETIC
		
		(If the identifier description of the numeric item being tested does not contain an operational sign (S), the field does not test numeric if there is an operational sign present at the time of test.)
		
		Example:
		05 NO-PURCHASES USAGE IS
		    DISPLAY PICTURE IS 999.
		05 NO-DIVIDENDS USAGE
		    IS DISPLAY PICTURE IS XXX.
		
		.
		.
		.
		
		IF NO-PURCHASES IS NUMERIC
		GO TO SALARY-PROC.
		IF NO-DIVIDENDS IS NUMERIC
		GO TO SALARY-PROC.
		
		(If NO-PURCHASES contains +123, it will test non-numeric. If NO-DIVIDENDS contains 12C, it will test non-numeric.)
			Different results will be obtained.
			
			(The ANS standard for the class test.)

Compound Conditions (implied subjects and relational operators)	When NOT is used in conjunction with a relational operator and an implied subject, the NOT is treated as part of the relational operator.
	
	Example:
	A > B AND NOT = C AND D
	
	  is equivalent to
	
	A > B AND A NOT = C AND A
	F NOT = D
		When NOT is used in conjunction with a relational operator and an implied subject, the NOT is treated as a logical operator.
		
		Example:
		A > B AND NOT = C AND D
		
		  is equivalent to
		
		A > B AND NOT A = C AND A = D
			In order to obtain the same results as in COBOL F, the relational statement must be expanded in accordance with COBOL F rules.
			
			(The ANS standard for implied subjects and relational operators.)

Language Element	D/E/F COBOL	ANS COBOL	Comments
MOVE statement (explicit move from numeric field to binary field) Arithmetic statements (implied move from numeric field to binary field)	COBOL D, E: Except in an arithmetic statement with no ON SIZE ERROR option, the contents of the sending field are truncated to fit the receiving field according to the size of their respective pictures, and then converted, if necessary. In an arithmetic statement with no ON SIZE ERROR option, the procedure described in "COBOL F" below is followed. Example: A PICTURE S99 COMPUTATIONAL. (The move of +1234 to A would result in A containing +34.)	Using the TRUNC compile time option, the contents of the sending field are truncated to fit the receiving field according to the size of their respective pictures, and then converted, if necessary. This corresponds to the COBOL D and E implementation except in arithmetic statements with no ON SIZE ERROR option. Example: A PICTURE S99 COMPUTATIONAL. (The move of +1234 to A would result in A containing +34.)	COBOL D, E: In arithmetic statements with no ON SIZE ERROR option, different results may be obtained when the sending field is larger than the receiving field. In other situations, no conversion is necessary if the TRUNC compile time option is used. COBOL F: Using the NOTRUNC compile time option, no conversion is necessary. Using the TRUNC compile time option, different results may be obtained when the sending field is larger than the receiving field. (The TRUNC option processing conforms to the ANS standard.)
	COBOL F: The contents of the sending field are converted to binary, if necessary, and then moved to the receiving field. If the contents are too large for the receiving field, they are truncated to fit. Example: A PICTURE S99 COMPUTATIONAL. (The move of +1234 to A would result in A containing +1234.)	Using The NOTRUNC compile time option, the contents of the sending field are converted to binary, if necessary, and then moved to the receiving field. If the contents are too large for the receiving field, they are truncated to fit. This corresponds to the COBOL F implementation. Example: A PICTURE S99 COMPUTATIONAL. (The move of +1234 to A would result in A containing +1234.)	
D E F			
MOVE statement (explicit move from numeric field to alphanumeric field) F	In the execution of a move from a binary or internal decimal field to an alphanumeric field, there is no conversion to another format.	In the execution of a move from a binary or internal decimal field to an alphanumeric field, the item is converted to external decimal format.	The results will be different under the ANS compilation.
Sign generation (explicit or implied move from unsigned to signed numeric field) C.	When an unsigned numeric literal is moved to a signed internal or external decimal field, the plus sign generated is an F, rather than the standard C. Example: The literal 1234 moved to a signed external decimal field would become F1 F2 F3 F4.	When an unsigned numeric literal is moved to a signed internal or external decimal field, the plus sign generated is a C. Example: The literal 1234 moved to a signed external decimal field would become F1 F2 F3 C4.	The display of a signed numeric field into which an unsigned numeric literal has been moved will be different under the ANS compilation.
D E			
Exponent overflow in arithmetic statements D E	An exponent overflow in an arithmetic statement causes execution of the ON SIZE ERROR statement.	An exponent overflow in an arithmetic statement does not cause execution of the ON SIZE ERROR statement.	Exponent overflow is not treated as a size error condition.
Computation Algorithms (MOVE, COMPUTE, DIVIDE) D E	a) In a MOVE from a floating-point field to an internal decimal field, no rounding is performed. b) In the execution of a COMPUTE statement, less accurate results are obtained for very large numbers. c) In the execution of a DIVIDE statement, the maximum scaled dividend is 30 digits.	a) In a MOVE from a floating-point field to an internal decimal field, rounding is performed. b) In the execution of a COMPUTE statement, more accurate results are obtained for very large numbers. c) In the execution of a DIVIDE statement, the maximum scaled dividend is 60 digits, yielding more accurate results with very large numbers.	The results of moves from floating-point to internal decimal fields could be different under the ANS compilation. The results of the execution of COMPUTE or DIVIDE statements for very large numbers could also be different.

COBOL Differences
Report Writer Feature
ANS COBOL New Features

The Report Writer Feature is new to users of D or E COBOL. The programmer can use the Report Writer Feature to specify the format of a printed report in the Data Division, thus reducing the amount of Procedure Division coding required. Special actions, such as the printing of page headings, footings, totals, and subtotals, can be performed automatically by specifying control breaks, such as the change in the month in a series of records, end-of-page, etc.

REPORT NAME AND SUBSCRIPTED OPERANDS. A report-name can appear in two report clauses, allowing one report to be written on two files; CONTROL and SUM clause operands can be subscripted or indexed.

C O B O L DIFFERENCES
REPORT WRITER FEATURE

Language Element	D/E/F COBOL	ANS COBOL	Comments
RECORD CONTAINS clause (File Description entry)	RECORD CONTAINS [integer-1 <u>TO</u>] integer-2 CHARACTERS (If the FD entry contains a REPORTS ARE clause, the RECORD CONTAINS clause has no effect on the number of characters in a line; 144 is assumed.) Example: RECORD CONTAINS 132 CHARACTERS REPORT IS PAYROLL-REPORT. F	RECORD CONTAINS [integer-1 <u>TO</u>] integer-2 CHARACTERS (If the FD entry contains a REPORTS ARE clause, integer-2 indicates the maximum size of the report line. The default size is 133.) Example: RECORD CONTAINS 144 CHARACTERS REPORT IS PAYROLL-REPORT.	If the FD entry contains a REPORTS ARE clause and the same output as produced by COBOL F is desired, a RECORD CONTAINS clause specifying 144 characters must be included.

PAGE clause
 	
(Report Description entry)
	a) If there is no PAGE clause, the following values are assumed:
	
	    heading = 1
	    first detail = 1
	    last detail = 48
	    footing = 48
	    page limit = 52
	
	b) If a PAGE clause is specified with some limits omitted, the omitted values are assumed to be as stated above.
	
	Example:
	PAGE LIMIT IS 55 LINES LAST DETAIL 46.
	    heading = 1
	    first detail =1
	F footing = 48
		a) If there is no PAGE clause, no values are assumed, and line control is not performed.
		
		b) If a PAGE clause is specified with some limits omitted, the omitted values are not fixed as in COBOL F. The procedure used to determine the values is described in the ANS COBOL Language manual.
		
		Example:
		PAGE LIMIT IS 55 LINES LAST DETAIL 46 FOOTING 48.
		    heading = 1
		    first detail = 1
			a) If there is no PAGE clause, the clause must be specified with the values assumed under COBOL F.
			
			b) If a PAGE clause is specified with some limits omitted, a new clause must be written with the omitted values the same as the assumed values for COBOL F.

NEXT GROUP clause (CONTROL FOOTING report group) (Report Group Description entry)	(Each time a CONTROL FOOTING report group with a NEXT GROUP clause is printed, the clause is activated.)	(Each time a CONTROL FOOTING report group with a NEXT GROUP clause is printed, the clause is activated only if the report group is associated with the control that causes the break.)	The format of a report produced under ANS COBOL may be different.
	Example: RD EXPENSE-REPORT CONTROLS ARE FINAL, MONTH, DAY. . . . 01 TYPE CONTROL FOOTING DAY LINE PLUS 1 NEXT GROUP NEXT PAGE. . . . 01 TYPE CONTROL FOOTING MONTH LINE PLUS 1 NEXT GROUP NEXT PAGE. 	Example: RD EXPENSE-REPORT CONTROLS ARE FINAL, MONTH, DAY. . . . 01 TYPE CONTROL FOOTING DAY LINE PLUS 1 NEXT GROUP NEXT PAGE. . . . 01 TYPE CONTROL FOOTING MONTH LINE PLUS 1 NEXT GROUP NEXT PAGE. 	
	EXPENSE REPORT . . January 31 . . . . 29.30 02 F	January total 131.40	EXPENSE REPORT . . January 31 . . . . 29.30 January total 131.40 02	

Language Element	D/E/F COBOL	ANS COBOL	Comments

SUM data-item clause (without UPON option)
 	
(Report Item Description entry)
	SUM data-name . . .
	
	(A data-name in the SUM clause must be a SUM counter in a CONTROL FOOTING report group at an equal or lower position in the control hierarchy, or an item defined in the File, Working-Storage, or Linkage Sections.
	
	Each time a GENERATE statement that refers to a Detail Report group in the report is executed, the values of all the data-names are added to the SUM-counter.)
	
	Example:
	FILE SECTION.
	    .
	    .
	    .
	02 NO-PURCHASES PICTURE 99.
	    .
	    .
	    .
	REPORT SECTION.
	01 DETAIL-1 TYPE DETAIL.
	    .
	    .
	01 DETAIL-2 TYPE DETAIL.
	    .
	    .
	01 TYPE CONTROL FOOTING DAY
	      LINE PLUS 2.
	    02 SUBTOTAL COLUMN 30
	       PICTURE ZZ9 SUM
	       NO-PURCHASES.
	    .
	    .
	
	(If either detail line is generated, SUBTOTAL is incremented by the contents of NO-PURCHASES.)
		SUM identifier . . .
		
		(A data-name in the SUM clause must be a SUM counter in a CONTROL FOOTING report group at an equal or lower position in the control hierarchy, or an item defined in the File, Working-Storage, or Linkage Sections that is also a SOURCE item in a DETAIL report group.
		
		A SUM counter is algebraically incremented just before presentation of the DETAIL report group in which the item being summed appears as a source item.)
		
		Example:
		FILE SECTION.
		    .
		    .
		    .
		02 NO-PURCHASES PICTURE 99.
		    .
		    .
		    .
		REPORT SECTION.
		01 DETAIL-1 TYPE DETAIL.
		    02 PICTURE Z9 SOURCE
		       NO-PURCHASES.
		    .
		    .
		01 DETAIL-2 TYPE DETAIL.
		    .
		    .
		01 TYPE CONTROL FOOTING DAY
		      LINE PLUS 2.
		    02 SUBTOTAL COLUMN 30
		       PICTURE ZZ9 SUM
		       NO-PURCHASES.
		    .
		    .
		
		(SUBTOTAL is incremented only when DETAIL-1 is generated. To achieve the same result as in the COBOL F example, NO-PURCHASES would have to be referred to as a SOURCE item in the DETAIL-2 group.)
			The item will be summed at a GENERATE statement only if it is a SUM counter in a CONTROL FOOTING report group as described or if it is a data item in the File, Working-Storage, or Linkage Sections that is a SOURCE item in the DETAIL report group being generated.

F

Language Element	D/E/F COBOL	ANS COBOL	Comments

GROUP INDICATE clause
 	
(Report Item Description entry)
	The GROUP INDICATE clause specifies that the elementary item is to be produced on the first occurrence of the item after a CONTROL break.
	
	Example:
	
	01 DETAIL-1 TYPE DETAIL.
	    02 COLUMN 2 GROUP
	       INDICATE PICTURE A(9)
	       SOURCE MONTHNAME OF
	       RECORD-AREA (MONTH).
	              .
	              .
	              .
	
	――――――――――――――――――――
	
	EXPENSE REPORT
	              .
	              .
	              .
	January A00
	                       A02
	
	――――――――――――――――――――
	Page 02
	                       A03
	                       A04
	              .
	              .
	              .
		The GROUP INDICATE clause specifies that the elementary item is to be produced on the first occurrence of the item after any PAGE break, as well as after a CONTROL break.
		
		Example:
		
		01 DETAIL-1 TYPE DETAIL.
		    02 COLUMN 2 GROUP
		       INDICATE PICTURE A(9)
		       SOURCE MONTHNAME OF
		       RECORD-AREA (MONTH).
		              .
		              .
		              .
		
		――――――――――――――――――――
		
		EXPENSE REPORT
		              .
		              .
		              .
		January A00
		                       A02
		
		――――――――――――――――――――
		Page 02
		January A03
		                       A04
		              .
		              .
		              .
			GROUP INDICATE items will be produced at PAGE breaks as well as at CONTROL breaks associated with them.

USE BEFORE REPORTING statement (CONTROL FOOTING report group) (Declaratives Section)	<u>USE BEFORE REPORTING</u> data-name (If a USE BEFORE REPORTING statement for a CONTROL FOOTING report group references a control item, it will access the new value of the item after the control break.)	<u>USE BEFORE REPORTING</u> identifier (If a USE BEFORE REPORTING statement for a CONTROL FOOTING report group references a control item, it will access the value of the item prior to the control break.)	The value of a control item accessed in a USE BEFORE REPORTING statement will be different.

Language Element	D/E/F COBOL	ANS COBOL	Comments

SOURCE clause
 	
(CONTROL FOOTING report group)
	SOURCE data-name
	
	(If a data item in a SOURCE clause in a CON-TROL FOOTING report group is also a control, the new value of the item after the control break will be printed.)
	
	Example:
	
	FILE SECTION.
	.
	.
	.
	01 INPUT-RECORD.
	   02 DAY PICTURE 99.
	.
	.
	WORKING-STORAGE SECTION.
	77 SAVED-DAY PICTURE 99
	     VALUE 0.
	.
	.
	REPORT SECTION.
	.
	.
	01 TYPE CONTROL FOOTING DAY
	    LINE PLUS 2.
	   02 COLUMN 27 PICTURE 99
	      SOURCE SAVED-DAY.
	.
	.
	PROCEDURE DIVISION.
	.
	.
	READATA. GENERATE DETAIL-LINE
	   MOVE DAY TO SAVED-DAY READ
	   INFILE AT END GO TO OUT.
	   GO TO READATA.
	
	(This coding ensures that when DAY changes, the date prior to the change will be printed with the subtotal for that date, rather than the new date.)
		SOURCE IS identifier
		
		(If a data-item in a SOURCE clause in a CON-TROL FOOTING report group is also a control, the value of the item prior to the control break will be printed.)
		
		Example:
		
		FILE SECTION.
		.
		.
		.
		01 INPUT-RECORD.
		   02 DAY PICTURE 99.
		.
		.
		REPORT SECTION.
		.
		.
		01 TYPE CONTROL FOOTING DAY
		    LINE PLUS 2.
		   02 COLUMN 27 PICTURE 99
		      SOURCE DAY.
		.
		.
		PROCEDURE DIVISION.
		.
		.
		READATA. GENERATE DETAIL-LINE.
		   READ INFILE AT END GO TO
		   OUT. GO TO READATA.
		
		(The coding to save the date is not necessary.)
			The value printed for the SOURCE data item will be different.

F

C O B O L   D I F F E R E N C E S
EXTRA PROGRAM FEATURES

Language Element	D/E/F COBOL	ANS COBOL	Comments
BASIS card	1 8 BASIS library-name. (Library-name is an external name.) Example: . . (control cards) . . 1 8 BASIS 'MAPROG' . F . .	1 8 BASIS library-name. (Library-name must follow the rules for forming a program-name.) Example: . . (control cards) . . 1 8 BASIS MAPROG . .	Quotation marks must be deleted from library-name. If library-name is a reserved word, it must be changed.
*DEBUG control card	1 8-11 *DEBUG location-name COBOL F: The TRY option can be added to instruct the compiler to ignore debug packet errors. Example (COBOL F): D E F 1 8-11 *DEBUG READ-A-CARD,TRY	1 8-11 DEBUG location-name (There is no TRY option.) Example: 1 8-11 DEBUG READ-A-CARD	The asterisk preceding DE- BUG must be deleted. The parameter, TRY must be deleted, if used.
Debug packets	COBOL D, E: There are no restrictions on GO TO, PERFORM or ALTER statement references from or to de- bug packets. COBOL F: In the body of a program, a PERFORM or ALTER statement may refer to a procedure- name in a debug packet. A GO TO statement in the body of a program or in a debug packet may refer to a procedure-name in a debug packet only if the paragraph or sec- tion associated with the referenced debug packet has been executed. A GO TO statement in a de- bug packet may refer to a procedure-name in the body of the program. A PERFORM or ALTER statement in a debug packet may refer to procedure-names in the body D E F of the program or in other debug packets.	In the body of a program, no references to pro- cedure-names in debug packets can be made. A GO TO, PERFORM or ALTER statement in a debug packet may refer to a procedure-name in the body of the program. A PERFORM or ALTER statement in a debug packet may refer to a procedure-name in another debug packet. A GO TO statement in a debug packet may not refer to a procedure-name in another debug packet.	Any references in the body of a program to procedure- names in debug packets should be removed. Any GO TO statement refer- ences in one debug packet to procedure-names in an- other debug packet should be removed.

COBOL Differences
ANS COBOL Additional Features

SORT/MERGE PROGRAM. In conjunction with entries in the Environment and Data Divisions describing the files to be sorted, the programmer can call the system Sort/Merge program with a SORT statement in the Procedure Division. He can perform special procedures on the records both before and after they are sorted. Within the limits of object-time storage, a program may have any number of SORT statements, and each SORT statement may have its own special procedures. Special registers provide communication with the Sort/Merge program.

SORT CHECKPOINTS. The Sort/Merge program will take checkpoints at logical intervals during the processing, if desired.

SORT SPECIAL REGISTERS. The programmer can communicate at object time with the system Sort/Merge program and optimize its performance through the following special registers:

SORT-FILE-SIZE is used to specify the estimated number of records to be sorted.

SORT-CORE-SIZE is used to specify the amount of storage available.

SORT-MODE-SIZE is used to specify the average record length in a file of variable-length records.

SORT-RETURN contains a code from the Sort/Merge program at the end of its operation, indicating success or failure.

CURRENT-DATE SPECIAL REGISTER. The programmer can obtain eight bytes from the CURRENT-DATE field containing the current month, day, and year.

TIME-OF-DAY SPECIAL REGISTER. The programmer can obtain six bytes from the TIME-OF-DAY field containing the current hour, minute, and second.

RETURN-CODE SPECIAL REGISTER. When control is returned from a called program, the main program can interrogate the special register RETURN-CODE as to the success or failure of the called program operations.

LABEL-RETURN SPECIAL REGISTER. The programmer can use the special register LABEL-RETURN to indicate to the system the validity of a nonstandard label at the end of USE BEFORE STANDARD LABEL PROCEDURE processing.

COMMENT LINES IN EVERY PROGRAM DIVISION. Any number of comment lines can be inserted within any part of a program. Each line has an asterisk in column 7. The asterisk and the comments are reproduced in the source program listing, but have no effect on the program.

CURRENCY SIGN SUBSTITUTION. A single-character nonnumeric literal can be substituted for the dollar sign ($) through the CURRENCY SIGN clause of the Special-Names paragraph.

REPLACING OPTION OF THE COPY STATEMENT. During the process of inserting text from a library into a program, words in the text can be replaced by data-names or literals through the REPLACING option of the COPY statement.

COPY STATEMENT FOR NEW FEATURES. Programmers can use the COPY statement to incorporate Report Description and Sort Description entries, as well as the Special-Names paragraph, from a source program library into their programs during compilation.

COPY STATEMENT FOR THE CONFIGURATION SECTION. Programmers can use the COPY statement to incorporate SOURCE-COMPUTER and OBJECT-COMPUTER statements from a source program library into their program during compilation.

COPY ENTIRE SOURCE PROGRAMS FROM A LIBRARY. An entire program can be retrieved from a source program library by a BASIS card for compilation. INSERT and DELETE cards can be used to make changes in the program as it is read in.

C O B O L   DIFFERENCES
ERROR-HANDLING DIFFERENCES

Language Element	Error Condition	Error-Handling D/E/F COBOL	ANS COBOL
RECORD KEY clause (File-Control paragraph) D E	The data-name specified in the RECORD KEY clause is not defined in a record of the selected file.	No diagnostic message is produced.	An E-level diagnostic message is produced.
LABEL RECORDS clause (File Description entry) D E	The clause is not specified.	LABEL RECORD IS STANDARD is assumed.	LABEL RECORD IS OMITTED is assumed.
VALUE clause (Record Description entry) D E	Literal exceeds maximum allowable length in PICTURE clause.	A W-level diagnostic message is produced, and the literal is truncated to fit.	A C-level diagnostic message is produced. The literal: 1. If it is an alphanumeric item is truncated to fit; 2. If it is an alphabetic item, is replaced by blanks; 3. If it is a numeric item, is replaced by zeros.
REDEFINES clause (Record Description entry) D E	The object of the clause is not the preceding data-name with the same level number.	No diagnostic message is produced. The preceding data-name with the same level number is assumed to be the object of the clause.	A C-level diagnostic message is produced. The preceding data-name with the same level number is assumed to be the object of the clause.
REDEFINES clause (Record Description entry) D E	The object of the clause is not defined.	No diagnostic message is produced. The preceding data-name with the same level number is assumed to be the object of the clause.	An E-level diagnostic message is produced, and the REDEFINES clause is deleted.
Label Processing Declarative (user labels) (Declaratives Section) D E	The declarative includes a branch out of the declarative.	No diagnostic message is produced.	A C-level diagnostic message is produced.

Language Element	Error Condition	Error-Handling D/E/F COBOL	ANS COBOL
OPEN statement D E F	NO OPEN statement is specified for a file.	COBOL D, E: No diagnostic message is produced. COBOL F: A W-level diagnostic message is produced.	A C-level diagnostic message is produced.
AT END phrase (READ statement, random access files) D E	AT END phrase present.	No diagnostic message is produced.	An E-level diagnostic message is produced, and the AT END phrase is deleted.
AFTER ADVANCING phrase (WRITE statement) D E	AFTER ADVANCING phrase missing where required.	No diagnostic message is produced.	A C-level diagnostic message is produced. AFTER POSITIONING 1 LINE is assumed.
INCLUDE statement D E	COBOL D, E: An INCLUDE statement is not immediately preceded by a procedure-name. ANS COBOL: A COPY statement is not immediately preceded by a procedure-name.	No diagnostic message is produced. The library entry specified in the INCLUDE statement is included.	An E-level diagnostic message is produced, and the COPY statement is deleted.
Continuation of nonnumeric literals D E	a) There is no hyphen in column 7 of a card containing the continuation of a nonnumeric literal. b) The first nonblank character following the hyphen on a card containing the continuation of a nonnumeric literal is not a quotation mark.	a) No diagnostic message is produced. A hyphen is assumed. b) A C-level diagnostic message is produced. The literal is assumed to end on the preceding card.	a) A C-level diagnostic message is produced. A hyphen is assumed. b) A C-level diagnostic message is produced. A quotation mark is assumed.

C O B O L   DIFFERENCES
RESERVED WORDS

The following keys appear to the left of the IBM ANS COBOL column:

Key	Explanation
(xu)	An IBM extension to ANS Standard COBOL taken from the CODASYL reserved word list.
(xuc)	An IBM extension to both the ANS standard and the CODASYL reserved word lists.
(cu)	A CODASYL reserved word that currently appears in neither the IBM ANS list nor the ANS standard list. The word may be used as a data-name or procedure-name without incurring a diagnostic message from one of the compilers described in this publication. However, the word should not be used because its use may incur diagnostic messages if it later becomes part of these lists.
(sp)	An IBM System/360 function-name used in the SPECIAL-NAMES paragraph. Function-name does not appear in the CODASYL reserved word list, but does meet CODASYL specifications.

C O B O L   DIFFERENCES
RESERVED WORDS

D, E	IBM ANS	F
ACCEPT	ACCEPT	ACCEPT
ACCESS	ACCESS	ACCESS
ACTUAL	ACTUAL	ACTUAL
ADD	ADD	ADD
	ADDRESS	
ADVANCING	ADVANCING	ADVANCING
AFTER	AFTER	AFTER
ALL	ALL	ALL
ALPHABETIC	ALPHABETIC	ALPHABETIC
ALTER	ALTER	ALTER
ALTERNATE	ALTERNATE	ALTERNATE
AND	AND	AND
APPLY	(xu) APPLY	APPLY
ARE	ARE	ARE
AREA	AREA	AREA
AREAS	AREAS	AREAS
	ASCENDING	ASCENDING
ASSIGN	ASSIGN	ASSIGN
AT	AT	AT
AUTHOR	AUTHOR	AUTHOR
	(xuc) BASIS	
	BEFORE	BEFORE

D, E	IBM ANS	F
BEGINNING	BEGINNING	BEGINNING
BLANK	BLANK	BLANK
BLOCK	BLOCK	BLOCK
BY	BY	BY
CALL	(xu) CALL	CALL
	(cu) CANCEL	
	CF	CF
	CH	CH
CHANGED	(xuc) CHANGED	CHANGED
CHARACTERS	CHARACTERS	CHARACTERS
CHECKING		CHECKING
	CLOCK-UNITS	CLOCK-UNITS
CLOSE	CLOSE	CLOSE
COBOL	COBOL	COBOL
	CODE	CODE
	COLUMN	COLUMN
	(xuc) COM-REG (DOS)	
	COMMA	COMMA
	COMP	
	(xu) COMP-1	
	(xu) COMP-2	
	(xu) COMP-3	
COMPUTATIONAL	COMPUTATIONAL	COMPUTATIONAL
COMPUTATIONAL-1	(xu) COMPUTATIONAL-1	COMPUTATIONAL-1
COMPUTATIONAL-2	(xu) COMPUTATIONAL-2	COMPUTATIONAL-2
COMPUTATIONAL-3	(xu) COMPUTATIONAL-3	COMPUTATIONAL-3
COMPUTE	COMPUTE	COMPUTE
CONFIGURATION	CONFIGURATION	CONFIGURATION
CONSOLE	(sp) CONSOLE	CONSOLE
	(cu) CONSTANT	
CONTAINS	CONTAINS	CONTAINS
	CONTROL	CONTROL
	CONTROLS	CONTROLS
COPY	COPY	COPY
	(xuc) CORE-INDEX	
	CORR	
	CORRESPONDING	CORRESPONDING
CREATING		CREATING
	(sp) CSP	
	CURRENCY	
	(xuc) CURRENT-DATE	
		CYCLES
	(xuc) CYL-INDEX (DOS)	
	(xuc) CYL-OVERFLOW (DOS)	
	(sp) C01	
	(sp) C02	
	(sp) C03	
	(sp) C04	
	(sp) C05	
	(sp) C06	

D, E	IBM ANS	F
	(sp) C07	
	(sp) C08	
	(sp) C09	
	(sp) C10	
	(sp) C11	
	(sp) C12	
DATA	DATA	DATA
DATE-COMPILED	DATE-COMPILED	DATE-COMPILED
DATE-WRITTEN	DATE-WRITTEN	DATE-WRITTEN
	DE	DE
	(xuc) DEBUG	
	DECIMAL-POINT	DECIMAL-POINT
DECLARATIVES	DECLARATIVES	DECLARATIVES
	(xuc) DELETE	
DEPENDING	DEPENDING	DEPENDING
	DESCENDING	DESCENDING
	DETAIL	DETAIL
DIRECT		DIRECT
DIRECT-ACCESS		DIRECT-ACCESS
	(xuc) DISP (OS)	
DISPLAY	DISPLAY	DISPLAY
	(cu) DISPLAY-n	
DISPLAY-ST	(xuc) DISPLAY-ST	DISPLAY-ST
DIVIDE	DIVIDE	DIVIDE
DIVISION	DIVISION	DIVISION
	DOWN	
	(xuc) EJECT	
ELSE	ELSE	ELSE
END	END	END
	(xu) END-OF-PAGE	
ENDING	ENDING	ENDING
ENTER	ENTER	ENTER
ENTRY	(xuc) ENTRY	ENTRY
ENVIRONMENT	ENVIRONMENT	ENVIRONMENT
	(xu) EOP	
EQUAL	EQUAL	EQUAL
	(cu) EQUALS	
ERROR	ERROR	ERROR
EVERY	EVERY	EVERY
EXAMINE	EXAMINE	EXAMINE
	(cu) EXCEEDS	
EXHIBIT	(xuc) EXHIBIT	EXHIBIT
EXIT	EXIT	EXIT
	(xuc) EXTENDED-SEARCH (DOS)	
FD	FD	FD
FILE	FILE	FILE

D, E	IBM	ANS	F
FILE-CONTROL		FILE-CONTROL	FILE-CONTROL
		FILE-LIMIT	FILE-LIMIT
		FILE-LIMITS	
FILLER		FILLER	FILLER
		FINAL	FINAL
FIRST		FIRST	FIRST
		FOOTING	FOOTING
FOR		FOR	FOR
FORM-OVERFLOW			FORM-OVERFLOW
FROM		FROM	FROM
		GENERATE	GENERATE
GIVING		GIVING	GIVING
GO		GO	GO
	(xuc)	GOBACK	
GREATER		GREATER	GREATER
		GROUP	GROUP
		HEADING	HEADING
HIGH-VALUE		HIGH-VALUE	HIGH-VALUE
HIGH-VALUES		HIGH-VALUES	HIGH-VALUES
	(cu)	HOLD	HOLD
I-O		I-O	I-O
I-O-CONTROL		I-O-CONTROL	I-O-CONTROL
IBM-360			IBM-360
	(xuc)	ID	ID
IDENTIFICATION		IDENTIFICATION	IDENTIFICATION
IF		IF	IF
IN		IN	IN
INCLUDE			INCLUDE
		INDEX	
	(cu)	INDEX-n	
INDEXED		INDEXED	INDEXED
		INDICATE	INDICATE
		INITIATE	INITIATE
INPUT		INPUT	INPUT
INPUT-OUTPUT		INPUT-OUTPUT	INPUT-OUTPUT
	(xuc)	INSERT	
INSTALLATION		INSTALLATION	INSTALLATION
INTO		INTO	INTO
INVALID		INVALID	INVALID
IS		IS	IS
		JUST	
JUSTIFIED		JUSTIFIED	JUSTIFIED
KEY		KEY	KEY
	(cu)	KEYS	
LABEL		LABEL	LABEL
LABELS			LABELS
	(xuc)	LABEL-RETURN (OS)	
		LAST	LAST

D, E	IBM	ANS	F
LEADING		LEADING	LEADING
	(xuc)	LEAVE (OS)	
		LEFT	LEFT
LESS		LESS	LESS
	(cu)	LIBRARY	
		LIMIT	LIMIT
		LIMITS	LIMITS
	(cu)	LINAGE	
	(cu)	LINAGE-COUNTER	
		LINE	LINE
		LINE-COUNTER	LINE-COUNTER
LINES		LINES	LINES
LINKAGE	(xu)	LINKAGE	LINKAGE
LOCK		LOCK	LOCK
LOW-VALUE		LOW-VALUE	LOW-VALUE
LOW-VALUES		LOW-VALUES	LOW-VALUES
	(cu)	LOWER-BOUND	
	(cu)	LOWER-BOUNDS	
	(xuc)	MASTER-INDEX (DOS)	
		MEMORY	
MODE		MODE	MODE
		MODULES	
MORE-LABELS	(xuc)	MORE-LABELS	MORE-LABELS
MOVE		MOVE	MOVE
		MULTIPLE	
MULTIPLY		MULTIPLY	MULTIPLY
NAMED	(xuc)	NAMED	NAMED
NEGATIVE		NEGATIVE	NEGATIVE
NEXT		NEXT	NEXT
NO		NO	NO
	(xuc)	NOMINAL	
NOT		NOT	NOT
NOTE		NOTE	NOTE
	(xuc)	NSTD-REELS (DOS)	
		NUMBER	
NUMERIC		NUMERIC	NUMERIC
OBJECT-COMPUTER		OBJECT-COMPUTER	OBJECT-COMPUTER
	(cu)	OBJECT-PROGRAM	
OCCURS		OCCURS	OCCURS
OF		OF	OF
		OFF	
	(cu)	OH	
OMITTED		OMITTED	OMITTED
ON		ON	ON
OPEN		OPEN	OPEN
		OPTIONAL	
OR		OR	OR
ORGANIZATION			ORGANIZATION

D, E	IBM	ANS	F
OTHERWISE	(xuc)	OTHERWISE	OTHERWISE
OUTPUT		OUTPUT	OUTPUT
	(cu)	OV	
	(cu)	OVERFLOW	OVERFLOW
		PAGE	PAGE
		PAGE-COUNTER	PAGE-COUNTER
PERFORM		PERFORM	PERFORM
		PF	PF
		PH	PH
		PIC	
PICTURE		PICTURE	PICTURE
		PLUS	PLUS
		POSITION	
	(xuc)	POSITIONING	
POSITIVE		POSITIVE	POSITIVE
	(cu)	PREPARED	
	(xuc)	PRINT-SWITCH	PRINT-SWITCH
	(cu)	PRIORITY	
PROCEDURE		PROCEDURE	PROCEDURE
PROCEED		PROCEED	PROCEED
	(cu)	PROCESS	PROCESS
PROCESSING		PROCESSING	PROCESSING
	(xu)	PROGRAM	
PROGRAM-ID		PROGRAM-ID	PROGRAM-ID
QUOTE		QUOTE	QUOTE
QUOTES		QUOTES	QUOTES
RANDOM		RANDOM	RANDOM
	(cu)	RANGE	
		RD	RD
READ		READ	READ
READY	(xuc)	READY	READY
RECORD		RECORD	RECORD
	(xuc)	RECORD-OVERFLOW (OS)	
RECORDING	(xu)	RECORDING	RECORDING
RECORDS		RECORDS	RECORDS
REDEFINES		REDEFINES	REDEFINES
REEL		REEL	REEL
RELATIVE (E)			RELATIVE
		RELEASE	RELEASE
		REMAINDER	
REMARKS		REMARKS	REMARKS
		RENAMES	
	(xuc)	REORG-CRITERIA (OS)	
REPLACING		REPLACING	REPLACING
		REPORT	REPORT
		REPORTING	REPORTING
		REPORTS	REPORTS
	(xuc)	REREAD (OS)	

D, E	IBM ANS	F
RERUN	RERUN	RERUN
RESERVE	RESERVE	RESERVE
RESET	RESET	RESET
RESTRICTED		RESTRICTED
RETURN	RETURN	RETURN
	(xuc) RETURN-CODE (OS)	
REVERSED	REVERSED	REVERSED
REWIND	REWIND	REWIND
REWRITE	(xuc) REWRITE	REWRITE
	RF	RF
	RH	RH
RIGHT	RIGHT	RIGHT
ROUNDED	ROUNDED	ROUNDED
RUN	RUN	RUN
	(cu) SA	SA
SAME	SAME	SAME
	SD	SD
SEARCH	SEARCH	SEARCH
SECTION	SECTION	SECTION
SECURITY	SECURITY	SECURITY
	SEEK	
	SEGMENT-LIMIT	
SELECT	SELECT	SELECT
	(cu) SELECTED	
SENTENCE	SENTENCE	SENTENCE
SEQUENTIAL	SEQUENTIAL	SEQUENTIAL
	SET	
	SIGN	
SIZE	SIZE	SIZE
	(xuc) SKIP1	
	(xuc) SKIP2	
	(xuc) SKIP3	
	SORT	SORT
	(xuc) SORT-CORE-SIZE	
	(xuc) SORT-FILE-SIZE	
	(xuc) SORT-MODE-SIZE	
	(xuc) SORT-RETURN	
	SOURCE	SOURCE
SOURCE-COMPUTER	SOURCE-COMPUTER	SOURCE-COMPUTER
SPACE	SPACE	SPACE
SPACES	SPACES	SPACES
	SPECIAL-NAMES	SPECIAL-NAMES
STANDARD	STANDARD	STANDARD
	(xuc) START	
	STATUS	
STOP	STOP	STOP
SUBTRACT	SUBTRACT	SUBTRACT
	SUM	SUM
	(cu) SUPERVISOR	
	(xuc) SUPPRESS	
	(cu) SUSPEND	

D, E	IBM ANS	F
SYMBOLIC		SYMBOLIC
	SYNC	
	SYNCHRONIZED	
	(sp) SYSIN (OS)	SYSIN
	(sp) SYSIPT (DOS)	
	(sp) SYSLST (DOS)	
	(sp) SYSOUT (OS)	SYSOUT
	(sp) SYSPCH (DOS)	
SYSPUNCH	(sp) SYSPUNCH	SYSPUNCH
	(sp) S01	
	(sp) S02	
TALLY	TALLY	TALLY
TALLYING	TALLYING	TALLYING
	TAPE	
	TERMINATE	TERMINATE
THAN	THAN	THAN
THEN	(xuc) THEN	THEN
	THROUGH	
THRU	THRU	THRU
	(xuc) TIME-OF-DAY	
TIMES	TIMES	TIMES
TO	TO	TO
	(xuc) TOTALED (OS)	
	(xuc) TOTALING (OS)	
TRACE	(xuc) TRACE	TRACE
	(xuc) TRACK (OS)	
TRACK-AREA	(xuc) TRACK-AREA	TRACK-AREA
	(xuc) TRACK-LIMIT (OS)	
TRACKS (E)	(xuc) TRACKS	TRACKS
TRANSFORM	(xuc) TRANSFORM	TRANSFORM
		TRY
	TYPE	TYPE
	(cu) UNEQUAL	
UNIT	UNIT	UNIT
UNIT-RECORD		UNIT-RECORD
UNITS		UNITS
UNTIL	UNTIL	UNTIL
	UP	
UPON	UPON	UPON
	(cu) UPPER-BOUND	
	(cu) UPPER-BOUNDS	
	(sp) UPSI-0 (DOS)	
	(sp) UPSI-1 (DOS)	
	(sp) UPSI-2 (DOS)	
	(sp) UPSI-3 (DOS)	
	(sp) UPSI-4 (DOS)	
	(sp) UPSI-5 (DOS)	
	(sp) UPSI-6 (DOS)	
	(sp) UPSI-7 (DOS)	
USAGE	USAGE	USAGE

D, E	IBM ANS	F
USE	USE	USE
USING	USING	USING
UTILITY		UTILITY
VALUE	VALUE	VALUE
	VALUES	
VARYING	VARYING	VARYING
WHEN	WHEN	WHEN
WITH	WITH	WITH
	WORDS	
WORKING-STORAGE	WORKING-STORAGE	WORKING-STORAGE
WRITE	WRITE	WRITE
WRITE-ONLY	(xuc) WRITE-ONLY	WRITE-ONLY
	(xuc) WRITE-VERIFY (DOS)	
ZERO	ZERO	ZERO
ZEROES	ZEROES	ZEROES
ZEROS	ZEROS	ZEROS

Ten Problems

Problem 1
SHAMPOO PAYROLL PROBLEM

In a beauty salon, operators are paid by the amount and type of work they do. The shampoo operators receive $1.00 per customer, the hair cutters receive $2.00 per customer, the hair setters receive $2.50 per customer, the stylists receive $4.00 per customer, and the permanent wave operators receive $5.00 per customer.

Given: Operator's name

Type of operator

Number of customers.

INPUT

Field	Card Columns
Name	1 - 25
Type	26
Customers	27 - 29
Blanks	30 - 80

FORMULA

Gross Pay = rate x customers.

PRINTED OUTPUT

```
TYPE OF OPERATOR.
      SHAMPOO - - - - - - 1
      HAIR CUTTERS- - - - 2
      HAIR SETTERS- - - - 3
      STYLISTS- - - - - - 4
      PERMANENT WAVE- - - 5


   NAME OF OPERATOR         TYPE    NO. OF CUSTOMERS      GROSS PAY

   SUSAN CALDWELL            1           100             $100.00

   MARGARET CUSHING          2           100             $200.00

   BARBARA HICKMAN           3           110             $275.00

   JOSEPHINE HOUSTON         4           050             $200.00

   MARY ANN PALMER           5           040             $200.00
```

Problem 2
DEPARTMENT STORE PROBLEM

Given: Customer's name
        Customer's address
        Customer's account no.
        Last month's balance
        Payments made
        Purchases made
on a card;

INPUT

Field	Card Columns
Customer's name	1 - 15
Customer's address	16 - 50

Account no.	51 - 55
Last balance	56 - 60
Month sales	61 - 65
Payments	66 - 70
Blanks	71 - 80

FORMULAS TO BE USED

Service charge = .015 * (last-balance − payments) (rounded)
Amount due = (last-balance − payments) + service charge + month's sales

OUTPUT

Field	Print Positions	
Blanks	1 - 3	
Name of Customer	4 - 18	
Blanks	19 - 20	
Address of Customer	21 - 55	
Blanks	56 - 57	
Customer Account	58 - 62	
Blanks	63 - 64	
Previous balance	65 - 71	(EDITED)
Blanks	72 - 73	
Sales this month	74 - 80	(EDITED)
Blanks	81 - 82	
Month's payments	83 - 89	(EDITED)
Blanks	90 - 91	
Service charge	92 - 97	(EDITED)
Blanks	98 - 99	
Amount due	100 - 106	(EDITED)
Blanks	107 - 120	

NAME OF CUSTOMER	ADDRESS OF CUSTOMER	ACCOUNT	PREVIOUS BALANCE	SALES	PAYMENT	SERVICE CHARGE	AMT DUE
DAVID ANDERSON	18745 MOBILE ST., RESEDA, CALIF.	62986	$100.00	$100.00	$20.00	$1.20	$181.20
BETTY L. BREWER	10321 LUNDY DR., INGLEWOOD, CALIF.	61477	$350.25	$50.00	$30.00	$4.80	$375.05
ARTHUR BROWN	12145 MADISON ST., L.A. 45, CALIF.	38940	$450.00	$30.00	$50.00	$6.00	$436.00

Problem 3
BANK BALANCE PROBLEM

Given: *in an 80 column card*

Account number

Type code: either a 1 punch or a 2 punch:

1 indicates a checking account
2 indicates a savings account

Deposits
Withdrawals
Last Balance

INPUT

Field	Card Column
Account no.	1 - 5
Type code	6
Blanks	7 - 8
Deposits	9 - 16
Withdrawals	17 - 24
Last balance	25 - 32
Blanks	33 - 80

FORMULAS

New balance = Last-balance – withdrawals + deposits.
Interest = rate x (last-balance – withdrawals + deposits)
New balance = Last-balance – withdrawals + deposits + interest.

OUTPUT

ACCOUNT NO.	NEW BALANCE
62986	$10,500.00
61788	$7,612.50
61003	$10,500.00
58440	$102,685.50

Problem 4
"AFRICA" PAYROLL PROBLEM

Each month a payroll is to be processed in the following manner:

A card file contains a master record for every employee in the company. Each record contains the employee's name, his number, the regular and overtime hours he has worked during the month, the wages he has earned so far this year, his rate of pay, and the number of dependents he has. The payroll is processed in the usual manner: computation of GROSS-PAY, FICA, WH-TAX and NET PAY. The results are used to print checks and to create new master records. These new records contain the new YTD-GROSS and zeros in the hours field (both regular and overtime). These new records create the CARD-OUT file which will be used next month as CARD-IN. (During the month the regular hours and overtime hours are added in by another program.)

This company has a subsidiary in Africa whose employees, though U. S. citizens, are not required to pay income tax. These employees have A's in front of their numbers—other employee numbers will have spaces in these character positions.

This program will use a table of income tax exemptions according to the number of dependents which looks like this:

DEPENDENTS

0	1	2	3	4	5	6	7	8	9	10
$0	$56	$112	$168	$224	$280	$336	$392	$448	$504	$560

Subtract from GROSS-PAY to find the taxable amount.

The formulas which the program will use are:

In America:

Gross-Pay = (regular hours * rate) + (overtime hours * 1½ rate).

FICA = .052 * gross pay (If YTD is less than $9000).

WH-TAX = .18 * (gross-pay − sub) sub is exemption according to dependents chart.

NET PAY = gross-pay − FICA − WH-TAX.

In Africa:

Gross-Pay = (regular hours * rate) + (overtime hours * 1½ rate).

WM-TAX = 0.

FICA = .052 * gross pay (If YTD is less than $9000).

NET PAY = gross-pay − FICA.

Card-In

Field	Card Columns	
Employee Name	1 - 29	
Employee Number	30 - 39	
Blank	40	
Rate	41 - 43	
Dependents	44 - 45	
Regular Hours	46 - 50	(xxx.xx)
Overtime Hours	51 - 55	(xxx.xx)
YTD-Gross	56 - 62	(xxxxx.xx)
Blanks	63 - 80	

Print-Out

Field	Print Positions
CHECK-LINE-1	
Name	1 - 29
Blanks	30 - 106
Date	107 - 114
Blanks	115 - 120
CHECK-LINE-2	
Blanks	1 - 90
Net-Pay	91 - 96
Blanks	97 - 120
CHECK-LINE-3	
Employee Name	1 - 29
Blanks	30 - 31
Employee Number	32 - 41
Blanks	42 - 43
Gross Pay	44 - 50
Blanks	51 - 52
Wh-Tax	53 - 57
Blanks	58 - 59
FICA	60 - 64
Blanks	65 - 66
Net-Pay	67 - 73
Blanks	74 - 120

AMES F. KING   12-8-72

AMES F. KING   A000053219 $1,061.27 $0.00 $0.00 $1,061.27 $1061.27

ILTON C. MORGAN   12-8-72

ILTON C. MORGAN   000064378 $464.00 $12.96 $24.13 $426.91 $426.91

OHN L. REED   12-8-72

OHN L. REED   000052887 $569.19 $82.29 $29.60 $457.30 $457.30

Problem 5
SALES AND COMMISSION PROBLEM

Commissions are paid to salesmen based upon the number of units that are sold. The unit commission varies with the product sold and the total commission is based upon the number of units sold of each particular product.

Sales are determined by the number of units sold times the individual product selling price.

Given:

Product	Commission Rate	Selling Price
1	$ .10	$ 16.00
2	$ .20	$ 30.00
3	$ .30	$ 43.00
4	$ .40	$ 60.00
5	$ .50	$ 75.00

INPUT RECORD FILE

Field	Card Columns
Territory Number	1 - 2
Salesman Number	3 - 5
Date	6 - 11
Name	12 - 30
Units Sold	31 - 35
Product Number	36

PROBLEM

1. Prepare a table of commissions for the five different products so that the product number itself will serve as a subscript.

2. Prepare a table of selling prices for the five different products so that the product number itself will serve as a subscript.

3. Write a COBOL program that will read both the commission table and price table and then process each data card to calculate the commission for each salesman. At the same time, prepare a report of the number of units sold and the amount of sales for each product by salesman, by territory and an overall total of sales.

OUTPUT

MONTHLY SALES AND COMMISSION REPORT
JANUARY 1973   PAGE   1

TERRITORY NUMBER	SALESMAN NUMBER	DATE	NAME	PRODUCT NUMBER	UNITS SOLD	TOTAL SALES	COMMISSION
10	111	010372	JONES HENRY	1	100	$1,600.00	$160.00
10	111	011072	JONES HENRY	2	2,301	$69,030.00	$13,806.00
10	111	011772	JONES HENRY	3	60	$2,580.00	$774.00
10	111	012472	JONES HENRY	4	20,502	$1,230,120.00	$492,048.00
					22,963	$1,303,330.00	$506,788.00
10	222	010372	SMITH ROBERT	1	55	$880.00	$88.00
10	222	010372	SMITH ROBERT	2	70	$2,100.00	$420.00
10	222	010372	SMITH ROBERT	3	800	$34,400.00	$10,320.00
					925	$37,380.00	$10,828.00
		TERRITORY TOTAL			23,888	$1,340,710.00	$517,616.00
		TOTAL SALES				$3,288,026.00 **	

Problem 6
PAYROLL REGISTER PROBLEM

P 281

Write a COBOL program that will calculate and print the Payroll Register as indicated. Also to punch a summary card with the information as indicated.

INPUT RECORD FILE

Field	Card Columns
Month	1 - 3
Day	4 - 5
Year	6 - 7

Department	14 - 16
Serial	17 - 21
Gross Earnings	57 - 61
Insurance	62 - 65
Withholding Tax	69 - 72
State UCI	73 - 75
Miscellaneous Deductions	76 - 79
Code (letter E)	80

CALCULATIONS

1. FICA = Gross Earnings x .052 (round to 2 places)
2. Net Earnings = Gross Earnings – Insurance – FICA – Withholding Tax – State UCI – Miscellaneous Deductions.
3. If the Net Earnings are zero or negative, go to error routine.
4. The Department Earnings value is the sum of the Net Earnings for each employee.
5. Calculate totals for all columns by department as well as an overall total for the entire payroll.

INPUT

Detail

Department	3 - 5	
Serial	10 - 14	
Gross Earnings	21 - 26	XXXX.XX
Insurance	33 - 37	XXX.XX
FICA	43 - 47	XXX.XX
Withholding Tax	54 - 58	XXX.XX
State UCI	65 - 68	XX.XX
Miscellaneous Deductions	76 - 80	XXX.XX
Net Earnings	92 - 97	XXXX.XX

OUTPUT RECORD — CARD

Field	**Card Columns**
Month	9 - 11
Day	12 - 13
Department Number	14 - 16
Department Net Earnings	17 - 22
Code (Character —)	80

PRINTED OUTPUT

	Field	Printing Positions
Heading		
Line		
1	WEEKLY PAYROLL REGISTER	40 - 62
2	WEEK ENDING	40 - 62
3	EMPLOYEE NO.	3 - 14
	GROSS	22 - 26
	WITHHOLDING	51 - 61
	STATE	65 - 69
4	DEPT.	2 - 6
	SERIAL	10 - 15
	EARNINGS	20 - 27
	INSURANCE	31 - 39
	FICA	44 - 47
	TAX	56 - 58
	UCI	66 - 68
	MISC. DEDNS.	74 - 85
	NET EARNINGS	89 - 100

```
                                WEEKLY PAYROLL REGISTER
                                WEEK ENDING SEP  3 1973                              PAGE    1

 EMPLOYEE NO.        GROSS                            WITHHOLDING  STATE
 DEPT.    SERIAL    EARNINGS   INSURANCE     FICA         TAX       UCI      MISC. DEDNS.    NET EARNINGS

  200    10670     $202.00      $3.10      $10.50      $28.00     $0.80       $0.00           $159.60
  200    10695     $203.00      $3.10      $10.56      $28.00     $0.90       $5.00           $155.54
  200    10700     $204.00      $3.10      $10.61      $28.00     $0.80       $0.00           $161.49
  200    10703     $205.00      $3.10      $10.66      $28.00     $0.80       $0.00           $162.44
  200    10725     $207.00      $3.10      $10.76      $28.00     $0.80      $10.00           $154.34
  200    10730     $208.00      $3.10      $10.82      $28.00     $0.80       $0.00           $165.28
  200    10742     $209.00      $3.10      $10.87      $28.00     $0.80       $0.00           $166.23
  200    10800     $210.00      $3.10      $10.92      $28.00     $0.80       $0.00           $167.18
  200    10890     $211.00      $3.10      $10.97      $28.00     $0.80       $1.00           $167.13

    DEPT            $1859.00    $27.90     $96.67     $252.00     $7.20      $16.00          $1459.23
```

Problem 7
UPDATED PAYROLL PROBLEM

Write a COBOL program to update a master tape file with a current card file. Both input files are in Social Security Number sequence. Input tape records are in blocks of ten 52-character records. The updated output tape blacks will be the same size.

The exception list shall be double spaced.

INPUT TAPE RECORD

Field	Positions
Employee Name	6 - 25
Social Security Number	26 - 34
Old Year-to-date Gross Earnings	35 - 41
Old Year-to-date Withholding Tax	42 - 47
Old Year-to-date FICA	48 - 52

INPUT CARD RECORD

Field	Card Columns
Department Number	1 - 2
Clock Number	3 - 5
Social Security Number	26 - 34
Current Gross Earnings	62 - 68
Current Withholding Tax	69 - 74
Current FICA	75 - 78
Code (Digit 1)	80

OPERATIONS TO BE PERFORMED

1. New Year-to-date Gross = Old Year-to-date Gross plus Current Gross

2. New Year-to-date Withholding Tax = Old Year-to-date Withholding Tax plus Current Withholding Tax.

3. New year-to-date FICA = Old Year-to-date FICA plus Current FICA.

4. If New Year-to-date FICA record exceeds $343.20, print Department Number, Clock Number, Employee Name, Social Security Number, New Year-to-date Gross, New Year-to-date Withholding Tax and Excess FICA amount.

OUTPUT UPDATED TAPE RECORD

Field	Positions
Department Number	1 - 2
Clock Number	3 - 5
Employee Name	6 - 25
Social Security Number	26 - 34
New Year-to-date Gross Earnings	35 - 41
New Year-to-date Withholding Tax	42 - 47
New Year-to-date FICA	48 - 52

OUTPUT PRINTED RECORD

Field	Print Positions	
Department Number	4 - 5	
Clock Number	9 - 11	
Employee Name	15 - 34	
Social Security Number	37 - 47	XXX-XX-XXXX
New Year-to-date Gross Earnings	52 - 60	XX,XXX.XX
New Year-to-date Withholding Tax	64 - 71	X,XXX.XX
Excess FICA	77 - 81	XX.XX

XX EMPLOYEES OVER $343.20.

```
                          EXCEPTION LIST
                     EMPLOYEES OVER $343.20                    PAGE  1

       DEPT CLOCK    EMPLOYEE NAME    SOC SEC NO.   YTD GROSS   YTD W/H   EX FICA

        15   425  JACKSON KENNETH    543-01-2232    7,300.00    685.00    16.80

        15   425  YOUNG SAMUEL       543-01-2234    7,450.00    700.00     6.80

        15   425  PHILLIPS ROBERT    543-01-2235    7,611.25    716.25     6.80

        15   425  SAWYER DAVID       543-01-2236    7,711.25    726.15     6.80

        15   425  HORNE ALBERT       543-01-2237    7,711.25    726.25     6.80

        15   425  FOX WILLIAM        543-01-2238    7,725.00    727.50     6.80

        18   565  HEPNER ELMER       543-01-2239    7,800.00    735.00     6.80

              7 EMPLOYEES OVER $343.20
```

Problem 8
SALES PROBLEM (REPORT WRITER FEATURE)

REPORT

DAILY SALES REGISTER

WEEK OF SEP 3   PAGE 1

ENTRY DAY	CUSTOMER NUMBER	SALESMAN NUMBER	SALE AMOUNT	
3	8257	71	$ 1,189.80	
3	11243	79	168.06	
3	29031	79	63.00	
3	29964	79	1,294.86	
3	79992	95	87.74	
3	85486	125	20.25	
		DAY 3 SALES	$ 2,823.71	*
4	1179	2	$70,711.29	
4	2965	37	12,716.92	
4	9002	1	842.17	
4	13605	1	3,092.72	
4	27654	9	217.90	
4	32007	22	429.65	
4	65952	16	223.35	
4	99003	58	4,000.00	
		DAY 4 SALES	$92,234.00	*
5	390	92	$ 27.00	
5	5006	56	897.32	
5	12125	181	371.98	
5	20239	145	18.16	
		DAY 5 SALES	$ 1,314.46	*

6	106	100	$ 1,494.73
6	298	24	2,020.60
		DAY 6 SALES	$ 3,515.33 *
7	256	3	$ 79.53
7	321	5	590.10
7	652	8	95.18
7	18569	90	421.15
7	20106	132	706.42
7	20902	27	55.80
7	25452	60	2,166.96

DAILY SALES REGISTER

WEEK OF SEP 3   PAGE 2

ENTRY DAY	CUSTOMER NUMBER	SALESMAN NUMBER	SALE AMOUNT
7	40764	43	$ 1,914.35
		DAY 7 SALES	$ 6,029.49 *
NUMBER OF SALES 28		TOTAL SALES	$105,916.99 **

INPUT RECORD FILE

Field	Card Columns
Month	1 - 2
Day	3 - 4
Year	5 - 6
Salesman Number	7 - 9
Customer Number	10 - 14
Sales Amount	51 - 57

CALCULATIONS

Compute the total sales values for each day of week.
Compute the total sales values for week.
Compute the number of sales for week.

Problem 9
COMMISSION PROBLEM (REPORT WRITER FEATURE)

REPORT

SALES COMMISSION REPORT

For Month of January 1973

SALES-MAN	CUS-TOMER	INVOICE	NET AMOUNT		RATE	COMMISSION	
2513	11110	12066	$ 9,850.40		8	$ 788.03	
2513	12129	13444	10,986.00		12	1,318.32	
2513	14983	14092	110.20		6	6.61	
			$20,946.60	*		$ 2,112.96	*
4490	15121	25930	$ 1,250.00		10	$ 125.00	
4490	49690	25220	12,359.20		11	1,359.51	
4490	72914	44873	690.70		14	96.70	
4490	78345	25118	8,255.12		8	660.41	
			$22,555.02	*		$ 2,241.62	*
TOTAL FOR MONTH OF JANUARY			$315,946.25	**		$30,642.51	**

INPUT RECORD FILE

Card Columns	Field
1	Code (digit 5)
2 - 6	Invoice Number
13 - 19	Customer Number
35 - 42	Net Amount
43 - 46	Salesman Number
54 - 55	Commission Rate
56 - 62	Commission Amount

CALCULATIONS

Find the total sales and total commissions for each salesman.
Find the total sales and total commissions for entire force for
month.

Problem 10
HOSPITAL PROBLEM (SORT FEATURE)

A card is punched for the number of patients in each hospital of the United States.

A report is prepared indicating the various patient totals for cities and counties within each state of the United States. An overall total is indicated for the entire United States.

INPUT RECORD FILE

Field	Card Columns
Date	1 - 6
State	7 - 8
County	9 - 11
City	12 - 14
Hospital Number	15 - 18
Number of Patients	70 - 75

OPERATIONS REQUIRED:

1. Sort data cards in the following sequence; major-State, intermediate-County and minor-City.

2. Prepare listing per output record format.

OUTPUT RECORD FORMAT.

```
                    HOSPITAL PATIENT REPORT
                       JANUARY 31,1968                    PAGE    1
```

STATE	COUNTY	CITY	NUMBER OF PATIENTS
AL	SEC	NBI	3,000
		COUNTY TOTAL	3,000
		STATE TOTAL	3,000
AR	ABA	CAL	2,500
		COUNTY TOTAL	2,500
		STATE TOTAL	2,500
CA	ORA	LB	486
		COUNTY TOTAL	486
CA	VEN	PH	2,000
		COUNTY TOTAL	2,000
		STATE TOTAL	2,486
DE	BAN	OXA	6,500
DE	BAN	RUN	2,000
		COUNTY TOTAL	8,500
		STATE TOTAL	8,500
FL	SD	AR	2,000
FL	SD	JUN	2,500
		COUNTY TOTAL	4,500
		STATE TOTAL	4,500
NE	CEN	FON	3,500
		COUNTY TOTAL	3,500
		STATE TOTAL	3,500
WN	BRE	WAS	1,500
		COUNTY TOTAL	1,500
WN	DUN	RED	1,500
		COUNTY TOTAL	1,500
		STATE TOTAL	3,000

Three Illustrative Problems

Illustrative Problem 1
"AFRICA" PAYROLL PROBLEM (SALARY)

Each month a payroll is to be processed in the following manner:

A card file contains a master record for every employee in the company. Each record contains the employee's name, his number, the regular and overtime hours he has worked during the month, the wages he has earned so far this year, his rate of pay, and the number of dependents he has. The payroll is processed in the usual manner: computation of GROSS-PAY, FICA, WH-TAX and NET PAY. The results are used to print checks and to create new master records. These new records contain the new YTD-GROSS and zeros in the hours field (both regular and overtime). These new records create the CARD-OUT file which will be used next month as CARD-IN. (During the month the regular hours and overtime hours are added in by another program.)

This company has a subsidiary in Africa whose employees, though U. S. citizens, are not required to pay income tax. These employees have A's in front of their numbers—other employee numbers will have spaces in these character positions.

This program will use a table of income tax exemptions according to the number of dependents which looks like this:

DEPENDENTS

0	1	2	3	4	5	6	7	8	9	10
$0	$56	$112	$168	$224	$280	$336	$392	$448	$504	$560

Subtract from GROSS-PAY to find the taxable amount.

The formulas which the program will use are:

In America:

Gross-Pay = (regular hours * rate) + (overtime hours * 1½ rate).

FICA = .052 * gross pay (If YTD is less than $9000).

WH-TAX = .18 * (gross-pay − sub) sub is exemption according to dependents chart.

NET PAY = gross-pay − FICA − WH-TAX.

In Africa:

Gross-Pay = (regular hours * rate) + (overtime hours * 1½ rate).

WM-TAX = 0.

FICA = .052 * gross pay (If YTD is less than $9000).

NET PAY = gross-pay – FICA.

Card-In

Field	Card Columns	
Employee Name	1 - 29	
Employee Number	30 - 39	
Blank	40	
Rate	41 - 43	
Dependents	44 - 45	
Regular Hours	46 - 50	(xxx.xx)
Overtime Hours	51 - 55	(xxx.xx)
YTD-Gross	56 - 62	(xxxxx.xx)
Blanks	63 - 80	

Print-Out

Field	Print Positions
CHECK-LINE-1	
Name	1 - 29
Blanks	30 - 106
Date	107 - 114
Blanks	115 - 120
CHECK-LINE-2	
Blanks	1 - 90
Net-Pay	91 - 96
Blanks	97 - 120
CHECK-LINE-3	
Employee Name	1 - 29
Blanks	30 - 31
Employee Number	32 - 41
Blanks	42 - 43
Gross Pay	44 - 50
Blanks	51 - 52
Wh-Tax	53 - 57
Blanks	58 - 59
FICA	60 - 64
Blanks	65 - 66
Net-Pay	67 - 73
Blanks	74 - 120

SALARY

1   IBM DOS AMERICAN NATIONAL STANDARD COBOL   CBF CL3-5   10/27/72

```
00001    001010 IDENTIFICATION DIVISION.
00002    001020 PROGRAM-ID. PAYROLL-CHECK.
00003    001030 AUTHOR. C. FEINGOLD.
00004    001040 DATE-WRITTEN.  JUNE 22 1972.
00005    001050 DATE-COMPILED. 10/27/72
00006    001060 REMARKS.
00007    001070     THIS REPORT PREPARES A PAYROLL CHECK.
00008    002010 ENVIRONMENT DIVISION.
00009    002020 CONFIGURATION SECTION.
00010    002030 SOURCE-COMPUTER.
00011    002040     IBM-360-H50.
00012    002050 OBJECT-COMPUTER.
00013    002060     IBM-360-H50.
00014    002070 INPUT-OUTPUT SECTION.
00015    002080 FILE-CONTROL.
00016    002090     SELECT MASTER-FILE
00017    002100         ASSIGN TO SYS009-UR-2540R-S.
00018    002110     SELECT MASTER-FILE-OUT
00019    002120         ASSIGN TO SYS005-UR-1403-S.
00020    002121     SELECT  MASTER-PUNCH
00021    002122         ASSIGN TO SYS006-UR-2540P-S.
00022    003010 DATA DIVISION.                              'SALARY'
00023    003020 FILE SECTION.                               'SALARY'
00024    003030 FD  MASTER-FILE                             'SALARY'
00025    003040     RECORDING MODE IS F                     'SALARY'
00026    003050     LABEL RECORDS ARE OMITTED               'SALARY'
00027    003060     DATA RECORD IS CARD-IN.                 'SALARY'
00028    003070 01  CARD-IN.                                'SALARY'
00029    003080     02 NAME PICTURE A(29).                  'SALARY'
00030    003090     02 EMP-NO.                              'SALARY'
00031    003100         03 NUM PICTURE 9(9).                'SALARY'
00032    003110         03 CODE-1 PICTURE A.                'SALARY'
00033    003120     02 FILLER PICTURE X.                    'SALARY'
00034    003130     02 RATE PICTURE 9V99.                   'SALARY'
00035    003140     02 NUMBER-1 PICTURE 99.                 'SALARY'
00036    003150     02 REG-HRS PICTURE 999V99.              'SALARY'
00037    003160     02 OVT-HRS PICTURE 999V99.              'SALARY'
00038    003170     02 YTD-GROSS PICTURE 99999V99.          'SALARY'
00039    003180     02 DATE PICTURE X(8).                   'SALARY'
```

2

```
00040    003190     02 FILLER PICTURE X(10).                'SALARY'
00041    003200 FD  MASTER-FILE-OUT                         'SALARY'
00042    003210     RECORDING MODE IS F                     'SALARY'
00043    003220     LABEL RECORD IS OMITTED                 'SALARY'
00044    003230     DATA RECORD IS RECORD-OUT.              'SALARY'
00045    003240 01  RECORD-OUT PICTURE X(133).              'SALARY'
00046    003250 FD  MASTER-PUNCH                            'SALARY'
00047    003260     RECORDING MODE IS F                     'SALARY'
00048    003270     LABEL RECORD IS OMITTED                 'SALARY'
00049    003280     DATA RECORD IS PUNCH-OUT.               'SALARY'
00050    003290 01  PUNCH-OUT.                              'SALARY'
00051    003300     02 FILLER PICTURE X.                    'SALARY'
00052    003310     02 NAME-OUT PICTURE A(29).              'SALARY'
00053    003320     02 FILLER PICTURE XX.                   'SALARY'
00054    003330     02 EMP-NO-3.                            'SALARY'
00055    003340         03 NUM-4 PICTURE ZZZ999999.         'SALARY'
00056    003350         03 CODE-4 PICTURE A.                'SALARY'
00057    003360     02 FILLER PICTURE XX.                   'SALARY'
00058    003370     02 RATE-1 PICTURE 9V99.                 'SALARY'
00059    003380     02 FILLER PICTURE XX.                   'SALARY'
00060    003390     02 NUMBER-2 PICTURE 99.                 'SALARY'
00061    003400     02 FILLER PICTURE XX.                   'SALARY'
00062    003410     02 FILLER PICTURE X(14).                'SALARY'
00063    003420     02 YTD-GROSS-1 PICTURE 99999V99.        'SALARY'
00064    003430     02 FILLER PICTURE X(6).                 'SALARY'
00065    003440 WORKING-STORAGE SECTION.                    'SALARY'
00066    003450 77  NONE PICTURE 99 VALUE 00.               'SALARY'
00067    003460 77  FICA-LIMIT PICTURE 9999V99 VALUE 9000.00. 'SALARY'
00068    003470 77  GROSS-PAY PICTURE 999V99 VALUE ZEROS.   'SALARY'
00069    003480 77  DEDUCTION PICTURE 999V99 VALUE ZEROS.   'SALARY'
00070    003490 77  KODE PICTURE A VALUE 'A'.               'SALARY'
00071    003500 77  FED-TX PICTURE 999V99 VALUE ZEROS.      'SALARY'
00072    003510 77  FICA-1 PICTURE 999V99 VALUE ZEROS.      'SALARY'
00073    003520 77  NET-PAY PICTURE 999V99 VALUE ZEROS.     'SALARY'
00074    003530 77  DIFFERENT PICTURE 9999V99 VALUE ZEROS.  'SALARY'
00075    003540 77  TX-AMOUNT PICTURE 999V99 VALUE ZEROS.   'SALARY'
00076    003550 77  COUNT PICTURE 999 VALUE 100.            'SALARY'
00077    003560 01  DEPENDENT-TABLE.                        'SALARY'
00078    003570     02 FILLER PICTURE 999V99 VALUE 056.00.  'SALARY'
```

```
00079   003580   02 FILLER PICTURE 999V99 VALUE 112.00.            'SALARY'
00080   003590   02 FILLER PICTURE 999V99 VALUE 168.00.            'SALARY'
00081   003600   02 FILLER PICTURE 999V99 VALUE 224.00.            'SALARY'
00082   003610   02 FILLER PICTURE 999V99 VALUE 280.00.            'SALARY'
00083   003620   02 FILLER PICTURE 999V99 VALUE 336.00.            'SALARY'
00084   003630   02 FILLER PICTURE 999V99 VALUE 392.00.            'SALARY'
00085   003640   02 FILLER PICTURE 999V99 VALUE 448.00.            'SALARY'
00086   003650   02 FILLER PICTURE 999V99 VALUE 504.00.            'SALARY'
00087   003660   02 FILLER PICTURE 999V99 VALUE 560.00.            'SALARY'
00088   003670   01 NO-DEPEND REDEFINES DEPENDENT-TABLE.           'SALARY'
00089   003680   02 DEPENDENTS OCCURS 10 TIMES, PICTURE 999V99.    'SALARY'
00090   003690   01 AREA-1.                                        'SALARY'
00091   003700   02 FILLER VALUE SPACE PICTURE X.                  'SALARY'
00092   003710   02 FILLER PICTURE X VALUE '1'.                    'SALARY'
00093   003720   02 FILLER VALUE SPACE PICTURE X(130).             'SALARY'
00094   003730   02 FILLER PICTURE X VALUE '1'.                    'SALARY'
00095   003740   01 PRINT-LINE.                                    'SALARY'
00096   003750   02 FILLER VALUE SPACE PICTURE X(27).              'SALARY'
00097   003760   02 FILLER PICTURE X VALUE '*'.                    'SALARY'
00098   003770   02 FILLER PICTURE X(11) VALUE SPACE.              'SALARY'
00099   003780   02 FILLER PICTURE X VALUE '.'.                    'SALARY'
00100   003790   02 FILLER PICTURE X(15) VALUE SPACE.              'SALARY'
00101   003800   02 FILLER PICTURE X VALUE '.'.                    'SALARY'
00102   003810   02 FILLER VALUE SPACE PICTURE X(16).              'SALARY'
00103   003820   02 FILLER PICTURE X VALUE '.'.                    'SALARY'
00104   003830   02 FILLER VALUE SPACE PICTURE X(17).              'SALARY'
00105   003840   02 FILLER PICTURE X VALUE '.'.                    'SALARY'
00106   003850   02 FILLER VALUE SPACE PICTURE X(13).              'SALARY'
00107   003860   02 FILLER PICTURE X VALUE '*'.                    'SALARY'
00108   003870   01 MONEY-TABLE.                                   'SALARY'
00109   003880   02 FILLER PICTURE A(13) VALUE '  ONE HUNDRED'.    'SALARY'
00110   003890   02 FILLER PICTURE A(13) VALUE '  TWO HUNDRED'.    'SALARY'
00111   003900   02 FILLER PICTURE A(13) VALUE 'THREE HUNDRED'.    'SALARY'
00112   003910   02 FILLER PICTURE A(13) VALUE ' FOUR HUNDRED'.    'SALARY'
00113   003920   02 FILLER PICTURE A(13) VALUE ' FIVE HUNDRED'.    'SALARY'
00114   003930   02 FILLER PICTURE A(13) VALUE '  SIX HUNDRED'.    'SALARY'
00115   003940   02 FILLER PICTURE A(13) VALUE 'SEVEN HUNDRED'.    'SALARY'
00116   003950   01 TABLE-MONEY REDEFINES MONEY-TABLE.             'SALARY'
00117   003960   02 HUNDRED OCCURS 7 TIMES PICTURE A(13).          'SALARY'


00118   003970   01 DOLLAR-TABLE.                                          'SALARY'
00119   003980   02 FILLER PICTURE X(25) VALUE 'ONE DOLLAR AND-----------'. 'SALARY'
00120   003990   02 FILLER PICTURE X(25) VALUE 'TWO DOLLARS AND----------'. 'SALARY'
00121   004010   02 FILLER PICTURE X(25) VALUE 'THREE DOLLARS AND--------'. 'SALARY'
00122   004020   02 FILLER PICTURE X(25) VALUE 'FOUR DOLLARS AND---------'. 'SALARY'
00123   004030   02 FILLER PICTURE X(25) VALUE 'FIVE DOLLARS AND---------'. 'SALARY'
00124   004040   02 FILLER PICTURE X(25) VALUE 'SIX DOLLARS AND----------'. 'SALARY'
00125   004050   02 FILLER PICTURE X(25) VALUE 'SEVEN DOLLARS AND--------'. 'SALARY'
00126   004060   02 FILLER PICTURE X(25) VALUE 'EIGHT DOLLARS AND--------'. 'SALARY'
00127   004070   02 FILLER PICTURE X(25) VALUE 'NINE DOLLARS AND---------'. 'SALARY'
00128   004080   02 FILLER PICTURE X(25) VALUE 'TEN DOLLARS AND----------'. 'SALARY'
00129   004090   02 FILLER PICTURE X(25) VALUE 'ELEVEN DOLLARS AND ------'. 'SALARY'
00130   004100   02 FILLER PICTURE X(25) VALUE 'TWELVE DOLLARS AND-------'. 'SALARY'
00131   004110   02 FILLER PICTURE X(25) VALUE 'THIRTEEN DOLLARS AND-----'. 'SALARY'
00132   004120   02 FILLER PICTURE X(25) VALUE 'FOURTEEN DOLLARS AND-----'. 'SALARY'
00133   004130   02 FILLER PICTURE X(25) VALUE 'FIFTEEN DOLLARS AND------'. 'SALARY'
00134   004140   02 FILLER PICTURE X(25) VALUE 'SIXTEEN DOLLARS AND------'. 'SALARY'
00135   004150   02 FILLER PICTURE X(25) VALUE 'SEVENTEEN DOLLARS AND----'. 'SALARY'
00136   004160   02 FILLER PICTURE X(25) VALUE 'EIGHTEEN DOLLARS AND-----'. 'SALARY'
00137   004170   02 FILLER PICTURE X(25) VALUE 'NINETEEN DOLLARS AND-----'. 'SALARY'
00138   004180   02 FILLER PICTURE X(25) VALUE 'TWENTY DOLLARS AND-------'. 'SALARY'
00139   004190   02 FILLER PICTURE X(25) VALUE 'TWENTY ONE DOLLARS AND---'. 'SALARY'
00140   004200   02 FILLER PICTURE X(25) VALUE 'TWENTY TWO DOLLARS AND---'. 'SALARY'
00141   004210   02 FILLER PICTURE X(25) VALUE 'TWENTY THREE DOLLARS AND-'. 'SALARY'
00142   004220   02 FILLER PICTURE X(25) VALUE 'TWENTY FOUR DOLLARS AND--'. 'SALARY'
00143   004230   02 FILLER PICTURE X(25) VALUE 'TWENTY FIVE DOLLARS AND--'. 'SALARY'
00144   004240   02 FILLER PICTURE X(25) VALUE 'TWENTY SIX DOLLARS AND---'. 'SALARY'
00145   004250   02 FILLER PICTURE X(25) VALUE 'TWENTY SEVEN DOLLARS AND-'. 'SALARY'
00146   004260   02 FILLER PICTURE X(25) VALUE 'TWENTY EIGHT DOLLARS AND-'. 'SALARY'
00147   004270   02 FILLER PICTURE X(25) VALUE 'TWENTY NINE DOLLARS AND--'. 'SALARY'
00148   004280   02 FILLER PICTURE X(25) VALUE 'THIRTY DOLLARS AND-------'. 'SALARY'
00149   004290   02 FILLER PICTURE X(25) VALUE 'THIRTY ONE DOLLARS AND---'. 'SALARY'
00150   004300   02 FILLER PICTURE X(25) VALUE 'THIRTY TWO DOLLARS AND---'. 'SALARY'
00151   004310   02 FILLER PICTURE X(25) VALUE 'THIRTY THREE DOLLARS AND-'. 'SALARY'
00152   004320   02 FILLER PICTURE X(25) VALUE 'THIRTY FOUR DOLLARS AND--'. 'SALARY'
00153   004330   02 FILLER PICTURE X(25) VALUE 'THIRTY FIVE DOLLARS AND--'. 'SALARY'
00154   004340   02 FILLER PICTURE X(25) VALUE 'THIRTY SIX DOLLARS AND---'. 'SALARY'
00155   004350   02 FILLER PICTURE X(25) VALUE 'THIRTY SEVEN DOLLARS AND-'. 'SALARY'
00156   004360   02 FILLER PICTURE X(25) VALUE 'THIRTY EIGHT DOLLARS AND-'. 'SALARY'
```

```
00157   004370      02 FILLER PICTURE X(25) VALUE 'THIRTY NINE DOLLARS AND--'.    'SALARY'
00158   004380      02 FILLER PICTURE X(25) VALUE 'FORTY DOLLARS AND--------'.    'SALARY'
00159   004390      02 FILLER PICTURE X(25) VALUE 'FORTY ONE DOLLARS AND----'.    'SALARY'
00160   004400      02 FILLER PICTURE X(25) VALUE 'FORTY TWO DOLLARS AND-----'.   'SALARY'
00161   004410      02 FILLER PICTURE X(25) VALUE 'FORTY THREE DOLLARS AND---'.   'SALARY'
00162   004420      02 FILLER PICTURE X(25) VALUE 'FORTY FOUR DOLLARS AND---'.    'SALARY'
00163   004430      02 FILLER PICTURE X(25) VALUE 'FORTY FIVE DOLLARS AND---'.    'SALARY'
00164   004440      02 FILLER PICTURE X(25) VALUE 'FORTY SIX DOLLARS AND----'.    'SALARY'
00165   004450      02 FILLER PICTURE X(25) VALUE 'FORTY SEVEN DOLLARS AND--'.    'SALARY'
00166   004460      02 FILLER PICTURE X(25) VALUE 'FORTY EIGHT DOLLARS AND--'.    'SALARY'
00167   004470      02 FILLER PICTURE X(25) VALUE 'FORTY NINE DOLLARS AND---'.    'SALARY'
00168   004480      02 FILLER PICTURE X(25) VALUE 'FIFTY DOLLARS AND--------'.    'SALARY'
00169   004490      02 FILLER PICTURE X(25) VALUE 'FIFTY ONE DOLLARS AND----'.    'SALARY'
00170   004500      02 FILLER PICTURE X(25) VALUE 'FIFTY TWO DOLLARS AND-----'.   'SALARY'
00171   004510      02 FILLER PICTURE X(25) VALUE 'FIFTY THREE DOLLARS AND---'.   'SALARY'
00172   004520      02 FILLER PICTURE X(25) VALUE 'FIFTY FOUR DOLLARS AND---'.    'SALARY'
00173   004530      02 FILLER PICTURE X(25) VALUE 'FIFTY FIVE DOLLARS AND---'.    'SALARY'
00174   004540      02 FILLER PICTURE X(25) VALUE 'FIFTY SIX DOLLARS AND----'.    'SALARY'
00175   004550      02 FILLER PICTURE X(25) VALUE 'FIFTY SEVEN DOLLARS AND--'.    'SALARY'
00176   004560      02 FILLER PICTURE X(25) VALUE 'FIFTY EIGHT DOLLARS AND--'.    'SALARY'
00177   004570      02 FILLER PICTURE X(25) VALUE 'FIFTY NINE DOLLARS AND---'.    'SALARY'
00178   004580      02 FILLER PICTURE X(25) VALUE 'SIXTY DOLLARS AND--------'.    'SALARY'
00179   004590      02 FILLER PICTURE X(25) VALUE 'SIXTY ONE DOLLARS AND----'.    'SALARY'
00180   004600      02 FILLER PICTURE X(25) VALUE 'SIXTY TWO DOLLARS AND-----'.   'SALARY'
00181   004610      02 FILLER PICTURE X(25) VALUE 'SIXTY THREE DOLLARS AND---'.   'SALARY'
00182   004620      02 FILLER PICTURE X(25) VALUE 'SIXTY FOUR DOLLARS AND---'.    'SALARY'
00183   004630      02 FILLER PICTURE X(25) VALUE 'SIXTY FIVE DOLLARS AND---'.    'SALARY'
00184   004640      02 FILLER PICTURE X(25) VALUE 'SIXTY SIX DOLLARS AND----'.    'SALARY'
00185   004650      02 FILLER PICTURE X(25) VALUE 'SIXTY SEVEN DOLLARS AND--'.    'SALARY'
00186   004660      02 FILLER PICTURE X(25) VALUE 'SIXTY EIGHT DOLLARS AND--'.    'SALARY'
00187   004670      02 FILLER PICTURE X(25) VALUE 'SIXTY NINE DOLLARS AND---'.    'SALARY'
00188   004680      02 FILLER PICTURE X(25) VALUE 'SEVENTY DOLLARS AND------'.    'SALARY'
00189   004690      02 FILLER PICTURE X(25) VALUE 'SEVENTY ONE DOLLARS AND--'.    'SALARY'
00190   004700      02 FILLER PICTURE X(25) VALUE 'SEVENTY TWO DOLLARS AND--'.    'SALARY'
00191   004710      02 FILLER PICTURE X(25) VALUE 'SEVENTY THREE DOLLARS AND'.    'SALARY'
00192   004720      02 FILLER PICTURE X(25) VALUE 'SEVENTY FOUR DOLLARS AND-'.    'SALARY'
00193   004730      02 FILLER PICTURE X(25) VALUE 'SEVENTY FIVE DOLLARS AND-'.    'SALARY'
00194   004740      02 FILLER PICTURE X(25) VALUE 'SEVENTY SIX DOLLARS AND--'.    'SALARY'
00195   004750      02 FILLER PICTURE X(25) VALUE 'SEVENTY SEVEN DOLLARS AND'.    'SALARY'
```

```
00196   004760      02 FILLER PICTURE X(25) VALUE 'SEVENTY EIGHT DOLLARS AND'.    'SALARY'
00197   004770      02 FILLER PICTURE X(25) VALUE 'SEVENTY NINE DOLLARS AND-'.    'SALARY'
00198   004780      02 FILLER PICTURE X(25) VALUE 'EIGHTY DOLLARS AND-------'.    'SALARY'
00199   004790      02 FILLER PICTURE X(25) VALUE 'EIGHTY ONE DOLLARS AND---'.    'SALARY'
00200   004800      02 FILLER PICTURE X(25) VALUE 'EIGHTY TWO DOLLARS AND---'.    'SALARY'
00201   004910      02 FILLER PICTURE X(25) VALUE 'EIGHTY THREE DOLLARS AND-'.    'SALARY'
00202   004920      02 FILLER PICTURE X(25) VALUE 'EIGHTY FOUR DOLLARS AND--'.    'SALARY'
00203   004930      02 FILLER PICTURE X(25) VALUE 'EIGHTY FIVE DOLLARS AND--'.    'SALARY'
00204   004940      02 FILLER PICTURE X(25) VALUE 'EIGHTY SIX DOLLARS AND---'.    'SALARY'
00205   004950      02 FILLER PICTURE X(25) VALUE 'EIGHTY SEVEN DOLLARS AND-'.    'SALARY'
00206   004960      02 FILLER PICTURE X(25) VALUE 'EIGHTY EIGHT DOLLARS AND-'.    'SALARY'
00207   004970      02 FILLER PICTURE X(25) VALUE 'EIGHTY NINE DOLLARS AND--'.    'SALARY'
00208   004980      02 FILLER PICTURE X(25) VALUE 'NINETY DOLLARS AND ------'.    'SALARY'
00209   004990      02 FILLER PICTURE X(25) VALUE 'NINETY ONE DOLLARS AND---'.    'SALARY'
00210   004900      02 FILLER PICTURE X(25) VALUE 'NINETY TWO DOLLARS AND---'.    'SALARY'
00211   004910      02 FILLER PICTURE X(25) VALUE 'NINETY THREE DOLLARS AND-'.    'SALARY'
00212   004920      02 FILLER PICTURE X(25) VALUE 'NINETY FOUR DOLLARS AND--'.    'SALARY'
00213   004930      02 FILLER PICTURE X(25) VALUE 'NINETY FIVE DOLLARS AND--'.    'SALARY'
00214   004940      02 FILLER PICTURE X(25) VALUE 'NINETY SIX DOLLARS AND---'.    'SALARY'
00215   004950      02 FILLER PICTURE X(25) VALUE 'NINETY SEVEN DOLLARS AND-'.    'SALARY'
00216   004960      02 FILLER PICTURE X(25) VALUE 'NINETY EIGHT DOLLARS AND-'.    'SALARY'
00217   004970      02 FILLER PICTURE X(25) VALUE 'NINETY NINE DOLLARS AND--'.    'SALARY'
00218   004980 01  TABLE-DOLLAR REDEFINES DOLLAR-TABLE.                           'SALARY'
00219   004990      02 AMOUNT OCCURS 99 TIMES PICTURE X(25).                      'SALARY'
00220   005010 01  PRINT-LINE-1.                                                  'SALARY'
00221   005020      02 FILLER PICTURE X(27) VALUE SPACE.                          'SALARY'
00222   005030      02 FILLER PICTURE X(25) VALUE ALL '*'.                        'SALARY'
00223   005040      02 FILLER PICTURE X(25) VALUE ALL '*'.                        'SALARY'
00224   005050      02 FILLER PICTURE X(25) VALUE ALL '*'.                        'SALARY'
00225   005060      02 FILLER PICTURE XXX VALUE '***'.                            'SALARY'
00226   005070 01  PRINT-LINE-2.                                                  'SALARY'
00227   005080      02 FILLER VALUE SPACE PICTURE X(27).                          'SALARY'
00228   005090      02 FILLER PICTURE X VALUE '*'.                                'SALARY'
00229   005100      02 FILLER VALUE SPACE PICTURE X(76).                          'SALARY'
00230   005110      02 FILLER PICTURE X VALUE '*'.                                'SALARY'
00231   005120 01  PRINT-LINE-3.                                                  'SALARY'
00232   005130      02 FILLER VALUE SPACE PICTURE X(27).                          'SALARY'
00233   005140      02 FILLER PICTURE X VALUE '*'.                                'SALARY'
00234   005150      02 FILLER PICTURE X(4) VALUE 'HRS.'.                          'SALARY'
```

```
00235   005160      02 FILLER VALUE SPACE PICTURE X.                              'SALARY'
00236   005170      02 TIME-1 PICTURE 999.9.                                      'SALARY'
00237   005180      02 FILLER PICTURE XXX VALUE ' . '.                            'SALARY'
00238   005190      02 FILLER PICTURE X(6) VALUE 'GROSS '.                        'SALARY'
00239   005200      02 GROSS PICTURE $$$9.99.                                     'SALARY'
00240   005210      02 FILLER VALUE SPACE PICTURE X.                              'SALARY'
00241   005220      02 FILLER PICTURE X(9) VALUE '. FED-TX'.                      'SALARY'
00242   005230      02 WH-TAX PICTURE $$$9.99.                                    'SALARY'
00243   005240      02 FILLER VALUE SPACE PICTURE X.                              'SALARY'
00244   005250      02 FILLER PICTURE X(10) VALUE '. FICA-TX '.                   'SALARY'
00245   005260      02 FICA PICTURE $$$9.99.                                      'SALARY'
00246   005270      02 FILLER VALUE SPACE PICTURE X.                              'SALARY'
00247   005280      02 FILLER PICTURE X(6) VALUE '. NET '.                        'SALARY'
00248   005290      02 NET-1 PICTURE $$$9.99.                                     'SALARY'
00249   005300      02 FILLER PICTURE XX VALUE ' *'.                              'SALARY'
00250   005310 01   PRINT-LINE-4.                                                 'SALARY'
00251   005320      02 FILLER VALUE SPACE PICTURE X(27).                          'SALARY'
00252   005330      02 FILLER PICTURE X(25) VALUE '*------------------------'.    'SALARY'
00253   005340      02 FILLER PICTURE X(25) VALUE '-------------------------'.    'SALARY'
00254   005350      02 FILLER PICTURE X(25) VALUE '-------------------------'.    'SALARY'
00255   005360      02 FILLER PICTURE XXX VALUE '--*'.                            'SALARY'
00256   005370 01   PRINT-LINE-5.                                                 'SALARY'
00257   005380      02 FILLER VALUE SPACE PICTURE X(27).                          'SALARY'
00258   005390      02 FILLER PICTURE XX VALUE '* '.                              'SALARY'
00259   005400      02 CHECK-NO PICTURE ZZ9.                                      'SALARY'
00260   005410      02 FILLER PICTURE X(26) VALUE SPACE.                          'SALARY'
00261   005420      02 FILLER PICTURE X(19) VALUE 'CRESTVIEW MOTOR CO.'.          'SALARY'
00262   005430      02 FILLER PICTURE X(26) VALUE SPACE.                          'SALARY'
00263   005440      02 FILLER PICTURE XX VALUE ' *'.                              'SALARY'
00264   005450 01   PRINT-LINE-7.                                                 'SALARY'
00265   005460      02 FILLER PICTURE X(27) VALUE SPACE.                          'SALARY'
00266   005470      02 FILLER PICTURE X VALUE '*'.                                'SALARY'
00267   005480      02 FILLER VALUE SPACE PICTURE X(30).                          'SALARY'
00268   005490      02 FILLER PICTURE X(18) VALUE '9240 WILSHIRE BLVD'.           'SALARY'
00269   005500      02 FILLER VALUE SPACE PICTURE X(28).                          'SALARY'
00270   005510      02 FILLER PICTURE X VALUE '*'.                                'SALARY'
00271   005520 01   PRINT-LINE-6.                                                 'SALARY'
00272   005530      02 FILLER VALUE SPACE PICTURE X(27).                          'SALARY'
00273   005540      02 FILLER PICTURE X VALUE '*'.                                'SALARY'
```

```
00274   005550      02 FILLER VALUE SPACE PICTURE X(32).                          'SALARY'
00275   005560      02 FILLER PICTURE X(13) VALUE 'BEVERLY HILLS'.                'SALARY'
00276   005570      02 FILLER VALUE SPACE PICTURE X(22).                          'SALARY'
00277   005580      02 DATE-1 PICTURE X(8).                                       'SALARY'
00278   005590      02 FILLER VALUE SPACE PICTURE X.                              'SALARY'
00279   005600      02 FILLER PICTURE X VALUE '*'.                                'SALARY'
00280   005610 01   PRINT-LINE-8.                                                 'SALARY'
00281   005620      02 FILLER VALUE SPACE PICTURE X(27).                          'SALARY'
00282   005630      02 FILLER PICTURE X(11) VALUE '*       PAY'.                  'SALARY'
00283   005640      02 FILLER VALUE SPACE PICTURE X(66).                          'SALARY'
00284   005650      02 FILLER PICTURE X VALUE '*'.                                'SALARY'
00285   005660 01   PRINT-LINE-9.                                                 'SALARY'
00286   005670      02 FILLER VALUE SPACE PICTURE X(27).                          'SALARY'
00287   005680      02 FILLER PICTURE X(15) VALUE '*       TO THE'.               'SALARY'
00288   005690      02 FILLER VALUE SPACE PICTURE X(62).                          'SALARY'
00289   005700      02 FILLER PICTURE X VALUE '*'.                                'SALARY'
00290   005710 01   PRINT-LINE-10.                                                'SALARY'
00291   005720      02 FILLER VALUE SPACE PICTURE X(27).                          'SALARY'
00292   005730      02 FILLER PICTURE X(24) VALUE '*       ORDER OF       '.      'SALARY'
00293   005740      02 NAME-PRINT PICTURE A(29).                                  'SALARY'
00294   005750      02 FILLER VALUE SPACE PICTURE X(16).                          'SALARY'
00295   005760      02 NET-2 PICTURE $$$9.99.                                     'SALARY'
00296   005770      02 FILLER PICTURE XX VALUE ' *'.                              'SALARY'
00297   005780 01   PRINT-LINE-11.                                                'SALARY'
00298   005790      02 FILLER VALUE SPACE PICTURE X(27).                          'SALARY'
00299   005800      02 FILLER PICTURE X(9) VALUE '*        '.                     'SALARY'
00300   005810      02 PRINT-HUNDRED PICTURE A(13).                               'SALARY'
00301   005820      02 FILLER PICTURE X VALUE SPACE.                              'SALARY'
00302   005830      02 FIFTY-PRINT PICTURE X(25).                                 'SALARY'
00303   005840      02 CENT PICTURE 99.                                           'SALARY'
00304   005850      02 FILLER PICTURE X VALUE '/'.                                'SALARY'
00305   005860      02 FILLER PICTURE XX VALUE 'XX'.                              'SALARY'
00306   005870      02 FILLER PICTURE X(26) VALUE '                         *'.   'SALARY'
00307   005880 01   PRINT-LINE-12.                                                'SALARY'
00308   005890      02 FILLER VALUE SPACE PICTURE X(27).                          'SALARY'
00309   005900      02 FILLER PICTURE X(21) VALUE '*       BANK OF THE U.S.'.     'SALARY'
00310   005910      02 FILLER VALUE SPACE PICTURE X(56).                          'SALARY'
00311   005920      02 FILLER PICTURE X VALUE '*'.                                'SALARY'
00312   005930 01   PRINT-LINE-13.                                                'SALARY'
```

```
00313   005940      02 FILLER VALUE SPACE PICTURE X(27).              'SALARY'
00314   005950      02 FILLER PICTURE X(23) VALUE '*   9250 WILSHIRE BLVD'.  'SALARY'
00315   005960      02 FILLER VALUE SPACE PICTURE X(35).              'SALARY'
00316   005970      02 FILLER PICTURE X(20) VALUE '--------------------*'.   'SALARY'
00317   005980  01 PRINT-LINE-14.                                     'SALARY'
00318   005990      02 FILLER VALUE SPACE PICTURE X(27).              'SALARY'
00319   006010      02 FILLER PICTURE X(26) VALUE '*    BEVERLY HILLS, CALIF'.  'SALARY'
00320   006020      02 FILLER VALUE SPACE PICTURE X(51).              'SALARY'
00321   006030      02 FILLER PICTURE X VALUE '*'.                    'SALARY'
00322   006040  01 LAST-RECORD.                                       'SALARY'
00323   006050      02 PAY.                                           'SALARY'
00324   006060         03 FIRS PICTURE 9.                             'SALARY'
00325   006070         03 SECOND PICTURE 99.                          'SALARY'
00326   006080         03 CENTS PICTURE 99.                           'SALARY'
00327   006090      02 FILLER VALUE SPACE PICTURE X(128).             'SALARY'
00328   006100 PROCEDURE DIVISION.                                    'SALARY'
00329   006110 BEGIN.                                                 'SALARY'
00330   006120      OPEN INPUT MASTER-FILE, OUTPUT MASTER-FILE-OUT, MASTER-PUNCH.  'SALARY'
00331   006130      GO TO BEGAN-JOB.                                  'SALARY'
00332   006140 TAX-ROUTINE-1.                                         'SALARY'
00333   006150      MULTIPLY GROSS-PAY BY .18 GIVING FED-TX ROUNDED.  'SALARY'
00334   006160 BEGAN-JOB.                                             'SALARY'
00335   006170      READ MASTER-FILE AT END GO TO LOCK-OUT.          'SALARY'
00336   006180      ADD 1 TO COUNT.                                   'SALARY'
00337   006190      COMPUTE GROSS-PAY ROUNDED = (REG-HRS * RATE) + (RATE * 1.5  'SALARY'
00338   006200      * OVT-HRS).                                       'SALARY'
00339   006210      IF CODE-1 EQUAL TO KODE GO TO AFRICA-PROCESS.     'SALARY'
00340   006220      IF NUMBER-1 EQUAL TO NONE GO TO TAX-ROUTINE.      'SALARY'
00341   006230      MOVE DEPENDENTS (NUMBER-1) TO DEDUCTION.          'JALARY'
00342   006240      IF GROSS-PAY IS GREATER THAN DEDUCTION SUBTRACT DEDUCTION  'SALARY'
00343   006250      FROM GROSS-PAY GIVING TX-AMOUNT, ELSE GO TO FICA-ROUTINE.  'SALARY'
00344   006260      MULTIPLY TX-AMOUNT BY .18 GIVING FED-TX ROUNDED.  'SALARY'
00345   006270      GO TO FICA-ROUTINE.                               'SALARY'
00346   006280 TAX-ROUTINE.                                           'SALARY'
00347   006290      PERFORM TAX-ROUTINE-1.                            'SALARY'
00348   006300 FICA-ROUTINE.                                          'SALARY'
00349   006310      IF YTD-GROSS IS LESS THAN FICA-LIMIT SUBTRACT YTD-GROSS  'SALARY'
00350   006320      FROM FICA-LIMIT GIVING DIFFERENT, ELSE GO TO STATE.  'SALARY'
00351   006330      IF DIFFERENT IS GREATER THAN GROSS-PAY MULTIPLY GROSS-PAY  'SALARY'
```

```
00352   006340      BY .052 GIVING FICA-1 ROUNDED, ELSE MULTIPLY DIFFERENT  'SALARY'
00353   006350      BY .052 GIVING FICA-1 ROUNDED.                    'SALARY'
00354   006360 STATE.                                                 'SALARY'
00355   006370      ADD GROSS-PAY TO YTD-GROSS.                       'SALARY'
00356   006380      COMPUTE NET-PAY = GROSS-PAY - FED-TX - FICA-1.    'SALARY'
00357   006390      GO TO PRINT-OUT.                                  'SALARY'
00358   006400 AFRICA-PROCESS.                                        'SALARY'
00359   006410      IF YTD-GROSS IS LESS THAN FICA-LIMIT SUBTRACT YTD-GROSS  'SALARY'
00360   006420      FROM FICA-LIMIT GIVING DIFFERENT, ELSE GO TO STATE-1.  'SALARY'
00361   006430      IF DIFFERENT IS GREATER THAN GROSS-PAY MULTIPLY GROSS-PAY  'SALARY'
00362   006431      BY .052 GIVING FICA-1 ROUNDED, ELSE MULTIPLY DIFFERENT  'SALARY'
00363   006450      BY .052 GIVING FICA-1 ROUNDED.                    'SALARY'
00364   006460 STATE-1.                                               'SALARY'
00365   006470      ADD GROSS-PAY TO YTD-GROSS.                       'SALARY'
00366   006480      COMPUTE NET-PAY = GROSS-PAY - FICA-1.             'SALARY'
00367   006490 PRINT-OUT.                                             'SALARY'
00368   006500      MOVE SPACE TO PUNCH-OUT.                          'SALARY'
00369   006510      MOVE NUMBER-1 TO NUMBER-2.                        'SALARY'
00370   006520      MOVE RATE TO RATE-1.                              'SALARY'
00371   006530      MOVE CODE-1 TO CODE-4.                            'SALARY'
00372   006540      MOVE YTD-GROSS TO YTD-GROSS-1.                    'SALARY'
00373   006550      MOVE NUM TO NUM-4.                                'SALARY'
00374   006560      WRITE PUNCH-OUT.                                  'SALARY'
00375   006570      MOVE NET-PAY TO PAY.                              'SALARY'
00376   006580      IF FIRS  IS NOT EQUAL TO ZERO MOVE HUNDRED (FIRS)  TO  'SALARY'
00377   006590      PRINT-HUNDRED.                                    'SALARY'
00378   006600      IF SECOND IS NOT EQUAL TO ZERO MOVE AMOUNT (SECOND) TO  'SALARY'
00379   006610      FIFTY-PRINT.                                      'SALARY'
00380   006620      IF CENTS IS NOT EQUAL TO ZERO MOVE CENTS TO CENT  'SALARY'
00381   006630      WRITE RECORD-OUT FROM PRINT-LINE-1 AFTER POSITIONING 1 LINES.'SALARY'
00382   006640      GO TO DESIGN-1.                                   'SALARY'
00383   006650 DESIGN.                                                'SALARY'
00384   006660      WRITE RECORD-OUT FROM PRINT-LINE AFTER POSITIONING 1 LINES.  'SALARY'
00385   006670 DESIGN-1.                                              'SALARY'
00386   006680      PERFORM DESIGN 2 TIMES.                           'SALARY'
00387   006690      MOVE REG-HRS TO TIME-1.                           'SALARY'
00388   006700      MOVE GROSS-PAY TO GROSS.                          'SALARY'
00389   006710      MOVE FED-TX TO WH-TAX.                            'SALARY'
00390   006720      MOVE FICA-1 TO FICA.                              'SALARY'
```

```
00391   006730          MOVE NET-PAY TO NET-1.                                          'SALARY'
00392   006740          WRITE RECORD-OUT FROM PRINT-LINE-3 AFTER POSITIONING 1 LINES.   'SALARY'
00393   006750          PERFORM DESIGN 2 TIMES.                                         'SALARY'
00394   006760          WRITE RECORD-OUT FROM PRINT-LINE-4 AFTER POSITIONING 1 LINES.   'SALARY'
00395   006770          GO TO DESIGN-2.                                                 'SALARY'
00396   006780 DESIGN-3.                                                                'SALARY'
00397   006790          WRITE RECORD-OUT FROM PRINT-LINE-2 AFTER POSITIONING 1 LINES.   'SALARY'
00398   006800 DESIGN-2.                                                                'SALARY'
00399   006810          PERFORM DESIGN-3.                                               'SALARY'
00400   006820          GO TO STOP-1.                                                   'SALARY'
00401   006830 GAP-1.                                                                   'SALARY'
00402   006840          MOVE SPACES TO AREA-1.                                          'SALARY'
00403   006850          WRITE RECORD-OUT FROM AREA-1 AFTER POSITIONING 1 LINES.         'SALARY'
00404   006860 STOP-1.                                                                  'SALARY'
00405   006870          WRITE RECORD-OUT FROM PRINT-LINE-1 AFTER POSITIONING 1 LINES.   'SALARY'
00406   006880          PERFORM DESIGN-3.                                               'SALARY'
00407   006890          MOVE COUNT TO CHECK-NO.                                         'SALARY'
00408   006900          MOVE DATE TO DATE-1.                                            'SALARY'
00409   006910          WRITE RECORD-OUT FROM PRINT-LINE-5 AFTER POSITIONING 1 LINES.   'SALARY'
00410   006920          WRITE RECORD-OUT FROM PRINT-LINE-7 AFTER POSITIONING 1 LINES.   'SALARY'
00411   006930          WRITE RECORD-OUT FROM PRINT-LINE-6 AFTER POSITIONING 1 LINES.   'SALARY'
00412   006940          PERFORM DESIGN-3.                                               'SALARY'
00413   006950          WRITE RECORD-OUT FROM PRINT-LINE-8 AFTER POSITIONING 1 LINES.   'SALARY'
00414   006960          WRITE RECORD-OUT FROM PRINT-LINE-9 AFTER POSITIONING 1 LINES.   'SALARY'
00415   006970          MOVE NAME TO NAME-PRINT.                                        'SALARY'
00416   006980          MOVE NET-PAY TO NET-2.                                          'SALARY'
00417   006990          WRITE RECORD-OUT FROM PRINT-LINE-10 AFTER POSITIONING 1         'SALARY'
00418   007010          LINES.                                                          'SALARY'
00419   007020          PERFORM DESIGN-3.                                               'SALARY'
00420   007030          WRITE RECORD-OUT FROM PRINT-LINE-11 AFTER POSITIONING 1         'SALARY'
00421   007040          LINES.                                                          'SALARY'
00422   007050          PERFORM DESIGN-3 2 TIMES.                                       'SALARY'
00423   007060          WRITE RECORD-OUT FROM PRINT-LINE-12 AFTER POSITIONING 1         'SALARY'
00424   007070          LINES.                                                          'SALARY'
00425   007080          WRITE RECORD-OUT FROM PRINT-LINE-13 AFTER POSITIONING 1         'SALARY'
00426   007090          LINES.                                                          'SALARY'
00427   007100          WRITE RECORD-OUT FROM PRINT-LINE-14 AFTER POSITIONING 1         BILLINGR
00428   007110          LINES.                                                          'SALARY'
00429   007120          PERFORM DESIGN-3.                                               'SALARY'
```

```
00430   007130          WRITE RECORD-OUT FROM PRINT-LINE-1 AFTER POSITIONING 1 LINES.   'SALARY'
00431   007140          MOVE ZERO TO NUMBER-1, FICA-1, NET-PAY, DIFFERENT, FED-TX.      'SALARY'
00432   007150          PERFORM GAP-1 4 TIMES.                                          'SALARY'
00433   007160          GO TO BEGAN-JOB.                                                'SALARY'
00434   007170 LOCK-OUT.                                                                'SALARY'
00435   007180          CLOSE MASTER-FILE, MASTER-FILE-OUT, MASTER-PUNCH.               'SALARY'
00436   007190          STOP RUN.                                                       'SALARY'
```

```
// EXEC
```

```
**********************************************************************************
*             .             .             .             .             .         *
*HRS. 160.0 . GROSS $753.75 . FED-TX  $95.36 . FICA-TX  $39.20 . NET $619.19 *
*             .             .             .             .             .         *
*             .             .             .             .             .         *
*------------------------------------------------------------------------------*
*                                                                              *
**********************************************************************************
* 101                       CRESTVIEW MOTOR CO.                                *
*                           9240 WILSHIRE BLVD                                 *
*                           BEVERLY HILLS                                      *
*                                                                              *
*        PAY                                                                   *
*        TO THE                                                                *
*        ORDER OF       JAMES RAINEY                              $619.19 *
*                                                                              *
*        SIX HUNDRED NINETEEN DOLLARS AND-----19/XX                            *
*                                                                              *
*                                                                              *
*        BANK OF THE U.S.                                                      *
*        9250 WILSHIRE BLVD                         ------------------- *
*        BEVERLY HILLS, CALIF                                                  *
**********************************************************************************
```

Illustrative Problem 2
USING READY TRACE DEBUGGING FEATURE

This is a "trigger" routine to compare STOCK LEVELS with quantity on hand in the LEVELS file. Input will be a LEVELS card containing the following:

Field	Card Columns
Identification Number	1 - 10
Level A	11 - 14
Level B	15 - 18
Level C	19 - 22
Quantity on Hand	23 - 26
Blanks	27 - 80

Assume that one card will contain all the data to be processed and that the quantity on hand is current.

Fields A, B, and C, represent stock levels. They are never equal. Find the field with the largest level and compare it with the quantity on hand. If the level is equal or less than the quantity on hand, all is well and the record is bypassed. If the level is greater than the quantity on hand, the material must be reordered. A record is punched into a card called OUTPUT RE-ORDER CARD as follows:

Field	Card Columns
Identification Number	1 - 10
Quantity on Hand	11 - 14
Blanks	15 - 17
Applicable Level	18 - 21
Blanks	22 - 80

The job is finished when the end-of-file is reached.
Write program to solve this problem.

```
00001   001010 IDENTIFICATION DIVISION.                                   LEVELSPR
00002   001020 PROGRAM-ID.                                                LEVELSPR
00003   001030     LEVELS-PROBLEM.                                        LEVELSPR
00004   001040 AUTHOR.                                                    LEVELSPR
00005   001050     C. FEINGOLD.                                           LEVELSPR
00006   001060 REMARKS                                                    LEVELSPR
00007   001070     THIS IS A TRIGGER ROUTINE TO COMPARE STOCK LEVELS WITH LEVELSPR
00008   001080     QUANTITY ON HAND IN THE LEVEL FILE.                    LEVELSPR
00009   002010 ENVIRONMENT DIVISION.                                      LEVELSPR
00010   002020 CONFIGURATION SECTION.                                     LEVELSPR
00011   002030 SOURCE-COMPUTER.                                           LEVELSPR
00012   002040     IBM-360-H50.                                           LEVELSPR
00013   002050 OBJECT-COMPUTER.                                           LEVELSPR
00014   002060     IBM-360-H50.                                           LEVELSPR
00015   002070 INPUT-OUTPUT SECTION.                                      LEVELSPR
00016   002080 FILE-CONTROL.                                              LEVELSPR
00017   002090     SELECT LEVEL-IN ASSIGN TO SYS009-UR-2540R-S.           LEVELSPR
00018   002100     SELECT LEVEL-OUT ASSIGN TO SYS005-UR-1403-S.           LEVELSPR
00019   002110     SELECT LEVEL-PUNCH ASSIGN TO SYS006-UR-2540P-S.        LEVELSPR
00020   003010 DATA DIVISION.                                             LEVELSPR
00021   003020 FILE SECTION.                                              LEVELSPR
00022   003030 FD  LEVEL-IN                                               LEVELSPR
00023   003040     RECORDING IS F                                         LEVELSPR
00024   003050     LABEL RECORDS ARE OMITTED                              LEVELSPR
00025   003060     RECORD CONTAINS 80 CHARACTERS                          LEVELSPR
00026   003070     DATA RECORD IS LEVELS-RECORDS.                         LEVELSPR
00027   003080 01  LEVELS-RECORDS.                                        LEVELSPR
00028   003090     02  IDENT-NO    PICTURE 9(10).                         LEVELSPR
00029   003100     02  LEVEL-A     PICTURE 9999.                          LEVELSPR
00030   003110     02  LEVEL-B     PICTURE 9999.                          LEVELSPR
00031   003120     02  LEVEL-C     PICTURE 9999.                          LEVELSPR
00032   003130     02  QTY-O-HAND  PICTURE 9999.                          LEVELSPR
00033   003140     02  FILLER      PICTURE X(54).                         LEVELSPR
00034   003150 FD  LEVEL-OUT                                              LEVELSPR
00035   003160     RECORDING MODE IS F                                    LEVELSPR
00036   003170     LABEL RECORDS ARE OMITTED                              LEVELSPR
00037   003180     DATA RECORD IS REORDER-CARD.                           LEVELSPR
00038   003190 01  REORDER-CARD    PICTURE IS X(133).                     LEVELSPR
00039   003200 FD  LEVEL-PUNCH                                            LEVELSPR
```

```
00040   003210     RECORDING MODE IS F                                    LEVELSPR
00041   003220     LABEL RECORDS ARE OMITTED                              LEVELSPR
00042   003230     DATA RECORD IS PUNCH-OUT.                              LEVELSPR
00043   003240 01  PUNCH-OUT       PICTURE IS X(80).                      LEVELSPR
00044   003250 WORKING-STORAGE SECTION.                                   LEVELSPR
00045   003260 01  EDITED-OUTPUT.                                         LEVELSPR
00046   003270     02  FILLER      PICTURE IS XXXX VALUE IS SPACES.       LEVELSPR
00047   003280     02  IDENT-OUT   PICTURE IS X(10).                      LEVELSPR
00048   003290     02  FILLER      PICTURE IS XXXX VALUE IS SPACES.       LEVELSPR
00049   003300     02  QTY-TO-ORDER PICTURE IS ZZZ9.                      LEVELSPR
00050   003310     02  FILLER      PICTURE IS XXXX VALUE IS SPACES.       LEVELSPR
00051   003320     02  LEVEL-SELECT   PICTURE IS ZZZ9.                    LEVELSPR
00052   003330     02  FILLER      PICTURE IS XXXX   VALUE IS SPACES.     LEVELSPR
00053   003340     02  Q-O-HAND    PICTURE IS ZZZ9.                       LEVELSPR
00054   003350     02  FILLER      PICTURE IS X(94) VALUE IS SPACES.      LEVELSPR
00055   003360 01  PUNCH-OUT.                                             LEVELSPR
00056   003370     02  ID-NO   PICTURE IS 9(10).                          LEVELSPR
00057   003380     02  Q-ON-H  PICTURE IS 9999.                           LEVELSPR
00058   003390     02  FILLER  PICTURE IS XXX VALUE IS SPACES.            LEVELSPR
00059   003400     02  THE-LEVEL   PICTURE IS 9999.                       LEVELSPR
00060   003410     02  FILLER PICTURE IS X(59) VALUE IS SPACES.           LEVELSPR
00061   003420 PROCEDURE DIVISION.                                        LEVELSPR
00062   003430     READY TRACE.                                           LEVELSPR
00063   003440 START-1. OPEN INPUT LEVEL-IN, OUTPUT LEVEL-OUT, LEVEL-PUNCH. LEVELSPR
00064   003450     MOVE SPACES TO REORDER-CARD.                           LEVELSPR
00065   003460 READ-1.                                                    LEVELSPR
00066   003470     READ LEVEL-IN; AT END GO TO END-OF-JOB.                LEVELSPR
00067   003480     IF LEVEL-A IS GREATER THAN LEVEL-B                     LEVELSPR
00068   003490     GO TO NEXT-1; OTHERWISE GO TO NEXT-3.                  LEVELSPR
00069   003500 NEXT-1.                                                    LEVELSPR
00070   003510     IF LEVEL-A IS GREATER THAN LEVEL-C                     LEVELSPR
00071   003520     GO TO HIGH-LEVEL-A; OTHERWISE GO TO NEXT-2.            LEVELSPR
00072   003530 NEXT-2.                                                    LEVELSPR
00073   003540     IF LEVEL-C IS GREATER THAN LEVEL-B                     LEVELSPR
00074   003550     GO TO HIGH-LEVEL-C; OTHERWISE GO TO NEXT-3.            LEVELSPR
00075   003560 NEXT-3.                                                    LEVELSPR
00076   003570     IF LEVEL-B IS GREATER THAN LEVEL-C                     LEVELSPR
00077   003580     GO TO HIGH-LEVEL-B; OTHERWISE GO TO NEXT-1.            LEVELSPR
00078   003590 HIGH-LEVEL-A.                                              LEVELSPR
```

3

```
00079    003600     IF LEVEL-A IS LESS THAN QTY-O-HAND GO TO READ-1.     LEVELSPR
00080    003610     MOVE LEVEL-A TO QTY-TO-ORDER, THE-LEVEL.             LEVELSPR
00081    003620     MOVE LEVEL-A TO LEVEL-SELECT.                        LEVELSPR
00082    003630     GO TO PRIN.                                          LEVELSPR
00083    003640 HIGH-LEVEL-B.                                            LEVELSPR
00084    003650     IF LEVEL-B IS LESS THAN QTY-O-HAND GO TO READ-1.     LEVELSPR
00085    003660     MOVE LEVEL-B TO QTY-TO-ORDER, THE-LEVEL.             LEVELSPR
00086    003670     MOVE LEVEL-B TO LEVEL-SELECT.                        LEVELSPR
00087    003680     GO TO PRIN.                                          LEVELSPR
00088    003690 HIGH-LEVEL-C.                                            LEVELSPR
00089    003700     IF LEVEL-C IS LESS THAN QTY-O-HAND GO TO READ-1.     LEVELSPR
00090    003710     MOVE LEVEL-C TO QTY-TO-ORDER, THE-LEVEL.             LEVELSPR
00091    003720     MOVE LEVEL-C TO LEVEL-SELECT.                        LEVELSPR
00092    003730     GO TO PRIN.                                          LEVELSPR
00093    003740 PRIN.                                                    LEVELSPR
00094    003750     MOVE IDENT-NO TO IDENT-OUT, IN-NO.                   LEVELSPR
00095    003760     MOVE QTY-O-HAND TO Q-ON-H, Q-O-HAND.                 LEVELSPR
00096    003770     WRITE REORDER-CARD FROM EDITED-OUTPUT,               LEVELSPR
00097    003780     WRITE PUNCH-OUT FROM PUNCH-OUT.                      LEVELSPR
00098    003790     GO TO READ-1.                                        LEVELSPR
00099    003800 END-OF-JOB.                                              LEVELSPR
00100    003810     CLOSE LEVEL-IN, LEVEL-OUT, LEVEL-PUNCH.              LEVELSPR
00101    003820     STOP RUN.                                            LEVELSPR
```


// EXEC

```
63
65
69
78
93  0123456789    1234    1234    234

65
69
78
65
75
83
93  1234567890 ·  1211    1211    211

65
75
83
65
75
69
72
88
93  2345678901    4411    4411    412

65
75
69
72
88
65
99
```

Illustrative Problem 3
INVOICE DESIGN AND BILLING PROBLEM

Customers invoices are prepared at the end of the month. Write a program to perform invoice billing and also design an invoice form.

Input will contain the following:

Data Item	Card Columns
Part Number	1 - 5
Blank	6
Item Description	7 - 19
Blank	20
Units	21 - 23
Blank	24
Unit Cost	25 - 29
Blank	30
Street	31 - 34
City and State	45 - 55
Blank	56
Date	57 - 64
Invoice Number	65 - 67
Name	68 - 80

```
00001    001010 IDENTIFICATION DIVISION.                                          BILLINGR
00002    001020 PROGRAM-ID. BILLING.                                              BILLINGR
00003    001030 AUTHOR. C. FEINGOLD.                                              BILLINGR
00004    001040 DATE-WRITTEN.   JUNE 19 1972.                                     BILLINGR
00005    001050 DATE-COMPILED. 10/27/72                                           BILLINGR
00006    001060 REMARKS.                                                          BILLINGR
00007    001070      THIS PROGRAM WILL PERFORM THE INVOICE BILLING FOR THE        BILLINGR
00008    001080      MONTH AND ALSO DESIGN THE INVOICE FORM.                      BILLINGR
00009    002010 ENVIRONMENT DIVISION.                                             BILLINGR
00010    002020 CONFIGURATION SECTION.                                            BILLINGR
00011    002030 SOURCE-COMPUTER.                                                  BILLINGR
00012    002040      IBM-360-H50.                                                 BILLINGR
00013    002050 OBJECT-COMPUTER.                                                  BILLINGR
00014    002060      IBM-360-H50.                                                 BILLINGR
00015    002070 INPUT-OUTPUT SECTION.                                             BILLINGR
00016    002080 FILE-CONTROL.                                                     BILLINGR
00017    002090      SELECT FILE-IN                                               BILLINGR
00018    002100           ASSIGN TO SYS009-UR-2540R-S.                            BILLINGR
00019    002110      SELECT FILE-OUT                                              BILLINGR
00020    002120           ASSIGN TO SYS005-UR-1403-S.                             BILLINGR
00021    003010 DATA DIVISION.                                                    BILLINGR
00022    003020 FILE SECTION.                                                     BILLINGR
00023    003030 FD  FILE-IN                                                       BILLINGR
00024    003040      RECORDING MODE IS F                                          BILLINGR
00025    003045      RECORD CONTAINS 80 CHARACTERS                                BILLINGR
00026    003050      LABEL RECORD IS OMITTED                                      BILLINGR
00027    003060      DATA RECORD IS RECORD-IN.                                    BILLINGR
00028    003070 01  RECORD-IN.                                                    BILLINGR
00029    003080      02 PART-NO PICTURE 99999.                                    BILLINGR
00030    003090      02 FILLER PICTURE X.                                         BILLINGR
00031    003100      02 ITEM-DESCRIPTION PICTURE A(13).                           BILLINGR
00032    003110      02 FILLER PICTURE X.                                         BILLINGR
00033    003120      02 NO-ORDERED PICTURE 999.                                   BILLINGR
00034    003130      02 FILLER PICTURE X.                                         BILLINGR
00035    003140      02 UNIT-COST PICTURE 999V99.                                 BILLINGR
00036    003150      02 FILLER PICTURE X.                                         BILLINGR
00037    003160      02 CUST-ADDRESS.                                             BILLINGR
00038    003170         03 STREET-1 PICTURE X(14).                               BILLINGR
00039    003180         03 STATE-CITY PICTURE A(11).                             BILLINGR
```

```
00040    003185      02 FILLER PICTURE X.                                         BILLINGR
00041    003200      02 DATE-1 PICTURE X(8).                                      BILLINGR
00042    003210      02 INVOICE-NO PICTURE 999.                                   BILLINGR
00043    003220      02 NAME PICTURE A(13).                                       BILLINGR
00044    003230 FD  FILE-OUT                                                      BILLINGR
00045    003240      RECORDING MODE IS F                                          BILLINGR
00046    003250      LABEL RECORD IS OMITTED                                      BILLINGR
00047    003260      DATA RECORD IS RECORD-OUT.                                   BILLINGR
00048    003270 01  RECORD-OUT PICTURE X(133).                                    BILLINGR
00049    003280 WORKING-STORAGE SECTION.                                          BILLINGR
00050    003290 77  COMPARE-1 PICTURE 999 VALUE ZERO.                             BILLINGR
00051    003300 77  COMPARE-2 PICTURE 999 VALUE ZERO.                             BILLINGR
00052    003310 77  COUNTER PICTURE 99 VALUE ZEROS.                               BILLINGR
00053    003320 77  DIFFERENT PICTURE 99 VALUE ZEROS.                             BILLINGR
00054    003330 77  TOTAL-ORDERED PICTURE 999 VALUE ZEROS.                        BILLINGR
00055    003340 77  SUM-O PICTURE 9999V99 VALUE ZEROS.                            BILLINGR
00056    003350 77  GRAND-SUM PICTURE 9999V99 VALUE ZEROS.                        BILLINGR
00057    003360 77  LIMIT-WS PICTURE 99 VALUE 19.                                 BILLINGR
00058    003370 01  DESIGN.                                                       BILLINGR
00059    003380      02 FILLER VALUE SPACE PICTURE X(31).                         BILLINGR
00060    003390      02 FILLER PICTURE X(71) VALUE ALL '*'.                       BILLINGR
00061    003400      02 FILLER VALUE SPACE PICTURE X(31).                         BILLINGR
00062    003410 01  DESIGN-1.                                                     BILLINGR
00063    003420      02 FILLER VALUE SPACE PICTURE X(31).                         BILLINGR
00064    003430      02 FILLER PICTURE X VALUE '*'.                               BILLINGR
00065    003440      02 FILLER PICTURE X(5) VALUE 'DATE.'.                        BILLINGR
00066    003450      02 FILLER VALUE SPACE PICTURE X.                             BILLINGR
00067    003460      02 DATE-1 PICTURE X(8).                                      BILLINGR
00068    003470      02 FILLER VALUE SPACE PICTURE X(40).                         BILLINGR
00069    003480      02 FILLER PICTURE X(11) VALUE 'INVOICE-NO.'.                 BILLINGR
00070    003490      02 FILLER VALUE SPACE PICTURE X.                             BILLINGR
00071    003500      02 INVOICE PICTURE 999.                                      BILLINGR
00072    003510      02 FILLER PICTURE X VALUE '*'.                               BILLINGR
00073    003520      02 FILLER VALUE SPACE PICTURE X(31).                         BILLINGR
00074    003530 01  DESIGN-2.                                                     BILLINGR
00075    003540      02 FILLER VALUE SPACE PICTURE X(31).                         BILLINGR
00076    003550      02 FILLER PICTURE X VALUE '*'.                               BILLINGR
00077    003560      02 FILLER VALUE SPACE PICTURE X(69).                         BILLINGR
00078    003570      02 FILLER PICTURE X VALUE '*'.                               BILLINGR
```

644

```
00079   003580      02 FILLER VALUE SPACE PICTURE X(31).                        BILLINGR
00080   003590 01 DESIGN-3.                                                      BILLINGR
00081   003600      02 FILLER VALUE SPACE PICTURE X(31).                        BILLINGR
00082   003610      02 FILLER PICTURE X VALUE '*'.                              BILLINGR
00083   003620      02 FILLER VALUE SPACE PICTURE X(24).                        BILLINGR
00084   003630   02 FILLER PICTURE A(20) VALUE 'GATLING SUPPLY HOUSE'.          BILLINGR
00085   003640      02 FILLER VALUE SPACE PICTURE X(25).                        BILLINGR
00086   003650      02 FILLER PICTURE X VALUE '*'.                              BILLINGR
00087   003660      02 FILLER VALUE SPACE PICTURE X(31).                        BILLINGR
00088   003670 01 DESIGN-4.                                                      BILLINGR
00089   003680      02 FILLER VALUE SPACE PICTURE X(31).                        BILLINGR
00090   003690      02 FILLER PICTURE X VALUE '*'.                              BILLINGR
00091   003700      02 FILLER VALUE SPACE PICTURE X(27).                        BILLINGR
00092   003710      02 FILLER PICTURE X(14) VALUE '221 SPRING ST.'.             BILLINGR
00093   003720      02 FILLER VALUE SPACE PICTURE X(28).                        BILLINGR
00094   003730      02 FILLER PICTURE X VALUE '*'.                              BILLINGR
00095   003740      02 FILLER VALUE SPACE PICTURE X(31).                        BILLINGR
00096   003750 01 DESIGN-5.                                                      BILLINGR
00097   003760      02 FILLER VALUE SPACE PICTURE X(31).                        BILLINGR
00098   003770      02 FILLER PICTURE X VALUE '*'.                              BILLINGR
00099   003780      02 FILLER VALUE SPACE PICTURE X(29).                        BILLINGR
00100   003790      02 FILLER PICTURE X(11) VALUE 'L.A. CALIF.'.                BILLINGR
00101   003800      02 FILLER VALUE SPACE PICTURE X(29).                        BILLINGR
00102   003810      02 FILLER PICTURE X VALUE '*'.                              BILLINGR
00103   003820      02 FILLER VALUE SPACE PICTURE X(31).                        BILLINGR
00104   003830 01 DESIGN-6.                                                      BILLINGR
00105   003840      02 FILLER VALUE SPACE PICTURE X(31).                        BILLINGR
00106   003850      02 FILLER PICTURE X VALUE '*'.                              BILLINGR
00107   003860      02 FILLER PICTURE X(8) VALUE 'SOLD TO.'.                    BILLINGR
00108   003870      02 FILLER VALUE SPACE PICTURE X.                            BILLINGR
00109   003880      02 NAME-1 PICTURE A(12).                                    BILLINGR
00110   003890      02 FILLER VALUE SPACE PICTURE X(48).                        BILLINGR
00111   003900      02 FILLER PICTURE X VALUE '*'.                              BILLINGR
00112   003910      02 FILLER VALUE SPACE PICTURE X(31).                        BILLINGR
00113   003920 01 DESIGN-7.                                                      BILLINGR
00114   003930      02 FILLER VALUE SPACE PICTURE X(31).                        BILLINGR
00115   003940      02 FILLER PICTURE X VALUE '*'.                              BILLINGR
00116   003950      02 FILLER VALUE SPACE PICTURE X(9).                         BILLINGR
00117   003960      02 STREET-NO PICTURE X(14).                                 BILLINGR
```

```
00118   003970      02 FILLER VALUE SPACE PICTURE X(46).                        BILLINGR
00119   003980      02 FILLER PICTURE X VALUE '*'.                              BILLINGR
00120   003990      02 FILLER VALUE SPACE PICTURE X(31).                        BILLINGR
00121   004010 01 DESIGN-8.                                                      BILLINGR
00122   034020      02 FILLER VALUE SPACE PICTURE X(31).                        BILLINGR
00123   004030      02 FILLER PICTURE X VALUE '*'.                              BILLINGR
00124   004040      02 FILLER VALUE SPACE PICTURE X(9).                         BILLINGR
00125   004050      02 CITY-STATE PICTURE X(11).                                BILLINGR
00126   004060      02 FILLER VALUE SPACE PICTURE X(33).                        BILLINGR
00127   004070      02 FILLER PICTURE X(16) VALUE 'TERM. 2/10/NET30'.           BILLINGR
00128   004080      02 FILLER PICTURE X VALUE '*'.                              BILLINGR
00129   004090      02 FILLER VALUE SPACE PICTURE X(31).                        BILLINGR
00130   004100 01 DESIGN-9.                                                      BILLINGR
00131   004110      02 FILLER VALUE SPACE PICTURE X(31).                        BILLINGR
00132   004120      02 FILLER PICTURE X VALUE '*'.                              BILLINGR
00133   004130      02 FILLER PICTURE X(69) VALUE ALL '.'.                      BILLINGR
00134   004140      02 FILLER PICTURE X VALUE '*'.                              BILLINGR
00135   004150      02 FILLER VALUE SPACE PICTURE X(31).                        BILLINGR
00136   004160 01 DESIGN-10.                                                     BILLINGR
00137   004170      02 FILLER VALUE SPACE PICTURE X(31).                        BILLINGR
00138   004180      02 FILLER PICTURE X VALUE '*'.                              BILLINGR
00139   004190      02 FILLER VALUE SPACE PICTURE X.                            BILLINGR
00140   004200      02 FILLER PICTURE X(8) VALUE 'ITEMS-NO'.                    BILLINGR
00141   004210      02 FILLER VALUE SPACE PICTURE X.                            BILLINGR
00142   004220      02 FILLER PICTURE X VALUE '.'.                              BILLINGR
00143   004230      02 FILLER VALUE SPACE PICTURE X.                            BILLINGR
00144   004240      02 FILLER PICTURE X(17) VALUE 'ITEMS-DESCRIPTION'.          BILLINGR
00145   004250      02 FILLER VALUE SPACE PICTURE X.                            BILLINGR
00146   004260      02 FILLER PICTURE X VALUE '.'.                              BILLINGR
00147   004270      02 FILLER VALUE SPACE PICTURE X.                            BILLINGR
00148   004280      02 FILLER PICTURE X(10) VALUE 'NO-ORDERED'.                 BILLINGR
00149   004290      02 FILLER VALUE SPACE PICTURE X.                            BILLINGR
00150   004300      02 FILLER PICTURE X VALUE '.'.                              BILLINGR
00151   004310      02 FILLER VALUE SPACE PICTURE X.                            BILLINGR
00152   004320      02 FILLER PICTURE X(10) VALUE 'UNIT-PRICE'.                 BILLINGR
00153   004330      02 FILLER VALUE SPACE PICTURE X.                            BILLINGR
00154   004340      02 FILLER PICTURE X VALUE '.'.                              BILLINGR
00155   004350      02 FILLER VALUE SPACE PICTURE X.                            BILLINGR
00156   004360      02 FILLER PICTURE X(10) VALUE 'TOTAL-COST'.                 BILLINGR
```

```
00157   004370      02 FILLER VALUE SPACE PICTURE X.              BILLINGR
00158   004380      02 FILLER PICTURE X VALUE '*'.                BILLINGR
00159   004390      02 FILLER VALUE SPACE PICTURE X(31).          BILLINGR
00160   004400 01   RECORD-PRINT.                                 BILLINGR
00161   004410      02 FILLER VALUE SPACE PICTURE X(31).          BILLINGR
00162   004420      02 FILLER PICTURE X VALUE '*'.                BILLINGR
00163   004430      02 FILLER VALUE SPACE PICTURE XXX.            BILLINGR
00164   004440      02 ITEM-NO PICTURE 99999.                     BILLINGR
00165   004450      02 FILLER VALUE SPACE PICTURE XX.             BILLINGR
00166   004460      02 FILLER PICTURE X VALUE '.'.                BILLINGR
00167   004470      02 FILLER VALUE SPACE PICTURE XXX.            BILLINGR
00168   004480      02 PART-DESCRIP PICTURE A(13).                BILLINGR
00169   004490      02 FILLER VALUE SPACE PICTURE XXX.            BILLINGR
00170   004500      02 FILLER PICTURE X VALUE '.'.                BILLINGR
00171   004510      02 FILLER VALUE SPACE PICTURE XXXX.           BILLINGR
00172   004520      02 AMOUNT-ORDER PICTURE ZZ9.                  BILLINGR
00173   004530      02 FILLER VALUE SPACE PICTURE XXXXX.          BILLINGR
00174   004540      02 FILLER PICTURE X VALUE '.'.                BILLINGR
00175   004550      02 FILLER VALUE SPACE PICTURE XX.             BILLINGR
00176   004560      02 PRICE PICTURE $$$9.99.                     BILLINGR
00177   004570      02 FILLER VALUE SPACE PICTURE XXX.            BILLINGR
00178   004580      02 FILLER PICTURE X VALUE '.'.                BILLINGR
00179   004590      02 FILLER VALUE SPACE PICTURE X.              BILLINGR
00180   004600      02 COST PICTURE $$,$$9.99.                    BILLINGR
00181   004610      02 FILLER VALUE SPACE PICTURE XX.             BILLINGR
00182   004620      02 FILLER PICTURE X VALUE '*'.                BILLINGR
00183   004630      02 FILLER VALUE SPACE PICTURE X(31).          BILLINGR
00184   004640 01   AREA-1.                                       BILLINGR
00185   004650      02 FILLER VALUE SPACE PICTURE X.              BILLINGR
00186   004660      02 FILLER PICTURE X VALUE '1'.                BILLINGR
00187   004670      02 FILLER VALUE SPACE PICTURE X(130).         BILLINGR
00188   004680      02 FILLER PICTURE X VALUE '1'.                BILLINGR
00189   004690 01   DESIGN-11.                                    BILLINGR
00190   004700      02 FILLER VALUE SPACE PICTURE X(31).          BILLINGR
00191   004710      02 FILLER PICTURE X VALUE '*'.                BILLINGR
00192   004720      02 FILLER VALUE SPACE PICTURE X(10).          BILLINGR
00193   004730      02 FILLER PICTURE X VALUE '.'.                BILLINGR
00194   004740      02 FILLER VALUE SPACE PICTURE X(19).          BILLINGR
00195   004750      02 FILLER PICTURE X VALUE '.'.                BILLINGR
```

```
00196   004760      02 FILLER VALUE SPACE PICTURE X(12).          BILLINGR
00197   004770      02 FILLER PICTURE X VALUE '.'.                BILLINGR
00198   004780      02 FILLER VALUE SPACE PICTURE X(12).          BILLINGR
00199   004790      02 FILLER PICTURE X VALUE '.'.                BILLINGR
00200   004800      02 FILLER VALUE SPACE PICTURE X(12).          BILLINGR
00201   004810      02 FILLER PICTURE X VALUE '*'.                BILLINGR
00202   004820      02 FILLER VALUE SPACE PICTURE X(31).          BILLINGR
00203   004830 01   TOTAL-RECORD.                                 BILLINGR
00204   004840      02 FILLER VALUE SPACE PICTURE X(31).          BILLINGR
00205   004850      02 FILLER PICTURE X VALUE '*'.                BILLINGR
00206   004860      02 FILLER VALUE SPACE PICTURE X(32).          BILLINGR
00207   004870      02 FILLER PICTURE X(14) VALUE 'TOTAL ORDERED.'. BILLINGR
00208   004880      02 FILLER VALUE SPACE PICTURE X.              BILLINGR
00209   004890      02 UNITS PICTURE ZZ9.                         BILLINGR
00210   004900      02 FILLER VALUE SPACE PICTURE X.              BILLINGR
00211   004910      02 FILLER PICTURE X(10) VALUE 'TOTAL AMT.'.   BILLINGR
00212   004920      02 GRAND-TOTAL PICTURE $$$$9.99.              BILLINGR
00213   004930      02 FILLER PICTURE X VALUE '*'.                BILLINGR
00214   004940      02 FILLER VALUE SPACE PICTURE X(31).          BILLINGR
00215   004950 PROCEDURE DIVISION.                                BILLINGR
00216   004960 BEGIN.                                             BILLINGR
00217   004970      OPEN INPUT FILE-IN, OUTPUT FILE-OUT.          BILLINGR
00218   004980      MOVE 200 TO COMPARE-1.                        BILLINGR
00219   004990 START-1.                                           BILLINGR
00220   005010      READ FILE-IN AT END GO TO LOCK-UP.            BILLINGR
00221   005020      MOVE INVOICE-NO TO COMPARE-2.                 BILLINGR
00222   005030      IF COMPARE-2 EQUAL TO COMPARE-1 GO TO CAL-1.  BILLINGR
00223   005040      IF COUNTER IS NOT EQUAL TO ZERO GO TO FIX-UP. BILLINGR
00224   005050 START-AGAIN.                                       BILLINGR
00225   005060      WRITE RECORD-OUT FROM DESIGN AFTER POSITIONING 2 LINES. BILLINGR
00226   005070 ROUTINE.                                           BILLINGR
00227   005080      WRITE RECORD-OUT FROM DESIGN-2 AFTER POSITIONING 1 LINES. BILLINGR
00228   005090 ROUTINE-1.                                         BILLINGR
00229   005100      MOVE DATE-I TO DATE-1.                        BILLINGR
00230   005110      MOVE INVOICE-NO TO INVOICE.                   BILLINGR
00231   005120      WRITE RECORD-OUT FROM DESIGN-1 AFTER POSITIONING 1 LINES. BILLINGR
00232   005130      PERFORM ROUTINE 2 TIMES.                      BILLINGR
00233   005140      WRITE RECORD-OUT FROM DESIGN-3 AFTER POSITIONING 1 LINES. BILLINGR
00234   005150      WRITE RECORD-OUT FROM DESIGN-4 AFTER POSITIONING 1 LINES. BILLINGR
```

7

```
00235   005160       WRITE RECORD-OUT FROM DESIGN-5 AFTER POSITIONING 1 LINES.    BILLINGR
00236   005170       PERFORM ROUTINE 2 TIMES.                                     BILLINGR
00237   005180       MOVE NAME TO NAME-1.                                         BILLINGR
00238   005190       WRITE RECORD-OUT FROM DESIGN-6 AFTER POSITIONING 1 LINES.    BILLINGR
00239   005200       MOVE STREET-1 TO STREET-NO.                                  BILLINGR
00240   005210       WRITE RECORD-OUT FROM DESIGN-7 AFTER POSITIONING 1 LINES.    BILLINGR
00241   005220       MOVE STATE-CITY TO CITY-STATE.                               BILLINGR
00242   005230       WRITE RECORD-OUT FROM DESIGN-8 AFTER POSITIONING 1 LINES.    BILLINGR
00243   005240       PERFORM ROUTINE.                                             BILLINGR
00244   005250       WRITE RECORD-OUT FROM DESIGN-9 AFTER POSITIONING 1 LINES.    BILLINGR
00245   005260       GO TO STOP-1.                                                BILLINGR
00246   005270 GAP-1.                                                             BILLINGR
00247   005280       WRITE RECORD-OUT FROM AREA-1 AFTER POSITIONING 1 LINES.      BILLINGR
00248   005290 STOP-1.                                                            BILLINGR
00249   005300       WRITE RECORD-OUT FROM DESIGN-10 AFTER POSITIONING 1 LINES.   BILLINGR
00250   005310       WRITE RECORD-OUT FROM DESIGN-9 AFTER POSITIONING 1 LINES.    BILLINGR
00251   005320       PERFORM ROUTINE-2 2 TIMES.                                   BILLINGR
00252   005330       GO TO CAL-1.                                                 BILLINGR
00253   005340 ROUTINE-2.                                                         BILLINGR
00254   005350       WRITE RECORD-OUT FROM DESIGN-11 AFTER POSITIONING 1 LINES.   BILLINGR
00255   005360 CAL-1.                                                             BILLINGR
00256   005370       ADD NO-ORDERED TO TOTAL-ORDERED.                             BILLINGR
00257   005380       ADD 1 TO COUNTER.                                            BILLINGR
00258   005390       MULTIPLY NO-ORDERED BY UNIT-COST GIVING SUM-O ROUNDED.       BILLINGR
00259   005400       ADD SUM-O TO GRAND-SUM.                                      BILLINGR
00260   005410       MOVE SUM-O TO COST.                                          BILLINGR
00261   005420       MOVE UNIT-COST TO PRICE.                                     BILLINGR
00262   005430       MOVE PART-NO TO ITEM-NO.                                     BILLINGR
00263   005440       MOVE ITEM-DESCRIPTION TO PART-DESCRIP.                       BILLINGR
00264   005450       MOVE NO-ORDERED TO AMOUNT-ORDER.                             BILLINGR
00265   005460       WRITE RECORD-OUT FROM RECORD-PRINT AFTER POSITIONING 1 LINES.BILLINGR
00266   005470       MOVE COMPARE-2 TO COMPARE-1.                                 BILLINGR
00267   005480       GO TO START-1.                                               BILLINGR
00268   005490 FIX-UP.                                                            BILLINGR
00269   005500       IF COUNTER IS LESS THAN LIMIT-WS SUBTRACT COUNTER FROM       BILLINGR
00270   005510       LIMIT-WS GIVING DIFFERENT, ELSE GO TO RETURN1.               BILLINGR
00271   005520       PERFORM ROUTINE-2 DIFFERENT TIMES.                           BILLINGR
00272   005530 RETURN1.                                                           BILLINGR
00273   005540       MOVE GRAND-SUM TO GRAND-TOTAL.                               BILLINGR
```

8

```
00274   005550       MOVE TOTAL-ORDERED TO UNITS.                                 BILLINGR
00275   005560       WRITE RECORD-OUT FROM DESIGN-9 AFTER POSITIONING 1 LINES.    BILLINGR
00276   005570       PERFORM ROUTINE.                                             BILLINGR
00277   005580       WRITE RECORD-OUT FROM TOTAL-RECORD AFTER POSITIONING 1 LINES.BILLINGR
00278   005590       WRITE RECORD-OUT FROM DESIGN AFTER POSITIONING 1 LINES.      BILLINGR
00279   005600       MOVE ZEROS TO COUNTER, DIFFERENT, TOTAL-ORDERED, SUM-O,      BILLINGR
00280   005610       GRAND-SUM.                                                   BILLINGR
00281   005620 START-2.                                                           BILLINGR
00282   005630       PERFORM GAP-1 10 TIMES.                                      BILLINGR
00283   005640       GO TO START-AGAIN.                                           BILLINGR
00284   005650 LOCK-UP.                                                           BILLINGR
00285   005660       PERFORM FIX-UP THRU RETURN1.                                 BILLINGR
00286   005670       CLOSE FILE-IN, FILE-OUT.                                     BILLINGR
00287   005680       STOP RUN.                                                    BILLINGR
```

```
***********************************************************************
*                                                                     *
*DATE. 11/21/71                                         INVOICE-NO. 100*
*                                                                     *
*                       GATLING SUPPLY HOUSE                          *
*                          221 SPRING ST.                             *
*                           L.A. CALIF.                               *
*                                                                     *
*SOLD TO. JUDGE STORE                                                 *
*         210 MAIN ST.                                                *
*         L. A. CALIF                                 TERM. 2/10/NET30*
*                                                                     *
*.....................................................................*
* ITEMS-NO . ITEMS-DESCRIPTION . NO-ORDERED . UNIT-PRICE . TOTAL-COST *
*.....................................................................*
*          .                 .            .            .             *
*  16724   .   GAS STOVES     .     4      .   $150.75  .   $603.00   *
*  26723   .   TABLES         .     7      .   $105.50  .   $738.50   *
*  87263   .   TOP CHAIRS     .    15      .    $10.00  .   $150.00   *
*  78642   .   BLACK DECKS    .     5      .   $110.00  .   $550.00   *
*          .                 .            .            .             *
*          .                 .            .            .             *
*          .                 .            .            .             *
*          .                 .            .            .             *
*          .                 .            .            .             *
*          .                 .            .            .             *
*          .                 .            .            .             *
*          .                 .            .            .             *
*          .                 .            .            .             *
*          .                 .            .            .             *
*          .                 .            .            .             *
*.....................................................................*
*                                                                     *
*                      TOTAL ORDERED.  31 TOTAL AMT.$2041.50*         *
***********************************************************************


***********************************************************************
*                                                                     *
*DATE. 12/21/71                                         INVOICE-NO. 101*
*                                                                     *
*                       GATLING SUPPLY HOUSE                          *
*                          221 SPRING ST.                             *
*                           L.A. CALIF.                               *
*                                                                     *
*SOLD TO. FRANK STORES                                                *
*         44 WILSHIRE ST                                              *
*         B.H. CALIF                                  TERM. 2/10/NET30*
*                                                                     *
*.....................................................................*
* ITEMS-NO . ITEMS-DESCRIPTION . NO-ORDERED . UNIT-PRICE . TOTAL-COST *
*.....................................................................*
*          .                 .            .            .             *
*  10024   .   MEN SUITS      .    25      .    $25.50  .   $637.50   *
*  14675   .   MEN SHIRTS     .    30      .    $35.00  . $1,050.00   *
*  42372   .   BLACK SHOES    .    50      .     $5.25  .   $262.50   *
*  36494   .   MEN SHORTS     .   250      .     $1.00  .   $250.00   *
*  16742   .   MEN SOCKS      .   225      .     $0.50  .   $112.50   *
*  13244   .   BLUE PANTS     .    20      .    $10.50  .   $210.00   *
*  24330   .   MEN COATS      .    25      .    $15.75  .   $393.75   *
*          .                 .            .            .             *
*          .                 .            .            .             *
*          .                 .            .            .             *
*          .                 .            .            .             *
*          .                 .            .            .             *
*          .                 .            .            .             *
*          .                 .            .            .             *
*          .                 .            .            .             *
*.....................................................................*
*                                                                     *
*                     TOTAL ORDERED. 625 TOTAL AMT.$2916.25*          *
***********************************************************************
```

IBM American National Standard Reserved Words

ACCEPT	COMP-2	DATE-WRITTEN
ACCESS	COMP-3	*DE
ACTUAL	COMPUTATIONAL	DECIMAL-POINT
ADD	COMPUTATIONAL-1	*DECLARATIVES
*ADDRESS	COMPUTATIONAL-2	DEPENDING
ADVANCING	COMPUTATIONAL-3	*DESCENDING
AFTER	COMPUTE	*DETAIL
ALL	COM-REG	DISP
ALPHABETIC	CONFIGURATION	DISPLAY-ST
ALTER	CONSOLE	DISPLAY
ALTERNATE	CONSTANT	DISPLAY-n
AND	CONTAINS	DIVIDE
APPLY	*CONTROL	DIVISION
ARE	CONTROLS	DOWN
AREA	CONVERSION	*EJECT
AREAS	COPY	ELSE
*ASCENDING	CORE-INDEX	END
ASSIGN	CORR	END-OF-PAGE
AT	CORRESPONDING	ENDING
AUTHOR	CSP	ENTER
BEFORE	CURRENCY	ENTRY
BEGINNING	CURRENT-DATE	ENVIRONMENT
BLANK	CYL-INDEX	EOP
BLOCK	CYL-OVERFLOW	EQUAL
BY	C01	EQUALS
CALL	C02	ERROR
CANCEL	C03	EVERY
*CF	C04	EXAMINE
*CH	C05	EXCEEDS
CHANGED	C06	EXHIBIT
CHARACTERS	C07	EXIT
*CLOCK-UNITS	C08	EXTENDED-SEARCH
CLOSE	C09	FD
*COBOL	C10	FILE
*CODE	C11	FILE-CONTROL
*COLUMN	C12	FILE-LIMIT
COMMA	DATA	FILE-LIMITS
COMP	DATE-COMPILED	FILLER
COMP-1		

*Indicates reserved words which are not contained in the S/360 ANS COBOL Subset compiler under the Disk Operating System.

*FINAL	LEAVE	ON
*FIRST	LEFT	OPEN
*FOOTING	LESS	OPTIONAL
FOR	LIBRARY	OR
FROM	*LIMIT	OTHERWISE
*GENERATE	*LIMITS	OUTPUT
GIVING	*LINAGE	OV
GO	*LINAGE-COUNTER	OVERFLOW
GOBACK	*LINE	*PAGE
GREATER	*LINE-COUNTER	*PAGE-COUNTER
*GROUP	LINES	PERFORM
*HASHED	LINKAGE	*PF
*HEADING	LOCK	*PH
HIGH-VALUE	LOW-VALUE	PIC
HIGH-VALUES	LOW-VALUES	PICTURE
HOLD	LOWER-BOUND	*PLUS
ID	LOWER-BOUNDS	POSITION
IDENTIFICATION	MASTER-INDEX	POSITIONING
IF	MEMORY	POSITIVE
IN	MODE	PREPARED
INDEX	MODULES	*PRINT-SWITCH
INDEXED	MORE-LABELS	PRIORITY
INDEX-n	MOVE	PROCEDURE
*INDICATE	MULTIPLE	PROCEED
*INITIATE	MULTIPLY	PROCESSING
INPUT	NAMED	PROGRAM
INPUT-OUTPUT	NEGATIVE	PROGRAM-ID
INSTALLATION	NEXT	QUOTE
INTO	NO	QUOTES
INVALID	NOMINAL	RANDOM
I-O	NOT	RANGE
I-O-CONTROL	NOTE	*RD
IS	*NUMBER	READ
JUST	NUMERIC	READY
JUSTIFIED	OBJECT-COMPUTER	RECORD
KEY	OBJECT-PROGRAM	RECORD-OVERFLOW
KEYS	OCCURS	RECORDING
LABEL	OF	RECORDS
LABEL-RETURN	OFF	REDEFINES
*LAST	OH	REEL
LEADING	OMITTED	*RELEASE

*Indicates reserved words which are not contained in the S/360 ANS COBOL Subset compiler under the Disk Operating System.

REMAINDER	*SORT	TOTALED
REMARKS	*SORT-CORE-SIZE	TOTALING
RENAMES	*SORT-FILE-SIZE	TRACE
REORG-CRITERIA	*SORT-MODE-SIZE	TRACK
*REPLACING	*SORT-RETURN	TRACK-AREA
*REPORT	SOURCE	TRACK-LIMIT
*REPORTING	SOURCE-COMPUTER	TRANSFORM
*REPORTS	SPACE	*TYPE
*REREAD	SPACES	UNEQUAL
RERUN	SPECIAL-NAMES	UNIT
RESERVE	STANDARD	UNTIL
RESET	START	UP
*RETURN	STATUS	UPDATE
RETURN-CODE	STOP	UPON
REVERSED	SUBTRACT	UPPER-BOUND
REWIND	*SUM	UPPER-BOUNDS
REWRITE	SUPERVISOR	UPSI-0 (DOS)
*RF	SUPPRESS	UPSI-1 (DOS)
*RH	SUSPEND	UPSI-2 (DOS)
RIGHT	SYMBOLIC	UPSI-3 (DOS)
ROUNDED	SYNC	UPSI-4 (DOS)
RUN	SYNCHRONIZED	UPSI-5 (DOS)
SA	SYSIN	UPSI-6 (DOS)
SAME	SYSIPT	UPSI-7 (DOS)
*SD	SYSLST	USAGE
*SEARCH	SYSOUT	USE
SECTION	SYSPCH	USING
SECURITY	SYSPUNCH	UTILITY
SEEK	S01	VALUE
*SEGMENT-LIMIT	S02	VALUES
SELECT	TALLY	VARYING
SELECTED	TALLYING	WHEN
SENTENCE	TAPE	WITH
SEQUENCED	*TERMINATE	WORDS
SEQUENTIAL	THAN	WORKING-STORAGE
SET	THEN	WRITE
SIGN	THROUGH	WRITE-ONLY
SIZE	THRU	WRITE-VERIFY
SKIP 1	TIME-OF-DAY	ZERO
SKIP 2	TIMES	ZEROES
SKIP 3	TO	ZEROS

*Indicates reserved words which are not contained in the S/360 ANS COBOL Subset compiler under the Disk Operating System.

COBOL Character Set

(In collating sequence, beginning with the highest value)

9 ⎫
  ⎪
  ⎬ (numbers)
  ⎪
0 ⎭

Z ⎫
  ⎪
  ⎬ (letters)
  ⎪
A ⎭

"   (quotation mark)

=   (equal sign)

'   (apostrophe, or single quotation mark)

>   (greater than)

,   (comma)

/   (slash, virgule, stroke)

—   (hyphen or minus symbol)

;   (semicolon)

)   (right parenthesis)

*   (asterisk)

$ (currency symbol)

+   (plus symbol)

((left parenthesis)

<   (less than)

.   (period or decimal point)

      (blank) (The notation frequently used to indicate a blank is b.)

Structure of <u>System-Name</u> in the ASSIGN Clause

SYSnnn-class-device-organization [-name]

nnn—a three-digit number between 000 and 221

class—a two-character field that represents device class.
    Allowable combinations are:

    DA   mass storage
    UT   utility
    UR   unit record

device—a four- or five-digit that represents device number.
    Allowable numbers for each device class are:

    DA   2311, 2321, 2314
    UT   2400, 2311, 2314, 2321
    UR   1442R, 1442P, 1403, 1404 (continuous forms only), 1443, 2501, 2520R, 2520P, 2540R, 2540P

organization—a one-character field that specifies file organization.
    Allowable characters are:

    S   for standard sequential files
    A   for direct files—actual track addressing
    D   for direct files—relative track addressing
    U   for direct files using REWRITE statement* —actual track addressing
    W   for direct files using REWRITE statement* —relative track addressing
    I   for indexed files
        *When the file is opened INPUT or OUTPUT, U and W are equivalent to A and D.

name—a one- to seven-character field that specifies the external-name by which the file is known to the system

Symbols Allowed in the PICTURE Clause

Symbol	Meaning
A	Alphabetic character or space
B	Space insertion character
P	Decimal scaling position (not counted in size of data item)
S	Operational sign (not counted in size of data item)
V	Assumed decimal point (not counted in size of data item)
X	Alphanumeric character (any from the EBCDIC set)
Z	Zero suppression character
9	Numeric character
0	Zero insertion character
,	Comma insertion character
.	Decimal point or period editing control character
+	Plus sign insertion editing control character
—	Minus sign editing control character
CR	Credit editing control characters
DB	Debit editing control characters
*	Check protect insertion character
$	Currency sign insertion character

Basic Formats

Identification and Environment Division—Basic Formats

IDENTIFICATION DIVISION—BASIC FORMATS

$\begin{Bmatrix} \underline{\text{IDENTIFICATION DIVISION.}} \\ \underline{\text{ID DIVISION.}} \end{Bmatrix}$
<u>PROGRAM-ID</u>. *program-name.*
<u>AUTHOR</u>. *[comment-entry]* . . .
<u>INSTALLATION</u>. *[comment-entry]* . . .
<u>DATE-WRITTEN</u>. *[comment-entry]* . . .
<u>DATE-COMPILED</u>. *[comment-entry]* . . .
<u>SECURITY</u>. *[comment-entry]* . . .
<u>REMARKS</u>. *[comment-entry]* . . .

ENVIRONMENT DIVISION—BASIC FORMATS

<u>ENVIRONMENT DIVISION.</u>
<u>CONFIGURATION SECTION.</u>
<u>SOURCE-COMPUTER.</u> *computer-name.*

<u>OBJECT-COMPUTER</u>. *computer-name* [<u>MEMORY</u> SIZE *integer* $\begin{Bmatrix} \underline{\text{WORDS}} \\ \underline{\text{CHARACTERS}} \\ \underline{\text{MODULES}} \end{Bmatrix}$]

    [<u>SEGMENT-LIMIT</u> IS *priority-number*] .
<u>SPECIAL-NAMES</u>. *[function-name* <u>IS</u> *mnemonic-name]* . . .
    [<u>CURRENCY</u> SIGN <u>IS</u> *literal*]
    [<u>DECIMAL-POINT IS COMMA</u>] .
<u>INPUT-OUTPUT SECTION.</u>
<u>FILE-CONTROL</u>.
    {<u>SELECT</u> [<u>OPTIONAL</u>] *file name*
    <u>ASSIGN</u> TO *[integer-1] system-name-1 [system-name-2]* . . .

        [FOR <u>MULTIPLE</u> $\begin{Bmatrix} \underline{\text{REEL}} \\ \underline{\text{UNIT}} \end{Bmatrix}$]

    <u>RESERVE</u> $\begin{Bmatrix} \underline{\text{NO}} \\ integer\text{-}1 \end{Bmatrix}$ ALTERNATE $\begin{bmatrix} \text{AREA} \\ \text{AREAS} \end{bmatrix}$

    $\begin{Bmatrix} \underline{\text{FILE-LIMIT}}\text{ IS} \\ \underline{\text{FILE-LIMITS}}\text{ ARE} \end{Bmatrix}$ $\begin{Bmatrix} data\text{-}name\text{-}1 \\ literal\text{-}1 \end{Bmatrix}$ <u>THRU</u> $\begin{Bmatrix} data\text{-}name\text{-}2 \\ literal\text{-}2 \end{Bmatrix}$

    [$\begin{Bmatrix} data\text{-}name\text{-}3 \\ literal\text{-}3 \end{Bmatrix}$ <u>THRU</u> $\begin{Bmatrix} data\text{-}name\text{-}4 \\ literal\text{-}4 \end{Bmatrix}$] . . .

    <u>ACCESS</u> MODE <u>IS</u> $\begin{Bmatrix} \underline{\text{SEQUENTIAL}} \\ \underline{\text{RANDOM}} \end{Bmatrix}$
    <u>PROCESSING</u> MODE <u>IS SEQUENTIAL</u>
    <u>ACTUAL</u> KEY <u>IS</u> *data-name*
    <u>NOMINAL</u> KEY <u>IS</u> *data-name*
    <u>RECORD</u> KEY IS *data-name*

$$\text{TRACK-AREA IS } \left\{ \begin{matrix} \textit{data-name} \\ \textit{integer} \end{matrix} \right\} \text{ CHARACTERS}$$

$$\text{TRACK-LIMIT IS } \textit{integer} \left[\begin{matrix} \text{TRACK} \\ \text{TRACKS} \end{matrix} \right] . \} \ldots$$

I-O-CONTROL

$$\text{RERUN ON } \textit{system-name} \text{ EVERY } \left\{ \begin{matrix} \textit{integer } \text{RECORDS} \\ [\text{END OF}] \left\{ \begin{matrix} \text{REEL} \\ \text{UNIT} \end{matrix} \right\} \end{matrix} \right\} \text{OF } \textit{file-name}$$

$$\text{SAME } \left[\begin{matrix} \text{RECORD} \\ \text{SORT} \end{matrix} \right] \text{AREA FOR } \textit{file-name-1} \; \{ \textit{file-name-2} \} \ldots$$

MULTIPLE FILE TAPE CONTAINS *file-name-1* [POSITION *integer-1*]
        [*file-name-2* [POSITION *integer-2*]] . . .
APPLY WRITE-ONLY ON *file-name-1* [*file-name-2*] . . .
APPLY CORE-INDEX ON *file-name-1* [*file-name-2*] . . .
APPLY RECORD-OVERFLOW ON *file-name-1* [*file-name-2*] . . .
APPLY REORG-CRITERIA TO *data-name* ON *file-name*

NOTE: Format 2 of the RERUN Clause (for Sort Files) is included with Formats for the
        SORT feature.

Data Division—Basic Formats

DATA DIVISION.
FILE SECTION.
FD *file-name*

$$\text{BLOCK CONTAINS } \textit{[integer-1 \underline{TO}]} \textit{ integer-2} \left\{ \begin{matrix} \text{CHARACTERS} \\ \text{RECORDS} \end{matrix} \right\}$$

RECORD CONTAINS *[integer-1 TO] integer-2* CHARACTERS
RECORDING MODE IS *mode*

$$\text{LABEL } \left\{ \begin{matrix} \text{RECORD IS} \\ \text{RECORDS ARE} \end{matrix} \right\} \left\{ \begin{matrix} \text{OMITTED} \\ \text{STANDARD} \\ \textit{data-name-1 [data-name-2]} \ldots \text{[\underline{TOTALING} AREA IS} \\ \textit{data-name-3} \text{ \underline{TOTALED} AREA IS } \textit{data-name-4}] \end{matrix} \right\}$$

$$\text{VALUE OF } \textit{data-name-1} \text{ IS } \left\{ \begin{matrix} \textit{data-name-2} \\ \textit{literal-1} \end{matrix} \right\} \text{ [\textit{data-name-3} IS } \left\{ \begin{matrix} \textit{data-name-4} \\ \textit{literal-2} \end{matrix} \right\} \text{]} \ldots$$

$$\text{DATA } \left\{ \begin{matrix} \text{RECORD IS} \\ \text{RECORDS ARE} \end{matrix} \right\} \textit{data-name-1 [data-name-2]} \ldots$$

NOTE: Format for the REPORT Clause is included with Formats for the REPORT WRITER
        feature.

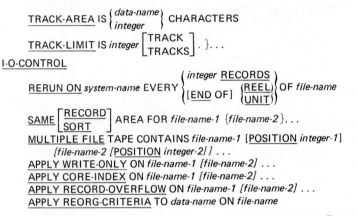

$$01\text{-}49 \quad \left\{ \begin{matrix} \textit{data-name-1} \\ \text{FILLER} \end{matrix} \right\}$$

REDEFINES *data-name-2*
BLANK WHEN ZERO

$$\left\{ \begin{matrix} \text{JUSTIFIED} \\ \text{JUST} \end{matrix} \right\} \text{ RIGHT}$$

$$\left\{ \begin{matrix} \text{PICTURE} \\ \text{PIC} \end{matrix} \right\} \text{ IS } \textit{character string}$$

$$\text{[\underline{SIGN} IS] } \left\{ \begin{matrix} \text{LEADING} \\ \text{TRAILING} \end{matrix} \right\} \text{ [\underline{SEPARATE} CHARACTER]}$$

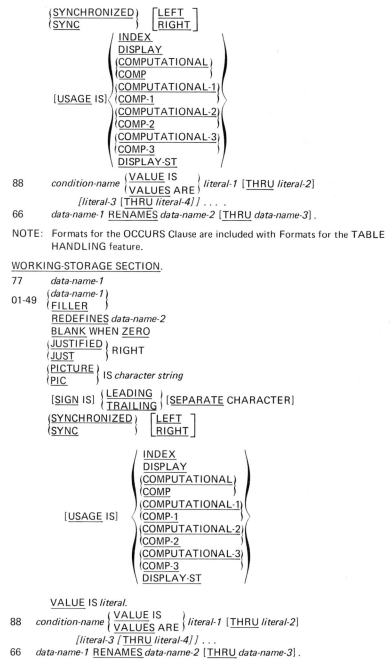

$\begin{Bmatrix} \text{SYNCHRONIZED} \\ \text{SYNC} \end{Bmatrix} \begin{bmatrix} \text{LEFT} \\ \text{RIGHT} \end{bmatrix}$

$[\text{USAGE IS}] \begin{Bmatrix} \text{INDEX} \\ \text{DISPLAY} \\ \begin{Bmatrix} \text{COMPUTATIONAL} \\ \text{COMP} \end{Bmatrix} \\ \begin{Bmatrix} \text{COMPUTATIONAL-1} \\ \text{COMP-1} \end{Bmatrix} \\ \begin{Bmatrix} \text{COMPUTATIONAL-2} \\ \text{COMP-2} \end{Bmatrix} \\ \begin{Bmatrix} \text{COMPUTATIONAL-3} \\ \text{COMP-3} \end{Bmatrix} \\ \text{DISPLAY-ST} \end{Bmatrix}$

88   *condition-name* $\begin{Bmatrix} \text{VALUE IS} \\ \text{VALUES ARE} \end{Bmatrix}$ *literal-1* [THRU *literal-2*]
     [*literal-3* [THRU *literal-4*]] . . . .

66   *data-name-1* RENAMES *data-name-2* [THRU *data-name-3*] .

NOTE: Formats for the OCCURS Clause are included with Formats for the TABLE
        HANDLING feature.

WORKING-STORAGE SECTION.

77   *data-name-1*

01-49 $\begin{Bmatrix} \textit{data-name-1} \\ \text{FILLER} \end{Bmatrix}$
        REDEFINES *data-name-2*
        BLANK WHEN ZERO
        $\begin{Bmatrix} \text{JUSTIFIED} \\ \text{JUST} \end{Bmatrix}$ RIGHT
        $\begin{Bmatrix} \text{PICTURE} \\ \text{PIC} \end{Bmatrix}$ IS *character string*

        [SIGN IS] $\begin{Bmatrix} \text{LEADING} \\ \text{TRAILING} \end{Bmatrix}$ [SEPARATE CHARACTER]

        $\begin{Bmatrix} \text{SYNCHRONIZED} \\ \text{SYNC} \end{Bmatrix} \begin{bmatrix} \text{LEFT} \\ \text{RIGHT} \end{bmatrix}$

        $[\text{USAGE IS}] \begin{Bmatrix} \text{INDEX} \\ \text{DISPLAY} \\ \begin{Bmatrix} \text{COMPUTATIONAL} \\ \text{COMP} \end{Bmatrix} \\ \begin{Bmatrix} \text{COMPUTATIONAL-1} \\ \text{COMP-1} \end{Bmatrix} \\ \begin{Bmatrix} \text{COMPUTATIONAL-2} \\ \text{COMP-2} \end{Bmatrix} \\ \begin{Bmatrix} \text{COMPUTATIONAL-3} \\ \text{COMP-3} \end{Bmatrix} \\ \text{DISPLAY-ST} \end{Bmatrix}$

        VALUE IS *literal.*

88   *condition-name* $\begin{Bmatrix} \text{VALUE IS} \\ \text{VALUES ARE} \end{Bmatrix}$ *literal-1* [THRU *literal-2*]
     [*literal-3* [THRU *literal-4*]] . . .

66   *data-name-1* RENAMES *data-name-2* [THRU *data-name-3*] .

NOTE: Formats for the OCCURS Clause are included with Formats for the TABLE
        HANDLING feature.

LINKAGE SECTION.
77   data-name-1

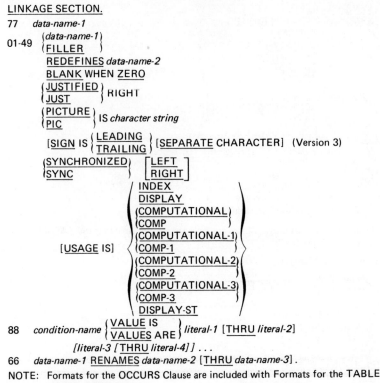

01-49   { data-name-1 }
        { FILLER   }
        REDEFINES data-name-2
        BLANK WHEN ZERO
        { JUSTIFIED }
        { JUST   } RIGHT
        { PICTURE }
        { PIC   } IS character string

        [SIGN IS { LEADING } [SEPARATE CHARACTER]   (Version 3)
                 { TRAILING }

        { SYNCHRONIZED }   [LEFT]
        { SYNC   }   [RIGHT]

                        INDEX
                        DISPLAY
                        { COMPUTATIONAL   }
                        { COMP   }
                        { COMPUTATIONAL-1 }
        [USAGE IS]   { COMP-1   }
                        { COMPUTATIONAL-2 }
                        { COMP-2   }
                        { COMPUTATIONAL-3 }
                        { COMP-3   }
                        DISPLAY-ST

88   condition-name { VALUE IS   } literal-1 [THRU literal-2]
                    { VALUES ARE }
        [literal-3 [THRU literal-4]] ...

66   data-name-1 RENAMES data-name-2 [THRU data-name-3] .

NOTE: Formats for the OCCURS Clause are included with Formats for the TABLE
       HANDLING feature.

Procedure Division—Basic Formats

{ PROCEDURE DIVISION.   }
{ PROCEDURE DIVISION USING identifier-1 [identifier-2] ...   . }

ACCEPT Statement

    ACCEPT identifier [FROM { SYSIN   }]
                           { CONSOLE   }
                           { mnemonic-name }

ADD Statement

FORMAT 1

    ADD { identifier-1 }   [identifier-2] ... TO identifier-m [ROUNDED]
        { literal-1   }   [literal-2   ]

        [identifier-n [ROUNDED]] ... [ON SIZE ERROR imperative-statement]

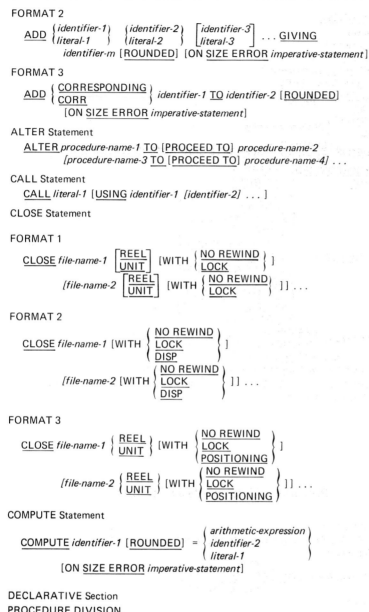

FORMAT 2

ADD $\begin{Bmatrix} identifier\text{-}1 \\ literal\text{-}1 \end{Bmatrix}$ $\begin{Bmatrix} identifier\text{-}2 \\ literal\text{-}2 \end{Bmatrix}$ $\begin{bmatrix} identifier\text{-}3 \\ literal\text{-}3 \end{bmatrix}$ ... GIVING
identifier-m [ROUNDED] [ON SIZE ERROR imperative-statement]

FORMAT 3

ADD $\begin{Bmatrix} \underline{CORRESPONDING} \\ \underline{CORR} \end{Bmatrix}$ identifier-1 TO identifier-2 [ROUNDED]
[ON SIZE ERROR imperative-statement]

ALTER Statement

ALTER procedure-name-1 TO [PROCEED TO] procedure-name-2
[procedure-name-3 TO [PROCEED TO] procedure-name-4] ...

CALL Statement

CALL literal-1 [USING identifier-1 [identifier-2] ...]

CLOSE Statement

FORMAT 1

CLOSE file-name-1 $\begin{bmatrix} \underline{REEL} \\ \underline{UNIT} \end{bmatrix}$ [WITH $\begin{Bmatrix} \underline{NO\ REWIND} \\ \underline{LOCK} \end{Bmatrix}$]
[file-name-2 $\begin{bmatrix} \underline{REEL} \\ \underline{UNIT} \end{bmatrix}$ [WITH $\begin{Bmatrix} \underline{NO\ REWIND} \\ \underline{LOCK} \end{Bmatrix}$]] ...

FORMAT 2

CLOSE file-name-1 [WITH $\begin{Bmatrix} \underline{NO\ REWIND} \\ \underline{LOCK} \\ \underline{DISP} \end{Bmatrix}$]
[file-name-2 [WITH $\begin{Bmatrix} \underline{NO\ REWIND} \\ \underline{LOCK} \\ \underline{DISP} \end{Bmatrix}$]] ...

FORMAT 3

CLOSE file-name-1 $\begin{Bmatrix} \underline{REEL} \\ \underline{UNIT} \end{Bmatrix}$ [WITH $\begin{Bmatrix} \underline{NO\ REWIND} \\ \underline{LOCK} \\ \underline{POSITIONING} \end{Bmatrix}$]
[file-name-2 $\begin{Bmatrix} \underline{REEL} \\ \underline{UNIT} \end{Bmatrix}$ [WITH $\begin{Bmatrix} \underline{NO\ REWIND} \\ \underline{LOCK} \\ \underline{POSITIONING} \end{Bmatrix}$]] ...

COMPUTE Statement

COMPUTE identifier-1 [ROUNDED] = $\begin{Bmatrix} arithmetic\text{-}expression \\ identifier\text{-}2 \\ literal\text{-}1 \end{Bmatrix}$
[ON SIZE ERROR imperative-statement]

DECLARATIVE Section
PROCEDURE DIVISION.
DECLARATIVES.
{section-name SECTION. USE sentence.
{paragraph-name. {sentence}... }... }...
END DECLARATIVES.

DISPLAY Statement

<u>DISPLAY</u> $\begin{Bmatrix} identifier\text{-}1 \\ literal\text{-}1 \end{Bmatrix}$ $\begin{bmatrix} identifier\text{-}2 \\ literal\text{-}2 \end{bmatrix}$ ... [<u>UPON</u> $\begin{Bmatrix} \text{CONSOLE} \\ \text{SYSPUNCH} \\ \text{SYSOUT} \\ mnemonic\text{-}name \end{Bmatrix}$]

DIVIDE Statement

FORMAT 1

<u>DIVIDE</u> $\begin{Bmatrix} identifier\text{-}1 \\ literal\text{-}1 \end{Bmatrix}$ <u>INTO</u> identifier-2 [<u>ROUNDED</u>]
　　　　[ON <u>SIZE ERROR</u> imperative-statement]

FORMAT 2

<u>DIVIDE</u> $\begin{Bmatrix} identifier\text{-}1 \\ literal\text{-}1 \end{Bmatrix}$ $\begin{Bmatrix} \underline{INTO} \\ \underline{BY} \end{Bmatrix}$ $\begin{Bmatrix} identifier\text{-}2 \\ literal\text{-}2 \end{Bmatrix}$ <u>GIVING</u> identifier-3
　　　　[<u>ROUNDED</u>] [<u>REMAINDER</u> identifier-4] [ON <u>SIZE ERROR</u> imperative-statement]

ENTER Statement

<u>ENTER</u> language-name [routine-name]

ENTRY Statement

<u>ENTRY</u> literal-1 [<u>USING</u> identifier-1 [identifier-2] ...]

ENTER Statement

<u>ENTER</u> language-name [routine-name]

EXAMINE Statement

FORMAT 1

<u>EXAMINE</u> identifier <u>TALLYING</u> $\begin{Bmatrix} \underline{\text{UNTIL FIRST}} \\ \underline{\text{ALL}} \\ \underline{\text{LEADING}} \end{Bmatrix}$ literal-1
　　　[<u>REPLACING BY</u> literal-2]

FORMAT 2

<u>EXAMINE</u> identifier <u>REPLACING</u> $\begin{Bmatrix} \underline{\text{ALL}} \\ \underline{\text{LEADING}} \\ \underline{\text{FIRST}} \\ \underline{\text{UNTIL FIRST}} \end{Bmatrix}$ literal-1 <u>BY</u> literal-2

EXIT Statement

paragraph-name. <u>EXIT</u> [<u>PROGRAM</u>] .

GOBACK Statement

<u>GOBACK.</u>

GO TO Statement

FORMAT 1

<u>GO TO</u> procedure-name-1

FORMAT 2

<u>GO TO</u> procedure-name-1 [procedure-name-2] ... <u>DEPENDING</u> ON identifier

FORMAT 3

<u>GO TO</u>.

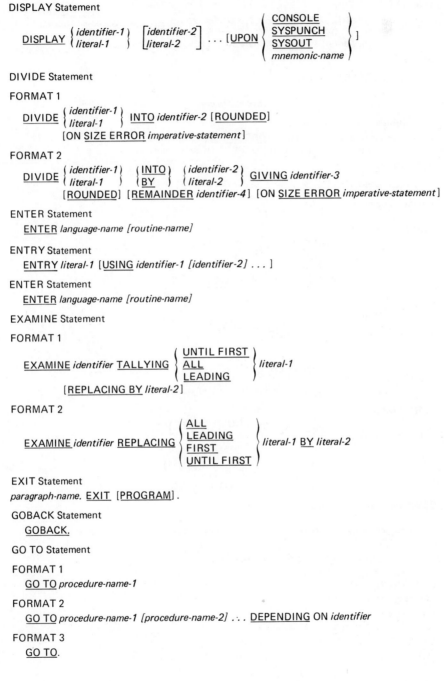

IF Statement

$$\text{\underline{IF} condition THEN } \begin{Bmatrix} \underline{\text{NEXT SENTENCE}} \\ \textit{statement-1} \end{Bmatrix} \begin{Bmatrix} \underline{\text{OTHERWISE}} \\ \underline{\text{ELSE}} \end{Bmatrix} \begin{Bmatrix} \underline{\text{NEXT SENTENCE}} \\ \textit{statement-2} \end{Bmatrix}$$

MOVE Statement

FORMAT 1

$$\underline{\text{MOVE}} \begin{Bmatrix} \textit{identifier-1} \\ \textit{literal-1} \end{Bmatrix} \underline{\text{TO}} \textit{ identifier-2 [identifier-3] } \dots$$

FORMAT 2

$$\underline{\text{MOVE}} \begin{Bmatrix} \underline{\text{CORRESPONDING}} \\ \underline{\text{CORR}} \end{Bmatrix} \textit{ identifier-1 } \underline{\text{TO}} \textit{ identifier-2}$$

MULTIPLY Statement

FORMAT 1

$$\underline{\text{MULTIPLY}} \begin{Bmatrix} \textit{identifier-1} \\ \textit{literal-1} \end{Bmatrix} \underline{\text{BY}} \textit{ identifier-2 } [\underline{\text{ROUNDED}}]$$

   $[\text{ON } \underline{\text{SIZE ERROR}} \textit{ imperative-statement}]$

FORMAT 2

$$\underline{\text{MULTIPLY}} \begin{Bmatrix} \textit{identifier-1} \\ \textit{literal-1} \end{Bmatrix} \underline{\text{BY}} \begin{Bmatrix} \textit{identifier-2} \\ \textit{literal-2} \end{Bmatrix} \underline{\text{GIVING}} \textit{ identifier-3}$$

   $[\underline{\text{ROUNDED}}] \quad [\text{ON } \underline{\text{SIZE ERROR}} \textit{ imperative-statement}]$

NOTE Statement

   $\underline{\text{NOTE}} \textit{ character string}$

OPEN Statement

FORMAT 1

$$\underline{\text{OPEN}} \left[\underline{\text{INPUT}} \left\{ \textit{file-name} \begin{bmatrix} \text{REVERSED} \\ \text{WITH } \underline{\text{NO REWIND}} \end{bmatrix} \right\} \dots \right]$$

   $[\underline{\text{OUTPUT}} \{ \textit{file-name } [\text{WITH } \underline{\text{NO REWIND}}] \} \dots]$

   $[\underline{\text{I-O}} \{ \textit{file-name} \} \dots]$

FORMAT 2

$$\underline{\text{OPEN}} \left[\underline{\text{INPUT}} \left\{ \textit{file-name} \begin{bmatrix} \text{REVERSED} \\ \text{WITH } \underline{\text{NO REWIND}} \end{bmatrix} \begin{bmatrix} \text{LEAVE} \\ \text{REREAD} \\ \text{DISP} \end{bmatrix} \right\} \dots \right]$$

   $$\left[\underline{\text{OUTPUT}} \left\{ \textit{file-name } [\text{WITH } \underline{\text{NO REWIND}}] \begin{bmatrix} \text{LEAVE} \\ \text{REREAD} \\ \text{DISP} \end{bmatrix} \right\} \dots \right]$$

   $[\underline{\text{I-O}} \{ \textit{file-name} \} \dots]$

PERFORM Statement

FORMAT 1

   $\underline{\text{PERFORM}} \textit{ procedure-name-1 } [\underline{\text{THRU}} \textit{ procedure-name-2}]$

FORMAT 2

$$\underline{\text{PERFORM}} \textit{ procedure-name-1 } [\underline{\text{THRU}} \textit{ procedure-name-2}] \begin{Bmatrix} \textit{identifier-1} \\ \textit{integer-1} \end{Bmatrix} \underline{\text{TIMES}}$$

FORMAT 3

   $\underline{\text{PERFORM}} \textit{ procedure-name-1 } [\underline{\text{THRU}} \textit{ procedure-name-2}] \underline{\text{UNTIL}} \textit{ condition-1}$

FORMAT 4

<u>PERFORM</u> *procedure-name-1* [<u>THRU</u> *procedure-name-2*]

<u>VARYING</u> $\left\{ \begin{array}{l} \textit{index-name-1} \\ \textit{identifier-1} \end{array} \right\}$ <u>FROM</u> $\left\{ \begin{array}{l} \textit{index-name-2} \\ \textit{literal-2} \\ \textit{identifier-2} \end{array} \right\}$ <u>BY</u> $\left\{ \begin{array}{l} \textit{literal-3} \\ \textit{identifier-3} \end{array} \right\}$ <u>UNTIL</u> *condition-1*

[<u>AFTER</u> $\left\{ \begin{array}{l} \textit{index-name-4} \\ \textit{identifier-4} \end{array} \right\}$ <u>FROM</u> $\left\{ \begin{array}{l} \textit{index-name-5} \\ \textit{literal-5} \\ \textit{identifier-5} \end{array} \right\}$ <u>BY</u> $\left\{ \begin{array}{l} \textit{literal-6} \\ \textit{identifier-6} \end{array} \right\}$ <u>UNTIL</u> *condition-2*

[<u>AFTER</u> $\left\{ \begin{array}{l} \textit{index-name-7} \\ \textit{identifier-7} \end{array} \right\}$ <u>FROM</u> $\left\{ \begin{array}{l} \textit{index-name-8} \\ \textit{literal-8} \\ \textit{identifier-8} \end{array} \right\}$ <u>BY</u> $\left\{ \begin{array}{l} \textit{literal-9} \\ \textit{identifier-9} \end{array} \right\}$ <u>UNTIL</u> *condition-3*]]

READ Statement

<u>READ</u> *file-name* RECORD [<u>INTO</u> *identifier*]

$\left\{ \begin{array}{l} \text{AT } \underline{\text{END}} \\ \underline{\text{INVALID}} \text{ KEY} \end{array} \right\}$ *imperative-statement*

REWRITE Statement

<u>REWRITE</u> *record-name* [<u>FROM</u> *identifier*] [<u>INVALID</u> KEY *imperative-statement*]

SEEK Statement

<u>SEEK</u> *file-name* RECORD

START Statement

FORMAT 1

<u>START</u> *file-name* [<u>INVALID</u> KEY *imperative-statement*]

FORMAT 2

<u>START</u> *file-name*

USING <u>KEY</u> *data-name* $\left\{ \begin{array}{l} \underline{\text{EQUAL TO}} \\ = \end{array} \right\}$ *identifier*

[<u>INVALID</u> KEY *imperative-statement*]

STOP Statement

<u>STOP</u> $\left\{ \begin{array}{l} \underline{\text{RUN}} \\ \textit{literal} \end{array} \right\}$

SUBTRACT Statement

FORMAT 1

<u>SUBTRACT</u> $\left\{ \begin{array}{l} \textit{identifier-1} \\ \textit{literal-1} \end{array} \right\}$ $\left[\begin{array}{l} \textit{identifier-2} \\ \textit{literal-2} \end{array} \right]$ ... <u>FROM</u> *identifier-m* [<u>ROUNDED</u>]

[*identifier-n* [<u>ROUNDED</u>]] ... [ON <u>SIZE ERROR</u> *imperative-statement*]

FORMAT 2

<u>SUBTRACT</u> $\left\{ \begin{array}{l} \textit{identifier-1} \\ \textit{literal-1} \end{array} \right\}$ $\left[\begin{array}{l} \textit{identifier-2} \\ \textit{literal-2} \end{array} \right]$ ... <u>FROM</u> $\left\{ \begin{array}{l} \textit{identifier-m} \\ \textit{literal-m} \end{array} \right\}$ <u>GIVING</u> *identifier-n*

[<u>ROUNDED</u>] [ON <u>SIZE ERROR</u> *imperative-statement*]

FORMAT 3

<u>SUBTRACT</u> $\left\{ \begin{array}{l} \underline{\text{CORRESPONDING}} \\ \underline{\text{CORR}} \end{array} \right\}$ *identifier-1* <u>FROM</u> *identifier-2* [<u>ROUNDED</u>]

[ON <u>SIZE ERROR</u> *imperative-statement*]

TRANSFORM Statement

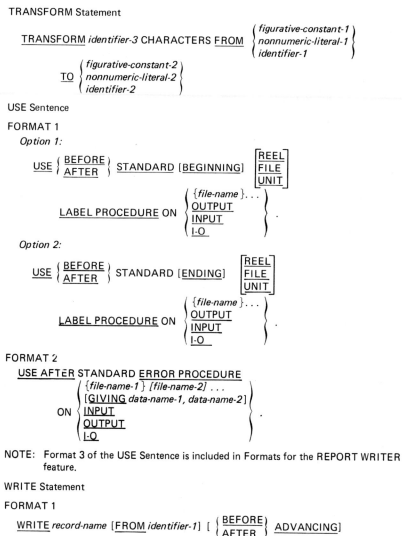

$\underline{\text{TRANSFORM}}$ *identifier-3* CHARACTERS $\underline{\text{FROM}}$ $\left\{ \begin{array}{l} \textit{figurative-constant-1} \\ \textit{nonnumeric-literal-1} \\ \textit{identifier-1} \end{array} \right\}$

$\underline{\text{TO}}$ $\left\{ \begin{array}{l} \textit{figurative-constant-2} \\ \textit{nonnumeric-literal-2} \\ \textit{identifier-2} \end{array} \right\}$

USE Sentence

FORMAT 1

Option 1:

$\underline{\text{USE}}$ $\left\{ \begin{array}{l} \underline{\text{BEFORE}} \\ \underline{\text{AFTER}} \end{array} \right\}$ $\underline{\text{STANDARD}}$ [$\underline{\text{BEGINNING}}$] $\begin{bmatrix} \text{REEL} \\ \text{FILE} \\ \text{UNIT} \end{bmatrix}$

$\underline{\text{LABEL PROCEDURE}}$ ON $\left\{ \begin{array}{l} \{\textit{file-name}\}\ldots \\ \underline{\text{OUTPUT}} \\ \underline{\text{INPUT}} \\ \underline{\text{I-O}} \end{array} \right\}$.

Option 2:

$\underline{\text{USE}}$ $\left\{ \begin{array}{l} \underline{\text{BEFORE}} \\ \underline{\text{AFTER}} \end{array} \right\}$ $\underline{\text{STANDARD}}$ [$\underline{\text{ENDING}}$] $\begin{bmatrix} \text{REEL} \\ \text{FILE} \\ \text{UNIT} \end{bmatrix}$

$\underline{\text{LABEL PROCEDURE}}$ ON $\left\{ \begin{array}{l} \{\textit{file-name}\}\ldots \\ \underline{\text{OUTPUT}} \\ \underline{\text{INPUT}} \\ \underline{\text{I-O}} \end{array} \right\}$.

FORMAT 2

$\underline{\text{USE AFTER}}$ STANDARD $\underline{\text{ERROR}}$ PROCEDURE

ON $\left\{ \begin{array}{l} \{\textit{file-name-1}\}\ [\textit{file-name-2}]\ \ldots \\ [\underline{\text{GIVING}}\ \textit{data-name-1, data-name-2}] \\ \underline{\text{INPUT}} \\ \underline{\text{OUTPUT}} \\ \underline{\text{I-O}} \end{array} \right\}$.

NOTE: Format 3 of the USE Sentence is included in Formats for the REPORT WRITER feature.

WRITE Statement

FORMAT 1

$\underline{\text{WRITE}}$ *record-name* [$\underline{\text{FROM}}$ *identifier-1*] [$\left\{ \begin{array}{l} \underline{\text{BEFORE}} \\ \underline{\text{AFTER}} \end{array} \right\}$ $\underline{\text{ADVANCING}}$]

[$\left\{ \begin{array}{l} \textit{identifier-2}\ \text{LINES} \\ \textit{integer}\ \text{LINES} \\ \textit{mnemonic-name} \end{array} \right\}$] [AT $\left\{ \begin{array}{l} \underline{\text{END-OF-PAGE}} \\ \underline{\text{EOP}} \end{array} \right\}$ *imperative-statement*]

FORMAT 2

$\underline{\text{WRITE}}$ *record-name* [$\underline{\text{FROM}}$ *identifier-1*] $\underline{\text{AFTER POSITIONING}}$ $\left\{ \begin{array}{l} \textit{identifier-2} \\ \textit{integer} \end{array} \right\}$ LINES

[AT $\left\{ \begin{array}{l} \underline{\text{END-OF-PAGE}} \\ \underline{\text{EOP}} \end{array} \right\}$ *imperative-statement*]

FORMAT 3

$\underline{\text{WRITE}}$ *record-name* [$\underline{\text{FROM}}$ *identifier-1*] $\underline{\text{INVALID}}$ KEY *imperative-statement*

Sort—Basic Formats

Environment Division Sort Formats

FILE-CONTROL PARAGRAPH—SELECT SENTENCE
SELECT Sentence (for GIVING option only)
    <u>SEL</u><u>ECT</u> *file-name*
       <u>ASSIGN</u> TO *[integer-1] system-name-1 [system-name-2]* . . .

         <u>OR</u> *system-name-3* [FOR <u>MULTIPLE</u> $\left\{ {\text{REEL} \atop \underline{\text{UNIT}}} \right\}$]

           [<u>RESERVE</u> $\left\{ {integer\text{-}2 \atop \underline{\text{NO}}} \right\}$ ALTERNATE $\left[{\text{AREA} \atop \text{AREAS}} \right]$].

SELECT Sentence (for Sort Work Files)
    <u>SEL</u>ECT *sort-file-name*
       <u>ASSIGN</u> TO *[integer] system-name-1 [system-name-2]* . . .

I-O-CONTROL PARAGRAPH
RERUN Clause
  <u>RERUN ON</u> *system-name*
SAME RECORD/SORT AREA Clause
    <u>SAME</u> $\left\{ {\underline{\text{RECORD}} \atop \underline{\text{SORT}}} \right\}$ AREA FOR *file-name-1* {*file-name-2*} . . .

Data Division Sort Formats

SORT-FILE DESCRIPTION
  <u>SD</u> *sort-file-name*
    <u>RECORDING</u> MODE IS *mode*
    <u>DATA</u> $\left\{ {\underline{\text{RECORD}} \text{ IS} \atop \underline{\text{RECORDS}} \text{ ARE}} \right\}$ *data-name-1 [data-name-2]* . . .
    <u>RECORD</u> CONTAINS *[integer-1* <u>TO</u>*]* *integer-2* CHARACTERS.

Procedure Division Sort Formats

RELEASE Statement
  <u>RELEASE</u> *sort-record-name* [<u>FROM</u> *identifier*]

RETURN Statement
  <u>RETURN</u> *sort-file-name* RECORD [<u>INTO</u> *identifier*]
    AT <u>END</u> *imperative-statement*

SORT Statement
  <u>SORT</u> *file-name-1* ON $\left\{ {\underline{\text{DESCENDING}} \atop \underline{\text{ASCENDING}}} \right\}$ KEY {*data-name-1*} . . .

  [ON $\left\{ {\underline{\text{DESCENDING}} \atop \underline{\text{ASCENDING}}} \right\}$ KEY {*data-name-2*} . . .] . . .
  $\left\{ \begin{array}{l} \underline{\text{INPUT PROCEDURE}} \text{ IS } section\text{-}name\text{-}1 \text{ [}\underline{\text{THRU}}\text{ } section\text{-}name\text{-}2\text{]} \\ \underline{\text{USING}} \text{ } file\text{-}name\text{-}2 \\ \underline{\text{OUTPUT PROCEDURE}} \text{ IS } section\text{-}name\text{-}3 \text{ [}\underline{\text{THRU}}\text{ } section\text{-}name\text{-}4\text{]} \\ \underline{\text{GIVING}} \text{ } file\text{-}name\text{-}3 \end{array} \right\}$

Report Writer—Basic Formats

Data Division Report Writer Formats

NOTE: Formats that appear as Basic Formats within the general description of the Data Division are illustrated there.

FILE SECTION—REPORT Clause

$$\begin{Bmatrix} \underline{REPORT} \text{ IS} \\ \underline{REPORTS} \text{ ARE} \end{Bmatrix} \text{ report-name-1 [report-name-2] } \ldots$$

REPORT SECTION

<u>REPORT SECTION.</u>

<u>RD</u> *report-name*

WITH <u>CODE</u> *mnemonic-name*

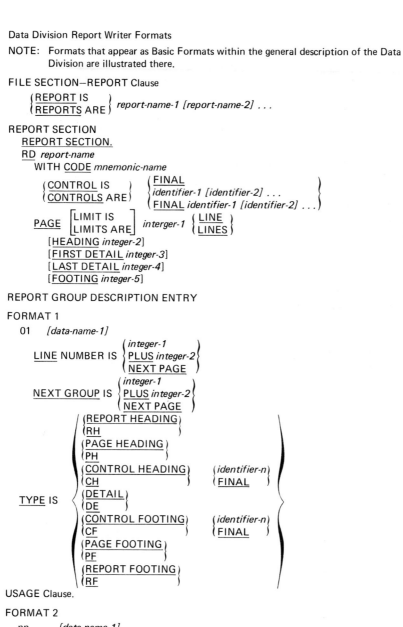

$$\begin{Bmatrix} \underline{CONTROL} \text{ IS} \\ \underline{CONTROLS} \text{ ARE} \end{Bmatrix} \begin{Bmatrix} \underline{FINAL} \\ identifier\text{-}1 \text{ } [identifier\text{-}2] \ldots \\ \underline{FINAL} \text{ } identifier\text{-}1 \text{ } [identifier\text{-}2] \ldots \end{Bmatrix}$$

$$\underline{PAGE} \begin{bmatrix} \underline{LIMIT} \text{ IS} \\ \underline{LIMITS} \text{ ARE} \end{bmatrix} interger\text{-}1 \begin{Bmatrix} \underline{LINE} \\ \underline{LINES} \end{Bmatrix}$$

[<u>HEADING</u> *integer-2*]

[<u>FIRST DETAIL</u> *integer-3*]

[<u>LAST DETAIL</u> *integer-4*]

[<u>FOOTING</u> *integer-5*]

REPORT GROUP DESCRIPTION ENTRY

FORMAT 1

01 *[data-name-1]*

<u>LINE</u> NUMBER IS $\begin{Bmatrix} integer\text{-}1 \\ \underline{PLUS} \text{ } integer\text{-}2 \\ \underline{NEXT PAGE} \end{Bmatrix}$

<u>NEXT GROUP</u> IS $\begin{Bmatrix} integer\text{-}1 \\ \underline{PLUS} \text{ } integer\text{-}2 \\ \underline{NEXT PAGE} \end{Bmatrix}$

<u>TYPE</u> IS $\begin{Bmatrix} \underline{REPORT HEADING} \\ \underline{RH} \\ \underline{PAGE HEADING} \\ \underline{PH} \\ \underline{CONTROL HEADING} \\ \underline{CH} \\ \underline{DETAIL} \\ \underline{DE} \\ \underline{CONTROL FOOTING} \\ \underline{CF} \\ \underline{PAGE FOOTING} \\ \underline{PF} \\ \underline{REPORT FOOTING} \\ \underline{RF} \end{Bmatrix}$ $\begin{Bmatrix} identifier\text{-}n \\ \underline{FINAL} \end{Bmatrix}$ $\begin{Bmatrix} identifier\text{-}n \\ \underline{FINAL} \end{Bmatrix}$

USAGE Clause.

FORMAT 2

nn *[data-name-1]*

LINE Clause—See Format 1

USAGE Clause.

FORMAT 3

nn *[data-name-1]*
   COLUMN NUMBER IS *integer-1*
   GROUP INDICATE
   JUSTIFIED Clause
   LINE Clause—See Format 1
   PICTURE Clause
   RESET ON $\left\{ \begin{array}{l} \textit{identifier-1} \\ \text{FINAL} \end{array} \right\}$
   BLANK WHEN ZERO Clause
   SOURCE IS $\left\{ \begin{array}{l} \text{TALLY} \\ \textit{identifier-2} \end{array} \right\}$
   SUM $\left\{ \begin{array}{l} \text{TALLY} \\ \textit{identifier-3} \end{array} \right\}$ $\left\{ \begin{array}{l} \text{TALLY} \\ \textit{identifier-4} \end{array} \right\}$ ... [UPON *data-name*]
   VALUE IS *literal-1*
   USAGE Clause.

FORMAT 4

01 *data-name-1*
   BLANK WHEN ZERO Clause
   COLUMN Clause—See Format 2
   GROUP Clause—See Format 2
   JUSTIFIED Clause
   LINE Clause—See Format 1
   NEXT GROUP Clause—See Format 1
   PICTURE Clause
   RESET Clause—See Format 2
   $\left\{ \begin{array}{l} \text{SOURCE Clause} \\ \text{SUM Clause} \\ \text{VALUE Clause} \end{array} \right\}$ See Format 2
   TYPE Clause—See Format 1
   USAGE Clause.

Procedure Division Report Writer Formats

GENERATE Statement
   GENERATE *identifier*

INITIATE Statement
   INITIATE *report-name-1 [report-name-2]* ...

TERMINATE Statement
   TERMINATE *report-name-1 [report-name-2]* ...

USE Sentence
   USE BEFORE REPORTING *data-name*.

Table Handling—Basic Formats

Data Division Table Handling Formats

OCCURS Clause

FORMAT 1

OCCURS *integer-2* TIMES
[$\left\{ \begin{array}{l} \underline{ASCENDING} \\ \underline{DESCENDING} \end{array} \right\}$ KEY IS *data-name-2 [data-name-3. . .] . . .*
[INDEXED BY *index-name-1 [index-name-2] . . .]*

FORMAT 2

OCCURS *integer-1* TO *integer-2* TIMES [DEPENDING ON *data-name-1*]
[$\left\{ \begin{array}{l} \underline{ASCENDING} \\ \underline{DESCENDING} \end{array} \right\}$ KEY IS *data-name-2 [data-name-3] . . .] . . .*
[INDEXED BY *index-name-1 [index-name-2] . . .]*

FORMAT 3

OCCURS *integer-2* TIMES [DEPENDING ON *data-name-1*]
[$\left\{ \begin{array}{l} \underline{ASCENDING} \\ \underline{DESCENDING} \end{array} \right\}$ KEY IS *data-name-2 [data-name-3] . . .] . . .*
[INDEXED BY *index-name-1 [index-name-2] . . .]*

USAGE Clause

[USAGE IS] INDEX

SEARCH Statement

FORMAT 1

SEARCH *identifier-1* [VARYING $\left\{ \begin{array}{l} index\text{-}name\text{-}1 \\ identifier\text{-}2 \end{array} \right\}$]
[AT END *imperative-statement-1*]
WHEN *condition-1* $\left\{ \begin{array}{l} imperative\text{-}statement\text{-}2 \\ \underline{NEXT\ SENTENCE} \end{array} \right\}$
[WHEN *condition-2* $\left\{ \begin{array}{l} imperative\text{-}statement\text{-}3 \\ \underline{NEXT\ SENTENCE} \end{array} \right\}$] . . .

FORMAT 2

SEARCH ALL *identifier-1* [AT END *imperative-statement-1*]
WHEN *condition-1* $\left\{ \begin{array}{l} imperative\text{-}statement\text{-}2 \\ \underline{NEXT\ SENTENCE} \end{array} \right.$

SET Statement

FORMAT 1

SET $\left\{ \begin{array}{ll} index\text{-}name\text{-}1 & [index\text{-}name\text{-}2] \ . . . \\ identifier\text{-}1 & [identifier\text{-}2 \ ] \ . . . \end{array} \right\}$ TO $\left\{ \begin{array}{l} index\text{-}name\text{-}3 \\ identifier\text{-}3 \\ literal\text{-}1 \end{array} \right\}$

FORMAT 2

SET *index-name-4 [index-name-5] . . .* $\left\{ \begin{array}{l} \underline{UP\ BY} \\ \underline{DOWN\ BY} \end{array} \right\}$ $\left\{ \begin{array}{l} identifier\text{-}4 \\ literal\text{-}2 \end{array} \right\}$

Segmentation—Basic Formats and Source Program Library Facility

SEGMENTATION—BASIC FORMATS

Environment Division Segmentation Formats

OBJECT-COMPUTER PARAGRAPH

SEGMENT-LIMIT Clause

$\quad$ <u>SEGMENT-LIMIT</u> IS *priority-number*

Procedure Division Segmentation Formats

Priority Numbers

section-name <u>SECTION</u> *[priority-number]* .

SOURCE PROGRAM LIBRARY FACILITY

COPY Statement

<u>COPY</u> *library-name* [<u>SUPPRESS</u>]

$\quad$ [<u>REPLACING</u> *word-1* <u>BY</u> $\begin{Bmatrix} word\text{-}2 \\ literal\text{-}1 \\ identifier\text{-}1 \end{Bmatrix}$ *word-3* <u>BY</u> $\begin{Bmatrix} word\text{-}4 \\ literal\text{-}2 \\ identifier\text{-}2 \end{Bmatrix}$] ...] .

Extended Source Program Library Facility and Debugging Language—Basic Formats

Extended Source Program Library Facility

BASIS Card

<u>BASIS</u>$\qquad$*library-name*

INSERT Card

<u>INSERT</u>$\qquad$*sequence-number-field*

DELETE Card

<u>DELETE</u>$\qquad$*sequence-number-field*

DEBUGGING LANGUAGE—BASIC FORMATS

Procedure Division Debugging Formats

EXHIBIT Statement

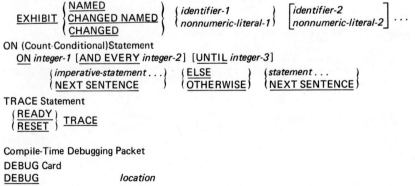

<u>EXHIBIT</u> $\begin{Bmatrix} \underline{NAMED} \\ \underline{CHANGED\ NAMED} \\ \underline{CHANGED} \end{Bmatrix}$ $\begin{Bmatrix} identifier\text{-}1 \\ nonnumeric\text{-}literal\text{-}1 \end{Bmatrix}$ $\begin{bmatrix} identifier\text{-}2 \\ nonnumeric\text{-}literal\text{-}2 \end{bmatrix}$ ...

ON (Count-Conditional)Statement

<u>ON</u> *integer-1* [<u>AND EVERY</u> *integer-2*] [<u>UNTIL</u> *integer-3*]

$\quad$ $\begin{Bmatrix} imperative\text{-}statement... \\ \underline{NEXT\ SENTENCE} \end{Bmatrix}$ $\begin{Bmatrix} \underline{ELSE} \\ \underline{OTHERWISE} \end{Bmatrix}$ $\begin{Bmatrix} statement... \\ \underline{NEXT\ SENTENCE} \end{Bmatrix}$

TRACE Statement

$\begin{Bmatrix} \underline{READY} \\ \underline{RESET} \end{Bmatrix}$ <u>TRACE</u>

Compile-Time Debugging Packet

DEBUG Card

<u>DEBUG</u>$\qquad$*location*

Glossary

ACCESS: The manner in which files are referenced by the computer. Access can be sequential (records are referred to one after another in the order in which they appear on the file), or it can be random (the individual records can be referred to in a nonsequential manner).

Actual Decimal Point: The physical representation, using either of the decimal point characters (. or ,), of the decimal point position in a data item. When specified, it will appear in a printed report, and it requires an actual space in storage.

ACTUAL KEY: A key which can be directly used by the system to locate a logical record on a mass storage device. An ACTUAL KEY must be a data item of 5 to 259 bytes in length.

Alphabetic Character: A character which is one of the 26 characters of the alphabet, or a space. In COBOL, the term does *not* include any other characters.

Alphanumeric Character: Any character in the computer's character set.

Alphanumeric Edited Character: A character within an alphanumeric character string which contains at least one B or 0.

Arithmetic Expression: A statement containing any combination of data-names, numeric literals, and figurative constants, joined together by one or more arithmetic operators in such a way that the statement as a whole can be reduced to a single numeric value.

Arithmetic Operator: A symbol (single character or 2-character set) or COBOL verb which directs the system to perform an arithmetic operation. The following list shows arithmetic operators:

Meaning	*Symbol*
Addition	+
Subtraction	—
Multiplication	*
Division	/
Exponentiation	**

Assumed Decimal Point: A decimal point position which does not involve the existence of an actual character in a data item. It does not occupy an actual space in storage, but is used by the compiler to align a value properly for calculation.

BLOCK: In COBOL, a group of characters or records which is treated as an entity when moved into or out of the computer. The term is synonymous with the term Physical Record.

Buffer: A portion of main storage into which data is read or from which it is written.

Byte: A sequence of eight adjacent binary bits. When properly aligned, two bytes form a halfword, four bytes a fullword, and eight bytes a doubleword.

Channel: A device that directs the flow of information between the computer main storage and the input/output devices.

Character: One of a set of indivisible symbols that can be arranged in sequences to express information. These symbols include the letters A through Z, the decimal digits 0 through 9, punctuation symbols, and any other symbols which will be accepted by the data-processing system.

Character Set: All the valid COBOL characters. The complete set of 51 characters.

Character String: A connected sequence of characters. All COBOL characters are valid.

Checkpoint: A reference point in a program at which information about the contents of core storage can be recorded so that, if necessary, the program can be restarted at an intermediate point.

Class Condition: A statement that the content of an item is wholly alphabetic or wholly numeric. It may be true or false.

Clause: A set of consecutive COBOL words whose purpose is to specify an attribute of an entry. There are three types of clauses: data, environment, and file.

COBOL Character: Any of the 51 valid characters (see CHARACTER) in the COBOL character set.

Collating Sequence: The arrangement of all valid characters in the order of their relative precedence. The collating sequence of a computer is part of the computer design—each acceptable character has a predetermined place in the sequence. A collating sequence is used primarily in comparison operations.

COLUMN Clause: A COBOL clause used to identify a specific position within a report line.

Comment: An annotation in the Identification Division or Procedure Division of a COBOL source program. A comment is ignored by the compiler. As an IBM extension, comments may be included at any point in a COBOL source program.

Compile Time: The time during which a COBOL source program is translated by the COBOL compiler into a machine language object program.

Compiler: A program which translates a program written in a higher level language into a machine language object program.

Compiler Directing Statement: A COBOL statement which causes the compiler to take a specific action at compile time, rather than the object program to take a particular action at execution time.

Compound Condition: A statement that tests two or more relational expressions. It may be true or false.

Condition:

- One of a set of specified values a data item can assume.
- A simple conditional expression: relation condition, class condition, condition-name condition, sign condition, NOT condition.

Conditional Statement: A syntactically correct statement, made up of data-names, and/or figurative literals, and/or constants, and/or logical operators, so constructed that it tests a truth value. The subsequent action of the object program is dependent on this truth value.

Conditional Variable: A data item that can assume more than one value; the value(s) it assumes has a condition-name assigned to it.

Condition Name: The name assigned to a specific value, set of values, or range of values, that a data item may assume.

Condition-name Condition: A statement that the value of a conditional variable is one of a set (or range) of values of a data item identified by a condition-name. The statement may be true or false.

CONFIGURATION SECTION: A section of the Environment Division of the COBOL program. It describes the overall specifications of computers.

Connective: A word or a punctuation character that does one of the following:

- Associates a data-name or paragraph-name with its qualifier
- Links two or more operands in a series
- Forms a conditional expression

CONSOLE: A COBOL mnemonic-name associated with the console typewriter.

Contiguous Items: Consecutive elementary or group items in the Data Division that have a definite relationship with each other.

Control Break: A recognition of a change in the contents of a control data item that governs a hierarchy.

Control Bytes: Bytes associated with a physical record that serve to identify the record and indicate its length, blocking factor, etc.

Control Data Item: A data item that is tested each time a report line is to be printed. If the value of the data item has changed, a control break occurs and special actions are performed before the line is printed.

CONTROL FOOTING: A report group that occurs at the end of the control group of which it is a member.

Control Group: An integral set of related data that is specifically associated with a control data item.

CONTROL HEADING: A report group that occurs at the beginning of the control group of which it is a member.

Control Hierarchy: A designated order of specific control data items. The highest level is the final control; the lowest level is the minor control.

Core Storage: Storage within the central processing unit of the computer, so called because this storage exists in the form of magnetic cores.

Data Description Entry: An entry in the Data Division that is used to describe the characteristics of a data item. It consists of a level number, followed by an optional data-name, followed by data clauses that fully describe the format the data will take. An elementary data description entry (or item) cannot logically be subdivided further. A group data description entry (or item) is made up of a number of related groups and/or elementary items.

DATA DIVISION: One of the four main component parts of a COBOL program. The Data Division describes the files to be used in the program and the records contained within the files. It also describes any internal Working-Storage records that will be needed (see "Data Division" for full details).

Data Item: A unit of recorded information that can be identified by a symbolic name or by a combination of names and subscripts. Elementary data items cannot logically be subdivided. Group data items are made up of logically related group and/or elementary items, and can be a logical group within a record or can itself be a complete record.

Data-name: A name assigned by the programmer to a data item in a COBOL program. It must contain at least one alphabetic character.

DECLARATIVES: A set of one or more compiler-directing sections written at the beginning of the Procedure Division of a COBOL program. The first section is preceded by the header DECLARATIVES. The last section is followed by the header END DECLARATIVES. There are three options:

1. Input/output label handling
2. Input/output error-checking procedures
3. Report Writing procedures

Each has its standard format.

Device-number: The reference number assigned to any external device.

Digit: Any of the numerals from 0 through 9. In COBOL, the term is not used in reference to any other symbol.

DIVISION: One of the four major portions of a COBOL program:
- IDENTIFICATION DIVISION, which names the program.
- ENVIRONMENT DIVISION, which indicates the machine equipment and equipment features to be used in the program.
- DATA DIVISION, which defines the nature and characteristics of data to be processed.
- PROCEDURE DIVISION, which consists of statements directing the processing of data in a specified manner at execution time.

Division Header: The COBOL words that indicate the beginning of a particular division of a COBOL program. The four division headers are:
- IDENTIFICATION DIVISION.
- ENVIRONMENT DIVISION.
- DATA DIVISION.
- PROCEDURE DIVISION.

Division-name: The name of one of the four divisions of a COBOL program.

EBCDIC Character: Any one of the symbols included in the eight-bit EBCDIC (Extended Binary-Coded-Decimal Interchange Code) set. All 51 COBOL characters are included.

Editing Character: A single character or a fixed two-character combination used to create proper formats for output reports.

Elementary Item: A data item that cannot logically be subdivided.

Entry: Any consecutive set of descriptive clauses terminated by a period, written in the Identification, Environment, or Procedure Divisions of a COBOL program.

Entry-name: A programmer-specified name that establishes an entry point into a COBOL subprogram.

ENVIRONMENT DIVISION: One of the four main component parts of a COBOL program. The Environment Division describes the computers upon which the source program is compiled and those on which the object program is executed, and provides a linkage between the logical concept of files and their records, and the physical aspects of the devices on which files are stored (see "Environment Division" for full details).

Execution Time: The time at which an object program actually performs the instructions coded in the Procedure Division, using the actual data provided.

Exponent: A number, indicating how many times another number (the base) is to be repeated as a factor. Positive exponents denote multiplication, negative exponents denote division, fractional exponents denote a root of a quantity. In COBOL, exponentiation is indicated with the symbol ** followed by the exponent.

F-mode Records: Records of a fixed length. Blocks may contain more than one record.

Figurative Constant: A reserved word that represents a numeric value, a character, or a string of repeated values or characters. The word can be written in a COBOL program to represent the values or characters without being defined in the Data Division.

FILE-CONTROL: The name and header of an Environment Division paragraph in which the data files for a given source program are named and assigned to specific input/output devices.

File Description: An entry in the File Section of the Data Division that provides information about the identification and physical structure of a file.

File-name: A name assigned to a set of input data or output data. A file-name must include at least one alphabetic character.

FILE SECTION: A section of the Data Division that contains descriptions of all externally stored data (or files) used in a program. Such information is given in one or more file description entries.

Floating-Point Literal: A numeric literal whose value is expressed in floating-point notation—that is, as a decimal number followed by an exponent which indicates the actual placement of the decimal point.

Function-name: A name, specified by the computer manufacturer, that identifies system logical units, printer and card punch control characters, and report codes. When a function-name is associated with a mnemonic-name in the Environment Division, the mnemonic-name may then be substituted in any format in which such substitution is valid.

Group Item: A data item made up of a series of logically related elementary items. It can be part of a record or a complete record.

Header Label: A record that identifies the beginning of a physical file or a volume.

High-Order: The leftmost position in a string of characters.

IDENTIFICATION DIVISION: One of the four main component parts of a COBOL program. The Identification Division identifies the source program and the object program and, in addition, may include such documentation as the author's name, the installation where written, date written, etc., (see "Identification Division" for full details).

Identifier: A data-name, unique in itself, or made unique by the syntactically correct combination of qualifiers, subscripts, and/or indexes.

Imperative-Statement: A statement consisting of an imperative verb and its operands, which specifies that an action be taken, unconditionally. An imperative-statement may consist of a series of imperative-statements.

Index: A computer storage position or register, the contents of which identify a particular element in a table.

Index Data Item: A data item in which the contents of an index can be stored without conversion to subscript form.

Index-name: A name, given by the programmer, for an index of a specific table. An index-name must contain at least one alphabetic character. It is one word (4 bytes) in length.

Indexed Data-name: A data-name identifier which is subscripted with one or more index-names.

INPUT-OUTPUT SECTION: In the Environment Division, the section that names the files and external media needed by an object program. It also provides information required for the transmission and handling of data during the execution of an object program.

INPUT PROCEDURE: A set of statements that is executed each time a record is released to the sort file. Input procedures are optional; whether they are used or not depends upon the logic of the program.

Integer: A numeric data item or literal that does not include any character positions to the right of the decimal point, actual or assumed. Where the term "integer" appears in formats, "integer" must not be a numeric data item.

INVALID KEY Condition: A condition that may arise at execution time in which the value of a specific key associated with a mass storage file does not result in a correct reference to the file (see the READ, REWRITE, START, and WRITE statements for the specific error conditions involved).

I-O-CONTROL: The name, and the header, for an Environment Division paragraph in which object program requirements for specific input/output techniques are specified. These techniques include rerun checkpoints, sharing of same areas by several data files, and multiple file storage on a single tape device.

KEY: One or more data items, the contents of which identify the type or the location of a record, or the ordering of data.

Key Word: A reserved word whose employment is essential to the meaning and structure of a COBOL statement. In this text, key words are indicated in the formats of statements by underscoring. Key words are included in the reserved word list.

Level Indicator: Two alphabetic characters that identify a specific type of file, or the highest position in a hierarchy. The level indicators are: FD, RD, SD.

Level Number: A numeric character or 2-character set that identifies the properties of a data description entry. Level numbers 01 through 49 define group items, the highest level being identified as 01, and the subordinate data items within the hierarchy being identified with level numbers 02 through 49. Level numbers 66, 77, and 88 identify special properties of a data description entry in the Data Division.

Library-name: The name of a member of a data set containing COBOL entries, used with the COPY and BASIS statements.

LINKAGE SECTION: A section of the Data Division that describes data made available from another program.

Literal: A character string whose value is implicit in the characters themselves. The numeric literal 7 expresses the value 7, and the nonnumeric literal "CHARACTERS" expresses the value CHARACTERS.

Logical Operator: A COBOL word that defines the logical connections between relational operators. The three logical operators and their meanings are:

> OR (logical inclusive—either or both)
> AND (logical connective—both)
> NOT (logical negation)

(See "Procedure Division" for a more detailed explanation.)

Logical Record: The most inclusive data item, identified by a level-01 entry. It consists of one or more related data items.

Low-Order: The rightmost position in a string of characters.

Main Program: The highest level COBOL program involved in a step. (Programs written in other languages that follow COBOL linkage conventions are considered COBOL programs in this sense.)

Mantissa: The decimal part of a logarithm. Therefore, the part of a floating-point number that is expressed as a decimal fraction.

Mass Storage: A storage medium—disk, drum, or data cell—in which data can be collected and maintained in a sequential, direct, indexed or relative organization.

Mass Storage File: A collection of records assigned to a mass storage device.

Mass Storage File Segment: A part of a mass storage file whose beginning and end are defined by the FILE-LIMIT clause in the Environment Division.

Mnemonic-name: A programmer-supplied word associated with a specific function-name in the Environment Division. It then may be written in place of the function-name in any format where such a substitution is valid.

MODE: The manner in which records of a file are accessed or processed.

Name: A word composed of not more than 30 characters, which defines a COBOL operand.

Noncontiguous Item: A data item in the Working-Storage Section of the Data Division which bears no relationship to other data items.

Nonnumeric Literal: A character string bounded by quotation marks, which means literally itself. For example, "CHARACTER" is the literal for, and means, CHARACTER. The string of characters may include any characters in the computer's set, with the exception of the quotation mark. Characters that are not COBOL characters may be included.

Numeric Character: A character that belongs to one of the set of digits 0 through 9.

Numeric Edited Character: A numeric character which is in such a form that it may be used in a printed output. It may consist of external decimal digits 0 through 9, the decimal point, commas, the dollar sign, etc., as the programmer wishes (see "Data Division" for a fuller explanation).

Numeric Item: An item whose description restricts its contents to a value represented by characters chosen from the digits 0 through 9; if signed, the item may also contain a + or −, or other representation of an operational sign.

Numeric Literal: A numeric character or string of characters whose value is implicit in the characters themselves. Thus, 777 is the literal as well as the value of the number 777.

OBJECT-COMPUTER: The name of an Environment Division paragraph in which the computer upon which the object program will be run is described.

Object Program: The set of machine language instructions that is the output from the compilation of a COBOL source program. The actual processing of data is done by the object program.

Object Time: The time during which an object program is executed.

Operand: The "object" of a verb or an operator. That is, the data or equipment governed or directed by a verb or operator.

Operational Sign: An algebraic sign associated with a numeric data item, which indicates whether the item is positive or negative.

Optional Word: A reserved word included in a specific format only to improve the readability of a COBOL statement. If the programmer wishes, optional words may be omitted.

OUTPUT PROCEDURE: A set of programmer-defined statements that is executed each time a sorted record is returned from the sort file. Output procedures are optional; whether they are used or not depends upon the logic of the program.

Overlay: The technique of repeatedly using the same areas of internal storage during different stages in processing a problem.

PAGE: A physical separation of continuous data in a report. The separation is based on internal requirements and/or the physical characteristics of the reporting medium.

PAGE FOOTINGS: A report group at the end of a report page which is printed before a page control break is executed.

PAGE HEADING: A report group printed at the beginning of a report page, after a page control break is executed.

Paragraph: A set of one or more COBOL sentences, making up a logical processing entity, and preceded by a paragraph-name or a paragraph header.

Paragraph Header: A word followed by a period that identifies and precedes all paragraphs in the Identification Division and Environment Division.

Paragraph-name: A programmer-defined word that identifies and precedes a paragraph.

Parameter: A variable that is given a specific value for a specific purpose or process. In COBOL, parameters are most often used to pass data values between calling and called programs.

Physical Record: A physical unit of data, synonymous with a block. It can be composed of a portion of one logical record, of one complete logical record, or of a group of logical records.

Print Group: An integral set of related data within a report.

Priority-number: A number, ranging in value from 0 to 99, which classifies source program sections in the Procedure Division (see "Segmentation" for more information).

Procedure: One or more logically connected paragraphs or sections within the Procedure Division, which direct the computer to perform some action or series of related actions.

PROCEDURE DIVISION: One of the four main component parts of a COBOL program. The Procedure Division contains instructions for solving a problem. The Procedure Division may contain imperative-statements, conditional statements, paragraphs, procedures, and sections (see "Procedure Division" for full details).

Procedure-name: A word that precedes and identifies a procedure, used by the programmer to transfer control from one point of the program to another.

Process: Any operation or combination of operations on data.

Program-name: A word in the Identification Division that identifies a COBOL source program.

Punctuation Character: A comma, semicolon, period, quotation mark, left or right parenthesis, or a space.

Qualifier: A group data-name that is used to reference a nonunique data-name at a lower level in the same hierarchy, or a section-name that is used to reference a nonunique paragraph. In this way, the data-name or the paragraph-name can be made unique.

Random Access: An access mode in which specific logical records are obtained from or placed into a mass storage file in a nonsequential manner.

RECORD: A set of one or more related data items grouped for handling either internally or by the input/output systems (see "Logical Record").

Record Description: The total set of data description entries associated with a particular logical record.

Record-name: A data-name that identifies a logical record.

REEL: A module of external storage associated with a tape device.

Relation Character: A character that expresses a relationship between two operands. The following are COBOL relation characters:

Character	Meaning
>	Greater than
<	Less than
=	Equal to

Relation Condition: A statement that the value of an arithmetic expression or data item has a specific relationship to another arithmetic expression or data item. The statement may be true or false.

Relational Operator: A reserved word, or a group of reserved words, or a group of reserved words and relation characters. A relational operator plus programmer-defined operands make up a relational expression. A complete listing is given in "Procedure Division."

REPORT: A presentation of a set of processed data described in a Report File.

Report Description Entry: An entry in the Report Section of the Data Division that names and describes the format of a report to be produced.

Report File: A collection of records, produced by the Report Writer, that can be used to print a report in the desired format.

REPORT FOOTING: A report group that occurs, and is printed, only at the end of a report.

Report Group: A set of related data that makes up a logical entity in a report.

REPORT HEADING: A report group that occurs, and is printed, only at the beginning of a report.

Report Line: One row of printed characters in a report.

Report-name: A data-name that identifies a report.

REPORT SECTION: A section of the Data Division that contains one or more Report Description entries.

Reserved Word: A word used in a COBOL source program for syntactical purposes. It must not appear in a program as a user-defined operand.

Routine: A set of statements in a program that causes the computer to perform an operation or series of related operations.

Run Unit: A set of one or more object programs which function, at object time, as a unit to provide problem solutions. This compiler considers a run unit to be the highest level calling program plus all called subprograms.

S-Mode Records: Records which span physical blocks. Records may be fixed or variable in length; blocks may contain one or more segments. Each segment contains a segment-descriptor field and a control field indicating whether it is the first and/or last or an intermediate segment of the record. Each block contains a block-descriptor field.

SECTION: A logically related sequence of one or more paragraphs. A section must always be named.

Section Header: A combination of words that precedes and identifies each section in the Environment, Data, and Procedure Divisions.

Section-name: A word specified by the programmer that precedes and identifies a section in the Procedure Division.

Sentence: A sequence of one or more statements, the last ending with a period followed by a space.

Separator: An optional word or character that improves readability.

Sequential Access: An access mode in which logical records are obtained from or placed into a file in such a way that each successive access to the file refers to the next subsequent logical record in the file. The order of the records is established by the programmer when creating the file.

Sequential Processing: The processing of logical records in the order in which records are accessed.

Sign Condition: A statement that the algebraic value of a data item is less than, equal to, or greater than zero. It may be true or false.

Simple Condition: An expression that can have two values, and causes the object program to select between alternate paths of control, depending on the value found. The expression can be true or false.

Slack Bytes: Bytes inserted between data items or records to ensure correct alignment of some numeric items. Slack bytes contain no meaningful data. In some cases, they are inserted by the compiler; in others, it is the responsibility of the programmer to insert them. The SYNCHRONIZED clause instructs the compiler to insert slack bytes when they are needed for proper alignment. Slack bytes between records are inserted by the programmer.

Sort File: A collection of records that is sorted by a SORT statement. The sort file is created and used only while the sort function is operative.

Sort-File-Description Entry: An entry in the File Section of the Data Division that names and describes a collection of records that is used in a SORT statement.

Sort-file-name: A data-name that identifies a Sort File.

Sort-key: The field within a record on which a file is sorted.

Sort-work-file: A collection of records involved in the sorting operation as this collection exists on intermediate device(s).

SOURCE-COMPUTER: The name of an Environment Division paragraph. In it, the computer upon which the source program will be compiled is described.

Source Program: A problem-solving program written in COBOL.

Special Character: A character that is neither numeric nor alphabetic. Special char-

acters in COBOL include the space ( ), the period (.), as well as the following:
$+ - * / = \$, ; ") ($

SPECIAL-NAMES: The name of an Environment Division paragraph, and the paragraph itself, in which names supplied by the computer manufacturer are related to mnemonic-names specified by the programmer. In addition, this paragraph can be used to exchange the functions of the comma and the period, or to specify a substitution character for the currency sign, in the PICTURE string.

Special Register: Compiler-generated storage areas primarily used to store information produced with the use of specific COBOL features. The special registers are: TALLY, LINE-COUNTER, PAGE-COUNTER, CURRENT-DATE, TIME-OF-DAY, LABEL-RETURN, RETURN-CODE, SORT-RETURN, SORT-FILE-SIZE, SORT-CORE-SIZE, and SORT-MODE-SIZE.

Standard Data Format: The concept of actual physical or logical record size in storage. The length in the Standard Data Format is expressed in the number of bytes a record occupies and not necessarily the number of characters, since some characters take up one full byte of storage and others take up less.

Statement: A syntactically valid combination of words and symbols written in the Procedure Division. A statement combines COBOL reserved words and programmer-defined operands.

Subject of entry: A data-name or reserved word that appears immediately after a level indicator or level number in a Data Division entry. It serves to reference the entry.

Subprogram: A COBOL program that is invoked by another COBOL program. (Programs written in other languages that follow COBOL linkage conventions are COBOL programs in this sense.)

Subscript: An integer or a variable whose value references a particular element in a table.

SYSIN: The system logical input device.

SYSOUT: The system logical output device.

SYSPUNCH: The system logical punch device.

System-name: A name that identifies any particular external device used with the computer, and characteristics of files contained within it.

Table: A collection and arrangement of data in a fixed form for ready reference. Such a collection follows some logical order, expressing particular values (functions) corresponding to other values (arguments) by which they are referenced.

Table Element: A data item that belongs to the set of repeated items comprising a table. An argument together with its corresponding function(s) makes up a table element.

Test Condition: A statement that, taken as a whole, may be either true or false, depending on the circumstances existing at the time the expression is evaluated.

Trailer Label: A record that identifies the ending of a physical file or of a volume.

U-mode Records: Records of unspecified length. They may be fixed or variable in length; there is only one record per block.

Unary Operator: An arithmetic operator (+ or −) that can precede a single variable, a literal, or a left parenthesis in an arithmetic expression. The plus sign multiplies the value by +1; the minus sign multiplies the value by −1.

UNIT: A module of external storage. Its dimensions are determined by the computer manufacturer.

V-mode Records: Records of variable length. Blocks may contain more than one record. Each record contains a record length field, and each block contains a block length field.

Variable: A data item whose value may be changed during execution of the object program.

Verb: A COBOL reserved word that expresses an action to be taken by a COBOL compiler or an object program.

Volume: A module of external storage. For tape devices it is a reel; for mass storage devices it is a unit.

Volume Switch Procedures: Standard procedures executed automatically when the end of a unit or reel has been reached before end-of-file has been reached.

WORD:
1. In COBOL: A string of not more than 30 characters, chosen from the following: the letters A through Z, the digits 0 through 9, and the hyphen (-). The hyphen may not appear as either the first or last character.
2. In the IBM System/360 or System/370: A fullword is four bytes of storage; a doubleword is eight bytes of storage; a halfword is two bytes of storage.

Word Boundary: Any particular storage position at which data must be aligned for certain processing operations in the IBM System/360 or System/370. The halfword boundary must be divisible by 2, the fullword boundary must be divisible by 4, the doubleword boundary must be divisible by 8.

WORKING-STORAGE SECTION: A section-name (and the section itself) in the Data Division. The section describes records and noncontiguous data items that are not part of external files, but are developed and processed internally. It also defines data items whose values are assigned in the source program.

Index